HITLER'S WAR AND THE GERMANS

Marlis G. Steinert

HITLER'S WAR AND THE GERMANS

PUBLIC MOOD AND ATTITUDE
DURING THE SECOND WORLD WAR

Edited and Translated by Thomas E. J. de Witt

OHIO UNIVERSITY PRESS : ATHENS, OHIO

CONTENTS

Those who forget
the past are condemned
to relive it.

Santayana

ACKNOWLEDGEMENTS

I OWE WARMEST GRATITUDE to numerous individuals and institutions, especially to Professor Jacques Freymond for his constant support, as adviser, critic, and example. The assistance and encouragement of the Graduate Institute of International Studies, directed by him, made possible the realization of this work.

At this time I also wish to express my sincere thanks to Professor Hans Mommsen, Ruhr-Universität Bochum, for his critical examination of the manuscript.

I owe further thanks to the officials of the various archives consulted for their courteous assistance in evaluating the documents in their files, especially chief archivist Dr. Heinz Boberach of the Bundesarchiv, Koblenz, whose suggestions were particularly valuable. I am also grateful to Professor Saul Friedländer for the initial stimulus leading to this inquiry.

MARLIS G. STEINERT

ABBREVIATIONS

AA	Auswärtiges Amt (Foreign Office)
ADAP	Akten zur Deutschen Auswärtigen Politik (Documents on German Foreign Policy)
AThH	August Thyssen Hütte (A. Thyssen Works)
BA	Bundesarchiv (Federal Archives)
BDM	Bund Deutscher Mädel (League of German Girls)
BHStA	Bayerisches Hauptstaatsarchiv (Bavarian Central Archives)
DNB	Deutsches Nachrichtenbüro (German News Service)
GBA	Generalbevollmächtigter für den Arbeitseinsatz (General Plenipotentiary for the Mobilization of Labor)
HA GHH	Historisches Archiv Gute-Hoffnungshütte (Archives of the Gute-Hoffnungshütte)
HJ	Hitlerjugend (Hitler Youth)
HStA	Hauptstaatsarchiv (Central State Archives)
HHStA Wbn	Hessisches Hauptstaatsarchiv Wiesbaden (Central State Archives of Hesse, Wiesbaden)
IBV	Internationale Bibelvereinigung (International Bible Association)
IfZ	Institut für Zeitgeschichte (Institute for Contemporary History)
IMT	International Military Tribunal (Case against the Major War Criminals)
IWM	Imperial War Museum
KdF	Kraft durch Freude (Strength through Joy)
KPD	Kommunistische Partei Deutschlands (Communist Party of Germany)

MA	Militärarchiv (Military Archives)
MGFA	Militärgeschichtliches Forschungsamt (Military Historical Research Branch)
NSDAP	Nationalsozialistische Deutsche Arbeiterpartei (National Socialist German Workers' Party)
NSDStB	Nationalsozialistischer Deutscher Studentenbund (N.S. German League of Students)
NSFO	Nationalsozialistischer Führungsoffizier (N.S. Guidance Officer)
NSV	Nationalsozialistische Volkswohlfahrt (N.S. People's Welfare)
Obb	Oberbayern (Upper Bavaria)
OKH	Oberkommando des Heeres (High Command of the Army)
OKL	Oberkommando der Luftwaffe (High Command of the Air Force)
OKM	Oberkommando der Marine (High Command of the Navy)
OKW	Oberkommando der Wehrmacht (High Command of the Armed Forces)
OLG	Oberlandesgericht (Provincial Court, Court of Appeal)
Pg	Parteigenosse (party member)
RFSS	Reichsführer SS (Reich Commander of the SS)
RGBl	Reichsgesetzblatt (Official Reich Journal)
RMVP	Reichsministerium für Volksaufklärung und Propaganda (Reich Ministry for Enlightenment and Propaganda)
RPÄ	Reichspropagandaämter (Reich Propaganda Offices)
RSHA	Reichssicherheitshauptamt (Reich Security Office)
SA	Sturmabteilung (Storm Troopers)
SD	Sicherheitsdienst (Security Service)
SPD	Sozialdemokratische Partei Deutschlands (Social Democratic Party of Germany)
SS	Schutzstaffel (Elite Guard)
Slg	Sammlung (Collection)
StA	Staatsarchiv (State Archives)
USNA	United States National Archives
V-Mann	Vertrauensmann (secret agent)
VfZG	Vierteljahreshefte für Zeitgeschichte (Journal of the Institute for Contemporary History)
Vg	Volksgenosse (German citizen)
WPr	Wehrmachtspropaganda (military propaganda)

INTRODUCTION

THE CONCEPT OF PUBLIC OPINION

EVERY STATE LEADERSHIP, be it democratic, authoritarian, or totalitarian, requires a certain degree of acclamation to exercise power in the long run. Without the consensus, whether forced or passive, of a broad social stratum, no government can long survive in the age of the masses. In western democratic forms of government, executive decisions are checked and corrected by elected public representatives, whereby public opinion plays a significant role in the creation of governmental as well as parliamentary will. Within coercive systems, on the other hand, attempts are made to obtain the requisite consent partly through rigorous formal and informal social controls and terror, partly by manipulation and influence of public opinion.[1] An exact knowledge of the prevailing climate and constellation of opinion is necessary for the successful influence of public opinion. As a substitute for the information obtained in democratic states through public opinion surveys or from the news services of parliaments, the press, radio, and television, totalitarian states draw mostly on the reports of surveillance and informer networks[2] that have a long historical tradition. Pharaohs and caesars, Chinese emperors, tyrants and public tribunes, absolute despots—all employed scouts and listeners who, following the example of Harun al Raschid, mingled with the people to learn their opinions. These methods were refined in time; whole police apparatuses and spy networks were established and inspired by Fouché's model.

From the beginning, the leadership of the Third Reich made full use of these sources of information. Yet one still frequently finds the assertion in sociopsychological treatises and textbooks as well as in public

1

opinion manuals that there is no noteworthy, or only weakly defined, public opinion in totalitarian societies, and that consequently the fascist states also had "only a very weak and ineffective instrument for public opinion research" at their disposal.[4] It is evident, at least since Heinz Boberach's publication of selections from the *Meldungen aus dem Reich*[5] compiled by the Security Service (SD), that this did not apply to the Third Reich. Moreover the SD reports had already been mentioned repeatedly in the Goebbels' diaries published shortly after World War II.[6] Less well known is the fact that Himmler's Security Service was not alone in furnishing the state and party leadership with information on the prevailing opinion of the German people; indications and communications concerning the public mood were also collected from the most varied organizations and institutions and transmitted through numerous channels.[7] It even appears as if hardly a National Socialist organization existed that did not, at least occasionally or in specific areas, deliver political situation reports. Naturally there were connections between the organizations and the Security Service to eliminate duplication and guarantee as comprehensive a presentation as possible. The same went for those state and military offices also reporting regularly on public attitude.[9] However, only in very few instances did it result in a lasting and continuous cooperation.

Many of the documents were lost through the effects of war or direct orders for their destruction;[10] other holdings have not yet been located in their entirety or made accessible.[11] The archival materials that have survived and can be consulted, however, are still more vast and informative than are usually available to the historian of other periods and subjects. Their existence and the various measures taken by top Nazi officials, especially by Martin Bormann in the second half of the war and by Joseph Goebbels in his planned propaganda campaigns, permit the conclusion that popular opinion in the Third Reich was by no means such a *quantité négligeable* as Ribbentrop represented to the Soviet chargé d'affairs in August, 1939.[12] While this may have been the case in part for the peaceful years, it changed fundamentally no later than the outbreak of war. Hitler's view of life, strongly influenced by the front-line experience and the lost war, made him fear a development akin to 1917-18 more than he feared foreign foes.

One of the roots for the striking interest of a totalitarian system in the mood of the nation should therefore be sought in the events of 1917-18. During the course of the war, comparisons were made again and again, both by political leaders and the public, to the time of the First World War. The Nazi elite tried its utmost to prevent a repeat of the so-called stab-in-the-back, based on the legend disseminated after the war that the homeland had undermined the front.

At this point the crucial question must be raised as to whether Hitler read the prepared reports of the various organizations and bureaus, or had himself informed of their content. Otto Ohlendorf, Chief of the Security Police (SD), testified at Nuremberg that the "*Meldungen aus dem Reich*" had not reached Hitler, with the exception of a few reports near the end.[13] No irrefutable documentary evidence to the contrary has been presented to date. In the "table-talks" edited by Henry Picker,[14] however, mention is made of one report with a notation by Hitler. Moreover, Goebbels, who had built his own opinion research apparatus using the activity reports of his Reich Propaganda offices, often drove to the Führer's headquarters where his press instructions, as well as those of Otto Dietrich, which frequently reflected direct reaction to opinion reports, were often inspired if not actually dictated by Hitler himself. Hitler's repeated intervention in the Church question, his attitude concerning the euthanasia action, his remarks about the population after Mussolini's fall all reveal an exact knowledge of the nation's mood. Naturally there were diverse possibilities for information available to the "Führer of the Greater German Reich." It is well known that he read foreign press reports and gleaned information from visitors. Beyond that he also seems to have read opinion research reports—although not daily and systematically—or was informed about them. Rudolf Hess, Reichsführer SS Heinrich Himmler, and his personal adviser, Dr. Rudolf Brandt, often used Martin Bormann's absence to acquaint Hitler with opinion trends; Bormann at times withheld these reports on the pretext that one could not burden Hitler with such questions.[15] This type of communication throws significant light on the unsystematic, disorganized, and desultory style characteristic of Hitler's work habits. Albert Speer, in his memoirs,[16] has again exposed dilettantism as one of Hitler's most characteristic peculiarities. Another feature was his moodiness, to which all his colleagues submitted, and which they included in their own power assessments. Hitler's knowledge of the national mood was consequently based on a sporadic appraisal which led to *ad hoc* reactions. These had only tactical significance; in his important decisions and calculations of strategic goals he did not allow himself to be influenced by the opinion of the populace. But his timing—the introduction and termination of policies—was often subject to it. On the other hand, the news and propaganda policy of the Third Reich, which will be discussed later and which was to mould and direct the opinion of the *Volk*, was not only a reaction to public opinion but was also frequently inspired by it, as well as often decisively forming the public mind. It can thus be confirmed, on the basis of the documents for National Socialist Germany analyzed in this study, that "public opinion and propaganda mutually limit and influence each other."[17]

The question of this inquiry is thus no longer whether there were any opinions in Hitler's Germany at all, but: 1. to what extent were these opinions differentiated, independent, and genuine, and to what extent were they manipulated or controlled; 2. which factors influenced them; and 3. how far did their influence reach?

It is of course a well-known fact that in democratic systems too, the mass of the population cannot manage without "accepted opinions." The bewildering variety of facts and events, the complexity of social, economic, and technical processes and situations, do not enable the average citizen, in most cases, to form his own opinion. Rather he accepts "coined phrases" or prepared views presented to him by the mass media or other information agencies. A certain manipulation thus also occurs here, although it has its limits, particularly when confronting an existing attitude relatively immune to all methods of persuasion. As this study will prove, such hardened and stereotyped opinions are also found in totalitarian states, and even the most massive influence produces minimal results. Obviously the spectrum of opinion in democratic states, due to the superabundance of news and information material, is more colorful and has more nuances than that of totalitarian states where news policies are uniform and represent a "conscious use of news for the purpose of creating opinions."[18] Nevertheless, in democracies there are also broad opinion trends, typical and representative opinions, and a widespread common mood. The latter can only be grasped incompletely and with difficulty using the numerical and quantitative methods suitable for demoscopic research. To explore it requires supplementary analytical research of the opinions disseminated by the media. Opinion polls of polling institutes thus provide only a very incomplete picture of the "climate," the atmosphere of a given period, or what Dovifat in referring to Bismarck calls the "undercurrent" or "common basis of opinion."[19] The strength of demoscopic inquiries rests on the percentage breakdown of concretely expressed opinions: what percent of the population supported or rejected a specific policy, had trust in a statesman, remained indifferent; what are the election chances of a party, an individual? Given additional qualitative interviews, it is also possible to show shadings of daily opinions and, by repeating specific questions at spaced intervals, to work out a trend. The totality of opinions naturally cannot be captured, only a representative sampling. Individual positions have to be ignored. This also applies to the statements of the German population's mood and attitude collected by the Third Reich's numerous political, military, and administrative agencies. They furnish typical widespread views, but beyond that also give some information about specific views of workers, peasants, and intellectuals as well as summary descriptions of regional variations. They do not, on the other hand, provide percentage breakdowns. In our era of faith in statistics this may be regarded as a serious shortcoming. It is compensated for in part, however, by the frequency and intensity of transmitted opinions. For the last phase of the war a few percentages are available, the result of American research teams questioning German prisoners of war. In dealing with the opinions of soldiers captured in the West, utmost caution must be used in evaluating them in view of what they represent.

The concept "public opinion" remains, especially in Germany, as controversial and unclear as ever; its scientific definition passes more or less for "squaring of the circle."[20] Moreover, it is used mostly in conjunction with demoscopic research methods. In this inquiry, therefore, with reference to the terminology of the period in question, the dual concept of "mood and attitude" [*Stimmung und Haltung*] will be used primarily. It has the advantage of incorporating both the emotional, spontaneous, often short-lived opinion and the lasting frame of mind determined by character, education, and experience, representing the actual starting point of all assessments and expressions of opinions.[21]

An instructional report of the NSDAP Reich Organization Directorate[22] indicates how opinion research at that time had to comprehend and deal with these twins. Mood was here defined as "a certainty of feeling," where emotions predominate and the individual allows himself to be led more by circumstances "than clarity of insight and rational understanding: he is, as it were, tuned by his surroundings like a musical instrument, instead of protecting his independence from them." Attitude, on the other hand, is explained most inadequately and in a completely orthodox party spirit: there are situations "which can no longer be mastered by mood but only by attitude." Consequently it falls mainly to the activist, the political leader, who can achieve such "a clear and firm attitude through the *Weltanschauung* which is in harmony with his blood inheritance, i.e., with his innermost being." "It bestows the essential viewpoint above and beyond daily concerns, because it tells us that struggle is the fundamental law of life, determining the history of nature and nations. . . . " This "attitude" is further based, according to the official party position, on "trust in the Führer" who knows no "bad moods."

This definition roughly conforms to the one given by Dovifat in 1937: "Today the concept 'public opinion,' which is still very evident in discussions about the press in Anglo-Saxon countries, and particularly in the United States, has fully receded in Germany. One no longer speaks of 'opinion' but rather of conviction and political faith. . . . "[23]

National Socialist reclassification of public opinion into mood and attitude thus encompasses the impulsive, spontaneous reaction to daily events and the "undercurrent" or "common basis of opinion" resulting from political indoctrination. In this manner both spontaneous, unconscious and irrational emotions, which also influence the formation of political opinion, as well as the inherited and acquired behavioral mechanisms were incorporated.

UNDERSTANDING DEEPER CAUSES

A commonplace example from the time of the Second World War, once used by Goebbels himself to characterize these two basic concepts, may elucidate the difference between mood and attitude while simultaneously permitting us to draw attention to motivations of opinions and behavioral patterns reaching far back into the past—motivations and patterns perhaps having etiological, historical, psychological, and sociological origins. As subtle a dimension as possible can thus be at least indicated for the mass of public opinion reports constantly used.

Any person is in a bad mood and ill-tempered if he spends nights in the cellar during air-raid alarms, possibly finding broken glass in his home, or worse, just rubble. For years many Germans endured this —as well as the poor nourishment, power stoppages and numerous deprivations—in good spirits; again and again they cleared, rebuilt, and persevered. Was it for "ideological" reasons or because they trusted the "Führer?" A contemporary diary, to begin with, gives a different, quite obvious explanation: "Neither sweeping rubbish nor salvaging pillows has anything to do with Nazi sentiments. No one thinks of Hitler while boarding up kitchen windows. Everyone, however, remembers that one cannot live in the cold. Before the evening comes and the air-raid sirens start howling, one has to have a hiding-place where he can stretch out his limbs. . . . "[24] This is only one of many simple reactions, based on the need for warmth, shelter, and security.

There is hardly any doubt that a not exactly quantifiable majority of Germans was "in agreement with National Socialist ideas of racism and authoritarian ideology" in the pre-war years of foreign and domestic successes.[25] Yet with increasing bombings and waning fortunes of war, fewer and fewer "Volksgenossen" were likely to be governed in their attitude by "Weltanschauung" and "faith in the Führer," as the Nazi leadership liked to publicize. This attitude corresponded far more, aside from purely instinctive behavior, to an educational ideal nurtured for generations, a basic spiritual attitude whose guideposts were obedience, performance of duty, and neatness: ideals that were usurped by National

Socialism, perverted by an unlawful state, and elevated from secondary to primary virtues. It was this incorporation of traditional values that also made it so difficult for the average German to comprehend Hitler's and his advisers' actual motives. The camouflage was so perfect, the mimicry so well done, that the Allies were also fooled into interpreting these initially Prussian virtues, which served the Nazis only as a façade behind which to achieve their goals of power politics more easily, as the root of National Socialist evils, and therefore increasingly began to regard Germans and Nazis as synonymous.

The mass of existing opinion reports and eye-witness accounts clearly prove, however, that the Third Reich was only rarely supported by a unanimous public vote; opinions were far less uniform, Germans did not favor aggression nor were they enthusiastic about war. They were more likely resigned, fearful of war, and yearning for peace. Hitler's brilliant victories naturally aroused enthusiasm—but that was only for a short time—whereas there were long months and years of submission. Severe criticism became increasingly vocal, especially of the anti-Church measures, of propaganda, of party dignitaries, also of inhumane measures, when they touched one's personal sphere of life; others, like the Jewish expulsion, were tolerated or ignored, and welcomed by some. Hitler, the main culprit, was admired up until the last months of the war by a considerable percentage of the population and stood beyond the pale of otherwise often numerous attacks against the regime.

The present state of social science offers a series of explanations for this. New experiments in human etiology—the comparative study of human behavior—have shown that man, once he has voluntarily submitted to an authority, acquiesces to a high degree and is almost blindly obedient.[27] The proverbial German obedience, then, is not just a Prussian inheritance but a general human phenomenon which was exaggerated by the particularly late German development in industrial, sociological, and national areas.

Social psychologists attribute the bond with Hitler to an identification of him as an ideal ego, a *pater patriae*. It was so strong that it explains not only the blindness in the face of his all too obvious lies and treachery, but also the widespread lack of opposition and revolutionary protest. For many Germans, destroying Hitler meant destroying oneself and Germany. All this had nothing to do with the real Hitler. Few knew and understood him.

Attempts have also been made to explain the background of the German mass delusion from historical and sociological perspectives. Its derivation from the German "national character" and the one-sided interpretation of a culmination of imperialistic intrigues of capitalism have meanwhile discredited themselves. The development of the German social structure and its traditions have offered further possible explanations. German family life, with the dominance of the father and blind submission to his will, is especially denounced as one of the cardinal evils and impediments to the evolution of a free will and personality.[28] Others see the root of authoritarian thought and susceptibility to authoritarianism and totalitarianism planted in the increasingly strong individuation of man, especially since the advent of capitalism. Emerging freedom had effected a radical change in the traditional social structures. Into this revolutionary situation, with its resulting vacuum, were thrust the teachings of Luther and Calvin, which seemingly produced, especially in Germany, an ambivalent attitude towards the godly and worldly authorities.[29] Luther himself was seen as a typical representative of that "authoritarian personality" whose characteristics were supposedly to be found especially in Germany, and whose inner insecurity gave the main impetus to the "escape from freedom." In a major study, Th. W. Adorno, Else Frenkel-Brunswik, Daniel J. Levinson, and R. Nevitt Sanford[30] characterized as essential factors of the authoritarian personality's totalitarian (fascist) syndrome: conventionalism, submission to authority, passion for authority, superstition and stereotyping, especially fatalism and a disposition to rigid categorization, power and robustness, destructiveness and cynicism, as well as projection, that is, transferring one's own impulses to the outside world. Meanwhile a few doubts and criticisms were voiced concerning these ideal-type characterizations of the authoritarian personality and its sado-masochistic impulses;[31] but we can count on further contributions to this theme, as the "sadistic state" thesis shows.[32]

History has recorded numerous cases of illusory excesses, be it the manias of witches, classes, or races, which include symptoms of mistaken reality, aggressiveness, and a relative incorrigibility—symptoms National Socialism exhibited on an unparalleled scale. A pseudo-messiah can often draw on all the suppressed hopes and expectations of masses frustrated by social conflicts and economic grievances. This "Führer" thus meets the needs of a group of psychologically unstable persons, tormented by fears and insecurities, who project onto him the archetype of the savior.[33]

An interdependence between the psychological construct of the chosen Führer and that of the masses, therefore, always exists. What happened in Germany in those twelve years of Nazi rule is not solely the fault of Hitler and his small clique. Hitler himself was aware of this interdependency, as he enunciated in a speech to the generals on January 27, 1944, in his headquarters at the *Wolfsschanze* [wolf's lair]: " . . . values that do not exist cannot be mobilized. It is therefore impossible to make of the Volk something other than is already present in its values. . . . "[34] The same naturally applies to "lack of values." Not only blind obedience or patience and opportunism, but also the wish, often unconscious, to be seduced should be seen as a reason for Germany's behavior as "a kind of mad dog among nations."[35] Hitler was a master in making the masses believe in the realization of "their infantile fantasies of omnipotence."[36]

With regard to the sociological origins of the "German catastrophe," to repeat Meinecke's popular characterization,[37] there are also numerous theses. Yet neither the failure of the German working class, which capitulated without a struggle even though it was the best organized in Europe, nor the extensive collaboration of the military elite and heavy industrialists is satisfactory as a single cause. The tremendous increase of the so-called "new" middle class with its philistine, narrow, petty-bourgeois horizon offers a far better explanation; Hitler knew how to effectively exploit its resentments and fierce appetite for compensation. Still most convincing remains Dahrendorf's thesis of the illiberalism of the overall German social structure. This present study provides further proofs and indices for the German's "structural immaturity." The assertion that Hitler first effected the transformation of German society, "which alone makes freedom possible,"[38] can only be accepted with reservation and must be taken up again in the conclusion.

The "German question" has therefore occupied many minds and called forth numerous interpretations, as this extremely short and summary resumé has attempted to indicate. The purpose of this book is less to examine the still acute question of origins and factors accounting for this development in such a highly civilized country than to present the behavior and reactions of Germans during the Second World War. In that respect numerous opinions and attitudes may certainly be classified as typically German; beyond that, however, there are basic attitudes which represent general human manifestations beyond the scope of the German situation, ideal for clarifying less the particularity of Deutschtum than the total human behavioral pattern in situations of stress and constraint.

MANIPULATION OF PUBLIC OPINION

In addition to the briefly discussed etiological, historical, psychological, and sociological origins, special mention should be made of the ideological and propagandistic techniques employed by the regime to create opinions. It was the task of propaganda to produce the unity of Volk and leadership postulated by National Socialism, to preserve it and extend it to ever larger circles. It was responsible for guaranteeing the requisite consensus of the population for the government's policies.

On March 15, 1933, having assumed control of the newly-created Reich Propaganda Ministry, Goebbels articulated these concerns: "The Volk is no longer to be left to its own resources, the government is no longer, as in the past, to be isolated from the Volk. . . . The Volk is to begin to think in unison, react in unison, and place itself whole-heartedly at the government's disposal."[39]

Even this virtuoso of propaganda technique learned how difficult was this task of influencing the Volk in the direction desired by the state leaders and what daily strains it cost.[40] Fragments of his diaries[41] and the ministerial conferences published by Willi A. Boelcke[42] provide a good insight into his tireless activity. Nothing failed to interest Goebbels and there was nothing he would not try to influence. His goal was absolute monopoly of control over opinion. He never achieved it; the war meant a further diminution of his power, so that in October, 1942, he refused "to accept responsibility for the public mood."[43] On the one side, in the area of foreign propaganda (which concerns us less), his main rival was the Foreign Office, with which he conducted a "tenacious guerrilla war;"[44] and on the other, in the area of military propaganda, the Supreme Command of the Armed Forces (OKW).[45] But even in the realm of news and press policy he was not the unchallenged master. The policies of Reich press chief Otto Dietrich, who usually stayed very close to Hitler, often did not agree with those of the Reich Propaganda Minister.[46] This annoyed Goebbels all the more because he regarded news policy in wartime as a central "weapon of war:" "One needs it in order to wage war, not to distribute information. . . . "[47] Divergent views at the top could therefore only have a negative effect and endanger his principle, summarized as follows: "Our total propaganda and political press efforts are oriented towards utility and results. Only what is expedient is done, and only that which benefits us is expedient. . . . "[48] Thus all statements by the press and radio were government-directed opinions. The German press for the years 1939-45 can therefore be ignored as a source for investigating public opinion. The "instructions," "orders" and "confidential information" of the Propaganda Ministry, the "daily slogans of the Reich press chief,"[49] Goebbels' ministerial conferences and material from the German News Service (DNB, since 1938 in Reich hands and subject to Propaganda Ministry instructions)—these determined down to the last detail what and especially what not to report, what commentaries to write, in what format, on what page, and in what scope. Therefore, a knowledge of the massive measures taken by the Nazi elite to influence opinion is far more important and indispensable for an evaluation of the extent to which German mentality was manipulated during World War II than is a study of newspapers.

Goebbels agreed with Bormann, the ever more powerful head of the Party Chancellory, concerning the importance of propaganda during wartime. A July 20, 1944, notation by one of Bormann's colleagues reads: "Next to the sword, propaganda is today an important and decisive weapon of war."[50] To Bormann, Goebbels' propaganda efforts did not always seem adequate and adept, so as the fortunes of war waned and the mood curve fell, he attempted to keep wavering party members and *Volksgenossen* in line with the help of party dignitaries whom he supplied generously with circulars and "confidential information."

In general, "public enlightenment" [*Volksaufklärung*], as it was called, played a crucial role alongside the actual propaganda. Nominally, Goebbels was also responsible for this. The training and briefing of party leaders, who in turn were responsible for the "emotional-ideological arming"[51] of the populace, were however in the hands of Reich Organization Leader Dr. Robert Ley and Alfred Rosenberg, Hitler's Deputy for the supervision of the overall spiritual and ideological education. Ley, as head of the German Labor Front, controlled one of the Third Reich's largest organizations, with thousands of employees and millions of marks in membership dues. The two quarreled fiercely over their jurisdictions—an opportunity which allowed Goebbels to establish a cultural office in his Reich Propaganda Directorate, which was also concerned with these questions. The areas of jurisdiction between Ley and Rosenberg were finally delineated in an agreement signed on October 15, 1942.[52] All party organizations, from the SS to the SA, BDM, HJ, and even less prominent institutions like the Nazi Peoples' Welfare Organization, were supplied with an abundance of propaganda literature for distribution among their local offices. But one should not draw the conclusion from this overlapping and squabbling that they neutralized each other, as was the case in other spheres, i.e., the economic sector. The opposite was the case: a sort of intensification resulted in a cascade of propaganda on an increasingly stupefied population, which exploded sporadically in anger when the rationalizations became too transparent.[53]

By the summer of 1938 state, party, and military authorities were already discussing and implementing measures to prepare the population for war. Even then the concept of "total war" had already surfaced—i.e., long before Goebbels officially released this slogan in 1943. Back during the Weimar Republic a host of publications dealing with the theme of total mobilization had appeared, attempting to prove that the national will only had to be properly prepared psychologically in order to make the nation invincible and make a new "stab-in-the-back" impossible. Most impressive in this respect was Ernst Jünger's essay, "Total Mobilization" in his 1930 volume *Krieg und Krieger*.[54] The catchword "total war" itself stems from General Ludendorff [quasi-military dictator during World War I], who complained in his war memoirs[55] that not the Army High Command but the Reich Chancellor had been responsible for enlightening the Volk and influencing its mood. For a future total war he recommended unified direction of press and film,[56] and the "word-of-mouth campaign" [*Mundpropaganda*] used by the Nazis during their struggle for power and intensified during World War II. Excerpts of Ludendorff's writings circulated in the Reich War Ministry and the OKW and inspired propaganda planning for a future war. Especially revealing about the propaganda objectives in a total war is the manuscript by Major (E) Dr. Ing. Albrecht Blau[57] of the Psychological Laboratory, War Ministry, Group V, which refers to both Ludendorff and Hitler: "Whoever employs propaganda makes use of a socio-psychological method, a vital technique geared towards exerting an emotional influence on others in such a way that they are given specific impulses to motivate them to perform specific actions. . . . One has to know the feelings and sensitivities of the group to be subjected to propaganda, the complexity of its social structure, the peculiarity of mass life, the existing tensions and *conflicting* forces *within* the masses, if one wants to apply propaganda properly . . . Propaganda is nothing more than the art of applied psychology . . . The goal of propaganda is therefore to *form the opinions* of the propagandized."

From August 30 to September 3, 1938, a course was organized by the OKW for press and censorship officers giving them a general view of the conduct of propaganda in wartime. In those lectures one already finds outlined the essential tasks of military propaganda and its delineation from the Reich Ministry for Enlightenment and Propaganda.[58] The military was responsible "for maintaining the mood, the emotional readiness for action and the will to victory" of the troops as well as "active propaganda in the combat area." It executed this task with the help of the newly introduced propaganda squadrons[59]—also in 1938 but first in the army—and the front newspapers.[60] One of its most effective propaganda weapons was the Armed Forces Report [*Wehrmachtsbericht*], in which the OKW, Hitler himself, and in special cases Goebbels, were involved. The final formulation came mostly from General Jodl.[61] The Wehrmacht was also responsible for the soldiers' indoctrination and attitude. All outside interference was resisted in principle—especially by the individual military services. In the hopes of strengthening his own position, Field Marshal Keitel signed a working agreement with Rosenberg on November 9, 1940, but nothing changed; Rosenberg continued to restrict his activity to the selection of educational material.[62] After the winter crisis of 1941-42, high-ranking military personnel increasingly worried about how to strengthen fighting morale.[63] On July 15, 1942, the army issued instructions to employ writers for military indoctrination.[64]

After the catastrophe of Stalingrad, efforts to inculcate a militaristic spirit were intensified. On May 28, 1943,[65] orders went out to military commanders of the reserve corps, the General Government of Poland, Prague, and Denmark to set up officers for this task. Special officers for "political-ideological indoctrination" were thus employed down to battalion level. Ultimately the party assumed greater control, beginning with Hitler's personal efforts in the fall of 1943. He distinguished ideological indoctrination by the Wehrmacht from that of the Soviets by the motto, "officers here—commissars there," which became the *leitmotiv*.[66] As a result, military indoctrination was renamed "National Socialist guidance." This cleared the way for the NSFO—the National Socialist guidance officer [*Führungsoffizier*]. By January, 1944, Hitler and Bormann had ordered the creation of an NSFO staff within the OKW and had secured close cooperation with a party directorate composed of representatives sent by Rosenberg, Ley, Goebbels, and Dietrich, and also the head of the party's racial office.[67] The NSFO was directly subordinate to the troop commander, who continued to bear sole responsibility for National Socialist leadership in the Wehrmacht. But by then the project aimed at creating the "political soldier" had already failed in practice. In the fourth and fifth years of the war little time or opportunity remained for ideological indoctrination, especially among combat troops. Personal example and a spirit of comradeship continued to be the most important motives for troop cohesion.

Another area of activity for Wehrmacht propaganda was the fostering of troop morale; they were supported in this by a special department within the Propaganda Ministry and the Nazi group, "Strength through Joy" [*Kraft durch Freude*].[68] Wehrmacht propaganda was also subject to military censorship carried out by officers of the OKW, Propaganda Ministry, and the military services.[69] All military reports, commentaries and notices—even obituaries—were subject to censorship both of content and style.[70] Finally, military propaganda was also responsible for the "moral confusion of the enemy" and "winning over friendly neutral countries as allies and preventing hostile neutrals from joining the enemy or damaging our country through economic blockade;" it had to conduct

propaganda among the enemy's forces and among the populations of occupied hostile territory.[71]

Just like the Wehrmacht in its domain, the NSDAP had, since 1938,
mapped out its plans in case of war, listing as duties especially the
"maintenance and improvement of the populace's mental capacity for
resistance in war" and sundry services. Preparatory work included above
all education in national defence and "preparation for a unified effort
by all German women."[72] Finally, measures were prepared for the
evacuation of the population from the western border regions to the
interior.[73]

Preparations for possible mobilization had therefore been made since
the summer of 1938—hardly surprising in view of Hitler's plans. Hand-in-
hand with this went the systematic preparation of the population for the
regime's warlike measures. While one finds a readiness at that time to
fight a total war among military and also party circles, Hitler's concept
was that of localized campaigns or *Blitzkriege*, whereby he accepted but
underestimated the risk of an enlargement of the war.

SOURCES: RELIABILITY AND VALUE

From the start, the suspicion emerges that opinion reports were doctored by the regime. One also cannot dismiss the fact that many sound
like executive reports and that phrases like "the whole German nation"
or "the entire population" and similar generalizations have to be regarded
with utmost scepticism. Hitler's Deputy countered such vague or tendentious expressions by reporters and the Security Service sharply, since successful influence could only be attained through objective information
about the true opinions of a majority of the population. Not embellishment but an "unsparing candor" was demanded of informants in "rendering observed shortcomings." In 1938, the "guidelines for the preparation of political situation reports" and "technical reports" already stated
that "the Führer's Deputy attaches great importance to a detailed, unadorned portrayal of the general public mood."[74] The same applied to
agents of the Security Service: "It is expected that the public mood will
be presented frankly, without embellishment or propagandistic make-up,
i.e., objectively, clearly, reliably, as it is, not as it could or should be."[75]
Goebbels also pressed for rectification of SD and Gauleiter reports when
the information proved too superficial or the description incorrect.[76]

These numerous demands for a critical evaluation of the situation
leave the impression that opinion reports were often too rosy; a comparison between a few local SD reports and the final version from the of-

fice of deployment analysis [*Einsatz-Auswertungsstelle*] in Berlin also shows that the "*Meldungen aus dem Reich*" were often "moderated." Anyone reading the reports, however, is struck by the increasingly critical tenor of the varying attitudes. Reports were therefore more likely to be colored "in favor of the state leadership," especially during the first war years. Ohlendorf, his assistant von Kielpinski, as well as Himmler and even Bormann would not accept the failure of National Socialism as party ideology and as a system of government. The actual attitude of Germans toward National Socialist reality must be evaluated rather more negatively than is revealed in reports utilized for this study. However, it must also be remembered that contemporary assessments of opinion generally stemmed from the ideal standpoint of a never-realized National Socialist utopia, and every deviation from this vision was immediately interpreted negatively.

Yet it did finally seem too dangerous to the regime's leading figures, above all Goebbels and Bormann, to hand over, as before, more and more pessimistic reports to a sizable circle of readers.[77] Both became more aware of the majority's power to form opinions. After June, 1943, the form of SD reports was changed; they were now called "*Berichte zu Inlandfragen*" [reports on internal affairs]. Seemingly from 1944 on, the number of recipients was reduced and specific topics were treated primarily. Furthermore, the number of agents was lowered. Bormann and Ley prohibited party and Labor Front functionaries from working with the Security Service; the SA had issued a similar ban earlier. In the autumn of 1944, Ohlendorf, head of the internal intelligence service (division III), warned his workers not to get too involved in details and individual assessments, but rather to evaluate events within a total context—and naturally from a National Socialist perspective.[78] His department received more and more new subjects in order to give it renewed justification for existence.[79] Beginning in June, 1944, we have only scattered Security Service reports, referred to either as "reports on the development of public opinion" or as reports about "the consequences of the Hitler assassination attempt," the so-called "Kaltenbrunner-reports."[80] They stem from the pen of *Obersturmbannführer* von Kielpinski, who conducted the investigation of the assassination attempt. A report "Volk and Leadership,"[81] dated approximately at the end of March, 1945, and one of March nineteenth concerning "mood and attitude of the working class"[82] can also be attributed to him. SD reporting continued until Hitler's death, and even later in Plön and Flensburg, under his successor Dönitz.[83]

But not only the SD had been reprimanded since 1943 for its negative reporting. In April-May, 1943, appeals court presidents and state attorneys-general, who sent situation reports regularly, first monthly and then every three months, to the Reich Justice Ministry, apparently received the suggestion to shift emphasis away from mood and toward attitude.[84] Based on a circular from the Party Chancellory,[85] reports of party dignitaries also increasingly expounded firm attitudes in place of fluctuating moods, faithful to Hitler's remark of March, 1942: "If what the people say were decisive, then everything would have been lost long ago. The true attitude of the Volk is rooted much deeper and is based on a firm inner resolve."[86] Reports of the Reich propaganda offices to the Reich Ministry for Public Enlightenment and Propaganda were likewise criticized for their negative rendering of opinion, supposedly based on insignificant or invalid evidence.[87] On March 10, 1943, Goebbels announced that "he does not wish the word mood to be used anymore because one cannot talk of mood when houses are burned to the ground and cities devastated. He only wants to hear of good attitudes."[88] As early as July of that year, however, SD offices had to report "manifestations of a weakening of attitude among the population."[89] The demands for unadorned reports and a de-emphasis of serious occurrences were difficult to reconcile; in a majority of cases, blunt descriptions of even the most negative utterances predominated more and more. Exceptions, such as doctored reports and obvious embellishments, will be noted frequently in this study.

A word remains to be said about those groups within the population encompassed by the opinion reports. The definition of the SD's domestic intelligence work stated that all aspects of life were to be included.[90] Information was collected from all sources, voluntary reporters to full-time paid collaborators, from every stratum and occupational sector of society—evaluations were made centrally by a few main-office employees. An excerpt from one circular of the Stuttgart SD section [Leitabschnitt] clarifies the scope and possibilities for reporting: "Make sure that all elements of the population are constantly watched for their attitude. Every V-Mann must take advantage of every opportunity, be it in his family, his circle of friends and acquaintances, especially his place of work to learn, through inconspicuous conversation, the actual effect on opinions of all important foreign events and domestic measures. Furthermore, conversations among Volksgenossen in workers' trains, street cars, in stores, at the barber, kiosk, at government offices (food and ration card distribution centres, labor exchanges, city halls, etc.), at weekly markets, in pubs, factories and canteens—all offer a great abundance of informative clues, often too little noticed."[91]

Thus no one was sure his words were not being passed on: the HJ reported on what was going on in the schools, in clubs, in religious groups.[92] The Catholic and Evangelical League of Women was spied upon by the N.S. *Frauenschaft*;[93] even coffee klatsches were no longer a place for idle gossip.[94] Reports of the Bavarian district presidents, based on communications from subordinate local bodies, district magistrate offices and free [*kreisfreie*] towns, provide remarks that originate from the "lower strata of the social pyramid," the sphere of the "little man."[95] Appeals court presidents' and public prosecutors' reports touch primarily on the area of justice and civil service but contain many valuable references to the general mood. These are probably the most subjective, personally biased reports, running the gamut from assertions by convinced Nazis to surprisingly open and courageous statements. Collectively it is possible to say of the mass of documents, given the tremendous variety of sources from informants to bureaucrats, officers, and even soldiers (specially deployed among the forces in 1944),[96] that they possess evidence of a remarkably high quality; critically evaluated, they do largely enable an objective representation. Reports of unknown and anonymous informers, moreover, give not only an insight into the average German's "public" opinion, how he expressed it while on public transportation, in queues outside stores, etc., but also "private" views uttered in the smallest gathering.

One can divide the population, or "opinion-holders,"[97] into five groups: 1. the general public, or masses; 2. the interested public; 3. the informed public; 4. the opinion elite or opinion-makers, i.e., communications elite, the representatives of mass media, interest groups, and social institutions; and 5. the political elite.[98] Using this division, one can ascertain that public opinion research in the Third Reich embraced mainly the first two groups, sporadically also the third. We are therefore dealing with a hard-to-define majority, extending from the mass of politically uninformed and often uninterested to the interested and informed, excluding however, the small percentage of opinion-makers[99] and political elite.

If, within this context, we now take up once more the concept of public opinion [*öffentliche Meinung*], having already discussed its ambiguity, it seems advisable to use the concept of the public's opinion [*Publikumsmeinung*], except for the division into mood and attitude for totalitarian states. In this way the existence of a national opinion [*Volksmeinung*], proved beyond a doubt by this study, is affirmed, while at the same time we emphasize that it is difficult to find it manifested openly. Such a distinction could even be valid for democratic states if one combines all manifestations of opinion discussed in the mass media and otherwise publicly under the rubric public opinion [*öffentliche Meinung*]; the expression *Publikumsmeinung* could be used for otherwise registered views, be they of a private nature, polls, or other inquiries as well as literature or archival sources.

The decision to make the war years instead of the peace years of

National Socialism the subject of this study about public mood and attitude was essentially conditioned by the nature of the sources.[100] In a brief synthesis, the chapter on the pre-war years is intended to focus on trends and problems, but it makes no claims to be a thorough or definitive presentation of those years. Rather it is hoped that this inquiry will provide an incentive for continued, more detailed research which will permit similarities and differences before and during World War II to be worked out—answering precisely, as well, a number of questions merely indicated here. In this attempt to provide a total overview of the essential contents of the German public's opinion during the Second World War, not all complexities can be discussed completely or satisfactorily, especially since our knowledge of Nazi rule remains incomplete, despite a literature which mounts daily. This inquiry represents an initial contribution to the elucidation of a subject still largely unknown.

Numerous excerpts from representative reports are quoted and partially fitted together like a mosaic in order to reproduce the originality and authenticity of reported opinions and to avoid possible reproach for manipulating or forcing the truth to suit personal judgments. Commentaries and explanations are kept to a minimum; the course of the war and military operations are mentioned only insofar as necessary for a complete understanding or illumination of the public's reactions. A chronological approach was chosen despite its manifold disadvantages for dealing with clearly arranged individual problems—except for the self-contained chapters on euthanasia and persecution of the Jews. Organization according to themes would have precluded:

1.   presenting the constant interaction, dovetailing, and mutual influence of propaganda and coercion on the one hand and the public's opinions on the other;

2.   showing the differentiation and fluctuation of opinions in a totalitarian state;

3.   reproducing the intensity and changes of mood and attitude in a temporal dynamic.

NOTES

1.   Lenin's and Stalin's writings prove convincingly how aware the Bolshevik leaders were of the need not only to influence but also to convince the masses. The study by Alex. Inkeles, *Public Opinion in Soviet Russia* (Cambridge, 1958), shows the Soviet-communist application of propaganda, the role of agitators as well as the mass media.

2. Parliamentary systems have also used similar sources of information in times of war, as the study the French historian Pierre Renouvin proves: "L'opinion et la guerre en 1917," *Revue d'histoire moderne et contemporaine*, tome XV (January-March, 1968), pp. 4-23. As the mood became critical in France in 1917, a so-called "bureau du moral" of the General Headquarters analyzed reports from prefects, commanders of corps areas, the police, gendarmes, public prosecutors and postal surveillance service.

3. See, for example, S. Stansfeld Sargent and Robert Clifford Williams, *Social Psychology* (New York, 1966), 3rd. ed., p. 473.

4. Peter R. Hofstätter, *Psychologie der Öffentlichen Meinung* (Vienna, 1949), p. 18.

5. Heinz Boberach, *Meldungen aus dem Reich* (Berlin, 1965), hereafter cited as Boberach.

6. *Goebbels Tagebücher aus den Jahren 1942 bis 1943*, edited by Louis P. Lochner (Zurich, 1948), pp. 114, 140, 171, 220, 303 (hereafter cited as *Tagebücher*).

7. See the detailed bibliography: sources, *infra*, pp. 345 ff.

8. See the Anordnung des Stellvertreters des Führers Nr. 201/38 of December 14, 1938: BA, NS 6/vorl. 231; and especially the Rundschreiben des Leiters der Parteikanzlei Nr. 26/43g of August 21, 1942 concerning "Zusammenarbeit der Parteidienststellen mit dem Sicherheitsdienst in Fragen der Berichterstattung und Nachrichtenbeschaffung": BA, NS6/344.

9. See, for example, the letter of the district president of Upper Bavaria to the Landräte and Oberbürgermeister of the district, Nr. 13 640/16 of July 12, 1940, concerning the cooperation with the Security Service, Munich section: HStA Oberbayern *Fasz.* 204, Nr. 3243; and the correspondence between the Chief of the SD, Heydrich, and General Reinecke, as well as the reply of Field Marshal Keitel (April 1 and 30, and May 23, 1940) to the demand for political situation reports: MGFA WO 1-5/180.

10. It is particularly regrettable that it has been impossible to locate the reports of the Berlin Polizeipräsidenten on the mood of Berliners. Berlin's mood was considered indicative and a determining factor for the overall mood, especially by Goebbels.

11. A part of the contemporary documents from lesser state authorities is still in the registries of the competent authorities and must still be transferred to state archives. One can therefore expect a yield of documents in coming years providing additional information about regional opinion trends and hopefully also facilitating detailed studies of individual social strata and problems. We can also assume that a number of these documents fell into the hands of the Soviet Union in 1945 and are in the DDR. The Deutsche Zentralarchiv in Potsdam informed the author in January, 1968, that they have no such material.

12. Telegram Nr. 166 (August 3, 1939) to von Schulenburg, German ambassador in Moscow: *Nazi-Soviet Relations, 1939-1941*. Documents from the Archives of the German Foreign Office, ed. by James Sontag and James Stuart Beddie (Washington, 1948), p. 38.

13. BA, *Alliierte Prozesse* L XXVII A 5/6, pp. 514, 515; mentioned by Boberach, p. xvii.

14. Henry Picker, *Tischgespräche im Führerhauptquartier 1941-1942*, rev. ed. by Percy Ernst Schramm (Stuttgart, 1967), pp. 206-7.

15. Letter of the former SS-Hauptsturmführer and long-time member of the Einsatz-Auswertungsstelle der SD in Berlin, Paul Neukirchen (October 6, 1969).
16. Albert Speer, *Erinnerungen* (Frankfurt, Berlin, 1969), p. 266.
17. Hofstätter, *Psychologie der Öffentlichen Meinung*, p. 148.
18. Emil Dovifat, *Zeitungslehre*, vol. II: *Theoretische Grundlagen—Nachricht und Meinung, Sprache und Form* (Berlin, 1937), pp. 97-98.
19. *Ibid.*
20. Franz Schneider, *Politik und Kommunikation. Drei Versuche* (Mainz, 1967), p. 48.
21. It corresponds to the concept "attitude" used by G. W. Allport in 1935 as a fundamental and essential concept of contemporary American social psychology; numerous studies attest to its continued use, and not only in the USA. Cf. Otto Klineberg, *Psychologie sociale* (Paris, 1967), pp. 541ff.; and Jean Stoetzel, "La conception de la notion d'attitude en psychologie sociale," *Sondages*, Nr. 2 (1963), pp. 20-50.
22. undated (1943?): BA, ZSg 3/424.
23. *op. cit.*, p. 108.
24. Ruth Andreas-Friedrich, *Schauplatz Berlin. Ein deutsches Tagebuch.* (Munich, 1962), p. 81.
25. Alexander and Margarete Mitscherlich, *Die Unfähigkeit zu trauern. Grundlagen kollektiven Verhaltens.* (Munich, 1968), p. 21.
26. Typical of this is, for example, the study by B. Schaffner, *Fatherland* (New York, 1948) based on the ICD Screening Center's analysis, culminating in the assertion that National Socialism was not a revolution of German life, but rather a continuation and intensification of a traditional way of life. The appendix includes an essay about the collective guilt of the German people (cf. pp. 80, 151 ff).
27. St. Milgram, "Behavioral Study of Obedience," *Journal of Abnormal Social Psychology*, No. 67, pp. 372, 378—commented upon by Irenäus Eibl-Eibesfeldt, *Grundriss der vergleichenden Verhaltensforschung* (Munich), pp. 434-38.
28. Schaffner, *op. cit.*, pp. 15 ff.
29. Erich Fromm, *Escape from Freedom* (New York, 1941).
30. *The Authoritarian Personality* (New York, 1950).
31. Cf. Hofstätter, *Einführung in die Sozialpsychologie* (Stuttgart, Vienna, 1954), pp. 446 ff.
32. Hermann Glaser, *Eros und Politik. Eine sozialpathologische Untersuchung* (Cologne, 1967), pp. 122 ff.
33. *Massenwahn in Geschichte und Gegenwart. Ein Tagungsbericht*, ed. by Wilhelm Bitter (Stuttgart, 1965), pp. 12 ff.
34. BA, Slg. Schumacher 365.
35. David Schoenbaum, *Hitler's Social Revolution: Class and Status in Nazi Germany* 1933-1939 (New York, 1966), p. xxii.
36. Mitscherlich, p. 34.
37. Friedrich Meinecke, *Die Deutsche Katastrophe* (Wiesbaden, 1946).
38. Ralf Dahrendorf, *Gesellschaft und Demokratie in Deutschland* (Munich, 1965), p. 442.
39. cited by Dovifat, pp. 101-2.
40. About the regime's techniques, i.e., silence, lies, distortions, etc., see

Walter Hagemann, *Publizistik im Dritten Reich* (Hamburg, 1948).

41. *Tagebücher.*

42. *Kriegspropaganda 1939-1941. Geheime Ministerkonferenzen im Reichspropagandaministerium,* ed. with introduction by Willi A. Boelcke (Stuttgart, 1966); later published as *"Wollt Ihr den totalen Krieg?" Die Geheimen Goebbels-Konferenzen 1939-1943 (1967),* by Boelcke.

43. *Ibid.,* p. 293.

44. *Kriegspropaganda,* pp. 126 ff.

45. Cf. pp. 11 ff. below.

46. Z. A. B. Zeman, *Nazi Propaganda* (London, 1964), 2nd. ed. 1965, p. 160.

47. *Tagebücher,* p. 197.

48. BA, ZSg 109/42, fol. 3a.

49. Cf. BA, ZSg 101, 102, 109.

50. BA, Slg, Schumacher 368.

51. Cf. *Buch-Hinweis Nr. 2 des Vertreters des Beauftragten des Führers für die Überwachung der gesamten geistigen und weltanschaulichen Schulung der NSDAP in Gau Baden,* of June 7, 1940: BA, NS Misch 1422.

52. See the draft of a letter by Reichsleiter Rosenberg to Robert Ley: BA, NS Misch 1421; and the "Vertrauliche Information" der Parteikanzlei, Beitrag 962, of November 13, 1942: BA, ZSg 3/1622.

53. See, for example, the letter of Ley to Hess, October 20, 1939, characterizing schooling [*Schulung*] as almost more important than propaganda: BA, NS 22/vorl. 713; or see diverse manuscripts in NS 22/vorl. 29 about Schulung of N.S. leaders to penetrate the broad strata of the Volk; or "Schulung für die praktisch-politische Menschenführung im Krieg" (Kreisleiter Paul Groh from Nürtingen), March 11, 1942 to Hauptschulungsamt Munich, which was already preparing post-war schooling.

54. Cf. Wolfgang Sauer, "Die Mobilmachung der Gewalt," in Bracher, Sauer, Schulz, *Die nationalsozialistische Machtergreifung* (Cologne-Opladen, 1960), pp. 808 ff.

55. Erich Ludendorff, *Meine Kriegserinnerungen 1914-1918* (Berlin, 1919), pp. 292 ff.

56. Ludendorff took up a project of Colonel Bauer, who in 1917 had already demanded a dictatorial direction of the press. Bethmann Hollweg had in fact dealt numerously with the problem of public opinion, but his efforts were torpedoed by the parties, OHL and the Kaiser. Cf. Wolfgang-Mommsen, "L'opinion allemande et la chute du gouvernement Bethmann Hollweg en juillet 1917," *Revue d'histoire moderne et contemporaine,* tome XV (January-March, 1968), pp. 39-53. For Bethmann Hollweg's earlier efforts to influence the public in the interests of war aims and peace negotiations, see Wolfgang J. Mommsen, "Die Regierung Bethmann Hollweg und die öffentliche Meinung 1914-1917," VfZG, Heft 2 (1969), pp. 117-59.

57. no date (1937-1938?), 35-page manuscript: MGFA WO 1-6/344. Cf. also "Wehrpropaganda und Wehrpolitik im wahren Staat," by Major (E) Dr. Hüsing, submitted at the beginning of 1938, 65-page manuscript.

58. Cf. MGFA WO 1-6/344 and 499, especially the lecture by Major Hielscher on August 26, 1938, on "Die vorbereitende Zusammenarbeit von Wehrmacht und Propaganda im Krieg."

59. The term was suggested by Colonel Ludewig and accepted by the OKW and RMVP on September 3, 1938, in the revised "Richtlinien für die

Zusammenarbeit zwischen Wehrmacht und Reichsministerium für Volksaufklärung und Propaganda in Fragen der Kriegspropaganda," in place of the original concept of "Propaganda-Einsatzstelle." See "Bericht über Tätigkeit als Reichsverteidigungsreferent im Reichsministerium für Volksaufklärung und Propaganda in der Zeit vom 15. Juli 1938 bis 31. Januar 1940," by Lieutenant-Colonel Wentscher: MGFA WO 1-6/349. For the creation and development of propaganda battalions see this report and the comprehensive presentation by Boelcke in *Kriegspropaganda 1939 bis 1941*, pp. 127-30.

60. The front newspapers obtained their information from: 1. the weekly correspondence of the OKW, "Stimme der Heimat"; 2. the "Mitteilungen für die Truppe," appearing twice weekly; 3. the daily "Nachrichten des Oberkommandos der Wehrmacht"; and 4. Bilderdiensten, DNB-Diensten, material of the propaganda battalions and troop comments. Cf. Merkblatt für Frontzeitungen, May, 1941: MGFA WO 1-6/391.

61. Cf. Erich Murawski, *Der deutsche Wehrmachtsbericht 1939-1945. Ein Beitrag zur Untersuchung der geistigen Kriegführung. Mit einer Dokumentation der Wehrmachtberichte vom 1. 7. 1944 bis 9. 5. 1945* (Boppard, 1962).

62. MGFA WO 1-6/324.

63. MGFA WO 1-5/179; and Volker R. Berghahn, "NSDAP und 'geistige Führung' der Wehrmacht," VfZG H. 1. (January, 1969), p. 29.

64. Oberkommando des Heeres Gen.z.b.V./H Wes.Abt. Az II Nr. 250/7 42 geh.—copy in BA, NS 6/vorl. 344.

65. Stab/Ic Nr. 3714/43 geh. BA NS 6/vorl. 344.

66. Berghahn, "NSDAP und 'geistige Führung' der Wehrmacht 1939 bis 1943," p. 51.

67. Copy of the Hitler order in BA, NS 6/vorl. 344. Cf. Anordnung 6/44 des Leiters der Partei-Kanzlei (January 7, 1944). *Ibid.*

68. Oberkommando der Wehrmacht AWA Az. 31-J(IIc) Nr. 1450/40 of March 23, 1940, regarding "Freizeitgestaltung . . ." MGFA Wo 1-6/179, and *Kriegspropaganda*, p. 130.

69. *Ibid.*, p. 132.

70. See, for example, MGFA WO 1-6/474, or the criticism of the manuscript "Kompanie-Tagebuch des 9. I.R. 43," which asserts in particular that there is more talk of the "horrors of war and its hardships" instead of "singing the praises of the brave soldiers." Cf. also General Jodl's criticism of an essay destined for the Japanese press (February 24, 1941); MGFA WO 1-6/479.

71. Cf. "Stichworte zur Besprechung der WPr O's und Führer der Prop. Komp," including Jodl's paragraphs: MGFA WO 1-6/498.

72. "Arbeitspläne der Reichsleitung der NSDAP für den Einsatz der Polizei und der angeschlossenen Verbände im A-Falle," issued by Abteilung M of Rudolf Hess' staff (May 16, 1938): BA, NS 6/vorl. 355.

73. Der Stellvertreter des Führers. Stab Abteilung M. I Az. 23/March 14, 1939, Tgb. Nr. 49/39g Rs. signed by SS-Brigadeführer Knoblauch. *Ibid.*

74. Der Stellvertreter des Führers. Stabsleiter, October 31, 1938. Added to the "Richtlinien" were precise directions and a detailed plan for the preparation of "Politische Lageberichte" by party functionaries; it covered general mood as well as the scope of NSDAP functions, those of Propaganda, Schulung, ecclesiastical matters, state enemies, Jewry, military, etc.—a total of thirty points. BA, NS 6/vorl. 231. An even more detailed plan cov-

ering forty points for a monthly "Tätigkeits- und Stimmungsbericht" was issued by Hess on December 21, 1934. Cf. Peter Diehl-Thiele, *Partei und Staat im Dritten Reich. Untersuchungen zum Verhältnis von NSDAP und allgemeiner Staatsverwaltung 1933-1945* (Munich, 1969), pp. 229 ff.

75. Sicherheitsdienst des RFSS SD-Leitabschnitt Stuttgart III C 4-Ry/ho Rundschreiben Nr. 168 (October 12, 1940): HStA Stuttgart K 750/38.

76. *Kriegspropaganda*, p. 211 (ministerial conference of October 26, 1939).

77. It was impossible to determine exactly which group of individuals received SD reports. Recipients included all Reich ministers and NSDAP Reich leaders. Individual reports, however, also seem to have been forwarded to interested administration offices and especially in the latter stages to the Wehrmacht. Cf., for example, the Vernichtungsprotokolle in BA, MA Wi/VIII 48.

78. "Aus dem Stenogramm der Ansprache von Amtschef III am 31. 10. 1944": BA, R58/990.

79. Cf. Heinz Höhne, *Der Orden unter dem Totenkopf. Die Geschichte der SS* (Gütersloh, 1967), p. 394.

80. Published in *Spiegelbild einer Verschwörung. Die Kaltenbrunner-Berichte an Bormann und Hitler über das Attentat vom 20. Juli 1944*. Geheime Dokumente aus dem ehemaligen Reichssicherheitshauptamt, by the Archiv Peter für historische und zeitgeschichtliche Dokumentation (Stuttgart, 1961). The actual records for these reports were stored in a bunker on the Prinz-Albrecht-Strasse and likely fell into Soviet hands. This information comes from Paul Neukirchen who also said that further holdings of the Inlandnachrichtendienst, stored in Kleistdorf, southeast of Frankfurt/Oder, must have been found by the Soviets.

81. Excerpts first published by Marlis G. Steinert in *Die 23 Tage der Regierung Dönitz* (Düsseldorf, Vienna, 1967), pp. 18-19.

82. BA, R55/625, fol. 129, 132.

83. Cf. Steinert, p. 147. Paul Neukirchen told the author that in the last days before Hitler's death, daily opinion reports were still delivered to Hitler's bunker and to fighting commanders in Berlin; Ohlendorf meanwhile moved with part of his staff first to Schwerin, then Eutin and finally Plön. Furthermore, reports of the Leiters Pro. in RMVP, still mention SD reports as their source in 1945 and a letter of Bormann to Kaltenbrunner (April 4, 1945) criticizes the SD report he had received that day as "typical" in its generalizations. BA, R58/976.

84. OLG-Präsident Zweibrücken (July 31, 1943), BA, R22/3389.

85. see below, p. 169.

86. Picker, p. 206.

87. The activity reports of Reich propaganda offices were only supposed to report the important aspects of the public's mood if it concerned the tasks and activity of the Propaganda Ministry. Its actual assignment was supposed to consist of: 1. an overview of the political-propaganda situation and 2. propaganda recommendations. Since these functions were difficult to isolate from the general mood—investigated by the SD—it was ordered that discussions concerning these reports with other offices and ministries be kept to a minimum. BA, R55/603, fol. 2, 3; and R55/620, fol. 186. Cf. also Rundschreiben of Propaganda Ministry to all RPÄ Propa 2061/27 (February 27, 1943): BA, R55/603, fol. 186.

88. *"Wollt Ihr den totalen Krieg?"*, p. 345.

89. Boberach, pp. 416 ff.
90. Cf. the copy of a report by Ohlendorf "Der innenpolitische lebensgebiets-mässige Nachrichtendienst in Deutschland," in Boberach, pp. 534 ff.
91. see footnote 75.
92. "SD-Leitabschnitt Stuttgart II 113-D 227-07 Rundschreiben Nr. 132 of August 21, 1940, Betr. Organisierung einer weltanschaulichen Gegnerbeobachtung in der HJ": HStA Stuttgart K750/38.
93. SD RFSS-Unterabschnitt Württemberg-Hohenzollern II 113 WD/Rdsch. 115 of June 30, 1939: HStA Stuttgart K750/36.
94. Report from Kreis Hanau for June-July, 1939: BA, NS Misch/1682, fol. 149,467.
95. *Die Kirchliche Lage in Bayern nach den Regierungspräsidentenberichten 1933-1943*. I. Regierungsbezirk Oberbayern, ed. by Helmut Witetschek (Mainz, 1966), pp. xi, xii. The preface by Dieter Albrecht provides a detailed report about the formation and value of the sources.
96. Cf. Volker R. Berghahn, "Meinungsforschung im Dritten Reich. Die Mundpropaganda-Aktion der Wehrmacht im letzten Kriegshalbjahr," *Militärgeschichtliche Mitteilungen* (Freiburg, 1/67), pp. 83-119; cf. also p. below.
97. Cf. James N. Rosenau, *Public Opinion and Foreign Policy*. An Operational Formulation (New York, 1961).
98. Gabriel Almond, *The American People and Foreign Policy* (New York, 1950), pp. 138 ff.
99. For the United States, Elmo Roper, separating opinion makers into "Great Disseminators" and "Lesser Disseminators," estimated 250-1000 for the former and 15,000-50,000 for the latter. See preface by Roper in Elihu Katz and Paul F. Lazarsfeld, *Personal Influence. The Part Played by People in the Flow of Mass Communications* (Glencoe, Illinois, 1955), p. vii.
100. Only fragmentary reports of the Gestapo, a few from Regierungsbezirke and Hoheitsträger der Partei and other Nazi organizations are available for the pre-war period. The documents of state offices pertain to only certain regions and times; SD reports as a tool of continuing public opinion research are only available from October, 1939, even though the SD began to collect reports of the public's mood as early as 1933. The annual report for 1938 and a quarterly report for the first quarter of 1939 were used for the pre-war chapter.

PROLOGUE

ON MARCH 5, 1933, after a campaign of unprecedented scope in Germany, Hitler succeeded in capturing only 17,277,180 votes (43.9 per cent), an increase of 5.5 million over the previous election, despite the use of thinly veiled street terror. The Social Democrats remained the second strongest party with 7,181,620 votes, followed by the Communists (4,848,058), the Center (4,424,900) and the German Nationalists with 3,136,760. Collectively therefore, the government coalition received only 51.9 per cent of the vote. Not even half the German electorate had supported Hitler in an election already tainted by intimidation.

Areas of political Catholicism and traditional labor strongholds remained largely faithful to their old parties: the Center, SPD and KPD. Minimal resistance was offered in Protestant-conservative districts. The NSDAP did enlarge its following in the Catholic-federalist regions of the Rhineland and also in Bavaria, but except for the Communists, already on the wane, the other parties had retained approximately the same number of votes. Increased Nazi returns came from newly eligible voters and those who had previously stayed at home.

Detailed vote analysis reveals that in March, 1933, there were still numerous electoral districts where the NSDAP had been unable to capture first place.[1] The Center Party, for instance, held its ground in the Catholic districts and communities of East Prussia, the electoral border district of Oppeln in Upper Silesia, the Catholic districts of Thuringia, particularly in Weser-Ems, and partly in South Hanover-Brunswick; its most triumphant results came in North and South Westphalia, Cologne-Aachen, Koblenz-Trier and also parts of Hesse-Nassau. While the

Catholic parties declined in Upper and Lower Bavaria, where the National Socialists had begun their victory march, communities in Upper Swabia and Baden generally resisted the NSDAP's pull. But neither here nor in Württemberg and Bavaria did the Center and its ally, the Bavarian People's Party, register the success achieved in the Catholic regions of northern Germany.

The parties of the Left held their ground, especially in the working class districts of Berlin and Potsdam, the electoral districts of Magdeburg and Merseburg, in Thuringia, and naturally in industrial Saxony. In Schleswig-Holstein, scene of National Socialist victories during the Weimar Republic's last days, the Left in four instances won majorities exceeding 60 per cent—this compared with success in one community in heavily Protestant East Hanover and several cases of Left and Center majorities in adjacent South Hanover-Brunswick. There were some majorities, but seldom as spectacular, in mixed confessional areas such as Hesse-Nassau and Hesse-Darmstadt. In any case, the NSDAP suffered its worst defeats in several of Württemberg's Catholic and industrial communities. In Düsseldorf's electoral districts, which had proven quite susceptible to National Socialism, only a residue of Center and Leftist support, more Communist than SPD, remained. Leftists could hold their own in a few areas of Franconia and the Pfalz, but they showed far greater strength in Hamburg and Bremen where the NSDAP also failed to win convincingly. Only the electoral district of Mecklenburg provided the Nazis with such a victory.

Remnants of the old geographical vote distribution were still evident in the pseudo-legal plebiscites of 1933/34, following the withdrawal from the League of Nations and Hitler's assumption of the Reich Presidency.[2] Clearly evident were the heavy losses of the confessional element, with only mild activity in its traditional strongholds of Koblenz-Trier, Cologne-Aachen and Westphalia. Protestant areas composed of small towns and agricultural hinterland were most susceptible to the state party's attraction and pressure.[3] Ultimately, bourgeois artisan towns and north German industrial cities proved most resistant, while Catholic cities and the south German region in general were more susceptible to the National Socialist virus. Overall one has to interpret these ostensibly legal acclamations more as a decline and as a further dispersion of the opposition's strength since March, 1933.

It is far more difficult to determine how much more support National Socialism obtained in subsequent years, and the degree and location of the remnants of opposition. Any meaningful answer to these questions requires, besides an interpretation of electoral trends, a recognition of the dual mandate of National Socialism—nationalism and socialism—

and of the expectations these evoked among the various social classes. The synthesis of these two great ideals or forces (the French "idée-force"), which gained strength primarily in nineteenth-century Europe, inspired people not only in the inter-war period nor solely in Germany. These intellectually and politically complex phenomena made demands which, reduced to their lowest common denominator, were greater social justice at home and an international image of a strong, united nation; this had a magnetic effect on a German society frustrated by its defeat in World War I, burdened with sole responsibility for the war, and shaken by inflation, hunger and deprivation.

The NSDAP's composition affords certain information about the strong attraction of these watchwords and ideas. Until 1930 the NSDAP was "by and large a party of völkisch provincialism;" after the outbreak of the economic crisis, it had become more "an organization of the desperate, with a considerable mixture of opportunism."[4] Party membership rose from the end of 1928 to the beginning of 1931 in proportion to the number of unemployed. Likewise, a relative increase in working-class members is evident, although, along with the peasants, they had the smallest representation, given total population figures; white-collar employees, meanwhile, were overrepresented by 90 per cent, as were the economically independent (100 per cent), civil servants, and teachers (each about 25 per cent).[5] The middle classes [*Mittelstand*] clearly dominated the movement. Since the turn of the century their growth had signalled a restructuring of society, without, however, building an adequate political base. By the end of the Weimar Republic, the NSDAP alone among the parties had been able to win over *en bloc* those previously apolitical, as well as the pro-conservative and pro-liberal among the *Mittelstand*. Anti-liberal, anti-democratic, anti-capitalist and anti-Semitic emotions played a significant role. A further striking characteristic of the NSDAP was its age grouping: it was primarily a party of the youth.[6] This social and age structure confirms one of the party's mandates—change of the status quo, of social conditions as well as of the establishment.

Unfortunately no comprehensive social history of the Third Reich exists which provides a thorough analysis of the relationship between National Socialist promises as contained in its program and their translation into reality. David Schoenbaum's *Hitler's Social Revolution*, Arthur Schweitzer's study, *Big Business in the Third Reich*, Robert O'Neill's *The German Army and the Nazi Party 1933-1939*, and Hans Mommsen's *Beamtentum im Dritten Reich*[7] give a tentative and partial explanation of the ties and interactions between the National Socialist state and the various elements of the population, of the realization or disregard of the party program. Karl Dietrich Bracher's *The German Dictatorship* provides an even deeper interpretation of these dimensions.[8] Still lacking is a synoptic study of the attitude of the intellectual elite.[9] Not a small number of them proved vulnerable to the Nazi watchwords[10] and failed miserably in their claim to spiritual leadership of the nation. Despite this "self-destruction" (Bracher), the results here also fell far short of the new governing elite's ideal conceptions. The annual situation report of the Reich Security Office for 1938 confirmed "the predominance of liberal attitudes in today's intellectual, scientific and university circles" and that "liberal influences have grown stronger in cultural spheres."[11] Although numerous intellectuals and artists paid public tribute to the new masters, in general an attempt was made to check party encroachments as far as possible and preserve the realm of science from ideological entanglements. "There are complaints at all universities about the passive behavior of lecturers who reject all political and philosophical issues which extend beyond the narrow confines of their specialties. One can speak of open and clear initiatives for National Socialism only among a small, particularly young, group of lecturers."[12] It is far more difficult to work out representative opinions and dispositions for this relatively small segment of the population, in comparison to other strata of German society, because individual attitudes are naturally more pronounced and thus more divergent here.[13]

To date little is known about the attitude of women towards this German variety of fascism,[14] except that true-blooded Nazis, with their delusions of masculinity, regarded them as second-class citizens and relegated them to the traditional three K's—*Kinder, Küche, Kirche.** The intellectual woman was despised; even more so the politicized woman.[15] Her only appropriate activities were motherhood, the household, and certain "natural" women's work. The majority of German women, furthermore, showed little inclination to greater freedom and went along with the views of the Third Reich. Despite mutual disregard for emancipation and conscious discrimination against women professionals during the years of high unemployment, the trend toward industrialization could not be arrested; the number of working women rose from 4.24 million in 1933 to 4.52 million in 1936, reaching 5.2 million by 1938.[16] Politically, women remained inactive. The Weimar Republic had given them the vote, but the splintering of parties and myriad economic and social stresses made the first German Republic appealing to few women. On the other hand, Hitler's emotion-tinged program and the pseudo-religious qualities attributed to his person as well as his "movement" brought many women under his spell.

* children, kitchen, church

It is evident today that the despairing, the hungry, and the dispos-
sessed who thronged to National Socialism during the economic crisis
realized only a modest change in the promised and hoped-for transformation of social circumstances. The severe social decline in terms of material essentials prevailed despite the heavy tribute paid by all segments
of society. The real losers were the "new" middle class and the previously disadvantaged lower classes, to whom the party was especially
indebted for its rise. Employees and small businessmen registered
meager gains. Artisan and middle class socialism flourished organiza-
tionally, but otherwise was lost in a smoke-screen of voluminous propaganda campaigns.

Anti-Semitic measures and Jew-baiting, particularly in the form of
the September 15, 1935, law for the protection of German blood,[17]
should therefore be considered not solely as a product of a Weltanschauung but as a conscious expedient to divert latent resentment among
the above classes away from the Nazi state. "The exposure of the Jewish
question in the press and in speeches has evoked a positive echo from
among all classes. More succinct propaganda against shopping in Jewish
stores will not only serve our principles but also lift the slightly depressed atmosphere within middle class circles. . . ."[18] This assertion
by the Cologne Gauleiter seems dubious and has at most a regional
validity. Yet it is mentioned as an indication of the tactical significance
of anti-Semitism, beyond merely gaining middle class support. Hitler
later confirmed this in his "table talks," in which he praised the achievements of Streicher, Gauleiter of central Franconia and publisher of the
gutter journal, *Der Stürmer*, for detaching the workers from the Jewish
leaders of the SPD and KPD through his continuous vituperation of the
Jews.[19]

Hitler's plans for German parity with other major European powers,
and an eventual continental hegemony, required an economic and
military recovery hardly compatible with social revolution, or, actually,
counter-revolution, as outlined in the original party program with its
pre-capitalist tendencies—tendencies which reflected middle class resentment against capitalism and the working class.[20] For tactical reasons,
the German dictatorship initially allied itself with the established powers
of big industry and the military against leftist social reformers and
traditional statists. Later Hitler achieved more complete subservience to
the state by playing off economic interest groups within industry and
repressing conservative elements within the officer corps.[21] Civil service
acquiescence promoted the consolidation of Nazi power. Many bureaucrats had anticipated a continuation of Brüning's "objective politics"
by the Third Reich; those initially not sympathetic to the regime were

won over through traditional loyalty to the state or through massive pressure:[22] in 1937, 63 per cent of all civil servants were party members, compared with 11 per cent in 1933.[23] Over the years, however, the civil service, in order to fight the "undermining of its competence" and an advancing "institutional degeneracy," found itself forced into conflicting roles as executor and antagonist of a Nazi hierarchy hostile to bureaucracy.[24] Dissenting civil servants, and particularly teachers, were pressured into active participation in the party by such means as non-promotion, arbitrary transferral, or dismissal. Clearly the consolidation of power through elimination of political opponents and collaboration with existing institutional and economic authorities, as well as the priority of national and foreign policy problems, left little room for social reforms.

Highly characteristic of this evasion of social promises is the National Socialist version of the much heralded "socialism of the deed." It consisted of a few welfare-state programs and a great number of regulations and policies designed to enhance the interest of the state. The means of production were not socialized—only the social relationships among the worker, artisan, and peasant were extolled, although they seldom enjoyed the "social gains." It was an honor to be a worker, to be a farmer living on his own soil, or to be a soldier offering himself to the fatherland. The importance that was given to these social groups was thus more of a psychological nature rather than the attribution of concrete social benefits. NSDAP membership figures reveal a caution, sympathy as well as opportunism: in 1935 workers were still 30 per cent underrepresented, the peasant as much as 100 per cent, while employees were overrepresented by about 65 per cent, independently self-employed by 100 percent and civil servants by 160 per cent.[25]

In the first years, the regime's prestige was enhanced considerably by declining unemployment. This success rested both on mounting rearmament and on a diminishing world economic crisis, with the regime adopting economic and financial measures already prepared or initiated during the last years of the Weimar Republic. While optically very convincing when compared with 1932, the conditions in the Third Reich did not stand favorable comparison with 1928: the share of salaries and wages in the national product was smaller, the share of industrial and commercial profits larger.[26] National Socialist economic and fiscal policies, which promoted this inequality of income and capital distribution, were geared primarily to the interests of forced rearmament, necessitating a reduction of social benefits through restrained consumption.[27] Workers, furthermore, had lost all their legal rights to freedom of movement, at the latest by 1938, with the building of the West

Wall; they had no right to organize, to negotiate independently on wages, or even to strike—but they had work and an element of security. Bitter resentment resulted over the salary differentials in the various economic sectors which conformed to the Nazi principle of "suitable wage." Mining and armaments were ranked at the top, while salaries were far too low in many other sectors. To achieve equalization through premiums proved difficult in most instances. Nevertheless, the Cologne Gauleiter, in 1935, believed he could ensure that the working class "was generally very decent and acted faithfully toward the state and the movement. Marxism had lost its fertile soil and its support. . . ."[28]

This last statement has only conditional validity. The traditionally marxist-oriented worker silently remained faithful to his old party. Through word of mouth, whispering campaigns, or leaflets, a minimum of agitation was maintained in an attempt to refocus discontent over social legislation against the Nazi regime.[29] "The KPD's objective was to create a reservoir of malcontents from all camps."[30] Like the Communist leaders, those of the Social Democratic Party also were imprisoned or had to emigrate. Contacts could only be maintained with difficulty and through illegal associations. "The goal of this illegal activity was to collect confidants of the working class from among its dissidents who would later form the nucleus for the coming day of liberation."[31] One can generally concur with the Reich Security Office: "The mood of the former marxist following in the Reich cannot be characterized as unified. Besides those circles for and against the Reich, there are also elements who rigidly refrain from all political involvement and devote themselves exclusively to their private interests."[32] Unable to articulate their displeasure on a political level, many workers were led to manifest loudly their dissatisfaction with social conditions. In a report for May, 1937, from the district of Bentheim, the Reich Women's League head, Mrs. Scholtz-Klinck, stated: "The discontent among the citizenry is greater than ever. They are holding the National Socialist regime responsible for the shortage of raw materials."[33] In the report for June, 1937, complaints of the Upper Silesian miners and the textile workers of Weser-Ems and North Westphalia were cited.[34]

Shortages of foodstuffs and daily essentials as well as rising prices, the effects of Hitler's autarchic policy, were considered oppressive by the 'little man.'[35] The governor of the Pfalz, on August 10, 1939, reported "heavy resentment among large segments of the population, in particular the workers, employees, and civil servants, over the unjustifiably high food prices."[36] Salary reductions in the building trade produced negative assessments of Nazi wage policy by construction workers; according to the report of one local party leader, "output declining, mood absolutely wretched."[37] Since the shortage of building materials had brought housing construction almost to a halt by 1939, disgruntlement extended beyond those unable to find decent housing to the artisans and small concerns who no longer received public contracts.[38] The indignation over the impact of the Four Year Plan is highlighted in the June, 1939, report from the district party leader of Biedenkopf-Dillenburg: "Among the working class there is large-scale discontent over the regulations arising out of the Four Year Plan, restricting freedom of individual movement much like compulsory military service, the directives establishing maximum wages and circumscription on a worker's right to terminate employment. The worker fails to understand why these regulations should adversely affect labor 90 per cent of the time while it hits the employer perhaps 10 per cent and the civil servants not at all. The worker is prepared to make any sacrifice if he can see that the burden is shared by the nation as a whole. . . ."[39]

Besides the workers, peasants and farmers were also disappointed and felt disadvantaged by the new regime. The party's blood-and-soil prophet, R. Walther Darré,[40] organized the farmers into a league, the *Reichnährstand*.[41] The Nazi farm program was based on the principles of control over markets and prices, stabilization of landed ownership in the form of an entailed estates law (*Reichserbhofgesetz*),[42] favorable credit for indebted farmers, and a land-planning scheme intended to redistribute population. Only the first principle was applied with any consistency— all the other provisions only in part or incompletely. Here, too, the privileged benefitted more than those at the bottom of the social pyramid; in 1938 Junker debts had already been reduced by 18.6 per cent, that of entailed peasants only by 15.5 per cent.[43] Large landowners, furthermore, were able to thwart original Nazi plans regarding their estates.[44] Despite price supports, peasant income in 1937 constituted only 8.3 per cent of the national income, down from 8.7 per cent in 1933. Propaganda notwithstanding, the ideal natural and simple rural life was enjoyed by only 18 per cent in 1939 compared with 20.8 per cent in 1933, while the percentage of employees in agriculture and forestry dropped from 28.9 to 26 per cent of the total work force. The consequences of sustained rural emigration, reflecting unrelenting industrialization, were longer hours and smaller profits for the farmer. Milk and butter production declined weekly to the extent that by the summer of 1939 the Reich was living off the cooking-fat reserves stored in September, 1938, in case of war.[45] Conditions looked just as bleak for the grain industry. Many a field lay fallow because of a rural labor shortage totalling 600,000 by 1938; there was also a need for some 333,000 marriageable women between the ages of seventeen and thirty-four. No wonder peasant attitudes fluctuated between despair and stupefaction: "This development creates a feeling of being crushed and tends towards an attitude partly of resignation and partly of a revolutionary discontent vis-a-vis the peasant leadership."[46] Passivity prevailed, however, in this social class, never noted for its revolutionary zeal: "The peasant population, according to reports, on the whole takes relatively little part in community life unless it involves material advantages. . . . The attitude toward the party is one of general disinterest. . . ."[47]

Employees and petty bureaucrats, no less than workers and peasants, lived under unfavorable economic conditions: "The petty civil servant, employee, secretary all increasingly complain about low salaries or wages compared to the high cost of living and shoddy quality of goods. Wages remain at the same level while taxes have gone up, rents are higher after every move, and food costs rise—less perceptibly, but noticeably over the years. . . ."[48]

This prevailing social injustice frequently seems to have been forgotten, for even today there are elements in the Federal Republic who praise Hitler's social measures and believe that National Socialism exhibited quite positive qualities. Yet on the basis of our present knowledge no doubt should remain that Hitler only conceived of, and used, the NSDAP as an instrument for the execution of his personal power and his demands for German hegemony; the objectives of "national Socialism" seemed secondary to him, only desirable, when occasion demanded, as a means of winning over the masses.

Complaints were voiced not only over the effects of Hitler's "guns before butter" policy. In areas traditionally loyal to the church—towns and countryside of Westphalia, the Rhineland,[49] southwest Germany, and Bavaria—criticism, especially by women, mounted against party and state anti-clerical policies.[50] Dissolution of monasteries and ecclesiastical institutions brought "passive resistance" to a head.[51] Initially Hitler had proclaimed freedom of worship and condemned all moral constraints; potentially hostile Catholic parties had been neutralized by the Concordat signed with the Vatican on July 20, 1933.[52] Although the Concordat secured special rights for Catholic associations, in effect recognition of the Nazi regime by the episcopacy had placed Catholics under moral obligation to obey this authority.[53] Clerics of both confessions sought to protect Christians from a struggle between their national responsibilities and their church loyalty. Clashes nevertheless became inevitable once the Nazis had conquered all the other bastions of power, political, industrial, and military.

Hitler, the "Catholic atheist,"[54] feared the Protestant Church far less than the Catholic Church, whose organization he had always admired and whose rituals had inspired Nazi ceremonies. His original desire, to supplant Christian doctrine methodically within the German heart, turned to hatred as he met popular and ecclesiastical resistance. Assuming that it would be easy to deal with the Protestant Church, he had encouraged Reich Bishop Ludwig Müller's "German Christian" movement in order to coordinate Lutherans and establish a German Protestant Reich Church. Failure of this plan was symptomatic of the conflicting tendencies and goals during the years 1933 to 1937. Efforts in 1935 by Hans Kerrl, Minister of Ecclesiastical Affairs, to arrive at a compromise between church and state were torpedoed by Himmler, Heydrich, Bormann, von Schirach, and Rosenberg; by 1937 it was evident that the attempt to establish a unified, Nazi-controlled church had failed. Pope Pius XI's encyclical of March 14, 1937, "Mit brennender Sorge" ("With Burning Sorrow"), which dealt with the threatened position of the Catholic Church in the German Reich, marked the end of a period of toleration. Leading churchmen, including Otto Dibelius and Dr. Martin Niemöller, were brought to trial or imprisoned. The July, 1937, conference of Gestapo church experts to work out a plan for intensification of anti-church measures signals the beginning of a bitter battle, ranging from outright disbandment of church organizations to surveillance, imprisonment, and selective bans on public speeches by clerics.[55]

In reading reports by Hess and other leading Nazis, as well as a flood of hate literature against the Protestant Church and 'political' Catholicism,[56] one is struck by the largely positive and conciliatory attitude of the churches. Only intense hatred and chicanery by the regime gradually turned church leaders of both confessions, albeit reluctantly, into cautious opponents who carefully sought to distinguish between their position toward the state and the party. Church critics and apologists generally suffer from a failure to appreciate the time factor and the slow, continuous shift in ecclesiastical position from supporter to critic. Typical of this progression is the case of Konrad Gröber, Archbishop of Freiburg, who had been a patron and member of the SS; he, like so many others, had hoped—far too long— that, as Heer subtly put it, "state totalitarianism and church totalitarianism could coexist without conflict."[57]

The Catholic Church's position deteriorated after the successful Austrian Anschluss; the Reich Security Office's annual situation report for 1938 noted "insecurity and massive confusion" in church circles. On the Catholic side, "a division had occurred between the Volk and the episcopacy, the episcopacy and the clergy, and the German and Austrian episcopacies," which seriously weakened the Church's fighting capacity.[58] Following a conference of deacons of the Paderborn diocese in the summer of 1938, the clergy was issued guidelines for the continued operation of Catholic Action: cooperation with Nazi organizations was recommended and membership was even suggested. The faithful, moreover, were to be influenced in accordance with party ideas.[59]

The Sudeten crisis in the Fall of 1938 and its temporary peaceful resolution by the Munich Agreement brought more people under the regime's spell. Episcopacy and clergy were now, according to SD reports, more than ever "concerned with refraining from anything that could incur political or police intervention. All potential public conflicts were avoided. . . ."[60] The Nazi state, meanwhile, continued its piecemeal regional dissolution of Catholic associations and prohibited the Catholic Youth League throughout the Reich. The Catholic League of Academics, the Catholic Academic Bonifatius Union, the Academic Mission Societies, and the Teutonic Order of Mary likewise disappeared.

Church activity was now limited to pastoral duties and youth care. However, notwithstanding this limitation, efforts were continuously deployed to seek rapprochement with the state.[61] One cannot resist the impression that until 1939 neither the Pope nor the German clergy had grasped the true nature of Hitler's regime. Reticence, it was hoped, would eventually moderate the Nazis; even Cardinal Faulhaber advocated a relaxation of tensions and an ignoring of Nazi aggressiveness.[62] But intransigent Nazis interpreted this development as a danger to their own position. In a letter of January 28, 1939, to the Military High Command, Martin Bormann, then head of Rudolf Hess' staff, labelled the clergy as potential political enemies of the Reich.[63] He therefore initiated stronger action for the "separation of state and party from the church,"[64] prohibiting on the one hand all political leaders and heads of affiliated party organizations from holding prominent positions in religious associations;[65] on the other hand, directing that all pastors who were high dignitaries of the party be relieved of their posts immediately, that clergymen holding other offices in the party and its formations be gradually replaced, and that no more pastors be entrusted with such offices.[66]

All this in due course provoked church resistance, especially at local and regional levels in traditionally religious areas, "using its myriad propaganda techniques to reestablish its diminished public image and undermining Catholic faith in the party leadership through systematic subversive activity. . . ."[67] The governor of Upper Bavaria, in his monthly report for December, 1938, believed that the "continuing cautious attitude towards the party and state among large segments of the population" was attributable to church influence.[68] Although the churches' maneuverability was circumscribed, they could still mobilize extensive public opinion in the event of a threat to their special interests and existence. But how did they respond to the regime's persecution of others, such as the Jews?

On May 26, 1932, prior to the Nazi take-over, the Berlin pastor

Joachim Hossenfelder had issued the "Guidelines for the German Christian Movement," which professed race, nation, and nationality, and rejected miscegenation—ideas already espoused since the mid-nineteenth century under the banner of Germano-Christian ideas of the future Reich.[69] Another Berlin pastor, von Rabenau, as a rebuttal, proposed twelve guiding principles stressing the freedom of the church. On January 11, 1933, followed the so-called Altona Confession, which established that it was the church's duty to heighten conscience and spread the gospel based on Holy Scriptures. With this, a schism between the völkisch-political and the theologically-oriented wings became evident, even before the Third Reich. These tendencies were accentuated extraordinarily after the take-over, when the Aryan paragraph played a considerable role.[70]

While the Catholic Church readily complied with the regulations of the Aryan paragraph—and even aided the Nazi state by engaging in research of ancestral church membership, which also meant racial membership,[71]— the young Reformed Church, forerunner of the Confessional Church, in May, 1933, issued a proclamation demanding that all decisions be made solely according to the spirit of the church. On the basis of the scriptures, they rejected the exclusion of non-Aryans. On September 27, two thousand pastors replied by opposing the introduction of such an Aryan paragraph. The *Pfarrernotbund*,* founded by Martin Niemöller in September, 1933, took over mutual assistance against illegal harassment. The Aryan paragraph had thus become a decisive factor in the internal disputes of the Protestant Church. Initially concerned mostly with theology, the rift eventually encompassed the so-called "Jewish-Christians," and only the Confessional Church eventually opposed the regime's illegal measures.[72] The preponderance of Protestant clergy, especially the radical Thuringian German Christians but also many representatives of the center, joined with the new masters and tolerated or welcomed anti-Semitic campaigns.[73] The Christian churches, therefore, carry perhaps a greater burden of the guilt than the public for the cruel fate of the Jews, failing to meet their obligations resolutely in view of their ability to influence public opinion. For wherever church authorities did speak out against this discrimination, there was reaction against it in the general population. Although the church was officially silent about the "night of crystal," propaganda leaders reported that the areas where pastors exercised their influence were the only pockets of resistance to the Jewish "solutions."[74]

Although the public had for years been subjected to a systematic Nazi hate campaign, one cannot assert that the "night of crystal," when stores were looted and synagogues burned all over Germany, was a spontane-

* Pastors' Emergency Alliance.

ous expression of national madness, *furor teutonicus*. The November 11, 1938, action was executed by controlled and directed elements. But Goebbels had staged the coup so perfectly that even the dullest fool realized what was going on: "The protest campaign against the Jews is frequently regarded by the public as orchestrated. The force applied in some cases has even given grounds for criticism among the rural population. . . ."[75] Judging from several reports,[76] this violence was almost unanimously rejected, although often because of the unnecessary destruction of goods—a sentiment shared by Göring. The churches, however, remained silent.

This period highlights the ineffectiveness of Nazi propaganda in arousing a broad anti-Semitic movement. Besides people motivated by genuine Christian charity, there were "liberal-pacifist elements," as the Reich Security Office noted, who labelled these measures as "barbaric" and "uncultured." Many believed, given their liberalism, that they had to intercede publicly for the Jews. The destruction of the synagogues was called irresponsible; some intervened on behalf of "poor suppressed Jews.." It was evident that the anti-Jewish policies were more forcefully rejected in the south (with the exception of Austria) and in the west (Catholic, densely populated, predominantly urban) than in the north (Protestant, scattered settlement, rural population).[77] In contrast, subsequent legal measures to exclude the Jews from economic life were generally regarded as "just" or accepted "with understanding" and even "with satisfaction."[78] Force was condemned less for humanitarian reasons than because it was unworthy of Germans. There were isolated cases of spontaneous sabotage, demolition and rioting, chiefly occasioned by euphoric events such as the Anschluss and the Munich Agreement. At such times, windows of private homes, businesses, and synagogues were smashed in several localities.[79]

One can find examples both of anti-Jewish riots and of goodwill toward Jews.[80] The present state of research, however, does not justify valid conclusions for the whole Reich, given its extreme regional variations. Accordingly it is difficult to say how many Germans there were who felt deep shame and helped their Jewish friends wherever possible, just as there were religious organizations and individual pastors who courageously interceded for the persecuted. In any case, the masses remained indifferent or passive. Hatred of the Jews at that time, as Speer aptly expressed it, "seemed so self-evident that it did not make an impression on me."[81]

If one disregards indignation of a social nature—above all from the proletariat, farmers, artisans, minor employees, and petty civil servants —as well as criticism from religious rural and small town areas, then from the opinion reports of 1938 and 1939, one can characterize the mood of the country as "good," "satisfactory," or "calm and reliable," but by no means enthusiastically pro-regime. There was one area, however, in which Hitler could count on a high consensus from among all segments, and that was his foreign and national "triumphs:" the return of the Saar, introduction of compulsory military service, re-occupation of the Rhineland. "The Saar victory with its celebrations had done more for consolidating volkisch unity and improving the general mood than a thousand rallies could have accomplished. . . ."[82] "The Olympics, Spain, and the results of the London talks are affecting the public mood beneficially and helping to overcome many unpleasant situations. . . ."[83] The Austrian Anschluss of February, 1938, marked a high point, judging from numerous reports of enthusiasm and jubilation: "Without a doubt the Führer has conquered many hearts previously cool toward him and the movement. The number still remaining aloof has visibly and markedly receded. . . ."[84] As a side benefit, the Anschluss shifted attention away from the military shakeup which had led to the strengthening of Hitler's control over the armed forces.*

The growing Sudeten crisis in the fall of 1938 was viewed with even greater reservations and fears of war. When, for the evening of September 27, Hitler ordered a "propaganda march" of motorized troops through Berlin's government quarter, these met everywhere with hostile and silent crowds. For hours the people stood silently in front of the Reich Chancellory where Hitler waited in vain for the customary ovations.[85] The American journalist William L. Shirer commented in his diary that this was the most impressive anti-war demonstration he had ever seen, and that this night's impressions renewed his faith a little in the German people.[86] But no mention was made of panic or resistance. The only results were larger bank withdrawals. In border regions, luggage makers did a good business; valuables were sent to the country's interior. To check these developments, the party coined the phrase "suitcase patriots,"[87] one that proved effective in exposing to ridicule those overly concerned with possessions.

Altogether one can best describe the mood as "serious and subdued;" the Security Office even spoke of a general depression and psychosis.[88]

---

* On February 4, 1938, Hitler announced the retirement of Generals von Fritsch (Commander-in-Chief of the Army) and von Blomberg (Minister of War and Commander-in-Chief of the Armed Forces). Hitler, already Supreme Commander of the Armed Forces, took over Blomberg's duties and abolished the War Ministry, replacing it with the new High Command of the Armed Forces (the OKW) headed by the pliable General Keitel. Fritsch's replacement was General von Brauchitsch. Ed.

In his report of September, 1938, however, the governor of Upper and Middle Franconia emphasized that "no hurrah patriotism existed, but perhaps honest readiness to follow the Führer's call to the bitter end." "Even in those days of momentous decisions, trust in the Führer remained steadfast despite the war scares. The Volk feels safe in his hands. . . ."[89] Trust in Hitler is mentioned in most reports, but the degree of prevailing tension can also be read in the reported "enthusiasm and jubilation" with which the Munich Agreement was received: "The peaceful solution of the Sudeten-German question found a happy response everywhere and released the population from its severe anxieties over the preservation of peace. The return of Sudeten Germans into the Reich is greeted everywhere with tremendous joy and the Führer receives heartfelt gratitude for achieving this success without warlike entanglements."[90] "The Führer's new bloodless European victory has strengthened extraordinarily the nation's faith in him and trust in his leadership. Even the grumblers and doubters are silent. . . ."[91]

Therefore, one cannot assess the Munich accord negatively enough; even Hitler himself did not regard it as a triumph but rather as a delay of his plans.[92] Not only was Hitler confirmed in his reckless policies and seduced into a miscalculation regarding the future posture of the western powers; it secured for him an almost legendary image among the German people, one which destroyed the basis for all criticism—even the most objective—of his policies. The hardest blow fell upon that small group of responsible officers who had collected around General Beck and who had been most hostile to Hitler and his war plans, especially after the dishonorable dismissal of General von Fritsch. Their opposition, initially arising out of military considerations and only gradually for moral reasons as well, had progressed to the point that a decision and preparations had been made for a coup d'état. Munich robbed them of any rationale, and far worse, aroused in some the uncertainty whether the dictator had not been right after all and they were only perpetual grumblers and know-it-alls.[93]

The same game was repeated in the spring: general nervousness and a war scare pervaded the atmosphere just as before the incorporation of Austria and the Sudetenland. After the "smashing" of Czechoslovakia and the annexation of Memel, again without bloodshed and without incurring sanctions by the West, enthusiasm and admiration for the Führer's "genius" was limitless. It is true that the Security office talks of "a relatively modest appreciation of the events and their national significance," and attributes this to "an economic strain wrought by materialism," which "leaves less and less room for the influence of ideals."[94] However, reports from the governors paint a different picture:

for example, "the public is aware that our Führer's foreign policy represents something unknown in world history insofar as he has succeeded in annexing large territories without shedding blood. . . ."[95]

It is impossible to list all the congratulations, from cities and universities, from classrooms, learned societies, and dignitaries of both confessions.[96] The words "deep devotion," "unconditional loyalty," "eternal love," and "gratitude" appear repeatedly. School children called him "General Bloodless" and believed that he cared for them "like a father." Even if one recognizes the pressure from the party and the high degree of social control exercised in totalitarian states, it does seem that in the spring of 1939 an identification with Hitler had taken place over broad segments of society.

Goebbels had worked for years on creating and strengthening this feeling of solidarity; from the outset he had presented a picture of Hitler as both one of the masses and yet standing above and apart from them. Press, radio, newsreels, Reich Party rallies, accompanied by thunderous "Heils!" and pseudo-religious flag consecrations, had imprinted on the public, day after day, hour after hour, an image of a man risen from a simple soldier to the radiant savior of the nation.[97]

In asking the question whether in the years 1933 to 1939 the National Socialist following had grown, diminished, or remained constant, the following factors have to be considered and weighed comparatively: 1. the acceptance or rejection of the regime's social measures; 2. the consequences of the church struggle; 3. the effects of anti-Semitic policies; 4. foreign policy successes; and 5. the personal admiration for Hitler. Even with economic improvement, the collective social expectations undoubtedly had been left far behind the regime's promises. Elements of the proletariat, a majority of the peasants, many small businessmen, employees, and civil servants had been disillusioned. Some of them would surely have turned to other parties in free elections, especially since the KPD and SPD did everything in their power through their illegal operations to incite dissatisfaction over the wage policy and blame it on the Nazis.

The campaign against the churches had assumed proportions especially repulsive to Catholic voters; the existence of Christian parties would certainly have deprived the Nazi party of further votes. The regime's racial policies were rejected by large numbers already hostile towards National Socialism: liberal, bourgeois, and Catholic classes, a few intellectuals, and a broad spectrum of the proletariat. The lower middle class, rural inhabitants of particular regions, and predominantly Protestant segments of the population welcomed or at least tolerated rigid economic discrimination and segregation of the Jews. Force was only supported by a minority of fanatics. Anti-Semitism must therefore be regarded as only *one* factor in the formation of political will and should not be overestimated.

Hitler's "national regeneration" and greater-German triumphs assured him of the acclaim of almost all citizens. "Reactionaries" such as the Pan-German League, the Stahlhelm, the Reichskriegerbund, and all those conservatives who had helped to prepare Hitler's policies— only to be outmaneuvered and subsequently to desert the movement— were just as animated as many patriotic representatives of the Left. The patriotic front was astonishingly broad. Revanchism netted Hitler personally an enormous increase in prestige, so that many misunderstandings were ultimately brushed aside as "growing pains" of the regime or excesses of party functionaries.

Thus an election around the time of Hitler's fiftieth birthday would perhaps, in a moment of national frenzy, have brought him a result similar to the March, 1933, election (although this must remain hypothetical until further research confirms or disproves it); it remains questionable whether a three-quarter majority could have been achieved or surpassed. Of course, if a plebiscite had taken place on the question of Hitler's personal accomplishments, the result would have been overwhelmingly in his favor.

The approaching Polish crisis hardly clouded relations between the leader and his followers. There was no trace of war psychosis from May until well into August. Everyone was convinced that the Polish question would be solved, and no one expected French or English intervention: "Despite the promised support, the public feels that neither France nor England will fight for Poland, if only because they had deserted former Czechoslovakia, which had represented a completely different bastion for the western powers than Poland could ever be. In any case, it is frequently said that crushing Poland is slowly becoming a compelling need."[98] The partition of Poland was being discussed without any precise notion of what this entailed. "Faith in the German military notwithstanding, people do not want to see another war. . . ."[99] Generally, reports emphasize the contrast with the September-October days of the previous year and its prevailing war psychosis.[100]

Thus, except for a minority, no one believed in a war; at most in a localized Polish campaign, but by no means in a new world war. The general climate of opinion thus corresponded to Hitler's own illusionary conception of a British retreat at the last minute. Naturally the press, itself caught up in the same spirit, abetted such thinking, as an illuminating report of July 5, 1939, proves: "In forming an opinion on the general situation, one cannot forget for a minute that both sides are bluffing just like last year. The English bluff now consists of the claim that they are not bluffing. There is absolute agreement by all participants on one point: even a victorious war is a worse business than giving way at an opportune time. We are thus witnessing solely a war of nerves which will, in the coming weeks and months, develop into a most serious crisis. But insofar as statesmen have ever controlled events in world history, a natural solution will be found in the form of a nervous collapse, which will then make the use of weapons superfluous. The English position is basically the same as in September. . . ."[101]

It goes without saying that in the meantime a relentless agitation against Polish "atrocities" was being conducted and swallowed by the population. "The terrible treatment and mistreatment of the German population by fanatic Polaks has aroused the greatest animosity and one repeatedly hears people remark that it is time the Führer intervened. . . ."[102] Also, a systematic campaign was conducted by press, radio, and rallies under the catchword "encirclement."[103] In the latter half of August a deterioration in mood becomes noticeable; numerous rumors were circulating, "encouraged by heavy troop call-ups. But until the end, the conviction prevailed that it would still be possible to avoid war. This hope was in fact encouraged by the agreement with Russia, breaking the encirclement of Germany.[104]

The pact with Stalin of August 23, 1939, surprised the world and, as later reports affirmed, was met with "mixed feelings"[105] or considered "necessary;"[106] given the tense situation at that time, it contributed to an improvement of the mood, at least among parts of the population, and also reinforced many hopes.[107] For the "alte Kämpfer" (party veterans) it represented, according to Rosenberg's political diary, "a moral diminution of respect in view of our twenty year struggle, the party rallies and Spain."[108] People took comfort in the knowledge that it was only a matter of "a simple community of interests."[109] But overall, Shirer observed, the pact was obviously popular since it destroyed the nightmare of encirclement and a two-front war.[110]

The generals voiced no protests when Hitler called his top commanding officers and their staff to the Berghof on August 22, 1939, and notified them of his intention to march against Poland.[111] This was very different from the Sudeten crisis when the dictator had met considerable resistance. Goebbels' skillful management of the press had fostered the erroneous assumption that the pact was merely a return to Bismarckian policies; traditional cooperation with Russia was emphasized and ideological differences were played down.[112] "We believe we can deal quickly with Poland and we honestly are looking forward to it," Edward Wagner, commander of the general quartermaster's staff, wrote to his wife on August 31. "The situation *has* to be settled."[113]

Meanwhile the fear of war gradually intensified: "Common sense tells everyone that we are, logically, step by step, being forced into war; and yet no one can admit that it is really coming."[114]

NOTES

1. For comparison see the exhaustive analyses and statistical data in Karl D. Bracher, Wolfgang Sauer, Gerhard Schultz, *Die nationalsozialistische Machtergreifung* (Cologne-Opladen, 1960), p. 94 ff.
2. *Ibid.* pp. 94 ff., 350 ff.
3. William S. Allen's study, *The Nazi Seizure of Power: The Experience of a Single German Town, 1930-1935* (Chicago, 1965), shows the unrelenting advance of National Socialism on this level of Protestant small-town society.
4. David Schoenbaum, *Hitler's Social Revolution* (New York, 1966), p. 40.
5. *Ibid.*, pp. 36-37.
6. In 1931, eighteen- to thirty-year-olds represented 61.3 per cent of the party membership while constituting only 31.1 per cent of the population; *Ibid.*, p. 38.
7. *Ibid.* Cf. also Arthur Schweitzer, *Big Business in the Third Reich* (London, 1964); Robert O'Neill, *The German Army and the Nazi Party, 1933-1939* (London, 1966); and recently Manfred Messerschmidt, *Die Wehrmacht im NS-Staat. Zeit der Indoktrination* (Hamburg, 1969) and Klaus Jürgen Müller, *Das Heer und Hitler. Armee und nationalsozialistisches Regime 1933-1940* (Stuttgart, 1969); Hans Mommsen, *Beamtentum im Dritten Reich* (Stuttgart, 1966).
8. Bracher, *Die deutsche Diktatur* (Cologne, 1969). The study appeared only after completion of this manuscript and could therefore be utilized only marginally.
9. Klaus Schwabe's study, *Wissenschaft und Kriegsmoral. Die deutschen Hochschullehrer und die politischen Grundfragen des Ersten Weltkrieges* (Göttingen, 1969) could serve as a model which pursues the similarities and disunion between annexationists and anti-annexationists through the various disciplines.
10. See Bracher, Schulz, Sauer, *Machtergreifung*, pp. 266 ff.; Léon Poliakov and Joseph Wulf, *Das Dritte Reich und seine Denker: Dokumente* (Berlin, 1959). Particularly illuminating about the attitude of historians is Karl Ferdinand Werner, *Das Nationalsozialistische Geschichtsbild und die deutsche Geschichtswissenschaft* (Stuttgart, 1967); cf. also Bracher, *Diktatur*, pp. 290 ff.
11. BA, R58/1094; fol.106.
12. BA, R58/1095; fol.6. See also Vierteljahreslagebericht 1939 des Sicher-heitshauptamtes: BA, R58/717; fol.61.
13. Aspects of this subject have already been investigated: Andreas Flitner, *Deutsches Geistesleben und Nationalsozialismus* (Tübingen, 1965), and Helmut Heiber, *Walter Frank und sein Reichsinstitut für Geschichte des neuen Deutschlands* (Stuttgart, 1966).

14. Material for this was available after completion of the manuscript in the documentation by Ursula von Gersdorff, *Frauen im Kriegsdienst 1914-1945* (Stuttgart, 1969).
15. See Goebbels' comments in his *Tagebücher aus den Jahren 1942 bis 1943*, ed. by Louis P. Lochner (Zurich, 1948), pp. 110, 192.
16. Schoenbaum, *op. cit.*, p. 185.
17. RGBl 1935, p. 1146.
18. Stimmungs- und Lagebericht des Gauleiters Grohé, Gau Cologne-Aachen, dated March 7, 1935 (BA, NS22/vorl. 583); cf. also his report of April 9, 1935.
19. Henry Picker, *Hitlers Tischgespräche im Führerhauptquartier 1941/42*, rev. ed. by Percy Ernst Schramm in collaboration with Andreas Hillgruber & Martin Vogt (Stuttgart, 1963), p. 262.
20. "National Socialism was a political protest against the economic realities of the twentieth century." Edward L. Homze, *Foreign Labor in Nazi Germany* (Princeton, 1967), p. 4.
21. One cannot generalize about the role of big industries; the role and assistance played by Bosch and Reusch in the resistance is already well known. In 1938 the Security Office, in its annual report, refers to the strong "liberal influences" within the economy. Leading roles both in industry and commerce "are usually played by those who reject all ties to nation and state." BA, R58/1094; fol.108. Cf. also Eberhard Czichon, *Wer verhalf Hitler zur Macht? Zum Anteil der deutschen Industrie an der Zerstörung der Weimarer Republik* (Cologne, 1967), for an analysis of German industry from a marxist viewpoint, with a subdivision of industries into pro-Nazi, right and left Keynesian and their individual share in Hitler's success.
22. See BA, NS6/vorl. 231; and H. Mommsen, *op. cit.*, pp. 62-90 for the discussion "Professional civil servant or political Administration."
23. Schoenbaum, *op. cit.*, p. 196.
24. Mommsen, *op. cit.*, pp. 15, 31, 147.
25. Schoenbaum, *op. cit.*, pp. 67-68.
26. *Ibid.*, p. 97.
27. See Rene Erbe, *Die nationalsozialistische Wirtschaftspolitik 1933 bis 1939 im Lichte der modernen Theorie* (Zurich, 1958), who calls Schacht's policies "a caricature" of Keynesian economic theory (p. 172).
28. Stimmungs- und Lagebericht of Gauleiter Grohé, Gau Cologne-Aachen, March 7, 1935 (BA, NS22/vorl. 583).
29. Recent publications prove that underground activity was more extensive than originally assumed: Kurt Klotzbach, *Gegen den Nationalsozialismus — Widerstand und Verfolgung in Dortmund 1930-1945* (Hanover, 1969), and Karl Schabrod, *Widerstand an Rhein und Ruhr, 1933-1945* (Herne, 1969).
30. Jahreslagebericht des Sicherheitshauptamts 1938. BA, R58/1094; fol.80.
31. *Ibid.*, fol. 89.
32. *Ibid.*, fol. 92; see also Bracher, *Diktatur*, pp. 401 ff.
33. BA, NS22/vorl. 860.
34. *Ibid.*
35. Economic report of general director Kellerman to the Regierungspräsidenten for January-March, 1939 (HA/GHH 4001 01 300/9).
36. BHStA, Abt. II. MA 106,676.
37. BA, NS Misch. 168; fol. 140,038.

38. See Vierteljahresbericht 1939 des Sicherheitshauptamtes. BA, R58/717; fol. 140.

39. BA, NS Misch 168; fol. 140,040

40. See, for example, the special edition of *Odal*/Monatschrift für Blut und Boden: "Neuordnung unseres Denkens," (Reichsbauernstadt Goslar, 1941), p. 28 in BA, ZSg 3/1120.

41. The law of September 13, 1933 (RGBl I, p. 626) empowered the Reich minister of agriculture to raise the level of German agriculture; this occurred with the decree of December 8, 1933 (RGBl I, p. 1060).

42. Decree of September 29, 1933 (RGBl I, p. 685).

43. Schoenbaum, *op. cit.*, p. 173.

44. Schweitzer, *op. cit.*, p. 200.

45. Informationsbericht Nr. 17 "Das Problem der Landflucht," BA, Zsg 101/34; fol. 75.

46. Jahreslagebericht des Sicherheitshauptamtes. BA, R58/1096; fol. 9; see also BA, NS Misch. 168, fol. 140,040.

47. Monthly report for February, 1939, by the district leader of Kissingen, Archiv Bischöfl. Ordinariat, Würzburg, *Nachlass Leier*/K2; See also May-June, 1939, political report, Kreisleitung Alzey, BA, NS Misch 1638, fol. 139 801, which has information concerning the growing friction among the rural population because of the labor shortage. Cf. SD-Unterabschnitt Württemberg-Hohenzollern: "Lagebericht des 2. Vierteljahres 1939." HStA Stuttgart, K750/46; and the monthly reports from December, 1937, to March, 1938; compiled by the NS-Volkswohlfahrt Office, BA, NS19/252 F48.

48. Political situation report for June-July, 1939, by the Kreisleiter of Kissingen. Bischöfl. Ordinariatsarchiv Würzburg: *Nachlass Leier*/K2.

49. See the reference material in Bernhard Vollmer (ed.), *Volksopposition im Polizeistaat. Gestapo und Regierungsberichte 1934-1936* (Stuttgart, 1957). One can apply the term "public opposition" only with appropriate care, since it was a one-sided evaluation. The Reich district Aachen, from which the reports stem, is furthermore a border region with a 90 per cent Catholic population. Nor had the national enthusiasm at the end of the decade taken hold by 1934-1936.

50. See, for example, the monthly report for May, 1937, by the Reichsleitung der NSDAP, Reichsfrauenführung. BA, NS22/vorl. 860.

51. Political situation report for May-June, 1939, by the Kreisleitung der NSDAP, Rheingau-St. Goarshausen. BA, Misch 1638, fol. 139 796. Cf. also, monthly report of the Regierungspräsidium for Lower Franconia and Aschaffenburg for February, 1939. BHStA, Abt. II MA 106,681.

52. See, for example, Hitler's government explanation to the Reichstag on March 23, 1933, in which he called both Christian confessions "important factors in the preservation of our national characteristics" and declared that "the rights of the churches would not be encroached upon, nor their relationship to the state changed." *Verhandlungen des Reichstags—Stenographische Berichte*, vol. 457, pp. 28B and 32A; or, the correspondence of the Reich minister of the interior, September 26, 1933, concerning the freedom of religion for civil servants and the decree of neutrality by Hitler's deputy on October 13, 1933. Cf. Friedrich Zipfel, *Kirchenkampf in Deutschland, 1933-1945. Religionsverfolgung und Selbstbehauptung der*

Kirchen in der nationalsozialistischen Zeit (Berlin, 1965), pp. 268, 270 (has the wrong date of October 17, 1933).

53. Gordon C. Zahn, *Die deutschen Katholiken und Hitlers Kriege* (Graz, 1965), p. 107.

54. Friedrich Heer, *Gottes erste Liebe. 2000 Jahre Judentum und Christentum* (Munich, 1967), p. 390; cf. also Guenther Lewy, *Die Katholische Kirche und das Dritte Reich* (Munich, 1965).

55. Cf. John S. Conway, *The Nazi Persecution of the Churches 1933-1945* (London, 1968), esp. pp. 169 ff. By November, 1937, seven hundred pastors had been imprisoned.

56. See Hess' circular "Die Deutsche Evangelische Kirche und ihr Verhältnis zum Nationalsozialismus seit seiner Machtübernahme," BA, Schumacher Collection 245/Bd. 1, found in Zipfel, *op. cit.*, pp. 384-441.

57. Heer, *op. cit.*, p. 412. The Gröber case is found in the correspondence of the Verwaltungschefs der SS Abt. V. Ch. R/57b/Dr. B./St. of January 19, 1938. A handwritten comment indicates that his membership was to be stricken quietly since the archbishop had not responded to a request that he make a personal statement regarding his withdrawal. BA, Schumacher Collection 445/Bd.2.

58. BA, R58/1094, fol. 45.

59. Confidential circular no. 103/38 of July 27, 1938 from Bormann to the Gauleiter. BA, NS6/vorl. 230.

60. Vierteljahreslagebericht 1939 des Sicherheitshauptamtes, BA, R58/717, fol. 27.

61. Monthly report of the governor for Upper Bavaria in *Die kirchliche Lage in Bayern*, p. 307.

62. See the protocol of the papal conference with the German bishops Bertram, Faulhaber, Schulte and Innitzer on March 6, 1939: *Actes et documents du Saint Siège relatifs à la Seconde Guerre Mondiale, vol. 2, Lettres de Pie XII aux évêques allemands 1939-1944* (Città del Vaticano, 1966), p. 414.

63. PS-117, *Nazi Conspiracy and Aggression* (Washington, 1946), vol. III, p. 169, cited by Conway, *op. cit.*, p. 217.

64. Letter of the SD-Oberabschnitts Süd, Unterabschnitt Mainfranken II 1131 of July 6, 1939. BA, Schumacher Collection 245 Bd.2. Similar orders had already been given since November, 1935, cf. Conway, *op. cit.*, p. 160.

65. Anordnung C422 63/38 of June 1, 1938, printed by Zipfel, *op. cit.*, pp. 449-50.

66. Rundschreiben Nr. 23/39 of January 23, 1939. BA, NS6/vorl. 232.

67. SD-Unterabschnitt Württemberg-Hohenzollern, Lagebericht (2. quarter of 1939) of July 1, 1939, HStA Stuttgart, K750/46.

68. *Die kirchliche Lage in Bayern*, p. 302.

69. *Der ungekündigte Bund. Neue Begegnung von Juden und christlicher Gemeinde*, ed. by Dietrich Goldschmidt and Hans Joachim Kraus (Stuttgart, 1963), 2nd ed., pp. 89 f.

70. Dated April 7, 1933 (RGBl. I, 1933), pp. 175.

71. See Lewy, *op. cit.*, pp. 308 ff.

72. The Confessional Church's charter, the Barmen Manifesto of May, 1934, was neither then nor later considered as a program of political protest, and there was no intention of initiating political opposition to the regime. The memorandum of June, 1936, took a courageous stand against the lead-

ership cult and concentration camps, but its publication was originally not intended. Bracher, *Diktatur*, pp. 417 ff.

73. See the list of Protestant bishops and presidents of state church offices who endorsed the foundation of an "Institute for the Detection and Elimination of Jewish Influence on the Church Life of the German People." The institute was established in Eisenach on May 6. Cf. Gesetzblatt der Deutschen Evangelischen Kirche (April 6, 1939), reproduced in "Mitteilungen zur weltanschaulichen Lage" Nr. 18, V, June 12, 1939. BA, ZSg 3/vorl. 1688.

74. Stimmungsbericht for November, 1938. Bischöfl. Ordinariatsarchiv Würzburg, *Nachlass Leier*/K2. Cf. also *Die kirchliche Lage in Bayern*, p. 301.

75. Regierungspräsident Oberbayern, December 10, 1938, BHStA, Abt. II, MA 106 671.

76. Report of governor of Lower Bavaria and Oberpfalz (December 8, 1938); report of governor of the Pfalz (December 9, 1938) and report of governor of Upper Bavaria (January 9, 1939) in BHStA, Abt. II, MA 106,673, MA 106, 676, MA 106,671.

77. Annual situation report for 1938, BA, R58/1096, fol. 110.

78. Laws of November 12, 1938 and November 28, 1938 (RGBl. 1938), I, pp. 1580, 1642 and 1676. Cf. Helmut Genschel, *Die Verdrängung der Juden aus der Wirtschaft im Dritten Reich* (Göttingen, 1967), *infra*. p. 236. Cf. also BA, R58/1096, fol. 31/32.

79. Governor of Lower Franconia and Aschaffenburg, monthly report for March 1938, and the monthly reports for May, September and October 1938 of the governor of Mainfranken, in BHStA, Abt. II, MA 106 681.

80. Cf. Franz Josef Heyen, *Nationalsozialismus im Alltag* (Boppard am Rhein, 1967), pp. 125 ff., for examples of isolated cases of excesses against the Jews, but also for contacts with Jews in the area Mainz-Koblenz-Trier.

81. Albert Speer, *Erinnerungen* (Frankfurt M., 1969), p. 126.

82. Stimmungs- und Lagebericht of Gauleiter Grohé (March 7, 1935) in BA, NS22/vorl. 583 (see also Vollmer, *op. cit.*, p. 165).

83. *idem*, of August 12, 1936.

84. Monthly report of the governor of Upper Bavaria (April 9, 1938), BHStA, Abt. II, MA 106,671; cf. also the monthly report of the governor of Schwaben and Neuburg (April 8, 1938), and governors of Upper and Lower Franconia, and Lower Bavaria-Upper Pfalz, BHStA, Abt. II, MA 106,638, 106,678, and 106,673.

85. Helmut Krausnick, "Vorgeschichte und Beginn des militärischen Widerstandes gegen Hitler," *Vollmacht des Gewissens*, vol. 1 (Frankfurt/Main, 1960), p. 365; and Ruth Andreas-Friedrich, *Schauplatz Berlin. Ein deutsches Tagebuch* (Munich, 1962), p. 9.

86. William L. Shirer, *Berlin Diary. The journal of a foreign correspondent 1934-1941* (New York, 1941), p. 143.

87. Governor of the Pfalz (October 10, 1938), BHStA, Abt. II, MA 106,676.

88. BA, R58/1094, fol. 110.

89. BHStA, Abt. II, MA 106,678.

90. Governor of Mainfranken (October 10, 1938), *ibid.*, MA 106,681.

91. Governor of Upper and Lower Franconia (November 7, 1938), *ibid.*, MA 106,678; cf. also reports of governor of Upper Bavaria (November 10, 1938), *ibid.*, MA 106,671, and the governor of Mainfranken for October 1938, *ibid.*, MA 106,681.

92. Cf. Keith Robbins, *Munich 1938* (Gütersloh, 1969), pp. 307 ff.

93. Krausnick, "Vorgeschichte und Beginn des militärischen Widerstandes gegen Hitler," *loc. cit.*, pp. 368-70; and O'Neill, *op. cit.*, p. 165. Cf. also Bracher, *Diktatur*, pp. 427 ff.

94. BA, R58/717, fol. 58.

95. Governor of Mainfranken (April 11, 1939); cf. also reports of the governor of Upper Bavaria (April 12, 1939) and the governor of the Pfalz (April 11, 1939) in BHStA, Abt. II, MA 106,681, 106,671, and 106,676.

96. BA, R54/vorl. 165c; see also BA, R54/vorl. 150, 151, 158.

97. Cf. Ernest K. Bramstedt, *Goebbels and National Socialist Propaganda 1925-1945* (London, 1965), chapter 9: "The projection of the Hitler image," pp. 194 ff.

98. SD-Unterabschnitt Mainfranken, Aussenstelle Aschaffenburg to the SD-Unterabschnitt Mainfranken, May 6, 1939. *Aus deutschen Urkunden 1935-1945* (printed shortly after the war by the British Foreign Office but never published; copy in IWM, London), p. 207.

99. *Idem*, May 11, 1939, *ibid.*, p. 208. Cf. also governor of Upper Bavaria (report of July 10, 1939), and the governor of Lower Bavaria and Upper Pfalz (report of August 7, 1939) in BHStA, Abt. II, MA 106,671 and 106,673.

100. Kreisleitung Bergzabern, Gau Hessen-Nassau, political report for May-June, 1939. BA, NS Misch 1638, fol. 139,800; Kreis Alsfeld-Lauterbach, political situation report for June, 1939, *ibid.*, fol. 139,803; Kreisleitung Wetzlar, July 24, 1939: BA, NS Misch 1682, fol. 159,309; Kreisleitung Büdingen, July, 1939, *ibid.*, fol. 149,301.

101. Informationsbericht Nr. 73, signed Dertinger—BA Zsg 101/34, fol. 269; cf. also report Nr. 74 which states "that armed conflict as such is not the goal of our policy, rather the peaceful solution of our eastern aspirations; at least, however, the localization of a conflict with Poland." *Ibid.*, fol. 373.

102. Kreisleitung Alzey, Monthly report for July-August, 1939, in *Aus deutschen Urkunden*, p. 211.

103. *Ibid.* Cf. also May-June, 1939, Kreisleitung Alzey, BA, NS Misch vorl. 1638, fol. 139,802, and Kreisleitung Wetterau, May-June, 1939, *ibid.*, fol. 139,804 and 139,897. Cf. Bramstedt,,*bop. cit.*, p. 183.

104. Governor of Upper and Middle Franconia (September 7, 1939), BHStA, Abt. II, MA 106,678.

105. Generalstaatsanwalt Naumburg/Saale, July 28, 1941: BA, R22/3380.

106. Oberlandesgerichtspräsident Ludwigshafen, October 8, 1940: BA, R22/3389.

107. Kreisleitung Darmstadt, monthly report (August, 1939), in *Aus deutschen Urkunden*, p. 211, and Kreisleitung Wiesbaden, (September, 1939), *ibid.*, p. 212.

108. *Das politische Tagebuch Alfred Rosenbergs 1934/35 und 1939/40*, ed. by Hans Günther Seraphim (Munich, 1964), p. 89.

109. Cf. Ausführungen des Kreisleiters Benda in Täglicher Inlandslagebericht des SD-Abschnittes Leipzig, September 28, 1939, in *Aus deutschen Urkunden*, p. 213.

110. *Berlin Diary*, p. 183.

111. Krausnick, "Vorgeschichte. . . ," *loc. cit.*, pp. 375-80; and O'Neill, *op. cit.*, p. 169.

112. Vertrauliche Information Nr. 183/39 of August 22, 1939, cited by Bramstedt, *op. cit.*, p. 195.

113. *Der Generalquartiermeister*. Briefe und Tagebuchaufzeichnungen des Gen.-quart.meisters des Heeres, General der Artillerie, Eduard Wagner, ed. by Elisabeth Wagner (Munich, 1963).

114. Jochen Klepper, *Unter dem Schatten Deiner Flügel. Aus den Tagebüchern der Jahre 1932-1942* (Stuttgart, 1965), p. 787.

I. BLITZKRIEG

Victory!
Germany is triumphant on all fronts
(*NSDAP motto of the week*)

1. OUTBREAK OF WAR AND THE POLISH CAMPAIGN

HELMUT KRAUSNICK, one of the leading experts on National Socialism, given his personal knowledge and command of the sources, has characterized the mood of the Germans as one of "reluctant loyalty."[1] Hardly a more fitting characterization can be made of the majority opinion at the outbreak of the war. Foreign and German eyewitnesses as well as sources within the party and state concurred at that time and subsequently that there was no evidence of war fever—but they did not confirm any opposition either. The American correspondent, William L. Shirer, observed a kind of defeatism and posed the question on August 31, 1939, as to how it was possible for a country to enter a major war with a population so dead set against it. Apathy seemed to him to be the most prominent characteristic among the Germans on September 1.[2] Another observer described the population as "harassed and depressed;"[3] historian Gerhard Ritter focused attention on the antithesis to the enthusiasm of 1914, which he attributed to systematic terror and militant propaganda that had numbed a population taught to be obedient.[4] Reports from state bureaus and SD sections speak of a calm and composed attitude, but even here there was no lack of comment on the depressed and indifferent behavior.[5] A precipitous stock market decline accompanied this depressed mood, hitting bottom on September 14 and only slowly beginning to recover after the Red Army had also marched into Poland on the nineteenth.[6] Mounting military success gradually dissipated the fear psychosis, and more positive remarks were heard. This gradual swelling of hope can easily be verified by still existing daily domestic reports of the Leipzig SD section for the first months of the war.[7]

The September declaration of war by England and France had been just as much of a shock to the population as to Hitler.[8] Germany suddenly found itself in a major war, one Hitler had not intended at this time and under these circumstances. His "program" provided for a series of campaigns over the years, eventually securing for Germany the necessary economic base for waging a world war. Thus Hitler had acted from purely German-national interests, failing to include in his calculations, or in the case of England fundamentally misunderstanding, the interests of foreign states. Now his bluff had been called and the intended localization made doubtful: "Optimists [still] believe that England has gone to the limits of its forbearance in honoring its obligations to Poland. England is too egoistic to risk human lives. It is therefore attempting to win the war simply by means of propaganda and blockade." Pessimists, though, believed that England and France were preparing for a massive strike against Germany.[9]

Why—and many a person has asked himself that question—why did the Germans silently and involuntarily follow Hitler to war and not resist joining this course into the abyss?

Recent studies show how well the Wehrmacht was already integrated into Hitler's state and how leading military figures such as Keitel and Jodl represented broad spectra of opinion.[10] In addition, paralysis induced by the system became evident, especially among the civilian population after many years of covert and open pressure by the regime, a practice which produced a combination of fear and resignation. Besides these factors, the following additional ones have to be considered: 1. Since the Versailles Treaty, the rearrangement of Germany's eastern boundaries had remained a constant goal of German foreign policy, even under Gustav Stresemann. Danzig, the Corridor, eastern Upper Silesia were all territories whose incorporation into the German Reich had been demanded repeatedly and advocated as a certain "legal claim" by influential military, conservative, and economic elements. Hitler's abrupt redirection of these traditional revisionist claims through the Non-Aggression Pact with Poland on January 26, 1934, was rather viewed with suspicion but finally accepted as a tactical, dilatory maneuver. 2. The "bloodless" settlement of the Anschluss of Austria, the incorporation of the Sudetenland and Memel, even the strategic defense of the Reich by the "destruction" of Czechoslovakia led most to believe and hope that the demands on Poland could also be satisfied by a kind of "*Blumenkrieg*" [flower war]. 3. For months massive propaganda had depicted a diabolical Poland. The fictitious attack on the Gleiwitz radio station, news of Polish atrocities against ethnic Germans [*Volksdeutsche*], and Hitler's explanations on September 1, 1939, that he had tried everything in the last two days to preserve the peace, had drummed into the population the belief that it was a justified, imposed war. On August 27, Shirer noted in his diary the isolation in which the German Volk lived. While the rest of the world was of the opinion that Germany was about to break the peace, the opposite was being asserted all over Germany.[11] The fiction of a dictated war was continually stressed even in the future by party, state, and the military.[12]

After the Germans had been thoroughly influenced accordingly by press and radio, "success reports" did not fail to materialize: "The population is largely informed about the causes of the war and the question of who is responsible for it. Not only enlightenment by the party but also Foreign Office announcements published in the press concerning efforts to preserve the peace are assisting in strengthening the will to resist and showing the public what it could expect if our spirit of resistance were to flag."[13] Another report stated that in general "the facts have reinforced a bitterness toward the western powers and on the other hand heightened belief in the enemy's war guilt. . . ."[14] Immediately after the outbreak of war, listening to foreign broadcasts was prohibited and severe penalties were imposed, in order to rob the German Volk of any opportunity to obtain information from other than state-controlled sources.[15] Anyone publicly doubting a German victory or questioning the legality of the war could expect to be arrested.[16]

It is therefore partly a misunderstanding of existing conditions to blame the Churches[17] either for acting cautiously and neutrally,[18] or even for calling for obedience to the "Führer" and performance of one's duty at home and at the front,[19] especially since most ecclesiastics were strongly nationalistic and patriotic, as previously emphasized. Moreover, in a letter of August 30, 1939, Goebbels had already circulated a notice through the Reich Ministry for Ecclesiastical Affairs expressing "the undesirability . . . of meetings at which views concerning the current situation are expressed."[20]

It is evident from reports of the papal nuncio in Berlin, Orsenigo, that a number of priests had nevertheless made negative statements about the war and had been imprisoned.[21] Orsenigo also clearly exposed the dissension among the Catholic clergy during the war in a report of April 13, 1940: "As long as the conflict only involved domestic policies, it was easy for anyone to distinguish between anti-National Socialist and subversive behavior; as was its duty, the clergy was against National Socialism but was not subversive. Now that it concerns foreign policy, this distinction is significantly more difficult; only a few understand that one can be against Hitler without being against the state, i.e., without being a traitor. . . ."[22]

Hitler's decision to postpone anti-church measures for the duration of the war and his call for a "*Burgfrieden*" [political truce] also help to explain the Churches' discretion or loyalty.[23] Having noted the negative reaction to his anticlericalism, he urged all party bureaus to avoid further friction between church and state, a "wish" which factions within the party struggling for control over ecclesiastical policies did not fully heed, despite repeated reminders.[24] However, oddly enough, this neutrality did not extend to surveillance, since reports on church activities were intensified.[25] A Burgfrieden was particularly compelling because most Germans remained faithful to the church and hostile to anti-clericalism; despite Rosenberg's efforts, by 1939 only 3.5 per cent of the population declared themselves "deists" and 1.5 per cent atheists, while the remaining 95 per cent of the eighty million Germans continued to register as church members, even including a majority of the three million Party members.[26] Regardless of Hitler's admonitions, both the churches and the Nazi state continued to claim the allegiance of the population without telling them that they would have to bear the burdens of this war. Both Christian Churches called for loyalty to the Führer, Volk, and Fatherland.[27]

Thus the Germans submitted to their seemingly-inescapable fate. Foodstuffs were rationed, textiles meant originally for three to four months had to last for years,[28] employment mobility was curtailed,[29] and a war economy decree issued[30] which was to introduce higher war taxes, reduce salaries and, if possible, also achieve price reductions. The goal, as Reich Economics Minister Funk announced at a special press conference on September 4, was to cover the cost of war in large part so that the rest could be obtained through credit without endangering the currency.[31]

Throughout the war one phenomenon can be observed in increasing proportions in Germany—the rumor. It is tempting to call it a typical expression or even a necessary product of a one-sided, state-controlled propaganda and information policy. In reality, however, rumors emerge everywhere and under all forms of government, especially in periods of insecurity, fear, and uncertainty. In the United States during the war so-called "rumor mills" were even established.[32]

The origins of these rumors can be traced to three complexes: 1. word-of-mouth and whisper campaigns by one's own or hostile propaganda offices which result in manipulated rumors; 2. facts, twisted and falsified by exaggeration and embellishment; and 3. wishes or anxieties often amplified by prophets and clairvoyants. Depending on the source, such rumors are encouraged or attacked by state authori.ies.[33] In the latter case one almost always finds references either to internal opponents or foreign radio broadcasts. A classic example of rumor fabrication already utilized in the first days of the war is mentioned in a correspondence of September 2, 1939, by the commander of corps area XIII.[34] Under the heading "I., Rumor-Mongering," he states: "It is obvious that rumor-mongers are at work again, and their activity is injurious to German defense measures. Purveyors of these rumors are primarily persons who have an improper or even hostile attitude towards the Nazi state because they lack the innate feeling, essential in every true German, for the eternal existential struggle by the German people for its vital necessities in war and peace."

As examples of existing rumors, he reported: excessive German troop losses, reports of mass hoarding, bombings, acts of sabotage, military set-backs, etc. Far more interesting are those opinions falling under his rubric "Demoralization":

> "a) Questioning the necessity of a war for Danzig and the Corridor;
> b) Passing on enemy war guilt lies and atrocity reports;
> c) Doubting German news, especially reports about cruelties against Germans by Poland and other enemy powers;
> d) Questioning German capacity to resist with regard to military arma- ments and strength, nutritional supplies, raw materials, etc.;
> e) Misgivings about the unanimity of leadership and Volk. . . ."

Each of these remarks proves that it had been impossible to stupefy all Germans despite massive propaganda; there were still persons who retained and asserted their critical judgments and firm ethical viewpoints. They further prove that despite all prohibitions and penalties, foreign radio broadcasts were heard by the public, troops, religious groups, and even within party circles. The Propaganda Ministry received numerous requests for special permissions.[35] Finally, on January 26, 1940, the OKW, on Goebbels' request, issued sharper directives.[36] Dangers to the fighting morale were sounded and the soldiers warned not to listen to foreign propaganda for fear of "spiritual self-mutilation." Lawyers explained to the public the heavy penalties for transgressions of the law, and the press reported several exemplary verdicts carrying a long period of penal servitude.[37]

In direct conjunction with these rumors, the question arises as to what degree they were believed or to what extent their factual content was regarded as proven. The answer to this question is especially signifi- cant with regard to "knowledge" of the regime's criminal practices. This particular aspect must be taken into consideration at this point; numer- ous references will be made later in the course of this study to deliber- ate rumors and distorted realities.

To illustrate this problem for the early period of the war, we will again use the correspondence of the corps area XIII commander. Under point V, "Atrocity Reports," it states: "Enemy propaganda still, as in 1914-18, does not shrink from reporting on supposed atrocities by German soldiers. . . . The German soldier knows his comrades and his countrymen (*Volksgenossen*). He knows they are incapable of *any* cruelties or injustices. From such reports he can clearly see how false *every* enemy propaganda statement is. . . ."[38]

In these few sentences one already finds expressed two basic opinions evident throughout the war and at all levels of society, excluding, of course, those who were well informed and responsible for the rumors: 1. This was the same enemy propaganda about German atrocities as during World War I, and 2. a "true" German was not even capable of such crimes. In reference to the first view, allied propaganda did circulate false reports, albeit often unintentionally, thereby enabling Goebbels to discredit the basic truths of most allied information by disproving just a few stories.[39] Foreign reports of the Third Reich's extermination program were immediately dismissed as heinous enemy slander. In one instance the Foreign Office collected and published foreign reports about German mistreatment of Polish ecclesiastics and intellectuals, and about mass executions, calling them "enemy propaganda."[40]

The press was repeatedly directed to take the most forceful stand against all atrocity reports and to reject them;[41] journalists were instructed to treat confidentially all information regarding the transport of Jews to the General Government,[42] just as in the pre-war years reports on concentration camps and the arrest of Jews had already been prohibited.[43]

The German citizen, therefore, had the choice of believing unverifiable rumors, enemy radio broadcasts that were sometimes lent credibility by hints from clergymen, or his own government. He had no proof. Everywhere there was a hunger for sensationalism, a desire for horror stories which naturally contributed to the dissemination of such rumors. But probably few really believed them during this initial period of the war; and that goes for the second opinion as well—who, without verification, would regard his neighbor, friend, even his father, brother, or husband as a murderer? Later, as rumors of atrocities intensified and men on leave told of mass executions, concealment became increasingly difficult and the whispering grew louder and louder.[44]

As a smoke-screen for its crimes, the Nazi regime from the beginning also served up a generous dose of enemy crimes. In response to the "British Government Blue Book" published in Basel in 1939, Goebbels ordered the fabrication of a blue book on "English Concentration Camps and Colonial Atrocities."[45] The racial struggle in Poland was concealed by endless reports of atrocities against ethnic Germans.[46] Thus initial reactions to executions in Poland reported by soldiers on leave were that "it is after all only fair and just that murderers of ethnic Germans had been shot just like the guerrillas."[47] Using an analogous argument, Hitler was also able in part to push the blame for "reprisals" onto the troops.

The deeper motivations underlying these propaganda campaigns can be explained partly in terms of a projection of innate drives onto others, just as the anti-Semitism of leading Nazis has been explained as a transference of their own guilt complexes to the Jews.[49] The chauvinism of Polish politicians in the thirties also aided German propaganda, much like the post-World War I war guilt question, which relieved the conscience and served as a political issue. It stimulated, moreover, feelings of hatred and aggression until then conspicuously absent from large segments of the population. The October 12, 1939, report of the Leipzig SD section indicates that such a policy seems to have produced results: "Press and radio informed the public extensively before and during the Polish campaign of the bestial Polish atrocities against ethnic Germans. . . . The result was a profound and vehement indignation by the German Volk, not only against the civilian Polish population but also against the military, which—as was reported—also widely engaged in atrocities. . . . There is general recognition of the fact that a civilized nation cannot retaliate measure for measure, but there is no appreciation for a situation in which the Poles are now better off under us than they were before. . . ."[50]

Germans, especially women, seem to have had friendly relations with the first prisoners of war from Poland—too friendly, according to a complaint in the November 20 domestic report, citing numerous cases of intimate relations between German girls and war prisoners. Contact was particularly close in the country, where Poles were taken into families and went dancing with the daughters. In many places Catholic clerics also gave preference to Poles.[51] State and military authorities reacted with a series of decrees forbidding, as "injurious to the Volk," social intercourse with war prisoners and setting penalties for it.[52] Extensive propaganda and police measures were unleashed, and the courts rendered deterrent verdicts: stiff penal servitude for women and death penalties for Polish war prisoners.

As a contrast to uninformed public opinion, a brief discussion of eyewitness reactions to German atrocities is useful, although the documents provide little information. Differentiating between those who "knew" and those who "participated," it is possible to categorize the mentality of concentration camp personnel according to three basic types: 1. the criminal element, found in all societies, but organized in the Third Reich;

2. the dedicated activists, from inquisitors to Heinrich Himmler and even scientists, all performing inhuman tasks for a higher purpose; and 3. myrmidons, the footsoldiers and stooges, whose twentieth-century variant is the *"Schreibtischmörder,"* the impersonal bureaucratic murderer who is often a mixture of 2 and 3.

But what about the German military, those soldiers and officers deployed in the Polish campaign? We do not know how many were and later became eyewitnesses to injustices, brutalities, and mass shootings, how many meted out "retribution" personally, and what their inner reactions were in the face of these events. The letter of Monsignor Splett, Bishop of Danzig, to Pope Pius XII on January 14, 1940, proves that many arrested priests, for example, were released through the intervention of generals, and that the real "fury of the Party organizations" only began after the soldiers had been withdrawn.[53] So far only individual cases have been recorded, such as the protests and actions of General Johannes Blaskowitz,[54] supreme commander in the East, who was subsequently recalled but later reinstated, and Field-Marshal von Küchler,[55] who was disciplined after the Polish campaign and relieved of his post as army commander. But even he demanded that his officers and soldiers refrain "from all criticism of the General Government's actions against the population, for example the treatment of Polish minorities, the Jews and church affairs."[56] The other commanders and top officers, alone capable of exerting influence, outwardly followed the OKW-recommended tactic of "non-involvement"[57] or later in the war sought to hinder the extermination policy by commandeering and employing Jewish labor. Ultimately all these attempts failed: "I have issued instructions to proceed severely," wrote Himmler on October 2, 1942, to Oswald Pohl, chief of the SS Economic Administration Office, "against all those who believe they can present ostensible arguments for armaments interests while in fact they merely want to assist the Jews and their enterprises."[58]

There were also German officers and soldiers who were appalled and very ashamed. In the words of one officer: "I am ashamed to be a German! The minority which sullies the German name with its murder, plunder, and ravagings will be the misfortune of the whole German Volk if we don't soon put a stop to them. . . ."[59] But nothing happened; most officers and soldiers tolerated or even condoned these actions, judging from a confidential report of October 23, 1939, by a journalist who had toured the provinces of Posen and West Prussia:[60]

". . . The streets are quiet and outwardly everything is normal in the cities and villages. Everyone is working. Seed grains have been distributed and the ground prepared. Lights are burning in all the cities; there is no blackout. . . . In short, the war *per se* is over.

"But the reorganization has begun. The new order appears extraordinarily complicated. It is not just a question of replacing the vanished Polish administration with Germans, but simultaneously a matter of cleansing those territories designated as Reich provinces 100 per cent of Poles and Jews and resettling them with returning Volksdeutsche from the Baltic, Volynia, etc. . . .

"In the liberation of German territory from the Poles, two methods are clearly distinguishable. In those areas where repatriated Balts are appearing, like Gotenhafen and the northern regions of the Corridor, the Poles are turned out on the spot. The procedure goes something like this: an arriving Balt, say a barber by profession, reports to the proper authorities with a request to open a barbershop. He receives the address of a Polish barber. Accompanied by an official of the Security Service, he proceeds to the place and tells the Pole to get lost . . . taking over the complete shop with inventory and personnel. . . . The Pole begins his journey, taking whatever portable possessions he has with him. His only directions are: Poland, east of Warsaw. . . . To avoid unpleasant scenes, these columns of refugees move solely after dark. During the day everything appears absolutely normal. . . .

"In those areas where compulsory transfer is less urgent, Poles, including all Jews, are presently being registered and, insofar as they are considered desirable inhabitants of the remaining Polish territory, are deported to their new homeland. . . . In those cases where a reappearance of contaminated individuals and the like in a future Poland seems undesirable, they are liquidated for reasons of expediency. This applies especially to Jews.

"The whole procedure is marked by speed and efficiency. To appreciate these matters, especially in their human context, one must keep in mind that these people in the East lack central European sentimentality anyway, and the individual as such has only minimal worth. . . ."

Liquidated for reasons of expediency, without central European sentimentality, the individual as such of little value—can one describe the National Socialist racial program any better?

Meanwhile the victorious troops returned home, and Hitler, on October 6, in a speech before the Reichstag, offered the Western Powers a peace proposal, one he admittedly made "only to place the enemy in the wrong."[61] Among the German population, however, the speech reawakened hopes for a speedy termination of the war[62] and gave rise to all sorts of rumors. One example had the British Government resigning, its King abdicating, and a cease-fire signed. In various firms, operations ceased because the work force flocked to discuss the reputedly new situation that had arisen. Joyous demonstrations occurred in Berlin, shoppers no longer wanted to register for rations since these would soon be unnecessary;

students staged enthusiastic rallies.[63] In the border regions of western Germany these hopes for peace were reinforced by the reopening of schools on both sides of the border.[64] Fortune tellers' and clairvoyants' business prospered when they predicted an early end to the war.

Goebbels' propaganda machine operated at full steam to infuse an intensified Anglophobia into a public mood that was slightly out of control. "Chamberlain rejects the German peace offer and refuses to understand the Führer's magnanimous gesture. They are defending, not the cause of nations, but of warmongers. . . ."[65] This smear propaganda bore fruit, according to official inquiries: "People are aware that England is Germany's main enemy and the *general mood* is so solidly *against England* that even children in the streets are singing satirical songs about England and especially about Chamberlain. Hopes for an early peace have not, however, completely vanished. . . ."[66]

"After Hitler, aware of Germany's power, had once more offered France and England peace in his great speech before the Reichstag on October 6, there was widespread confidence that the enemy would not reject the proffered hand. After this did occur, the Volk realized that England only wants Germany's annihilation; thus trusting completely in the Führer, the Volk has resolved more than ever to see this imposed war through to the victorious end. . . ."[67]

2. THE FIRST WINTER OF WAR

The time from the end of the military campaign in Poland—the actual racial war had just begun—to the surprise attack on Norway was the period so aptly characterized by the French as "drôle de guerre." It was a kind of cold war, without engagements, a hiatus between two lightning campaigns—due largely to weather conditions and not to Hitler's intentions.[68] During this time the German public became aware of a deterioration in its hardly opulent lifestyle and, since nothing exciting was happening, it became a period of austerity and boredom. Laborers and employees complained about inadequate food allocations,[69] idle soldiers were bored and publicly derided as "vacation warriors" ["*KdF-Krieger*"], "firemen on the West Wall," "bunker sleepers," and "potato warriors."[70] There was grumbling about provisions: "Horst Wessel butter—marching along in spirit*" or "have you read what it says for butter in the new Meyers dictionary? 'Spread from the Weimar days.' "[71]

* Horst Wessel, a Berlin SA leader, was killed in a street brawl in February, 1930, and made into a national hero by Propaganda Minister Goebbels. The official SA song, or Horst Wessel Lied, "Die Fahne Hoch" was dedicated to his 'spirit,' which marched along. *Ed.*

The only incident of late autumn, 1939, that was a topic of conversation was the assassination attempt on Hitler in the Bürgerbräukeller on November eighth: "The attempted assassination in Munich has strengthened the Volk's feeling of solidarity. Public interest in the results of the special commission's inquiry into the event is very great. The question of how it could have happened remains the number one topic of conversation in all social circles. Love for the Führer has grown even stronger, and the attitude towards the war has become more positive in many circles as a result. . . ."[72]

At first the Catholic Church refrained from taking a position. ". . . By contrast, the Protestant Church sharply condemned the Munich assassination attempt and took a clear stand." In various regions of the Reich, thanksgiving services were held which, to take an example from Stuttgart, ran something as follows:

> Within all of us who have gathered today, emotions are still quivering over the diabolical attempt on our Führer's life. At the same time our gratitude for God's unending mercy is great and sustains us. Amidst the hail of bullets in the World War, in his courageous path on November 9, 1923, in the ensuing years of struggle for political power, and now during this infernal attack, almighty God again and again has held His protective hand over him; and we should beseech God every morning to protect our Führer, grant him victory and thereby also us, so that we can attain a good peace and our Volk be granted Lebensraum and a chance to live.[73]

Finally the Catholic Church also took a stand. In a letter, the Pope congratulated Hitler on his deliverance.[74] According to a November 22, 1939, SD report,[75] the public mood played a role in this, "being very agitated in individual districts over the passivity of the clergy and the Church." The diocesan paper for the archdiocese of Freiburg therefore published an article on November 19 in which the usual thanks were given God and special reference was made to the work of supposed foreign elements. Other Catholic papers followed suit.

Unofficially, however, strong doubts seemingly prevailed among a large segment of the Catholic clergy about the background of the assassination attempt as propagated by Goebbels' apparatus. While the newspapers had already been directed on November 9 to lay the blame not on domestic groups but on foreigners,[76] which ultimately led to accusations against the Secret Service, a sizable percentage of the Catholic priests seemed inclined to accept the opinion of the Strasbourg broadcasts that it was an attempt from within the Party.[77]

The public also expressed doubt about the veracity of the Propaganda Ministry's thesis, as communicated by a domestic situation report of the

Leipzig SD section in connection with the arrests of November 9, 1939: ". . . for example, the view is still held that it is not right to arrest former Stahlhelm members, Catholics, etc., while the Reich asserts that the culprits are to be sought within the Secret Service or international Jewry. The opinion exists that this wave of arrests will take the 'wind out of the sails' of German propaganda."[78]

It is evident that in late autumn, 1939, there was considerable dissatisfaction, unrest, and dissonance among the population. All SD reports register intensified activity by marxist and communist groups.[79] Pamphlets and propaganda leaflets calling for the overthrow of the regime were distributed. An SD report of November third claims that this activity resulted from the communist attitude that it was less dangerous now because the state, eager to retain Russia's friendship, could not impose a heavy hand. Another report[80] talks of two opinion trends within German marxist circles: "One side is of the opinion that Stalin betrayed the workers, and that communism must now be carried forward independently of Russia. Trotsky's followers propagandize within these groups. They are attempting to win over those communists disillusioned with Stalin. Another segment hopes that communism will gain ground again as a result of the Berlin-Moscow Pact."

In Berlin, the night following the abortive assassination attempt, the show windows of Hitler's personal photographer Hoffmann were smashed. Only pictures of the Führer were being displayed in the showcases.[81] These communist disruptions inside the old Reich ranged far behind those in newly annexed areas in scope and intensity. Especially the Austrian Communists came alive.[82]

Brisk activity was also noted within religious circles: "Opposition by political Catholicism continues. Special interest is being devoted to the youth and the soldiers."[83] A few reports also provide concrete examples from sermons and speeches of the Protestant Church and in particular from members of the Confessional Church, more or less publicly against Nazi practices.[84] In such cases there always followed the ominous sentence that the state police had been notified.

"One can generally say that within the Reich the attitude of the Protestant Church to events is more positive, with the exception of the radical Confessional wing, than that of the Catholic Church. In Protestant services one finds now and then genuine and sincere prayers for the Führer and the German Volk, coming from an inner affirmation of events. Generally speaking in the Catholic Church, by contrast, Germany's present destiny is either completely ignored or presented as a time of particular hardship, one of the most severe tests and chastisements God has sent in order that those Germans alienated from Christianity might find their way back to God and the true Church."[85]

The Catholic Church's attitude at this point was probably influenced by the papal encyclical *Summi Pontificatus* of October 20, 1939,[86] which spoke with reference to Luke 22:53 of a true "hour of darkness," without emphasizing German aggressions. Among intransigent Nazis the encyclical was viewed as an attack exclusively against Nazi Germany.[87] Subsequent editorials of the international press were considered particularly damaging to Germany's image. Nazis argued that the Pope, on the basis of Catholic natural right, had directly assailed the National Socialist Weltanschauung and, in referring to international law, characterized National Socialism "as an expression of naked egotism which knows no regard for the welfare of nations. . . ."[88]

There is no doubt, despite an official policy of neutrality towards the Churches, that hatred within the Party leadership continued to grow. Göring, Goebbels, Bormann, and Rosenberg never missed an opportunity to curtail the Churches' power. Rosenberg quite correctly defined the nature of this showdown as "spiritual warfare."[89] It was assumed that the clergy's attitude was centrally dictated and controlled. The following measures and mottos, directed centrally, were attributed to the Catholic Church: 1. they would welcome Germany's defeat, and thereafter they hoped for a partition of Germany into Catholic states; 2. they were increasingly equating National Socialism with Bolshevism;[90] 3. they were disseminating and discussing news from foreign broadcasts; 4. they were preparing the way for discrediting the Reich government and leading personalities in Germany by spreading bad jokes; and 5. they were presenting the war as God's punishment for the "moral depravity of the German Volk."[91]

One can discern the Catholic Church's strength and perhaps even its increasing influence on the populace just from this constant mistrust of the Catholic Church by Party leaders. Its strength lay especially in the fact that people could speak their minds freely to their priests about unpleasantness and worries, and seek the consolation not possible from Party offices. A typical example is offered by the behavior of the population evacuated from the Western zone at the outbreak of war. Although evacuation plans had been drawn up since 1938, the measure was carried out precipitously and with little coordination: "The removal of the population from the Western red zone unfortunately did not work out as well as was required in the interests of the participants . . . the returnees were thrown together and some arrived at destinations not intended for them. Especially unpleasant was the separation of family members. Thus it occurred that fathers wandered the country in despair, searching for wife and children. In some areas transport trains also arrived without supervisors, so that terrible confusion reigned. . . ."[92]

There was consequently a great deal of anger, and many people refused to remain where they had been sent, particularly in cases where urban residents ended up in rural or underdeveloped areas. The SD report of November 8, 1939,[93] talks about 80 per cent of the evacuees "leaving the transport without authorization and making their way home or wandering aimlessly." Furthermore, they were often taken in only grudgingly[94] and called "Saar French," "Frenchies" and "Gypsies."[95] Such expressions must have produced bitter reactions from the very nationalistic Saar population. Since they could not complain to the Party, which was guilty of the disorganization of the "evacuation," the predominantly Catholic Saarlander sought consolation from the Church.[96]

Aside from the clergy and the faithful, the attitude of the students also annoyed Party officials. Apparently the academic youth was little impressed by the momentous times and the Party's mission. They were having a good time despite the war and ideological bombardment; numerous complaints came from the university towns of Marburg, Göttingen, Breslau, and Jena about classroom antics and disrespect for student leaders.[97]

Following these reports Goebbels condemned the young people's behavior in his December, 1939, ministerial conference and ordered preparation of a report on students at Göttingen.[98] The situation soon deteriorated and reports about unruly juveniles multiplied. The Leipzig SD section, in the spring of 1940, reported a rise in store thefts and especially heavy frequenting of dance-halls in which about half the clientele danced "dances of a jazz-like nature despite clearly posted notices prohibiting the Swing and Lambeth Walk." About 20 per cent of the visitors were youth under eighteen, or even under sixteen.[99] On March 9, 1940, a "police decree for the protection of youth" was promulgated ordering those under eighteen to clear the streets by nightfall. They were prohibited from staying in pubs, cinemas, and cabarets after 9 p.m.; youths under sixteen were not allowed to drink alcohol or to smoke in public.[100] About a month later another report on "oppositional youth" appeared, while in Leipzig a court case against a group of ninety-two, the "Reeperbahn gang," resulted in lengthy prison terms for some. There were also political groups not merely motivated by youthful exuberance calling themselves "Red X," "Red G," and the like.

Teenage girls cared little for private or state associations; of those employed in the Junker Works, for example, only eight of sixty belonged to the League of German Girls (BDM). Parents who were asked why they refused to send their daughters replied "because the BDM ruins them. . . ."[101] This attitude was typical of many parents whose daughters were *pro forma* members of the League but were seldom permitted to attend meetings.

Actually, women often aroused the regime's ire. Representatives of the

upper-middle and upper classes especially made efforts to liberate themselves from the Party's influence and remain aloof. To avoid working for
the Nazi League of Women, they collected privately for charity and did
volunteer work through the Red Cross.[102] This distancing from the
"Volksgemeinschaft" was not well received by Nazi functionaries, who
were also irritated by the fact that not all women had been won over to
the war effort—the original decree for compulsory service had been withdrawn since previous normal mobilization of female labor had sufficed.[103]
Many women now also had time to scour the shops for non-rationed foods;
here, too, resentment was directed in particular against the more affluent
people who could afford additional restaurant meals or delicacies.[104]
Envy, a "pivotal question of social existence"[105] fully exploited by the
Nazis to gain power, was to give the Third Reich a great deal of trouble.

The dominant topic of the first winter of war, however, was the coal
crisis. Beginning November sixth and continuing late into the spring,
complaints never ceased. This bottleneck in provisioning both the population and industry resulted from transportation difficulties. For years, transport vehicles, particularly freight cars of the Reich Railway, had been
neglected and their replacement postponed in favor of more vital war
goods. The Polish campaign took more rolling stock out of circulation.
In the mines, shifts were dropped and the Rhenish-Westphalian Coal
Syndicate was forced to store 1.2 million tons of coal in November, 1939,
alone. At fourteen sites in the Saar, thirty-eight shifts were cancelled
in the first weeks of November.[106] The situation was aggravated, especially in the cities, when severe frost set in after Christmas.[107] There
were stormy scenes in front of coal yards, coal trucks were stopped and
coal dealers threatened; eventually the police had to be called in.[108]
Coal shortages became noticeable everywhere, but especially in northern
and central Germany; it was worst in East Prussia and those areas which
had previously heated with wood.[109]

Transportation problems furthermore caused temporary work stoppages[110] which only added to worker unrest already aggravated by the
coal crisis, inadequate food supplies, and notably poor potato deliveries.[111]
Unrest was particularly evident in those plants where workers had remained faithful to their old marxist ideals.[112] In many cities "communist
graffiti" appeared as the winter came to a close. At the Leuna Works
the inscriptions "Down with Hitler" and "Red Front" were found; at
one plant in Schwandorf, Upper Palatinate, someone wrote: "Nazis
murder workers. Hitler is a murderer of workers. Down with Hitlerism."
Reports of similar occurrences came from Dortmund, Bielefeld, Dresden,
Plauen, and Würzburg.[113] Berlin reported dissemination of Social Democratic literature printed abroad.[114]

Unfavorable reports also emanated again from farming communities.[115] As spring approached, the state wanted to replace about one million laborers required for the agrarian economy with Polish workers.[116]

Rural and city inhabitants complained most about the poor supply of shoes and sole-leather. The Düsseldorf economic operations staff was forced to admit that "the shoe issue (is beginning) to become a political question of the first order."[117] Shortage of footwear resulted in repeated refusals to work.

Given these developments, the tenor of discontent running through all the opinion reports is not surprising: "Lately the general mood of the public has to be judged as hardly favorable or optimistic. . . ."[118] Almost all reporters agreed that no war enthusiasm was yet evident.[119] "Everyone is waiting for something to happen . . .";[120] the capture of the German tanker "Altmark" by the British destroyer "Cossack" and the release of three hundred English prisoners transferred from the "Graf Spee" only briefly diverted public opinion from its workaday worries.[121] Life quickly returned to its bleak routine.

3.   BLITZKRIEG IN NORWAY AND FRANCE:
     HITLER TRIUMPHANT

The occupation of Denmark on April 9, 1940, and the landing of German troops in Norway suddenly caused "all other questions to recede into the background, and otherwise normal debates over economic worries and restrictions grew silent."[122] "Developments in Scandinavia and engagements with English sea and air forces completely dominate the mood of the whole Reich. All events are followed with an interest and involvement not seen since the beginning of the war. One finds uniformly strong approval and enthusiasm among all segments of society. There is a general conviction that the Führer again acted 'at the right moment' . . . and German propaganda arguments are being endorsed. . . . *Denmark's loyal conduct* is generally respected and has awakened a certain sympathy for the Danish people. Norway's resistance, on the other hand, is seen by many as proof of its strong ties to England. . . ."[123]

Thus, almost no one entertained moral reservations; only the "Meldungen aus dem Reich" for May 20[124] mentioned an edition of the monthly foreign pamphlet *Das wahre Deutschland* which had an editoral entitled "New Desecration of the German Name." Domestic presses, however, heeded the special instructions of the Reich Press Chief which spoke of "defending" Denmark and Norway, and a "lightning-like German reply" to the British attempt to make Scandinavia a theatre of

war against Germany. German operations were supposedly only unleashed by England's action,[125] even though in fact Hitler's decision was
made previously and quite independently. Although the details of Hitler's
plans were unknown to the German public, the explanations provided by
the propaganda network seemed plausible, and Germans were delighted
that they had beaten England to the punch. Their vision, however, was
so blurred that they saw as their main accomplishment "the moral impression made on the remaining neutral countries, especially Holland,
Belgium, and the southeast."[126] The report also spoke of a "proud mood,"
and in fact the Germans were proud at this point of their might, their
military achievements, and "their" Führer, for whom they expressed
"boundless admiration."[127]

Goebbels sensed the danger of this sudden exuberance and urged
avoidance of "hyper-optimism";[128] and indeed, the buoyant mood
quickly gave way to harsh realities.[129] The usual invectives over poor
foodstuffs, vegetables, and high prices were heard.[130] There were also renewed reports of busy activity by the Catholic Church.[131] This observa-
ble reversal was finally so radical—the public was alarmed at the losses
in Norway and complained about poor and inadequate press and radio
coverage—that there was talk of a downright "collapse of morale" at
Goebbels' ministerial conference.[132] How critical Goebbels' assessment of
the mood was can be seen by his remark that under no conditions could
there be a shortage of vital foodstuffs "since it would be impossible in
that case to maintain morale in Berlin."[133]

Germany's Western offensive quickly produced a renewed upswing in
morale. At the end of the Polish campaign and again at the turn of the
year, rumors had already appeared here and there about a possible occupation of Holland, only to disappear again. As late as May 8 the DNB
officially denied that two German armies had massed on the Dutch
border.[134] On May 10, however, at 5:30 a.m., German troops marched
into Holland and Belgium without a declaration of war, although Hitler
had repeatedly promised to respect their neutrality. In similarly worded
notes, the Dutch and Belgians were accused of having directed their
defenses exclusively towards the east and having conducted military talks
with the Western Powers. Germany had to assume the protection of
these neutral states and avert the danger of an attack on the Ruhr region.
The press received instructions "to convince the whole Volk that Holland and Belgium actually broke the neutrality."[135]

An SD report four days later was already able to register a clear success for this propaganda: "It must be emphasized that there were never
any illusions about Belgium's attitude and that the detentions[136] by the security police have made the strongest impression. From public conversa-

tions we gather that these pronouncements are not only viewed as an act of skillful propaganda; the opinion also exists that here a 'doublecross of the German Volk' has been uncovered. . . ."[137]

Germans were fully aware "that this time progress would be slower than in the Polish campaign or Norway. . . ."[138] In the same spirit, the Propaganda Minister had also instructed and advised the press on the first day of the offensive not to succumb "either to exaggerated optimism or to wild panic"[139] in its reports of the western drive.

However, the center of interest, according to SD reports, was Adolf Hitler, and anxiety over his welfare: "The Führer's personal participation has again made a particularly deep impression on all levels of society. Reports from all over the Reich concur that this announcement has the whole Volk worried about the Führer's life. Even if it has generally strengthened confidence in a successful Western operation, one possible reversal is emphasized, namely the loss of the Führer. . . ."[140]

As in the case of the Norwegian campaign, all other events again receded into the background. Neither Chamberlain's fall and the formation of a national government under Churchill nor the occupation of Iceland by British troops received much attention. Those events were too far removed from the direct sphere of interest. Switzerland's mobilization created a far greater stir, especially in southern Germany, and many believed Germany would not tolerate this "provocation" for long.[141] In early June, many people in southwestern Germany expected a speedy entry[142] into the small neighboring country, and even in July a certain unrest over this issue persisted.[143]

The Propaganda Ministry meanwhile swung its operations into high gear. Goebbels established the principle "that all enemy information incorrect or possibly harmful must be denied immediately. It is not necessary to examine the reports in detail as to their accuracy; crucial is only whether enemy assertions can in any way become damaging to us. . . ." Furthermore, he ordered activation of the war guilt question and enemy atrocity stories.[144]

Holland capitulated after five days of fighting, and Belgium surrendered two weeks later. Enthusiasm was very high, though Germans still resented "neutral" and supposedly friendly Holland's conduct, more so because the Dutch successor to the throne had married a German prince.[145] Victory over Belgium was seen as a blow to the morale of British and French troops. General respect and praise was voiced for the Belgian monarch who ceased hostilities in order to prevent further bloodshed and who stayed with his troops until the very end, unlike other heads of state.[146]

If the public was not always in agreement with the news services during the Norwegian campaign, reports of the start of the Western offensive aroused general admiration and respect. Agreement between regime and public seemed so secure, success of the Wehrmacht so complete, that Goebbels decided nothing had to be done at present to remind the population of the ban against listening to enemy broadcasts.[147]

Instead a new indoctrination campaign was launched to mobilize latent hatred against France or just to arouse new hatred in general. Memories of the Rhineland and Ruhr occupation were rekindled and the French branded as "niggerized sadists."[148] Again the SD report can be considered a successful one, stating on June 10 a "complete reversal of sentiment toward France." "Almost everywhere, France is being placed on a level with England. . . ."[149] A further report a few days later points to discrepancies in reports of the French and British and their "fighting value." Thus for example a few reports emphasized the cowardly flight of the English from Flanders, while others noted the brave evacuation of soldiers under heavy fire. "At times the French are presented as braver fighting opponents than the British. Especially in reports from the front, one hears that the average Poilu is a decent fighter. This is compared with German propaganda material about French atrocities against German prisoners. . . ."[150] Coordination between state-controlled propaganda and reports reflecting events just wasn't always successful, and Goebbels still had work in the future to eliminate positive accounts of the enemy's conduct. To be sure, the French campaign did create what the Nazi leadership had missed so far: "a true war spirit."[151] Bound up with this was the "confident expectation of a glorious and perhaps even imminent termination of the war."

Probably the German Volk had seldom stood as solidly behind the Nazi leadership and Adolf Hitler: "The reputation of the Führer has risen immeasurably even among the half-hearted and grumblers, because of the tremendous successes. Clergymen who seldom bothered to give the 'German greeting' now greet orally and in writing with 'Heil Hitler'."[152] "Not loud jubilation but deep inner joy testifies to the proud confidence of all citizens in a victorious conclusion to this battle forced on us by the Western Powers. . . ."[153]

On June 10, Mussolini announced Italy's entry into the war, postponed a few days on Hitler's express wishes:[154] "Italy's entry into the war has so far met with *no uniform reception*. Everywhere it produced different reactions and provoked the most lively discussions. Reports cite 'spontaneous enthusiasm,' 'joy,' 'satisfaction' and 'profound satisfaction' on the one hand, and 'surprise despite tense expectations,' 'reserved expectations,' 'no special pleasure' . . . on the other. Trust and mistrust are affecting people's feelings equally. 'Now comes Italy, after the war has almost been won and the hardest battles already fought,' is voiced repeatedly. . . . Although opinions not actually unfavorable to Italy are circulating we must point out that there are also, not just isolated, voices of mistrust. It shows that the breach of alliance from the World War has still not been forgotten completely. . . ."[155]

In his conference of June 16, 1940, Goebbels immediately reacted to this hardly friendly attitude towards Italy: "We must prevent the German Volk from getting the wrong impression of Italy's war capacity, which would only insult and discourage Italians."[156] But this time the result of word-of-mouth propaganda was long in coming. The national stereotype of the unreliable, unenthusiastic ally was too deeply rooted to be overcome by a few slogans. Latent mistrust forced Goebbels to insist once more a week later that it was vital "that the press tactfully redirect into reasonable avenues the emerging anger and hatred against Italy. It must explain to the Volk just how Italy helped us by remaining inactive. . . . The military angle had best be ignored."[157]

On June 10, the day Italy entered the war, the French government left Paris for Tours; June 14, German troops marched into Paris, which had been declared an open city. "News of *German troops entering the French capital, surrendered without a battle*, sent the population throughout the Reich into ecstasy to a degree never before experienced. On many squares and streets there were joyous demonstrations. . . ."[158] Everywhere there was an expectancy of early capitulation. The capture of Verdun in so short a time made the strongest impression. The city's name was still tied in everyone's mind to memories of long and bloody battles that had cost 300,000 lives in World War I.

"The surprising tempo of military and political developments these last days continues to dominate public opinion. *Discussion of non-military things has for weeks receded into the background.* There is talk everywhere of this most incredible performance by German soldiers. This enthusiasm of late always gives the impression that further intensification is not possible, and yet the public expresses greater enthusiasm with each new development. . . ."[159]

For Hitler, as for most Germans, especially those who had experienced Germany's defeat in 1918, victory over France represented the greatest triumph, erasing a blemish[160] so deeply felt that the stab-in-the-back legend had been disseminated as an excuse. Now, however, it was expunged, Germany's shield of honor shone again, and the world seemed right to many Germans. People were therefore prepared to exercise magnanimity. Things, however, developed quite differently than expected; like Hitler, most Germans had their own interests in mind and no understanding for the interests and mentality of the rest of the world.

The French request for a cease-fire was generally interpreted as a sign of an early end to the war in the West and an early settlement with England as well, though Hitler was still worried about the effect of Italy's possibly high demands on France. To avoid Pétain's continuation of the war from the African colonies, Hitler met with Mussolini on June 18 to persuade him to defer his territorial demands until the expected peace negotiations with France and England took place.[161] The public followed this meeting of the two fascist leaders with great excitement: "Enthusiasm among the Munich inhabitants has never been as great as today. In the rest of the Reich the consultations with Mussolini concerning the terms of the cease-fire were, as before, received with the same divided opinion. . . . On the one hand, the Duce's participation is seen only as a polite gesture, on the other a majority accuses Italy of seeking its share of the spoils too soon after entering the war. Generally people begrudge Italy the successes it will obtain so cheaply. It assumes the same role as Russia in Poland. The suggestion is made from various sectors which correctly recognize and evaluate Italy's assistance, that a modification of the attitude of the majority of the people be undertaken. . ."[162]

In the eyes of the regime, public opinion was consequently nothing more than an instrument to be manipulated at will. Yet even at this juncture it did not always have a unified ring. For example, at the time two opinion trends were evident toward France. One wanted to accord the vanquished the chivalrous custom of magnanimous and honorable treatment; the other was filled with resentment and hatred, the one for which Goebbels made himself spokesman: "We owe it to the German people that the French do not, through false sentimentality, get away with just a black eye. We can only emphasize again and again, with utmost clarity, that negotiations are totally out of the question, that first of all France's army, navy, and armaments must be handed over and that this was the last time, for the next three hundred to four hundred years, that France can attack a peaceful Volk without cause. . . ."[163]

The "Meldungen aus dem Reich" summarized the attitudes toward France as follows: "Hard terms are unanimously demanded for France, as hard as possible but still just, compared to Versailles. Several elements in society even allow France a few concessions. But predominantly, given the memory of the shameful conduct of French rulers in 1918, the demand is that France must be 'made so small' that it cannot ever again contemplate a war against Germany. In detail, the majority is of the opinion that France must return the German colonies, surrender its fleet, give up Alsace-Lorraine, permit erection of military bases along its coast, and hand over to Italy Tunisia, Savoy, Corsica, and a piece of the Riviera. Other combinations deal with the establishment of a protectorate over Flanders;

some even go so far as to envisage all of France as a German protectorate. . . ."[164]

On June 22 the cease-fire was signed.[165] "The public's attention was directed mainly to the *cease-fire negotiations in Compiègne*. With satisfaction and emotion it was noted that negotiations were being conducted at the same place as in 1918. The gentlemanly behavior of the Germans, in sharp contrast to the arrogant vindictiveness of the French delegation the last time, elicited general respect and support. The emphatic and refined manner in which the Führer once and for all wiped out from history the shame of 1918 met with unrestrained admiration. The Führer's presence at the talks had a special reassuring effect. . . ."[166]

At this time Hitler stood at the zenith of his political career. Even to the older German officers, who at times had been more than critical of him, he had now truly become the "Führer" of Germany.[167] Thereby the German resistance and its planned coup—taken up again after the Polish campaign,[168] temporarily postponed when Hitler threatened to eradicate the "spirit of Zossen," and finally pursued by means of Halder's tactic of departmental resistance—also lost its impetus for a long time due to a lack of support. Only a heterogeneous, socially isolated opposition remained.

Even traditionally leftist groups seemed, insofar as reports permit a sweeping conclusion, to have been less negatively disposed to Hitler after his victory over France; many previous opponents spoke highly of Hitler, gave more to war relief, and adorned their homes with flags.[169] The June 24 SD report also mentioned a new inner resolve among the German people: "One can no longer speak of organized resistance within former communist and marxist circles. . . ." Now defeatist influences were attributed only to church elements.[170] Under the pretense of religious welfare, they were supposedly attempting to "create unrest and discord among the population through *clever oral propaganda*," especially the Catholic Church. "Within both confessional circles concern is voiced '*that after the conclusion of the war harsh and decisive measures will be taken against the Churches*'."[171] Yet the opposition could not have accomplished much since only a decreasing number of clergymen were reported for refusing to fly the flag on holidays.

Further indication of minimal resistance among the Germans in the early summer of 1940 was the decreasing number of criminal cases relating to the war.[172] The Landrat of Mainz wrote in his report for April-June, 1940, that "the domestic position of the state has never been so strong." Of course he knew of a few grumblers who had not considered it necessary to fly the flag, and others who were more worried "about how to obtain ration cards than about the results of military battles."[173] But even for these Germans, considered too materialistic by the Nazis, the military triumphs brought better provisioning. After July 1, an additional quarter of a pound of butter per person was issued; furthermore, an improvement in the quality of beer was introduced by raising the basic wort from 6 per cent to 9-10 per cent to create a better disposition among those numerous German beer drinkers who frequently criticized the quality of their favorite beverage.

The only unrest these days was in western Germany, created by the numerous bombings and the first daylight raids by British planes, whereby the population of several localities was exposed to fire from dive bombers.[174]

4. OPERATION SEA LION

After the cease-fire with France, Hitler and his closest military advisers believed that final victory was only a question of time. Hitler sent out peace feelers to England—one official contact ran through Sweden, another via the German and English ambassadors in Madrid. The German dictator entertained the view that it would now be possible to come to terms with England over a division of spheres of interest in the world. As victor it seemed natural for him to rule the European continent unchallenged. He expected England not only to withdraw from her traditional sphere of influence in the Mediterranean; a total revision of the African colonies was also planned. This illusionary phase lasted until about the middle of July. During these three weeks propaganda had to pursue its previously envisaged double goal: suppress rising sympathies for France and maintain a certain Anglophobia.

Both trends are easily documented in Goebbels' ministerial conferences and press instructions. On June 24, he declared that "the journalistic struggle against England must continue with undiminishing vigor."[175] On July 1 and 2 he was at Hitler's headquarters; on the third the word came that peace rumors were to be ignored. Neither precise information nor deadlines were to be announced, only the demand for continuation of the struggle must be kept alive.[176] Regarding France, Goebbels faced the dilemma of fostering Francophobia while suppressing all news from that war zone favorable to the enemy; repeated instructions called for a "cool reception" of pro-French sentiments and a revival of Italian popularity.[177] Everything was to await Hitler's speech. Instruction no. 462 of July 5 stated: "We still don't want to give the impression that for Germany no more bridges exist to the English people. It is still the intention of German propaganda to divide the English people from their government. A certain political interlude is still anticipated, presenting new possibilities after diplomatic relations between France and England are broken off. How long this interlude will last depends solely on the Führer. . . ."[178]

On the evening of July 6: "The Führer, after arriving in Berlin, expressed the wish to a few dignitaries that the German press should not become aggressive towards the English people, only toward Mr. Churchill and his clique. This is presently very important. Also, we do not want to give the impression that the French are decent people and would fit nicely into the German scheme of things. . . ."[179]

A "fundamental directive" followed at noon on July 9: "The editorial staffs are alerted that all future reports of conflicts between England and France (i.e., Martinique and Dakar) are not to be interpreted so as to arouse more sympathy for France. This would be a totally undesirable development. Germany will sign no 'gentlemanly' peace with France. . . . In the future, France will play the role of an 'enlarged Switzerland' in Europe, a vacation land and possibly also a producer of certain fashionable items. . . ."[180]

We know what new European order National Socialist leaders had in mind. Its extravagance emerges from a strictly confidential bulletin of July 12, 1940: "Europe's new order is a conscious part of Germany's general direction. Guidelines of the Prop(aganda) Min(istry) already indicated that France, in the future, will only play the role of a small Atlantic state. One has to imagine this quite concretely: apart from Italian territorial demands on France, our demands will also be quite extensive. The Führer has not issued the final word and we have to assume the extent of German demands in the peace treaty with France. It seems certain, however, that besides Alsace-Lorraine we will also add sizable portions of Burgundy, including the plateau of Langres and Dijon as capital, to the Reich. There is talk here and there of a 'Reich Gau Burgundy.' Channel ports like Dunkirk, Boulogne, etc., will at least become German naval bases, if not Reich territory. Territorial discussions of the northwestern border states Holland and Belgium have not been held. King Leopold will be given the opportunity to rule as sovereign of an autonomous Flanders, incorporating both Belgian and French Flanders. If King Leopold refuses to go along, Holland and Belgium would become protectorates of some sort. Norway and Denmark are not very different. We can work with the Danish king. In Norway, preparations are being made to retain a functioning administration—after removal of King Haakon. All these countries will receive purely administrative self-rule, but Germany will determine all military, economic, and nationality questions. . . . The peace treaty will eliminate France not only as a major power but generally as an influential political European state. Concerning the colonial question, there is still no clear final position. It can only be viewed within the greater context of the English dominions. This brings us to the interesting problem of German *military objectives against England*. These last fourteen days of battle lull have brought a sizable number of people in Berlin to the conclusion that the battle for the Isles will not begin because England will accept, in some form, Germany's basic demands. This is operating on the assumption that Lloyd George or someone else will be found to assume Churchill's unfortunate legacy under the maxim 'to salvage what is still salvageable.' German and Italian demands should run something like this: England must withdraw completely from the Mediterranean, abandon all its bases, relinquish Egypt, the Sudan and the near East, furthermore withdraw from Africa and retain only the three empire-states of India, Australia, and Canada; finally it must dismantle its fleet in home waters and retain only squadrons for the protection of the three empire-states. . . ."[181]

It was obvious on July 15 that England would not accept these imperialistic demands, which can only be described as a sheer utopia. The 'interlude' was over: "We can now no longer count on delaying the very hard and costly war against England. Here in Berlin doubt exists whether there will be a landing immediately. Probably the bombings will be so intense as to raise the possibility that the English people will weaken prior to a complete showdown and invasion. . . ."[182]

Hitler had issued instructions to the OKW as early as July 2, setting in motion preliminary plans for a landing in England. Given Great Britain's negative response to the peace feelers, he issued order no. 16 for Operation "Sea Lion" on July 16, though he secretly continued to hope it would never have to be executed. During these days the fateful decision to break his tactically motivated alliance with Russia matured, and he returned to his original concept of annihilating Bolshevism and seizing land in the east. As his remarks at the time clearly reveal, he hoped simultaneously to eliminate England's last support on the continent.[183] Not until July 19 did he hold his repeatedly postponed Reichstag speech, in which he officially made Great Britain a peace offer.[184] Within an hour the journalist Sefton Delmer rejected the offer in a trenchant statement on the BBC, followed within a few days by the government's rejection through its Foreign Minister, Halifax. German propaganda, in reply to the hostile commentaries of the English press, threw itself into an orgy of hate against England.

The desired echo reverberated throughout the German public. While the SD report of July 4 still reflected indecisive propaganda concerning Britain, and Shirer observed on July 20 in his diary that Germans still desired peace,[185] after July 25 Anglophobia became more defined: "Halifax's speech and ostentatiously intensified air raids by English airmen against German cities following Hitler's speech fanned hatred of England even more. The final reckoning is yearned for more than ever. . . ."[186]

On August 1—the day Hitler issued order no. 17 for an intensified sea and air war against England—the Propaganda Minister emphasized the need for the state media, the press and newsreels, "to see us through the present waiting period in such a way that the Volk does not sink into stagnation but rather maintains its present level of tension. The situation has become more difficult insofar as the Volk today no longer asks *when* but *why* the attack has not yet taken place. . . ."[187]

Without military accompaniment, however, the barrage of propaganda only increased widespread indifference. People were just fed up being served "the *same reports* with *almost identical commentary* in various broadcasts."[188] Again Joseph Goebbels reacted immediately and castigated the "monotony of arguments" two days after this report appeared. A few days later he demanded that "our" remaining newspaper content, besides official announcements, must "also be the result of freely formed opinions, at least within limits."[189] Naturally this was a white lie; and thus growing uncertainty spread about the course of the war. The public divided into two camps, optimists and pessimists: "One side still believes that England will be defeated within a few weeks of the actual outbreak of hostilities, and that the war will still end this year. The other, however, whose numbers are increasing with every additional day, fears that the war will drag on into next year. . . ."[190]

Certainly there was no real collapse of public confidence. There was some concern over a second winter of war, inadequate coal supplies,[191] poor footwear—complaints about these had increased again—but not a real depression. Attempts were made to revive public morale by special announcements of successful air and naval activity. But the barometer of opinion did not climb until Göring, on August 12, issued the order to begin the air war over England. "The regime's announcement of a *total blockade* of the Isles has had a very animating effect on the whole population, according to available reports." The number of optimists grew, and many Germans again believed in an early end to the war.[192] To certain military authorities, however, these hopes seemed premature and exaggerated, given the still incomplete landing preparations and emerging doubts about the seriousness of Hitler's intention to carry out the landing in England. Major-General Walter Warlimont, head of the national defense division (L) within the OKW, therefore recommended a correction of the previous propaganda line.

A secret note of August 19, 1940, containing Keitel's handwritten comments, begins with the following words: "The tone of our press and radio has led to a belief by the people in a rapid conclusion to the war. An early landing in England is generally expected. Add to this the fact that the Volk is spoiled by our quick successes in Poland and France, and does not credit the English with much. Should the war extend beyond the winter and then probably for an unforeseeable period, a setback in morale is unavoidable. Effective counter-action is the responsibility not only of the Party and its propaganda offices, but also of the *Wehrmacht leadership.*" To this paragraph Keitel added: "Guidelines for propaganda in general come from the Führer. Thus I request revision of this note so that its recommendations sound less like criticism of existing methods than *future military* needs."[193]

In addition to criticism of the direction of propaganda, the note also contained a suggestion that was to play a role later in the course of the war, namely the deployment of soldiers at home to improve morale. As outlined by Warlimont's section, it read: "The Wehrmacht collapsed in World War I due to failure at home. It can never recur in this form because of today's government, quite apart from the advantageous military situation. The Volk blindly trusts the leadership and is tightly organized, through and through, by the Party." Nevertheless, suggestions were made to mobilize the "source of strength" of the military spirit for the second winter and to let soldiers talk freely of life in the army to small gatherings. The OKW head characterized this as just one more "wave of meetings." Moreover, it would place the Wehrmacht in a kind of opposition to the Party. "Then more 'military request concerts' followed by 'social evenings' would be better," Keitel remarked.

His rejection was not unfounded. Goebbels previously had categorically declined a similar request, emphasizing "that the Party is alone responsible for political and cultural leadership of the German Volk, and has the sole right to appeal to the people at meetings." He rejected "old admirals and generals" talking to the German people in factories, especially since they did not always have the correct feeling for the people.[194] An order to this effect, reserving leadership of the Volk to the Party, followed at the close of the year.[195] We can assume, however, that the OKW's recommendation, rewritten to suit Keitel, was transmitted to the Propaganda Minister, since Goebbels in his conference of August 23 did point "to the need for acquainting the Volk gradually with the fact that the war may drag on beyond the winter." While still arguing for a possible termination in 1940, Goebbels wanted to avoid dashing unfounded hopes as well as to prepare for the eventuality of a longer war.[196]

Preparing for a protracted war while simultaneously sustaining hopes for an early end—which aptly reflects the degree of uncertainty among

Germany's war leaders during these weeks—proved to be a bad tactic. One can no longer speak of unified public opinion as it existed during the French campaign. Opinion fluctuated between the extremes of hope for an early end to the war and a growing fear and anxiety of another winter of war.[197] Once more Hitler was able to lift morale in his speech at the start of the second war year, particularly by his assurance of a massive attack on England: "relax, it's coming" became a familiar quote. It gave the impression, "only a man who is past the biggest obstacles and has victory securely in his pocket can speak that way."[198] But when nothing happened during September aside from bombing raids on English cities, a certain indifference slowly spread as more and more people began to accept the idea of a second winter of war.[199]

The signing of the Tripartite Pact by Germany, Italy and Japan—delineating spheres of influence and providing for mutual support in case of attack by powers presently not involved in either European or Asian conflict—resulted once more in a short improvement in morale. Again many Germans began to reckon with a major assault on England in the immediate future.[200] But when nothing happened again, the disappointment became evident in numerous expressions of displeasure.[201] Then came the first heavy raid on Berlin, on August 24, which was a profound shock to Berliners. Shirer noted that they were dumbfounded, hardly believing it possible that something like this could happen. At the start of the war, Göring had boasted that no plane could penetrate the outer or inner air defenses of Berlin—and naive Berliners had believed him.[202] The "messages" from the press conference of August 29 stated: "The Reich's prestige will not permit nightly English raids on Berlin. . . ."[203] But as a precaution, evacuation of women and children from endangered areas was begun. This evacuation, in turn, gave rise to all sorts of talk, as related by Bamberg's Public Prosecutor General: "That segment of the population without real political insight or positive political behavior has not proven to be so insignificant. This group, which previously shared a common optimism, given the brilliant military victories and particularly given their insulation from events, is now viewing a second winter of war with mistrust and pusillanimity after these little air raid alarms and bombings. . . ."[204]

Opinion during the latter half of 1940 was not only divided among the public but also among groups within the Churches, especially the Catholic clergy. "Meldungen" increasingly focused on the adverse impact of this unrelated conflict.[205] A July 15 report dealt with the influence of Protestant clergymen on the public;[206] its "religious propaganda" was less negative largely because of a divided leadership and internal dissension. Only remarks by individual pastors, primarily members of the Confessional Church, were noted: de-emphasizing the historic world role of the German Volk, and *"focusing on confessional life."* Often the unity of all Christians was also being highlighted, irrespective of their nationality. Both Churches explained the war as God's punishment: "Overall it has been established that only *after a complete victory in the West* did the Protestant Church attempt to stress its national reliability. . . ."

An August 22 SD report[207] returned to the problem of the Catholic clergy's influence, especially among the rural population, and listed their most common slogans and themes: 1. citing the decline of great empires, particularly Napoleon's, as an example for Germany; 2. minimizing the significance and authority of the Third Reich and its leaders; 3. utilizing Nazi concepts such as community fellowship for its own purposes; 4. persecutions of Christians and displacement of spirituality in Germany; and 5. the war as God's punishment.[208] A report of September 26, 1940, gave further examples of anti-Nazi propaganda, including a) that one could not wish a final victory for National Socialism, b) that Communism is in any case better than Nazism.[209] An inevitable consequence was that "various farmers, some women and laborers . . . publicly repeated the statement of an itinerant Catholic preacher: *'It would be better if Germany lost the war since victory for Hitler would mean the end of the Catholic population.'* Others said that England was fighting justly in the name of Christianity, for when National Socialism has conquered the Island, there, just as here, the crucifixes would be removed from schools and public buildings. . . ."[210]

In addition to these more or less open attacks on Nazi Germany, there were also efforts "to document the positive attitude of Catholicism towards the state, its willingness to cooperate. . . ." The report of the Reichsstatthalter of Hesse had no complaints about the Churches' behavior.[211] Upper Bavaria reported continued discretion by the clergy, although a lack of enthusiasm for military victories was evident.[212] Far more aggravating, from a Nazi viewpoint, was the observation of the Hamm Public Prosecutor General in a report of September 30 to Reich Justice Minister Dr. Gürtner: " . . . The treacherous activity of Catholic priests had largely ceased after the outbreak of war. Unfortunately a change is becoming very evident. Recently, instances of hostile remarks against the National Socialist state, be they from a pulpit or at other opportunities, are increasing. . . . One pleasant note is that large numbers of Catholics also apparently no longer show much sympathy for their clergy's behavior. . . ."[213]

Judging from these reports, there were two currents of opinion within the Catholic Church over the position to be taken vis-à-vis the Nazi state. The two camps clashed at the Fulda Conference of Bishops, held August

21-24. The militant group was represented by Cardinal Faulhaber of Munich, Archbishop Gröber, Freiburg, Bishop Preysing, Berlin, Bishop Galen, Münster, and Bishop Rackl, Eichstädt. The conciliatory group, with Bishops Wienken, Berlin, Bertram, Breslau, and Schele, Cologne, believed in the need for compromise. They based their argument on Pope Pius XII's letter to the German episcopate on the occasion of the Conference in which he had admonished them to unite.[214] Their position was furthermore determined by the view that too rigid a stance vis-à-vis the state would alienate a considerable segment of the faithful, particularly during wartime. The Conference nevertheless failed to overcome the disagreements between the two wings,[215] so the Reich's Catholics found no unified position within their Church. Public opposition to one program, however, received support from the Churches, and it was this opposition from both sides which caused its termination or at least forced its later continuation in greatest secrecy.

5. ELIMINATION OF "WORTHLESS LIFE": EUTHANASIA

Professor Dr. Karl Brandt, Public Health Inspector General in the Third Reich, testified at the Nuremberg Doctors' Trial that in 1935 Hitler had already expressed his intentions of taking up and solving the euthanasia question during the war because such a problem was easier to handle then.[216] In July, 1939, a number of professors and psychiatrists were informed in the Führer's Chancellory in Berlin of his intention to initiate a euthanasia program to kill the mentally ill in Germany.[217] At the end of October, 1939, Hitler signed a letter dated back to September 1 in which he ordered Reich Leader Bouhler and Dr. Brandt "to extend the authority of doctors we will name later in such a way that patients, deemed probably incurably ill after a most critical examination can be granted a merciful death."[218] In compliance with the Führer's order, which was never enshrined in legal form, the Reich Union of Sanatoriums and Nursing Homes was established, comprising about fifty persons including lawyers and doctors. An initial trial euthanasia was carried out in 1939; from January, 1940, to August, 1941, 70,273 mentally ill fell victim to "mercy killings." Afterwards the next of kin received a letter with approximately the following wording, except for varying illnesses: "We regret to have to inform you that your ——, who had to be transferred for a while to our institution, died here unexpectedly on —— as a result of influenza accompanied by pneumonia and ensuing circulatory weakness. All our medical efforts were unfortunately in vain. He passed away gently and without pain. With his severe, incurable illness, death was a release for him. On police orders, due to existing danger of epidemic here, we had to have the body cremated immediately. . . ." Next, special requests were solicited with regard to the burial of the urn; otherwise this would take place on the spot without charge. The belongings had been destroyed for reasons of epidemic policy.[219]

Notifications such as these sometimes resulted in embarrassing blunders. Patients died of an inflamed appendix that had been surgically removed years ago; one family received two urns instead of one. In other cases the public became suspicious, for example when, in one community, death notices gradually arrived from the same institution with the same cause of death. In some cases tragic scenes also occurred when victims were picked up, scenes that did not remain concealed.[220]

The earliest available report of the public's awareness of the euthanasia action comes from Gertrude Scholtz-Klinck, Reich Women's Leader, concerning reports received from Baden for August, 1940: "Districts Bühl and Mannheim further report that their sanatoriums and nursing homes are being phased out. Next of kin complain that they received no news of their relatives' whereabouts. Most often, they were informed that the charges had died of some illness and that the ashes could be picked up at a specified place. The wildest rumors are circulating."[221] According to her September report, institutions were still being vacated, and worried next of kin were running to their pastors for help. "Some people claim that the state first eliminates older people, pensioners, so that their money could be used for other purposes. . . . What can I reply," the district women's leader for Emmendingen wrote, "to calm these people without running the danger of damaging the Party in some way?"[222]

Continued secrecy produced even more incredible rumors. One commentary on this[223] asserts that "the Volk is not resisting the idea per se but rather its present execution, without any selection or legal basis . . . at least any known to the people." This comment, however, surely had only limited applicability, as will be shown. Above all, next of kin were naturally incensed in most cases and offended by the hypocritical tone of the notifications. The various religious institutions of both confessions, with long traditions of care for the sick and elderly, as well as leading church figures including among others Cardinals Bertram and Faulhaber, the bishops of Cologne, Paderborn, and Limburg, and the head of the Bethel Institutions, Friedrich von Bodelschwingh, all turned to state authorities in protest or demanded redress.[224]

How the action affected staunch Nazis is seen in a letter of November 25, 1940, from a district women's leader to the wife of Walter Buch, chief justice of the Party: " . . . At first we instinctively resisted believing the matter or at least considered the rumors excessively exaggerated. At the last meeting of the Gau school in Stuttgart in mid-October, I was still assured by a 'well informed' source that it concerned only absolute cretins and that 'euthanasia' was only being applied in carefully examined cases. Now it is quite impossible to convince anyone of this version; absolutely proven isolated cases are sprouting like mushrooms. Maybe one can discount 20 per cent, but even if 50 per cent were discounted the situation would not improve. The dreadful and dangerous thing is not so much the fact itself; if there were a law like the sterilization law with established criteria and the strictest expert tests, I am convinced the initial unrest would die down. . . . Most dreadful in this situation is the 'open secret,' which produces a feeling of terrible insecurity. . . . Now people are clinging to the hope that the Führer is unaware of these things, that he *could* never know, otherwise he would intervene; certainly he has no idea of its scope and manner of execution. But I have a feeling it cannot continue for long or this trust will also shatter. . . ." Therefore the author demanded: "This matter must be brought to the Führer's attention before it is too late, and there *must* be a way for the voice of the German people to reach the ear of its Führer. . . ."

The letter, however, never reached the actual architect of this action, but rather Heinrich Himmler, who subsequently wrote to Bouhler's deputy, Stabsleiter Viktor Brach, that there was probably no choice but to terminate use of the Grafeneck Institution. "In any case, we should enlighten [the public] in an intelligent and sensible manner by showing films about the mentally ill and those with hereditary diseases, especially in that area."[225]

This did not end the scandal, and the program continued, reaching the attention of an ever widening audience. At the beginning of 1941, reports began to multiply. Bamberg's Appeals Court president communicated on January 2, 1941: "The elimination of incurable mentally ill has now also filtered down here and caused bitter indignation. It began when a few insane asylums in the district were vacated and inmates were reportedly transferred to distant institutions. Now next of kin are continually receiving news that inmates have suddenly died, cremation has already taken place and the ashes are being sent on request. Obviously these things become general gossip, and without official explanations, leave the door open for the worst rumors. One can hear that for the time being it may only affect insane asylums, but that later, the incurably ill will also be eliminated in hospitals, after which it would only be a small step to render politically undesirable healthy persons harmless."[226]

No one realized at the time how accurate this assumption would turn out to be. Meanwhile reports continued to reach the Justice Ministry, administered by State Secretary Schlegelberger after Gürtner's death, from the senior prosecutor of Düsseldorf,[227] from Bamberg, this time from the public prosecutor general,[228] from the president of the District Court at Wiesbaden,[229] from the Appeals Court president of Nuremberg,[230] and from Munich's OLG-president.[231] Returning to the subject in his situation report of March 1, Bamberg's Appeals Court president said: "There is great unrest among large groups of the population because of this situation, and not only among citizens with mentally ill patients in their families. Such conditions are intolerable in the long run because they involve a number of the most dangerous uncertainties and also provoke the most absurd rumors, which in turn become a source of constant unrest among the population. . . ."[232]

In March, 1941, State Secretary Dr. Schlegelberger turned to the head of the Reich Chancellory to call his attention to the numerous consequences for justice of the euthanasia measures.[233] To reach a unified Reich policy as well as to inform those still in the dark, Schlegelberger assembled the heads of German justice in Berlin on April 23 and 24, 1941, and instructed them to inform their subordinates orally about Hitler's authorization and the program; all charges and protests were to be presented to the Reich Justice Ministry immediately, without processing.

The Catholic Church, meanwhile, took an official interest in the matter. On May 15, the fiftieth anniversary of Pope Leo XIII's encyclical "Rerum Novarum," Pius XII in his Pentecost message referred to this letter and Pius XI's "Quadragesimo anno" of 1931, saying that the state should not have power over the beginning and end of human life.[234] On July 28, 1941, Bishop Clemens August von Galen filed a declaration with the public prosecutor's office of the district court and also the police chief in Münster. In his sermon in the St. Lamberti Church on August 3, he publicly denounced the euthanasia program as a violation of the fifth commandment.[235] Subsequently he issued a pastoral letter comparing Bolshevism and National Socialism, and, like Pius XII and Pius XI's encyclical, pleading for the right to life. On November 2, Bishop Preysing pointed to the sanctity of life and stated: "We do not want to sink back to the viewpoint of primitive or, better said, decadent peoples where the slaughter of old disabled parents is permitted. . . ."[236] On December 31, suffragan Bishop Dr. Kolb also condemned the program in the Bamberg cathedral: "I maintain, on the basis of the laws of our faith and belief in Providence, *that man is not permitted to destroy human life because of incurable suffering. . . . I further maintain that the sick, whose way of life is conditioned by*

physical suffering, and also the insane have a right to life. . . ."[237]
Prominent doctors such as Professor Büchner in Freiburg and Professor
Sauerbruch also protested against the measures.

Excerpts of Galen's pastoral letter were added as appendix to the
September 22 "Meldungen aus dem Reich."[238] This was the first time
SD reports indirectly took up the topic of euthanasia. Only on January
15, 1942, in a comprehensive report dealing with public reaction to the
film "I accuse," which had examined the problem of medical mercy
killing, was the matter gone into more closely.[239] At this stage the
program had already been severely curtailed, if not completely halted.[240]
This reticence is all the more apparent since accounts of all other factors affecting morale were rendered. From jurists' reports[241] we know of
the alarm in many parts of the Reich during the summer and fall of
1941, aggravated considerably by the Bishop of Münster's sermon.[242]
The press, on the other hand, was prohibited from broaching the
subject.[243] It is, therefore, always possible that instructions existed not
to mention it in the "Meldungen" either, for they also reached a wider
reading audience; perhaps special reports were prepared as secret
Reich business for a very small group and then destroyed. But since the
problem had been so widely discussed, a solution was found within
the context of the film, permitting an observation "that generally the
implementation of euthanasia is endorsed." If this had truly been the
case, then why the secrecy? Goebbels had similarly remained silent,
with one exception,[244] and reviews of the film "I accuse" were blocked
for a while.[245] Finally the film could be mentioned, but without com-
menting either positively or negatively on euthanasia per se.[246]

The Party oligarchy, led by Hitler, had undoubtedly failed to calculate—or had miscalculated—the effects of the euthanasia program. For
future plans they did draw this conclusion from their experience: the
need for greater secrecy and removal of the scenes of official mass
murder to distant regions where the German population was precluded
from observation and control.

6. BETWEEN SEA LION AND BARBAROSSA

On September 17, 1940, Hitler postponed the target-date for the
landing in England "until further notice;" on October 12, he administered the death-blow to Operation "Sea Lion." Clearly, the disunited
war and propaganda policy of the regime had not been without effect on
public opinion. Reports from the various Gaus revealed "completely
incomprehensible and ill-mannered behavior among large segments of

the population that day. . . . Impatience prevails because the 'great battle' against England still has not occurred (e.g., Allenstein). People are already switching to other topics (e.g., Dresden). Regrettably, even interest in military events has declined. The population is reluctant to contemplate a second winter of war, thus daily cares, especially about fuel, were definitely emphasized more. . . ." Complaints were again voiced mostly over the "monotony" of reports. "People are now accustomed to hearing that the last attacks were stronger than those before and again had a devastating effect." The war against England "is being fought primarily by the press, and with a great expenditure of mighty words. . . ."[247]

Goebbels found the SD report of a "deteriorating public mood a bit too pessimistic" but thought it advisable "for the press to exert itself more so that interest in military affairs does not decline further."[248] Three days later, however, Nazi demoscopy had to present another negative diagnosis: "According to available reports, the public's present mood is marked by a certain nervousness, traceable firstly to ubiquitous fears of a prolonged war, and also to what for most is an uncertain political situation. . . ." This insecurity promoted rumor-mongering such as the talk in many places of German troops having marched into Rumania to seize control of the important oil wells; others believed that Wehrmacht units were en route to Greece; that first England had to be defeated in the Mediterranean before the Island itself would be attacked. This rumor-mongering confirmed the suspicion "that foreign broadcasts are again being heard in increasing numbers by the German population these past few weeks. . . ."[249]

In the middle of Europe in the twentieth century, it was simply impossible to isolate a population from the outside world in such a way that it was solely at the mercy of a totalitarian state's indoctrination and propaganda. The tedium and ennui of official information policy, Goebbels' principle of "appealing to instinct, not intellect,"[250] and "the principle of endless repetition of propaganda slogans"[251] only drove information-hungry people to secretly tune in foreign news services.

At times, however, this interception of foreign stations had its advantages for the regime. Rumors arising in this fashion, for example, accounted for the lack of public alarm when a "training detachment" [*Lehrtruppe*] of motorized infantry in division strength as well as air force units were sent to Rumania.[252] These troops were to reform Rumania's forces and "protect" the oil fields in light of Russia's ultimatum to Rumania in late June to cede Bessarabia and northern Bukovina. The German public had shown great interest but little understanding for Rumanian politics—King Carol's abdication and the establishment of an authoritarian regime under General Antonescu with Carol's son Michael as figurehead.[253] Attention, however, was riveted too much on the conflict still expected with England; as soon as interest was no longer captured by military events, it turned to routine worries.

For some time, but especially since October, 1940, the public and particularly the working classes had been complaining about fixed wages and rising living costs. First hit were textiles, footwear, essential commodities, and various foods: "This fact aroused general dissatisfaction and apprehension. Press comments of only a 4 per cent price rise were actively discussed and noted with indignation."[254] On September 21, 1940, labor trustee Daeschner had already issued a strong indictment of Nazi wage policy as well as employer practices. He declared "that National Socialist social policy existed only in the imagination. All reforms in the field of social policy had bogged down at the start." In reality everything was as it had been, "even if in the somewhat prettier National Socialist garb."[255] From other sources within the German Labor Front, reports of discord among the workers also emanated, with the cause to be found in the wage freeze and higher living costs.[256] A dovetailing of criticism regarding propaganda and social conditions is evident in reports from Hamburg, Munich and Cologne:[257] the political mood was reserved, public skepticism of an early end to the war was intensified by unrealistic propaganda, and social discontent now surfaced due to economic and class disparities and rising prices. Early in 1941, Bamberg's Appeals Court president indirectly condemned the price rise which hit the little man and civil servants most, those who lacked good connections and sufficient funds.[258] The SD report of November 21, 1940, had observed that prices and food supplies were "a vital factor in the general mood."[259] A catalogue of annoyances included "difficulties with cooking fat and meat allotments, a reduction of bread rations, inadequate market deliveries of fruits and vegetables, as well as the complete elimination of game, poultry, and fish deliveries." Not only high prices but also poor quality were deplored. Sausages, a favorite food in Germany, were often unpalatable. No wonder the mood was sour, particularly among workers, as manifested by a declining "work morale" and increasing absence from work without excuse.[260]

Reich propaganda was called upon to "walk on eggs" during this period of "lethargy."[261] The press had to "captivate the Volk and buoy its mood with interesting reports; political and diplomatic affairs will occur these days which, although of keen interest to the Volk, cannot be printed."[262] These interesting affairs were Hitler's efforts, which ultimately backfired, at fashioning a "continental bloc" against the Anglo-

Saxon Powers. More conciliatory policies toward France, and Spanish participation, were required.[263] Consequently Hitler held October meetings with Mussolini, acting French Premier Laval, General Franco, and Marshal Pétain. But efforts to induce Franco to join failed.[264] Coverage of these meetings was sparse and commentaries were not welcome.[215] Nor were Germans supposed to learn a bit later of Hitler's intention to transfer the remains of the Duke of Reichstadt, Napoleon's son, to Paris from Vienna on December 14; nevertheless it did leak out, though no mention could be made of the fact that the Duke had been King of Rome![266] Hitler's gesture might have revived sympathies for France and angered Italians. The upshot of all this news suppression was that even Goebbels found German newspapers boring.[267]

Just as thorny a problem for Nazi propaganda during the summer and fall of 1940 was relations with the Soviet Union. As mentioned briefly, Soviet demands on Rumania had created unrest among the German population and doubts about Russo-German friendship were heard.[268] In eastern Germany especially, all Soviet actions were followed closely: the erection of memorials for the war dead—contrary to usual practice; the restoration of Sundays in place of a free sixth weekday; the reintroduction of rank insignia for officers and obligatory salute in the Red Army. "Everyone is convinced that given its present regime Russia is hardly tolerable as a permanent neighbor for Germany, and people doubt whether Russo-German friendship can really last all that long under existing circumstances."[269] A further cause of unrest was the annexation by Russia of the Baltic states on July 21, 1940. The completely casual treatment of this topic by press and radio was criticized as "incomprehensible belittlement."[270]

To those responsible for directing opinion, it was a matter of presenting relations with the Soviet Union as being as detached as possible, and to forestall undesirable parallels or analogies between the two systems. Two orders emanating from press conferences of mid-1940 are particularly revealing in this respect: " . . . We are pursuing a common foreign and economic policy, but intend to maintain a conscious intellectual demarcation between Bolshevism and National Socialism, even if we no longer take daily active issue with Bolshevism. We must no longer blur the boundaries between these two Weltanschauungen. . . ."[271] " . . . All reports about domestic developments in the Soviet Union, as for example the introduction of officer ranks in the army, the elimination of political commissars, and the like should only be quoted verbatim without special emphasis because otherwise the impression will be created that Russia is marching along the same road as National Socialism."[272]

The November 12, 1940, Berlin visit of Soviet Commissar for Foreign Affairs, V.M. Molotov, demonstrated German ambivalence toward the Soviet Union. Initially Hitler had sought to win Russia over to the "continental bloc" and persuade her to forsake her eastern and southeastern goals in favor of expansion in Asia, but the fiasco of Mussolini's impetuous attack on Greece on October 28 made Hitler skeptical even beforehand of the outcome of these approaching talks as he began to lean more and more toward an eastern conflict. Consequently the press was issued instructions for "muffled drums" after an initial fanfare about the great significance of this visit so as to avoid arousing too much sympathy.[273] Reports were not to exceed two columns, and no commentaries were permitted.[274] The closing communiqué confirmed the need for cooperation and an intensification of relations,[275] but despite these cautious words, the public was pleased and "Meldungen aus dem Reich" registered a "buoyant mood."[276]

Hitler's efforts backfired. Molotov presented firmer Soviet demands for influence in Turkey, Bulgaria, and Rumania.[277] Nor had Hitler realized his hopes of inducing Spain to enter the war as soon as possible in order to cushion mounting Italian reverses. Instead, Hungary, Rumania, and Slovakia joined the Tripartite Pact on November 20, 23, and 24 respectively. These accessions, combined with intensified Luftwaffe attacks on England, revived hopes for an early end to the war. These were so strong that the press repeatedly received instructions to make no reports of peace feelers and peace rumors emanating from the Anglo-Saxon camp so as to create no illusions.[278] The public received Hungary's accession to the Tripartite Pact with mixed feelings —people had reckoned more with Spain as a partner after the visit to Obersalzburg on November 18 of Spanish Foreign Minister Serrano Suner.[279] Mistrust of Hungary was based on its treatment of the German minority. In numerous Reich cities, doubt about the sincerity and loyalty of Hungarian politics was publicly registered. One heard remarks such as: Hungary joined the Pact just in the nick of time to "inherit" something.[280] At the same time the leadership diagnosed with displeasure that the reputation of the English was growing slowly and steadily. Instead of hatred, "a certain respect for the persistence"[281] of the island nation appeared. This crumbling of the enemy's image hit the propaganda sources all the more severely because it was in no position to stem this tide with reports of a growing crisis mood in England; such information would only have given rise once more to dangerous optimism,[282] which in turn could have led to "undesirable reversals in mood" if British resistance continued.

The Nazi bosses of Germany found the steadily mounting resentment among the Volk against their main ally even more embarrassing. As in the period after Italy entered the war, critical voices were raised again: "Italians are daily losing respect as a result of their defeats in Greece. . . . The old anti-Italian prejudices have reappeared with a bang. One can hear repeatedly 'that the Germans will have to pull them out of this mess now'. . . ."[284] Or: "All reports indicate increasing discussion among the whole population about *Italy*. Their defeat at the hands of the Greeks met with amazement and contempt, but no fear of any negative impact on Germany's war effort. Newest developments in the war in North Africa, however, awakened a certain alarm, since the fate of the Suez Canal and thereby vital Mediterranean predominance depends on an Italian attack on Egypt. And practically no one today believes in Italian hegemony over the Mediterranean. Embitterment is growing daily against the Italians, who are characterized as 'incompetent and unreliable.' The public has not forgotten 1915, and just now Italy's conduct during the Great War is being discussed again everywhere. . . ."[285]

Based on this alarming report, Goebbels suggested that the Italian subject be handled with greater care—reports not only from Greece but also from Italy itself, "in order to allow the numerous Italian jokes to die down."[286] He expressly warned that "those things resented by the German people must never appear in press and radio."[287] English propaganda already used every conceivable means to incite the two peoples against each other. The task of the German press was to emphasize "German loyalty to the alliance and the concept of the Axis, even if it is presently unpopular."[288]

These efforts did not, however, produce the desired results; thus the Reich Propaganda Minister on December 23 again demanded "support for Italians by press and radio."[289] On December 27 he called for a flood of Axis friendship material to be issued by the Propaganda Ministry. It is "an old mistake of Germans to let resentment influence foreign policy."[290] Yet despite his efforts Italophobia grew. Italian military reports were popularly called "spaghetti reports": long and thin.[291]

It would be false to conclude from the disappointment over the postponed invasion of England, the growing restrictions on life, and the failure of the Axis partner, that it was more than mere weariness or that it was a broad trend toward anti-regime hostility. A few jokes along these lines did circulate, according to Shirer, but neither the American journalist nor Goebbels mistook the nature of opinion.[292] At the time Goebbels described the German frame of mind quite correctly as one of "slight depression."[293] The observation of the Cologne appeals court president concerning "the increasing emotional strain and irascibility among wide circles of the population"[294] is also accurate. The "Führer's" prestige, however, was in no way affected; likewise, hardly anyone doubted a victorious end to the war.[295] Hitler's message, "the year 1941 will consummate the greatest victory in our history,"[296] also furnished the motto and prelude for the new year.[297]

This year, however, also did not begin without any rumors. Gossip of all kinds spread about a possible American entry into the war; there was unrest in East Prussia over the "mysterious" relations with Russia.[298] Whether foreign reports were again the cause is difficult to say, but it lies within the realm of the possible, given the hardening of America's attitude. Furthermore, the Wehrmacht again reported intensified reception of foreign broadcasts and demanded harsher penalties for this infraction.[299] Anxiety over German-Soviet relations can be attributed partly to excessive discretion by the German press on this subject. German newspapers had been instructed to provide no commentaries or details about the signing of a new German-Soviet economic agreement for the time being: "The agreements are thus to be considered as purely political and discussed with requisite discretion."[300] The reasons are to be found in a tense grain situation. Reports of increasing Russian grain deliveries could easily have produced too optimistic an assessment of the situation. The grain harvest of 1940 had been far worse than those of both previous years, to which must be added that the German cereal grain stockpile, according to a Reich Food Ministry source, "has experienced considerable unforeseen demands because we took over a completely pillaged Alsace. Lorraine also had to be provided totally with cereal grains. Belgium, Luxembourg, the Protectorate, especially Norway, all together no longer permit us to view the overall cereal grain balance with the optimism of the first war year."[301]

Also, much as during the first winter of war, a number of grievances reappeared whose causes were rooted not only in the military situation but also in socio-political conditions. Alongside the previous elite a "brown" Party elite had established itself; otherwise little had changed in the social structure. For representatives of the NSDAP's left wing, the failure to carry out a social revolution remained the most bitter disappointment: "The 'social stratification' can hardly be presented more strikingly than here. Private clubs, alumni gymastic squads with a heavy reactionary bent, 'better' family social intercourse, the social club "Harmony," among other establishments, all give a picture of a torn society."[302]

If you wanted to get ahead but belonged neither to the old established leading groups nor to the new high society, you had it as tough as ever. Only the Party book and a ruthless use of elbows frequently brought relief. Such manifestations were described by minor party functionaries, who took offense, as careerists and opportunists: "While on the one hand a large number of Party members still do their duty without fuss and turn down all other jobs which might have brought additional hard cash or provided the basis for improved professional standing, on the other hand there are numerous hangers-on only out for their own gain by relying on their Party membership. They get ahead, receive civil service posts and senior positions of authority with absolutely no guarantee that they will maintain the ideological orientation in these offices and departments. . . . What we are meticulously establishing in faith and trust among the public, those with Party badges are demolishing because they just don't work responsibly. . . ."[303]

This touching lament by a subordinate official ignored NSDAP patronage and the continuous pressure from the Party executive to place Nazis in secure positions. Bamberg's solicitor general spoke, for example, of a blunt resort to "connections."[304] If the civil service was able to marshal tough and delaying opposition against these efforts, it was primarily because the Party lacked qualified candidates.[305]

Rebellious juvenile behavior, diagnosed in almost all industrial nations after the Second World War, was already increasingly worrying authorities in the Third Reich before and during the first winter of the war. There were numerous reports on juvenile crime.[306] Burglaries and nightly "roamings" were among the most frequent offenses of male youths. The Chief of the Security Police and Secret Service sent out a ten-page memorandum in January, 1941, about the "neglect of female juveniles," with numerous enclosures.[307] He attributed the reasons for these deteriorating signs partly to developments before 1933. In addition, lack of parental supervision and an absence of paternal authority were cited since fathers were at the front. Greatest cause for concern, however, was the sexual precocity and aggressiveness of young girls. Fourteen- to seventeen-year-olds were taken from barracks and hotels where they had been "for purposes of prostitution."[308]

Since the Third Reich sought to suppress all criticism, in view of its claim to totalitarian infallibility, the Churches above all were made responsible for all grievances, mounting insecurity, and bewilderment. "In general, the adverse impact of the clergy on the population's mood still continues"[309] was the title of a five-page addendum to the December 12, 1940, SD report. Only the remarks of Bishop Rackl of Eichstädt were noted as being positive, from the Nazi hierarchy's point of view; however, his comments only concerned a recommendation of Winter Relief and gratitude to the soldiers. A few church newspapers also received good marks. But otherwise only negative judgments were made, especially in reference to Christ being called the highest "Führer," to which Goebbels responded that the word had never been applied to Christ before it was coined by the Party.[310] Reports from ranking Justice sources also spoke in part of a growing political Catholicism and Protestantism, of subversive attitudes, hopes for a German defeat, and even insults against the head of state;[311] others told of closing of monasteries.[312] Indeed, from December to the summer of 1941, a large number of monasteries were seized partly as "enemy property," partly to house Party offices or evacuees.[313] These measures aroused the indignation of the Catholic population to the utmost. There were new problems with Party bureaus, as reported, for example, by the Reich Women's League leaders for Silesia and Swabia. The effective range of Nazi organizational functions was checked by the unbreachable boundaries created by the continued activity and existence of the Churches. "Pastors still have such an influence in our Gau that even new membership drives for the German Women's League and youth groups is very difficult. . . . Parents, out of regard for the pastor, do not dare admit their daughters to any Party organization. . . ."

Gau Baden complained about "insidious agitation" by "blacks" [Catholics] in episcopal letters and described the Lioba Sisters as especially dangerous because of their "harmful work within the family."[314] Similar reports by the Nazi Women's League in other Gaus clearly reveal a basic professional jealousy at the root of this conflict with the Churches. Members of the Reich Chancellory were also envious of "noticeably higher church collections," often far surpassing Winter Relief results.[315] Church youth work was viewed with particular alarm, and a circular from the Reich Youth Directorate of March 19, 1941, repeated demands that any situation tending to aggravate the "confrontation of ideologies" was to be avoided.[316]

Martin Bormann offered the most articulate statement of the Party's monopolistic claim not only to the outer but also the inner man. In his well-known letter of June 6, 1941, to the Gauleiter of Münster, sent three days later to all Gauleiters as a circular, he defined the "relationship of National Socialism to Christianity."[317] In his opinion they were mutually exclusive; Christianity was based on human uncertainty, National Socialism on "scientific foundations." For centuries the Church had ruled the people, now "for the first time in German history the Führer had taken over public leadership. . . . All influences that could impair, or even damage, the Führer's and the Party's rule must be eliminated. More and more the Volk must be wrested away from the Churches and their agents, the pastors. . . ."

In their eagerness to neutralize their opponents, Party bureaus made numerous tactical errors which often produced the opposite of the desired effect. Such a blunder was the decision to observe traditional religious celebrations, processions, pilgrimages, etc., on Sundays or holidays instead of weekdays. Refusal to comply could result in prohibition of the event.[318] Postponement especially of the Ascension of Christ and Corpus Christi Days to Sundays aroused strong feelings. "The vast majority of the rural population, which clings to these customs, shows no understanding for these measures. Despite explanations that it is a matter of military exigency, they regard these measures as anti-religious and anti-ecclesiastical, and fear that the struggle against the Church will really commence once the war is over. Postponement of the pilgrimages until Sunday also had an undesirable effect in that many more persons participated than had been usual on previous weekday pilgrimages. . . ."[319] In one Silesian locality, women reportedly retaliated by boycotting Mothers' Day celebrations put on by the Women's League.[320]

Gauleiter Wagner's order of April 23, 1941, to remove all crucifixes from classrooms and end school prayers, provoked further indignation. Everywhere demonstrations, litigations, and riots resulted—even *Mutterkreuze** were returned. Women pushed their way into schools and threatened to keep their children at home. There was talk of a work strike and, as an indication of the atmosphere, even threats to bring their complaints to the Führer. When in early September Wagner rescinded his order under the pressure of events, protests at first continued because the cancellation had occured secretly and it took time for the lifting of these restrictions to spread.[321] This subject will be discussed again later in conjunction with the attack on the Soviet Union.

Another area in which reactionary social policies and war demands made themselves felt increasingly strongly was the wage and price sector. A further complication arose from the fact that the German economy had been unprepared for a long war, since everything was geared to Hitler's concept of Blitzkrieg. Just as there was no long-term strategic military planning, so there was also a lack of systematic planning for a war economy. Every war exigency had to be met by changing priorities within the war productions sector without expanding or restructuring the existing transitional stage in such a way that it would result in a real war economy.[322] One of the fundamental reasons for delaying this imperative reorganization was to avoid curtailing the consumer industry for as long as possible for fear of repercussions on the public morale. Just as they sought to postpone reduction of food rations as

* Mothers' Honor Crosses (three classes for fertile mothers: bronze for bearing more than four children, silver for over six, and gold for over eight). *Ed.*

long as possible by reducing quality instead, they also attempted to hide a shortage of consumer goods through a wage freeze. Even though total production of commodities did not drop until December, 1941, and even increased in some industries, it is a fallacy to conclude that "the burden of the war on the German people over these years was very small."[323] This ignores the fact that a large percentage of the consumer goods went to the Wehrmacht, leaving much less for civilian needs; it also disregards the normal growth rate and especially the destruction of goods by bombings. A "survey of the overall economic situation," originating in Göring's Bureau as Commissioner for the Four Year Plan and compiled on the basis of situation reports from provincial governors and economic operations staffs, tells us about actual shortages in the consumer sector at the beginning of 1941. It includes the following: "There is still no adequate supply of finished industrial goods of all kinds that comes close to meeting existing demands. In contrast to previous months, one notes how serious is the emphasis in present reports on the urgency of further deliveries of textiles and household goods (cf. Düsseldorf, Vienna, Karlsruhe, Dresden, Reichenberg, Stuttgart, Breslau, Berlin). . . . In Düsseldorf and Bonn, textile and furniture vouchers distributed to ca. five hundred bombed-out citizens could not be redeemed and had to be recalled. . . ." There was concern that it would hardly be possible to come close to meeting the demand resulting from the second Reich clothing voucher. "Some operations staffs reported drastic scenes where contingency consumption had forced unavoidable rejection of perfectly valid needy cases. Rejected applicants often tried to put pressure on economic offices through Gau administrations or the NSV. . . ."[324]

Concerning wage and price conditions, the report continued: "The intensification of the wage and price squeeze, repeatedly stressed here in the past, has continued during the period of this report. While wages in the old Reich [*Altreich*] have climbed an average of only 4 to 5 per cent since the outbreak of war, comparatively high increases and bonuses paid to laborers in the East (Warthegau, Reich Gau Danzig-West Prussia, the General Government) as well as in the West (especially Lorraine and Luxembourg) have aroused the desire among their fellow workers at home for similar wage hikes, given the more intensive work conditions required by war demands. In addition, there are widely varying efficiency bonuses in some key industries. Stettin reports, for example, that technical staff and other workers in the aircraft industries, especially in Peenemünde, receive bonuses as high as 30 to 50 per cent of their regular salary. Repercussions were soon noticed among workers at vital military shipyards. . . ." But according to opinions of consulted operational staffs, a further increase in purchasing power was regarded as useless. The report therefore closed with the demand, that "if necessary, authorities must again stipulate the fundamental adherence to the wage freeze."

This assessment is doubly revealing. First, it explains why the impression so frequently existed, and in part still exists today, in countries conquered by Germany, that Germans lived in a land of milk and honey during World War II. Many occupying troops and administrative units were far better off there than at home because of higher salaries, black marketeering, requisitioning and an extremely advantageous exchange rate for the mark.[325] Within the "*Altreich*," to use the contemporary term, things were quite spartan. Previously mentioned circumvention of wage freeze instructions by means of bonuses, premiums, etc., also illustrates the basic error both of Nazi economic policy and political leadership: namely, the reluctance at all levels to tackle the problem at its roots and thoroughly stabilize the situation instead of muddling through with extraordinary decrees and *ad hoc* solutions. In place of the much heralded German organization, there evolved a maze of contradictory regulations.

How wretchedly poor some individuals were can be illustrated by one example. Youths, ages eighteen to nineteen, who already had to work as hard as adults, received an hourly wage of thirty-three to forty-four pfennigs. If such a young man lived a distance from his work and had to provide for himself, one can picture his "employee morale" and his attitude towards the war. One district shop steward from the Labor Front, who had reported this and other hardship cases, then posed the justifiable question, "whether such workers could possess any enthusiasm for work, or any sympathy for our military situation."[326] Pensioners were no better off, according to an SD report of January 30, 1941: the cost of living index has risen from 117.2 in January, 1933, to 130.8 by December, 1940, a rise mostly accounted for by clothing prices, less by food, and hitting lower incomes worst.[327] Clearly the little man who had expected National Socialism to improve his situation markedly and provide a more equitable distribution of the national product had backed the wrong horse. To prevent further deterioration of morale, Goebbels, on February 12, ordered that "cost of living indexes, which are based on misleading data, are no longer to be made public."[328] Nevertheless, reports from Frankfurt, Stettin, and Carlsbad provide further indices[329] permitting general conclusions: dominant themes were poor worker morale, tense working conditions, the attitude of employers, exhaustion, poor wages and excessive prices.

Otherwise the interval between the end of the French campaign and the beginning of the Russian was characterized by much the same absence of German publications as during the news dry spell between the Polish and Norwegian campaigns. Censorship was especially strict again at the start of 1941. Nothing could be reported. The Reich Press Chief's daily watchword on February 4 stated that "treatment of *all* nonessential questions possibly oppressive or irritating to the German people must be scrupulously avoided. This includes primarily those matters which ridicule the idiosyncracies, customs, habits, or dialects of individual tribes. It is prohibited to play off one tribe against another, one city against another, or one part of the Reich or Volk against another, no matter how well-meaning the intentions."[330] On February 9 the demand was for "the subject of 'invasion' to vanish from press discussions" in order to avoid raising unnecessary hopes for a landing in England.[331] The watchword for February 13 stated: "Information about the *wages of foreign workers* and how much they are permitted to send home is not desired in the Reich press."[332] Thus there were not many topics available, and the panacea of polemics could hardly hide this dearth. It seems even Hitler criticized the German press at the time for its tedium, thereby angering some editors who considered this unfair. International and military events in the spring of 1941 finally offered the press a bit more material, but at first this gave little cause for improvement of the depressed and irritable mood.

Bulgaria joined the Tripartite Pact on March 1; on the second, German troops entered the country via Rumania to prepare to assist hard-pressed Italians with a northern Greek campaign. Bulgaria's accession also finally offered Hitler an opportunity to bring Yugoslavia into Germany's sphere of influence. Secret negotiations were begun on March 4 at the Berghof with Prince-Regent Paul, followed by the ceremonial signing in Berlin of Yugoslavia's adherence to the Pact, as well as supplementary agreements, on March 25. Two days later General Simovic overthrew Paul's government and placed the minor Peter II on the throne. There was no doubt of the new regime's pro-western orientation; anti-German demonstrations were held in Belgrade and other Serbian cities. Hitler's impulsive decision to destroy the Yugoslavian state and simultaneously to delay his Russian campaign was to contribute significantly to the subsequent failure of this "Blitzkrieg." The German public meanwhile registered surprise and bewilderment at the turn of events in Yugoslavia. For the first time in months a segment of society feared that a grave situation had developed to the disadvantage of the Axis powers.[334]

Hitler privately admitted that he had miscalculated developments and was at the mercy of events:[335] the continental bloc against England had failed to emerge, and Italy had suffered reverses in the Mediterranean which forced German intervention in Africa and the Balkans. Yet Hitler's luck held. Where the Italians had faltered, partly due to insufficient motorization and a lack of modern tank battalions and antitank defenses, German soldiers emerged as victors. The Tenth Air Corps was transferred to Sicily, bringing British convoy traffic to a halt. On January 11, Hitler ordered the creation of an antitank unit, later named the "German Africa Corps," for deployment in Tripoli. Initially only a light division with plans for a panzer division to follow in May, it began its counter-offensive against England on March 31 under the command of the "desert fox," General Rommel. Tobruk, lost by the Italians, was encircled on April 11, and Rommel's forces penetrated to the Libyan-Egyptian border in May, while the balance of power in the Mediterranean again shifted in favor of Italy. Meanwhile the Yugoslavian campaign had begun on April 6; Belgrade was occupied on the twelfth and an unconditional surrender was signed on the seventeenth. German troops had simultaneously opened a wide front in Salonika, bringing about Greece's final collapse on April 24.

These successes—far more rapid and complete than expected—"unleashed wave upon wave of enthusiasm. Everywhere amazement and gratitude were expressed to our victorious soldiers."[336] Generally one had anticipated from six to eight weeks—propaganda, like Hitler's calculations, had been geared to two months.[337] Again hardly anyone had doubted an eventual victory. Nevertheless, the Balkan campaign was far less popular than the one in France.[338] Enthusiasm waned rapidly, much like the successes of the Africa Corps. Naturally people were proud of the German soldiers, but propaganda had great difficulty in justifying the need for these military operations. Hatred of England, which the leadership tried to stir up again at this time, also refused to take proper hold. Germans had had enough of war. They had achieved more than they had dared to envisage in their wildest dreams. Further expansion and prolongation of hostilities was not to their liking, and their anger once more turned against Italy, seen as the cause of this highly undesirable development.[339]

Increasingly, however, another topic forced its way into the forefront: the Soviet Union. Hitler's silence concerning German-Soviet relations in his speech on January 30, 1941, had not gone unnoticed,[340] nor had press and radio silence.[341] As is customary in such circumstances, a bevy of rumors circulated about "the possibility of hostilities with Russia," and there was even conjecture about the date of a German offensive.[342] Rumors were strongest in the eastern provinces, according to Allenstein's senior prosecutor: "For some weeks, 'Russia' has been the main topic of conversation. One gets the feeling that 'something is amiss' with our neighbor to the east, and one hears the most absurd rumors. There is, for instance, talk of recent sharp differences within the Council of Commissars between Stalin and Molotov over whether or not to continue the pro-German course of Soviet foreign policy. Supposedly it even came to blows between followers of the two camps. The intent of heavy troop concentrations in East Prussia is supposedly to strengthen Molotov's position and if necessary to 'intervene' in Russia. According to other rumors, the Soviets are preparing to commence hostilities against us. Consequently opinions also differ about the purpose of certain German military measures, whether they are only preventive or are designed as a defense against an impending Russian invasion. Frightened people, especially women, already fear the worst. Even those less timid are following developments with concern. Recently instituted air-raid drills hardly help to calm the population."[343]

The visit to Berlin on March 26-27 of the Japanese Foreign Minister, after his stop in Moscow on the twenty-fourth, created a stir and was interpreted solely in the light of German-Soviet relations: "Most speculation surrounding Matsuoka's mission[344] in Germany centers on a settlement of all antagonisms between Russia and the Axis powers. . . ."[345] Similar observations were reported throughout the Reich.[346] The subsequent Moscow signing of the Russo-Japanese friendship pact on April 13 could only be reported in small print on the second or third page, "for specific reasons."[347] Keen observers, who in the meantime had learned to interpret even such small signs, became suspicious at this belittlement and drew their own conclusions with the help of existing rumors. Such was the case with Reich Finance Minister Count Schwerin von Krosigk, who despite his high office had not been initiated into Hitler's strategic plans. Schwerin von Krosigk felt obliged to caution against such a reckless policy and wrote to Göring on April 4, probably counting on better chance of a reply from him. Basing his remarks on Göring's own warnings to preserve at all cost the Volk's strength and will to resist, the Finance Minister pointed to an increasing stress on the labor supply, noticeable signs of fatigue, and a barely adequate food supply. He worried about the dangerous jolt to peace hopes if Germany attacked Russia and brought on a two-front war. "Don't you believe," he asked, "that we are expecting too much from this willing, loyal, and trusting Volk if this treaty with Russia, once celebrated . . . as *the* greatest guarantee of victory, as *the* greatest political achievement, as *the* security against English blockade plans . . . is perverted? I fear that most people will not be equal to so severe a test."[348] His assessment was substantiated by many SD reports; many people thought Germany would one day collapse under the weight of its own victories.[349]

On May 8, "Meldungen aus dem Reich" issued a special report entitled "Rumors about Russia and their Effect,"[350] which also showed that for the past three months rumors of a clash between the USSR and the Reich had grown steadily. The bases for such assumptions were the erection of the so-called East Wall and troop concentrations along the Russo-German border. If these developments were initially viewed with apprehension, everything changed under the impact of events in southeast Europe: "Since the termination of the Balkan campaign, most people are convinced that Russia is also easily beatable. At the same time, however, the wish is expressed that perhaps a peaceful solution will still be found. Many citizens express the reservation that Germany presently lacks the population to hold the vast Russian expanse for any length of time. . . ."

It was common at the time to underestimate Russia's military potential. Estimates of the Red Army's fighting strength were far too low everywhere: "There is talk within military circles of an invasion within, at the latest, eight weeks and that the war—if it can be called that—will be conducted with little bloodshed. The 'Red Army' is only a number without head or will. Russia's brains are all in Russian concentration camps or have been eliminated. All told, some sixteen million people are supposedly imprisoned in Russian camps, that is ca. 10 per cent of the total population. The German army is more likely awaited as a liberator than as an enemy. . . ."[351]

This grotesque miscalculation was not limited to the poorly informed. Major-General Marcks' study of an eastern campaign, released August 5, 1940, estimated nine weeks at best and seventeen weeks at worst in order to occupy the Soviet Union up to a line stretching from the lower Don to the middle Volga and northern Dvina Rivers and to smash the main body of the Red Army. Hitler characterized this army to Bulgaria's Ambassador in Berlin as "nothing more than a joke."[352]

The above Leipzig report deserves our attention for another remark; it reported from intelligence sources that these were of the opinion "that the Führer will proceed with his program and realize his eastern expansionist plans (they speak of the bread basket of Europe). . . ." It seems this awareness of the real situation was at first confined to the well-informed. At the beginning of May, the great mass still believed in aggressive Soviet intentions, according to detailed reports from various cities and regions, because "Russia disapproves of Germany's expansionist policy, but especially because it was not given prior notification of the entry of German troops into Hungary, Bulgaria and Yugoslavia. . . ."[353]

To confirm this view, people pointed to the fact that the friendship pact between Yugoslavia and the Soviet Union, concluded on April 5—one day before Germany's invasion—had only been given minimal coverage by the press. "In all areas of the Reich the consensus is that the *erection of the East Wall* is confirmation that Germany's leaders, too, anticipate an attack by Russia at any time."[354] Despite the wildest rumors, most Germans could not and would not believe that their "brilliant" Führer would deliberately plunge Germany into that much-feared two-front war. Additional rumors circulated after Stalin dismissed Molotov;[355] the probable number of invading German divisions was also bandied about as more and more voices accused Germany of responsibility for tensions with Russia.[356] Most rumors stemmed from letters sent home by soldiers stationed along the Russo-German border.

Amidst this swarm of rumors and guesses, the news of Rudolf Hess' flight to England hit like a bombshell. Hitler's deputy had boarded a modified Me110 and flown it to Scotland in a last-ditch effort to prepare the way for peace between England and Germany. The unsuccessful attempt by this dreamer, completely devoted to Hitler, whom Goebbels had called a "fuzzy front man,"[357] induced Hitler to disavow his previous deputy. On May 12 he issued the version that Hess suffered "delusions." In the Reich Press Chief's daily instructions for May 13, there was also talk of "mental disorder."[358]

Reports on the effect of this development on the population noted "a real shock" among those positively oriented toward the regime, "while among those critical of the regime a thinly concealed malicious glee was observed. . . ."[359] For many Party members it was a "blow to the very foundations of National Socialism and the Party."[360] Superlatives such as "paralyzing horror"[361] and "deepest dismay"[362] were not uncommon. It was even considered a "lost battle."[363] Without exception, official explanations were sharply criticized and dismissed as incredible. German propaganda, attacked from all sides as clumsy and boorish, was largely responsible for the Hess affair receiving such public attention[364] and for promoting another wave of rumors.[365] One satirical verse made the rounds everywhere:[366] "There is a song all o'er the land:/we're setting out t'ward Angelland./But if one should arrive by plane,/he'd surely be declared insane. . . ."*

Clearly the version of a deranged idealist[367] found no support. Most assumed treason,[368] which resulted in a wave of sympathy for Hitler,[369] "who is not spared any blow of fate."[370] But as Goebbels had predicted on May 13, it was only an episode with no lasting adverse effects on

---

*"Es geht ein Lied im ganzen Land:/Wir fahren gegen Engelland./Doch wenn dann wirklich einer fährt,/So wird er für verrückt erklärt . . . "

German propaganda.[371] The excitement died down quickly,[372] and the public again turned to other topics of conversation.

In general a relatively "listless and flat mood"[373] prevailed during the late spring of 1941. A lack of patriotic spirit was evident in the behavior of the women. During World War I, the female population had rushed to the service of the fatherland. In World War II they avoided it where possible. In place of a growing female labor force, one finds a decline; from May 31, 1939, to May 31, 1941, the number of German women employed dropped by 287,500.[374] Coincidentally, there was a shift from the factory to administration. While agriculture, industry, handicrafts, retail trade (business, banking, insurance, tourism), and housekeeping lost 835,000 women, communications, energy, and administration absorbed 554,000 female workers. Most unemployed women whose husbands had been drafted strove to make life as comfortable as possible. Their indolence and enjoyment of life aroused the anger and envy of their less fortunate sisters who had to work for a living. These could not and would not understand why in wartime not every idle worker was conscripted.[375] After the Nazi Women's League had obviously failed,[376] Goebbels, who concerned himself with everything, tackled the problem and on February 13 gave his approval to an order that girls and women without children between the ages of fourteen and forty report to labor exchanges. "The practical significance of such a measure is evident in view of a considerable labor shortage. But the psychological side to compulsory female labor also matters, since it is ideal for lifting significantly the working spirit of women who have already been laboring in German armaments factories for months or years. Furthermore, it offers an effective means of totally overcoming an antiquated class concept, traces of which are still evident, particularly among the better classes. . . ."[377]

On March 14, the Reich Propaganda Office ordered the opening of the campaign, "German women help us win."[378] Later, in his speech of May 4 following the Balkan campaign, Hitler—who basically remained an opponent of female work—personally encouraged an additional effort by women and girls on behalf of the war economy.[380] But neither the propaganda campaign nor the "Führer's" words found "much response."[381] The "Meldungen aus dem Reich" of May 26, 1941, had to report "that even after the Führer's speech, reports of volunteers ready to take up work have not reached expected levels."[382] News from many cities made one thing very clear: hardly any women had volunteered for work.[383] Party officials were informed on June 18 by "confidential information" from the Party Chancellory about instructions concerning wartime deployment of wives of officers, army officials, and non-commissioned officers, issued by the reserve army commander at the beginning of the war and elaborated upon by the OKH on December 28, 1940. The voluntary principle was maintained, but emphasis was placed on the moral duty to assist the Volk community. These appeals were just as fruitless. Also contributing to a listlessness in the late spring of 1941 were the "almost simultaneous developments of an aggravated food situation—lowering of meat rations, cutting of bread distributions, sensitive rationing of beer—with all its side effects," and the "nearly certain outlook, since Hitler's May 4 Balkan speech, of a prolongation of the war beyond 1941 ('next year our Wehrmacht will possess even better weapons')."[384]

As early as May 14, 1941, the press had received instructions on how to impart to the Volk the scheduled June 2 reduction in meat rations: each normal user's ration was cut by one hundred grams, that of heavy laborers and self-supporters by two hundred grams. The explanation was that since the beginning of the war the total consumption of meat had risen constantly despite unchanged rations. This rising consumption was attributed to a preparation "for the historic decisions of the war," which called for an enlargement of the Wehrmacht and armaments industries to a new high. Consequently the number of heavy laborers would have to be increased by several million and additional foreign workers and war prisoners would also have to be fed.[385]

"Meldungen aus dem Reich"[386] reported some discord and concern over the future food situation. Individual voices were already heard "stating that in comparing present meat rations to those of the World War, things now are 'just like then' . . . " The DAF district shop steward in Freiburg presented the same argument: "One can talk and preach all one wants, there is still a great fear among the people stemming from the last war, especially among older citizens."[387] Without a doubt, "unpleasant fluctuations"[388] were noticeable in the public mood. There was little spirit of self-sacrifice; "confidence in the Führer is dwindling."[389] People believed that the reduction in rations was due to the need to feed the occupied territories as well, and they generally argued "that supplies for the Reich must first be guaranteed, while the enemy could starve if need be . . . "[390] The Reich government's policy of exploiting occupied countries could thus rely on the consensus of a broad spectrum.

The death of ex-Kaiser Wilhelm II on June 4, 1941, in Dorn, Holland, aroused hardly any interest;[391] the press had previously been instructed to play down the event and avoid reawakening the monarchist issue.[392] Only a victory on Crete provided a little lift and took the public's mind off Russia.[393] Goebbels deliberately promoted rumors of a possible landing in England at his conference of June 5; the June 13 edition of the *Völkischer Beobachter*, containing his article "The Example of

Crete," was seized by his order shortly after it was published.[394] An engineered whisper campaign spread more wild rumors, including Stalin's impending visit to Berlin and Russia's willingness to cede her border lands to Germany for settlement by German farmers.[395] A minority remained unconvinced by such talk of an agreement, particularly the clever Berliners and eastern Germans[396] who could hardly be fooled when there were 153 divisions, i.e., 75 per cent of the army, and over three million men and 3580 tanks massed on the Russian border.

The mood was charged with expectancy as all of East Prussia became a military camp.[397] On Sunday, June 22, the "period of Russo-German indecision"[398] came to an end.

NOTES

1. Helmut Krausnick & Hermann Graml, "Der deutsche Widerstand und die Allierten," *Vollmacht des Gewissens*, Vol. II (Frankfurt/Main, 1965), p. 482.
2. Shirer, *Berlin Diary*, pp. 189, 191, 197.
3. Klepper, *Unter dem Schatten Deiner Flügel*, p. 797.
4. Ritter, *Carl Goerdeler und die deutsche Widerstandsbewegung*, p. 245.
5. See, for example, Regierungspräsident of Upper Bavaria, September 11, 1939; of Lower Bavaria and the Upper Palatinate, October 9, 1939; of the Palatinate, September 19, 1939; of Upper and Middle Franconia, October 6, 1939. BHStA, Abt. II, MA 106,671, 106,673, 106,676, and 106,678, and SD section Leipzig of September 5, 1939. IWM FD 332/46.
6. Inlandslagebericht of the SD section Leipzig. IWM 271/46, CIOS 4233.
7. *Ibid.* Cf. also *Aus deutschen Urkunden*.
8. Paul Schmidt, *Statist auf diplomatischer Bühne 1923-1945* (Bonn, 1953), p. 473.
9. SD section Leipzig, September 11, 1939. IWM 271/46 CIOS 4233.
10. Cf. Manfred Messerschmidt and Klaus-Jürgen Müller.
11. *Berlin Diary*, p. 172.
12. Cf. Foreign Office White Books, *Urkunden zur letzten Phase der deutsch-polnischen Krise*, and *Dokumente zur Vorgeschichte des Krieges* (Berlin, September 7 and December 12, 1939). Cf. also Az.W. Pr.O.Mob. Nr. 8712/39 geh. Betr. Geistige und Seelische Betreuung der Truppe. MGFA WO 1-5/179.
13. Monthly report of the Regierungspräsident of Mainfranken for January, 1940, dated February 10, 1940. BHStA, Abt. II, MA 106,681.
14. "Meldungen aus dem Reich," April 5, 1940. BA, R58/150. Cf. Monthly report of the Regierungspräsident of Upper and Middle Franconia for March, 1940, of April 7, 1940, concerning the German publication of 'secret' Polish documents verifying German claims.
15. RGBl. I, p. 1683.

16. Decree of the Chief of Security Police pp II Nr. 223/39g of September 3, 1939, mentioned in the Gestapo letter, Staatspolizeistelle Munich, B.Nr. 206, 47/39 II of November 20, 1939. StA Obb. Fasz. 204, Nr. 3243.
17. Cf. Gordon C. Zahn, *Die deutschen Katholiken und Hitlers Kriege* (Vienna, 1965).
18. *Die kirchliche Lage in Bayern*, pp. 313, 315.
19. Monthly report of the Regierungspräsident of Upper and Middle Franconia, October 6, 1939. BHStA, Abt. II, MA 106,678; cf. also "Erklärung der deutschen Bischöfe zum Kriegsausbruch, September, 1939," in Ferdinand Strobel, *Christliche Bewährung* (Olten, 1946), p. 268, and Zahn, *op. cit.*, pp. 87, 97, 99, 102, 134, 148, 173, 174, 197.
20. Cf. Letter of the Munich Staatspolizeistelle, B.Nr. 34 158/39, II, B/Pf of November 15, 1939, to the Polizeipräsident of Munich and the Landräte of Upper Bavaria. StA Obb. Nr. 1875.
21. *Die Briefe Pius XII. an die deutschen Bischöfe*, p. 353.
22. *Ibid.*
23. Zipfel, *Kirchenkampf in Deutschland, 1933-1945*, p. 226. Cf. also Alexander Werth, *Russland im Kriege 1941-1945* (Munich, 1965), p. 305: Stalin used similar tactics and ceased all anti-religious propaganda shortly after the outbreak of war. This maneuver seemed an "imperative for Soviet government policy" to the dictator.
24. Picker, *Hitlers Tischgespräche*, pp. 154, 176. Cf. Klaus Scholder, "Die evangelische Kirche in der Sicht der nationalsozialistischen Führung bis zum Kriegsausbruch," VfZG, H. 1, January 1968, p. 22. Cf. also the Verfügung of the Reich Interior Minister I Ö 1067/40 i of July 24, 1940, copy in the correspondence of the SS section XV. Abt. II. Az i m— Hamburg, August 9, 1940: BA, Slg. Schumacher 245/vol. 2.
25. BA, NS Misch/474, fol. 112,809.
26. Conway, *The Nazi Persecution of the German Churches*, p. 232.
27. *Ibid.*
28. Informatorische vertrauliche Bestellungen from the economic press conference of September 12, 1939: BA, ZSg 101/46, fol. 543.
29. RGBl. I, p. 1685.
30. *Ibid.,* p. 1609.
31. BA, MA Wi I F 5/357.
32. Sargent and Williams, *Social Psychology*, p. 551. An inquiry in the USA during the war named hate, fear, and wishful thinking as psychological motives. Robert H. Knapp, "A Psychology of Rumor," *Public Opinion Quarterly*, VIII (1944), No. 1, pp. 22-37. Cf. as supplement, Gordon Allport & Leo Postman, "The Basic Psychology of Rumor," *The Process and Effects of Mass Communication*, ed. by Wilbur Schramm (Urbana, 1954).
33. In the ministerial conference of November 2, 1939, Goebbels demanded, for example, that party offices be made aware of rumor mongering and that a short film in the form of a comedy be made. *Kriegspropaganda*, p. 216. Cf. also the ministerial conference of June 6, 1940, in which the creation of rumors was again discussed. *Ibid.*, p. 378.
34. Cf. correspondence of the commander of corps area XIII, fn. 12, above.
35. Cf. copy of a Vortragsvermerks, W Pr II c of September 30, 1939, and a letter of the Propaganda Ministry 328/39g (38 Rf 3000) of October 22, 1939, to the OKW. MGFA Wo 1-6/351.

36. Cited by Boelcke, *Kriegspropaganda*, p. 259.
37. *Ibid.*, pp. 263-64.
38. Cf. fn. 12.
39. See, for example, a brochure put together in the late fall of 1939 by Fritz Reipert, *In acht Kriegswochen 107mal gelogen, Dokumente über Englands Nachrichtenpolitik im gegenwärtigen Kriege* (Berlin, no date).
40. See the numerous reports "über polnische Presse- und andere Feindpropaganda betr. Polen," MGFA WO 1-6/350-52.
41. *Kriegspropaganda*, pp. 342, 351, 355, 361, 367.
42. *Ibid.*, p. 268.
43. Hagemann, *Publizistik im Dritten Reich*, p. 168.
44. Cf. *infra*, pp. 140 ff.
45. *Kriegspropaganda*, p. 217.
46. The Foreign Office authorized publication of a documentary White Book, *Die polnischen Greueltaten an den Volksdeutschen in Polen*, ed. by Hans Schadewaldt. MGFA WO 1-6/323.
47. "Bericht zur innenpolitischen Lage" of April 29, 1940, in Boberach, *Meldungen aus dem Reich*, p. 63.
48. Helmut Krausnick, "Hitler und die Morde in Polen," VfZG, H. 2 (1963), pp. 196-209.
49. G. M. Gilbert, *The Psychology of Dictatorship*, based on an examination of the leaders of Nazi Germany (New York, 1950).
50. IWM FD 332/46.
51. BA, R58/145. Cf. also the report of November 10, 1939, BA, R58/144.
52. See, for example, the decree of the Bavarian Interior Ministry of December 2, 1939: Bayerisches Gesetz- und Verordnungsblatt, Nr. 37, of December 11, 1939, p. 341. Or, the memorandum of the OKW, *Kriegsgefangene* (Berlin, 1939);—copy in BHStA, Abt. I, Akt. Nr. 2085 b, command of the OKW concerning "Verkehr Kriegsgefangener mit deutschen Frauen." A2 2 Nr. 69/40 24 iia AWA/Kriegsgef. I c, January 10, 1940, in which ten-year imprisonment and possibly the death penalty were threatened. MGFA WO 1-6/342, order of Himmler, May 11, 1940, dealing with the handling of war prisoners. RGBl. I, Nr. 86, of May 17, 1940, p. 769.
53. *Actes et documents du Saint Siège relatifs à la Seconde Guerre Mondiale*, vol. 3: *Le Saint Siège et la Guerre en Europe* (Città del Vaticano, 1967), pp. 194-95.
54. Léon Poliakov and Josef Wulf, *Das Dritte Reich und seine Diener. Dokumente* (Berlin, 1956), pp. 516 f. See also Hans von Krannhals, "Die Judenvernichtung in Polen und die Wehrmacht," *Wehrwissenschaftliche Rundschau*, No. 10 (1965), pp. 570-81, for the Wehrmacht's activities in Poland; also cf. Krannhals' testimony before a Düsseldorf court on November 12, 1964, about "Die Judenpolitik in Polen" (MS, 21p.).
55. IfZ Rep. 501, IV F. 2. Verteidigungs-Dokumentenbuch I für Georg von Küchler.
56. Der Oberkommandierende der XVIII Armee (ic Nr. 2489/40 geheim), July 22, 1940. Copy in Poliakov-Wulf, *Das Dritte Reich und seine Diener*, p. 385.
57. Cf. Krannhals, "Die Judenvernichtung . . . " *loc. cit.*, p. 571.
58. *Reichsführer. Briefe an und von Himmler*, ed. by Helmut Heiber (Stuttgart, 1968), p. 151 (hereafter cited as *Reichsführer*). For the Wehrmacht's attitude, cf. also *infra*, p. 141.

59. Letter of Stieff, head of division III of operations in the General Staff, dated November 21, 1939, cited in Graml, "Die deutsche Militäropposition von Sommer 1940 bis zum Frühjahr 1943," in *Vollmacht des Gewissens*, vol. II, p. 428. Cf. also the remarks of General of the Infantry Ulex, and Major von Tschammer und Osten, Poliakov-Wulf, *Das Dritte Reich und seine Diener*, p. 518.

60. This "confidential information" constitutes a sort of short protocol of the daily Berlin press conferences. They only exist in the form of journalists' notes. The present report was taken down by Georg Dertinger, Foreign Minister of the DDR from 1949 to 1953, then imprisoned for spying; pardoned in 1964, he died in Leipzig in January, 1968. BA, ZSg 101/34, fol. 535-39.

61. Hitler made this remark in a discussion with Count Ciano on October 1, 1939. Cf. *Staatsmänner und Diplomaten bei Hitler: Vertrauliche Aufzeichnungen über Unterredungen mit Vertretern des Auslandes 1939-1941*, ed. by Andreas Hillgruber (Frankfurt/Main, 1967), p. 41.

62. Shirer, *Berlin Diary*, p. 217.

63. Boberach: "Bericht zur innenpolitischen Lage," October 11, 1939, p. 9.

64. "Bericht zur innenpolitischen Lage," October 23, 1939: BA, R58/144.

65. Press instructions of October 13, 1939: Hagemann, *op. cit.*, p. 243.

66. "Bericht zur innenpolitischen Lage," October 16, 1939: BA, R58/144.

67. Monthly report of the Regierungspräsident for Upper and Middle Franconia, November 7, 1939. BHStA, Abt. II, MA 106,678. Cf. also "Inlandslagebericht des SD-Abschnittes Leipzig" of October 22, 1939. IWM 271/46 CIOS 4233.

68. Already on September 29, 1939, Hitler told the three branches of the military he still planned to attack in the West in the fall. Hans-Adolf Jacobsen, *Fall Gelb. Der Kampf um den deutschen Operationsplan zur Westoffensive 1940* (Wiesbaden, 1957), pp. 8 f.

69. SD Leipzig section, October 31 and November 20, 1939. IWM FD 332/46 and CIOS 4233.

70. 268th Division to XXIV A.K., December 4, 1939, regarding the mood of the home front and its effects on the troops. MGFA WO 1-5/180.

71. Kreisleitung Wilhelmshaven, November, 1939. Niedersächsisches Staatsarchiv 277-10/2. For the foul mood of the troops and its adverse effects on discipline, cf. also SD section Leipzig, November 18, 1939, IWM CIOS 4233. Goebbels also exclaimed on December 9, 1939, that the most difficult problem was occupying the soldiers. *Kriegspropaganda*, p. 238.

72. "Bericht zur innenpolitischen Lage," November 13, 1939: BA, R58/144. Cf. also the report of November 10, with similar tenor: Boberach, p. 18. Cf. "Stimmungsmässiger Überblick über die Gesamtpolitische Lage," Kreis Wiesbaden, November 1939: BA, NS Misch 1792.

73. "Bericht zur innenpolitischen Lage," November 15, 1939: BA, R58/144.

74. Conway, *op. cit.*, p. 240.

75. BA, R58/145.

76. *Kriegspropaganda*, p. 222.

77. "Bericht zur innenpolitischen Lage," November 22, 1939: BA, R58/145. Georg Elser alone was involved in the assassination attempt. Cf. Anton Hoch, "Das Attentat auf Hitler im Münchner Bürgerbräukeller," VfZG, No. 4 (October, 1969), pp. 383-413.

78. Report of November 15, 1939: IWM 271/46 CIOS 4233. In Leipzig the

following were arrested: forty-three Jews, sixteen KPD leaders, ten SPD leaders, one SAP leader, four members of the resistance, two members of the "Black Front," two WO leaders, three Catholic Action, two subversive theologians, one Freemason, two JBV members: *Aus deutschen Urkunden*, p. 216.

79. Cf. "Berichte zur innenpolitischen Lage," of October 9, 13, 16, 25; November 3, 13, 15, 24; December 1, 4, 12, 1939, as well as "Meldungen aus dem Reich" of December 22, 1939: BA, R58/144-146 and Boberach, pp. 4-5, 19, 20, 23.

80. SD report of October 16, 1939: both reports in BA, R58/144.

81. "Bericht zur innenpolitischen Lage," October 16, 1939: *Ibid.*

82. "Bericht zur innenpolitischen Lage," November 24, 1939: BA, R58/145. Cf. also Boberach, p. 21.

83. "Bericht zur innenpolitischen Lage," October 13, 1939: BA, R58/144.

84. "Bericht zur innenpolitischen Lage," October 23, 1939: *Ibid.*, and of December 1, 1939: Boberach, p. 21.

85. "Bericht zur innenpolitischen Lage," December 6, 1939: BA, R58/145.

86. Cf. Saul Friedländer, *Pius XII und das Dritte Reich. Eine Dokumentation* (Reinbek b. Hamburg, 1965), pp. 37-38.

87. Letter by Heydrich to Lammers, November 10, 1939, signed by Gestapo chief Müller; and *Mitteilungen zur weltanschaulichen Lage*. (No. 1, VI of Feb. 11, 1940), issued by Rosenberg's bureau, in Friedländer, *op. cit.*, pp. 37-38 and BA, ZSg 3/vorl. 1689, respectively.

88. *Mitteilungen zur weltanschaulichen Lage, ibid.*

89. *Das politische Tagebuch Alfred Rosenbergs*, p. 110.

90. See especially "Meldungen aus dem Reich," February 21, 1940: BA, R58/148.

91. "Meldungen aus dem Reich," January 19, 1940: Boberach, pp. 39, 40; and that of February 5, 1940, that the cold front was God's punishment: BA, R58/148.

92. Monthly report of the Regierungspräsident of Upper and Middle Franconia of September, 1939: BHStA, Abt. II, MA 106,678.

93. Boberach, p. 15.

94. Report of the appeals court president for Ludwigshafen, January 8, 1940: BA, R22/3389.

95. Boberach, p. 17.

96. *Das politische Tagebuch Alfred Rosenbergs*, p. 106.

97. "Bericht zur innenpolitischen Lage," November 24, 1939 (III Kulturelle Gebiete): BA, R58/145.

98. On December 9 and 10, 1939. *Kriegspropaganda*, p. 239.

99. Inlandslagebericht of March 4, 1940: IWM 271/46 CIOS 4233.

100. About other clubs, cliques and gangs, see: Werner Klose, *Generation im Gleichschritt. Ein Dokumentarbericht* (Oldenburg/Hamburg, 1964), pp. 222 ff. The annual SD report for 1938 proves that this was not only a war manifestation; it also speaks of "wild groups": BA, R58/1095, fol. 123, 124.

101. "Meldungen aus dem Reich," of April 5, 1940: BA, R58/150.

102. "Stimmungsmässiger Überblick über die Gesamtpolitische Lage," Kreis Wiesbaden, November 1939: BA, NS Misch/vorl. 1792, fol. 307, 316.

103. Economic press conference of September 22, 1939: BA, ZSg 115/1939.

104. SD Leipzig section: "Lage auf den Lebensgebieten," September 18, 1939: IWM 271/46 CIOS 4233.

105. Helmut Schoeck, *Der Neid. Eine Theorie der Gesellschaft* (Freiburg, 1966), p. 7.
106. "Meldungen aus dem Reich," December 4, 1939: Boberach, p. 24.
107. "Meldungen aus dem Reich," January 8, 1940: *ibid.*, p. 34.
108. Minister President Göring, Commissioner for the Four Year Plan V.P. 3891g. "Übersicht über die wirtschaftliche Gesamtlage" of February 25, 1940, signed Kiderlen: IWM FD 4809/45 File 2. Cf. also propaganda instructions of December 22, 1939; January 11, 12, 27, and 30, 1940; February 1 and 2, 1940; and April 30, 1940: *Kriegspropaganda*, pp. 249, 261, 263, 264, 274, 277, 279, 280, 337.
109. For this topic see the following reports of the appeals court (OLG) presidents or public prosecutors general (PPG) to the Reich Justice Ministry: OLG-president Kiel, January 9, 1940: BA, R22/3373; PPG-Königsberg, February 8 and April 14, 1940: R22/3375; OLG-president Bamberg, February 26, 1940: R22/3355; OLG-president Dresden, March 6, 1940: R22/3362; PPG-Celle, April 1, 1940: R22/3359; and Kreisleiter of Wetzlar and Worms: BA, NS Misch/1726, fol. 303,934 and 303,974-83.
110. See, for example, "Meldungen aus dem Reich," February 16, 1940: Boberach, p. 49.
111. "Meldungen aus dem Reich," January 12, 1940: *ibid.*, p. 36.
112. Public Prosecutor General of Düsseldorf, March 1, 2, 31, 1940: BA, R22/3363.
113. "Meldungen aus dem Reich," March 29, 1940: BA, R58/149.
114. "Meldungen aus dem Reich," April 3, 1940: BA R58/150. For the distribution of hate literature, see also "Meldungen" of April 10, 1940: *ibid.*
115. Monthly report of the Regierungspräsident for Upper and Middle Franconia of April 7, 1940: BHStA, Abt. II, MA 106,678.
116. Economic press conference of March 19, 1940: BA, ZSg 115/1940. Unemployment figures at the end of the winter were 250,253 of which 64,603 were employable. The women numbered 64,246 of which, however, only 557 were employable. Highest unemployment figures came from Silesia and the Rhineland with 38,087 and 24,231 respectively: press conference of Infantry General Thomas of March 5, 1940: BA/MA Wi/IF 5.357.
117. Minister President Göring, Commissioner of the Four Year Plan, V.P. 4996g, "Übersicht über die wirtschaftliche Gesamtlage" of March 15, 1940: IWM FD 4809/45 File 2.
118. Appeals court president Cologne, March 13, 1940: BA, R22/3374. Similarly Public Prosecutor Munich, January 20, 1941: R22/3379.
119. See, for example, OLG-president Bamberg, January 4, 1940: BA, R22/3355; OLG-president Ludwigshafen, January 8, 1940: R22/3389; OLG-president Brunswick, March 5, 1940: R22/3357; OLG-president Kiel, October 9, 1940: R22/3373.
120. *Ibid.*
121. Cf. H. Knackstedt, "Der 'Altmark'-Zwischenfall," *Wehrwissenschaftliche Rundschau* (1959), pp. 391-411, 466-486. Cf. also Boberach, p. 52.
122. "Meldungen aus dem Reich," April 10, 1940: Boberach, p. 59.
123. "Meldungen aus dem Reich," April 12, 1940: BA, R58/150.
124. BA, R58/184.
125. *Kriegspropaganda*, pp. 315-16.
126. "Meldungen aus dem Reich," April 15, 1940: Boberach, p. 60.
127. Public Prosecutor General Königsberg, April 14, 1940: BA, R22/3375.

128. *Kriegspropaganda*, p. 322.
129. "Meldungen aus dem Reich," April 24, 1940: BA, R58/150.
130. "Meldungen aus dem Reich," May 3, 1940: Boberach, p. 87.
131. "Meldungen aus dem Reich," April 22, 1940: BA, R58/150.
132. *Kriegspropaganda*, p. 322.
133. *Ibid.*, p. 337.
134. Mentioned by Boelcke, *ibid.*, p. 344.
135. *Ibid.*, p. 345.
136. This refers to the inquiry of the kidnapping of the British officers Best and Stevens with the help of Walter Schellenberg.
137. Boberach, p. 66.
138. *Ibid.*
139. *Kriegspropaganda*, p. 344.
140. Boberach, p. 66 (May 14, 1940). Cf. also, SD Leipzig section, May 22, 1940, *Aus deutschen Urkunden*, p. 221.
141. Boberach, p. 67.
142. *Ibid.*, p. 71, footnote 5, p. 82.
143. *Ibid.*, p. 84.
144. *Kriegspropaganda*, pp. 346, 349-51, 355, 367. Cf. also, Auswärtiges Amt, strictly secret information, May 28, 1941: "Feindliche Hetzpropaganda betr. die besetzten und angegliederten Gebiete" Nr. 19/1941, esp. p. 19, "Polen. Bilddokumente deutscher Grausamkeit in der Times:" MGFA-WO 1-6/357.
145. Boberach, pp. 68-69.
146. "Meldungen aus dem Reich," May 30, 1940: BA, R58/151.
147. *Kriegspropaganda*, pp. 362-63. This restraint did not, however, last long; already on June 26 warnings against hearing foreign broadcasts began again. Cf. *Ibid.*, p. 407.
148. *Ibid.*, pp. 369, 370.
149. Boberach, pp. 74, 75.
150. "Meldungen aus dem Reich," June 13, 1940: BA, R58/151.
151. Public Prosecutor General of Bamberg, May 30, 1940: BA, R22/3355.
152. Public Prosecutor General of Darmstadt, June 6, 1940: BA, R22/3361.
153. Public Prosecutor General of Nuremberg, June 21, 1940: BA, R22/3381; cf. also, PPG of Naumburg/Saale, June 6, 1940: BA, R22/3380.
154. ADAP, IX, Dok. 357, pp. 396-98.
155. "Meldungen aus dem Reich," June 13, 1940: BA, R58/151. Similar remarks were already made prior to Italy's entry into the war, cf. SD Leipzig section, May 22, 1940: *Aus deutschen Urkunden*, p. 222. For further critical opinions, see "Meldungen aus dem Reich," June 27, 1940: Boberach, p. 81.
156. *Kriegspropaganda*, p. 392.
157. *Ibid.*, p. 402. On June 23.
158. "Meldungen aus dem Reich," June 17, 1940: BA, R58/151.
159. "Meldungen aus dem Reich," June 20, 1940: BA, R58/151.
160. The war diary of the SA-Sturm 33/5 Bamberg said characteristically for June 19, 1940: "The shame of November, 1918, is nearing its end:" StA Bamberg, Rep. M31.
161. Cf. "Aufzeichnung über die Unterredung zwischen dem Führer und dem Duce in München am 18 Juni 1940," in *Staatsmänner und Diplomaten bei Hitler*, pp. 139-43; and Hillgruber's explanation on p. 138.
162. "Meldungen aus dem Reich," June 20, 1940: BA, R58/151.

163. *Kriegspropaganda*, pp. 395-96 (June 18, 1940). Cf. also SD Leipzig section, Aussenstelle Oschatz, June 18, 1940: *Aus deutschen Urkunden*, p. 223.

164. "Meldungen aus dem Reich," June 20, 1940: BA, R58/151.

165. Cf. Hermann Böhme, *Der deutsch-französische Waffenstillstand im Zweiten Weltkrieg*, Part I: "Entstehung und Grundlagen des Waffenstillstandes von 1940" (Stuttgart, 1966).

166. "Meldungen aus dem Reich," June 24, 1940: BA, R58/151.

167. Hermann Graml, "Die deutsche Militäropposition vom Sommer 1940 bis zum Frühjahr 1943," *loc. cit.*, p. 418; and Andreas Hillgruber, *Hitlers Strategie. Politik und Kriegsführung 1940-1941* (Frankfurt/Main, 1965), p. 61.

168. Erich Kosthorst, *Die deutsche Opposition gegen Hitler zwischen Polen- und Frankreich Feldzug* (Bonn, 1957), 3rd. ed.

169. Report of the Regierungspräsident for Upper and Middle Franconia for June, 1940, on July 8, 1940: BHStA, Abt. II MA 106,678; cf. also OLG-president Bamberg, July 1, 1940: BA, R22/3355.

170. Boberach, pp. 77-78.

171. "Meldungen aus dem Reich," of July 4, 1940—esp. IV "Gegner-Kirche and Krieg" with a number of examples; cf. also Anlage I to "Meldungen" of July 15, 1940: BA, R58/152.

172. Cf. for example, Public Prosecutor General for Bamberg, July 26, 1940: BA, R22/3355; Senior Prosecutor for Darmstadt, July 27, 1940: BA, R22/3361.

173. BA, NS Misch 1726, fol. 303,807.

174. "Meldungen aus dem Reich," June 24, 1940: BA, R58/151; cf. also Meldungen of July 4, 1940: Boberach, p. 88.

175. *Kriegspropaganda*, p. 403. These instructions were repeated June 28, *ibid.*, p. 410.

176. *Ibid.*, p. 412.

177. *Ibid.*, pp. 413, 416, 417, 418, 421, 422.

178. BA, ZSg 101/17, fol. 9.

179. *Ibid.*, fol. 13.

180. *Ibid.*, fol. 16.

181. Informationsbericht of July 12, 1940: BA, ZSg 101/36, fol. 39-41.

182. *Ibid.*, fol. 51.

183. Walter Warlimont, *Im Hauptquartier der deutschen Wehrmacht 1939 bis 1945. Grundlagen. Formen. Gestalten* (Frankfurt/Main, 1962), pp. 128-29.

184. Domarus, II, 1. half volume, pp. 1540-59.

185. *Berlin Diary*, p. 457.

186. "Meldungen aus dem Reich," July 25, 1940: BA, R58/152. Cf. Aussenstelle Oschatz, July 25, 1940: *Aus deutschen Urkunden*, p. 25; and monthly report for July, 1940, of the Regierungspräsident for Upper and Middle Franconia: BHStA, Abt. II MA 106,679. Cf. also, *Kriegspropaganda*, p. 40.

187. *Kriegspropaganda*, p. 443.

188. "Meldungen aus dem Reich," August 5, 1940: BA, R58/153.

189. August 7 and 10, 1940: *Kriegspropaganda*, pp. 449, 453.

190. "Meldungen aus dem Reich," August 12, 1940: Boberach, p. 95.

191. In his conference of August 14, Goebbels reported that extraordinary unrest existed in Berlin concerning coal supplies. Cf. *Kriegspropaganda*, p. 460. Cf. also, "Meldungen aus dem Reich," August 26, 1940, referring to the issue of shoes: Boberach, p. 98.

192. "Meldungen aus dem Reich," August 19, 1940: BA, R58/153.
193. MFGA WO 1-6/354.
194. *Kriegspropaganda*, p. 284 (February 12, 1940).
195. RGBl. 1941, I, p. 45.
196. *Kriegspropaganda*, pp. 474-75.
197. "Meldungen aus dem Reich," August 26, 1940: Boberach, pp. 97-98. Cf. also Nuremberg's Public Prosecutor General, October 14, 1940: BA, R22/3381.
198. "Meldungen aus dem Reich," September 9, 1940: BA, R58/154.
199. "Meldungen aus dem Reich," September 23, 1940: *ibid.*
200. "Meldungen aus dem Reich," September 30, 1940: Boberach, p. 103.
201. *Ibid.*, pp. 104-9 (October 7, 1940).
202. *Berlin Diary*, p. 486.
203. Anweisung No. 850: BA, ZSg 101/17, fol. 1.
204. October 5, 1940: BA, R22/3355.
205. "Meldungen" of April 22, 29, and June 24, 1940.
206. BA, R58/152.
207. BA, R58/153.
208. A very similar list of themes is found in Rundschreiben No. 143 of the SD Stuttgart section, September 5, 1940. It also included atrocity reports of cruelties committed against Poles by German soldiers. Cf. HStA Stuttgart, K 750/38.
209. BA, R58/154.
210. Examples are Pastor Dietrich Bonhoeffer, leading figure within the resistance, and Pastor Hellmut Gollwitzer. Both were prohibited from speaking publicly at the end of August, 1940, for "demoralizing activity." StA Obb. No. 1875.
211. BA, NS Misch 1726, fol. 303,751-53.
212. *Die kirchliche Lage in Bayern*, p. 321.
213. BA, R22/3367.
214. *Die Briefe Pius XII. an die deutschen Bischöfe*, pp. 85 ff. This confrontation between the two wings had almost resulted in Bishop Preysing's withdrawing from the Fulda Conference in June or his resignation from Berlin's bishopric because he did not concur with Cardinal Bertram's congratulatory letter to Hitler on his birthday on April 20. Cf. *ibid.*, pp. xxxi f. and 74 f.
215. Cf. three informative letters of the Chief of the Security Police and SD, Heydrich, to Foreign Minister Ribbentrop on September 10 and October 17, 1940, and January 13, 1941: AA Inland II 6/45.
216. Protocol p. 2413, cited in Alexander Mitscherlich and Fred Mielke, *Wissenschaft ohne Menschlichkeit. Medizinische und Eugenische Irrwege unter Diktatur, Bürokratie und Krieg* (Heidelberg, 1949), p. 176.
217. *Ibid.*, p. 177, note 1.
218. IMT, vol. XXVI, p. 169 (doc. 630-PS).
219. The *Schumacher Collection*/401, BA, contains a letter of Standartenführer Schiele from Munich, November 22, 1940, to Obergruppenführer Jüttner with a comprehensive report and copies of various letters concerning the subject of euthanasia. Cf. also BA, NS19 neu/1578.
220. Cf. the correspondence of the Kreisleiter for Weissenburg, Bavaria, of March 6, 1941, to the Gauleitung Franconia, re. "Beunruhigung der Bevölkerung von Absberg durch auffälliges Wegschaffen von Insassen des Ottilienheimes," including enclosures: BA, NS Misch 1916.

221. BA, NS22/vorl. 860.
222. *Ibid.*
223. see footnote 219 above.
224. Conway, *op. cit.*, pp. 269 f.
225. All documents in BA, Slg. Schumacher/401. The letter to Brach published in *Reichsführer! Briefe an und von Himmler*, ed. by Helmut Heiber (Stuttgart, 1968), p. 83, (cited in future as *Reichsführer*). Cf. also Léon Poliakov, *Le breviaire de la haine* (Paris, 1951), pp. 212 f.
226. BA, R22/3355.
227. BA, R22/3363 (February 3, 1941).
228. BA, R22/3355.
229. BA, R22/3364 (February 15, 1941).
230. BA, R22/3381 (March 3, 1941).
231. OLG-president, March 5, 1941: BA, R22/3379.
232. BA, R22/3355.
233. Mitscherlich & Miele, *op. cit.*, pp. 194 ff.
234. Translated with National Socialist commentary in "Vertraulicher Mitteilungsdienst zusammengestellt von der Dienststelle des Reichsschulungsbeauftragten der NSV-Hauptstelle Theoretische Schulung," No. 1, September, 1941: BA, NS Misch/1525.
235. Zahn, *op. cit.*, p. 122.
236. Cited in *Die Briefe Pius XII. an die deutschen Bischöfe 1939-1944*, p. 174, footnote 1.
237. Monthly report for December by the Regierungspräsident for Upper and Middle Franconia, BHStA, Abt. II, MA 106,679.
238. BA, R58/164.
239. Boberach, pp. 207-11.
240. Hitler supposedly already gave a verbal order to halt the program in August, 1941. Mitscherlich and Miele, *op. cit.*, p. 198.
241. Report of the OLG-president of Hamm, August 7, 1941: BA, R22/3367. Celle's General Public Prosecutor reported on August 1, 1941: "In one locality the matter even became the object of a children's game." BA, R22/3359. Cf. also, OLG-president Celle, September 2, 1941: BA, R22/3359; Düsseldorf, November 1, 1941: BA, R22/3363.
242. General Public Prosecutors, Hamm, September 30, 1941, and Düsseldorf, December 1, 1941.
243. *Kriegspropaganda*, p. 711.
244. *Kriegspropaganda*, p. 711.
245. BA, ZSg 109/20, fol. 23, 28, 61.
246. BA, ZSg 109/24, fol. 1/2. Sonderinformation No. 43/41 of August 23, 1941.
247. "Meldungen aus dem Reich," October 7, 1940: Boberach, pp. 104-6.
248. *Kriegspropaganda*, p. 543.
249. "Meldungen aus dem Reich," October 10, 1940: BA, R58/155.
250. *Kriegspropaganda*, p. 311.
251. *Ibid.*, p. 313.
252. "Meldungen aus dem Reich," October 14, 1940: BA, R58/155.
253. Cf. for example, "Meldungen aus dem Reich," July 15, 1940: BA, R58/152.
254. "Meldungen aus dem Reich," October 14, 1940: BA, R58/155.
255. BA, ZSg 115/1940.
256. Kreisverwaltung der DAF, Freiburg, October, 1940: BA, NS5 I/58.
257. BA, R22/336, 3374, 3379.

258. BA, R22/3355.
259. Boberach, pp. 111-14.
260. Cf. an announcement by the works manager for GHH in Oberhausen of November 12, 1940: HA GHH 400101/3.
261. Goebbels in his conference of October 14, 1940: *Kriegspropaganda*, p. 549.
262. Conference of October 23, 1940: *ibid.*, p. 555.
263. Cf. Eberhard Jäckel, *Frankreich in Hitlers Europa. Die deutsche Frankreichpolitik im Zweiten Weltkrieg* (Stuttgart, 1966).
264. *Staatsmänner und Diplomaten bei Hitler*, pp. 230-47. Cf. also ADAP, vol. IX, p. 513.
265. Bestellungen from the press conference of October 23, 1940, Anweisung No. 244: BA, ZSg 101/18, fol. 47.
266. Bestellungen from the press conferences: a) November 12, 1940, Anweisung No. 717, and b) December 14, 1940, Anweisung No. 735, BA, ZSg 101/18, fol. 163, 169.
267. *Kreigspropaganda*, p. 557; and BA, ZSg 101/18, fol. 51. Cf. also *Kriegspropaganda*, p. 567 (November 13, 14, 1940).
268. "Meldungen aus dem Reich," July 4, 1940: Boberach, p. 83.
269. "Meldungen aus dem Reich," July 15, 1940: BA, R58/152.
270. "Meldungen aus dem Reich," July 25, 1940: *ibid.*
271. Bestellungen from the press conference of August 12, 1940, Anweisung No. 705: BA, ZSg 101/17, fol. 76.
272. Bestellungen from the press conference of August 22, noon, Anweisung No. 797: *ibid.*, fol. 99.
273. Bestellungen from the press conference of November 11, 1940, Anweisung No. 412, daily slogan: BA, ZSg 101/18, fol. 88.
274. *Kriegspropaganda*, p. 566; and Bestellungen from the press conference of November 13, 1940, Anweisung No. 428: BA, ZSg 101/18, fol. 92.
275. *Kriegspropaganda*, p. 566.
276. BA, R58/156 (November 14, 1940).
277. Cf. the report of his talk with Hitler in *Staatsmänner und Diplomaten bei Hitler*, pp. 295-319; and his discussion with Ribbentrop, ADAP, XI, pp. 472-78.
278. BA, ZSg 101/18, fol. 73, 156, 158, 193, 204.
279. *Staatsmänner und Diplomaten*, pp. 320, 330.
280. "Meldungen aus dem Reich," November 25, 1940: BA, R58/150.
281. Goebbels in his conference of October 24, 1940: *Kriegspropaganda*, p. 557.
282. *Ibid.*, pp. 576, 578.
283. *Ibid.*, p. 580.
284. "Meldungen aus dem Reich," November 25, 1940: BA, R58/156.
285. "Meldungen aus dem Reich," December 16, 1940: BA, R58/156. Cf. also OLG-president of Bamberg, January 2, 1941: BA, R22/3355, and OLG-president of Brunswick, January 4, 1941: BA, R22/3357.
286. *Kriegspropaganda*, p. 582 (December 5, 1940).
287. *Ibid.*, p. 587 (December 16, 1940).
288. *Ibid.*, p. 589 (December 19, 1940).
289. *Ibid.*, p. 593.
290. *Ibid.*, p. 594.
291. "Meldungen aus dem Reich," January 27, 1941: BA, R58/157.
292. The head of Berlin's civil air defense had advised Berliners to go to bed

early in order to catch a few hours sleep before air raid alarms began. Some followed his advice, and they entered the cellar with "good morning." Those who had not yet slept answered "good evening"; and there were those who replied "Heil Hitler." Of those it was said that they were asleep all the time.
Or: A plane carrying Hitler, Göring, and Goebbels crashes. Sixty-four dollar question: Who is saved? Answer: the German people. *Berlin Diary*, p. 563; cf. also p. 581.

293. *Kriegspropaganda*, p. 558.
294. On November 10, 1940: BA, R22/5374.
295. See, for example, OLG-presidents of Bamberg and Brunswick, January 2 and 4, 1941: BA, R22/3355 and 3357. The SD report of November 28, in its section "current film programs" had commented about the interest created by pictures of Hitler. Boberach, p. 116.
296. Hitler's New Year message, mentioned in the SD report of January 9: Boberach, p. 117. Cf. also monthly report for January, 1941, by the Regierungspräsident for Lower Franconia and Aschaffenburg: BHStA, Abt. II, MA 106,681.
297. Cf. "Meldungen aus dem Reich," January 16, 1941: BA, R58/157; and February 3, 1941: Boberach, p. 126. Cf. also Domarus, II, 2. Halbband, pp. 1657-64.
298. Rumors of a possible altercation with the USSR were already reported from there in December. Cf. "Meldungen aus dem Reich," December 16, 1940: BA, R58/156. Public prosecutor general, Königsberg, February 10, 1941: BA, R22/3375.
299. Cf. Chef des Oberkommandos der Wehrmacht No. 25/41g WR (II/6) of January 11, 1941, about "Abhören feindlicher Sender durch Wehrmachtangehörige." MGFA WO 1-6/325 and Goebbels' conference of February 26, 1941: *Kriegspropaganda*, p. 626.
300. BA, ZSg 109/18, fol. 28, 30.
301. Economic press conference, February 4, 1941: BA, ZSg 115/1941.
302. SD section Leipzig, Aussenstelle Oschatz. II 225. Tgb. No. 42/41: IWM FD 332/46.
303. Ortsgruppenleiter Wilhelmshaven, cited in the report of the Kreisleitung Wilhelmshaven for October, 1940: Niedersächsisches Staatsarchiv 277, 10/2.
304. August 1, 1941: BA, R22/3355.
305. Cf. Hans Mommsen, *passim*.
306. President of the Hanseatic Appeals Court, November 7, 1940: BA, R22/3366. OLG-president, Cologne, November 10, 1940: BA, R22/5374. Public prosecutor general, Celle, January 27, 1941: BA, R22/3359.
307. III A Z ST/GT of January 6, 1941, to Major-General Reinecke, OKW: MGFA WO 1-/180.
308. Public prosecutor general for Königsberg, February 10, 1941: BA, R22/3357.
309. BA, R58/156.
310. *Kriegspropaganda*, p. 592. Cf. also "Meldungen aus dem Reich," January 23, 1941: Boberach, pp. 118-21.
311. Public prosecutor general for Königsberg, December 9, 1940, February 10 and April 2, 1941: BA, R22/3357.
312. OLG-president Kassel, January 4, 1941, concerning closing of·the Franciscan monastery Frauenberg in Fulda: BA, R22/3371; and early March about

closing the St. Boniface monastery of the Host of the Pure Virgin Mary in Hünfeld.

313. Cf. Boberach, p. 119, footnote 1.

314. BA, NS22/vorl. 860.

315. "Vertrauliche Informationen" of May 28, 1941: BA, ZSg 3/1621. Cf. also *Die kirchliche Lage in Bayern*, No. 373.

316. Cf. Boberach, p. 79, footnote 1, and BA, NS Misch/474, fol. 112,808.

317. This letter was presented to the Major War Trials at Nuremberg as Prosecution document D75: IMT, vol. XXXV, pp. 9 f., and comes from one of the Confessional Church's leaflets confiscated by the Gestapo in Munich. Bormann's defense counsel questioned the authenticity of the document: IMT, vol. XIX, p. 137. Zipfel, *op. cit.*, p. 511, reports about various copies and transcribed the one of the Reich Propaganda Office. A copy of the Party Chancellory circular is in the Bundesarchiv, NS Misch 6/vorl. 336.

318. Cf. the correspondence of the Secret State Police, Munich office, B. No. 40400/41-II of April 23, 1941, to the Polizeipräsidium Munich, concerning processions and pilgrimages as well as church festivities. StA Obb., No. 1876.

319. Monthly report for May, 1941, by the Regierungspräsident for Upper Bavaria: *Die kirchliche Lage in Bayern*, pp. 327-28.

320. Report of the NSDAP Reich Women Executive for the months April-May (June, 1941): BA, NS22/vorl. 860.

321. *Die kirchliche Lage in Bayern*, pp. 328, 330-31; and report of the Regierungspräsident for Upper Bavaria, October 8, 1941: BHStA, Abt. II, MA 106,674.

322. Cf. Alan Milward, *The German Economy at War* (London, 1965).

323. *Ibid.*, p. 29.

324. V.P. 1197/41 g. RS, of November 23, 1941: IWM FD 4809/45, file 2; J 004147; 004155.

325. For example, at the beginning of the French campaign the exchange rate was 1 RM=20Frs.

326. Arbeits- und Lagebericht der Kreisverwaltung Freiburg for May, 1941: BA, NS5 I/58, fol. 78698. Cf. also reports of January and February, fol. 78727 f.

327. Boberach, p. 122.

328. *Kriegspropaganda*, p. 618.

329. Cf. Boberach, pp. 135, 137.

330. V.I. No. 30/41: BA, ZSg 109/18, fol. 102.

331. *Ibid.*, fol. 118.

332. *Ibid.*, fol. 130.

333. Cf. Notes from the press conference of February 10, 1941: BA, ZSg 101/19, fol. 106.

334. "Meldungen aus dem Reich," March 27, 1941, and March 31, 1941; Boberach, pp. 127, 129.

335. *Staatsmänner und Diplomaten bei Hitler*, p. 417.

336. "Meldungen aus dem Reich," April 10, 1941: Boberach, p. 133.

337. *Kriegspropaganda*, p. 658.

338. *Ibid.*, p. 686.

339. "Meldungen aus dem Reich," April 10, 1941: Boberach, p. 134.

340. Boberach, p. 126.

341. SD section Leipzig, March 22, 1941: *Aus deutschen Urkunden*, p. 238.

342. Public prosecutor general, Naumburg, March 31, 1941: BA, R22/3380.
343. Cited in Königsberg's public prosecutor general's report of April 2, 1941: BA, R22/3375.
344. Cf. *Staatsmänner und Diplomaten bei Hitler*, pp. 503-14.
345. "Meldungen aus dem Reich," March 27, 1941: Boberach, p. 127.
346. Cf. for example, the report of Allenstein's senior prosecutor, *Ibid.*, p. 128.
347. Statement by Goebbels in *Kriegspropaganda*, p. 677; and V.I. No. 93/41 of April 14, 1941: BA, ZSg 109/20, fol. 42.
348. BA, R2/24243. Cf. also Steinert, *op. cit.*, pp. 134 f.
349. BA, R58/160.
350. *Ibid.*
351. Security Service of RFSS, SD section Leipzig, Aussenstelle Leipzig, May 3, 1941: *Aus deutschen Urkunden*, pp. 240-41.
352. Hillgruber, *Deutschlands Rolle in der Vorgeschichte der beiden Weltkriege*, pp. 105, 107.
353. "Meldungen aus dem Reich," May 8, 1941: BA, R58/160.
354. *Ibid.*
355. "Meldungen aus dem Reich," May 12, 1941: Boberach, p. 143.
356. *Ibid.*, pp. 143, 144.
357. *Kriegspropaganda*, p. 729.
358. *Ibid.*, and BA, ZSg 109/21, fol. 33.
359. Report of the Regierungspräsident for Central Franconia, June 11, 1941: BHStA, Abt. II, MA 106,681.
360. Report of the Regierungspräsident for Swabia and Neuburg, June 10, 1941: BHStA, Abt. II, MA 106,684.
361. Public prosecutor general, Naumburg, May 30, 1941: BA, R22/3355 and SD-Aussenstelle Bünde, May 13, 1941: Höhne, *op. cit.*, p. 390.
362. OLG-president Bamberg, June 25, 1941: BA, R22/3355 and OLG-pres. Rostock, July 1, 1941: BA, R22/3385.
363. OLG-president Frankfurt, June 26, 1941: BA, R22/3364, and Security Service of the RFSS, SD section Leipzig, Aussenstelle Leipzig, May 17, 1941: *Aus deutschen Urkunden*, p. 245.
364. *Ibid.*, p. 243 and also OLG-president Königsberg, June 6, 1941: BA, R22/3375.
365. Cf. *Aus deutschen Urkunden*, p. 244; OLG-president Bamberg, June 25, 1941: BA, R22/3355; Monthly report of June 10, 1941: BHStA, Abt. II, MA 106,671; B. No. 27309/41-II, May 31, 1941: StA Obb. No. 1877.
366. Andreas-Friedrich, *op. cit.*, p. 50.
367. There is still debate about Hess' motives: the version from former Nazi and SS circles is that Hess acted with Hitler's knowledge (Paul Neukirchen) while Albert Speer saw it as part of a distancing between the two men and Hess' attempt to regain stature in Hitler's eyes (*Erinnerungen*, p. 190). In contrast, Karl Dietrich Bracher sees it as a "sacrifice." (*Die deutsche Diktatur*, p. 307).
368. *Aus deutschen Urkunden*, p. 245.
369. *Ibid.*, p. 46, and OLG-president Königsberg, June 6, 1941: BA, R22/3375. Monthly report of the Regierungspräsident for Upper and Central Franconia, June 8, 1941: BHStA, Abt. II, MA 106,679.
370. Boberach, p. 146.
371. *Kriegspropaganda*, p. 728.

372. Public prosecutor general, Naumburg/Saale, May 30, 1941: BA, R22/3380. Public prosecutor general, Nuremberg, May 31, 1941: BA, R22/3381. Public prosecutor general, Düsseldorf, May 31, 1941: BA, R22/3363.
373. Public prosecutor general, Königsberg, June 6, 1941: BA, R22/3375.
374. BA/MA Wi I F 5/3690.
375. See, for example, report of the NSDAP Reich Directorate, Reich Women's League for the months January-March, 1941: BA, NS22/vorl. 860.
376. Hess Anordnung A 44/40 (not for publication): BA, NS6/vorl. 331.
377. Kriegspropaganda, p. 618.
378. Ibid., p. 640, and Sonderinformation No. 14/41 of March 19, 1941, about the campaign "Frauen helfen siegen," Pressepolitischer Arbeitsplan: BA, ZSg 109/19, fol. 67-69.
379. See 181, footnote 283; p. 231 ff.
380. Domarus, vol. II, 2. Halbband, p. 1708.
381. Public prosecutor general, Königsberg, June 6, 1941: BA, R22/3375.
382. Boberach, p. 148.
383. Folge 27. BA, ZSg 3/1621.
384. Regierungspräsident for Swabia and Neuburg, June 10, 1941: BHStA, Abt. II, MA 106,679.
385. V.I. No. 120/41: BA, ZSg 109/20, fol. 36.
386. May 22, 1941: Boberach, p. 147.
387. BA, NS5 I/58.
388. Monthly report for June, 1941, of the Landkreis Aachen, June 30, 1941: BA, NS 1714, fol. 301,608. Cf. also "Übersicht über die wirtschaftliche Gesamtlage," Göring. V.P. 9499/41 g. Rs. of June 21, 1941, which speaks of a "pressure on the general mood." IWM F.D. 4809/45, file 2.
389. See footnote 365 above.
390. Boberach, p. 147.
391. Ibid.
392. Cf. V.I. No. 135/41 of May 31, 1941: BA, ZSg 109/21, fol. 100-101.
393. The beginning of the Crete operation had been kept from the public. Kriegspropaganda, pp. 744, 749. Cf. also BA, ZSg 109/21, fol. 67, 69, 75, 96. "Meldungen aus dem Reich," June 9, 1941: Boberach, p. 151.
394. Kriegspropaganda, pp. 746 and 765; and "Wollt ihr den totalen Krieg?", p. 180.
395. "Meldungen aus dem Reich," June 12, 1941: BA, R58/161.
396. "Meldungen aus dem Reich," June 16, 1941: Boberach, p. 153.
397. OLG-president, Königsberg, June 23, 1941: BA, R22/3375; BA, ZSg 101/120, fol. 237.
398. BA, ZSg 101/20, fol. 130.

II. WORLD WAR

No problem is so great
that it could not be
solved by a German.

Hermann Göring

1. OPERATION BARBAROSSA

HITLER BEGAN THE SECOND PHASE of his war plan with the June 22
attack on the Soviet Union. After a period of localized lightning strikes,
the real world war,[1] which had originally been planned as a series of
world "Blitzkriegs," began. Now the very nature of war changed. From
a "normal war"[2] as had been conducted in the West, and a "racial war"
initiated after cessation of military operations in Poland, a new type of
"war of annihilation" emerged, unknown in European military annals
for its unspeakable brutality and horror. Its goals were threefold: 1) to
acquire "Lebensraum" in the East; 2) as a by-product of the war, to rob
England of her last continental support and break her status as a world
power; and 3) to annihilate the "Jewish-Bolshevik" enemy, including
the Soviet elite and all Jews. At the so-called "generals' conference"
of March 30, 1941, Hitler had already announced his disregard for all
conventions of international law in his impending Eastern campaign.[3]
His intention to exterminate the Soviet political elite is documented in
the famous commissar order of June 6, 1941, in which he instructed
that all political commissars "be shot immediately;"[4] in Hitler's name,
Göring formulated the order of July 31, 1941, to exterminate all Jews,
directing Reich SD Chief, Reinhold Heydrich, "to make all necessary
preparations for a final solution of the Jewish question . . . with the
participation of all competent central German authorities."[5] This occurred
at a time when Hitler believed a victory over Russia had already been
achieved. The two developments, the battle in the East to conquer
needed "living space" and the solution of the Jewish question, are
directly and inseparably related. Both are axiomatic demands formu-

117

lated by Hitler between 1919 and 1925, which he now wanted to realize.[6] Directly on the heels of three million German soldiers followed SD extermination squads [*Einsatzgruppen*] and police units; during the months to come, over one million Jews fell victim to these "cleansing operations" in western Russia.

To justify this pillage and murder in the eyes of the German public, the enemy was blamed again, much as was done following the surprise attacks on Poland, Holland, and Belgium. Hitler's proclamation of June 22 talked about a "conspiracy by Jews and democrats, Bolsheviks and reactionaries."[7] Germany was therefore forced to save and secure Europe. From the first day, the theme of a German "mission" rang out. Goebbels and Reich Press Chief Dietrich initiated an enormous propaganda campaign. The greatest difficulty for Hitler, as he said in a later dinner conversation, was "turning the wheel 180 degrees."[8] The press was given detailed instructions on how to change the public's mind without creating the impression that this attack on a former ally was a sudden "about-face." "National Socialism began as a movement against Bolshevism. It conquered and restructured the German Reich under this banner. After completing these tasks within the Reich, the struggle against Bolshevism was postponed for almost two years by an apparent *Burgfrieden* ["castle peace," i.e., domestic truce.] Now that the Führer has uncovered the treachery of the Bolshevik dictator, National Socialism, and with it the German people, return to the principle of its origin, the fight against plutocracy and Bolshevism."[9] It was further suggested that "psychologically" the press proceed "very carefully." "It is obviously impossible to jump right into an anti-Bolshevik line immediately; they should rather calmly point out, in a series of transitions, that Germany remained silent against Bolshevism for political reasons. . . . Furthermore, and that would be the next stage of the propaganda, plutocracy and Bolshevism have the same origin, namely a Jewish origin. . . ."[10] In various forms, this equation of capitalism and Bolshevism, of plutocracy and communism, all under Jewish domination, became the leitmotif of German propaganda until the last stages of the war,[11] when an attempt was made to separate these odd partners.

Reports both from state and Party sources on the German public's first reactions were almost uniformly ones of surprise and dismay; a few spoke of shock, paralysis, or a bombshell effect.[12] The first available SD report correctly attributed this subdued shock effect to long-time rumors of tensions with Russia.[13] The timing, above all, surprised people. Apparently the whisper campaign of Stalin's impending visit and similar chimeras had ensured disbelief in an immediate conflict. People were also alarmed more by the prospect of further prolongation of the war than by its expansion, awareness of which was still incomplete, or than the fear of losing.[14] Most concerned were the women: "The war with Russia has made such an impression on our women because, until recently, we pointed to complete accord with Russia in our meetings. In these local groups the news of our entry into Russia consequently hit like a bombshell. . . ."[15]

Uninformed or uninterested people, and dedicated Nazis as well, all quickly came to terms with the new situation.[16] Most decided, without need for lengthy propaganda, "that a conflict with the world's enemy would have to come sooner or later. . . ."[17] And as absurd as it might sound today, a wave of sympathy engulfed Hitler for having kept his silence: "His patience and willingness to sacrifice himself are described as superhuman."[18] Thus the war with the Soviet Union was viewed as a new but unavoidable burden to be borne with the "Führer's" help. There was less talk than ever of a war spirit. Only the appeals court presidents of Rostock and Nuremberg reported that the war had been greeted with "joy" or as "a liberating act."[19] One can safely credit these statements to ardent Nazis.

For the remainder of the population, the observation of Bamberg's public prosecutor was far more apt: "Generally the expansion of the war into a world war surpasses the imagination and energy of a large segment of the population." The objective of uniting all Germans had been quite understandable at the beginning of the war. A few vague ideas did exist concerning the acquisition of colonies, but no one had conceived of the need or possibility of a world war. "Now the drive into Russia has, in the opinion of the Volk, only accentuated the problem of how to pacify and satisfy the people in presently occupied areas, i.e., the former Poland, by extending it to other areas as well. Germany's future role, according to propaganda, as leading state in Europe, and the direct incorporation of Eastern territory remain incomprehensible to a large portion of the population. Basically, the concept of a greater German Reich as a pure racial state (in which even Bohemia and Moravia represent alien bodies) within the framework of essentially equal European nations was firmly rooted in the general consciousness. Naturally, numerous co-existing desires for German supremacy raise concern about how such a condition can be maintained without prolonged tensions and anxiety. . . . A clash of current conceptions and emerging developments is obvious. . . ."[20] This appropriate analysis is confirmed by the fact that unlike previous military campaigns, there was no crescendo in the public mood, coupled with a simultaneous drop in preoccupation with domestic political events and daily hardships. The Reich Security Office glibly explained the lack of enthusiasm, when compared with the Western campaign, as earlier public overindulgence in victories and the incomparable vastness of the two war arenas. Yet successes were every bit as astounding: German armies penetrated deep into Russia, reaching the Dnieper and Smolensk by mid-July—little more than two hundred miles from Moscow and 450 miles from the starting point of Bialystok. Two encirclements around Bialystok and Minsk alone produced 323,898 prisoners, and there was talk of a quick end to the war.[22] It was, therefore, not a lack of victories which can be blamed for the absence of enthusiasm.

It was the changing situation, an increasing harshness, that accounted for a diminishing spirit. "*The general mood* of a broad public spectrum —as previously mentioned in a July 9 report—continues to deteriorate. Even if confidence in victory and trust in the leadership and military still exists, citizens are depressed, embittered, and angered by the severity of the Eastern struggle, the criminal conduct of the Red Army, the evident losses appearing in casualty reports, and finally also due to provisioning difficulties. . . ."[23]

Without any sense of balance, press and radio presented German readers and listeners with a picture of a Soviet state full of perverted brutalities. The Propaganda Ministry's information service had collected materials on Soviet Communism's crimes and offenses—persecutions of clergy and intellectuals, the various party and army purges, GPU activities, etc.—and directed the press to serve them *en masse* to the German public, together with pictures and accounts of primitive living conditions in the USSR,[24] compared to the social achievements of the Third Reich. Newspapers were to reject sharply all reports from Moscow of crimes and inhuman treatment by German officers and soldiers.[25]

Soviet efforts to smear German troops were regarded with disdain as unoriginal and simplistic:[26] "In their counter-propaganda, the Soviets accept the authenticity of German photographs but claim they are victims who had been shot by German troops. As star witnesses they produce German soldiers, supposedly defectors, named Meier, Müller, and Schulz. This Soviet propaganda is very primitive." It is hardly surprising, therefore, if the German public was incensed by the "inhumane Bolshevik conduct of the war" and if the large numbers of prisoners elicited comments such as: " . . . 'one might eliminate more and capture fewer,' feeling that 'we will get even less to eat if we burden ourselves with this Russian riffraff and have to feed them'."[27] It is also understandable given press instructions not to discuss the subject of "special German economic interests in Russian territory. The impression of material gain resulting from the occupation of any territory must be avoided."[28]

Newsreels showed scenes of GPU atrocities, Red Army crimes, and columns of unshaven, unkempt, and starving Soviet prisoners, described as rabble and usually depicted as criminal types. Many people could not accept the pictured riflewomen as prisoners of war, and thought such types should be shot. Scenes of Jewish prisoners, arrested and forcefully employed for German clean-up operations, met with great satisfaction.[29] The Nazi leadership was masterful in mobilizing baser instincts, projecting their own sadistic urges onto others, and exposing the human abyss. Treatment of Soviet prisoners during the first months of the Eastern campaign was based on the motto of "survival in the struggle between two irreconcilable ideologies," as Hitler had declared to his generals on March 30. Russian soldiers did not receive the "special treatment" for commissars, but OKW decrees also demanded "ruthless and energetic action" against them; millions died of starvation and exhaustion.[30] Only after the lightning strikes had proven a failure and Germany required additional manpower for its armament industries, was slightly more humane treatment considered. On December 18, the OKW issued a decree for the "restoration and maintenance of Soviet war prisoners' fitness to work," with demands for adequate food, heated lodgings, medical supervision, and sufficient clothing.[31] However, until this order eventually took effect, exhausted prisoners were simply shot. When criticized by a propaganda department about the impact of these shootings on the German image of justice and authority, General Jodl admitted the need for keeping more soldiers alive as laborers but also called for counter-propaganda to present such cases as "prisoners who refused to march on, not because they *could* not but because they *would* not. . . ."[32] The general, along with other high-ranking officers, was free of that "sentimentality" which Nazi propaganda repeatedly tried to eradicate among the Germans.

The mood in Germany was certainly not rosy[33] and continued to deteriorate, fluctuating from week to week depending on the news from Russia but overall remaining appreciably below the level of 1940. At no time did domestic political events disappear from view. "In conversations among urban residents the 'catastrophic food situation' oftentimes takes up more space than military events. Latest reports from Stuttgart, Esslingen, Reutlingen, Tübingen, Ludwigsburg, Horb and Göttingen collectively point to indignation among wide segments of society over shortages, prices and preferential distribution of fresh vegetables, fruits, and potatoes, reaching proportions that give cause for concern; it affects the desire to work and the fighting resolve of citizens so adversely that it 'just can't go on like this'."[34] The above report on mounting "irritation" in Swabia is reinforced by reports from elsewhere, particularly the July 7 SD report on poor food provisioning.[35] Göring's office for the Four Year Plan also pointed to severe food shortages in the Ruhr, while Berlin's police chief noted rising resentment against administrative agencies and "derisive comments about the huge organizational apparatus existing everywhere today; there is a feeling that all this organization stifles life and in this case prevents proper provisioning of food. . . ."[36]

The DAF district shop steward in Freiburg wrote on July 31, 1941: " . . . In short, the mood among the working class is very bad at present! One hears remarks that are very reactionary, provoked by 1) price and wage developments, and 2) the food situation. One fact that has emerged is that citizens from regions endangered by air attacks have remained with us for weeks and months now and pay daily board representing one-third to one-half of the average wage of our workers; these people can afford the best meals on meatless days and pay cutthroat, profiteering prices under the table for foodstuffs. . . ." With some justice the Nazi functionary declared: "The working population is again the one which has to bear the whole brunt of the economic struggle. . . ."[37] A little later the Stuttgart SD reported: "Everywhere one finds the opinion that 'in this war *the little people are the losers once more.*' They must work, do without and keep their mouths shut while others can afford anything with money, connections, license, and ruthlessness. '*Everything is just like it was before*: here big shots and plutocrats . . . there the good-natured, stupid and laboring people. Can one still speak of a *Volksgemeinschaft* [people's community]?' . . ."[38]

In its "Vertrauliche Informationen," the Party Chancellory directed itself toward numerous rumors of further food reductions and asserted that they lacked any foundation as far as meat, fats, and cake rations were concerned. Complaints about potatoes and vegetables were justified, but due to a strained transportation situation no decisive action could be taken.[39] When anxiety persisted,[40] Göring ordered at a conference on September 16, 1941, that rations could not be reduced under any circumstances. He would never tolerate it "since in wartime the mood at home is a considerable factor in the defense of the Reich. The enemy knows exactly that he can no longer defeat the German people militarily. His only hope is to wear down the mood of the home front."[41]

Economic issues were not the only source of irritation affecting the public mood; there were anti-Church policies and the previously discussed euthanasia measures. Two events which aroused particular excitement were the removal of crucifixes and the distribution of the Fulda Bishops' letter. Protests against anticlerical measures took on a new dimension and a new harshness, especially in the rural areas, with the war against Russia: "A few women thought it incomprehensible 'that we fight Bolshevism and its godlessness on the one hand and the Church on the other'. . . ."[42] Hamm's appeals court president presented various judicial reports of bitterness among the Catholic population following the closing of institutions belonging to the Jesuits, Claretians, and Benedictines. While the monks of the Benedictine monastery in Gerleve near Coesfeld were being removed, a mass of demonstrating people assembled, singing hymns. The Benedictines had enjoyed great popularity among the 95 per cent Catholic population. "The whole population is in deep mourning over the actions of the state secret police. People feel it is a great injustice that the monks, accused of no crime, nor sentenced by judicial decision, were expelled by the state secret police and robbed of their possessions. They view this with particular bitterness and grief since thirty members of this order are soldiers in the field, as is generally known. . . ."[43]

In Herzogenaurach, in eastern Bavaria, the rector of the girls' school was forced to seek refuge in the city hall from protesting mothers and school children for authorizing the removal of crucifixes.[44] Women wrote their husbands in Russia that they had better "come home to fight Bolshevism *here*."[45] The Reich Women's League reported similar complaints as well as "deep unrest" and "a sizable number of resignations" from Nazi women's organizations.[46]

In his sermons of July 13 and 20, 1941, in the Lamberti Church, the Bishop of Münster issued a strongly-worded protest: "The Gestapo at this very moment is continuing to throw innocent fellow citizens out into the street, exile them from the country, and incarcerate irreproachable, highly respected Germans without a trial or defense;" he called the closing of monasteries an outrageous injustice. His sermons added to the tension,[47] much like the Fulda Bishops' letter of June 26, 1941, which was read from almost every pulpit on July 6. This pastoral letter, which to the great disappointment of the Nazis said nothing about the attack on Russia, focused in great detail on the restrictions in the area of religious education, literature, special spiritual care and the closing of monasteries. It failed to comprehend such measures at a time "when the unity of the Volk should be preserved and not strained and endangered by offending the religious feelings of a large part of the population." Leading Catholic clergy thereby adroitly exploited Nazi propaganda themes. On the other hand, the point was also made that the "survival of Christianity and the Church in Germany" was at stake, and attention was directed to Rosenberg's *Der Mythus des XX. Jahrhunderts* [*The Myth of the Twentieth Century*], which contained the statement that Germans had to choose between Christ and the German Volk. Responding, the German bishops stated: "We German Catholics reject such a choice with burning indignation. We love our German people and serve them, if need be, to the death. At the same time we also live and die for Jesus Christ and want to remain united with him, now and for all eternity. . . . If we take pains to preserve Christianity among our people, we thereby also stand for the individual right and dignity of every German. . . ."[48]

This pastoral letter is typical of the attitude among the German Catholic hierarchy during the Second World War, one "both of support and opposition," of patriotism combined with protest.[49] The impact on the public was considerable: " . . . The reception of the pastoral letter in most crowded churches depended partly on the local situation; the *rural population became much more agitated* than the urban. The effect also depended heavily on the style of the delivery; where the reading was monotonous or too fast the unrest was not too great, but since the clergy as a rule used rhetorical devices such as conspicuous emphasis, pauses for effect, etc., and often became very excited, it was able to carry along the audience accordingly. As several reports indicate, women frequently wept. . . ." Seldom did anyone walk out of the church demonstratively; following the service there was lively discussion. Only a small percentage of the church-goers thought the tone of the letter was too harsh. Most reacted positively to the content and negatively to the Nazi state and the official Party. A few typical remarks were:

> "Finally the Church isn't putting up with everything anymore;"
> "That should have been said long ago;"
> "Let's hope the people at the front hear of this, how religion is being treated; it is high time that the war is ended;"
> "Party and state can say and do as they please, we stand by our Church;"
> "I'd rather be shot than renounce my faith."[50]

Within Party circles the pastoral letter was viewed "as the most dangerous and underhanded thing committed by the Catholic Church in a long time." Appropriate reaction was anticipated "because not only the prestige of Party and state has suffered a severe blow from the reading of the pastoral letter, but the clergy has also acquired certain authentic material resulting from the official accusations by the bishops which it will undoubtedly use to the fullest in a demoralizing whisper propaganda."[51] But Hitler, highly disturbed by the unrest, ordered suspension of church property expropriations on July 30.[52]

Without doubt the war with Russia had considerably strengthened the Catholic Church's position in Germany.[53] But it simultaneously placed the Church in a kind of dilemma. In his encyclical *Divini Redemptoris* of March 19, 1937, Pope Pius XI had unequivocally condemned atheistic Communism. Pope Pius XII had remained silent about the German-Soviet Pact. After the attack on the Soviet Union, the Pope carefully avoided speaking of a crusade.[54] Yet a few German bishops openly welcomed the struggle against Communism. In his pastoral message, the militant Bishop Clemens August von Galen said: " . . . For us it was a release from a serious concern and relief from a heavy burden when, on June 22, 1941, the Führer and Reichchancellor declared the expiration of the so-called 'Russian Pact' signed in 1939 with the Bolshevik rulers in Moscow, and when his proclamation to the German people uncovered the mendacity and perfidy of the Bolsheviks."[55]

Germans were roused to fight Bolshevism by their Catholic and Protestant leaders.[56] But this ruthless war was being waged by a regime whose acts of despotism were the equal of its enemy. Thus in the second part of his letter, Bishop Galen condemned the teachings of naturalism and materialism in Germany as forerunners of Communism. Thereby he confronted the same duality of patriotism and opposition which robbed the churches and resistance movements of their ability to act decisively.

Abuses and shortages in the economic sector and measures against the Churches were the domestic causes for mounting unrest. Added to these were dissatisfaction and discord among the female population which also constituted the sustaining element of protests against inadequate foodstuffs and discrimination against the Churches. Women, along with youths, were reproached for their lack of discipline and their aversion to work.[57] Their "dawdling" had a contagious effect on some male associates.[58] But low wages and exclusion from the incentive system hardly motivated the women. Idleness among a broad segment of their sisters had an even more detrimental effect. Few women voluntarily reported for work for the fatherland even after the proclamation of a "European crusade against Bolshevism."[59] The report of the Reich Women's Leader for the months of August and September, 1941, contained the following under "Gau Reports" for Swabia: "If it is impossible to get all the wives of political leaders into the Nazi Women's League, and we already face difficulties within our own ranks, it is hardly surprising that basically antagonistic elements are creating a very bad morale. . . ." Gau Düsseldorf returned to the topic of exemptions from war service by the well-to-do. "There were apparently cases of factory owners claiming their daughters for their offices, but then these girls never worked seriously." This reportedly had a negative effect on working women and mothers.[60] Similar egoistical conduct and shirking were observed by the Kreisleiters of Pinneberg[61] and Lübeck.[62] Where women were indirectly pressured into volunteering for work, it was mostly among the working classes, sometimes including wives of political bosses but seldom touching the upper strata.

The actions of women evacuated from western and northern regions of the Reich were observed just as sullenly by the lower classes. Especially on the farm, the city dwellers aroused displeasure when they hoarded and took their marital vows lightly;[63] as the appeals court president in Munich reported: " . . . They indulge their laziness for months and, instead of working and helping the fatherland in its time of need, they turn the heads of farmers and flirt with them."[64] Social tensions were thus aggravated by jealousy and mistrust between town and country. In many cases the old Bavarian resentment of Prussia was also a factor.

In the eyes of Nazi leaders, the domestic political scene claimed too much attention and influenced morale unfavorably during the early battles in the East. The Reich Propaganda Leader, therefore, in agreement with the head of the Party Chancellory, turned on August 4 to all NSDAP Reichsleiters and Gauleiters in a personal and strictly confidential letter, urging them to take necessary steps "to bring the German people closer and closer together, and absolutely to refrain from actions which only lead to differences of opinion. The war demands the absolute concentration of the people's entire material, spiritual, and emotional strength on victory. Therefore issues not directly related to this and problems whose solutions do not seem urgent for achieving victory have no place in public discussion. Raising questions or problems whose open treatment only causes unnecessary trouble and harmfully inflames the public is expressly prohibited. . . ." There was to be no discussion of the danger of nicotine at a time when soldiers smoked by the millions; especially the religious and denominational issue was no longer to be a subject of debate, or be attacked at all, for that matter. "The Führer has instructed me to see that these topics and the like disappear completely from public discussion. Insofar as issues have to be raised within the context of executing the National Socialist program, the most expedient solution will ensue after the war. . . ."[65]

This example shows again that Hitler was exactly informed about anti-Church activities and their effects. Much occurred in the Third Reich without his knowledge, but there was nothing truly decisive about which he was not informed. The frequently heard heartfelt sigh, "if the Führer only knew this," was a sign of a complete misjudgment of the situation.

There were, of course, unauthorized actions and abuses within the lower echelons of authority; in many areas there was incredible chaos over who was responsible. But when it came to fundamental issues, such as the continued existence of the Churches during the war, only Hitler decided.

Finally on August 6, after a period of very meager news, the OKW issued a special report about further major advances in the East and large numbers of prisoners. The population had awaited such information impatiently, and its absence had contributed to a depressed mood.[66] Earlier optimistic expectations of a rapid collapse of the "clay colossus" had proven a disappointment. The special report acted as a release. Most impressive were "the figures of the enemy's material losses. The feeling abounds that Russia now has only men but no weapons, especially tanks and aircraft. It is lost. . . ."[67]

But meanwhile the press had been furnished secret information on August 2 to counteract inflated hopes; no date for the termination of the Eastern campaign had yet been set. The leadership no longer ignored massive Russian reserves in manpower and heavy weapons. The Soviet Union's low standard of living had enabled accumulation of a vast reserve over the past two decades. Nor were Soviet troops surrendering by the thousands, as previously reported; the most active divisions were composed of dedicated Bolsheviks. "Of course for the time being the German people cannot be told this quite so bluntly, although it would help considerably to clarify matters. . . ."[68]

In the meantime, Army Group Center had broken through the "Stalin Line" and by August 8 captured 348,000 men and 3,250 tanks plus much other equipment, primarily in battles around Smolensk and Roslawl. Leningrad was besieged on the tenth, and Hitler confidentially informed the press that Leningrad and Moscow were to be levelled. "Petersburg [Leningrad] will therefore not be stormed. We want to avoid creating a new Verdun . . . It is the first time in world history that a city of two million will literally be levelled to the ground. These things have nothing to do with morality, but rather represent a military and political decision by the rulers of Petersburg themselves. . . ."[69]

Yet it soon became evident that the Soviets could not be overrun by a Blitzkrieg. Hopes dwindled for an end to the war in 1941, and despite a supposed buildup for a landing in England before the winter, the expectation of American aid to Britain and possible US intervention in Ireland, Portugal, and the West African coast gave cause for concern.[70]

On August 21 Hitler's fateful order followed, against the advice of Army Commander-in-Chief von Brauchitsch and Chief of the General Staff

Halder, to redirect Army Group Center southward to destroy the enemy around Kiev and to enable Army Group South to move on Kharkov and Rostov. This decision to delay the final battle for Moscow, considered vitally important for the success of the campaign by most generals, in favor of the Ukrainian grain region, the Crimea, and the coal and industrial districts of the Donets Basin, cost Hitler crucial weeks.

Many Germans began the third war year with a "certain anxiety."[71] The press received instructions to avoid mentioning the subject of two years of war before September 3.[72] Nevertheless, some newspapers carried commemorative articles on September 1, provoking another explanation from the Reich Press Chief "that September 1 was only the beginning of a police action against Poland, where Germany had countered opposing force. The actual day war broke out was September 3, when English aggression began. . . ."[73]

Self-confidence began to crumble week by week. The average German was no longer capable of visualizing the situation.[74] "There is now more talk of having underestimated the enemy. Citizens no longer seem nearly as self-confident as during the first weeks of the war. Isolated reports of battles and successes at sectors along the whole front allow no coherent overview, and for the most part were received without enthusiasm. People generally conclude that the tempo of the advance has slowed. . . ."[75]

For the first time since the beginning of the war, "Meldungen aus dem Reich" mentioned alarm caused by letters from the front. Until then all SD reports as well as those from Party and high justice officials had always talked of the elevating influence on morale of mail from the front. What had apparently applied to the German soldier until then, and for many would apply for some time to come, was that "there is no 'mood' among us soldiers," as a German war correspondent had replied to a question about the mood. Soldiers considered that a civilian question.[76] Growing military victories had contributed to the feeling among soldiers that despite great hardships they were well led militarily and politically.[77] But now the "Meldungen" of September 11, 1941, stated: "According to several reports, letters from the front have lately contributed to an impairment of public morale. While extremely optimistic news reached home and circulated widely at the start of the Eastern campaign, we have had to observe for some time that soldiers are writing of 'increasing difficulty with provisionings,' of 'incredibly great Soviet Army reserves in manpower and materiel,' and of 'the hopelessness of a decision in the near future.' Reports of this kind are spreading like the wind and add significantly to an increase of uncertainty among the population over the course of the Eastern campaign."[78] In fact, German soldiers received "dreadful impressions"[79] which in turn provoked them to ask in their letters home whether "the people could imagine all the hardships and fierce battles and thus the achievements of the troops out there."[80]

It was clearly shown for the first time how superior such personal communications were to the impact of propaganda. More recent findings of public opinion research are confirmed here: the influence of inter-personal relations and opinions of like-minded individuals, or those regarded in small circles as an authority on a problem, often weigh more heavily than the opinions disseminated by the communications media.[81] This insight, achieved in the United States, seems even more valid for a totalitarian system with its artificial, uniform opinion—the influence of just the clergy in the Third Reich is convincing proof of this thesis. The Nazi regime knew how to utilize this intuitively grasped phenomenon in later war years. But first, opinion reports had to discover that the public morale is "determined less by the public direction of propaganda than by these concerns about the Eastern front and the hundred small daily cares."[82] The tone of conversations was defined by thoughts of "those poor soldiers."

Fake optimism and palliative propaganda got on the Germans' nerves as the life and death struggle for existence gradually hit home. Churchill was frequently cited as an example of someone who "told his nation 'the truth' and apparently had no illusions about the intensity and sacrifice of the struggle. 'We should not be treated as immature children or fools'. . . ."[83] After November, 1941, when the drive had come to a stop as winter descended on Russia, Goebbels drew the necessary conclusions and attempted to inject more realism into propaganda.[84]

With regard to the attitude of Germans towards their European allies in the struggle against Bolshevism, only the Finns were viewed with respect.[85] Rumanians, particularly General Antonescu, but even more the Italians, were regarded with mistrust.[86] The English opponent inspired partly respect, partly growing hatred.[87] Propaganda seems to have made Hitler's conception of the Russian struggle plausible to some Germans as the last stage before the final conflict with England.[88]

Otherwise that high degree of inner accord between Hitler and the Germans, prevalent during most previous campaigns, no longer existed since the attack on Russia; there was also no impulse for enthusiasm. That decision, which Hitler called the most difficult of his life,[89] represented the turning-point in his relationship with the German people. He did continue to retain the trust of large segments of the population, as evidenced by the great interest and upswing in the mood caused by his meeting with the Duce,[90] as well as his speech on October 31;[91] but his goals no longer meshed with the desires of the broad masses. To continue to count on their support, it was necessary to fall back on deeply rooted complexes and resentments. Continuity could be drawn between 1918 and Hitler's project to conquer land in the East for the economic and strategic security of the Reich,[92] but this represented only the ideas of the old elite and was no object of mass longing, such as the union with Austria or the victory over the French foe had been. Contrary to these elite views, anti-Slavic emotions also had a widespread historic legacy in Germany and Austria. They had been nourished again by the fear of Communism, that bourgeois bogeyman, since 1918. Hitler could therefore only justify his "drive to the East" by repeatedly resorting to the motto of the struggle against the cultural enemy, presenting it as a compelling necessity.

In any case, Hitler considered the campaign won by early October.[93] The Kiev encirclement had destroyed powerful Soviet armies and resulted in 665,000 more prisoners. Army Group Center was reinforced for the drive on Moscow; on October 3, Hitler declared the enemy beaten and unable to rise again.[94] The impact on the Volk was spectacular, since many offices had previously reported dejection, indifference, and crumbling confidence in the course of the war.[95] Suddenly victory seemed much closer, even if the end was not yet in sight. The leitmotif of propaganda during these weeks was "the war in the East has been decided, the struggle is not over."[96]

The offensive against Moscow—Operation Typhoon—began on October 2; soon further victories around Bryansk and Wjasma inflicted devastating losses on the Soviet Union. According to military reports, Russia lost seventy-three infantry divisions, seven tank divisions, and manpower, bringing the total number of Russian prisoners-of-war to over three million. On October 9, Reich Press Chief Dietrich declared before the German and foreign press that the Soviet Union was "militarily finished." Amplifying on this theme, Hans Fritzsche (a well-known radio commentator) stated on October 13 that the "military decision of the war has taken place. What remains now is primarily of domestic and foreign political character. At some point the German armies will stop, and we will draw a new border to guard greater Europe and the European interest bloc under German leadership against the East. It is possible that military tensions and smaller conflicts *may still last eight to ten years*, but this changes nothing in the German rulers' resolve to build a European continent and organize it according to our dictated laws. True, it is a '*Europe behind barbed wire*,' but this Europe will be economically, industrially, and agriculturally completely self-sufficient and practically unassailable militarily. . . ."[97]

These statements, assuredly on orders from the highest source, clearly reveal how close to his goal Hitler thought he was. Also symptomatic is the public reaction both to his October 2 order of the day, that the enemy must be "smashed before the advent of winter,"[98] and to the remarks of Otto Dietrich: "It was observed that without exception the impact on the citizenry had been turned inward and that nowhere was there cause for celebration. . . ." Dietrich's statement was often seen as a tactical anticipation "to deter the United States from entering the war at the last moment."[99] For weeks the public had followed "*current difficulties with America*. Many citizens believe they recognize in the handling of this issue the German government's intention to prepare the people for an American entry into the war; others interpret the heightened tone of German propaganda as provocation with the objective of persuading America to declare war now, since the active participation of the USA in the war can no longer be delayed anyway once it reaches its full military potential."[100]

The assumption that the Volk was to be prepared for a military conflict with the USA is correct, as proven by the "confidential information" to the press on October 11: " . . . Since we have slowly accustomed the German people to the possibility of an American entry into the war, we do not want to expose them to the fluctuations of American opinion. . . ."[101] Yet many people could not quite get used to the thought and were frightened: memories of the impact of American entry into World War I remained vivid.[102] However, by continually emphasizing German strength and the quality of her arms, Nazi propaganda was able to reduce the fear of American potential.[103]

Not all Germans in the fall of 1941 were pessimistic about the war in Russia. "One segment of the population was gripped by exaggerated optimism at the Reich Press Chief's statement that the campaign in the East had been decided. . . ."[104] But as battles continued with undiminished fierceness, disappointment set in. "Despite recognition of the outstanding accomplishments of the German troops and the tremendous difficulties confronting the German advance, a certain disappointment still prevails among a broad segment of the population because the final destruction of Bolshevism has not occurred with the desired speed and because an end to the Eastern campaign is still not foreseeable. In discussions among citizens about the military situation in the East, the question continually posed is how an end to the war against Russia is even possible. On the one hand, the impossibility of a peace or cease-fire with Stalin is recognized; on the other, they also consider it impossible to occupy all of Russia with German troops, since there would not be enough. . . ." The population was also struck by an absence of further results from the northern and central sectors of the front; suddenly, after destroying 260 of Russia's best-equipped divisions, German armies were unable to advance. Fourteen days earlier, German troops had been reported sixty kilometers from Moscow; then nothing.[105]

The offensive against Moscow slowly ground to a halt as roads turned into mud; only track-driven vehicles could tediously advance, supplies and reinforcements could not be moved up, and fuel ran low. The Soviet government had moved its center to Kuibyshev on the Volga. Stalin sent new Siberian troops, outfitted for a winter campaign, into the battle. A last drive for Moscow penetrated to within thirty kilometers; then came the unexpectedly early Russian winter. Motorized vehicles and automatic weapons broke down, and deaths from exposure surpassed combat losses because German troops had been poorly outfitted for such cold—Hitler had counted on winter quarters in Leningrad and Moscow. On December 1, the Commander of Army Group Center, Field Marshal von Bock, reluctantly informed Hitler that final efforts to smash Russian forces before Moscow had collapsed. The attack was halted on December 8, followed on the sixteenth by Hitler's order to stop; the Blitzkrieg in Russia had failed a year after its conception.

2. PERSECUTION OF THE JEWS

Animus meminisse horret are the opening words of Virgil's Aeneas in his report about Troy, and indeed it continually requires a supreme effort to relate this abysmal and horrible chapter of Nazi crimes and to analyze the disgraceful role of the Germans. The facts are largely known today; a wealth of documents, eye-witness accounts, and monographs have been published on this topic; therefore, a summary of the vital aspects should suffice.

The Third Reich's anti-Semitic policy developed in several waves, beginning with force and then ebbing only to revive with renewed vigor. In its formulation, several authors and tendencies interacted: the sadistic-pornographic with Julius Streicher and the *Stürmer*; the mystical-theoretical with Alfred Rosenberg; the cold, rational, SS experts such as Adolf Eichmann's predecessor, Leopold von Mildenstein, who promoted the exodus to Palestine initiated by the 1933 Haavara Agreement, and who expanded cooperation with Zionist organizations;[106] the economic-financial with Schacht and Schwerin von Krosigk, who wanted to make a profit for Germany from Jewish emigration; and above all, naturally,

Hitler, Goebbels, Göring, and Bormann, who blended political calculations with "genuine" and "false" anti-Jewish resentment.[107]

In the first years after the take-over of power, from 1933 to 1935, Nazi
policy was primarily geared to expelling the Jews little by little from
public life, via laws and regulations. A two-edged and shady tactic was
employed, giving Jews and particularly the outside world the illusion of
dissociation but not expulsion. After the 1936 Olympics, however, the
last courtesies were dropped,[108] and with the forceful Aryanization of the
economy beginning in 1937-38, assisted by extortion and threats, the
Jews found their "Lebensraum" increasingly restricted. With the unfolding of a completely fascist state in 1938, the pressure became unbearable. A wave of arrests ensued in June; in October seventeen thousand
were deported to Poland, and in November was the notorious pogrom.
The objective of all these actions was to drive the Jews from the Reich.
Emigration, however, was too slow for Nazi rulers, reaching only about
129,000 by 1937. From then until emigration was halted in October,
1941, an additional 170,000 left, making a total of around 300,000.[109]

If one analyzes the figures and keeps in mind that Jews composed
about 1 per cent (383,000) of the population in 1871, only 0.90 per cent
(568,000) at the height of the Weimar Republic when Germany was supposedly completely dominated by Jews,[110] and finally just 0.32 per cent
(222,000) in 1939,[111] it becomes evident that objective social tensions
could only have provoked real hatred of the Jews in certain professions
or urban centers. Yet the latent anti-Semitism found primarily in Protestant middle-class circles was hardly as virulent as one would assume
on the basis of Nazi propaganda; Goebbels' staged "night of crystal"
fell far short of the response anticipated by the regime. Therefore, after
the outbreak of war the role of the Jew as scapegoat, as symbolic antithesis of the Germanic-Aryan, was amplified more than ever; Communists
and capitalists were presented more consistently and distinctly than before as closely related to and contaminated by the Jews. In this extreme
form of anti-Semitism, as practised and preached by National Socialists, sociological and religious elements, psychological motives and
political tactics were fused into such an unprecedented mania of destruction that derivation from a single causal link seems impossible.

For those Jews who remained in Germany despite the chicanery and
persecutions, Hitler's war brought new and unexpected sufferings. If
"voluntary" emigration was followed by forceful eviction, deportation to
the General Government came next. Paul de Lagarde's plan to resettle
the Jews in Madagascar, suggested initially during Bismarck's time,
was discussed again for a while in the mid-thirties. This was the last
utopian concept of the SS for a rationalistic, bureaucratic solution to

the Jewish emigration problem. For Hitler the decision to achieve his territorial ambitions through a war with Russia was tied to a final settlement of the Jewish Question. SS emigration specialists now became the agents of the final solution.

Until they were transported East, the average day during the war for the Jewish population in Germany meant primarily forced labor in the armaments industries, continuous fear of the Gestapo, and denial of the last amenities of life. Their curfew began at 8 P.M., and certain areas were off-limits at all times for them; they had no protection from evictions and were only permitted to shop during certain hours.

Given all this discrimination and the beginnings of 'evacuation,' a euphemism for deportations, the average German's lack of reaction and general indifference towards his Jewish neighbor is conspicuous, especially if one recalls the emotions and unrest produced by the crucifix campaign, the expulsion of monastic brethren, and, above all, euthanasia. Reactions in extant documents are also extremely sparse. Now and then one does find references to individual acts, especially within the context of Security Service and Gestapo counter-measures, when there existed a basis for public support of the Jews. Judicial practice offers additional material; "Meldungen aus dem Reich" sporadically also reported such details, but these hardly seem conclusive.[112]

More revealing for our topic than isolated cases are overall reactions to the introduction on September 1, 1941, of the Star of David, a badge made of yellow cloth with the imprinted word "Jew," to be worn on the left breast.[113] The "Meldungen aus dem Reich" of October 9 reported: "*The Star of David regulation* was welcomed and received with satisfaction by a vast majority of the population, particularly since many had expected such an identification for some time. Only from a small group, mostly Catholic and bourgeois, did isolated voices of compassion emanate. There were also individual references to 'medieval methods.' Fear exists, mainly in these circles, that hostile nations will identify Germans living there with a swastika and resort to further reprisals against them. Everywhere the first appearance of labelled Jews was actively observed. People were surprised to learn how many Jews are actually still in Germany. . . ."[114]

On October 1, 1941, there were still 163,692, mostly urban residents concentrated most heavily in Frankfurt and especially in Berlin. Other reports from the Reich Women's leader also substantiate the positive receptions to these measures in Gau Hesse-Nassau and Berlin; in both areas, as well as in Gau Saxony, references were made to the stupidity of excluding Jewish wives of Aryans from this regulation.[115] The SD report of February 2, 1942, provides the first comprehensive overview of the impact of this police decree: "The promulgation of the decree to identify Jews in the population has generally worked out favorably. It is noted everywhere that this decree has answered a long-held desire of a wider section of the public, especially in areas with still a great number of Jews. These reports, however, also unanimously show that the special treatment of Jews married to those of German blood has given rise to amazement and anger within the population. These exceptions in the ordinance are often even criticized as a 'half measure' by citizens. We have especially been able to ascertain that a radical solution of the Jewish problem generally found more understanding than any compromise, and that in most circles the desire exists for a clear outward distinction between the Judaic and the German citizen. It is indicative that the identification decree is often seen not as a definitive measure but as a prelude to further decisive decrees with the goal of a final settlement of the Jewish Question. . . ." The report closes with the comment: "However, most welcome would be an early deportation of all Jews from Germany."[116]

The manner of noting discrimination is characterized by the monthly report for April, 1942, by the governor for Upper and Central Franconia, in which he referred to the "evacuation" of 781 Jews in March and 105 in April with the comment: "Except for a few suicides and attempted suicides, no disturbances occurred."[117] His remarks on the police ordinance in his September report also included neither public disturbances nor resentment except for the special treatment of some Jews. For November, he informed authorities that in one village near Ansbach a gallows was erected for the young wife of a watchmaker with the inscription "for the Jewess."[118] Mainfranken's governor omitted any mention of the decree in his September report; Augsburg's police president communicated that the action had met with great satisfaction except for the shopping options for Jews which had not yet been suitably regulated.[119] A subsequent report in December noted that the prohibition of Jews from the weekly market was welcomed—but not by all Germans, as it was established that "non-Jews are doing the Jews' shopping."

The state secret police too had to report repeatedly the existence of non-conformist behavior in regard to the Jewish Question. There were still "persons of German blood" who "continued to have friendly relations with Jews" and appeared in public with them. "Since those of German blood still seem to remain unsympathetic to the most elementary concepts of National Socialism and behave in what can be regarded as a disdainful manner toward state policies, I order that in such cases the German partner temporarily be placed in protective custody for educational purposes; in difficult cases they should be assigned to a concentration camp, first level, for up to three months. The Jewish partner should in any case be arrested and sent to a concentration camp for the time being."[120]

To comment briefly on all these reports, it is clear that the amazement about the number of Jews still in Germany points to the little contact Germans had had with them. This also explains in part the indifference of many. Under the burdens of wartime, the attention of most Germans was focused first on the development of the military situation, upon which the nation's fate hung, and then on the private sphere with all its daily worries and dangers, as well as on anxieties over the fate of one's own family. This withdrawal into privacy is not exclusively a German characteristic,[121] only it had catastrophic consequences in Germany with regard to the Jewish Question.

The vague statement that the identification of Jews "generally worked out favorably" and was a "long-held desire of a wider segment of the public, especially in areas of Jewish concentration," may be interpreted as a lack of visible opposition, with public support in only a few cities. Global assertions about the attitude of Germans towards the Jews should be regarded with caution since, as previously emphasized, strong regional variations existed. If some real anti-Semitism appeared in some crowded urban centers such as Frankfurt, there were whole regions in which the regime's Jew-baiting was viewed merely as a Party slogan and ignored. The population persisted in its rejection of Nazi propaganda attempts to play up hatred of Jews and showed its indifference. Symptomatic of this, for example, are the varying reactions to euthanasia and the Jewish Question, as shown by a small observation in the weekly report from the Kreisleitung in Kiel, December 8, 1941—a few weeks after the introduction of the Star of David. It states that the film "I accuse" had been extraordinarily well received while "The Eternal Jew" registered below average attendance.[122] Euthanasia occupied their minds; the Jewish Question was considered annoying and boring.

The beginning of deportations therefore seemed to many a good solution because it relieved them of the need to worry about the future fate of the Jews. "It should be considered whether the possibility exists of deporting these unpleasant fellows to the East so that they disappear completely from the urban landscape of our Gau."[123] The public prosecutor general of Nuremberg's court of appeals communicated that on November 15, 1941, the first transport of Jews had left for the East: "The population, from whom this operation was not concealed, took approving note of the fact." This "approval" was achieved partly because rumors were circulating at the time—from what source is not difficult to guess—that Jews had informed the other side about how few anti-aircraft guns were stationed in the Nuremberg area. Air raids were attributed to this fact.[124]

Aside from this broad mass of approving, indifferent, and instigating Germans, there were two small minorities: one small group of brutal and primitive elements who participated and took delight in persecutions and genocide, and the numerically not-very-large section of individuals—be they intellectuals, church members, workers, or members of the upper middle class—who were bitterly ashamed but undertook no action out of fear for their own existence and that of their families, but also that of their Jewish friends. Only a very few actually helped. They usually paid with loss of their freedom if not their lives.[125]

To those few, whose readiness to help has been documented, some church organizations belonged, with special mention of Pastor Grüber in Berlin. With the help of pastors and members of the Confessional Church, he founded his Bureau, which together with other relief agencies stood by many Jews and helped them to emigrate.[126] On December 19, 1940, in the midst of Christmas preparations, Grüber was arrested and was forced to spend more than two years in the concentration camps of Sachsenhausen and Dachau. His friend, the half-Jewish Pastor Werner Sylten, could only continue the work for a short period before also being arrested, leaving only private and illegal relief actions for the Jews. Such assistance took not only the courage of one's convictions but also a willingness to face death.[127]

On November 15, 1941, Joseph Goebbels published in *Das Reich* one of his many demagogic articles, "Jews are to blame." Here the introduction of the Star of David is presented as "an extraordinarily humane regulation, a hygienic prophylactic so to speak, to prevent Jews from sneaking into our ranks unrecognized and sowing the seeds of discord." The isolation of the Jews from the racial community is "an elementary rule of racial, national, and social hygiene." There were good people and bad people, good animals and bad animals. "The fact that the Jew still lives among us is no proof that he also belongs with us, just as a flea becomes a domestic animal because it lives in the house." Thereby the Jew was degraded once more by official channels from human being to insect, and zoological criteria were being applied to humans. "If Mr. Bramsig or Mrs. Knöterich, upon seeing an old woman with the Star of David, are moved to sympathy, they should kindly not forget that a distant cousin of this old woman is sitting with Nathan Kaufmann in New York and has prepared a plan according to which the German population under age sixty is to be sterilized; her distant uncle's son stands behind Mr. Roosevelt as warmonger, using the names Baruch, or Morgenthau, or Untermayer, inciting him to war. Remember also that if war came about, an American soldier might possibly kill the only son of Mr. Bramsig or Mrs. Knöterich, all to the greater glory of Judaism, to which this old woman belongs, no matter how fragile and piteous she may seem."

One has to read these perfidious concoctions in order to comprehend the atmosphere in which repeated efforts were made to stifle sympathy, demeaning it as "foggy humanitarianism."[128] "People" then also considered it "intolerable," "that even now, when the struggle of Judaism against the German Reich is raging at its height, emigrated Jews whose attitude toward the Reich is well known are paid pensions and living allowances. . . . Things have gone so far that German agencies even seek out missing Jews abroad in order to pay them their assistance. . . ." Only recipients living in "hostile foreign countries" naturally received no such payments.[129]

This witch hunt took on more and more ugly forms. As Jews were more completely identified, they were prohibited from using public means of transportation, their homes were marked, and their housing space decreased. They could no longer inherit from Germans, have telephones, subscribe to newspapers. Gradually they no longer received fish nor ration cards for meat, clothing, milk, tobacco, cake, white bread, or scarce commodities. "Meldungen aus dem Reich" felt they could diagnose with satisfaction "a clear-cut attitude among the public against Judaism." Newsreel depictions of Jewish prisoners often evoked remarks such as: "It would be better to shoot these guys immediately."[130] German courts were forbidden to "continue to sacrifice time and money to treat purely Jewish matters."[131] It was only a few steps from this to the exclusion of Jews from normal legal proceedings and placing them under the police law as established by Regulation Thirteen of the Reich Citizenship Law of July 1, 1943.[132]

After the United National Church of German Christians, in April 1939, had already demanded the purification of the Church from Jewish elements in its notorious Godesberg Declaration, many Christians, following the identification of Jews, petitioned their clergy for separate religious services, since "one could not be expected to receive Communion next to a Jew."[133] As a result, members of the Confessional Church distributed a pamphlet which read that it was a Christian's duty not to exclude Jews, who had the same rights as other congregational members, from their divine service; the question was posed rhetorically whether church officials ought not to take special care of these Jews. The Protestant consistory of the church province of Silesia, however, felt itself compelled to dissociate itself from this pamphlet because it was based

on an appeal signed by a curate of Breslau. Soon other Protestant
Churches also deserted their Jewish co-religionists. In January, 1942,
Evangelisches Deutschland reported: "Concerning the canonical position
of Protestant Jews, the Protestant churches and church leaders of Saxony,
Hesse-Nassau, Schleswig-Holstein, Thuringia, Mecklenburg-Anhalt,
and Lübeck have issued a declaration and corresponding church law:
church membership of Christian Jews will accordingly be cancelled in
those church areas."[134]

The Catholic Church took a very cautious position on "Christian
Jews." Speaking with a confidential agent on November 13, 1941, the
papal nuncio in Berlin "declared that special religious services could
not be authorized in view of the small number of Jews." Furthermore,
the nuncio considered the German attitude toward the Jews to have
"become noticeably more benevolent" since the introduction of the
Star of David. As example, he mentioned an incident in a Berlin street-
car: "After a young man had called on an old Jewess to vacate her seat
for him, two gentlemen immediately rose conspicuously to offer their seat
to the Jewess. . . ."[135] In a letter of September 17, 1941, Cardinal Bertram, Archbishop of Breslau and chairman of the Fulda Bishops Conference, urged avoidance of hasty measures such as the creation of Jewish pews and the like. Cardinal Innitzer, Archbishop of Vienna, issued
a similar appeal cautioning against the introduction of separate services
until absolutely necessary. The SD report referring to this whole question closed with the comment that Church support for the religious segregation of Jews was not to be expected.[136] In fact, the number of Jews
in the Reich had declined to only 131,823 by January 1, 1942,[137] thus
making the problem of special religious services superfluous.

On January 20, the infamous Wannsee conference took place, at which
the "organizational, technical, and material matters for the final solution of the European Jewish Question" were discussed by all participat-
ing central offices. Whoever was not eliminated by "natural attrition"
while working was to be "treated accordingly" since he belonged to the
robust group.[138]

Combatants and specially privileged Jews were sent to Theresien-
stadt—the "model concentration camp"—the rest were sent East and put to
work or "given special treatment." Systematic and planned genocide
now followed "chaotic executions"[139] in Poland and Russia.[140] Having
learned from the example of euthanasia, the leaders shifted the scenes
of horror to the East. The first death camps, Belzec, Sobibor, Treblinka,
and Lublin (Maidanek) emerged, using carbon monoxide gas tested by
the superintendent of the criminal division, Christian Wirth, in the
euthanasia program. The extermination machine began operating in

Belzec on March 17, 1942, with six gas chambers. But the method was considered imperfect and too slow; it was finally replaced in Auschwitz by using the prussic-acid derivative Zyklon B. This assembly-line murder was to be kept as secret as possible; whoever talked was shot.[141] All orders were either given orally or designated as secret Reich matter to be destroyed if the enemy approached.

Hitler, the instigator of this inferno, reportedly never visited an extermination camp. Only Himmler was permitted to bring him the results. We know of the Reichsführer SS, that he became ill at a mass shooting of two thousand Jews but subsequently found lofty words to exort his SS men to such executions.[142] What did the German people know about these crimes? The question has often been posed and is still very difficult to answer conclusively. An attempt will at least be made here to give a somewhat differentiated answer avoiding global accusations or argumentation.

For many Wehrmacht members in the East—it is impossible to estimate their exact number—the shootings could not remain secret. Based on a report by Major Freiherr von Gersdorff, who toured the front in the area of Army Group Center from December 5 to 12, 1941, we know that executions of Jews, prisoners, and commissars "were widely known" and met sharp criticism from among the officer corps. These executions were viewed as "injurious to the honor of the German Army." The question of responsibility was vehemently discussed. These measures furthermore helped to strengthen enemy resistance.[143] Similar remarks by officers were reported from the area commander for the rear sector, Army Group North.[144] Numerous other eye-witness accounts reveal that German soldiers were unwilling witnesses, or watched deliberately, or even assisted in these massacres.[145]

The Nazi regime always found new believable excuses to justify these gruesome actions, such as arson, attacks on the Wehrmacht, sabotage, espionage, and above all the formation of guerrilla bands. Even Germany's most competent General Staff officer, Field Marshal von Manstein, had accepted Hitler's thesis of a war of extermination and with it the elimination of the Jews: "This struggle against the Soviet armed forces is not being waged solely according to traditional European military rules. Fighting continues behind the front. Partisans, guerrillas in civilian dress, surprise individual soldiers and small detachments, seeking to disrupt supply lines by means of sabotage using mines and time bombs . . . Judaism constitutes the middleman between the enemy in the rear and remaining fighting forces of the Red Army and Red leadership. It occupies here, more than in Europe, all key positions of political leadership and administration, of trade and commerce, and furthermore forms the cell for all unrest and potential rebellions. The Jewish-Bolshevik system must be exterminated once and for all. It must never again interfere in our European living space. . . ."[146]

There were, however, also some officers, as previously mentioned,[147] who tried their utmost to save their "Wehrmacht Jews" from the clutches of Himmler's police squads and *Einsatzgruppen*.[148] They had to anticipate immediate or later sanctions, since little escaped the attention of Himmler's spies.

Under the rubric of fighting partisans, units of the Wehrmacht were involved in these crimes.[149] Occasionally the army enlisted the support of *Einsatzgruppen* to fight straggling enemy formations. Good relations therefore often developed between leaders of the *Einsatzgruppen* and front units. The more the Soviet partisan activity intensified, the more these special forces were requested. For better camouflage, separate "guerrilla task forces" [*Bandenkampfverbände*] were created; their leaders were named C.O.'s who were ultimately subordinated to a Chief of Bandenkampfverbände, Erich von dem Bach-Zelewski. Combined Jewish and partisan operations were mounted, such as "action malaria," "operation harvest festival," "operation Hamburg," etc., serving primarily to destroy the Jews. Simultaneously, other unfortunates were rounded up in ghettos and concentration camps to be gassed.

Men on leave brought reports of shootings back to Germany and rumors multiplied. Finally, in October, 1942, Bormann felt obliged to furnish Gauleiters and Kreisleiters with a kind of linguistic guideline: "In the course of working on the final solution of the Jewish Question, we have heard of recent discussions among the population in various regions of the Reich about 'very strict measures' against Jews, especially in the Eastern territories. These findings revealed that such ideas—mostly distorted and exaggerated—are spread by persons on leave from various units stationed in the East who have had occasion to witness such measures. It is conceivable that not all citizens fully appreciate the necessity for such action, especially not those segments of the public which have not had the opportunity to form their own opinion of Bolshevik atrocities. . . ." To combat these rumors, "often deliberately tendentious," the head of the Party Chancellory offered an argument which recounted National Socialist anti-Semitic policy. Cleansing the Reich of Jews through emigration had become untenable as Germany's territory expanded and the number of Jews increased. Fearing that the coming generation would not share the Nazi perception of the problem, the leaders demanded that a solution had to be found now, by the present generation. "Therefore, the complete displacement, that is the elimination, of millions of Jews living in the European economic area is an imperative rule in the struggle to secure the existence of the German people. It is in the nature of things that these somewhat difficult problems can only be solved with ruthless severity. . . ."[150] The tenor of this statement corresponds with Goebbels' diary entries which repeatedly refer to consultations with Hitler.[151]

As Bormann noted, there were Germans who showed no understanding for this brutal racial policy. Hitler, in his table-talks, commented on the so-called middle classes which "now lament" when Jews, who after all had perpetrated the "stab-in-the-back" in their day, "were deported to the East."[152] Goebbels made similar observations: "Unfortunately it is again evident that the better classes, especially the intellectuals, do not understand our Jewish policy and to an extent support the Jews. Consequently our scheme was prematurely disclosed, so that quite a number of Jews escaped our grasp. . . ."[153] However, not only intellectuals protested, many of whom, by the way, surrendered all too easily to the regime. Only a few days later, Goebbels noted: "Somewhat unpleasant scenes regrettably took place in front of a Jewish home for the aged, where a large crowd assembled and in some instances even sided with the Jews. . . ."[154] Soon thereafter: "The evacuation of Jews from Berlin did lead to many unpleasantries. Unfortunately Jews and Jewesses in privileged marriages were at first included in the arrests, leading to great fear and consternation. The planned arrest of all Jews on one day proved a flop, owing to the shortsighted behavior of industrialists who warned the Jews in advance. In all, we failed to seize four thousand Jews. They are now wandering about Berlin, homeless and unregistered, and naturally present a great danger to the public. . . ."[155] Not the Jews but the regime's policies posed a public threat. At the time of almost critical post-Stalingrad atmosphere, the Nazi elite had to maneuver very carefully on the racial question. When Jewish partners of mixed marriages were also seized, a demonstration of Aryan spouses occurred in Berlin, in front of the collection point in the Rosenstrasse, where conscripts for the armaments industries had been locked up. The protest was not dispersed by force for fear of unexpected consequences, and the imprisoned Jewish spouses were released again several days later. SD reports make no mention of such incidents and protests, and they probably did not become known to the general public. Consequently no one in Germany learned the lesson—either from this event or from the reaction of the Nazi elite to the issues of the crucifixes and euthanasia —of the power inherent in public protest, even in a totalitarian state. Yet critical remarks did multiply. One could hear from evacuated Berliners as early as 1942 that the Jewish Question could have been solved more humanely. No one has the right to exterminate a people, especially since those Jews who had damaged Germany had emigrated between 1933 and 1941.[156] Declining fortunes of war may have contributed to growing fears among many that "one day we shall have to pay dearly" for things done to the Jews.[157]

In April, 1943, as Nazi propaganda began an ambitiously-planned campaign with clearly inflammatory anti-Jewish slogans concerning the discovery of mass graves in Katyn with four thousand bodies of murdered Polish officers, one heard frequent expressions in Germany that there was hardly cause for excitement over the crimes of the Soviets since "Poles and Jews were eliminated on a far larger scale by our side."[158]

Such remarks came from intellectual and confessional circles, according to SD reports. The uncovering of mass graves in Vinnitsa in July, 1943, was hardly noticed and again triggered similar—if any—comments, namely that "our side also eliminated all hostile elements in the East, especially the Jews."[159] Additional commentary from SD reports to these two events suggests complicity on the one hand—people endured the Katyn propaganda campaign "without batting an eye";[160] on the other hand, it reveals widespread apathy and insensibility, largely caused by "now almost daily losses of life through enemy bombers in the west and north. . . ."[161] These uninterrupted heavy air raids not only produced indifference but also fomented hatred among the more primitive while awakening the insight among the thoughtful "that it was irresponsible of the regime and the NSDAP to take such steps against the Jews. . . ."[162]

The fact that the mass executions occurred in connection with the Russian campaign erased for many the stench of murder. Destruction of the enemy in war was deemed—and still is—legitimate, particularly when it was a *bellum justum*, a "righteous" war. The denunciation of the Jew as the real culprit responsible for the war therefore actually served the purpose of making the extermination program acceptable as an elimination of a military opponent. One incident in the Berlin subway, described by an eye-witness, makes this very clear: "In the subway four German soldiers with Russian campaign decorations and iron crosses read about the discovery of Katyn and were appalled. Only one remained calm and just said dejectedly: 'If you dig a hundred kilometers farther on, you'll find ten thousand Jewish corpses. War is war, after all.' The whole subway heard it and no one said a word."[164] Mounting guilt complexes and silent criticism such as this induced the regime to issue new inflammatory slogans.[165] Goebbels now made sure that the press received a daily "Jewish theme."[166]

In May, 1943, propaganda sought to counter growing public criticism of insufficient German safety precautions following heavy attacks on the

Ruhr dams[167] by again emphasizing the Jew as author of the bombings; this clumsy maneuver was sharply rejected by many.[168] Even within Party circles this diversionary tactic was considered so inept and exaggerated that they dismissed any effect on the German people.[169]

Did the regime retreat in the face of this mounting restlessness in the public mood and stop its policy of destruction? On the contrary: it only became determined to accelerate and conceal it even more. On April 9, after having received the statistical report from the inspector for statistics, Pg. Koherr, about the final solution of the Jewish Question, Himmler wrote to the Chief of the Security Police and SD: "As far as I'm concerned, the most important thing is still that as many Jews as is humanly possible now be transferred East. . . ."[170] At the same time Koherr was instructed to use the term "transport of Jews" instead of "special treatment."[171] Bormann also sent a secret letter to all Gauleiters in effect rescinding his instructions of nine months earlier. The Führer had instructed him that the future final solution of the Jewish Question no longer be discussed; instead mention could be made of the complete mobilization of Jewish labor.[172]

Beginning in the summer of 1943, one finds almost no reference to public reactions to the persecution of Jews. One cannot dismiss the possibility that highly secret reports existed which were destroyed in 1945.[173] At his ministerial conference of December 12, 1942, Goebbels had already remarked on the strong use of "ostensible Jewish horrors in the East" by English propaganda and the need to do something about it. The subject "is quite delicate and we had better not engage in polemics; instead English atrocities in India, Iran, and Egypt ought to be emphasized. . . ."[174]

Correspondence of Württemberg's Archbishop Wurm to the Ministry for Ecclesiastical Affairs on March 12 and to Hitler on July 16 reveal that the fate of Jews was worrying more and more people in Germany. Archbishop Wurm, a leading spokesman for the Confessional Church, intervened at this point on behalf of the privileged Jews, now also threatened. "These intentions, like the extermination of other non-Aryans, are also inconsistent with God's commandment and violate the basis of all Western thought and life: the God-given primeval right to human existence and human dignity. . . . Facts that have become known in our homeland and are widely discussed burden most heavily the conscience and strength of countless men and women among the German people; they suffer more from some measures than from the sacrifices they make every day. . . ."[175] Another letter followed in December. Archbishop Bertram, who had already intervened against the planned compulsory divorce of mixed Jewish marriages, also protested to the Interior Ministry and the

Reich Security Office against the inhumane actions to which non-Aryan deportees were subjected in camps and which had resulted in the death of many.[176] These protests, as well as others, proved totally ineffectual. By September 1, 1944, the number of Jews registered in Germany had dropped to 14,574. Public notices prohibiting Jews from using park benches, telephone booths, swimming pools, restaurants, etc., were now superfluous and "gradually removed." The same applied to gypsies.[177] Although the propaganda machine continued to vilify Jews, it became increasingly difficult to keep anti-Semitic feelings alive or to interest the public in the subject.[178]

Given the lack of further SD reports on propaganda results, the only sources providing information on the direct impact of this continual Jew-baiting are scattered records of a number of letters addressed to the Propaganda Ministry. In these often quite crude epistles of the last two war years, the suggestion was made, for example,—and not just once—that all Jews in cities endangered by air attack be collected and denied access to shelters, publicizing the number killed after the bombings. "Should this method prove ineffectual against this terror from the skies, this pest of humanity would at least be partially exterminated by order of their own kind in enemy countries."[179] Other suggestions aimed at "informing American and British governments that tenfold the number of Jews would be shot for civilians killed after every terror attack."[180] A number of these and similar outbursts by simple people, but also by academics, have been preserved.[181] They hardly make for elevating reading, but they do permit the following conclusions: 1. that they are spontaneous reactions to the Nazi hate campaign, given their bulk at specific times and their similarity in wording; 2. that ostensible Jewish culpability for the war was largely accepted, with many letters suggesting texts for leaflets for Americans and Englishmen which posed the question whether they were unaware or incapable of understanding that they were being used, fighting and dying merely for the Jews;[182] 3. that all proceed on the assumption that many Jews were still at liberty; and 4. that if there is any response to the subject of the murder of Jews, only shootings are mentioned. Neither here nor elsewhere are there any references to developments in concentration camps or gassings.

It is now immaterial how these murders took place. What should be clarified is that in Germany itself only a very few people knew about the monstrous scope of the crimes, that many were befuddled by propaganda. Among the many millions of Germans at home and at the fronts, a large number was also unsuspecting. Moreover, rumors, talk, and hints about mass executions were, for many individuals, ideas beyond rational comprehension. Approximately six million Jews bestially exterminated

—today, after uncontestable proof, it still remains incomprehensible. On February 4, 1945, a Berliner who helped many Jews wrote in her diary: " 'They are forced to dig their own graves,' people whisper. 'Their clothing, shoes, shirts are taken from them. They are sent naked to their death.' The horror is so incredible, that the imagination refuses to accept its reality. Something fails to click. Some conclusion is simply not drawn. Between knowledge in theory and practical application to individual cases . . . there is an unbridgeable gulf. . . . We don't permit our power of imagination to connect the two, even remotely. Could we continue to live if we realized that our mother, our brother, our friend, our lover, enduring inconceivable suffering, was being tortured to death?

"Is it cowardice that lets us think this way? Maybe! But then such cowardice belongs to the primeval instincts of man. If we could visualize death, life as it exists would be impossible. One can imagine torture, horror, and suffering as little as death. . . . Such indifference alone makes continued existence possible. Realizations such as these are bitter, shameful and bitter. They admit that we also do not belong to the strong and proud who arise to begin a great crusade against injustice. Who in the world stood up to revenge the agony of a hundred thousand murdered Armenians? Who rebelled against the tortures of the Inquisition? The news of the massacre of Jews spread around the world. Did breakfast agree less with a single person as a result? Did living become impossible for anyone because the plight of the martyred choked them and tore at their conscience? . . ."[183]

This diary entry is not cited as an excuse; Germany must bear the responsibility before history for this bestial genocide. But it does offer *one* explanation for widespread passivity—enough has been presented in preceding pages about complicity and ethical brutalization. It is supported by the findings of Louis de Yong, Director of the Netherland "Rijkinstitut vor Oorlogsdocumentatie," who reports that even eye-witnesses from Birkenau refused for weeks to accept the truth about the gas chambers. The monstrosity of mechanized mass murder defied human imagination.[184]

Other explanations are based upon far more elementary causes. If only a few Germans dared what the Dutch, Danish, French, and Italians undertook for their Jewish minorities, it was because Germans had to act against their own state, nation, and leaders, while resistance in occupied countries was simultaneously an act of rebellion against a foreign enemy. In Germany, compassion for and aid to Jews was considered a direct attack on the Third Reich. Every ethnologist, sociologist, and social psychologist is familiar with the phenomena of defensive reactions of group members against those outside the group and against foreign elements within it. Another known fact of social science is that inhibitions to killing are developed extraordinarily strongly almost only when it comes to group members and are very difficult to overcome; the same does not apply toward outsiders. More recent experiments, as already briefly mentioned,[185] have shown that orders by freely elected and recognized authority were carried out by a high percentage of tested individuals, irrespective of the content of the deed and without any reservations of conscience, even when they could recognize that the consequences of their obedience were gruesome. These findings of the humanities and social sciences surely permit an emotionless approach. However, they can only partially explain a phenomenon such as anti-Semitism.

Documentary material available to us is meagre, but its tendencies seem quite clear. Did the Jewish Question perhaps concern the broad masses far less than previously assumed, and does the modest space devoted to this chapter, given the scope of our study, correspond to the importance due this problem within the limits of developing German opinion? This is a perplexing question. In the response by the German people to Hitler and his Weltanschauung, anti-Semitism hardly played the key role which it unquestionably did in Hitler's ideology.

3.   WAR IN THE BALANCE: DECEMBER 1941 TO DECEMBER 1942

From December, 1941, to December, 1942, prospects in the battle of the Axis powers against the Soviet Union and Anglo-Saxons were about even. But thereafter the fortunes of war tilted irrevocably in favor of the "strange alliance" between Capitalism and Communism.

Public opinion in Germany during this period was unusually irregular and oscillated back and forth like the index of a scale. Its essential trends are difficult to delineate due to confusion and contradictions of opinion. Unrest among youth, dissatisfaction among women, growing disapproval by the faithful, and mounting criticism of propaganda policy were all evident and spreading. There were indications of a cooling between the leadership and large segments of society. Causes for this process of alienation and this unfolding reversal of opinion are to be found essentially in the constantly deteriorating military situation and the length of the war, which was viewed more and more as a burden.

After the beginning of the third winter of war, Germans, accustomed to victory, for the first time saw themselves confronted with serious military difficulties. German soldiers in Russia met an opponent who defended himself with a tenacity previously unknown and poured in new reserves again and again. The German infantryman, absolutely inadequately equipped for a hard winter and severe cold, had to endure the worst hardships. Tens of thousands suffered from frostbite.[186] But Hitler had prevented any possible spread of defeatism at an extremely critical juncture with his order to stand firm; every voluntary retreat was prohibited, instructing that "troops be compelled to offer fanatical resistance where they stand without regard to the advancing enemy on their flanks and rear."[187] The significance of this turn of events, from attack to defense, did not quite dawn on the Germans at home. But two events in the meantime troubled them profoundly and made them realize that the Eastern campaign was not proceeding as planned: Goebbels' appeal for collection of winter clothing and the change of supreme command of the army.

As late as November 18, Goebbels had told the press to inform the public that the necessary winter clothing for the troops had already been procured during the summer and lay ready at railway terminal points. Distribution was already proceeding; only the transportation situation was still causing some delays. When the Reich Propaganda Minister then called for a collection drive on December 21 and labelled it as a "Christmas present from the German people to the Eastern front," he triggered surprise, astonishment, shock, and sharp criticism.[188] Accounts of equipment shortages from men on leave and from army mail were now given much greater credence.[189]

The resignation of von Brauchitsch and Hitler's assumption of the OKH could not be discussed by the press.[190] Still, according to an SD report, it unleashed the strongest surprise among the public, often bordering on consternation because this was, after all, the Christmas season and a time when the most difficult battles were being waged on all fronts. The publicized heart condition of the former commander-in-chief of the army was widely rejected as the real cause in favor of some deep ulterior motive of great importance to Hitler.[191] This was encouraged by the fact that Hitler had neither mentioned nor praised Brauchitsch in his proclamation. Speculations concerning the actual reason began immediately. By far the largest group connected Goebbels' announced winter clothing drive with the dismissal, assuming that Hitler had made Field Marshall von Brauchitsch responsible for the poor provisioning. Another group assumed that the threatening situation at the front was the cause. Then there were those who expressed sympathy for the Führer, who now had to assume an additional responsibility. "Trust in the Führer is so unshakeable that initial dismay over the resignation of the former supreme army commander soon gave way to a more confident assessment of the situation and by now the event has already receded largely into the background. . . ."[192]

This last assertion of the SD report proved false. Unrest continued because the same day that the ailing Brauchitsch resigned, the commander of Army Group Center, Field Marshal von Bock, was relieved "for health reasons," and word leaked out that the commander of Army Group South, Field Marshal von Rundstedt, had already been replaced by Field Marshal von Reichenau on December 3.[193] Then, when Hitler sent Brauchitsch wishes for a speedy recovery, Rundstedt represented the Führer at the state funeral of the suddenly deceased von Reichenau, and Hitler appeared in a published picture with von Bock, the public began to wonder who was leading the troops and why the "sawed-off field marshals" were being treated so cordially.[194] Two days later Goebbels still described the mood as "so-so," with continued uncertainty about the fate of Brauchitsch. In any case, the matter had certainly not died down completely.[195] Leftists and class-conscious workers welcomed the change in army command and remarked "that these *reactionaries* must be replaced little by little."[196]

Hitler's crude response, to blame the generals for his own failure to provide strategic leadership and proper provisioning for the troops by removing top military personnel as scapegoats, did bring him renewed sympathy and expressions of public trust, but at the same time it also increased existing insecurity. People expected clarification from him about the background to the Brauchitsch affair and the fiasco surrounding the winter supplies—that is clear from the SD reports of February 2, 1942.[197] Instead, those just relieved of their posts were being treated with kindness. But no intelligent person could miss the fact that the Wehrmacht had suffered a further loss of power. The army was not only directly subordinated to Hitler; its general staff had to submit to a further curtailment of its jurisdiction. It was now only responsible for the East; all other theaters of operation were removed from its competence and entrusted to the OKW.[198]

Aside from this mistaken fragmentation, the dismissal of Brauchitsch had still another consequence. According to Ulrich von Hassell's dairy entry of December 22, 1941, it undid the work of many months.[199] Von Brauchitsch was no man of resistance, but neither was he a dedicated Nazi: he wavered continually between his conservative ideals and admiration for the Führer. After repeated efforts by the opposition group around Canaris, Oster, and Dohnanyi, he finally seemed more amenable to their argument for the removal of Hitler after witnessing personally

Hitler's strategic blunders. Brauchitsch's removal thus robbed the opposition of its contact man in the highest military circles and dealt a decisive blow to plans for a coup.

Military fortunes failed Germany not only in the East, where it lost Kalinin to the Russians on December 17, and soon thereafter Kaluga; bad news also came from North Africa where Bengasi was retaken by the British and Rommel's forces had to retreat to Mersa-el-Brega. These results produced an extreme pessimism at home: "Here and there people already regarded the whole North African theater as lost for the Axis powers. There were also expressions of fear concerning the possibility of an invasion of Sicily, Sardinia, and southern Italy by British forces. An optimistic assessment of the situation reemerged only after the announcement of successful resistance by German-Italian troops in the area around Agedabia, even if there was still apprehension that the Africa Corps would be unable to withstand the pressure of British forces indefinitely because of inadequate reinforcements of men and material."[200]

The full import of Hitler's declaration of war against the United States was not grasped at first, because of the impression of unfavorable developments in the offing and news of the first Japanese successes: "The declaration of war against the USA was certainly not startling and often viewed as official confirmation of an existing state of affairs. Only in rural areas were isolated cases of surprise and a certain concern over an additional enemy registered. The creation of clearly defined fronts, as one segment of society described the new situation—particularly after the superlative victories of our Japanese ally—has eased and relieved tensions according to most reports. Often noted with satisfaction was that this time Germany had taken the initiative and thereby convincingly demonstrated its strength and certain assurance of final victory to the outside world, unlike during the World War. . . ."[201] As during the Eastern campaign, most people could no longer get a clear picture of the real situation: "For the time being the public is unable to form a clear idea of the repercussions of the state of war with America. They anticipate primarily defensive warfare and a long-drawn-out overseas war. . . ."[202]

On Hitler's express wish, the press was urged "that the question of responsibility for the outbreak of war with the United States be treated with utmost forcefulness by overall German propaganda and without interruption under constant repetition of the German theses."[203] Germans were daily bombarded with slogans and phrases such as "Roosevelt, the warmonger and world criminal, henchman of the Jews . . . ," the Jewish-Bolshevik clique and the Jewish-plutocratic "war criminals."[204] Hitler's vision of war guilt was at first received with astonishment but then accepted. He convinced the public of his reluctant but necessary declaration provoked by American interference in European affairs. Guilt therefore lay solely with the USA.[205] It had meddled in Japanese interests, *ergo* it was responsible for the Japanese attack on Pearl Harbor; similarly, it had encouraged and supported Germany's enemies. Of course it was true that Hitler had not desired a confrontation with the USA at that time—it was to remain for the future when Germany's position as a world power was secured[206]—but he naturally did not advertise this fact.

The propaganda theme for the third winter of war was "realistic optimism."[207] The goal, as Goebbels explained, was "to toughen the German people and give them the impression that the government demanded toughness but in return would lead them firmly and justly. . . ." At home there should no longer be any talk of "sacrifices" but only of "inconveniences." "The presentation of the overall situation to the German public must absolutely correspond to actual conditions. Only then can we omit isolated facts whose public knowledge could lead to precipitous or false conclusions. We must therefore make certain that such items as are not made public, but still are found out in other ways by one person or another, fit into the total view held by German propaganda. . . ."[208]

The "other ways" in which undesirable details were publicized were stories by soldiers reporting about conditions in Russia; as a result numerous rumors emerged, nourished, moreover, by foreign news broadcasts. In January and February, 1942, Goebbels in his diary often brought up the subject of the defeatist mood within the OKW and OKH. Hitler demanded a written report which apparently was prepared, and on the basis of this Goebbels thought it was time that "examples be made, for if such tendencies are represented within the officer corps, how can one blame the Volk if it becomes disheartened in time and hangs its head."[209] The Reich Propaganda Minister was basing himself *expressis verbis* on the SD report that day:[210] "Citizens have the feeling that public agencies always maintain an "official face" when there are negative events. A situation has therefore developed where many people, under such circumstances, no longer consider the press the best source; rather they construct 'their view' from rumors, stories by soldiers and individuals with 'political connections,' military mail and the like, so that often the most absurd rumors are accepted with a surprising lack of discrimination. . . ."[211]

The SD report continued that many soldiers "write home, without any scruples, the most outrageous stories about the hardships, cold, poor food, etc., they endure." Goebbels commented: "It is just indescribable what our soldiers at the front write home about. It is partly attributable to a desire for self-importance. Boasting plays a large role. . . . I urge once more that the OKW instruct its soldiers regarding this point, but I have no great hopes. A general human weakness is at work here against which we are powerless."[212] Yet, in fact, the German soldier did have to endure merciless cold; at 40° below zero, they were incapable of using weapons, companies disintegrated, soldiers hobbled along on their weapons, their feet wrapped in rags. Apathy did spread, but only because many had reached the end of their endurance, exhausted physically and mentally.[213] Hitler later admitted to his Propaganda Minister: "Thank God, the people learned only a fraction of this. . . ."[214]

Goebbels' suggestion to instruct the troops on the content of army mail was acted upon by the OKW in an article entitled "The Art of Writing Letters" in *Mitteilungen für die Truppe*. Emphasis was placed on "manly, hard and clear letters . . . differentiating between impressions best locked deeply in the heart because they only concern soldiers at the front and those which can be and should be related at home to keep them informed about the war. . . . Anyone who complains and bellyaches is no true soldier. . . ."[215] Partial results of these "admonitions" were reported already by February 19: "Incoming army mail increasingly contains more favorable portrayals of the overall situation at the Eastern front";[216] "Meldungen" on March 2, 1942, stated: "Overall, the negative influence of army mail from the East has diminished, the letters have become more optimistic."[217] Morale among the soldiers improved during February, due to some easing of the frost, arrival of reserves, and a gradual improvement in the military situation and billeting. Self-confidence and a feeling of superiority over the Russians reemerged. Yet a front inspection report for the area of the Fourth Army distinguished between the mood of the military leadership, operating under unabating mental strain from shifting developments, and that of the troops from regimental commanders down, who could recover after a few days of rest, often merely a local slackening of enemy pressure. Military leaders were resentful over military developments and winter provisioning: "The winter catastrophe would have been avoided if someone had listened to us. We warned them as clearly as we could. No one listened, read our reports, or they failed to take them seriously. They do not want to know the truth. . . ." When decisions were taken, the critics continued, they came too late and were too general to apply to a particular situation. Individual initiative was not encouraged. The troops, on the other hand, were not burdened with these concerns, and their spirits were remarkably buoyant, largely due to hopes of relief, furloughs, and a spring offensive, bringing back the "good times of summer." Though Hitler's dismissal of the generals was welcomed, the bond of trust between officers and men remained firm, and all criticism of the leadership ceased when it came to Hitler.

This report from the front, therefore, confirmed Goebbels' entry about severe unrest—interpreted by him as defeatism—among military leaders. But then the Reich Propaganda Minister also found defeatists, "alarmists," and "gripers"[218] in Berlin, in the ministries and highest Reich agencies. Foreign broadcasts and the information services of various organizations were seen as causes. The distribution system was consequently rigorously tightened.[219] Based on Hitler's order of January 15, 1942, only Göring, Ribbentrop, Keitel, the commanders of the three services, as well as the ministers Goebbels, Ohnesorge, Frick, and Lammers were permitted to listen to foreign stations; all other Reich ministers required special permission from the Führer.[220] Those with such permission were allowed to grant similar rights to a small number of persons within their area of responsibility. In his diary, Goebbels complained on February 11 that it was "terrible how many prominent persons are now trying to prove to me that they cannot continue their work without permission to tune in foreign stations."[221]

In an effort to improve the poor relations between the armed forces and the Party, Keitel sent a letter to the three service commanders on March 2, calling for closer and more dedicated cooperation between offices of the two sides during this total war.[222] Evidently Hitler, after taking over supreme command of the army, had complained about the lack of National Socialist attitude among the officer corps, and Keitel had made it his principal task to make this message more immediate to his subordinates. "A close involvement of the army with the whole Volk will undoubtedly strengthen both the will to see it through and faith in the final victory at the front and at home." Since Keitel hardly had an opportunity to see his commanders personally, he couched the Führer's thoughts in the form of instructions and guidelines to command posts.[223] In his regulations concerning the "responsibility of the German officer" of May 31, 1942, he stated categorically: "Thus the officer must also be capable of educating his soldiers to become convinced representatives of this Weltanschauung, which—stemming from the front experience of 1914-1918—was brought to singular heights by the Führer. . . ." The mood of army mail was taken as one indicator of the officers' attitude.[224]

Goebbels' remarks and Keitel's actions reveal that segments of the officer corps had an indifferent or even critical attitude towards National Socialism. During 1942 indications also grew of a certain "lack of appreciation" for the Party's task and its representatives, whose behavior elicited numerous reproaches. The police president of Augsburg reported, for example, that many parents showed no understanding for either the goals or the work of the Hitler Youth, and that he had been told by a Landrat "that attendance at churches was greater and greater while at Party meetings it was declining steadily."[225]

From an interesting investigation of German readers' wishes and habits in the third year of war,[226] we learn that primarily light reading was requested, a dearth of which forced them to fall back on more elevated fiction, while the so-called political writings were least popular—with the exception of "standard works of the Movement" such as *Mein Kampf* and *The Myth of the Twentieth Century*, which were bought for gift purposes. Everything recognizable by title and appearance as official literature was avoided. This also corresponded to the "attitude of the population towards lectures on ideological issues."[227] "Numerous reports submitted from all over the Reich make the same observation, *that for some time interest in lectures about ideological issues has slackened considerably among large sections of the public. . . .*" This "steadily declining interest" was explained as the result of "excessive exposure" and "weariness," though clumsy speakers merely repeating platitudes were also partly to blame. "Several reports also mention that *interested listeners in particular sense certain contradictions at such lectures between the old National Socialist principles and practical political and military developments these last years.*" The survival of the Nazi state and racial concepts in their original form were questioned, and some people had difficulty reconciling the creation of the Protectorate, incorporation of alien areas, and the immigration of foreign workers with existing ideology.

One can assume on the basis of this report that an increasing number of Germans began to see through Hitler's policies. Another report four months later gives an even clearer picture of this: ". . . To be sure, there is frequently a lack of appreciation for the course the war has now taken. If they were still convinced at the outbreak of war that it was a necessary defensive action against impending danger, now citizens often clearly oppose the *new European order*, inevitably linked with the war, and regard it as imperialism. A concept of vast territorial acquisition is still far from the minds of most. . . ."[228] An addendum to the SD report, entitled "diplomatic households," referred to rumors about the rather cosy life of prominent personalities of Party, state, and the military. Such rumors had been circulating for some time, but were given impetus by Bormann's decree of March 30, 1942, which demanded an exemplary standard of living from lower echelon Party leaders, particularly in view of food rationing.[229] In part these rumors stemmed from systematic English propaganda initiated by the British journalist Sefton

Delmer to discredit Nazi functionaries.[230] Stories about the life style of German Party and administrative personnel in Poland also nourished talk of a sybaritic existence. "The citizen considers himself dying of work here while 'the big shots' enjoy a life of pleasure and abundance in Poland. It causes bitterness and leads to observations such as: 'So those are members of our leading class!' . . ."[231]

Similar comments were heard from the Rhineland as well. In the Cologne-Aachen area, rumors of widespread graft by a Kreisleiter and other heads of the NSV abounded since the beginning of December, 1941, spurred on by the sentencing of those responsible for this talk.[232] One often heard: "It is much worse today than during the Second Reich. Almost all leading figures have great holdings and property today and none of them have to starve. . . ." This partially justified criticism[233] was directed equally against Reich ministers, Reichsleiters, and Gauleiters, but especially against Robert Ley and his opulence.

The spartan life of the vegetarian and abstainer Adolf Hitler stood in marked contrast to the criticized life-style of many Nazi functionaries, and this helped considerably to solidify the image of the selfless and devoted son and Führer of his people while placing the blame for all wrongdoings, failures, and abuses on others. Although the Party was mistrusted more and more, his word still counted with many. Thus he consoled the despondent when he predicted on January 30, 1942, that this year, too, the enemy would be beaten as before,[234] particularly since he invoked parallels between the Party's struggle and eventual victory and the present war situation. Goebbels referred to a "vibrant mood" in the Berlin Sportpalast. Hitler had "charged the people like a generator. . . ."[235] His derisive comments about Churchill, whom he called a "deceitful subject" and a "loafer of the first order," and his reference to the "accomplice in the White House," Roosevelt, found a positive response according to an SD report.[236] Only a man of Hitler's stature could take such liberties and expose the weakness of his enemies. Repeated reference to Germany's superior position today in contrast to that of Frederick the Great strengthened confidence in Hitler and ultimate victory. Hitler's eulogy at the death of his Armaments Minister, Fritz Todt, following shortly after the Sportpalast speech, moved many women to tears. "Comments by citizens indicate that 'the Führer had never shown his human side to that degree,' or that 'the German people have never felt as deeply united with the Führer' as at this time. . . ."[237]

On Memorial Day, March 15, 1942, Hitler spoke again.[238] "The strongest and unquestionably the most lasting impression was made by the sentence: 'But one thing we already know now: the Bolshevik hordes, which could not vanquish German and allied soldiers this winter, will be annihilated by us this coming summer.'[239] This word of the Führer strengthened considerably the hopes of most people that Bolshevism would yet be destroyed this year. Numerous citizens, in this regard, observed that the Führer had never expressed himself in this way if he was not himself completely convinced and certain that his predictions would turn out to be true. . . ."[240]

Most of these remarks must be regarded as kowtowing before Hitler by SD officials, since "Meldungen aus dem Reich" noted "no significant upswing in the mood." Public interest was captured by growing rumors about an imminent reduction of food rations. At the ministerial conference of February 3, ministerial director Brandt of the propaganda section had already informed Goebbels that Hitler had authorized a reduction in food distribution beginning in April. Bread shortages had to be attributed to relief deliveries to Finland[241]—which was true for once, because naked hunger was raging through this small allied country and Germany provided at least some help. Despite orders for utmost secrecy by Goebbels, the news leaked out and immediately had an extremely adverse effect on morale. The Reich Propaganda Minister, who had just recently observed that the German people enjoyed a standard of living impossible in any other European country,[242] now feared that the new rations would "no longer suffice for the absolute guarantee of health and preservation of reserves. We are now slowly reaching conditions similar in some respects to those of the third year of the World War. . . ."[243] One typical report from Berlin stated: "The feeling of being unable to eat one's fill anymore simply because enough cannot be obtained depresses working people above all, people from whom high productivity is expected in the factories. But it also depresses housewives, on whom the burden of feeding their families falls, who spend hours daily—often in vain—at markets and in stores to buy a few, partly spoiled, potatoes, a few turnips or slightly frozen white cabbage. . . ." Serious "deterioration in morale" was also reported from the Ruhr area and southern Germany due to a complete absence of fish, eggs, vegetables, legumes, and baby food. Particularly in cities the search was on for "the guilty one." "According to reports reaching us, interest in military happenings and preoccupation with food supply problems counterbalance each other in predominantly rural areas as well as in smaller and medium-sized towns, while in the larger towns and especially in the cities, provisioning difficulties override everything. . . ."[244]

Goebbels collected all kinds of conceivable arguments to explain the reduction in food rations. "They are very powerful, but I doubt their efficacy to a certain extent because no one listens to well-thought-out arguments when his butter and meat are taken away."[245] By comparing the situation to a similar food crisis in England, Goebbels sought to create the impression that the British blockade was responsible for shortages, and that it was a consequence of war. Press allusions to England prior to the cuts were regarded by the public as confirmation of prevailing rumors. Germans had slowly learned to interpret such innuendos. The upshot of these efforts was thus more often negative, and they further substantiated "the reliability of rumors and all non-official news sources."[246]

The impact of the announcement to cut rations surpassed worst expectations. "Several reports mentioned that the news of 'drastic' food reductions had an absolutely 'crushing' effect on a large segment of the population, to a degree in fact hardly matched by any other event of the war. . . . Workers in cities and industrial areas especially, who often viewed previous food supplies as rather meager, have, according to observations thus far, adopted an attitude which lacks any appreciation for the necessity of these new measures. The morale within these groups has reached an all-time low for the war. . . ."[247]

This report reached Hitler and elicited the previously cited remark minimizing the mood manifested in public conversations and pointing to the people's firm inner resolve.[248] Even Goebbels consoled himself by considering SD reports too negative and those of propaganda offices too rosy.[249] But a subsequent report substantiated the accuracy of the SD assessment: Germans were beginning to view the whole war, including German endurance, military capacities, and prospects for victory, from the perspective of food requirements.[250]

Inadequate food supplies thus provoked many Germans to wonder about the future course of the war in a way they had not when war was declared on America in December, amidst a constant shower of propaganda. The Leipzig SD section reported drastically: "Since the stomach is the determining factor not only for the overall health of the individual but also for the well-being of the people as a whole, a general depression is discernible. Confidence in victory and the will to see it through have begun to falter seriously. . . ."[251] In addition, the activity of British bombers was increasing, which aroused doubts about Germany's own production capacities. On March 28-29, a series of area bombardments was launched with a terror attack on Lübeck, followed by one on Augsburg on April 17, this time in broad daylight without substantial hindrance from German fighters or flak.[252] Hitler was "hit very hard" by the news of the assault on Lübeck,[253] and Goebbels said, "Thank God, it is the north German population, which is generally far more resilient than that of the south and southeast. Nevertheless, it is unmistakable that the English air raids have increased in intensity and significance and if they continue at this pace would have a demoralizing effect on the German population. . . ."[254] For a time he was right. Enemy air raids mounted from week to week and became a "determining factor in morale," along with the daily cares. Even during the summer, when the military situation had improved, it ranked well above military events.[255]

It appears that some leading Nazi functionaries capitalized on the general unrest to alter the existing duality between Party and state in favor of the Nazi movement, particularly in the area of justice. Goebbels repeatedly suggested personnel changes in the Justice Ministry after the death of Gürtner, since it had become necessary for the Party to propose legal reforms, revisions, and the like in the face of silent sabotage from within various ministries.[256] An SD report[257] on the effect of criminal justice on the public mood observed that criticism of wartime justice could seriously affect the public's attitude. There was talk of a crisis of confidence arising from the double standard of justice, one for the rich and influential and another for the average citizen. Prosecution of illicit trading and profiteering became a gauge of the degree of trust in the state—the more the state prosecuted these crimes, the greater the respect for the law. Signs of procrastination invariably produced a rift in the social fabric, declining faith in an equitable distribution of the burden, and a deteriorating morality as the average citizen felt himself entitled to engage in similar dealings on the black market.

The thrust of this report suggests fine tailoring, handled on Himmler's urging by Ohlendorf's office in the Reich Security Office. In any case, Hitler, supposedly informed by Bormann,[258] went into a long derisive monologue on the administration of justice and lawyers in general.[259] Goebbels at the same time published an article in *Das Reich*, entitled "Open Discussion," in which he attacked black marketeering,[260] but the public remained skeptical—even after two capital verdicts were handed down against food racketeers.[261] This was followed three weeks later, on April 26, by Hitler's scathing attack in the Reichstag on the administration and justice, demanding authorization—immediately granted of course—for him to circumvent existing laws to punish every German who misused his office or failed to carry out his duties.[262] This invoked public surprise, one SD report noted, only because Hitler already had legal and personal authority as Führer and Reichchancellor. It did, however, confirm to the average German that Hitler was indeed informed of developments and renewed public trust in his ability to correct the abuses.[263]

The apparent artificial formulation of the above report contrasts sharply with the tone of a report by the Leipzig SD, stating that the word dictator was heard being used by representatives of the older generation as well as the working classes.[264] A subsequent report did confirm a strong positive response to Hitler's speech, but it also noted the general public attitude that this was "*a very serious situation* . . . forcing the entire Volk and every individual to write off all personal wishes and considerations and adjust *to a total war*." Justice officials were naturally "shocked"; no event produced such a flood of commentaries from them nor crushed them as much.[265] They now felt insecure and misrepresented to the public.

The "crisis of confidence" became a "crisis of justice" in SD terminology, and to that extent the maneuver by Goebbels, Himmler, Bormann, and others had worked.[266] Previous isolated references to interference by non-judicial organs in the criminal process now became more common, thus heightening fears of arbitrary verdicts.[267] Justice was characterized "as the whipping boy of the present state," amidst fears of an end to independent, impartial judgments.[268] Eventually Goebbels suggested a "small stimulant," since there was no sense in humbling civil servants and lawyers until they lost all interest in the war and their work.[269] But unrest subsided slowly after Hitler's deep incursion into the realm of justice. At the end of August, a new Reich Justice Minister was named, the former Justice Minister of Saxony, Thierack, who was simultaneously made head of the Nazi League for the Protection of Justice and President of the German Academy of Law. His task, as formulated by Bormann, "was primarily political, to bring the administration of justice and justice officials in line with National Socialism."[270] Reports on the reception of the appointment were generally positive, partly because no one dared to voice objections and partly because Thierack was the lesser of two evils in view of Freisler's candidacy.

The "crisis of justice" would never have reached such dimensions had it not been fueled by the resentment of Party officials whose hostility stemmed from their unfavorable dealings with the courts in their 'time of struggle'; during the Weimar Republic these petty officials lacked any sensitivity for the law or judges, given their own background and education. This incompetence within the new political elite was at the root of the failure by the Party bureaucracy to dislodge the state apparatus. It was the Third Reich's key problem—the lack of specialists in the administration of everything from the economy to the military. Instead of making a *tabula rasa*, as the Communists had done in Russia, the Nazi legal revolution left many bulwarks of the established order untouched. To advance more rapidly or remain unmolested, many technocrats did put on brown uniforms, but without any dedication to the new ideology. Ohlendorf had recognized the necessity for an evolutionary approach,[272] but now, during the third year of war, it became obvious to idealists of

Ohlendorf's stripe that the Party's position of predominance had not emerged as planned, and they sought to delineate it dramatically. Hitler's decision in favor of *divide et impera*, sealing the dualism of Party and state, destroyed years of effort by lower, middle, and higher Party officials who had endeavored to fuse Party and state posts through personal union.[273] Bormann defined the NSDAP as the "organization to guide and supervise all Germans politically, ideologically and culturally." After offering examples differentiating between the administration and guidance of society, he closed by rejecting the fusion of both functions in one office, "no matter how appealing this personal union of Party offices and state bureaus may seem at first."[274] But this decision by Hitler to cooperate with the old, traditional political and social forces prevented a complete radicalization of German society. The conception of using the traditional elite for the dual function of legitimatizing the Nazi revolution and serving as its instrument underestimated the old leadership's assertiveness and the weight of the existing social structure.

Increasing signs of a process of disillusion and disassociation were evident on both sides. A growing number of Germans were sobered and disappointed by National Socialism, on whose eclectic program so many hopes had been pinned.[275] Even Hitler showed his dissatisfaction. Already in January, 1942, he had remarked: "If the German Volk is not prepared to assert itself for its own survival, fine: then let it vanish!"[276] Suited to this cooling atmosphere was the new image of Hitler, propagated by the regime, as "the great King" alone and far above the masses, an allusion to Frederick the Great instead of the crusader in shining armor.[277]

The basic mood among Germans around the middle of 1942 was one of "wait and see."[278] The public had been troubled by renewed anticlericalism and mounting antagonism between Church and Nazi leaders. The Churches had taken a strong stand on the issue of mixed marriages[279] and reacted unfavorably to a "church bell campaign" which required delivery of all but the most valuable church bells to the Reich Office for Metals by April, 1942.[280] Nazis on their part were incensed by "slanderous sermons" and critical pastoral letters chastising state anticlericalism, atheism, and misuse of power—whereby Roosevelt and Churchill were depicted as defenders of Christendom—without, however, condemning the war *per se*, particularly the struggle against Bolshevism.[281] But there was no real opposition to the regime despite increasing signs of anxiety and nervousness among women, who constituted the Churches' strongest but unpolitical support.[282] As a result, Hitler and Göring continued to discourage compulsory employment of women,[283] ignoring vigorous protests by the Propaganda, Finance, and Armaments Ministers based on the principle of no work, no food.[284]

Gradually better news from the East and from Africa during June stimulated a "slowly growing interest" in military events.[285] It was the navy which received the most recognition and support among the armed forces this year. While the slogan "empty Atlantic,"[286] used the previous summer to cloak waning U-boat successes, still had to be employed, the submarine weapon could be deployed with greater success after the declaration of war on the USA.[287] "Meldungen aus dem Reich" frequently reported great admiration produced by special announcements of enemy sinkings.[288]

"In discussions among citizens a keen satisfaction was often expressed with the fact that England and America are seemingly incapable of effectively countering the systematic German U-boat campaigns. The increasing number of sinkings should, in the opinion of many citizens, gradually make itself felt not only in the provisionings for England and America but also especially in the British and American public's morale. In Reich areas endangered by air attacks, there is even hope that the British will soon be forced to halt or at least limit their attacks due to heavy tanker losses."[289] Ultimately Germans became so accustomed to a steady stream of victory announcements that they were hardly noticed.[290]

Hidden behind this growing indifference was, besides the factor of habit, a deep anxiety. "Although the general mood has remained unchanged despite positive and negative influences, there has been increasing evidence lately of efforts by citizens to accept positive news from the fronts more guardedly. To be sure, sustained sinkings by our U-boats are still discussed enthusiastically, but in a kind of nervous eagerness to try and figure out how long the war can still last, given the increasing number of sinkings. Now and then citizens attempt to calculate when the obvious damage to the enemy will make itself felt. Developments around Kursk and Kharkov, actively discussed by everyone of late, were generally celebrated as a great German victory. But even here a large segment of the population is asking itself where the enemy gets its mass of men and material. One can sense at times a certain resignation in the way the public follows the struggle of our brave Wehrmacht against a numerically far superior opponent. Even men on leave have repeatedly called the vast expanse of Russian soil our strongest enemy. To some it therefore seems impossible to penetrate so vast an area and bring a quick end to Soviet rule. As a result there is a certain insecurity and caution with which even great German victories are noted. . . ."[291] Similar growing inner unrest can be read from other reports: war weariness,[292] skepticism about the future despite the conquest of Sevastopol and 240,000 Soviet prisoners of war from the battle around Kharkov, and more trenchant political jokes slowly losing their last vestiges of humor.[293]

To what extent the malicious tendency of jokes can be credited to foreign propagandists was and is difficult to determine. In any case, it is a fact that Communist propaganda, severely circumscribed by the German-Soviet Pact, was given new impetus by the war against Russia. While British propaganda avoided attacking Hitler directly and preferred discrediting the Party bosses, German Communist emigrants geared their attack to the real culprit, exposing not only his criminal policies but also his stupidity. Thus one propaganda piece signed by Wilhelm Pieck and Walter Ulbricht reads: "Hitler attacked the Soviet Union to rob it and exploit its raw materials and wealth for the war against England and to prepare for his war against the United States. . . . In his policies Hitler has shown himself not only as an oppressor of peoples but also as a shortsighted and stupid politician. His stupidity and shortsightedness resulted in the formation of a common front of the Soviet Union, England, and the United States of America. . . ."[294]

Naumburg's public prosecutor remarked in January, 1942, how difficult it was to ascertain "the extent of influence of enemy propaganda on morale . . . ; the assumption that this is the case cannot be ruled out, and it is certain that the number of listeners to foreign stations is far greater than the number of reported cases. Gossip or nebulous diffusion of these enemy broadcasts does the rest, since—as shown by the facts in several cases of political crimes—there is still hidden sympathy for Communism among the people and an incomprehensible misunderstanding of the true nature and danger of Bolshevism."[295] The increasing number of air raids provided Communist propaganda with more fuel. Pieck, Ulbricht, and other emigrated KPD members used the bombing of Essen and Cologne for a June 12 German-language broadcast over Radio Moscow with an appeal to "the German working population." German workers were urged to leave the endangered war production centers along with the "Nazi bigwigs" and the privileged and flee to the countryside. However, it remained unclear what they were supposed to live on, since all changes of employment were prohibited. A further suggestion was that the workers overthrow the state leadership and Hitler by force.[296] This was followed on June 14 by ten rules calling on Germans not to aid the war effort, to prepare for armed resistance, to commit acts of sabotage, overthrow Hitler, etc. Pamphlets and leaflets as well as other German-speaking radio stations pointed to the futility of the struggle and exposed contrasts between the workers and plutocrats to emphasize the theme of the class struggle.[297]

This extreme, direct form of propaganda tended to be less effective than the more subtle form of British psychological warfare. It is common knowledge that no peoples' committees were created nor the regime toppled. The only results were isolated acts of sabotage, revolutionary slogans on walls, and class-warfare-tinged expressions of discontent. The Soviet model was not attractive to the German worker. In addition, the Russian standard of living was too low in comparison with the German, the conditions too primitive. But what did result—and not due to Communist propaganda—was a change in the commonly accepted image of the Russian.

On July 10, the Third Reich's propaganda leaders felt compelled to issue a fundamental statement to the press, given the danger that it too might, "on the basis of latest military events, reflect on the reasons why the Soviet soldier fights so fiercely."[298] It was "completely inappropriate" to wonder about the "Russian soul" because it did not exist, just as there was no Russian people, since the Soviet Union was composed of a mixture of races. Even less appropriate was writing that the Soviet soldier was fighting "heroically." "After all, what is heroic? There is the courage of the hero and the criminal . . . the rule of the elite with heroic thoughts sustained by the moral strength of a great ideology, and the rule of the inferior, where the word heroic is completely misused. . . ."[299]

Apparently the problem was so critical that the next week Goebbels published an article, "The so-called Russian soul," in *Das Reich*, with suggestions to all officials, propagandists, and public speakers on "our attitude towards all erroneous portrayals and opinions regarding the military and heroic quality of the Bolshevik masses."[300] The thrust was identical to that of the press instructions: racial mixture, animalism, only capable of defensive warfare. "In official eyes the individual hardly counts as much as say a bicycle. . . ."

Goebbels' noticeable insistence is explainable by reports of a changing public mood as to the national stereotype of the Russian. It probably has to do with as yet undiscovered reports from Party officials and propaganda offices which provoked the Reich Propaganda Minister, in his July 15 conference, to comment on them and add: "Our thesis, according to which Commissars hold the Russian army together with whips, is no longer believed; on the contrary, the conviction is gaining ground daily that the Russian soldier is sold on Bolshevism and is fighting for it."[301] This was confirmed by SD reports on the growing amazement at Soviet resistance and emerging contradictions between the official picture of a primitive, disorganized, chaotic, and brutalized Soviet society and Russia's human and materiel strength and potential.[302] Conscripted Russian workers often proved to be intelligent, resourceful, and far more educated than expected.[303] It became obvious to more and more Germans "that the previous uniform picture did not, at least not any more, correspond to a complex reality. . . ."

It should be added that Goebbels, who had always had a secret liking for Communism, had expressed at his July 28 conference a willingness to conclude an eventual peace with Russia, should Stalin, who was angered at the absence of the second front, offer generous territorial terms guaranteeing Germany's security.[304] This comment was possibly provoked by an alleged proposal for a separate peace on behalf of dissidents within the ruling Soviet, Molotov, Kalinin, and others.[305] In any case, it is striking how many rumors abounded in the summer of 1942 of an alleged cease-fire offer by Stalin.[306]

A similar reassessment of the image of Britons can be detected. Their persistence and tenacity shown in the face of German air bombardments inspired reluctant respect. The attempt on March 28, 1942, to destroy the German submarine base at St. Nazaire, which ended with a partial success and capture of a few English soldiers, had also aroused respect by its recklessness. The term "arrest" instead of capture of English soldiers in the report of the event met with criticism and was regarded as a diminution of one's own achievement.[307] At first the public also felt a "soldierly respect" for English pilots, as for example in their attack on Augsburg on April 17, particularly for their "smart approach to the anticipated target and their 'perfectly calculated bombings' which had targeted and hit almost exclusively strategic installations. . . ."[308]

But the increase in area bombings in order to demoralize the population nurtured the desire for reprisals and a hatred of England which German propaganda had been unable to really stimulate. After the heavy raid on Hamburg during the night of July 26-27, 1942, one again heard questions like, "when will England no longer be an island?" or "when will English terror raids be repaid a thousandfold and English cities rubbed out?"[309] Outrage rose even more when the OKW announced that German soldiers had been captured and shackled in the otherwise unfortunate Anglo-Canadian landing attempt at Dieppe on August 19.[310] In retribution, 1,376 English prisoners of war were placed in chains, which in turn led to the shackling of the same number of German prisoners.[311] The escalation of hatred was to continue.

Two major trends of opinion can again be detected in regard to France. A majority, difficult to quantify, was of the opinion "that one cannot count in the foreseeable future on a positive attitude toward the Reich by the French, as well as the peoples of other conquered and occupied countries. A willingness to cooperate in the creation of a new Europe has to be compelled by Germany with more or less strong pressure. Another

segment of the population, however, has hopes that the French government shake-up will result in France's adherence to the policies of the
Axis powers, whereby great stock is placed in the appointment of Darlan
to supreme commander of all French forces; and we are even toying
with the idea of an eventual French entry into the war on the side of the
Axis powers."[312]

This illusion, entertained by only a smaller segment of the population,
was heavily shaken as British and American troops, on November 8,
initiated Operation "Torch" in North Africa, landing at Casablanca,
Oran, and Algiers. The whole venture, designed to prepare for the thrust
against the Axis' "soft underbelly," shocked the Germans. After the
landing at Dieppe had been repulsed so effectively, the public had been
lulled too much into a sense of security. Now people were unclear about
the seriousness of the hour. Some rightly feared a threat to the Africa
Corps; others saw in it the "second front," which at first had been scorn-
fully torn apart by German propaganda, then silenced by Hitler only to
be later taken up again by propaganda.[313] German entry into the unoccupied part of France on November 10 was taken as confirmation of this
opinion.

"In this connection, the assumption is also that no special significance
should be attributed to French resistance in North Africa since it was
probably only for show, because the French would inwardly always lean
more to the Americans and English than to Germany. French behavior
toward the Anglo-American attack on North Africa has not met with
satisfaction. . . ."[314] When German news services finally came out with
the story that Admiral Darlan had ordered the suspension of hostilities,
assumed supreme governmental power in French North Africa, and
joined the Allies, there was little surprise. It seems many had expected
such "treason."[315] Marshal Pétain's evasive and inconclusive December 5
reply to Hitler's belated offer of an alliance was "generally" labelled as
"rather late and non-committal," by some as "impudent." Pétain, by
his retarded and impolite reply, had shown no understanding for Germany's position; his popularity and the widespread Francophilia which
Goebbels had observed in August[316] had dwindled.

If Operation "Torch" lessened sympathy among those Germans who
had misjudged the true feelings of a defeated arch-enemy, it contributed
to greater American prestige. Americans were no longer regarded as
"military dilettantes."[317] But above all it was just the thing to revive
latent mistrust of the Italian ally. "In particular, people are asking how
the Americans had been able to pass through the strait of Gibraltar with
such a strong force without this operation being noticed in time by Italian
strategic reconnaissance. In this respect the question is also posed as to

where the much-vaunted Italian fleet was. . . ."[318] Overestimating Germany's strength and the strategic capabilities of the Desert Fox, people also blamed the Italian infantry for the loss of Egypt, Montgomery's capture of Tobruk on November 13, and the fall of Bengasi on the twentieth. There was general fear of an Italian collapse, in view of rumors of war weariness on the part of the Italian population.[319]

In sharp contrast was the average German's image of Japan, based on World War I remembrances. Initial victories at Pearl Harbor, Sumatra, and Singapore all evoked admiration. Repeated comparisons with the Italian fleet did not flatter the latter.[320] "It is evident that the Japanese are rated much higher as allies than the Italians. Seldom are even friendly feelings towards Italians registered."[321] The dimension of further victories in East Asia was difficult to comprehend and led to an overestimation of allied achievements, thus creating a picture of the Japanese warrior "which no longer does justice to the accomplishments of our own soldiers," as the SD report bitterly noted.[322] Completely in contrast to the feelings of superiority over Italians, a kind of inferiority complex set in: "The Japanese present themselves as so-called 'super Teutons.' There is a feeling that one can still find qualities in the Japanese which our legendary heroes possessed many hundred years ago. . . . A certain insecurity about our own direction, our own possibilities and models can no longer be ignored. . . ." It seems the comparison with Japanese valour provoked a very pessimistic view of European disunity in many Germans.

Mounting pessimism on the one hand and exaggerated hopes on the other defined the basic constellation of opinion for the remainder of the year. Favorable developments on the Eastern front shifted the mood from an "uneasy wait for the great offensive"[323] in June to a cautious optimism in July. Yet "considerable differentiation"[324] in opinion was registered. Only some people followed military happenings with real interest and were confidently disposed; others could form no real idea and took rather indifferent notice of developments; and yet another group was increasingly "influenced by the cares and burdens of daily living, the food difficulties and fears of intensified enemy air raids. . . ." We are thus dealing with a typical spectrum of public opinion: the undecided, the wavering masses in between two polar opposites.

After the successes of Army Group A in the Caucasus, the party of optimists grew, "still believing in the possibility of Soviet Russia's collapse this year. . . ." Hitler and Goebbels were troubled by these escalating expectations. Press and radio were urged to draw attention to the global scope of the war and to ensure that "the illusionary mood in the

Reich is dampened somewhat."[325] The SD report of August 31, however, still pointed to *"the irregularity of the general mood among the population, which oscillates between exaggerated optimism and serious concern. . . ."*[326]

At the beginning of the fourth year of war, newspapers were instructed as before to mention September 3 as the start of the war in their lead articles.[327] The SD report made no special mention of public reaction to this fact. Referring to the basic morale, it stated: "After the end of three years of war, the position of a large majority can be widely characterized by a certain resignation, partly reflected in an even stronger degree of war weariness and frequently also expressed in remarks of the following nature: 'Who would have thought, after the great victories at the beginning of the war, that the war would take this course and drag on so long?'; or 'How much longer will the war last? An end is still not in sight!'; or 'What still awaits us?' Growing food supply problems, three years of restrictions in all areas of daily life, the intensity and scope of daily increasing enemy air attacks, the fear for the lives of family members at the front, and civilians at home who fall victim to enemy air raids are all factors having a greater and greater impact on the mood of many individuals and increasingly resulting in the desire for an early end to the war. . . ."

Reports also spoke of a downright "psychotic fear" of air raids in numerous cities which superseded everything else.[328] Exaggerated rumors about the extent of damage and about allied leaflets heralding further destruction contributed to a deepening psychosis. The press receive instructions to lift morale by publishing pictures and descriptions of the "brave behavior of the population in stricken cities." Photographs and references to damage and destruction, on the other hand, were to be avoided if possible.[329] The population, at this time and later, in fact demonstrated exemplary behavior during numerous nights of horror. Here one could see sincere readiness to help and compassion for one's fellow man, especially in working class districts and among women.[330] If the Germans ever deserved praise during World War II, it was for their courage and compassion in the midst of a hail of bombs.[331] Here a real *"Volksgemeinschaft* and solidarity," "comparable to the military concept of comradeship," developed. The threat to life and property contributed to the elimination of the typical anonymity of the industrial age and promoted neighborly, human contact. The intended demoralizing effect of air raids—in 1942 alone, 41,440 tons of bombs were dropped on Germany—thus failed and was only achieved when the overall situation had become hopeless. At first, however, it fostered increasing hate and stubborn resistance which benefitted the Nazi regime.

On August 31, "Meldungen aus dem Reich" mentioned Stalingrad for the first time[332] and the significance attached to this battle even by the populace: "The vast majority of citizens are turning their attention primarily to the *battle for Stalingrad*. People assume that the capture of this most crucial cornerstone will at least bring about a decisive military turnabout. . . ."[333]

Naturally this opinion was the product of news information and propaganda—but only in part. In short order Stalingrad took on an almost magical significance—every subsequent SD report underlined this,[334] and on September 28 one even stated that most listened "as if hypnotized" to reports of developments there; one is thus tempted to believe in a heightened consciousness which made Stalingrad a symbolic turning point in more than a military sense.

This almost maniacal fixation was temporarily lessened[335] by Hitler's annual address opening the Winter Relief campaign.[336] In his rather lacklustre speech he had exclaimed that he "would storm and take Stalingrad." Göring achieved a further marked relaxation on Thanksgiving Day[337] with his announcement of an increase in food rations and a special Christmas distribution.[338] Furthermore, due to Göring's homey style, the "little man" felt himself addressed, particularly since respect was being shown to the lower classes by decorating deserving farmers and agricultural laborers and drawing attention to the services of miners whose pensions were to be raised. Battles in the East and in North Africa suddenly receded into the background once more, and the improvement in the material necessities of life was interpreted as a lasting measure and turn for the better.[339] Rumors were already circulating again of cease-fire negotiations with Russia. "A persistent inner willingness for a compromise peace is also frequently reported, the more so because very few citizens have any accurate conception of the actual military objectives and many feel that the conquest of the vast eastern territories exceeds our capacities. . . ."[340]

Then, allied landings in North Africa took center stage and many observed a change in the situation to Germany's disadvantage. "The general conviction has taken hold that the most recent developments are not militarily decisive but will prolong the war. Belief in final victory remains unshattered," in large measure, no doubt, due to Hitler's speech.[341] But a majority was "still incapable of comprehending events in the Mediterranean clearly and therefore they assess the military situation with a feeling of uneasiness. A certain gloominess and anxiety exists among many people because they 'cannot quite cope' with events any more and fear an unknown danger which they cannot quite grasp. . . ." At the same time concern over Stalingrad intensified once more.

The offensives in Africa and Russia were seen as part of a "gigantic plan to overwhelm the Axis powers." And the wildest rumors blossomed again, as always during times of uncertainty.[342]

The special Christmas distribution did guarantee that Germans could bake their holiday specialties and even spread a bit of Christmas cheer,[343] even though the news leaked out via soldiers' letters that the Sixth Army was encircled in Stalingrad. Secretly, however, the increasingly evident disenchantment of Germans with Hitler, which began with the Russian campaign in 1942, grew further. The Nazi leadership became more and more aware that the old established powers and groups, whose influence it thought it had checked if not rendered harmless, continued to be active on the German scene and to broaden their sphere of operations. This applied not only to political Catholicism and Protestantism but also to the conservative middle classes, heavy industry, and even the army, i.e., representatives of Right and Center with whose help Hitler had gained power and with whose expertise he could still not completely dispense. The Left, robbed of its leaders, remained far more powerless and only entered the picture at the local or regional level.[344]

Signs of a radical upheaval in the situation by the end of 1942 become very obvious from Bormann's letter to all Gauleiters on December 18, 1942. In it the head of the Party Chancellory referred to Gau administration reports of an increasingly negative reaction from the public.[345] According to Bormann, a closer investigation proved that these were isolated manifestations of strained nerves and inveterate pessimists which should not be viewed as symptomatic of general unrest. Mistaken generalizations had encouraged assessments which Bormann now attempted to minimize. There was no doubt "that despite the changing mood . . . the attitude of our people remains sound in contrast to 1917/18 . . ." Bormann called on the party to be more active, remain in constant contact with the masses and take the lead in displaying unshakeable optimism: "Any doubts about a German victory and the justice of our cause must be silenced immediately by unassailable arguments and—if that does not help—by stronger methods using the example of our own struggle. As before the takeover of power, we find ourselves in the hardest of struggles; our old adversaries have gathered again and are now using their old tactics against us. *The Führer expects the Party to apply on its own the spirit and methods from the time of our struggle, which are not only to administer and govern but to lead.*"[346]

This recognition and admonition was a signal for further, harder measures by the regime, thereby introducing a new phase of the war.

National Socialism, increasingly placed on the defensive, had to ward off not only its enemies abroad but also growing counterforces from within.

NOTES

1. This interpretation is based on A. Hillgruber's concepts in *Hitlers Strategie, Politik und Kriegsführung*, and *Deutschlands Rolle in der Vorgeschichte der beiden Weltkriege*.
2. Ernst Nolte, "Ebenen des Krieges und Stufen des Widerstandes," in *Probleme des zweiten Weltkrieges* (Cologne, 1967), p. 203.
3. Cf. diary notes of Halder, cited in Hans-Adolf Jacobsen, *Der Zweite Weltkrieg. Grundzüge der Politik und Strategie in Dokumenten* (Frankfurt, 1965), pp. 109-10.
4. *Ibid.*, p. 110. Concerning details and origins of the commissar order, see Heinrich Uhlig, "Der verbrecherische Befehl. Eine Diskussion und ihre historisch-dokumentarische Grundlagen," in *Vollmacht des Gewissens*, vol. II, pp. 289-410.
5. IfZ.-IMT Document No. 2586=PS-710 (photocopy).
6. Cf. Eberhard Jäckel, *Hitlers Weltanschauung. Entwurf einer Herrschaft* (Tübingen, 1969), p. 79.
7. Domarus, vol. II, 2 Halbband, p. 1726.
8. Night of February 22, 1942: Picker, *op. cit.*, p. 181, and compare p. 344.
9. Vertrauliche Informationen, 1. Ergänzung, BA, ZSg 109/22, fol. 51. Cf. also *"Wollt ihr den totalen Krieg?,"* p. 182.
10. Press conference of June 22, 1941: BA, ZSg 101/20, fol. 40.
11. Further press arguments provided by Otto Dietrich, who can be considered a more direct mouthpiece of Hitler, included uncovering Bolshevik sabotage and keeping Germans free of sentimentality. Cf. V.I. No. 156/41: BA, Zsg 109/22, fol. 78, 79.
12. Monthly report of the Regierungspräsident for Swabia and Neuburg, July 8, 1941: BHStA, Abt. II, MA 106,684; Gau Schleswig-Holstein, general political report: BA, NS Misch/1722, fol. 301, 521; report of SD-Aussenstelle Minden, June 24, 1941: Höhne, *op. cit.*, p. 391; public prosecutor general, Nuremberg, August 1, 1941: BHStA, Abt. II, MA 106,681.
13. "Meldungen aus dem Reich," June 23, 1941: Boberach, p. 155.
14. Report of the Regierungspräsident for Lower Franconia and Aschaffenburg, July 11, 1941: BHStA, Abt. II, MA 106,681.
15. Report of NSDAP Reichsleitung, Reichsfrauenführung, for the months April-June, 1941. Meldungen aus den Gauen, Gau Magdeburg-Anhalt: BA, NS22/vorl. 860.
16. Regierungspräsident for Swabia and Neuburg, July 8, 1941; BHStA, Abt. II, MA 106,684.
17. Monthly report by the Regierungspräsident for Upper and Central Franconia: BHStA, Abt. II, MA 106,681; cf. also OLG-president Königsberg, July 5, 1941: BA, R22/3375. Public prosecutor general, Naumburg, July 28, 1941: BA, R22/3381; PPG, Nuremberg, August 1, 1941: BA, R22/3381. "Mel-

dungen aus dem Reich," June 23, 1941: Boberach, p. 156. Cf. further-more, Jochen Klepper, who wrote as a soldier in Rumania: "Everyone's first thought is the length of the war, but then the conviction of the need for this conflict with Russia sooner or later." *Überwindung. Tagebücher und Aufzeichnungen aus dem Kriege* (Stuttgart, 1958), p. 50.

18. "Meldungen aus dem Reich," June 23, 1941: Boberach, p. 155.

19. July 1, 1941: BA, R22/3385 and 3381.

20. August 1, 1941: BA, R22/3355.

21. "Meldungen aus dem Reich," July 7, 1941: Boberach, pp. 158, 160.

22. Cf. comment by Halder in Jacobsen, *Der Zweite Weltkrieg*, p. 114.

23. Sicherheitsdienst RFSS, Leitabschnitt Stuttgart III A 4-, July 15, 1941: HStA Stuttgart, K 750/47.

24. Cf. Boelcke, "*Wollt Ihr den totalen Krieg?*," p. 183; and BA, ZSg 109/23, fol. 26.

25. *Ibid.*, fol. 32.

26. *Ibid.*, fol. 34, 43.

27. Cf. footnote 23 above.

28. BA, ZSg 109/22, fol. 84.

29. "Meldungen aus dem Reich," July 24, 1941, "Zur Aufnahme der Wochen-schau vom 19.-26. Juli 1941," Boberach, p. 165.

30. In total, almost four million Soviet prisoners-of-war died by the end of the war. Cf. Gerald Reitlinger, *Ein Haus auf Sand gebaut. Hitlers Gewalt-politik in Russland 1941-1944* (Hamburg, 1962), pp. 114 ff.

31. Az 2 f24. 12a AWA/Kriegsgef. ID of December 18, 1941: No. 8648/41.

32. Propaganda-Abteilung W beim Befehlshaber des rückwärtigen Heeres-gebietes Mitte: "Stimmungsbericht für die Zeit vom 1. bis 15. Novem-ber 1941:" MGFA WO1-6/359.

33. Höhne, *op. cit.*, p. 391.

34. Cf. footnote 23 above.

35. Boberach, p. 162.

36. "Übersicht über die wirtschaftliche Gesamtlage," Göring's Dienststelle für den Vierjahresplan, August 20, 1941: V.P. 13495. IWM FD 4809/45/ file 2, J.004096. Cf. also Public prosecutor general, Düsseldorf, July 31, 1941: BA, R22/3363 and public prosecutor general, Bamberg, August 1, 1941: BA, R22/3355.

37. BA, NS5 I/58, fol. 78679. Further complaints in August in fol. 78663.

38. Sicherheitsdienst RFSS SD-Leitabschnitt Stuttgart, III. A 4 September 1, 1941: HStA Stuttgart, K750/48.

39. Folge 31, July 19, 1941, Punkt 303 "Gerüchte über weitere Einschränkungen in der Lebensmittelzuteilung," BA, ZSg 3/1621.

40. See, for example, "Meldungen aus dem Reich," August 21, 25, September 1, 11, 1941: "Weitere Meldungen über Schwierigkeiten in der Kartoffel-versorgung und Klagen über die derzeitigen Brotrationen," Boberach, pp. 171, 176 f.

41. Copy of a report of September 18, 1941: BA, R26 IV/vorl. 51.

42. See footnote 23 above, and also OLG-president Munich, July 3, 1941: BA, R22/3379 and public prosecutor general Bamberg, August 1, 1941: BA, R22/3355.

43. August 7, 1941: BA, R22/3367. Cf. also Nuremberg, July 1, 1941: BA, R22/3381.

44. OLG-president Nuremberg, September 2, 1941: *ibid.*
45. Public prosecutor general Munich, September 26, 1941: BA, R22/3379.
46. BA, NS22/vorl. 860. Cf. also the war diary of SA-Sturm 33/5 Bamberg, which mentions the crucifix matter on September 10, October 8 and 15, 1941: StA Bamberg, Rep. M31 No. 11. fol. 61, 63, 64.
47. Public prosecutor general Hamm, September 30, 1941: BA, R22/3367.
48. Addendum to "Meldungen aus dem Reich," July 21, 1941: BA, R58/162.
49. Zahn, *op. cit.*, pp. 109, 94
50. "Meldungen aus dem Reich," July 21, 1941, "Auswirkungen der Verlesung des Hirtenbriefes des gesamten Episkopats Deutschlands:" BA, R58/162. Many of the quotes come from the Stuttgart SD section report of July 15, 1941: HStA Stuttgart, K750/47.
51. "Meldungen," July 21, 1941. Cf. also the letters of Heydrich to Ribbentrop, August 18 and October 7, 1941, about the Fulda Bishops' Conference and the declaration of loyalty by the German episcopate to the pope, in which reference is made to the attacks on the Church in Germany and euthanasia. AA Inland II g/45.
52. *Documents on German Foreign Policy*, Series D, vol. XIII, p. 536.
53. In September the Gestapo was again expressly directed to curtail matters relating to the Church. Conway, *op. cit.*, p. 285 f.
54. *Die Briefe Pius XII. an die deutschen Bischöfe*, pp. xxxiii f.
55. "Hirtenwort des Bischofs Clemens von Münster über Bolschewismus und Nationalsozialismus," addendum to "Meldungen aus dem Reich," September 29, 1941: BA, R58/164.
56. See a similar response from the Protestant Church, Conway, *op. cit.*, appendix 18.
57. Reichsmarschall Grossdeutsches Reich, Beauftragter für den Vierjahresplan, VP 11594/41 g. Rs., July 23, 1941: "Übersicht über die wirtschaftliche Gesamtlage," IWM 4809/45 file 2, J 004,107.
58. HA GHH No. 4001026/10: "Niederschrift über die Vertrauensratssitzung am Dienstag den 26.8.41."
59. This proclamation was issued on June 26, 1941, on suggestion of the Foreign Office. Cf. BA, ZSg 109/22, fol 107, and "*Wollt ihr den totalen Krieg?*," p. 182. Goebbels at first was not enthusiastic about the term crusade since it could be associated with failures and bloodshed. *Ibid.*, and ZSg 109/22, fol. 118.
60. BA, NS22/vorl. 860.
61. September 25, 1941: BA, NS Misch 1722, fol. 301434, 301435. Cf. also the long Arbeitsbericht of the Gaufrauenschaftsleiterin Kiel, November 29, 1941: *ibid.*, fol. 300885.
62. *Ibid.*, fol. 301117, 301118.
63. Monthly report of the Regierungspräsident for Upper and Central Franconia for June, 1941: BHStA, Abt. II, MA 106,679.
64. September 3, 1941: BA, R22/3379.
65. BA, Schumacher Collection 382.
66. "Meldungen aus dem Reich," August 4, 1941: Boberach, p. 167.
67. SD Leipzig section, August 7, 1941: *Aus deutschen Urkunden*, p. 248.
68. BA, ZSg 101/40, fol. 135 and 137. Cf. also SD Leipzig section, domestic political report of August 12, 1941: *Aus deutschen Urkunden*, p. 249.
69. BA, ZSg 101/40, fol. 287. Ca. 260,000 people died of cold and starvation

in Leningrad. The situation improved in the first months of 1942 when connections via Lake Ladoga were established, enabling foodstuffs to be sent across the lake. About one million civilians could be evacuated. Cf. Dimitrij W. Pawlow, *Die Blockade von Leningrad 1941* (Stuttgart, 1967), and Alexander Werth, *Russland im Kriege 1941-1945* (Munich, 1965), pp. 222 ff.

70. "Meldungen aus dem Reich," August 21, 1941: Boberach, p. 170. Cf. also Funkspruch of SD Leipzig section, August 6, 1941, reporting on public unrest and the reservations about the huge number of "Bolshevik-infected subhumans" taken prisoner: *Aus deutschen Urkunden*, p. 247. Cf. furthermore the report of August 12, 1941, about growing numbers of pessimistic voices concerning the possibility of a final accounting with England before the winter. *Ibid.*, p. 249.

71. "Meldungen aus dem Reich," September 4, 1941: Boberach, p. 172.

72. V.I. No. 227/41 of August 31, 1941: BA, ZSg 109/24, fol. 134.

73. V.I. No. 228/41 of September 1, 1941: BA, ZSg 109/25, fol. 1.

74. Cf. "Meldungen aus dem Reich" of August 4, 1941: "Aufnahme und Auswirkung der allgemeinen Propaganda-, Presse- und Rundfunklenkung in der Zeit vom 1. bis 4. August 1941:" Boberach, p. 169.

75. "Meldungen aus dem Reich," September 8, 1941: *ibid.*, p. 173.

76. Hans Gert Freiherr von Esebeck, "Schlachtfeld Nordafrika. Kampf und Sieg des Deutschen Afrika-Korps" (typed manuscript), Berlin, p. 192. BA, NS Misch/460.

77. See, for example, the report of Major Bürker about his impressions on the visit of Pz Gr. 2 des XXXXVI. A.K. and 10. Pz-Div (July, 1941): MGFA WO1-6/411.

78. "Meldungen aus dem Reich," September 11, 1941: BA, R58/164.

79. *Mitteilungen für die Truppe*, No. 157 (November, 1941): BA, MA WO1-6/9.

80. *Idem.*, No. 163 (December, 1941), *ibid.*

81. Cf. Elihu Katz and Paul F. Lazarsfeld, *Personal Influence. The part played by people in the flow of mass communication* (Glencoe, Illinois, 1955).

82. "Meldungen aus dem Reich," September 8, 1941: Boberach, p. 174.

83. September 1, 1941: HStA Stuttgart, K750/48.

84. Cf. page 132 of the text and "*Wollt ihr den totalen Krieg?*," p. 196.

85. "Meldungen aus dem Reich," September 4, 8, 1941: Boberach, pp. 173, 174.

86. "Meldungen aus dem Reich," June 26, July 7, September 4, 1941: *ibid.*, pp. 156, 161, 173.

87. *Ibid.*, p. 159. Cf. also SD Stuttgart section, September 1, 1941: HStA Stuttgart K750/48.

88. See, for example, "Meldungen aus dem Reich," July 3, 1941, which states that opinion was "that the offensive against Russia is only an intermediate phase in the great war against England . . .": BA, R58/162.

89. Speech of October 3, 1941: Domarus, vol. II, 2. Halbband, p. 1762.

90. "Meldungen aus dem Reich," September 11, 1941, "Zur Aufnahme der Wochenschau vom 6. bis 12. September 1941:" BA, R58/164.

91. "Meldungen aus dem Reich," October 6, 1941: Boberach, p. 180. Monthly situation report, Kreisleitung Norder-Dithmarschen, October 23, 1941: BA, NS Misch/1722, fol. 301245.

92. Hillgruber, *Deutschlands Rolle in der Vorgeschichte der beiden Weltkriege*, pp. 58 ff.
93. Otto Dietrich, *Zwölf Jahre mit Hitler* (Cologne, 1955), p. 102.
94. Domarus, vol. II, 2. Halbband, pp. 1758-67.
95. "Meldungen aus dem Reich," September 15, 18, 1941: BA, R58/164; October 6, 1941: Boberach, p. 180.
96. "*Wollt ihr den totalen Krieg?*," p. 188.
97. *Ibid.*, p. 189.
98. Domarus, vol. II, 2. Halbband, p. 1756.
99. "Meldungen aus dem Reich," October 13, 1941: Boberach, p. 183.
100. "Meldungen aus dem Reich," September 15, 1941: BA, R58/164.
101. BA, ZSg 109/26, fol. 41. Cf. Saul Friedländer, *Auftakt zum Untergang. Hitler und die USA 1939-1941* (Stuttgart, 1965), for policies toward the USA until its entry into the war.
102. Public prosecutor general, Nuremberg, October 1, 1941: BA, R22/3381.
103. Cf. Boberach, p. 187.
104. "Meldungen aus dem Reich," October 27, 1941: *ibid.*, p. 184.
105. "Meldungen aus dem Reich," November 6, 1941: Boberach, pp. 185-86.
106. See Höhne, *op. cit.*, pp. 198 ff.
107. For this, see Eva G. Reichmann, *Die Flucht in den Hass. Die Ursachen der deutschen Judenkatastrophe* (Frankfurt/Main, 1956).
108. Compare Hans Mommsen, "Der nationalsozialistische Polizeistaat und die Judenverfolgung vor 1938," *VfZG* (January, 1962), No. 1, pp. 68-87.
109. Compare Wolfgang Scheffler, *Judenverfolgung im Dritten Reich 1933 bis 1944* (Berlin, 1960), p. 26.
110. H. G. Adler, *Die Juden in Deutschland. Von der Aufklärung bis zum Nationalsozialismus* (Munich, 1960), p. 148.
111. *Ibid.*, p. 13.
112. Cf. "Meldungen" of July 15, 1940; November 28, 1940; November 27, 1941, in BA, R58/152, 156, 166. Cf. also report for January 29, 1942: Boberach, p. 215.
113. RGBl I, p. 547; and Decree of Reich Interior Minister, September 15, 1941. Cf. Addendum in "Vertraulichen Informationen" of the Party Chancellory, November 22, 1941: BA, ZSg 3/1621a. For press propaganda instructions, see V.I. Nr. 217/41 of August 28, 1941: BA, ZSg 109/24, fol. 101; Nr. 252/41 of September 26, 1941: BA, ZSg 109/25, fol. 84.
114. "Meldungen aus dem Reich," October 9, 1941: BA, R58/165.
115. Monthly report for August-September, 1941: BA, NS 22, vorl. 860.
116. "Meldungen aus dem Reich," February 2, 1942: Boberach, p. 220.
117. BHStA Munich, Abt. II, MA 106,679. Cf. also public prosecutor general, Düsseldorf, BA, R22/3363.
118. Monthly report for September, 1941: *ibid.*
119. BHStA, Abt. II, MA 106,694, 106,683.
120. Geheime Staatspolizei, Staatspolizeistelle Nürnberg-Fürth, No. 7479/41 II B4 of November 3, 1941, concerning attitude of Germans of pure blood towards Jews. StA Bamberg, Rep. K9/Vers. XV. No. 1301.
121. Gabriel A. Almond, in his informative study *The American People and Foreign Policy*, pp. 30 ff, points out as the outstanding characteristic of Americans the emphasis on material and private value which is a signifi-

cant cause for widespread lack of interest in foreign policy. Even in foreign crisis situations, Americans quickly return to their private concerns after a temporary diversion.

122. BA, NS Misch/1722, ff. 33049.
123. Kreisleitung Lübeck (early November ?): *ibid.*, ff. 301121/22.
124. Report of October 4, 1941: BA, R22/3381.
125. A percentage breakdown of the individual groups is not possible on the basis of reports. Nevertheless, the following result of a private, unrepresentative questionnaire of party members from various occupations and social strata is presented, with all its reservations.
After the November 1938 pogrom, the following groups emerged:
5 per cent fanatics who supported the use of force,
32 per cent cautiously reserved or indifferent,
63 per cent unreservedly indignant.
A second poll in the fall of 1942 showed the following result:
5 per cent supported the right to racial destruction,
69 per cent were indifferent,
21 per cent were in favor of a Jewish state or Lebensraum,
5 per cent clearly rejected anti-Semitism.
Michael Müller-Claudius, *Der Antisemitismus und das deutsche Verhängnis* (Frankfurt/Main, 1948), pp. 162-75.
126. Zipfel, *op. cit.*, pp. 218 ff.; "Kämpfer gegen Diktatoren," *Die Welt* (June 12, 1968).
127. Erich Maria Remarque, *Die Nacht von Lissabon* (Cologne, 1962), p. 116.
128. Cf. "Vertrauliche Informationsbericht" about a trip through the Polish "General Gouvernement" including Galicia, of October 5, 1941: "If there are still people who have compassion for the Jews, we recommend they take a look in such a ghetto: the sight of a rotting, depraved race decayed to the bone destroys all sentimental humanitarianism. . . ." BA, ZSg 101/41, ff. 55.
129. "Meldungen aus dem Reich," October 27, 1941: BA, R58/165.
130. "Meldungen aus dem Reich," November 27, 1941: BA, R58/166.
131. "Meldungen aus dem Reich," January 29, 1942: Boberach, pp. 215-16.
132. RGBl. I, p. 372.
133. "Meldungen aus dem Reich," November 24, 1941: Boberach, p. 195.
134. Cited by Klepper, *Unter dem Schatten Deiner Flügel*, p. 1019.
135. Chef Sipo and SD. IV Bl-930/41g. Rs. of December 18, 1941, to Reich Foreign Minister: AA Inland IIg/44.
136. "Meldungen aus dem Reich," November 24, 1941: Boberach, p. 197.
137. Scheffler, *op. cit.*, p. 43.
138. See the "Wannsee-Protokoll," *Der Nationalsozialismus. Dokumente 1933-1945*, ed. with commentary by Walter Hofer (Frankfurt, 1957), pp. 303-5.
139. Saul Friedländer, *Kurt Gerstein ou l'ambiguité du bien* (Paris, 1967), pp. 93 f.
140. Concerning the extent of the crimes, see Reinhard Henkys, *Die nationalsozialistischen Gewaltverbrechen. Geschichte und Gericht* (Stuttgart, 1964).
141. Friedländer, *Kurt Gerstein*, p. 94; and Höhne, *op. cit.*, p. 347.
142. *Ibid.*

143. Photocopy in IfZ. Cf. Karl Demeter, *Das deutsche Offizierskorps in Gesellschaft und Staat, 1650-1945* (Frankfurt, 1965, 4th revised ed.), pp. 22, 223.

144. Chef der Sicherheitspolizei und SD-Adjutant, Cd. 5. B. No. 58422/42 gh. Rs., February 13, 1942: BA, NS19 neu/2030.

145. Gerald Reitlinger, *Die Endlösung. Hitlers Versuch der Ausrottung der Juden Europas 1939-1945* (Berlin, 1956), pp. 220 ff. Raoul Hilberg, *The Destruction of the European Jews* (Chicago, 1961), pp. 215 ff. Léon Poliakov and Josef Wulf, *Das Dritte Reich und die Juden* (Berlin, 1955), pp. 519 ff. Scheffler, *op. cit.*, p. 107; *Der Nationalsozialismus*, pp. 300 ff. Cf. also the position taken by the Chief of the General Staff of OKW II, July 22, 1941: Poliakov-Wulf, *Das Dritte Reich und seine Diener*, p. 357.

146. Armeeoberkommando II., Abt. 10/AO Br. 2379/41, November 20, 1941: Poliakov-Wulf, *Das Dritte Reich und seine Diener*, p. 451. Cf. a similar remark by Field Marshal von Reichenau, Armeeoberkommando 6 Abt.1a-Az. 7 A.H., October 10, 1941: *ibid.*, p. 455.

147. See page 57.

148. Cf., for example, the steps taken by Major Liedke and especially Lieutenant Dr. Albert Battel regarding the evacuation of Jews in Pizenysl on July 23-24, 1942. Himmler ordered that Battel be imprisoned after the war and a Party legal proceeding be initiated. BA, NS19/1765.

149. Höhne, *op. cit.*, pp. 337 ff.

150. BA, ZSg3/1622; presented in extract form in Scheffler, *op. cit.*, pp. 55-56.

151. *Op. cit.*, pp. 114, 122, 134-43.

152. Picker, *op. cit.*, p. 348.

153. *Tagebücher*, p. 237.

154. *Ibid.*, pp. 251-52.

155. *Ibid.*, p. 267.

156. IWM Fd 332/46. Report of SD Leipzig section of August 19, 1942.

157. Letter of March 27, 1943, by a corporal from a reserve hospital to the head of the propaganda section in the Ministry for Propaganda and Enlightenment. The author thought that there were few dedicated Nazis who still believed in a final victory and that many disapproved of measures in the East. BA, R55/583. Cf. also Max Geiger, *Der deutsche Kirchenkampf 1933-1945* (Zurich, 1965), cited in Friedländer, *Kurt Gerstein*, p. 133.

158. "Meldungen aus dem Reich," April 19, 1943: Boberach, p. 383. Cf. also the monthly report by the Regierungspräsident for Swabia and Neuberg of May 10, 1943, which asserts that the Katyn propaganda also "unleashed discussions about the treatment of Jews in Germany and the Eastern territories." BHStA. Abt. II. MA 106/684.

159. "SD-Bericht zu Inlandfragen," July 26, 1943; "Meldungen über die Entwicklung der Öffentlichen Meinungsbildung:" BA, R58/186.

160. "Aufnahme und Auswirkung der allgemeinen Propaganda-, Presse- und Rundfunklenkung in der Zeit vom 16. bis 19. 4. 1943," "Meldungen aus dem Reich," April 19, 1943: Boberach, pp. 385, 386.

161. Cf. footnote 159 above.

162. Report of the SD section, Halle, of May 22, 1943: BA, NS6/406.

163. Medal "Winterschlacht im Osten 1941/42" (May 26, 1942).

164. Paula Stuck von Reznicek, Streng Persönliche Tagebuchnotizen in BA/MA Slg. 106/vol. 19, fol. 19.

165. Cf. BA, ZSg 109/42, fol. 33, 34, 37, 40, 41, 45, 63, 69, 73-76, 85, 97, 130.

166. BA, ZSg 102/43, fol. 152.
167. Cf. page 202.
168. Reports from Gaus Halle-Merseburg, Kurhessen, Brandenburg, in Partei-Kanzlei II B 4: "Auszüge aus Berichten der Gauleitungen u.a. Dienststellen. Zeitraum 23.-29.5.43:" BA, NS6/415.
169. *Ibid.*
170. Tgb. No. 1573/43: BA, NS19/neu 1570.
171. SS-Obersturmführer Brand on April 10, 1943, to the Inspector for Statistics: *ibid.* The report itself is 16 pages long.
172. No. 33/43: BA, NS6/vorl. 344.
173. Cf. correspondence of the Reichsverteidigungskommissar for the district of Berlin of March 20, 1945: BA, NS 19/118 F42. All documents dealing with the final solution of the Jews were to be destroyed and a short indication to the nineteenth report about "Sondereinsatz Berlin" for the period February 14-20, 1945, shows this was largely done. Berghahn, "Meinungsforschung im Dritten Reich," *loc. cit.*, p. 110.
174. *"Wollt ihr den totalen Krieg?,"* pp. 312-13. Cf. also V.I. (confidential information) of December 8, 1942, No. 315/42: BA, ZSg 109/40, pp. 21 ff., 222; No. 323/42, December 17, 1942: ZSg 109/40, fol. 43.
175. In Scheffler, *op. cit.*, pp. 110-11.
176. Lewy, *op. cit.*, pp. 316-18.
177. Reich propaganda office, Bayreuth, beginning of July, 1944, concerning "öffentliche Juden-Verbote:" StA Bamberg. Rep.K.9/Verz. XV, No. 2.
178. Cf. slogan no. 9 for April: BA, ZSg 3/1540.
179. BA, R55/570, fol. 60.
180. BA, R55/571, fol. 46; see also fol. 6.
181. See, for example, *ibid.*, fol. 94, 95, 114, 123-25, 145, 240; BA, R55/577, fol. 89, 90, 221, 222, 232-37.
182. BA, R55/578, fol. 210, 214; R55/579, fol. 35, 37, 50, 77-79, 82, 97-112, 118, 119, 122, 123, 187-88, 204, 223-24, 236-39. Typical of such attitude is a letter of a worker from Tangerhütte (Stendahl) to an English worker, in which he calls on him to be mindful of his race and refuse the Jews all war service. He asked him if he had thought about the race to which he belonged, that he was Aryan and Germanic. The letter closed: "With pure Germanic feelings, your German comrade." R55/570, fol. 181.
183. Andreas-Friedrich, *op. cit.*, pp. 83-84.
184. Louis de Jong, "Die Niederlande und Auschwitz," *VfZG*, No. 1 (January, 1969), p. 15.
185. See page 7.
186. Fifty thousand light and severe cases had been reported by January 20, 1942. *Goebbels' Tagebücher*, p. 73.
187. *Entscheidungsschlachten des Zweiten Weltkrieges*, ed. by Hans-Adolf Jacobsen & Jürgen Rohwer (Frankfurt/Main, 1960), p. 171.
188. Cf. OLG-president Bamberg, January 5, 1942: BA, R22/3355; Hanseatic OLG-president, same date: R22/3366; public prosecutor general, Naumburg/Saale, January 27, 1942: R22/3380; public prosecutor general, Königsberg, February 19, 1942: R22/3375; monthly report for December, 1941, by Regierungspräsident for Upper and Central Franconia: BHStA, Abt. II, MA 106679; monthly report for December, 1941, by Regierungspräsident for Swabia and Neuburg: MA 106684.
189. "Meldungen aus dem Reich," January 5, 22, 1942: Boberach, pp. 202, 212.

190. Geheime V.I., No. 336/41 of December 22, 1941: BA, ZSg 109/28, fol. 66. Cf. also ZSg 101/22, fol. 271 and "*Wollt ihr den totalen Krieg?*," p. 201.

191. All sources reported this skepticism; almost all commented on the belief in an interconnection between both events. Cf., for example, the report of Aussenstelle Oschatz to SD Leipzig section, December 29, 1941: *Aus deutschen Urkunden*, p. 253; monthly report for December, 1941, of the Regierungspräsident for Upper and Central Franconia: BHStA, Abt. II, MA 196679; monthly report of the Regierungspräsident for Swabia and Neuburg: MA 107684.

192. "Meldungen aus dem Reich," January 5, 1942: Boberach, p. 204.

193. Also dismissed were General Guderian (December 25) and General Hoepner (January 8).

194. "Meldungen aus dem Reich," January 22, 1942: Boberach, p. 212.

195. *Tagebücher*, p. 52.

196. Sicherheitsdienst des RFSS, SD Leipzig section, Aussenstelle Oschatz, December 29, 1941: *Aus deutschen Urkunden*, p. 253.

197. Boberach, p. 217.

198. Warlimont, *op. cit.*, p. 232, footnote 23.

199. *Vom anderen Deutschland* (Frankfurt/Main, 1964), pp. 212, 217. Cf. also O'Neill, *op. cit.*, p. 146.

200. "Meldungen aus dem Reich," January 5, 1942: Boberach, p. 206.

201. "Meldungen aus dem Reich," December 15, 1941: *ibid.*, p. 198.

202. *Ibid.*, p. 199.

203. "*Wollt ihr den den totalen Krieg?*," p. 198. See also teletype message HB2 107157 by OKW/WPr Ia to the propaganda section, Ostland, about military commander of Ostland, which included: "I. Responsibility for the outbreak of war lies solely with the old warmonger Roosevelt. . . .": MGFA, WO1-6/344.

204. V.I. No. 322/41 (December 8, 1940): BA, ZSg 109/28, fol. 19; and fol. 22, 33, 37; 109/30, fol. 30, 87; 109/33, fol. 45; ZSg 101/22, fol. 234. Cf. also Party Chancellory instructions of the evening of December 11, 1942: No. 854 TP, BA, ZSg 101/22, fol. 229.

205. "Meldungen aus dem Reich," December 15, 1942: Boberach, p. 198.

206. Hillgruber, *Deutschlands Rolle in der Vorgeschichte der beiden Weltkriege*, p. 123. This farreaching plan was not plotted until it became evident that the war with Russia would not end as quickly as anticipated. On July 25, Hitler had still stated to Admiral Raeder that he had "reserved a sharp conflict against the USA as well" after the termination of the Eastern campaign. *Ibid.*, p. 121.

207. "*Wollt ihr den totalen Krieg?*," p. 200.

208. *Ibid.*, pp. 201-2.

209. *Tagebücher*, p. 46.

210. *Ibid.*, p. 47; "Meldungen aus dem Reich," January 22, 1942: Boberach, pp. 211-13. Cf. also SD-Hauptaussenstelle Erfurt, January 12, 1942: cited in Höhne, *op. cit.*, p. 391.

211. Boberach, p. 211.

212. *Tagebücher*, p. 47.

213. "Auszugsweise Abschrift aus dem Bericht des Major Oehmichen über den Frontbesuch der 4. Armee vom 9. bis 24.2.1942:" MGFA, WO1-6/326.

214. *Tagebücher*, p. 128.

215. Copy in Party Chancellory: "Vertrauliche Informationen," Folge 20, March 11, 1942, Beitrag 258. Feldpostbriefe: BA, ZSG 3/1622.
216. "Meldungen aus dem Reich," February 19, 1942: Boberach, p. 226.
217. *Ibid.*, p. 229.
218. *Tagebücher*, pp. 45, 49.
219. Cf. *Tagebücher*, p. 55; and *"Wollt ihr den totalen Krieg?,"* p. 212.
220. *"Wollt ihr den totalen Krieg?,"* p. 211.
221. *Tagebücher*, p. 80 (February 11, 1942). Cf. also V.I. in Party Chancellory, Folge 20 (March 11, 1942), Beitrag 260: "Kampf dem Gerücht," BA, ZSg 3/1622.
222. OKW, Az ln AWA/J (Ia), Berlin, March 2, 1942, concerning cooperation between Wehrmacht and NSDAP: BA, NS 6/vorl. 337.
223. OKH, PA(2) Ia Az.21 No. 6290/42g H.Q., June 1, 1942: BA, Slg. Schumacher/367.
224. OKH, No. 6350/42g PA2 (Ib/Ia), Berlin, May 31, 1942: BA, NS6/vorl. 339, fol. 12426-12427. Cf. also No. 6660/429 Az14 PA 2(Ia), H. Qu. June 11, 1942: *ibid*, fol. 12409-12411.
225. April 10, 1942: BHStA, Abt. II, MA 106684.
226. "Meldungen aus dem Reich," February 23, 1942, "Zur Lage im Schrifttum:" BA, R58/169.
227. This is the exact title of the addendum. *Ibid.*
228. SD Leipzig section, June 24, 1942: IWM FD332/46.
229. April 21, 1942. Goebbels mentioned Bormann's intention concerning such a decree as early as February 22, but was quite skeptical about its success. *Tagebücher*, p. 98. Cf. also Boberach, p. 251.
230. Sefton Delmer, *Die Deutschen und ich* (Hamburg, 1962), pp. 474 ff.
231. SD Leipzig section, May 6, 1942: *Aus deutschen Urkunden*, p. 254.
232. Public prosecutor general, Cologne, February 4, 1942: BA, R22/3374.
233. Numerous NSV officers had, for example, taken foodstuffs and textiles after the massive air attack on Rostock which they sold illegally. Cf. BA, NS19/252 F48. Cf. also SD Leipzig section report, July, 1942: *Aus deutschen Urkunden*, pp. 258-59, about the splendid life style of leading individuals. Speer, *op. cit.*, pp. 231, 546 footnote 6.
234. Domarus, II, 2. Halbband, p. 1826-34.
235. January 31, 1942: *Tagebücher*, p. 67.
236. "Meldungen aus dem Reich," February 2, 1942: Boberach, pp. 218-19.
237. "Meldungen aus dem Reich," February 16, 1942: BA, R58/169.
238. Domarus, II, 2. Halbband, pp. 1848-52.
239. *Ibid.*, p. 1850.
240. "Meldungen aus dem Reich," March 19, 1942: Boberach, p. 239.
241. *"Wollt ihr den totalen Krieg?,"* p. 213.
242. *Tagebücher*, p. 68.
243. *Ibid.*, pp. 78, 79.
244. "Meldungen aus dem Reich," March 2, 1942: Boberach, p. 228; cf. also pp. 230; 231.
245. *Tagebücher*, p. 83.
246. "Meldungen aus dem Reich," March 22, 1942: Boberach, pp. 244, 245.
247. *Ibid.*, pp. 242-43.
248. See page 16.
249. *Tagebücher*, p. 140. Reports of Reich propaganda offices are only available

from March 15, 1943 on, in the Bundesarchiv. See bibliography. It is not impossible that earlier reports are located in East German archives.

250. "Meldungen aus dem Reich," April 20, 1942: Boberach, pp. 253, 254.
251. April 8, 1942: IWM FD332/46.
252. Cf. "Meldungen aus dem Reich," April 2, 20, 1942: Boberach, pp. 252, 255.
253. Picker, *op. cit.*, p. 22.
254. *Tagebücher*, p. 151.
255. Cf. "Meldungen aus dem Reich," July 30, 1942: Boberach, p. 273.
256. *Tagebücher*, p. 124 (March 19, 1942).
257. "Meldungen aus dem Reich," March 26, 1942: Boberach, pp. 246-50.
258. Letter of Paul Neukirchen of October 19, 1969. Albert Speer was also informed accordingly by Ohlendorf. (Information given the author).
259. Picker, *op. cit.*, pp. 222-25.
260. "Meldungen aus dem Reich," April 2, 1942: Boberach, pp. 250-51.
261. Domarus, II, 2. Halbband, pp. 1865-76.
262. RGBl. I, p. 247.
263. "Meldungen aus dem Reich," April 27, 1942: Boberach, p. 259.
264. "Meldungen aus dem Reich," SD Leipzig section, April 27, 1942: IWM FD 332/46.
265. "Meldungen aus dem Reich," April 30, 1942: BA, R58/171. Cf. also Hanseatic OLG-president, May 11, 1942: R22/3366; public prosecutor general, Naumburg (Saale), May 24, 1942: R22/3380; public prosecutor general, Brunswick, May 31, 1942 (signed by chief district attorney): R22/3357; public prosecutor general, Darmstadt, June 6, 1942: R22/3361; public prosecutor general, Celle, May 31, 1942: R22/3359.
266. "Meldungen aus dem Reich," October 6, 1942: BA, R22/3355.
267. "Meldungen aus dem Reich," April 30, 1942: BA, R58/171. Cf. also OLG-president, Königsberg, June 29, 1942: R22/3375; OLG-president, Hamm, July 7, 1942: R22/3367.
268. OLG-president, Cologne, July 2, 1942: BA, R22/3374 and OLG-president, Kiel, July 18, 1942: R22/3373.
269. *Tagebücher*, p. 199 (May 13, 1942).
270. Rundschreiben No. 131/42 by head of the Party Chancellory, August 27, 1942: BA, NS6/vorl. 38, fol. 11899-11901.
271. Cf. analysis of OLG-president, Karlsruhe, December 3, 1942: BA, R22/3370. In the margin of further critical comments about "the guidance of criminal law," Thierack wrote "completely misunderstood."
272. Cf. Ohlendorf's reminder to his staff: "Aus dem Stenogramm der Ansprache von Amtschef III am 31. 10. 44" (handwritten): BA, R58/990.
273. Cf. Diehl-Thiele, *Partei und Staat im Dritten Reich*.
274. Rundschreiben No. 121/42 of August 7, 1942, about separation of leadership of Party and state offices. BA, NS6/vorl. 338, fol. 11779-11783.
275. Typical is the remark in the war diary of the SA troop 33/5, Bamberg (August 21, 1942) which makes repeated reference to the hostility of farmers: "Blatantly the German farmer opposes the Third Reich and does the exact opposite. . . . Yes, yes, the farmer is reactionary. We have to enlighten him. . . ." StA Bamberg, Rep. M31, No. 11, fol. 91.
276. Picker, *op. cit.*, p. 171.
277. *Wollt ihr den totalen Krieg?*, pp. 220, 228; "Meldungen aus dem Reich," May 28, 1942: BA, R58/172.

278. SD Leipzig section, May 6, 1942: *Aus deutschen Urkunden*, p. 225; "Meldungen aus dem Reich," February 4, 1942: Boberach, p. 262.

279. SD report, March 30, 1942: BA. R58/170.

280. "Meldungen aus dem Reich," Boberach, p. 232, footnote 1.

281. "Meldungen aus dem Reich," March 22, April 6, 1942: BA, R58/171. Cf. also Boberach, pp. 235, 236; *Tagebücher*, pp. 141, 138, (March 26, 1942); "Meldungen aus dem Reich," July 6, 1942: R58/173, August 24, 2942: R58/174, August 31, 1942: R58/174; Delmer, op. cit., pp. 474.

282. "Meldungen aus dem Reich," July 23, 1942: Boberach, p. 272; Friedrich Percival Reck-Malleczwen, *Tagebuch eines Verzweifelten*. Zeugnis einer inneren Emigration (Stuttgart, 1966), p. 154; SD Leipzig section, April 8, 1942: IWM FD 332/46.

283. "The Führer has decided not to employ women directly in the production process. Instead they should bear children." Economic conference of November 19, 1942, lecture by Sauckel: BA, ZSg 115/1942. Göring used the analogy of "thoroughbreds and work horses." Highly valued women should concern themselves primarily with "the preservation of the species." Cf. Correspondence of Chef des SS-Hauptamtes Berger, CdSS HA/Be/Bo/T66. No. 150/42, of April 2, 1942: BA, NS19/neu 1963. Cf. also Speer, *op. cit.*, pp. 234-35, 547-48, footnotes 11, 14, 15.

284. *Tagebücher*, pp. 48, 150. Cf. also the letter by the Reich Finance Minister to Göring on March 4, 1942: BA, R2/24243.

285. "Meldungen aus dem Reich," June 22, 1942: Boberach, p. 262.

286. Oberkommando der Kriegsmarine M I Pa B. No. 10641/41 of October 4, 1941: MGFA WO1-6/395.

287. For details of the U-boat warfare, see Jürgen Rohwer, *Die U-Boot-Erfolge der Achsenmächte 1939-1945* (Munich, 1968) and Bodo Herzog, *60 Jahre deutsche U-Boote, 1906-1966* (Munich, 1968).

288. "Meldungen aus dem Reich": February 19, March 2, 19, July 9, August 17, 1942: Boberach, pp. 227-29, 241, 268, 284.

289. "Meldungen aus dem Reich," April 23, 1942: BA, R58/171.

290. "Meldungen aus dem Reich," September 10, 1942: Boberach, p. 298. The most successful month during World War II was November, 1942, in which 118 trading vessels were sunk with total tonnage of 743,321.

291. SD Leipzig section, May 23, 1942: *Aus deutschen Urkunden*, p. 225.

292. Monthly report for May, 1942, by the Regierungspräsident for Upper and Central Franconia: BHStA, Abt. II, MA 106679; "Meldungen aus dem Reich," July 30, 1942: Boberach, p. 274.

293. "Meldungen aus dem Reich," June 22, 1942: BA, R58/172; similar tendencies are also in the reports of June 29 and July 9, 1942: Boberach, pp. 264-67.

294. Sent by OLG-president, Königsberg, on January 5, 1942: BA, R22/3375.

295. January 27, 1942: BA, R22/3380.

296. RSHA Amt IV. "Meldung wichtiger staatspolizeilicher Ereignisse," No. 10 of June 22, 1942: BA, R58/205. Cf. also No. 11 of June 24, 1942: *ibid*; No. 1 of July 1, 1942: R58/206.

297. "Meldungen wichtiger staatspolizeilicher Ereignisse," No. 4 of July 8, 1942: R58/206; No. 2, October 6, 1942: R58/208; No. 5, December 15, 1942: *ibid*. Cf. also Gilles Perrault, *L'orchestre rouge* (Paris, 1968); Fabian Schlabrendorff, *Offiziere gegen Hitler* (Zurich, 1951), pp. 97 ff.

298. Berghahn, "NSDAP und 'geistige Führung' der Wehrmacht 1939-1943," p. 47.
299. Blatt 2 of V.I. No. 177/42: BA, ZSg 109/35, fol. 31.
300. Sonderdienst der Reichspropagandaleitung. Sonderlieferung 28/42 of July 18, 1942: BA, ZSg 3/1671.
301. *"Wollt ihr den totalen Krieg?"*, p. 261.
302. Report of August 17, 1942: Boberach, pp. 286-89.
303. Contacts intensified with time and came to an exchange of opinions between German and Soviet miners about working conditions. The comparison did not always favor Germany, which troubled Goebbels immensely. *"Wollt ihr den totalen Krieg?"*, p. 281 (conference of September 16, 1942).
304. *Ibid.*, p. 266.
305. This is the story by regimental commissar Josef Kerness, who ran across German troops on June 18, 1942 at Kharkov. Cf. *Kriegstagebuch des Oberkommandos der Wehrmacht* (Wehrmachtführungsstab) 1944-1945, kept by Helmut Greiner and Percy Ernst Schramm (Frankfurt/Main, 1961), II, pp. 1287 f.
306. "Meldungen aus dem Reich," August 13, 17, 20: Boberach, p. 284; *"Wollt ihr den totalen Krieg?"*, pp. 294, 298.
307. "Meldungen aus dem Reich," April 2, 1942: Boberach, p. 252.
308. "Meldungen aus dem Reich," April 20, 1942: *ibid.*, p. 256.
309. "Meldungen aus dem Reich," July 30, 1942: *ibid.*, p. 276.
310. "Meldungen aus dem Reich," October 22, 1942: *ibid.*, p. 315.
311. Cf. *"Wollt ihr den totalen Krieg?"*, pp. 289, 291.
312. "Meldungen aus dem Reich," April 20, 1942: Boberach, p. 253.
313. *"Wollt ihr den totalen Krieg?"*, pp. 232, 240, 262, 267.
314. "Meldungen aus dem Reich," November 12, 1942: Boberach, pp. 316-17.
315. "Meldungen aus dem Reich," November 19, 1942: *ibid.*, p. 322.
316. *"Wollt ihr den totalen Krieg?"*, p. 276.
317. Boberach, p. 323.
318. "Meldungen aus dem Reich," November 12, 1942: *ibid.*, p. 317.
319. "Meldungen aus dem Reich," November 19, 1942: *ibid.*, pp. 320, cf. 323.
320. Public prosecutor general, Naumburg, January 27, 1942: BA, R22/3380.
321. Hanseatic OLG-president, March 12, 1942: BA, R22/3366.
322. "Meldungen aus dem Reich," August 6, 1942, "Die Sicht Japans in der Bevölkerung": *ibid.*, pp. 278-83.
323. "Meldungen aus dem Reich," June 22, 1942: BA, R58/172.
324. "Meldungen aus dem Reich," July 30, 1942: Boberach, p. 273.
325. *"Wollt ihr den totalen Krieg?"*, pp. 271, 273.
326. BA, R58/174.
327. V.I. No. 221/42 of August 28, 1942: Tagesparole des Reichspressechefs. BA, ZSg 109/36, fol. 91. Cf. also V.I. No. 226/42, of September 2, 1942: Tagesparole des Reichspressechefs. BA, ZSg 109/37, fol. 7. At the end of November, Goebbels began anew a heavily prepared propaganda campaign, "that we did not want this war and did not start it"; Churchill "started it." *"Wollt ihr den totalen Krieg?"*, p. 307.
328. "Meldungen aus dem Reich," September 3, 1942: Boberach, pp. 295, 296. Cf. also diary entry for SA troop 33/5, Bamberg, of September 27, 1942, which talks about a general war weariness making itself widely felt. StA Bamberg, Rep. M31, No. 11, fol. 95.

329. V.I. No. 108/42 of August 13, 1942: BA, ZSg 109/36, fol. 42. Cf. also, *"Wollt ihr den totalen Krieg?"*, p. 270.
330. See, for example, "Meldungen aus dem Reich," July 30, 1942: Boberach, p. 227; or "Kriegschronik des Kreises Duisburg der NSDAP," Monthly report for July 1942: BA, NS Misch/1866.
331. Goebbels placed the number of civilian deaths on October 2, 1942, at 10,900. *"Wollt ihr den totalen Krieg?"*, p. 287.
332. General Paulus on August 19 issued the order for the attack on Stalingrad. The Sixth Army then crossed the Don on August 21 and reached the Volga north of Stalingrad on the twenty-third.
333. BA, R58/174.
334. "Meldungen aus dem Reich," September 3, 10, 28, 1942: Boberach, pp. 297, 300.
335. "Meldungen aus dem Reich," October 5, 1942: Boberach, p. 304.
336. On September 30, 1942. Domarus, II, 2. Halbband, pp. 1912-24.
337. "Meldungen aus dem Reich," October 8, 1942: Boberach, pp. 306-09.
338. The increase in food rations at the beginning of the fourth war year was only possible because of a massive exploitation of occupied areas. Increases were: fifty grams of meat per week, bread rations back to pre-April 6 levels of 2,250 grams per week. Cf. Göring's discussion with the Reich Commissars for the occupied territories and the military commanders about the food situation on August 6, 1942: Poliakov-Wulf, *Das Dritte Reich und seine Denker*, pp. 471 ff.
339. "Meldungen aus dem Reich," October 22, 1942: *ibid.*, p. 315.
340. *Ibid.*, p. 314.
341. Reference is to Hitler's speech at the Munich Beer Hall on November 8, in which he had said that he would not allow Stalingrad to become a second Verdun. The Germany of 1918 had laid down its arms at a quarter to twelve; he would only stop five minutes after twelve. Domarus, II, 2. Halbband, p. 1935. For the report of the mood, see "Meldungen aus dem Reich," November 12, 1942: Boberach, p. 318.
342. "Meldungen aus dem Reich," November 26, 1942: *ibid.*, pp. 323-26. Cf. also "Meldungen," December 3, which refer again to public anxiety: BA, R58/178.
343. "Meldungen aus dem Reich," December 29, 1942: Boberach, p. 329.
344. Cf., for example, *Widerstand an Rhein und Ruhr*.
345. See a typical report from Kreisleitung Schlüchtern, Gau Hesse-Nassau, of December 16, 1942: BA, NS Misch/1641. "Naturally, as elsewhere, there are a few types who, we know, inwardly reject the present regime and are always ready to lend an ear to enemy news swindels. Such swine are despised by the whole population except for pastors and their close friends. . . ."
346. Anordnung A91/42 by head of the Party Chancellory: BA, NS6/vorl. 338. Originally intended as No. 198/42 from the Führer's headquarters. Copy by the Chef des SS-Hauptamtes Gottlob Berger on January 18, 1942, with Verteiler IV. BA EAP-2050-a/1. Reich propaganda offices also received the circular. Propa 2061/27.2.42.23.2.3, BA, R55/603, fol. 186.

III. TOTAL WAR

All-out effort for victory.
Joseph Goebbels

1. DEFEATS: STALINGRAD AND TUNISIA
(JANUARY TO JUNE, 1943)

THE SIXTH ARMY under General Paulus and the Fourth Army under General Hoth penetrated Stalingrad between the first and fifteenth of September, 1942; from then until the middle of November a bitter house-to-house battle ensued. General Paulus and later the new Army Chief of Staff, General Zeitzler, recommended suspending the attack, but Hitler was determined to take Stalingrad at any cost. Supposedly the vital oil fields of Maikop and Grozny were at stake; "without them," Hitler had told Paulus before the summer offensive of 1942, "I would have to liquidate this war."[1] But in fact it was a matter of prestige, since this objective had already been attained when German troops reached the Volga and cut off river traffic. Nevertheless, Hitler repeated his position in his Munich Beer Hall speech on November 8, also stressing Stalingrad's significance as a grain transportation center.[2]

Stalin placed the same importance on the city and formed three new army groups from reserves in the area: the "Stalingrad front" south of the city under General Jeromenko, the southwest "Don front" under General Rokossovsky, and the adjoining western army forming the "Southwest front" along the Don under General Watutin. The Russian counteroffensive began on November 19, breaking though the Sixth Army's left flank, which was held by Italian and Hungarian forces. By the twenty-second most of the Sixth Army and segments of allied troops, totalling about 250,000 men, were encircled.[3]

While Paulus wanted to attempt a break-through toward the southwest, Hitler, after slight hesitation, issued the command for the Sixth Army to hold out in Stalingrad. Hitler's decision was influenced signif-

184

icantly by Göring's assurance that he could supply the encircled troops by air. Hitler furthermore hoped that Field Marshal Erich von Manstein, with Army Group Don, would succeed in "bringing enemy attacks to a halt and recapturing positions held prior to the attack."[4] Delays in raising new troops, strong Russian counterattacks, and fuel shortages frustrated all efforts. On December 25, the fate of the Sixth Army and accompanying units was essentially sealed and the last struggle began. If, aside from motives of prestige and Hitler's increasingly inflexible strategy of holding firm, we seek any military sense in this episode, one blown to epic proportions by Nazi propaganda, it is perhaps to be found in the ability of this Stalingrad pocket to tie down large enemy forces and thus contribute to saving parts of the southern German front as well as facilitating the necessary retreat of the army group from the Caucasus. But, as we shall see, Stalingrad was to serve another function.

The last Soviet attack began on January 10 under the direction of Marshal Voronov. On January 25 the remaining forces in this totally destroyed city were split into two pockets. Paulus surrendered on the thirty-first, the day after being promoted to Field Marshal. In vain he had sought Hitler's authorization to capitulate. The northern pocket surrendered on February 2. About 42,000 wounded soldiers and specialists could still be flown out; about 100,000 died, and about 90,000 were captured, of whom only a few thousand survived.[5]

The German propaganda machine began as early as January 23 to twist these events to its purposes. The Reich Press Chief's daily slogan proclaimed: "1. In connection with the immediately forthcoming cumpulsory labor service for women and other sweeping organizational policies for the conduct of total war, the great and stirring heroic sacrifice of *German troops encircled in Stalingrad* will become, for the German nation, the moral driving force for a truly heroic stand by the German people and the beginning of a new phase of the German will to victory and marshalling of all resources. . . ."[6]

On Hitler's instructions, Goebbels intended to take advantage of the Stalingrad catastrophe "to psychologically fortify our people."[7] Every word about this heroic struggle, so he thought, had to become part of history. The OKW report should "be so worded as to move hearts for centuries to come." As examples he suggested Caesar's speeches, Frederick the Great's appeal to his generals before the battle of Leuthen, and Napoleon's call to his Guard. "These few phrases about the epic song of Stalingrad must be unpretentious, clear, and simple as if chiseled in rock." The heroic was to be featured, the horrors and despair moderated.[8] Paulus' capture could not be mentioned by the German press.[9] Following the announced end of the battles on February 3, there was a three-day national commemoration; all theaters, cinemas, and entertainment spots were closed. Hitler ordered preparation of a commemorative book to be composed in part of confiscated and copied mail from Stalingrad soldiers.[10]

Local Party groups were instructed to collect such letters and forward them to district offices.[11] But the result, it seems, failed to satisfy expectations, and Goebbels apparently declared it as "intolerable for the German people."[12] Evidently only 2.1 per cent of those letters analyzed by the army information bureau proved positive, 4.4 per cent were doubtful, 57.1 per cent completely critical, 3.4 per cent in opposition, and 33 per cent without opinion.[13] A small selection of these letters was published. They are evidence of the deepest human despair and abandonment, devoid of any of the pathos normally confronted quite often in this war—well within the tradition of German idealism.[14] "We are told our struggle is for Germany, but there are few here who believe that this senseless sacrifice can be of value to our homeland."[15] "We are completely alone, without outside help. Hitler has left us in the lurch. . . ."[16] "If what we were promised is false, then Germany is lost because in that case no one's word can be trusted. Oh, this doubt, this terrible doubt, if it could only be lifted soon!"[17]

For Germans at home doubts also began to creep in more and more. Gradually they became more piercing, more urgent, as the level of consciousness was raised from a latent state. The common phrase of the previous fall about a turning-point of the war re-emerged, and there was talk of this as the beginning of the end.[18] The "new formulation"[19] of military reports, such as "flexible defense and well planned evacuation,"[20] caused alarm. Many believed that "a low point in this war" had been reached. Nevertheless, the immediate reaction to the bad news from Stalingrad was quite calm—or was it more numb? The SD report claimed that there was no question of a mood of despair; on the contrary, "the situation in a broad segment of the working population is quite favorable for a turn toward a total war effort in all spheres of life. . . ."[21]

This observation and assessment was either the answer to a probe ordered from the top or—and this seems just as plausible given the preparation of SD reports—the result of knowledge about decrees prepared in the meantime for a far-reaching incorporation of all available national resources. The "Meldungen aus dem Reich" added that the public expected Hitler to announce appropriate policies in a speech marking the tenth anniversary of the accession to power. Germans, however, "oppose larger festivities, particularly in view of the situation of Stalingrad's defenders." But Hitler did not speak personally on January 30. His silence befitted the pose of a solitary[22] "great king," surrounded by trag-edy. The Reich Propaganda Office issued Goebbels' interpretation of the figure of Hitler and events at Stalingrad, evoking images of the *Nibelun-gen*.[23] As symptomatic of its self-image, the Nazi elite compared this stage of the war with the crucial period of Frederick the Great, when the situation, far more catastrophic than Stalingrad, nevertheless ended victoriously.

Was it in keeping with this symbolism that Hitler abandoned the title of Reich Chancellor sometime during 1943 and now merely signed laws and decrees as "The Führer" instead of "The Führer and Reich Chan-cellor"? In any case, from his secluded heights Hitler turned directly to his people less and less often. His proclamation of January 30 was read by Goebbels and contained no reference to stronger measures. In his speech, however, Goebbels dealt exhaustively with regulations and de-crees for total war mobilization.[24] Propaganda for the total war com-menced on January 4. In his ministerial conference,[25] Goebbels spoke not only of his "propaganda for total war" but also of the need to pro-ceed to "total warfare" now that the difficulties were so great. It was thus necessary "to enunciate a few firm principles routinely and continuously at every opportunity and to drum them into the minds of the people." These principles, which he compared to the leitmotifs of Wagnerian operas, were to ring out in all possible variations. Most important of these were: "1) The war was forced on the German people; 2) This war is a matter of life and death; 3) We are dealing with total warfare."

Only the last of these basic phrases presented something new. The first leitmotif was reminiscent of the first days of the war, the second began with the Russian campaign, and reflected Hitler's pseudo-Darwin-ian interpretation of the life struggle. The new battle-cry, an exaggerated amplification of the second, was now to serve as license for the introduc-tion of all kinds of domestic and foreign policies. The guiding principles signaled the escalation of the war from a local struggle, which had been both desired and provoked—a theme now quietly ignored—to a great battle for existence and ultimately a brutal war of self-assertion [*Behauptungs-kampf*]. The proclamation of total war was not a consequence of the Allied statement on "unconditional surrender" of January 24, 1943, and had been prepared well prior to the latter. Total war—that is, the mobiliza-tion of all resources, economic,[26] military, psychological and human—had long been demanded or anticipated by Goebbels, by certain elements within the armed forces, by Albert Speer, who had been named Arma-ments Minister on February 9, 1942, and by a large majority of the working population. Hitler did not opt for this course until his Blitzkrieg strategy had long proven untenable and he began to realize that the fortunes of war now favored the other side.[27] At the previously mentioned ministerial conference, Goebbels had addressed himself for the first time to those who dismissed the idea of military defeat and suggested that the war might indeed be lost if all resources were not mobilized. A committee composed of Bormann, Lammers, and Goebbels was set to work on the necessary plans which projected an additional call-up of a million soldiers to the front, the closing of numerous shops and luxury establishments, and the introduction of compulsory labor.[28] The first result of this effort appeared on January 13 in the form of a decree by the Führer "about the full employment of men and women for the task of Reich defense." It began with the words: "Total war presents us with duties which have to be mastered immediately in the interests of as early a victorious peace as possible. . . ."[29] A release of manpower for the military and the armaments industry was scheduled; vacated positions were to be filled by individuals from less vital sectors of the economy. The Chief of the OKW was to check all indispensable positions and terminate all preparations and planning for future peacetime programs. All men from ages sixteen to sixty-five and all women ages seventeen to fifty had to report for labor allocation. A profusion of regulations[30] for the implementation of this total mobilization followed. On January 17, *Das Reich* carried an explanatory article by Goebbels called "Total War," which was welcomed by large segments of society: "We promise whole-heartedly to the working population, especially mobilized women, that sponging loafers who don't want to relinquish any of their peacetime comforts, despite the war, will be 'pressed hard.' But it will hardly suffice to brand 'outsiders of the nation' with words. Gentle exhortation and contempt will accomplish nothing. . . ."[31] Many of those who were willing to make sacrifices either felt these measures were late in coming or questioned the feasibility of coordinating such a complex society with dispatch and vigor. The premier concern was whether the burden of war would now really be distributed equitably.[32] The wording of the regulation of January 27[33] was considered "weak" and "inconsequential," and most continued to wait in suspense for the introduction of these policies to see whether they would embrace members of the upper classes. Skepticism was reportedly high, and there were numerous accounts of exceptions and violations—that the "prominent people" were avoiding them somehow.[34] "Executions of these measures without loopholes is seen by a large percentage of the population as a direct criterion for the existence of a real *Volksgemeinschaft* and for the leadership's determination to put into practice indiscriminate mobilization for all. . . ."

Thus it was primarily the working population and especially its radical elements who demanded and welcomed total mobilization. Most of all, however, mobilization stirred those women not previously integrated into the work process. The egalitarian struggle for equality, based largely on envy tinged by a spirit of class-struggle, accounted for the opinion of the lower strata. Joseph Goebbels loved to hear such notes: "The Minister will see to it that daughters of plutocrats cannot shirk this obligation. . . ."[35]

On February 18 he gave his famous speech in the Berlin Sportpalast, presenting the audience with ten leading questions including whether the public believed in final victory, whether it would endure all hardships until then, accept the mobilization of all women and the death penalty for shirkers and profiteers, in short whether it wanted a total war. It was a masterpiece of demagogery, prepared to the last detail, based on analyses of opinion surveys, and deliberately manipulating radical currents. Particularly reliable Party members were brought to Berlin and drilled for the mass spectacle.[36]

The initial impact of the speech was, according to an SD report, "unusually great and generally very favorable."[37] In the last analysis, however, its reception was uneven, as indicated by other observations. Results of opinion research pointed to a positive reaction on the part of the broad masses of employees as well as "devoted" Nazi followers. It did, however, bewilder timid souls because of its ruthless hardness.[38] Obviously the most impressive fact for many was "that the leadership was precisely informed about the true mood of the people."[39] But the more removed people became from the speech, the more subtle the evaluations. Among the civil service and upper classes there was criticism of its "class-struggle" tendency. In northern Germany, especially in Pomerania but also in northern Westphalia, the speech was dismissed as pure propaganda and "theatrics." Swabians above all resented presentation of the answers to the ten questions as a plebiscite; in Saxony they thought "that probably no one dared to disagree even if he was of a different opinion."[40]

These and similar critical remarks deeply offended the vain Propaganda Minister whom Hitler had just praised for his handling of public opinion at this crucial moment.[41] On February 27, therefore, the Propaganda Ministry, basing its position on Bormann's letter of December 18,[42] and interested in results, not reports of public disgruntlement, demanded harsher counter-measures for dealing with discontent, including the use of corporal punishment for hostile students. Digressing briefly to the question occasionally raised, as to whether supposedly objective television reporting would have damaged the regime, one should not forget that Goebbels and Hitler were masters of the art of manipulation. Hitler's conscious poses for pictures and his hypnotic qualities exercised in personal interviews and at mass meetings could just as easily have been utilized on the screen. An SD report confirms this thesis in its comment on the tremendous impact of Goebbels' speech on theater newsreel audiences captivated by the charged atmosphere at the Sportpalast.[43] In his ministerial conference of February 26, Goebbels announced that he had received a flood of mail in response to his speech. Ninety per cent demanded more radical measures. Included were a few insulting letters "which were obviously written by Jews."[44] This comment reconfirms the Propaganda Minister's inability to handle criticism, shifting the blame onto the Jews instead.

The defeat at Stalingrad was thus to be used in recapturing public opinion, which had slipped from the regime's control, and in diverting attention from the Reich's increasingly dangerous foreign situation by exploiting widespread working class resentment of continued evidence of class distinctions. With a steady flow of opinion reports, the Nazi leadership was well informed on the ever increasing centrifugal currents within public opinion away from the manipulated mainstream. On January 18, 1943, SD reports had confirmed a growing independence in the formation of public opinion. Few Germans were satisfied with official information; as previously mentioned, they had learned to interpret every nuance and to read between the lines. Still the most reliable sources were army mail and stories from soldiers on leave from the front. Independent thoughts and news gained from foreign broadcasts added to the growing uncertainty in public opinion and the increasingly irregular mood.[46] At the same time, fear for the fate of relatives created a much more far-reaching anxiety; the opinion was voiced more frequently that time was working in favor of the enemy. The Western Allies had every opportunity to mass men and materiel at their leisure.[47] The main topic of discussion was the war's duration. "Today the question is no longer one of how long victory will take but of how long we can last with any chance for a favorable termination of the war. A third Russian winter under conditions similar to the first two, especially in view of the enemy's fighting strength, is unthinkable. The war in the East must be decided this summer. . . ."[48]

Thus, while a part of the population viewed the decision in the East as being decisive, another part parroted the proposed thesis that this conflict could only be understood—in terms of Hitler's reasoning of 1940-41—as a stage preceding the conflict with the West.[49] Such remarks, however, only aroused more anxieties among the better informed. There was little reason for an optimistic assessment of the situation. "Presently only faith in the still untapped but certainly also the last reserves and the justness of fate can provide the basis for our will to endure and our hopes for victory."[50] Yet opinions were voiced drawing comparisons with 1918.[51] The very serious tone of propaganda and newspapers only deepened the depression. A frank assessment from Gau East-Hanover read: "Plain, unadorned press coverage and propaganda have produced extremely serious alarm among the populace. The public observes with a certain bitterness the great contrast between former and present reporting. They reproach newspapers and propaganda as well for having underestimated the opponent in the East; a completely false picture was painted of his strength and armaments potential. Now we have gone to the other extreme and are painting everything black, causing a considerable crisis of confidence in regard to press and propaganda. In view of this exceedingly sombre reporting, the danger exists that out of this crisis of confidence may develop a far more serious crisis of military and political leadership. . . ."[52]

In order to satisfy the demands of Party and state leaders to emphasize the people's firm attitude instead of the fluctuating mood, public opinion reports were now frequently introduced with observations that were later chastized as lies in the course of the ensuing detailed presentation. For example, one began as follows: "What has proven more decisive than the mood is again, especially in the last weeks, the attitude of the population, which as usual is sustained by trust in the Führer and faith in final victory. . . ."[53] A few pages later, however, we read that "in certain circles" criticism had emerged with increasing force. In particular, Hitler, at whom more direct aim was now being taken, was blamed for having promised too much. There were bitter comments regarding his words that no power on earth could dislodge the Germans from Stalingrad or the Volga. General Halder's dismissal was attributed to his opposition to a simultaneous attack on Stalingrad and the Caucasus; others failed to see how the military leadership could have overlooked Soviet offensive power. The Gau administration for Westphalia-South reported "that in trains the Führer was being called the mass murderer of Stalingrad without the perpetrator being arrested or soundly thrashed. There were also comments blaming Party leaders for the war and its concomitant misery. Talk is also going around, reportedly from officers, that Brauchitsch had to go last winter, but that as this time the Führer was responsible, who goes now? Unfortunately such baseness does not immediately meet with the requisite massive reply. It shows how bourgeois and soft large elements within the Party membership are. . . ." Do comments such as these suggest that elements within the military, even within the Party itself, were no longer completely trustworthy from the Nazi elite's point of view?

For the great majority of front-line soldiers, particularly those in the

East, this did not apply.[54] Hitler's strategic inflexibility, his holding firm at any price, the winter crisis of 1941-42, and now the catastrophe at Stalingrad had awakened the desire in many a high-ranking military commander—and not only in the East—for the creation of a unified armed forces command or at least a supreme commander for the East, since Hitler would not relinquish the overall supreme command of the army anyway. Field Marshal von Manstein had suggested this to Hitler on February 6; Field Marshal Milch, General Guderian, and General Zeitzler sought to achieve a similar solution—naturally all in vain. These efforts and even some sharp criticism of Hitler did not by any means represent disloyalty or even opposition, but rather merely an attempt to avoid future military miscalculations. Only a very small group of younger officers around the first general staff officer for Army Group Center, Colonel von Tresckow, decided to strike at the root of the evil and cooperated actively in a planned coup d'état to remove Hitler by assassination. The plan miscarried for technical reasons. Hitler emerged from his plane on March 13 unscathed.[55] If Henning von Tresckow and his friends had not dealt with the ever-vacillating Field Marshal von Kluge, and if they had not constantly been aware of the example of the front-line soldier, whose mood was by far the best and most confident, they might have looked for other contacts and intensified their assassination efforts. In their isolation, however, they knew nothing of the rapidly spreading defeatism during those months,[56] the mounting discontent toward the regime. In military areas behind the lines and in some of the occupied territories, the mood and attitude of soldiers and officers was often already fundamentally different from those at the front.[57] There were frequent indications of mounting tension between members of the armed forces and representatives of civilian authorities, most of whom had been made Party members. Reports arriving from all possible local Party groups and Gau administrations referred to complaints from soldiers on furlough.[58] They were bitter about the free and easy life of young Party functionaries, both at the front and in occupied regions, particularly in France, who were arrogant and corrupt and were having affairs with secretaries.[59]

Rumors and stories of intolerable conditions abounded. Talk was that military offices were overstaffed by up to 40 per cent with every ploy being used to resist cuts. Food and luxuries destined for the troops were intercepted and sent home to relatives.[60] Veritable dens of corruption were reported from some Gaus, and even Goebbels noted this fact in occupied areas.[61] Reserve army officers also reported the poor mood and a "defeatist attitude" to Party officials, but these were discounted as overly pessimistic—or merely too sober and realistic—and elicited bristling replies from incensed Nazis that they had misunderstood the "sensitivity of the situation."[62]

There was an increasing number of Gau reports about a "defeatist attitude and anti-Party mood spreading here and there in military circles. . . ." The mood in the barracks was not good, according to Gau Württemberg-Hohenzollern; veiled suggestions that the Führer lacked leadership qualities came from within officers circles.[63] Further confirmation of deteriorating relations between the Nazi state and segments of the officer corps comes from a string of commands, decrees, and exhortations aimed at intensifying ideological indoctrination.[64] Officers were reminded of their responsibility for proper behavior not only in front of the troops but also in public, where they were expected to serve as examples of confidence instead of contributing to lower morale during critical periods.

In this connection, we should mention a letter of February 10, 1943, from the Chief of the SS-Hauptamt, SS-Gruppenführer Gottlob Berger, to Himmler. Berger referred to the political indoctrination within the Red Army and suggested similar steps for the Waffen-SS: "I therefore request even more strongly, since we cannot wait until after the war and since we now have also received many young volunteers whose homes have failed miserably and whose relatives are often not attuned to National Socialism, that we now authorize and introduce with all available means the ideological and political education of the Waffen-SS as a part of the service schedule; furthermore [I suggest] that ideological education be assigned the place it should claim within the overall training." Enclosed was a draft decree, which was reformulated by Himmler and issued as an SS order on February 24, 1943, with emphasis on the personal example of troop commanders in addition to specialized instruction.[65]

Whereas Hitler had originally welcomed the lack of military involvement in politics, he now felt it necessary to promote "political officers" —in other words, actively committed National Socialist officers—based secretly on the Soviet example. In its *Mitteilungen für das Offizierskorps*, the OKW elaborated: "The driving force of the Bolsheviks is a political idea, that of a Marxist world revolution, which has to be opposed by an even stronger political dynamic of the German military. . . . Today the military and political demands placed on the Volk are one. It is impossible for the officer to think other than politically, thus also as a National Socialist. . . ."[66] The introduction at this time of specialists for military indoctrination mentioned in the introduction,[67] was the next step in the creation of a political officer corps whose "ideological training" Hitler had endeavored to hasten after assuming supreme command of the army.[68]

But not only the armed forces and the Waffen-SS were to be tied more closely to the Nazi state and activated in its interests. The NSDAP, the actual instrument for penetrating the people in all its classes and spheres, was also spurred on to greater activity—and was more strictly controlled. As early as November 22, 1942, copies of all speeches and addresses by Party officials were ordered in advance for Hitler's inspection.[69] Then, on May 19, 1943, a Führer's decree was issued "concerning the removal of men with international ties from important positions in the state, Party, and Wehrmacht." Family connections abroad, it stated, had proven harmful to the general welfare. Such individuals were therefore to be excluded from the start from promotions to vital posts: "1. If they are married to women from countries at war with us or politically hostile, or 2. if they belong to groups which may be regarded as international because of familial ties to presently or previously influential social or economic circles in hostile countries."[70] In the meantime, Bormann had elaborated on his letter of December 18, 1942, reminding all leading Party officials that "the time is past for teas, receptions, and gala dinners" for which the public no longer had any sympathy. "We have to expect that there will be more gossip about one night of carousing than a hundred nights of working. . . ."[71]

All these measures for the complete mobilization of the population, the efforts for an intensified indoctrination of the Wehrmacht and the Waffen-SS, the mobilization of the Party, are significant not only for their objective of welding a national body firmly together in the face of increasing foreign dangers and the mustering of all conceivable reserves. They are simultaneously a symptom of the further alienation of the Hitler regime from a great many Germans, promoted by an inner crisis within the Party. In his diary, Goebbels talks about prominent individuals from Party and state involved in profiteering, about "refractory Gauleiters" and a "leadership crisis."[72] Stalingrad not only symbolized a turning point in the military situation but also contributed to raising an existing subliminal process of alienation to the threshold of consciousness among wider circles and thus deepened the rift between the Nazi elite and its subjects.

The NSDAP and its representatives increasingly became targets of discontent. If all young people in reserved positions in industry, agriculture, and railways were already viewed with scorn and envy, accusations of shirking were hurled especially at men in Party uniforms who were serving in the homeland. "The latest measures regarding the change to total warfare have furthermore led to more vociferous public expressions of opinion *to the effect that no one has the right to be a political leader who has not also done his stint at the front and thus*

proven that he is prepared to give his health and life for National Socialist Germany. . . ." Women whose husbands had been killed or were at
the front were especially insistent on this point. When one political
leader of the NSDAP remarked to a woman who had parted with "Auf
Wiedersehen" that she had forgotten the greeting "Heil Hitler," he received in reply: "You, young man, have forgotten to relieve my aging
husband in Russia."[73]

This criticism initially still diffuse, began to concentrate noticeably
and ultimately turned not only against lower Party elements but against
the movement leaders as well. We have seen how jokes and rumors had
already become more malevolent and sharp in 1942. Now they become
downright hateful and—from the leadership's point of view—destructive.
According to reports from various Party officials, the old opposition was
rearing its head once more, even attacking the Führer himself.[74] Party
Chancellory reports compiled from Gau information leave no doubt that
Hitler's greatness and infallibility had suffered severely in the eyes of
many Germans. "Particularly dangerous is the fact that people now
even dare to criticize the person of the Führer openly and attack him in a
hateful and spiteful way."[75] Albert Speer, in his memoirs, recalls that
Goebbels spoke to him not of a "leadership crisis" but a "leader crisis."[76]

An example of the spiteful tone of jokes is contained in the following
story: "The Führer drove to the Tannenberg memorial and called out to
Hindenburg: 'Hindenburg, you great fighter, here stands a private at
the end of his tether!' "* Rumors of Hitler's insanity or nervous collapse
also refused to die.[77] Commentaries by the Party Chancellory on this
and much other gossip noted that it stemmed "without exception, unless taken from enemy broadcasts, from groups and elements within our
people, whose only goal remains the overthrow of the National Socialist
regime."[78] This last comment seems too extreme and fails to discount
sufficiently the significance of these jokes; Goebbels once described their
frequent function as a "faeces of the soul." In its "confidential information" of March 22, the Party Chancellory directed Gau offices to
combat enemy propaganda which was capitalizing on domestic unrest
with the tried methods of the Weimar days and to call on the Gestapo
and SD for support.[79]

The Führer's speech on Memorial Day—this time belatedly on March
21—worked as a momentary damper on rumors.[80] But like Goebbels'
speech of February 18 and the rousing mobilization appeal, Hitler's

---

* "Hindenburg, du grosser Streiter, hier steht ein Gefreiter und kann nicht
mehr weiter!"

exhortation had only a passing stimulating effect on the public mood. If there were signs here and there of a slight improvement in the mood, they rested on the ephemeral hope of a stabilization of the Eastern front[81] and a return of the initiative to German troops. It was true that the southern front had held, and that outwardly the winter campaign of 1942-43 had ended with a German victory when Kharkov was retaken on March 14 and Byelograd a week later. German troops stood approximately along the line where they had begun the 1942 summer offensive—only that one German and three allied armies, a total of fifty divisions, had been lost in the process. Additional losses totalled approximately twenty-five divisions, while a fundamental shift in power relationships was also underway. The Soviet armament industry, transferred behind the Urals, continuously produced new war materials: tank production alone reached about two thousand per month in 1943. By March, 159 German divisions were facing some six hundred Soviet divisions of comparable size. Army Group South, with thirty-two divisions, had to hold a 450-mile front and contain 341 Soviet divisions, a relationship of about one to seven, while Army Groups North and Center were at about a one to four disadvantage.[82]

When the Wehrmacht report announced on March 12, 1943, that Soviet hopes of recapturing the Ukraine had been frustrated and on March 14 that Kharkov had been retaken by German troops, many in Germany who had no real overview of actual losses again took heart: "The opinion now prevails widely that the reported tightening of the front is really based on an overall strategic plan and that thus there was no cause for alarm. . . ." This report therefore admits indirectly that the regime's attempts to disguise the failures had not worked.[83]

Short periods of buoyancy were triggered mostly by the confidence and attitude of the front-line soldiers.[84] They were the staunchest supporters of Hitler and the regime. Mobilization of officers and soldiers to raise the public mood, a step rejected by Goebbels during the first and second winters of war,[85] had long since been introduced. Numerous opinion probes had shown that objective and personal information found a far more favorable response than ringing propaganda slogans. Thus, for example, a campaign called "the front speaks to the homeland" was prepared in late summer of 1942, in close cooperation between military authorities in Gau Cologne-Aachen and the propaganda office; beginning on January 9, twelve non-commissioned and twenty-four commissioned officers spoke at five hundred gatherings attended by 245,846 persons. Similar ventures were undertaken in other regions with the cooperation of Party and OKW representatives and proved more successful than Goebbels' new hard line,[86] which appeared to be an obvious propaganda maneuver to mobilize women for labor service. "The large majority of citizens is clearly in favor of a manly and militaristic speech. There is generally little toleration for polemics with the enemy. At present anything that portrays the opposition as divided, weak, and ridiculous not only fails to be convincing, it also awakens a strong intuitive opposition and appropriate remarks by citizens."[87] Even the once popular newsreel had lost its attraction, "no longer a leading factor in influencing opinions and moods."[88]

Agitation and motivation of baser instincts by the Propaganda Minister were rejected not only by those critical or indifferent toward the regime but also by Party members. In a compendium of Gau reports, the Party Chancellory commented: "As already indicated in the last report, various press releases and remarks by leading Party members— in part also the sharp attacks on certain propertied elements by Pg. Dr. Goebbels—have aroused destructive individuals who are using this opportunity to vent their proletarian instincts and inject class-struggle tendencies into the Volk. . . ." In this connection, the report of Gau Halle-Merseburg sent on March 11, 1943, was considered "remarkable" and cited: "Among loyal National Socialists, who also allow themselves some just criticism, downright antipathy toward the so-called Goebbels method is becoming evident. *They have become suspicious of National Socialist propaganda because it is possible to go from one extreme to the other within a few weeks,* and therefore they are wary of every new regulation. The Minister's every remark is pulled to pieces and criticized in every possible way. Frequent contradictions between the real mood and attitude and the picture presented in newspapers and on radio —obviously for the outside world—are occasionally so manifestly gross that one turns away in exasperation. . . ."[89]

In Saxony, a traditional bastion of Communism, remarks tending to stimulate the class struggle were naturally followed with special interest by the Party. There it was observed extremely critically that Goebbels, in his speeches and in his article of February 7, 1943, "The hard lesson," was increasingly emphasizing a distinction between the fate to be expected by the German elite of the Wehrmacht, sciences, economy, and culture at the hands of Soviet rulers and that of the masses. The Gau administration of Saxony warned: "From this example it is once more evident that our propaganda cannot be too careful, all the more so *because enemy propaganda and political opponents within the Reich use the argument that the general masses don't have to fear Bolshevism because they have nothing to lose!*"[90]

Such arguments had been heard more than once. The SD report of February 15 had already drawn attention to their existence all over the

Reich: "From the working classes one hears the opinion that workers would not be much worse off under Bolshevism than at present. Older workers who formerly belonged to the red groupings remarked that they had had to work hard under the Kaiser, during the Republic [*Systemszeit*], and in the Third Reich, and could expect nothing different under Bolshevism, probably nothing worse than lots of work and little pay. . . ." Southern and western regions of the Reich, on the other hand, reported that elements within all parts of the population, especially "Catholics and the extremely materialistic," thought they had less to fear since they belonged to the "Anglo-American sphere." SD reports still qualified such remarks as isolated occurrences but did feel compelled to suggest that they were the "beginnings of a crisis of confidence."[91]

How strongly the middle and upper classes viewed the "Goebbels method" and total war mobilization measures as a vehicle of class hatred emerges from reports and warnings by various *Chefpräsidenten*. They observed growing unrest within the civil service. Goebbels' renewed attacks against this professional group in his Sportpalast speech led to fears among them for the continued existence of the bureaucracy.[92] There was concern in middle-class circles that the mobilization to work of so-called "fine ladies" was motivated less by attempts to maximize war production than by a desire to encourage gutter instincts and class hatred which, once released, might one day turn in a different direction.[93] Overall, one can say that Goebbels' propaganda at the beginning of the total war phase was widely condemned as "maladroit,"[94] if not dangerous, bringing discredit to its promoter as well as to the regime's radio commentator, Hans Fritzsche.[95]

Of course these irritations and sharp criticisms of propaganda methods and their protagonists were basically nothing more than fits of frustration in an increasingly hopeless situation. And the less spectacular the events on the military side, the worse the mood. A short time after the loss of Stalingrad, those at the Führer's headquarters had apparently deluded themselves into believing they had successfully prevented a serious collapse of morale.[96] An SD report of February 8 had reported that the first shock had been cushioned.[97] However, it quickly became obvious that it had not been a matter of overcoming shock, but of recuperating from a kind of blackout produced by a severe blow. As consciousness slowly returned, the effects became more evident as the weeks passed. There were no signs of the "moral impetus" which propaganda had sought to arouse; the sacrifice of Stalingrad had not fired the "heroic will to victory" among Germans.

Essentially, three factors can be cited as reasons for this failure. The flamboyant announcement of domestic total war measures was not matched by a forceful implementation of policies, nor was the loud propaganda in keeping with actual results. As could be expected, the mobilization of women proved somewhat problematical. Even the regulations for its implementation demonstrated a watering down of the original concept and authorized a whole catalogue of exceptions, so that the *vox populi* spoke of "rubber regulations."[98] Included in the exemption from registration, besides those already working, were mothers with one child under six years of age or at least two under fourteen, advanced women students, and school children. Numerous questions remained open, such as, for example, the matter of weighing volunteer work for charitable organizations or the employment of domestic servants. The maximum age for compulsory registration was eventually reduced to forty-five years, so that a large number of women above that age quit their jobs. The pressure of applications for jobs with the post office, the military, economic agencies, in short all offices promising easy work, was enormous.[99] Until this time, the number of working women in greater Germany had been placed at 8.6 million, but only 968,000 worked in the armaments industry by the end of 1942.[100]

After the introduction of compulsory female labor, champions and protagonists of the regime's anti-emancipation policy for women found themselves at a disadvantage. The "housewife" had been the ideal until then, partly due to a natural inclination and partly out of a desire to reduce unemployment, but primarily to secure the biological survival and growth of the Volk; the working woman was pitied, ignored, or considered second class. Once compulsory labor was introduced, representatives of this general ideal suddenly found themselves objects of increasing reproach and at the mercy of ridicule or malicious joy from their working sisters.[101] A wave of hostility at their newly assigned places of employment made the unaccustomed work and surroundings even more loathsome.

Sauckel, the Plenipotentiary for the Mobilization of Labor, felt compelled to instruct the DAF to counteract such abuses, but Dr. Ley, Reich Organization Leader, in a speech in East Prussia, only aroused more resentment both inside and outside the Party when he remarked that formerly non-employed persons "had wronged Germany for three and a half years."[102] Several Gau administrations observed that Ley was misguided, since it had been an official policy to keep women away from jobs. The Party's task was to correct this tactical error and remedy the backward women's policy, not to abuse those who had supported it.

Many industrial firms were hardly pleased by the new increases in the labor force resulting from the new law. A lack of enthusiasm for the work among newcomers, frequent job changes, and half-day shifts adversely affected the general working atmosphere and particularly the attitude of women working full-time. Many firms were compelled to create new jobs to meet these requirements. Some abruptly rejected these policies as unprofitable for the production process and as completely idiotic.[103] Women sent by labor exchanges to mines were also often turned back for lack of suitable jobs and the absence of separate sanitary facilities.[104]

Young girls and women who had reported to the military and were employed as "news assistants"—regardless of their reasons, be they patriotism, economic necessity, or easy occupations—confronted problems of quite a different nature. Partly with justification, most often not, this new profession fell more and more into disrepute; some parents even refused to permit their daughters to accept such employment. The girls were commonly described as "camp-followers" accompanying soldiers much like former canteen-women. Slanderous expressions such as "officer's mattress" were also widespread.

In reports about such gossip one senses a growing uneasiness within the system regarding the question of women's rights. On the one hand there was the desire to uphold an antiquated feminine ideal of purity and womanliness, on the other hand there were all those efforts to promote reproduction and protect unwed mothers. Himmler, in an SS order at the start of the war, had declared that it was also "a noble duty" of young German women to bear the children of soldiers leaving for the front, even out of wedlock, though "not frivolously but rather in deepest moral earnestness."[105] His breeding plans in the form of operation "Lebensborn" are too well known to require repeating. Nevertheless, the "mother animal" ideal of women prevailed and collided with the coercive policies of total war.

Party literature in 1943 still denounced the intellectual and erotic woman.[106] The ideal of womanhood, as spread by official propaganda, included simplicity and unaffectedness. Make-up and extravagant fashions were taboo. "Women in pants and war paint" scandalized the public and provoked abusive language,[107] to which Goebbels reacted quite negatively. "Total war has nothing to do with a conscious and deliberate cult of primitivism."[108] Simplicity was not a virtue or a necessity, and the press was expressly instructed to avoid arousing baser instincts, particularly in such externals as dress and mannerisms.[109] The planned prohibition of permanent waves and hair coloring could not be executed and was thus replaced by a silent decision to eliminate the supply of hair dyes and other essentials for beauty care and to discontinue the manufacture of parts for the repair of hairdryers.[110]

But even these steps eventually came under attack, since in fact little had changed in the opinion of the public. Initial enthusiasm for total war turned to indifference and skepticism.[111]

Once launched, the campaign to close businesses also proved quite a failure in its impact on morale. Those involved often felt that they had been treated unjustly when compared with neighbors who probably had better connections or harder elbows and managed to keep their shops open. Others saw it as a product of an economic policy whose goal was total state regimentation: "People are rather of the view that the war is only a pretense to eliminate free enterprise and private initiative once and for all and to implement a radical socialization of our economic life. Repeatedly expressed in these circles is the comment that we are rapidly conforming to economic conditions in Soviet Russia. . . ."[112]

Since the policy hit the lower middle class hardest, that group which had given the NSDAP its strongest voting support, the program ultimately worked against the regime. Fear crept into circles of former supporters that the whole middle class was to be socialized.[113] Gau Thuringia reported: "Despite Party propaganda that the closing of businesses is only a war measure, the attitude constantly re-emerges that the middle class is to be systematically eradicated. Those affected often remark that they would prefer to receive an official explanation guaranteeing the later re-establishment of their livelihoods. Since middle class enterprises control a vast circle of friends, they have the ability, given their fear for their survival, to infect other sections of the population with their distressed and angered mood."[114]

Above all, however, it was the irregularity and variability in the implementation of this policy in various cities and Gaus which aroused ill feelings among the public and Party members alike. In Mecklenburg, for instance, Party officials and economic agencies found it difficult to enforce regulations strictly after it became known that execution was lax in Berlin and other surrounding Gaus.[115] As Gauleiter of Berlin, Goebbels had taken a pragmatic approach, avoiding hostile reactions by instructing those offices responsible for the enforcement of total war to act generously and leniently. Similar decisions had been made in Saxony, Thuringia, and Bavaria; given the surplus of unsuitable manpower, many stores were not closed down, while owners of closed enterprises turned their anger toward the Party. Government agencies were indifferent as to which shops were shut down, telling owners to "go to the Party, it probably wanted you closed."[116]

The second factor accounting for the lack of enthusiasm over total war measures was the increasing English and American attacks on and bombings of German cities. The population attributed the escalation of the air war directly to total warfare: "According to reports from western Germany, but also from other regions of the Reich, the public sees the enemy air offensive as the result of the declaration of total war. Many citizens understand by total war not so much the total mobilization of all manpower for armaments purposes, but rather the transition to a total mobilization of all means, even the most extreme, in the struggle against the enemies. The proclamation of total war was therefore interpreted by many citizens as a challenge which could not remain unanswered by the enemy. This misunderstanding has led to a certain public antagonism toward the capital, from where total war has been declared. Characteristic of this attitude is the following verse, already commonly heard in the industrial region:

> Dearest Tommies, do fly on,
> We're all miners put upon.
> To Berlin would be our guess,
> They're the ones who shouted 'yes'.*[117]

Women found it particularly difficult to cope with precision bomber attacks which left inadequate warning time to collect the children and reach shelters. Consequently an increasing number of people began to stream toward air raid shelters between six and seven p.m. and to remain until nine and ten p.m. Restaurants became noticeably emptier during this period. After massive raids on Berlin (repeatedly), Hamburg, Düsseldorf, Cologne, Wilhelmshaven, Munich, and Essen during the period January to March, 1943, people were asking fearfully every day, "is it our turn tonight?"[118] Terror began to spread to regions so far spared from bombings.[119] Without immediate press coverage rumors exaggerated the casualty figures tenfold.[120] As previously mentioned,[121] these attacks radicalized the mood, but seldom called up any anti-Jewish tendencies. Hatred grew particularly against the Anglo-Saxons, and demands for immediate retaliation were heard again.[122] There was also general consternation at the enemy's ability to hit the Ruhr dams; German propaganda efforts to blame the Jews were rejected out of hand.[123] It was instead viewed as an unavoidable outcome of war, although the question was raised why so little flak had been stationed along these vital military points; cries for the punishment of the guilty parties were even heard.[124]

The actual "combined bomber offensive," agreed upon at the Casa-

* "Lieber Tommy fliege weiter,/wir sind alle Bergarbeiter./Fliege weiter nach Berlin,/die haben alle 'ja' geschrien."

blanca Conference, began in June with "round the clock bombing." As a result, the public assumed that "American production is now going at full steam and has become almost inexhaustible. What has been feared for one and a half years has now finally happened, namely that we have no way of preventing British-American cooperation or of disrupting it appreciably. Concerning the air war, the doubt is frequently expressed as to whether 'our inactivity in the West is still tactical or already a sign of our own immobility'. . . ."[125]

Until this time the much praised "attitude," in contrast to the mood, was still emphasized as good. But even here the first symptoms of a deterioration were now being diagnosed. "After the attacks, the population is completely exhausted and apathetic. But most totally bombed-out citizens were happy and felt lucky to have escaped with their lives. Tragic cases of individual fates at first overshadowed all concerns. While the population of bombed areas *generally* displays an *exemplary attitude* and quietly bears its fate, there was, however, also evidence on a *small scale of a poor attitude*. In these isolated instances, opponents voiced comments against the state, the Party, and the leadership."[126] These "subversive remarks" were attributed in part to a simple loss of nerves—people had declared that they didn't know how they could have uttered such remarks as: "We can thank our Führer for this." Clearly such remarks, made under stress, should not be taken too seriously, but they do indicate an increasing circulation of slogans openly blaming Hitler and the Party, as confirmed by other reports:

"It is also apparent that the German greeting ["Heil Hitler"] is seldom used in those cities after an attack, one is morely likely to hear an explicit "good morning" instead. . . . A more adverse effect, however, was created by widely disseminated stories about the reportedly poor morale and hostile attitude of people who had suffered from the bombings. . . ." Stories about the erection of gallows with effigies of the Führer hanging from them circulated everywhere. In many regions the following joke was also passed by word of mouth: "A Berliner and an Essener were discussing the extent of their damages. The Berliner exclaimed, the bombardment had been so bad in Berlin that window-panes were still shattering five hours after the attack. The Essener replied, that's nothing; in Essen Führer-pictures were still flying out of windows fourteen days after the last attack."

The lodging of bombed-out victims from the north and the west in less endangered regions of central Germany spread the fear and anxiety of heavy raids. With all available means, Goebbels tried to counter the enemy's planned demoralization of the public's spirits and to turn pent-up feelings of aversion and aggression into a hate psychosis against the enemy.[127] Beginning in the middle of March, British flyers were systematically labelled "British incendiaries;"[128] later the expression "air gangsters" was added. After March, retaliation emerged for the first time as a propaganda theme to fortify the mood. On March 10, Goebbels had still warned against making "big promises of reprisals."[129] But in an article in *Das Reich* on March 21, he did announce that Germany still possessed a great number of trumps which it would play at the proper time. Then, in a mass rally in the Sportpalast on June 5, 1943, the Propaganda Minister declared that the German people were now obsessed by the idea of "tit for tat" reprisals.

But this hate and retaliatory propaganda did not generate a positive response everywhere according to a report on his speech in Wuppertal: "Now and then Dr. Goebbels' words were called 'cheap consolation' for the survivors. In part, people are of the opinion that things went too far here and that a hate litany was unsuitable for a funeral service. Appealing to the conscience of the English and Americans was useless anyway; they would not now cease their operations. Only appropriate revenge would do any good. Speeches about future reprisals were now slowly becoming superfluous; we must finally take action. . . ."[130]

Nevertheless, there was hardly a report these days which did not take up the issue of retaliation: "Here and there reports indicate that besides a strong hatred of the English and the Americans, reproaches against leading German personalities were also being voiced by certain elements of the population. They no longer want to hear anything about reprisals from Dr. Goebbels. Herman Göring, or 'Meier'[131] as he is also being called already, should finally open a pigeonry, as promised." Cited as typical of the general mood was a worker from a suburb of Erfurt: "Belief in retribution won't help any more if it is not soon, very soon, supported by action. Haste is imperative!"[132] From northern regions came reports of the "need for revenge" and a distinct "desire for retaliation."[133] Accounts from bombed out areas were devoured with a mixture of sensationalism and fear.[134] The SD report on domestic affairs of July 1, 1943,[135] synopsized the rising hatred against the Allies and the growing need for action while in typical fashion omitting all reference to attacks on leading German figures. This RSHA report, much more cautious than individual SD accounts or those of Party officials on matters involving the Party, rested not only on Heydrich's earlier prohibition of digging into Party affairs (December 8, 1935),[136] but also Goebbels' and Bormann's repeated displeasure with these reports[137] and the fact that Ohlendorf himself could not always face realities.

Instead, the SD report contained a long section on rumors regarding new weapons. Modern guns with a range of 125 to 375 miles were being discussed both in secret and in public, guns which would even reach the British mainland. There was talk of rocket projectiles, new planes, and a new kind of bomb based on the principle of atomic fission. "Smoke shells" were mentioned, and the use of Japanese kamikazes against England was prophesied.[138] Experiments with novel remote-controlled bombs and rocket-propelled planes were in fact underway. Hitler, moreover, had signed an order on December 22, 1942, for the production of apparatus A-4, later the V-2 weapon.[139] A long time was to pass, however, before their final introduction, and they were preceded by the air force's use of the V-1. Developments in the field of atomic fission, by contrast, lagged in Germany, partly due to a shortage of materials, poor organization, and the exigencies of war, but also partly because important scientists in the field had been driven out by Hitler's anti-Jewish policy.[140]

Rumors about new weapons reveal clearly how gossip develops from real facts, is fueled by whisper propaganda, often becomes sheer phantasy, and yet sometimes approximates the truth. Another rumor which persistently resurfaced was the possibility of a "gas war." The Third Reich had conducted experiments with humans on the effects of poison gas.[141] Moreover, special units had been formed for eventual engagement and placed under the command of the general for secret troops [Nebeltruppen]. Because of the double-edged nature of this weapon—in unfavorable weather it could work against one's own troops or, in the hot North African climate, dissipate too quickly, quite apart from the possibility of enemy reprisals, considering their air superiority—its introduction was apparently never seriously contemplated before the autumn of 1944. At that time Reich Minister Speer was to order the closing of firms producing the gases tabun and sarin.[142] But rumors about the possible use of a "gas war" did not cease either in 1943 or 1944[143] and were fanned by news from the Eastern front and reports of gas mask drills.[144] Intensification of the air war, particularly the use of phosphorous canisters, only strenghtened the general conviction—especially after the devastating attack on Wuppertal on May 30, 1943—that these new terror methods were already a form of chemical warfare.[145]

Another example of the impact of the air war and the public's reaction to propagandistic exploitation of attacks is offered by the bombardment of Cologne on June 29, 1943, during which the Cathedral was badly damaged. "From Catholic Eichsfeld, which is hardly positive in its general political-ideological attitude, comes the following report: The bombardment of Cologne, which also hit the Cologne Cathedral, has unleashed the greatest indignation here, especially in

Catholic circles. For the first time in a long while, Catholics of Eichsfeld were agreed that only the National Socialist state with its own ruthlessness and resoluteness can repay an enemy like the English which 'dared to attack the Cologne Cathedral'. . . ." In less confessional circles, outrage and disgust were also registered at this deed, notably among women, but a certain detachment was noticeable. Here the regret for the Cathedral was for the destruction of one of the most prominent monuments of German culture and history.

Armaments workers from Suhl commented shortly after the news, "better the Cologne Cathedral smashed than a hundred people killed."[146] Uninterrupted coverage of the event on the radio soon got on many people's nerves. One farm worker from a rural region remarked: "Now we get fourteen days of nothing but the Cologne Cathedral on radio. This will be the same story as Katyn."[147] The Halle SD section had made similar observations regarding public reaction to the thrust of propaganda directed at the loss of irreplaceable cultural monuments instead of the enormous loss of human life, when it was the latter which really incensed the German public against the English. Typical is the reaction of one working-class woman that propaganda was getting to be too much. The Cathedral was important, "but the poor people who lost their lives on that occasion are not mentioned," she asserted; "that matter is silently ignored. The individual apparently has no more value in present-day Germany!"[148]

Aside from such insights, there were also positive assessments of the propaganda campaign on the destruction of cultural monuments. "The bombing of the Cologne Cathedral has aroused more emotions than all previous reports from badly hit cities. . . . The Cathedral was never so highly valued as a national shrine as after its severe damage." Many voices thus encouraged full use of this propaganda theme. "The response which this attack has evoked in the whole civilized world is viewed with great interest in this case. As far as can be ascertained, there is also no evidence that continuous reference to the Cologne Cathedral is regarded as exaggerated propaganda. This is all the more remarkable since today many people declare at every opportunity that 'it is all just propaganda!'. . . ."[149] Halle noted seeming approval of official arguments both among Catholics and "egg-heads," more in fact than among the general public and especially among industrial workers.[150] But there was relatively strong agreement among all sections in a desire for revenge. "In the present phase of their hatred of England, the German people still show a willingness to make the greatest sacrifice if it would result in the final punishment of English crimes. . . ." The mood fluctuated between "hope and despondency. But in general the Volk is presently unified in its hatred of England. . . ."[151]

As had been the case in the past, strong criticism of the Reich Propaganda Minister was expressed again. His articles aroused growing disgust: " . . . people today are simply not willing to 'be comforted by these well-chosen words'. . . ."[152] Many took the following position on Goebbels' article, "Of Speaking and of Silence," which appeared in issue number twenty-five of *Das Reich*, June 20, 1943, and gave the first indications of a concern over the possible alienation of the masses from the regime: "The opinion is that, regardless of how good the majority of Goebbels' articles are, it does seem appropriate to take a break and let other leading figures have their say at this time. . . ."[153] "From all regions of the Reich there are reports of evacuees saying that Dr. Goebbels should not show himself, lest he be stoned, lynched, or hooted. . . . When Dr. Goebbels was in the west, air raid sirens were sounded in the cities so that the population would head for the shelters, for fear that they might do something to Goebbels. Amidst the ruins of devastated cities, signs were erected reading 'We have the Führer to thank for this.' Here and there it came to uprisings against the regime, but the SS suppressed them brutally. . . ."[154]

We know little about such oppositional activity. The only known public protest and resistance against the regime was the "White Rose" action of February 18, 1943.[155] Within four days, brother and sister Hans and Sophie Scholl, who had distributed handbills at the University of Munich, were sentenced to death by the People's Tribunal. Rumors about events in Munich circulated all over Germany but especially in the south. There was talk of "larger demonstrations by Munich students"[156] and of "mass executions."[157] It seems there were also stories of graffiti and leaflets with a Marxist content scrawled on or affixed to public buildings in Berlin and other cities, which people were not immediately destroying but rather reading and passing on.[158] According to a report of March 12, numerous arrests took place in Düsseldorf, Dortmund, Stettin, Magdeburg and Görlitz because of dissemination of Communist literature.[159]

More and more Germans began to listen to foreign radio; no one admitted listening, but there were animated discussions about how Englishmen were allowed to tune in German stations. While those in the west and southwest preferred the Swiss station Beromünster,[160] those with relatives either missing or captured in Russia listened to Radio Moscow, particularly after Stalingrad, since it read the names, occupations, and addresses of prisoners, which the USSR refused to furnish to representatives of neutral powers.[161] These programs naturally contained a heavy dose of propaganda, some with religious overtones and many with suggestions for sabotage.[162] The number of Communists indicted in the so-called "treason trials" [*Heimtückeprozessen*][163] seems to have been small, though the public prosecutor general of Naumburg (Saale) suspected that the number of old or newly-recruited Communist supporters should not be underestimated.[164] At any rate, denunciations for tuning in foreign radio stations became more rare,[165] and there were fewer people who considered it a punishable offence,[166] in contrast to the start of the war, when long prison sentences had been considered just.[167]

A favorite topic of propaganda was the denunciation of and contempt for Bolshevism, which "through constant repetition of propaganda slogans was to focus on the broad masses and not on small select groups."[168] Again Stalingrad was the starting point for a new, intensified campaign. "From now on, every radio talk, every report, every speech and every weekly slogan has to close with the stereotype phrase that the struggle against Bolshevism is our great task." Goebbels then pointed to Cato and his famous call for the destruction of Carthage.[169] The new propaganda was to mobilize all European nations and also Eastern peoples against Soviet Russia: there was to be an exact differentiation of individual nations within the Soviet Union and a discontinuation of Germany's settlement claims and colonial policy, which could only play into the hands of enemy propaganda.

The Reich Propaganda Minister was thus recommending a policy long demanded in vain by the military and foreign office.[170] The defeat at Stalingrad was necessary to win wider support within the Party, though the aggravated military situation alone did not give rise to the new propaganda campaign.[171] On February 17, Goebbels expressly mentioned domestic opinion reports[172] from which four slogans circulating in Germany could be deduced which required counteraction: 1) "Bolshevism has changed"; 2) "The English and Americans will prevent bolshevization"; 3) "One can't do more than work anyway"; 4) "The Bolsheviks will only hang Nazis."[173]

The press and radio received detailed instructions on how to discredit these slogans, while the Party Chancellory simultaneously started a massive word-of-mouth propaganda action. Bolshevism had not mellowed and become democratic; that assertion was to be exposed as an Anglo-Saxon propaganda ploy. The claim that workers who had to work anyway had nothing to lose was to be countered by accounts of concentration camps and deportations. Ultimately it was not a question of who would be hanged—the assumption was that only Nazis would swing—but whether victory and national self-preservation against Jewish Bolshevism could be achieved. With Britain and America betraying Europe, only Adolf Hitler could save western civilization from Bolshevism.[174]

If one consults opinion surveys in the Third Reich for the success of this propaganda, one finds that the impact was minimal. The public's image of Russia had shifted even more than had been reported by the SD in August, 1942.[175] In April and July, 1943, the SD's domestic intelligence service devoted two more reports to this topic. The first, on April 15,[176] is particularly interesting for the deliberate emphasis on how the picture of an "inhuman and soulless system of oppression" and of "stupefied, half starved, dulled masses," as painted by Nazi propaganda, had been shaken by first-hand impressions of Russians working in Germany and had thus brought German propaganda into question. The following observations concerning Soviet workers had impressed Germans the most:

1. Contrary to a widespread notion of the atheistic attitude of the Russian population, one often discovered a deep piety.
2. Workers from the east are no "mechanical robots" but rather show a high level of intelligence and prove to have excellent technical gifts.
3. Only a small percentage are illiterates. The level of education of the population of the USSR must be far above that of the Csarist empire.
4. Bolshevism has in no way destroyed the family. Strong family ties and a pronounced morality, especially among women, were praised. Even the cleanliness of eastern workers, a matter held in high esteem in Germany, was attested to.
5. Soviet workers were unfamiliar with forced labor and corporal punishment.

"Such revelations have radically changed the image of the Soviet Union and its people. . . . Where anti-Bolshevik propaganda continues to use the old and well-known arguments, it no longer creates the interest or belief that it did at the start of the war. . . ."

The second report[177] confirms this trend. It became increasingly difficult for propaganda to drive home to workers the point "that Bolshevism is really the danger it has always been made out to be. . . ." More and more the conviction took hold that the little man, unlike the establishment, had no reason to be afraid. On the basis of the Soviet Union's tremendous industrial achievements, fighting spirit, level of education, and religious tendencies, many Germans were drawing comparisons between working-class conditions under the Csars and Bolsheviks and under the Republic and National Socialism, not always detrimental to the former, given due consideration to the diverse cultural levels of the European peoples in the USSR. "The appeal of a stirring propaganda under the slogan 'Victory or Bolshevism' has not been very great," according to the Regierungspräsident for Swabia and Neuburg.[178] Personal impressions obtained from contacts with Eastern workers and Soviet military advances carried far more weight and exerted far greater influence on public opinion than tendentious Nazi propaganda.

The third and decisive reason for the failure of Goebbels' mobilization campaign was the difficult military situation. In previous years the discontent, grief, and daily worries had been cushioned and counterbalanced by news of victories. But now the generally hoped-for and anticipated successful spring offensive did not materialize, and the summer offensive also failed to meet expectations. "Meldungen aus dem Reich" had reported on April 5 how many Germans adopted the fixed idea "that it is 'do or die' this summer, when 'everything must be staked on one card because a third winter battle in the East would be tantamount to losing the war'. . . ."[179]

To Goebbels this thesis seemed extremely dangerous, but he decided to forego any action until the proper time,[180] which as usual meant waiting for the right moment to ridicule "those of little faith." But this time the results were a long while in coming. On April 15, Hitler had given the order for operation "Citadel," a tank movement north of Byelograd to encircle extended Soviet forces near Kursk. Hitler's decision to delay the attack until the arrival of new panther and tiger tanks, over the opposition of von Kluge and von Manstein, gave the Soviets ample warning to counter German strategy and bring the operation to a halt with heavy German losses.[181] On July 11, the Soviets began their offensive from the north and east against the German flank around Orel, breaking through the tank army. Since in the meantime Anglo-American forces had landed in Sicily on July 10, and fresh reserves were urgently needed there, operation "Citadel" was terminated. The initiative on the Eastern front passed irrevocably to the Soviets, and from then on a multi-front war determined military events, even in the East.

The campaign in North Africa, meanwhile, developed even more adversely for the Axis powers. Italy lost the last remnant of its colonial empire when Field Marshal Montgomery entered Tripoli, capital of Libya, on January 21. On February 4, his army crossed the Tunisian border, making possible operational coordination with Eisenhower's forces and placing all Allied armies in North Africa under the command of General Alexander. Rommel's army, only poorly resupplied and strengthened by Italian infantry divisions, finally came to a halt at the French Mareth Line, built before the war to protect Tunisia. Although the "Desert Fox" achieved minor break-throughs against the Americans to the northwest, his troops had to retreat to the original line of departure and were forced to cancel a counterattack on the British in early March. On March 10,

Rommel flew to the Führer's headquarters with a proposal for the evacuation of the Tunisian bridgehead; Hitler refused to budge an inch, ordered Rommel to attend to his deteriorating health in Germany, and replaced him with General von Arnim. A renewed British attack and the union of British and American armies on April 7 led to the defeat of the remaining Axis forces; only seven hundred men escaped and the rest, 252,000, were captured.

As previously indicated, the public tried to comprehend the individual stages of military development in the East and in Africa less in their detail than with a view to the whole perspective.[182] When little occurred in the East, interest in this military theatre slackened; instead of the refrain sung by soldiers at the Eastern front, those whose positive attitude was repeatedly emphasized—"Everything passes, all is o.k., retreat in December, offensive in May"—one heard ". . . first goes the Führer and then the Party."[183] Concerning North Africa, fear increasingly set in that in the long run Italian and German forces would not be a match for the enemy[184] and would be unable to hold their position.[185] The latter opinion was slowly being suggested by press and radio, though official comparisons with Stalingrad were painstakingly avoided. Nevertheless, the concept of "Tunisgrad" quickly came into use; one even heard the term "German Dunkirk." The possibility of an attempted landing by Anglo-Americans on Sicily or Sardinia was also frequently discussed.

Thus, when the armed forces news service announced the loss of Africa on May 13, no special reaction was provoked, only a further downward slide in morale. Main items of conversation were the losses and the fate of prisoners, whereby most people were relieved that their relatives were captured by the West "because there prisoners would be treated according to the principles of the Geneva Convention, while nothing was known about the fate of prisoners-of-war in Bolshevik hands."[187]

The course and losses of the North African campaign as well as the Allied landing on Sicily again caused Germans to concern themselves more intensively with their Italian ally. Italophobia had been revived by events at Stalingrad; many had blamed the catastrophe on the failure of Italian troops.[188] The situation in Italy itself also gave cause for alarm. One Berlin report spoke of altercations between German and Italian soldiers. "German soldiers, in their travels through Italy and conversations with Italians, got the impression that Fascism was scarce, while the so-called royal party, the group around the crown prince, and above all the Vatican with all its unpleasant auxiliaries, were throwing their weight around. . . ."[189]

Hostility toward Italy intensified by June, as confidence in the Axis partner sank with rumors of a possible separate peace between the

Americans and the Italian king. "The general view is that Italy would have left the Axis were it not for the presence of so many German troops. . . ."[190] But even this did not hinder an unfriendly Italian attitude towards German soldiers, some of whom were on occasion stoned after a bombing attack, for which they were held responsible. Rumors of Mussolini's ill health abounded. He was seen as the "sole guarantor of Italian loyalty to the alliance."[191] Of all the Italian armed forces, only the fascist militia in southern Italy was still regarded as trustworthy.

Although the German public had speculated for weeks about a possible Allied landing in southern Italy, the announcement by the OKW "did to some extent trigger alarm." Remarks about Italian "cowardice" and "softness" were heard more than ever. The observation of a farm worker was cited as typical: "Here the Italians have nothing else to do but defend their own mess. What do they do? They let the English and Americans land on their own soil. If the English invade Italy, then for the Italians the war is over."[192]

On the basis of reports, the Reich Security Office believed it could discern three groups within the population: positive-thinking Party members who were of the opinion that the Allies were permitted to enter Sicily in order to destroy them completely; a second and much larger group which believed it would require long and difficult battles, massive troop reinforcements, and aid for Italy to drive out the intruders; and finally a group, either indifferent or negatively disposed toward National Socialism and recruited largely from confessional circles, which regarded the landing as "the beginning of the end."[193] While propaganda argued that Stalingrad had represented the heavier loss of men and materiel, most people considered the loss of Tunisia far more serious since it was seen as the "springboard to Europe," leading to the invasion of Sicily which opened "the door to Europe."[194]

The military situation thus gave rise to pessimism. By the beginning of summer it was already crystal-clear that the U-boat—the weapon on which such high hopes had been pinned in 1942-43—had passed the zenith of its success. The "Anti-U-Boat Warfare Committee," founded in 1942, had done its work well. But it was primarily the new radar position finder which forced the German navy to halt its U-boat group operations in May, 1943. The German public, which had taken increasing delight in the sinkings,[195] had to bury its hopes as of May for a favorable turn in the war by means of this weapon.[196]

Analyzing the opinion reports from May to June, 1943, one finds an unprecedented low in public opinion. Reading these reports must have created unrest and concern among the Nazi elite. One concrete measure in reaction was to further intensify the surveillance of "all dangerous elements."[197] Hitler belatedly saluted Stalin's purges of the Red Army; unlike his Soviet counterpart, Hitler still had to cope with potentially dangerous forces within the military, the Churches, and social circles, although publicly he tried to dismiss his almost manic fear of assassination or a new November Revolution.[198] Yet no popular revolution, no *levée en masse*, ensued even in the months of crisis after Stalingrad. Opinion surveys do permit the conclusion, however, that a military coup at this time would have found a broad consensus among the population and was even expected by many. A susceptibility to foreign propaganda, previously unknown, and a severe criticism of the Party, its cadres, and the military leadership, were noticed at this time, as well as a considerable crumbling of the Führer cult. The crisis of confidence arising out of Stalingrad had reached an initial culmination point. The "poison" of enemy "insinuations" had begun "slowly to seize the inner recesses of the German soul." Attempts to neutralize this intoxication had failed.[199] Albert Speer writes that the meaning of Stalingrad lay in the fact that Goebbels had begun "to doubt in Hitler's star and thus in victory— and so had we."[200] How much more valid was this for the majority of the population, whose interpreter and modulator Goebbels regarded himself to be?

As early as the last week in May, the Party Chancellory had to draw the conclusion from Gau reports that morale had deteriorated so badly that it began to affect the formerly still positive attitude.[201] People were not only asking how the war was to be won (Kurhessen), but also adopting the position that it would be lost (Mainfranken). Especially intellectuals (Upper Silesia, Westphalia-South), but also all kinds of businessmen openly abused the Party and its Führer. " 'I didn't vote for Hitler!' has become a kind of catchphrase among businessmen. . . ." (Westphalia). The Führer's authority began to slip (Halle-Merseburg, Upper Silesia). No report omitted reference to severe attacks against propaganda; since it was fatal to attack Hitler, state, and Party directly,[202] criticism was focused on the manipulation of public opinion.[203] Indicative is the public's assessment of leading Nazis in the form of a "new theatre program":

"1.   'The Autocrats,' with Adolf.
 2.   'Stars shine brightly,' with Hermann.
 3.   'Lots of Lies,' with Joseph.
 4.   'To new shores' or 'The Way to Freedom,' with Hess.
 5.   'The Saint and the Fool,' with Rosenberg.
 6.   'The Liar and the Nun,' with Himmler.
 7.   Gala evening—all together in 'The Robbers'."[204]

The first signs of soldiers infected by poor morale at home also appeared at this time; soldiers on leave were more prone to be critical than before.[205] Stalingrad had been a learning experience; despite a generally positive attitude among the front-line soldiers, there were instances of dejection—"we're only good for cannon fodder"—and defeatism: "The opinions of comrades are all the same, namely that peace, spelled 'collapse,' is nigh. . . ." But the June 28 SD report from Halle also noted that almost all letters from soldiers expressed relief at the prospect of leaving the homeland and returning to their comrades at the front.[206]

Adding to the disquieting military situation and the incessant air attacks was the inadequate food supply according to several reports.[207] Meat rations were reduced at the end of May while bread and fats were raised minimally.[208] The new rations were considered too meager, particularly among the working-classes: "Instead of one hundred grams of meat we get only a piece of bread with spread."[209] The supply of vegetables and fruits was also felt to be insufficient.[210]

One nevertheless gets the impression that these worries lay far behind other burdens and no longer dominated discussions as they did in the first war years when there was little other cause for complaint. In retrospect, we can view these expressions of discontent in the first years as a kind of safety-valve for inadmissable criticism. Only among a minority did the disapproval take the shape of deliberate political opposition to the regime. Now, however, in larger circles as well, criticism became more than a matter of material dissatisfaction. The crisis reached far deeper, particularly in regard to the Churches: "It is evident that everything ideological is crumbling under the impact of military events and in the face of death, which is suddenly confronting thousands of families."[211] Cancellations of church membership, never large at any time, declined further, and many Germans who had left returned to the fold. The Party Chancellory commented bitterly already in February: "In any case, it confirms a hundred times over the old experience, that for the Church, times of need are times of plenty."[212] Hitler had to admit that the pithy biological phrases of the strength of blood and the survival of the Volk through its descendants had found few sincere supporters. "It would be wrong to underestimate the tremendous psychological impact which the belief in the hereafter with its promises has had on many citizens."[213] Nevertheless, relying on the masculine attraction of the Führer of the Third Reich, and given its contempt for the clergy's spiritual and pastoral qualities, the Party Chancellory still believed in April, 1943, that it could claim: "We have to be very clear on this, that *in the conquest of the German individual's mind preeminence will be guaranteed to those who are also in a position to present the best men* *as spokesmen of their idea*! It will thus depend not only solely on *what* the leadership of both sides has to say but also on *who* says it!"[214] In view of the Party leadership crisis, acknowledged even by Goebbels, this faith in its own ranks hardly seemed justified. It was already evident who enjoyed more public respect on the basis of the kind of greetings exchanged. Southern Germany reported a clear-cut "Grüss-Gott* move-ment;"[215] "Heil Hitler" was used less and less, while Party badges steadily vanished from lapels.[216] Himmler noted the complete failure of the Hitler Youth to "instill idealism and an understanding for the great-ness of our times" among the youth.[217]

Hitler and the Party had to observe, to their own disadvantage, a phenomenon from which they had profited in the early thirties and during the initial stages of the take-over: the rapidity with which majority opinions were accepted and the fickleness of public opinion. If, during the years of national successes, the characteristic dynamics of be-havioral conformity within specific groups favored the Nazis, the trend of developing majority public opinion now began to have detrimental consequences for the Third Reich.

2.   THE DEFECTION OF ITALY

In this atmosphere, probably the most ominous for the Nazis since their take-over, the news of Mussolini's "resignation" struck "like a thunderbolt."[218] The head of the fascist sister state, the only "guarantor" of Italian allegiance, had left Italy's political scene. The shock[219] and confusion within Germany's Party and state leadership, reflected in the extreme aridity of news, was probably even greater than that of the average citizen. It was impossible, Goebbels noted, "to enlighten" the Volk "that in Rome it was not a matter solely of Mussolini's resignation, but of a profound organizational and ideological crisis of fascism, possibly even its liquidation."[220] Hitler's first priority was to bring the Duce to Germany as quickly as possible and to arrest the Italian gov-ernment under Badoglio. Then Mussolini was to be reconfirmed in his earlier posts.[221]

Given the critical attitude of public opinion, the Nazi elite, as could be expected, worried about the possibilities of a similar development at home. Himmler was directed to deal ruthlessly with any such attempt. To all outward appearances, however, Hitler was confident and uncon-cerned. He remarked to Goebbels that he hardly feared subversive ac-tivities, since the Germans were so ill-disposed towards Italians and had

* traditional south German greeting

already foreseen and expected these events.[222] This remark shows again how well Hitler was informed of public opinion reports. He apparently did not consider betrayal from within his own ranks, and he judged correctly the military leaders closest to him. On the other hand, the populace in many areas certainly did not exclude the possibility of a "military dictatorship"[223] for Germany.

As the first brief reports about the Italian revolution became known, the masses, accustomed to long-winded interpretations by the regime, felt itself to be "without political leadership." As always in times of uncertainty, the wildest combinations and rumors circulated. Consequently there were again heavy fluctuations in opinion. Every person changed his mind several times a day. "A searching and groping for the truth is clearly evident. The change in government has not yet made itself felt in the behavior of the population. But their attitude has been strongly affected insofar as considerable segments of the population have so lost heart that they no longer believe the war can be won."[224]

It is noteworthy that Security Service reports established for the first time a new category in addition to the previously used mood and attitude: behavior [Verhalten]. With this distinction they sought to obscure the true extent of dissatisfaction among the populace. Even if the mood was miserable and the attitude had visibly deteriorated, behavior towards the totalitarian rulers remained loyal-to-passive. The basic mood was equivalent to a deep depression. Profound dismay spread among National Socialists in "that the collapse, within a few hours, of a regime at least twenty years old could be possible."[225] Dedicated Party members closed ranks, resolving "to forestall with all means at their disposal any kind of impact" on Germany. Another part of the population "viewed the Italian incidents as an encouraging sign for the reintroduction of so-called democratic freedom. . . . Finally there is a group of so-called Party members who no longer dare to use the greeting 'Heil Hitler' publicly and have downright fits of fear that as members of the NSDAP they are on a so-called black list like the one in Italy. Domestic events in Italy have affected Germany so as to force responsible offices to realize that a portion of the population has turned away from National Socialism, that another element can only be described as fellow-travellers, and that it is now clear where true National Socialists still exist among the people."[226] At this point, the last could hardly have constituted more than one-third of the population. The Reich Security Office confirmed this; while optimists still kept up spirits with the rationale that Germany did not need Italy, pessimists were now in the majority and prepared for the worst.[227] Clearly the alienated, the despairing, the idealists, and National Conservatives as well as former members of the Center and Bavarian People's Parties, who had all thronged to National Socialism during the critical years of the Weimar Republic and had been blinded by Nazi promises and early successes, now increasingly turned away.

The commitment to Hitler did, however, remain very strong. One could hear quite a few opinions that Hitler would now perhaps also have to go, but these were in no way meant maliciously as the RSHA emphasized. Rather one could detect numerous expressions of sympathy: "In several of the reports the point is made that the Führer also suffered a loss of prestige insofar as the disloyalty of his personal friend Mussolini, in whom he had publicly placed the greatest trust, represented a failure of fascism. But these observations diminished in face of the deep sympathy felt by wide segments of the population that the Führer had again been dealt a bitter disappointment from among his circle of closest friends."[228]

Hitler's silence on events in Italy had unfavorable repercussions. Just at this moment of doubt and uncertainty, a word from Hitler, as reports reveal, would have brought many people closer to the regime again. Now, however, political tension snowballed.[230] The possibility of a parallel development in Germany and the establishment of a military dictatorship were increasingly discussed. Since the Propaganda Office restricted itself to publicizing the expediency of continued military cooperation with Italy,[231] the public was left to its own devices. Rumors about the flight of Göring, Ribbentrop, and Schirach abounded. Spiteful jokes made the rounds: Hitler was writing a new book, entitled "My Mistake;" or, he had been lost in a submarine along with Goebbels, and they had not been saved, but the German people had.[232] More Party badges vanished from lapels and "Heil Hitlers" became scarcer as well. More and more people were discussing the question "whether 'something could still be salvaged' by a change in regime. . . .," and the cry was heard, "We need a new government!"[233] From heavily bombed cities came reports of a "November mood."[234] Conditions for a revolutionary attempt had probably never been better.[235] But resistance circles wanted to secure backing from the enemy before risking chaos at home[236]—this at a time when the Allies, due to Germany's declining military fortunes, were less disposed than ever to believe promises from opposition groups and fearful of possibly sowing the seeds of a future stab-in-the-back legend. Thus chances were missed on both sides to remove Hitler and his closest cohorts and to end the war.

Instead the torrid pace continued but with renewed force. The bombardment of Hamburg from July 24 to August 3 gave a foretaste of the suffering awaiting the populations of German cities, which reached its peak in the fire-bombing of Dresden in February, 1945. In the "Report of the Hamburg Police Commissioner acting as local air raid leader, about the heavy air blitz on Hamburg in July-August 1943," one reads: "An almost utopian picture of a metropolis, suddenly devastated, without gas, water, electricity, and transportation, with stone ruins of once flourishing residential areas, became reality. The streets were covered with hundreds of bodies. Mothers with children, men young and old, burned, charred, or uninjured, clothed or naked in waxen pallor like store window mannequins, lay in every position, calm and peaceful, or cramped, the agony of death on their faces. Shelters presented the same picture, even more gruesome in its effect since it showed here and there the last desperate struggle against a merciless fate. If in one place the occupants were sitting on their chairs, contented and uninjured, as if asleep, killed unsuspectingly and painlessly by carbon monoxide gas, the positions of bones and skulls in other shelters indicated how its occupants tried to escape to safety from the underground prison. No imagination will ever be able to comprehend and describe the scenes of terror and horror that took place in many sealed AR-shelters. . . ."[237]

Knowledge of such attacks weighed like a "nightmare"[238] on the German population and intensified the feeling of "insecurity and hopelessness." The impression of complete helplessness had a particularly depressing effect, as the Appeals Court President of Hamm stated in a lengthy report on August 31: "Our Volk is composed not only of heroes but also of a goodly portion of faint-hearted people not suited to heroism."[239] To the faint-hearted, the military situation appeared dim: "We are on the defensive and struggling against an overwhelmingly superior force. Italy will defect as soon as it receives certain concessions from the enemy. Then the Italian front will collapse and a new one form along the Alps, bringing southern Germany and our relocated industry into effective range of enemy aircraft. . . ."[240]

This forlorn situation only strengthened belief in the ultimate defection of Italy,[241] and yearnings for "peace at any price" were heard from many.[242] The German government's silence, which—as Goebbels announced—had "nothing to do with embarrassment or helplessness," but was due instead "solely to a law of political expediency,"[243] prompted many Germans to listen even more to enemy broadcasts. This in turn resulted in an increasing number of violations of the treason law and the radio decree.[244] Reports do not indicate to what extent wishes for revolution, heard here and there, were inspired by the establishment of the "National Committee for a Free Germany"[245] in Moscow on July 12 and 13, and by the reports of Radio Moscow and the "German National Radio" [Deutscher Volkssender] about the goals of this union of captive German officers and soldiers and German Communist emigrants.

How Germans felt towards the regime in the summer of 1943 is further illustrated by an SD report on the "attitude of youth toward the Party."[246] The report was compiled by the official in charge of youth on the basis of information provided by SD head offices and presented to Ohlendorf. Since the report was too negative, it had to be rewritten under the direction of von Kielpinski. But even this milder version apparently aroused Bormann's ire.[247]

The thermometer for the attitude of juveniles was based in the SD report on behavior during the annual initiation ceremony into the NSDAP, in this case for the generation of 1924 and 1925. From the relatively high number of applications alone, a positive attitude toward the leadership was concluded—a conclusion deliberately ignoring the pressure exerted by social, state, and Party controls. The following extremely cautious qualifications reveal the use of smoke-screen tactics previously mentioned. From all regions, it stated, there were reports which gave cause for concern. There were expressions of an attitude hardly gratifying to state and Party leaders that showed "indifference and lack of inner preparedness" on the one hand and even "intentional rejection of admission to the Party" on the other. To many juveniles, admission to the NSDAP did not seem "an especially worthwhile goal," but rather was considered "in fashion" or even a "necessary evil." Motives given for rejecting the Party ranged from vague arguments of wanting to remain free—there was still time later—to remarks considered defeatist, namely that they wanted to await the outcome of the war, and even more negative utterances. In these cases the reporter concluded that either parental or especially religious influences were at work.[248] The number of youths attempting to escape the clutches of the totalitarian power structure in this way was "so great that it must not be overlooked." To eliminate this "serious flaw," or even "grave threat"—in the eyes of the Nazi leadership—to the future existence of the Party, the SD urgently recommended intensified ideological "orientation and penetration" of the three oldest Hitler Youth classes by reliable Party members or soldiers.

Concerning the basic causes for such an attitude among German youth, the point was made that they were not to be found in the juveniles themselves but rather in three sets of experiences:

"1. Those youths presently in the Hitler Youth have always experienced the Party as a historical fact. They are not tied to it through the experience of a political struggle which would illustrate to them that the Party had to fight for the present state and thus had won the right to make demands on this state and its people and to claim ideological leadership. For many of these juveniles, the Führer is not the representative for the Party, but is first of all Führer of the state and above all Commander-in-Chief of the Armed Forces.

Therefore, they have no inhibitions in being critical of the Party just as of every other state institution. *They lack the naturally developed loyalty to the Party* of older Party members . . .

2.   *The youth expects from the Party that it will also enforce in practice its claim to leadership.* The experiences of youth frequently contradict this. Juveniles are bored by those endless Party speeches, those parades and festivities already frozen into routine. Very often they were shocked by the discrepancy between demands and behavior on the part of Party functionaries.

3.   Finally, reserve toward the Party finds further nourishment from the unsolved question of Party-Church relations. Since a large segment of the youth, and above all their parents, still have religious affiliations, remarks against a 'former holy faith' by Party members, officials, and Hitler Youth leaders would only be repellant. This is particularly the case at present because the youth is also partly aware, due to the existing military situation, that the Church, for instance, very thoroughly concerns itself with the dependants of the war dead, and the clergy gives clear answers to questions of life and the present. . . ."

The first experience clearly indicates a generational problem. For the "teens" and "twens" of the war years, the period of Party struggle and take-over of power, the Versailles peace treaty and the Weimar Republic were already "history."[249] The Party embodied the "establishment" with all its undesirable phenomena of unconditional recognition of its "acquired" rights. The religious content of the Party and the Führer myth were felt by many to be "stale" or "rubbish," as it was called, and only tolerated *nolens volens*. The second experience, the Party's claim to leadership, was weighed coolly against reality, and the comparison was often disadvantageous to party officials. The arrogance and exclusivity of Party and state officials—and here we come to the third experience—contrasted noticeably with the helpfulness and humanity of the Churches.

Viewed as a whole in 1943, a majority of youths outwardly behaved loyally toward state and Party. A smaller percentage, though one still not to be ignored, made no bones about its disapproval of existing conditions. Within this minority, four groups are discernible: 1) the 'wild' groups, partly with anarchistic overtones, whose destructive activities and criminal manifestations were the result of the war as well as a degenerate part of civilization arising from a permanent industrial revolution;[250] 2) youth groups influenced by the ideology of the Youth Leagues whose origins date from the beginning of the century, seeking to recover a piece of juvenile romanticism amidst the ruins of larger cities; 3) the cliques of political opposition emerging in the west, the "Edelweiss" or "Skull Pirates," also influenced by youth league concepts but more hostile toward the Party and regime;[251] and 4) the liberal and democratically oriented groups with preference for the English language, music, and clothing. Membership was mostly from the upper middle class; they met for parties and discussion, rejected the Hitler Youth and military service, had little interest in the war, and despised National Socialism.[252] An almost "epidemic appearance" of juvenile bands of all stripes was observed in 1943-44. As a sign of recognition the youths wore edelweiss, a skull, or a colored pin imprinted on wallets, purses, belts, or lapels; their "uniform" was composed of Scottish plaid shirts, short pants, white scarves, white socks, hunting knife, and often also firearms. Their rendezvous were public establishments, air raid bunkers, street corners, archways, and pubs. As nicknames they preferred primarily those of American Western heroes: "Johnny," "Texas Jack," "Alaska Bill," and "Whiskey Bill."

The secret police intervened in advance of the law, resorting to "special treatment," the mildest form of which was a warning. The courts, for their part, sentenced juveniles to prison terms ranging from several months to years, depending on the severity of the crime, from high treason to resisting the state, breach of the peace, or just disorderly conduct; another determining factor was whether the youth was a ringleader, active participant, or camp follower. Aside from resistance, serious crimes included formation of new parties and violation of the decree on compulsory youth service.

Criminal offenses continued to be in a minority in 1943. Compared with 1942, a 0.6 per cent decrease in the juvenile delinquency rate was noted, while overall criminality had risen by 0.3 per cent. Fraud and moral crimes had decreased among juveniles, while fatal assaults, homicides, and arson had climbed; in other words, a drop in the number of offenses had been registered, but concomitantly also a shift from misdemeanors to felonies.[253]

To check this increasingly "subversive" behavior—"on trains there were occasional conversations hardly concealing revolutionary ideas. . ."[254] —and to prevent deterioration of the public mood to the "danger zone" which existed even for totalitarian states, the Nazi regime adopted a number of counter-measures. First was an anti-rumor campaign initiated by the Reich propaganda offices. Based on experience from Gau East Hanover and with consent of the Party Chancellory, school children were manipulated; they were told, either by the school or the Party, of certain facts, rumors, and also political events in a manner appealing to their imagination and urged to relate these at home. "Mothers and fathers set store by these reports from their children and consequently an adroit propaganda can be conducted through children, one that can possibly have excellent results. Codeterminate is parental pride in the fact that their children are already concerning themselves with political happenings and can join in conversations. If children are so influenced that they can report enthusiastically on military developments or the self-sacrifices on the home front, then it will undoubtedly have a major impact on the public mood."[255]

In addition to this attempted indoctrination of school children, authorized by directives sent down via district governors to school superintendents and teachers, intensified word-of-mouth propaganda was conducted through Reich propaganda offices. This was primarily to counter exaggerated rumors about air raid casualties, news regarding the whereabouts of prisoners-of-war in Russia, and similar talk, based in most cases on foreign sources.[256] Further anti-rumor slogans dealt, for example, with the alleged withdrawal of meat rations from the elderly, ostensible ration reductions, confiscation of double windows for shipment to the Ruhr, or other stories described as absurd by authorities.[257]

Aside from these moves, which should be interpreted as a reaction and counter-measure to slogans considered by the state as detrimental to public opinion, a number of more active steps were undertaken. Once again army mail had to be enlisted as positive testimony for the public; local propaganda leaders had to collect letters expressing "confidence in victory" and display them in suitable showcases. They anticipated a special impact from letters sent by soldiers previously "not firmly rooted in National Socialism" but now radiating optimism and confidence.[258]

The most vital campaign, however, was to be a "general appeal to the propaganda activization of Party members," suggested by the Party Chancellory at the end of August. A proposal to this effect, prepared on August 27, 1943,[259] constitutes a noteworthy document for its blunt candor, not only confirming pessimistic opinion reports but also substantiating the ongoing process of corrosion. The loss of confidence had crept right into the midst of the NSDAP.[260] Open and manipulated propaganda tactics were deemed inadequate to counteract the devastating impact of intensified air attacks, the Italian episode, and various military reverses. False predictions and numerous gross errors by press and radio had discredited them with the public. "Steadfastness at home, therefore, has never been so critically dependent on the firm attitude and sure leadership of the Party as today." A considerable number of Party members, however, had not fulfilled their duties as opinion leaders, instead floating helplessly themselves. Many lacked the courage to confront gossip and softness with vigor, while Party activists were inundated with routine work which diverted them from their primary function of leadership. Goebbels' propaganda efforts, his almost exclusive reliance on "mechanical official propaganda," and poor staffing of offices also came under attack and provided the basis for a more active role on the part of all Party members. To this end, rallies and meetings were recommended to revitalize each member and reconfirm him in his leadership role.

Bormann, on August 31, initialed the submission with the order that it be implemented "as soon as possible" with the participation of the Main Educational Office [*Hauptschulungsamt*] and the Reich Propaganda Office. Simultaneously, the Party Chancellory indirectly attempted to break through the silence of the Reich Propaganda Leader concerning events in Italy by informing Party officials. On August 18, Bormann forwarded to all Gauleiters a circular prepared by the Foreign Office for German missions abroad,[261] in which a detailed "report on the Italian situation" was enclosed. The report merits attention in that it is written by an Italian and throws light on a few interesting parallels—or contrasts—between Fascism and National Socialism, without expressly enunciating them. The first fact, considered basic, namely that the revolution "had not swept away the old institutions and organizations," applied to both regimes. Then with regard to the Italian Fascist Party: "It intervened rather as a new force among existing forces. The cooperative movement did improve living conditions for the workers, but in no way eliminated the *plutocracy*; on the contrary, it strengthened it. The Fascist regime strove to infiltrate the military and placed the Duce at its head. But it did not touch the monarchy, to which the military was actually subordinate. Youth organizations and new schools tackled the new Fascist education. However, this education continually had to reckon with Catholicism. . . ." A further power, never crushed by Fascism, was Judaism. What is more, a certain "changing of the guard" had occurred within the Party.

Now Mussolini had been betrayed by elements from big business, the military, Party leaders, and bureaucrats. Industrialists had maintained organizational and intellectual ties to the Anglo-Saxon world; officers had come from the army general staff and in lesser numbers from the navy; defected Party leaders were convinced from the outset of the war that Italy was insufficiently prepared: that is why they had demanded a "position of neutrality." After analyzing the individual incidents relating to the *coup d'état*[262] and the creation of the Badoglio government, the Italian expert came to the conclusion that after two weeks in office the new regime had already disappointed all those who had placed their hope in it and in an early peace. The only enthusiasts were the Jews.

Based on the political constellation in Italy, the assertion was finally made that the present regime only constituted an intermediate phase. "Either it will end in a slide towards Bolshevism or it will lead to a new Fascism." The report closed with the consideration that perhaps it was quite beneficial that the "Badoglio experiment" had been given freedom to develop.

In the light of this information sent to Party officials, both the silence of the propaganda machine for reasons of "political expediency" and Hitler's opinion regarding a possible parallel development in Germany become understandable. Party officials undoubtedly reflected on the fact that in Germany preference had also been given to a "graduated" process of organization over one of a complete destruction of the old structure, though much more progress had been made in a shorter period of time. Neither an independent head of state nor a potent general staff remained. An additional security guarantee against an armed putsch was the existence of a second military arm, the Waffen-SS.[263] Furthermore, the maneuverability and foreign ties of big business were increasingly circumscribed, and the Jews had either been deported or murdered. Only political Catholicism had held its own, even strengthening its position after a temporary weakness—but there was no fear of revolutionary activity from it. Discontent among the public could be held in check, the leaders thought, by increased propaganda and intensified terror.[264] To make this curtailment of the margin of freedom plausible, inner and outer freedom were contrasted and declared antithetical. On the basis of recent German history, by juxtaposing the freedom of November, 1918, with resulting foreign enslavement, propaganda argued that only a "certain amount of coercion" at home could bring outward freedom for a people.[265]

Under these tighter restrictions, the fourth anniversary of the war met with a dreary reception.[266] There was no hope as yet of an eventual breach in the East-West alliance confronting Germany, thanks to Goebbels' propaganda of "complete unity between the Jews in Washington, London, and Moscow. . . ."[267] Few were convinced by the official argument that victory was still in sight now that Hitler had employed superior strategy to break the stranglehold in which Germany had been held at the start of the war. On the contrary, disappointment was observed over the failure of both Hitler and Göring as well as other leading figures to speak up. "We are, after all, a people's state and have a popular government. We therefore hoped that on this fateful day marking the outbreak of war, a few words 'from above' would have been directed at all those difficult and troubling questions touching each and every one."[268]

Once again the mass media's limited range of possible influence became evident. Not until Hitler spoke on September 10 and the Italian scene began to change did the decline of public spirit come to a halt. *What* the Führer said to the masses—Italy's capitulation had been more or less expected in any case—was less important than *how* he said it. "Upon hearing the calm voice of the Führer, who delivered his arguments with an unshakable confidence in victory, this peace communicated itself to many citizens. People exclaimed that 'as long as the Führer keeps his nerve, everything is o.k. with us. . . ."[269] No indication exists as to how many Germans were still affected by Hitler; particularly striking is the absence of reference either to a majority or to the general public.

Hitler's remarks[270] about the Duce's domestic political difficulties surprised most. Until then the conviction had more or less prevailed that Mussolini had rejected the alliance. The biggest impression, however, was made by Hitler's reference to revenge. Many who had lost faith gathered fresh hope. Hitler also knew how to elicit understanding for the need to wait a while longer before revenge could be realized. The Party Chancellory contributed its efforts to strengthening hopes for retribution and thus also to the public's ability to hold out. Officials were instructed to avoid any mention of specific target dates and to stop idle gossip about the extent and nature of this retribution, about "new weapons . . . etc., so that the enemy is not carelessly offered valuable hints. It must suffice that the citizen knows: retribution will come. . . ."[271]

Partly animated by Hitler's speech, the public further recovered its spirit with the arrival of new reports from Italy. On September 10, the OKW informed the public of the disarming of Italian troops in the area of Rome and northern Italy after brief skirmishes. Italian units in southern France and the Balkans had also laid down their arms. On the following day the capitulation of Italian garrisons on Rhodes was announced, as well as the occupation by German troops of Milan, Turin, Padua, and Pola. A sign of relief finally swept through the German population, and Italian jokes suddenly reemerged.[272]

The special operation of September 12 which liberated Mussolini gave rise to a further upswing in the mood "as numerous citizens were shaken out of their lethargy and displayed a confidence not seen for some time. The way in which the situation, initially regarded as critical, was mastered by the German command is seen as a sign of German resourcefulness and strength and of the Wehrmacht's unimpaired striking force. The latter had completely swept away the prolonged uneasiness that Germany had been forced to relinquish the initiative to the enemy. . . ." Although the overall military situation remained serious, Allied capitulation demands on Italy did strengthen the will to hold out. "In case of a German defeat," the explanation went, "the demands would likely be stiffer. . . ." The crescendo of peace slogans waned, particularly in southern Germany[273] where the general assumption had been that the Western powers would check Bolshevism and impose a relatively easy occupation. "Apparently a less humane" treatment of Italians by Anglo-Americans had given these circles a jolt.[274] In the wake of an improving mood and of disappointment over Allied cease-fire conditions in Italy, attacks against the NSDAP and leading figures of the Nazi regime diminished appreciably.[275] The Duce, on the other hand, was now regarded as little more than a Gauleiter taking his orders directly from Hitler; in the eyes of the Germans, Italy had forfeited its position as an ally with equal rights.[276]

Not since the fall of Stalingrad had the regime received such a good rating. "Amidst all the unpleasant developments, the news of the energetic and successful intervention by our military in Italy and the bold stroke to free the Duce swept in like a cleansing rainstorm. In the face of all the cares and fears, the effect of these two factors was a downright relief. Confidence in the Führer and our military strength was suddenly raised enormously. . . ."[277] This assessment by the public prosecutor may be too optimistic; nevertheless, a certain upswing in the mood was unmistakable.

3.   WHAT HARDENS US BE PRAISED: FALL, 1943, TO JUNE, 1944

The first signs of a "gradual flagging"[278] of spirits were again detected near the end of September. At fault were accounts from the Eastern theatre of operations, an arena which had been pushed into the background by the spectacular events in Italy.

The Soviet summer offensive had begun on July 17 with a pincer movement in the Donets basin; the German lines were penetrated south of Kursk and east of Stalino, and on August 22 German troops finally evacuated Kharkov. Hitler was finally forced to act on Field Marshal von Manstein's entreaties to evacuate the region and fall back behind the Dnieper. An exposed Army Group Center forced its retreat to the line Melitopol-Dnieper-Desna. Russian pursuit was to be impeded by a "scorched earth" policy and the forceful evacuation of all able-bodied inhabitants. On September 30, German armies stood completely behind the Dnieper, over which the Soviets held two bridgeheads. In addition, contact to Army Group Center had been cut by the Soviet breakthrough in the direction of Kiev. In the course of September, Bryansk, Smolensk, and Roslawl had been lost. By October 9, Germans had also been forced to evacuate the Kuban bridgehead and pull back to the Crimean Peninsula through the streets of Kerch.

Reports of these withdrawals unleashed "serious concern." That segment of the population which continued to trust blindly in National Socialist political and military leadership "regarded these German measures as a strategic maneuver in accordance with a brilliant plan of the Führer's, envisaging a concentration of all forces in order to initiate the appropriate counter-attack in the spring of 1944." However, besides these "faithful" there were a growing number of skeptics. "Such attitudes were supported by reports from front-line soldiers who talk about an enormous Soviet superiority and speak of the German front as 'pitifully undermanned'. . . ."[279] There was no question as to their accuracy; German infantry divisions had suffered heavy losses and were reduced to one-half or even one-third their fighting strength. Hardest hit were the constantly deployed tank units which lost 1560 tanks from July to September. On October 1, 8,400 Soviet tanks faced only seven hundred combat-ready German tanks.[280]

SD reports on the mood from the front in the fall of 1943[281] made the same distinctions between front-line troops, members of the armed services behind the lines, and those stationed in occupied areas north and west and in the Balkans. "While soldiers from *occupied regions* never influenced the home front all that positively before, at times even provoking unrest with stories of camp life, it is striking that now a growing number of those *on leave from the eastern front* are coming home with pessimistic views, while a few months ago they still had an almost unshakeable confidence and complete faith in the triumph of our arms. In remarks by soldiers from the Eastern front it is primarily *statements about the relative strength* of Germany and the Soviet Union which *have a depressing effect* on the population. . . . Lately men on leave have also spread an increasing number of unfavorable reports on the *relationship between officers and men*." Reports of declining officer authority, inexperienced junior officers, and rumors of carousing, sexual license, and black marketeering created impressions of a gradual demoralization along the front, analogous to the final stages of the First World War. Reports of defeatism from the western regions were even worse.

If we can rightly assert that responsible Nazis, and Hitler in particular, had delayed or, when possible, avoided making important decisions, we must also note that they acted swiftly when it concerned the eradication of abuses endangering their own existence. After the reports of raucous living in occupied areas and their adverse effects on public opinion continued to mount, Hitler issued a long decree on fundamentals [*Grundsatzbefehl*] on November 27, 1943, aimed simultaneously at strengthening the front, freeing labor for armaments,[282] and stemming signs of demoralization: "The struggle for the existence of the German people and for the future of Europe is nearing its climax. . . . The ranks of fighting soldiers have been considerably thinned by death, injury, and illness. The disparity between fighting troops and the large numbers of soldiers behind the lines has risen to such a degree that it threatens to become not only a purely military but also a psychological danger.—We know it from the last war by the name of 'camp life.' The words have been abolished but the manifestations have remained." Hitler declared his resolve to restore the fighting strength of front-line troops with "the most ruthless methods." All resistance was to be broken by "draconian penalties."

The Wehrmacht and Waffen-SS had to transfer one million men from their ranks to the front. In home and rear-guard regions all individuals not engaged in critical military work were to be drafted "without regard to age and medical qualification." The number of offices and units exempt from service was to be reduced. Special controls were to be introduced into all cities to eradicate signs of high living and to direct civilian laborers, including women, to the Wehrmacht. Fitness criteria were to be simplified. Hitler closed the long decree with the threat: "If, after January 1, 1944, I am informed of cases where for reasons of indifference, egotism, and disobedience the decrees to strengthen the front are not executed, I will treat the responsible superior as a war criminal. . . ."[283] This phase of total mobilization of the military sector temporarily came to a close with the previously mentioned Führer's decree of December 22, 1943, which introduced a Nazi command staff into the OKW and into the supreme commands of the three separate military branches.[284]

On the economic front, the transition from a "peace-like wartime economy" to a full-fledged war economy was finally made in the fall of 1943. Speer assumed control from the Reich Economics Ministry over the areas of raw materials and industrial and handicraft production. His title, commensurate with the new tasks, was now no longer Reich Minister for Arms and Munitions, but rather for Mobilization and War Production.[285] As a result, almost the entire production system of Greater Germany was now consolidated in one hand. Only air force armaments remained outside his competence; jurisdiction over naval armaments had already been transferred on June 26. Speer thus also controlled *de facto* the economies of occupied areas. Beginning in the

fall of 1943, the German consumer industry was to be radically curtailed for the first time in the war. But in the interests of political
expediency, only half-way measures were applied.

In the area of propaganda, Goebbels attempted to deal with criticism
of the Nazi regime by issuing "Thirty War Articles for the German
Volk,"[286] a kind of negative *Magna Charta*. Beginning with the article
that the very thought of capitulation was treasonous, it went on to
speak of the "right to life" of the German people, the treachery of
foreign propaganda in asserting that the leadership "has it better than
the people," and the need for greater sacrifice for the sake of future
generations. This became the basis of the Party activization program
which began with rallies for Party members in November, 1943,[287] and
was supplemented by the revived theme of revenge.[288] Even religious
overtones were employed. In his traditional speech at the Munich beer
hall on November 8,[289] Hitler cleverly described himself as "innerly
deeply religious," frequently "bowing in gratitude before the Almighty."
If his comments undoubtedly evoked ridicule from church circles, his
speech made a profound impression on a majority of his listeners,
according to SD reports.[290]

Another means of averting undesirable criticism and forestalling an
irrevocable rift between the rulers and the ruled was the use of brutal
repressive tactics. In his speech Hitler had stated that he would not
shrink from "sending a few hundred criminals to their death without
further ado." Penalties for "defeatism" were in fact stiffened considerably
and certain crimes transferred from special courts to the People's Tribunal [*Volksgerichtshof*] which originally had only been competent in
matters of high treason.[291] The intention was to achieve a greater degree
of uniformity in the sentencing of political "subversion." By their relative mildness judgments of the regular courts had often aroused the
indignation of hard-line Nazis.[292] While the People's Tribunal pronounced death penalties, the lower courts sentenced individuals of
equal stature and crimes only to varying prison terms.[293]

The best-known case involved state councillor Theodor Korselt of
Rostock. He was sentenced to death by the People's Tribunal for having
expressed the opinion, in the wake of Mussolini's "resignation," that
the same thing should happen in Germany. Hitler should step down,
since there was no longer any prospect for victory. After all, not everyone wanted to be burned alive.[294] The sister of Erich Maria Remarque,
Frau Scholz, was also sentenced to death.[295] Such verdicts were deliberately communicated to the German public as a deterrent. On November 6, Goebbels wrote in his diary: "I believe, at any rate, that we
can expect no difficulties from the moral attitude of the German Volk.

Our Volk is presently in a splendid frame of mind. This is attributable to our good propaganda, but in part also to the severe measures we are taking against defeatists. . . ."[296]

Comparing the present mood with the catastrophic one between spring and autumn, one has to agree with Goebbels, albeit with some reservations; "excellent" would hardly be the word to describe the state of opinion, but it was far better than some months back. The fact that Mussolini's fall ultimately had a less adverse effect than feared, that a large part of Italy was still in German hands, and that Anglo-American treatment of Italians was quite severe—all these had once more raised the heavily damaged prestige of the regime in some people's eyes. A further consolidation was achieved by combining hope for retribution with intimidation through terror. Critics became more cautious and met with less approval.[297] Now the pendulum increasingly swung between apathy, "the opinion that we absolutely have to win because otherwise all would be lost,"[298] and blind fatalism.

Least interested and most indifferent were the women.[299] Weighed down by the cares of daily life, their horizon no longer extended beyond the routine. Only those with family at the front followed military events in that specific sector. Marriages suffered from long separations: "combat soldiers on leave often failed to show any understanding for how domestic affairs were conditioned by war, and were uninterested in many of the daily cares on the home front. As a result, a certain drifting apart of couples occurred more often." When the husband finally came home on leave, instead of expected honeymoons there were scenes and clashes.

Evacuation of women and children from endangered zones was also far from conducive to harmonious family relations. Some women took it in stride; others constantly fretted about their husbands' welfare. Living alone, without familial attention and laughing children, it was not surprising that men lost their zeal and strength for work. "Especially within working-class circles, the comment is frequently heard that if there is any interest in maintaining their ability and zest for work, their wives should remain with them. . . . Married men in particular declare that family life is the only compensating factor for their hard work. We should not take away even this last thing that makes life still seem worth living. . . ."[300]

Not the least of the problems created by enforced separation was the sexual. Here the needs of men were considered natural and necessary for Germany's survival;[301] therefore, the Wehrmacht tried to meet them with the creation of bordellos, but for the female sex such needs were declared immoral and denied when possible. However, the relaxation of morals and separation of couples, common to all wars, soon made it evident that not only men possessed erotic desires and felt the need for sexual release. The SD felt compelled to issue a report on this matter, entitled "The Immoral Behavior of German Women."[302] According to its findings, the decline in morals was no longer confined to isolated cases, "but rather involved a *large number of women and girls* who were more and more inclined *to enjoy sexual life to the full.* Many places have notorious bars where soldiers' wives go to meet men who will accompany them home. With mothers running around, *the children* are often left to themselves and are *in danger of running wild. . . .*"

According to SD statements this phenomenon concerned predominantly women from the lower strata of society, but similar tendencies were also emerging within other circles.[303] For *upper society*, it was naturally easier to receive visitors discreetly into the home. And not only lonely wives were starved for love. The SD also found "a strong inclination toward sexual abandonment" among single people, a fact that led to numerous pregnancies among 14- to 18-year-olds and to the spread of venereal diseases. As a last unpleasant consequence of deficient moral stature, the report cited intercourse with prisoners-of-war and "alien workers."

This free life-style among women presented a strain for the Nazi leadership. On the one hand, sexual libertinism on the part of men was heightened since "every woman is available today;" on the other, the fighting morale of soldiers was weakened by anxiety over the sexual excesses of their wives. Among the reasons cited for this lack of virtue among women were the absence of former social activities such as dances, vacations, sports, and fashions; basic sexual need; relatively high family support payments which enabled women to frequent pubs and coffee houses; daily threats of air attack, creating an attitude of instant gratification while possible; erotic films and literature; the poor example of the elite with its divorces and affairs; and the desire for the luxury goods of occupied countries: coffee, chocolates, alcohol, and stockings which soldiers brought back with them. That the regime's anti-church policy had contributed to the breakdown of previous moral tabus was never suggested.

Lack of equality in the sexual realm was matched by discrimination in the socio-political sector. This was quite apparent in matters pertaining to wage policy. In this case we possess a document which clearly proves that Hitler was the one who blocked every improvement.

At a conference attended by Reich Organization Leader Dr. Ley, Plenipotentiary for the Allocation of Labor Sauckel, Lord Mayor Liebel in place of Reich Minister Speer, Price Commissioner Dr. Fischböck, Ambassador Abetz, and Reich Minister Dr. Lammers—who took the minutes[304]—Ley proposed an equalization of salaries for men and women on the principle of "equal pay for equal work and equal efficiency." Hitler countered with a "statement of principle" that: "Wages in the National Socialist state serve two functions: a) remuneration for productivity per se, but beyond that b) wages also have to fulfill a social function, i.e., to consider the rank of the worker in the Volk community. For the latter reason the man, from whom the state demands that he marry and build a family, must receive higher remuneration than the single man and the woman. It would be impossible to gear wages purely to performance. If one did this, the end result would be that the younger man who is probably more productive, is better paid than the older man. . . ." In the case of women, the principle of equal pay for equal work could not be solved during the war anyway, since a true performance comparison would be impossible as long as younger, more productive men were in the field. Hitler was therefore again presenting the principle of "commensurate salary." Hereto came the fear resulting from the world economic crisis of a new wave of unemployment in peace years, which to him seemed to make desirable the future exclusion of women as competitors for work. A final motive was ultimately his biologically slanted conception of the natural inferiority of women.

The principle of wage equality was, in his opinion, "in complete contradiction to the National Socialist principle of support for the *Volksgemeinschaft.*" This ideal, which he wanted to realize in peacetime, envisaged that "only the man would earn money, and that even the lowliest worker would have a three-room dwelling for himself and his family. The woman would then have to stay at home to look after the house and the family. . . ." Hitler wanted to cling to these principles even during the war, otherwise "peacetime work would obstruct National Socialist designs." If a woman did perform a man's work and in addition had to care for her children, equalization could be achieved through wage premiums or tax relief—but not by raising the basic pay. This obvious discrimination against female laborers and the underlying delusion of male superiority become especially clear in Hitler's closing remarks: "regarding peacetime, one should also consider that certain occupations should be closed to men, occupations such as the job of waiter which could just as well be filled by a woman, and even more so that of a hairdresser; it is nothing short of unworthy for a man to do a woman's hair. . . ."

These social attitudes came from a man preoccupied by military command and thus more and more removed from the public eye. Domestic affairs were left to his ambitious Chief of the Party Chancellor, Bormann—the actual head of the NSDAP—, and to Goebbels and Himmler, a triumvirate governed by jealousy and rivalry. Completely independent of them, yet growing in power and responsibility, was Albert Speer, who was unencumbered by any ideological criteria or considerations other than efficiency, thus incurring the mistrust of intransigent Party leaders. Then there was Hermann Göring, steadily losing prestige and influence, and a number of "demigods" as well as some political ciphers.

Hitler slowly stepped into the background, as evidenced by the weak response and negligible impact of his New Year's speech;[305] Hitler jokes continued to abate as did personal attacks on him—criticism was directed mainly against the regime personified by him and against its policies.[306] Goebbels was partly to blame, always aiming to place Hitler in historical perspective. As the waning fortunes of war were to be seen *sub specie historiae*, likewise the figure of the Führer was to be measured by the standard of history. Again Frederick the Great served as model. What his contemporaries had thought of him between 1760 and 1763 was very different from present judgments of the great king.[307] Bormann encouraged this distancing of Hitler from the people by attempting to give him quasireligious stature. The concept "Führer" was to take on cosmic significance and thus had to be reserved for Hitler alone.[308]

Meanwhile the Volk bent under the knout of war. During the winter and spring of 1943-44, the Eastern theatre claimed far more attention than military developments in Italy. Soviet troops renewed their attacks on November 3 in the direction of Kiev, though their actual winter offensive did not begin until December 24. Crossing the Russo-Polish prewar border, General Watutin's troops reached Rovno and Luzk on February 5 and then turned southward to Uman to endanger the German Dnieper frontal arc. Hitler rejected Manstein's recommended evacuation of the area because of the ore mines of Krivoi Rog and Nikopol, and Manstein was subsequently able to smash the Soviet spearhead against Vinnitsa and Uman. Some fifty thousand Germans were nevertheless encircled; without informing Hitler, Manstein ordered a breakout towards the southwest, and about two-thirds fought their way to freedom on the night of February 17.

Those segments of the population who followed the Eastern campaign attentively were alarmed at the loss of Rovno and Luzk. Newspapers carried articles with the heading, "Extremely Bizarre Developments on the Eastern Front," and pointed to "strange line formations and a severe indentation of the front." Many Germans were worried about expected further "alignments of the front" and asked themselves "how far our military command actually intends to withdraw, or whether we no longer possess the freedom and opportunity to decide this ourselves." Far more bewildering for the public, however, was the fact that the press and radio neglected the Eastern theater more and more, labelling instead the West and the "anticipated invasion as militarily decisive and as the first front."[309]

Since December, Hitler's conception of an invasion in the West had been played up by propaganda. The dual themes of revenge and invasion were now to dominate the scene and to instill new courage and will to resist in a German people increasingly cornered by results in the East and by an intensified air war.

Revenge and termination of the war were increasingly viewed synonymously. "As a third element, add the 'invasion,' whereby some people mean the English-American landing attempt in the west, others a German operation against the British Isles." The date for this retaliation, considered militarily decisive, was set by those who believed in it at all for the spring: "Some citizens even completely doubt any retaliation. It is nothing more than a grandiose propaganda maneuver by the German leadership with the purpose of frightening the population in England and inducing the Anglo-American leadership to implement prematurely their not fully matured plans. In contrast, there are opponents who characterize the retribution propaganda as a technique on the part of the leadership to continue to 'bring people up to scratch' and to prolong this hopeless war a while longer. Reprisal jokes, of which there are quite a number, probably stem chiefly from these circles. For example: "Retribution will come when homes for the aged post signs, 'closed due to induction!'" "1950. Conference in the Führer's headquarters about the date for retaliation. It is adjourned for lack of agreement on the question of whether the two planes should fly beside or behind each other. . . ." Also typical is the following joke: "During the last attack on Berlin, the English dropped hay for the jackasses who still believe in revenge. . . ."[310]

Goebbels reacted to such reports with a campaign which presented the German situation as far rosier than that of the enemy, leaving no doubt as to the outcome of the anticipated invasion.[311] Available documents confirm the effectiveness of propaganda in combining invasion, retribution, and air attacks in such a way as to raise public morale and to instill a greater sense of common fate, a more intense hatred of England, and the will to keep on fighting.[312] The condition of helpless and defenseless victims caught in a hail of bombs proved fertile soil for propagating hopes of revenge and retribution. Growing dissatisfaction with the regime was skillfully diverted to the enemy. The objective of the Allied bombing offensive backfired; instead of demoralizing the German population, one can almost say the new wave of terror saved the Nazi regime from a most explosive domestic situation. Opponents of the regime were probably not reduced in numbers, but they were now silent. All resistance to the regime surely seemed suicidal in the light of the foreign threat.

"The people have surpassed themselves as a result of the bombing raids, heroically overcoming fear. One can say that the bourgeoisie is dead or at least in its death throes. Pettiness, meanness, a clinging to possessions, that soup-plate horizon, stalwart egotism, intellectual narrow-mindedness, the mixture of perpetual fear and feeble hopes, the whole gamut of wretchedness that characterizes the bourgeois and philistines—have vanished into thin air. Inwardly and outwardly most people present an image inconceivable just a while ago. Germans are on the verge of becoming a real Volksgemeinschaft. Just as this Volksgemeinschaft closes ranks as a matter of course, during and after bombing raids, it is also determined to see the battle through to victory."[313] Similar observations were made by the public prosecutors of Darmstadt; Kiel—who described public attitude as "superb"[314]—; Hamburg, who spoke of a sense of "security" exuded by citizens even in the shelters;[315] and Düsseldorf: the blame for the casualties "is not charged to the state but to the enemy."[316]

SD reports commented on the "disgust," "contempt," and "bitterness" felt towards enemy pilots.[317] On the other hand, a certain "conflict of feelings" toward the enemy was also indicated: "The vast majority of the population, to be sure, steadfastly maintains that the Führer must ruthlessly 'exterminate' England because the misery which the English have heaped upon us can only be repaid in kind. In contrast, however, the comment is also repeatedly made that one should remember the women and children in England who would perish as a result. After all, we are Germans who condemn Anglo-American air terror and therefore cannot resort to similar methods." From among more religiously oriented groups came the question of whether one had a right to hate one's enemy and exterminate him. Bishop von Galen commented on that issue, stating that "retaliation against non-military objectives not only conflicted with Christian thinking, but also contradicted the tradition of military chivalry which prided itself on rising above primitive and basic lust for revenge."[318] But such notions of Christian charity were hardly evident among all confessional groups. The population of the severely plagued western regions exhibited more vindictiveness than that of other areas. No uniform image of the British emerged, despite Goebbels' hate campaign. "Hate-filled remarks about England are more often expressions of despair or indignation and of the view that the destruction of England offers the only road to our own deliverance. Furthermore, anti-British hatred is directed more against individuals, the air gangsters for example, and the Jewish-plutocratic leadership personified by Churchill, to whom, however, a certain reluctant tribute is paid at times. One cannot speak of hatred for the English people as a whole. The argument is also frequently made that the English people were dragged into the war by their warmongers. . . ." Uniformity of opinion was made more difficult by stories from German prisoners-of-war of humane treatment at the hands of the English during World War I. Among the intelligentsia there was no evidence of hatred; Churchill was frequently judged a capable man who had to be taken seriously.

This report serves as a reason for introducing three digressions which throw further light on public opinion during the first half of 1944. If the view was often expressed that the British people had been innocently driven to war by warmongers, it was a conscious or subconscious allusion to one's own situation. A number of observations indicate a growing public concern with the problem of war guilt. Goebbels received letters from the public expressing the opinion that "the Führer and his National Socialist movement carry the blame for the outbreak of this war,"[319] or that considerable doubt existed "as to whether Russia would have independently started the war against Germany and Europe if Germany had not beaten her to it. . . ."[320] The head of the Reich propaganda office in Berlin wrote on June 2, 1944, to Sondermann, deputy head of the propaganda division in the Reich Ministry for Propaganda and Public Enlightenment: "From various quarters, especially the Party membership, one learns in talks with the public and conversations in air raid shelters that the belief frequently exists that Germany carries a certain measure of responsibility for the outbreak of war in 1939, and the burdens and worries of this war were therefore to a considerable extent the fault of the Reich."[321] Two days later, obviously due to public pressure, Goebbels released an article in *Das Reich*, "Was this War Avoidable?" Here Goebbels renewed his attempts to explain how the enemy had begun its military preparations well before the war, waiting only for an opportune moment to strike. Enemy assertions that Germany could have avoided a confrontation presupposes German acquiescence to their aggressive intentions. "We must defend our very life, for the enemy is not attacking the Party nor the Wehrmacht nor industry nor the state, his attack is directed at us as a people. . . ."[322]

The second digression relevant to the report on public attitudes toward the English concerns the treatment of allied pilots shot down. Here the Nazi regime conducted an ugly smear policy. In an announcement of March 22, 1944, to all Gauleiters regarding the "treatment by the

German population of British and American air crews forced to land," Bormann informed them that the population was indeed arresting allied flyers but "not maintaining a distance in keeping with the severity of the war." Thus they were to be enlightened accordingly. "Whoever behaves in an undignified manner towards air crews who have crash landed, be it from malevolent intentions or misconstrued sympathy, will be ruthlessly called to account. In blatant cases it will result in assignment to a concentration camp and disclosure in the newspapers. In petty instances, a minimum of fourteen days imprisonment will result at the local head offices of the state police who will give preference to these citizens for clean-up work in damaged areas." This directive could only be passed on verbally.[323]

At the end of May, Goebbels published two articles in the *Völkische Beobachter* and *Das Reich* inciting downright murder; in "Now is Enough" and "A Comment on Enemy Air Terror," he demanded that strafers be killed like mad dogs. There were those who supported his position.[324] Low-level attacks by British fighters on individuals were an especially dubious aspect of the air war, affecting the rural population more than any other. The Reich Propaganda Minister received a number of letters with demands that the flyers either be shot, hanged or tied to trees near vital industrial targets so they could see what their comrades were doing.[325] Among the intelligentsia, however, there were reservations, according to a report from Schwerin,[326] "that reckless treatment of air gangsters could easily lead to reprisals against German prisoners-of-war or parachuting German pilots; but generally, and particularly in principle, there is support for Dr. Goebbels even within these circles. Individual citizens, however, warn against permitting such 'executions' in public; the impression could then arise that it was only state or Party-employed instigators who brought the people's emotions to the boiling point. Thus, if one wanted to accomplish something without simultaneously endangering captured Germans, then 'it' must be done cleverly ('shot while attempting escape' for instance) by discrete individuals. . . ."

This perfidious piece of advice, already tested in practical operations, was later employed when allied pilots escaped from the camp near Sagan and then were recaptured. As far as we know the practice was not adopted by the population.

The third digression concerns the attitude of intellectuals. Here, as in many previous reports, their critical or hostile position was emphasized. As already mentioned in the introduction, many members of this segment of society had paid tribute to the new regime, partly from misguided idealism, partly from opportunism, but partly also from conviction. The annual situation report for 1938 and the quarterly report by the SD, from which an excerpt was cited, point to a reticent if not procrastinating attitude among university professors.[327]

We also have two reports for the period of total warfare concerning the Technical Institute at Darmstadt and the University at Giessen. Aside from strong reproaches against state and military for gross neglect of research in the natural and especially the physical sciences, the substance of the observations is about the same as that of the immediate pre-war period. Known Nazi activists were "shunned, praised until they left for elsewhere, or rejected for technical reasons." The attitude of various academics is described as "impenetrable"; furthermore, they had—in the Third Reich of all places—given preference to non-Aryan colleagues.

"Reserved neutrality can serve as the common denominator of all observations at universities in this region concerning mood, attitude, and outlook on war developments among professors." However: "Academics who might publicly dare a negative opinion do not exist. . . ." University professors were literally accused for their "objectivity" and also their largely pessimistic basic tendencies. But only a small group was marked as being indifferent to National Socialism; for most, however, one has to conclude opportunism, even if the word was never employed. "The present lack of publications is partially attributable to the fact that people don't know how the war will end; therefore, aside from medicine, engineering, and the natural sciences, only the humanities can publish something very neutral. . . ." The reporter's comment reveals the discontent of a convinced Nazi: "It seems bad form to work ideological questions into the sciences," whereby his sights were aimed particularly at the medical faculty with its professional exclusivity and disregard for National Socialist issues. "Our new recruits, types who in a purely technical sense have now reached a certain stature, have learned from National Socialist problems only that they have to be in the Party so they can at least outwardly show that they know how to go along with the times."[328]

We thus find here a behavioral model typical of a broad spectrum of public servants and employees; Buchheim termed it "structural opportunism,"[329] to be found among all segments of society, and likely in all totalitarian societies, since it guarantees a relatively undisturbed existence in an environment one neither necessarily endorses nor respects but one that, if challenged, would mean loss of possessions if not loss of freedom and life.

Returning from this digression to the SD report on the public image of the enemy, most Germans resented the United States' entry into the war, which they regarded as self-serving, but were either indifferent toward Americans individually or saw in them a contemptible "dollar imperialism," plutocracy, and cultural inferiority. While Russia's awesome power still aroused irrational fears, the sacrifices and achievements of the Russian people increasingly won respect and evoked, in reaction, criticism of the German military command for failing to implement the same tough war measures as existed on the home front. "From front-line soldiers comes the expression: 'The Russians are conducting total war, we are fighting an elegant war.' "[330] Italians meanwhile remained the logical choice as recipients of the public's scorn and anger.[331] Mussolini's attempt to reestablish the Italian Fascist state was given little credence, and attention soon shifted once more to the East in anticipation of the annual German spring offensive.

Despite setbacks which forced evacuation of the Crimea, the overall attitude both at the front and at home remained better in the spring of 1944 than in the previous year. Since this was unwarranted by military developments, the cause is largely to be found in public apathy;[332] more and more people took flight into an irrational fatalism,[333] waiting for the "great miracle" which would change everything at one stroke. An "existential anxiety" [Lebensangst] became quite evident; others were "fed up." Discontent and listlessness gained ground. But reports about "Party weariness," disappearance of Party badges, were far scarcer[334] and criticism of propaganda was kept more in bounds.[335] A good and unmalicious joke involved the two well-known Cologne originals, Tünnes and Scheel: "Tünnes chanced upon Scheel in the Cologne Cathedral with a radio. When asked what he was doing with a radio in here, Scheel replied: the radio has to go to confession, it has lied too much in recent weeks."[336]

Oberbefehlsleiter Friedrichs of the Party Chancellory was therefore justified in reporting with some pride on the Party's success in the past year to a meeting of Reichsleiters and Gauleiters at the Führer Haus in Munich on March 23, 1944. "When the war ceased to roll on according to a minute by minute program last year, when we suffered military reverses, when we experienced Stalingrad, later Tunisia, then the betrayal of the Duce and beyond that we encountered heavier and heavier air raids on the Reich, there stood the Party; but one did learn here and there that individual Party members became weak in the knees, tired, lax, uninterested and unable to achieve the bearing which we must demand from a Party member." With the help of the general appeal, Party rap sessions, and word-of-mouth propaganda, not just the NSDAP was being revived; the public was also instilled with new courage. "In this way it was really possible, for example, to call a halt to the rumors, jokes, etc., spread during the past year, so that we can declare today that jokes about leading Party members, about the Party . . . are practically as good as gone; those one does hear are exceptions. . . ." After reciting future tasks, Friedrichs closed with the words: "If the Party is operating, the mood in the nation will, without a doubt, be sustained, the attitude at home will be irreproachable, the front will have the necessary support, it will get the necessary weapons; we must therefore employ all our resources for the conservation of the combat effectiveness and fighting strength of the movement at home. . . ."[337]

A new wave of meetings swept over an increasingly indifferent population in the spring of 1944.[338] People wanted no more slogans, no more prognoses; they wanted a decision arising from a matching of strength with the Anglo-Americans. To cite all the voices concerning the widespread hopes for an invasion and for revenge is impossible, since not one report, be it from the Justice Ministry, the SD, or Party officials, fails to mention them. Nor can one determine the extent to which these reports responded to directives or actual facts. In the ups and downs of opinion, three trends crystallized and were summarized by the SD section in Schwerin in mid-May as follows:[339]

    a)   The invasion takes place and succeeds to the extent that the enemy forms a number of bridgeheads at various points along the European seacoast. From there, long, bloody positional warfare breaks out (example Nettuno) to which the Reich must eventually succumb for lack of men and raw material, especially since the enemy air force can further increase its activity by using newly-won positions. Even a partially successful invasion leads to defeat, since German reserves no longer permit a long war.

    b)   The invasion fails and is superbly repulsed everywhere. Tremendous enemy losses from new German weapons. Army and air force pursue and begin their invasion of the British Isles. Retribution sets in. Mood in England—already heavily burdened by numerous strikes—collapses. England has to capitulate.

    c)   For the present the invasion does not take place; continuation of enemy attempts to demoralize the German people by means of a war of nerves (invasion threat). Further assistance for Bolshevism. Continuation and intensification of air attacks. In June a new Soviet offensive, thus the departure of more forces from the west; then suddenly enemy landing operations to deliver the death-blow to German resistance.

The majority of the masses shared the hopes enunciated under b), that it would be possible to repulse Allied landings and reach a settlement with England. Word-of-mouth propaganda and massive indoctrination undoubtedly had a lot to do with creating this optimistic vision. More critical elements, especially intellectuals, took a more pessimistic view, either a) or c), on the premise that time was working against Germany.

If we compare this convincing report on overall public opinion with an SD study of November 22, 1943: "Basic Questions on the Mood and Attitude of the German People, re: Total Victory, Negotiated Peace or Peace at any Price?,"[340] a certain conformity and continuity become apparent. It is quite evident that after the collapse in morale in the spring and summer of 1943, the large masses were optimistic from the end of the year until the invasion. Only two minority opinions dissented: a relatively small percentage of Germans who favored a peace at any price and a somewhat larger percentage in favor of a compromise peace. Their constituency came from all sectors of society and generally reckoned with "leniency" from the enemy. Some hoped for a pact with the Allies against Bolshevism, others counted on an agreement with Stalin.[341]

But beginning in May, the state and Party leadership as well as the public reckoned with an invasion any day: "The chance for a decisive turn in the military situation in our favor within the foreseeable future allows most citizens to await an invasion with great hopes. They refer to it as the last opportunity to turn the tide. There is hardly any evidence of a fear of invasion. On the contrary, they assume a severe defeat for the enemy. . . ."[342] Those voices which usually suggested a propaganda trick had diminished considerably.

Final preparations began with the daily slogan for May 11, which called on all public media to awaken the people to the gravity of the situation.[343] Bormann simultaneously placed the Party on alert: " . . . every person manning a responsible post must be available every hour of the day and night."[344] The Party was once more summoned to be on its best behavior and "to render with revolutionary fervor a decisive contribution to victory."[345] The hour of "total Weltanschauung"[346] had come.

NOTES

1. IMT, vol. VII, p. 290. Testimony of Paulus.
2. Domarus, II, 2. Halbband, pp. 1937 f.
3. Dahms, op. cit., pp. 507-8.
4. This was the OKH order cited in Erich von Manstein, Verlorene Siege (Bonn, 1955), p. 326.
5. Lothar Gruchmann, Der Zweite Weltkrieg (Munich, 1969), p. 194.
6. BA, ZSg 109/40, fol. 117. Cf. also fol. 120.
7. "Wollt ihr den totalen Krieg?," p. 329 (January 27),
8. Ibid.

9. *Ibid.*, pp. 332-33.
10. The mail censorship bureau for the tank company AOK 4 issued reports that provide a partial impression: MGFA WO1-6/367.
11. Rundschreiben No. 8/7/43 of January 29, 1943, by the district propaganda leader for greater Frankfurt/Main: BA, NS Misch/1648, fol. 142916.
12. Heinz Schröder, *Stalingrad "bis zur letzten Patrone"* (Lengerich, West-phalia, n.d.), p. 68. This book was to replace the one declared "intolerable" by Goebbels.
13. *Letzte Briefe aus Stalingrad* (Gütersloh, n.d.), p. 68.
14. See, for example, *Kriegsbriefe gefallener Studenten 1939-1945*, ed. by Walter Bähr and Dr. Hans W. Bähr (Tübingen, 1952), and the reports of Feldpostprüfstellen in MGFA WO1-6/367.
15. *Letzte Briefe aus Stalingrad*, p. 8.
16. *Ibid.*, p. 12; see also pp. 15-16.
17. *Ibid.*, p. 23.
18. "Meldungen aus dem Reich," February 4, 1943: Boberach, p. 346.
19. *Ibid.*, p. 340 ("Meldungen," January 21, 1943).
20. Regierungspräsident of Regensburg, March 10, 1943: BA, NS19/246.
21. Boberach, p. 341.
22. A document of Amt I in the RSHA, Tgb. No. 256/42 of December 3, 1942, mentions, from indirect sources, that panic had gripped the German leadership, including Hitler. For a time he secluded himself and refused to speak. BA, NS19/neu 1641.
23. "Zwischenbilanz der Winterschlacht:" BA, ZSg 3/1672.
24. *Archiv der Gegenwart*, ed. by Siegler Verlag (n.d.) 5808 F (AG 13/1943).
25. *"Wollt ihr den totalen Krieg?,"* pp. 315 ff.
26. For the delays, missed opportunities and splintering of economic mobiliza-tion beginning in the first years of the Nazi regime, see Wolfgang Sauer, "Die Mobilmachung der Gewalt" in Bracher, Sauer, and Schulz, *Die Na-tionalsozialistische Machtergreifung*, pp. 818 ff.; Milward, *op. cit.*; Gregor Janssen, *Das Ministerium Speer. Deutschlands Rüstung im Krieg* (Berlin, 1968); and Dieter Petzina, *Autarkiepolitik im Dritten Reich. Der National-sozialistische Vierjahresplan* (Stuttgart, 1968).
27. Cf. Alfred Jodl, "Der Einfluss Hitlers auf die Kriegsführung," *Krieg-stagebuch des Oberkommandos der Wehrmacht*, vol. IV (Frankfurt/Main, 1961), p. 1721 (cited in future as KTB/OKW).
28. *"Wollt ihr den totalen Krieg?,"* pp. 317, 318.
29. Hans-Adolf Jacobsen, *1939-1945. Der Zweite Weltkrieg in Chronik und Dokumenten* (Darmstadt, 1959), 4th. ed., p. 373.
30. RGBl. 1943, I, pp. 67, 75. See also BA, ZSg 3/1623 and NS Misch/1727.
31. "Meldungen aus dem Reich," January 18, 1943: Boberach, pp. 335, 336.
32. "Meldungen aus dem Reich," January 28, 1943: *ibid.*, pp. 342, 343.
33. Order issued by Sauckel, RGBl. I, p. 67.
34. "Meldungen aus dem Reich," February 4, 1943: Boberach, p. 347.
35. *"Wollt ihr den totalen Krieg?,"* p. 322 (January 21, 1943); see also p. 329 (January 28).
36. Walter Hagemann, *Publizistik im Dritten Reich*, pp. 464, 465.
37. "Meldungen aus dem Reich," February 22, 1943: Boberach, p. 359.
38. Monthly report of the Regierungspräsident for Lower Franconia and Aschaffenburg, March 10, 1943: BHStA, Abt. II, MA 106681. Cf. also

Regierungspräsident Regensburg, same date: BA, NS19/346; Partei-
Kanzlei II B4: "Auszüge aus Berichten der Gauleitungen und anderer
Dienststellen," period February 21 to February 27, 1943, in BA, NS 6/414;
and report "about the first impression of the Minister's speech, representing a summary of presently available reports from Reich propaganda
offices" by the Propaganda Chief of the Propaganda Staff, dated February
19, 1943: BA, R55/61, fol. 1-5.

39. Underlined in the original. See footnote 38 above, Partei-Kanzlei II B4.
40. *Ibid.*
41. "The Minister learned that the Führer expressed his particular satisfaction
    with German propaganda, especially the topic of Stalingrad."—February 8,
    1943. *"Wollt ihr den totalen Krieg?,"* p. 235.
42. Propa 2061/February 27, 1943/23-2,2(h): BA, R55/603, fol. 187.
43. "Zur Aufnahme der Kriegswochenschau vom 27. 2. bis 5. 3. 1943" in
    "Meldungen aus dem Reich," March 4, 1943: Boberach, p. 365.
44. *"Wollt ihr den totalen Krieg?",* p. 343.
45. "Meldungen aus dem Reich," January 18, 1943, "Aufnahme und Aus-
    wirkung der allgemeinen Propaganda-, Presse- und Rundfunklenkung:"
    Boberach, pp. 334 ff.
46. The following reported intensified interception of enemy radio broad-
    casts: compendium of Party Chancellory reports for the period February 21
    to 27: BA, NS6/414; report of the Regierungspräsident for Upper and
    Central Franconia, dated March 8, 1943: BHStA, Abt. II, MA 106679;
    "Meldungen aus dem Reich," January 18, March 15: Boberach, pp. 339,
    372.
47. "Meldungen aus dem Reich," January 11, 1943: *ibid.*, pp. 331, 332.
48. "Meldungen aus dem Reich," February 8, 1943: *ibid.*, p. 353.
49. *Ibid.*, p. 354.
50. *Ibid.*, p. 355.
51. Partei-Kanzlei II B4: "Auszüge aus Berichten der Gauleitungen u. a.
    Dienststellen" for the period January 24-30, 1943: BA, NS6/414; and
    "Meldungen aus dem Reich," February 15, 1943: Boberach, p. 357.
52. Partei-Kanzlei, *ibid.* See also the milder report from the Gauleitung
    Weser-Ems.
53. Partei-Kanzlei, *ibid.*, period February 14-20, 1943.
54. See, for example, "Briefe deutscher Kriegsgefangener" in BA, R55/583,
    fol. 2, 5, 6. And, Partei-Kanzlei, *ibid*, period February 14-20, 1943, and
    April 4-10, 1943; as well as numerous excerpts of reports of OKW Gen
    z.B./H Wes Abt., of April 19, 21, 1943, which all confirm a good, confident,
    and at times excellent mood. MGFA WO1-6/591.
55. Schlabrendorff, *op. cit.*, pp. 114 ff.
56. There was even gloom and doom in the OKW and AHA, according to a
    report by Berger to Himmler. Cd SS HA/Be/Ra/Vc-Tgb. No. 390/43
    GKdos. Chef Adjtr. Tgb. No. 202/43 GKdos of April 18, 1943: BA,
    NS19/398.
57. "A wavering mood, yes even the mere questions, if and how the enemy
    can be beaten, only begins 1000 kilometers behind the front. . . ." Partei-
    Kanzlei II B4: "Auszüge aus Berichten der Gaue u.a. Dienststellen.
    Zeitraum 4.4. bis 10.4.43:" BA, NS6/414.
58. *Ibid.*, for the period January 10-16, 1943.

59. See a letter addressed to the Reich Propaganda Office of Württemberg-Hohenzollern from France, in Partei-Kanzlei, *ibid.*, for the period February 14-20, 1943.

60. *Ibid.*, for February 21-27, 1943.

61. *Ibid.*, for April 4-10, 1943; and *Tagebücher*, p. 282 (March 19).

62. Cited in Partei-Kanzlei, for the week February 14-20, 1943, *ibid.*

63. See footnote 60.

64. See especially the order by General Schörner of February 1, 1943, to all troops, distributed by the OKH. Rundschreiben No. 102/43 of the Party Chancellory distributed it on July 7, 1943, to Reichsleiter and Gauleiter: BA, NS 6/vorl. 342. A further decree was issued on March 29, 1943, by the army personnel office of the OKH, "Haltung des Offiziers im Heimats-kriegsgebiet" concerning the bad mood in the barracks. Ag P 2 Chefgr. Az. 21 No. 3900/43 signed by General Schmundt, copy in BA, NS6/vorl. 344.

65. BA, Slg. Schumacher 439.

66. See Partei-Kanzlei II B 4, "Vertrauliche Informationen," May 14, 1943: BA, ZSg 3/1623, fol. 23.

67. See page 7.

68. See page 153. See also Partei-Kanzlei, "Auszüge . . . June 20-26, 1943," BA, NS6/415.

69. Order A81/42 by the head of the Party Chancellory: BA, NS6/vorl. 338.

70. Führer's headquarters: BA, NS 6/vorl. 345.

71. A call for the "mobilization of the home front," No. 37/43, March 1, 1943: BA, NS6/vorl. 340. Even Himmler found his additional food coupons for his mess withdrawn since one wanted to pull the rug out from under rumors of extraordinary allowances to leading individuals. See the correspondence with Backe of February 10 and 20, 1943: BA, NS19/neu 280.

72. *Tagebücher*, pp. 277, 281, 296.

73. Partei-Kanzlei II B4, "Auszüge aus Berichten der Gaue u.a. Dienststellen," March 7-20, 1943: BA, NS6/414.

74. See report of Regierungspräsident for Swabia and Neuburg, February 11, 1943: BHStA, Abt. II, MA106684; and Regierungspräsident for Upper and Central Franconia, March 8, 1943, *ibid.*, MA 106679.

75. Underlined in the original. Partei-Kanzlei II B4, "Auszüge . . ." for March 7-20, 1943: BA, NS6/414. See also, OLG-President, Bamberg, March 29, 1943, and OLG-president, Kassel, March 31, 1943: BA, R22/3355 and 3371.

76. Speer, *op. cit.*, p. 271.

77. Partei-Kanzlei II B4, "Auszüge . . ." for March 7-20, 1943: BA, NS6/414. See also "Meldungen aus dem Reich," March 15, 1943: Boberach, p. 371. Cf. the weekly activity report of Reich propaganda offices by the Head Pro, sent to Goebbels on March 16, 1943: BA, R55/601, fol. 4-5. Furthermore, Goebbels noted on March 20 that Hitler felt in best form. He had had trouble with his stomach, but Professor Morell had been able to take away the pain. *Tagebücher*, p. 287.

78. See footnote 75. Cf. the telegram of Reich propaganda office, Danzig, March 23, 1943, about a whole group of rumors. In his reply the next day, Goebbels indicated that the rumor that the Führer had laid down his su-preme command came from an English radio station. Himmler's supposed assassination was an old rumor, and "as for other rumors reported by you,

they are so stupid that no further comments are required." BA, R55/613, fol. 25, 26.
79. BA, ZSg 3/1623.
80. Partei-Kanzlei II B4, "Auszüge . . ." for March 21-27, 1943: BA, NS6/414. "Meldungen aus dem Reich," March 22, 1943: Boberach, p. 375. OLG-president, Kassel, March 31, 1943: BA, R22/3371.
81. Partei-Kanzlei II B4, "Auszüge . . . ," for February 21-27, 1943: BA, NS6/414.
82. Gruchmann, *op. cit.*, pp. 235 ff.
83. "Meldungen aus dem Reich," March 15, 1943: Boberach, pp. 370, 371.
84. See report of Gau Pommern. Partei-Kanzlei II B4, "Auszüge . . . ," from April 4-10, 1943: BA, NS6/414.
85. See page 76.
86. Cf. "Erfahrungsbericht über die Versammlungsaktion" of February 1, 1943: BA, R55/610, fol. 6-23. See also, for example, the letter of DAF, Strength through Joy organization, Gau Essen, of February 8, 1943, to Gefolgschaftsführer of Gute-Hoffnungshütte in Oberhausen: HA/GHH No. 400 1026/2.
87. "Aufnahme und Auswirkung der allgemeinen Propaganda-, Presse- und Rundfunklenkung in der Zeit vom 26. 1. bis 28. 1. 1943": Boberach, pp. 233, 344, 345.
88. "Zur Aufnahme der Kriegswochenschau vom 27. 2. bis 5. 3. 1943": *ibid.*, p. 365.
89. "Auszüge aus Berichten der Gaue u.a. Dienststellen," period March 7-20, 1943: BA, NS6/414.
90. Partei-Kanzlei II B4, "Auszüge . . ." for March 21-27, 1943: *ibid.*
91. Boberach, p. 358. Similar remarks also in "SD-Berichte zu Inlandfragen," July 26, 1943: "Einstellung der Bevölkerung zur Propaganda über den Bolschewismus," *ibid.*, p. 421.
92. OLG-president, Bamberg, March 29, 1943: BA, R22/3355.
93. OLG-president, Zweibrücken, April 1, 1943. This report like many others had Thierack's signature. BA, R22/3389.
94. Word of OLG-president, Hamm, March 31, 1943: BA, R22/3367.
95. Fritzsche was head of the German press section in the Propaganda Ministry and as of October, 1942, "Beauftragter für die politische Gestaltung des Grossdeutschen Rundfunks." See *Kriegspropaganda*, pp. 61 ff. See also the comments about Fritzsche's boring voice and "twaddling" in the report of Gau Kurhessen. Partei-Kanzlei II B4, "Auszüge aus Berichten . . ." for March 21-27, 1943: BA, NS6/414.
96. Stabsleiter Sündermann reported February 4: "We have to be clear on this: we have accomplished that the German people have accepted the not joyful news for Germany well and with courage . . ." BA, ZSg 101/42, fol. 30.
97. Boberach, p. 352.
98. "Erste Stimmen zur Verordnung über die Meldung von Männern und Frauen für Aufgaben der Reichsverteidigung" of January 27, 1943: Boberach, p. 349.
99. "Meldungen aus dem Reich," February 8, 1943: *ibid.*, p. 356.
100. Confidential report from the economic conference of February 26, 1943. Figures are those of the labor mobilization chief in the Reich Ministry for Munitions and Armaments, Colonel Nikolai. BA, ZSg 115/1942.

101. See the letter of the head of the SS main office, G. Berger, of April 2, 1943, concerning Göring's attitude to the women's labor question. BA, NS 19/neu 1963.
102. Partei-Kanzlei II B4, "Auszüge . . . ," for March 21-27, 1943: BA, NS6/414. Cf. also OLG-president, Jena, April 1, 1943: BA, R22/3369.
103. See AThH 3021/17. It includes a number of pamphlets of large industrial firms about the difficulties of employing those with limited skills.
104. Opinion report of the SA, Troop 23/143, Erkenschwick, March 25, 1943: BA, NS Misch 1047.
105. SS order for all SS and police, October 28, 1939, and the letter of Himmler to all SS men and police of January 30, 1940, which included an undated letter of Hess to an unwed mother. StA Bamberg, Rep. K17/XI, No. 398. Hess has suggested that the bureau of vital statistics should record "war father" in cases of unwed mothers.
106. Schulungsbrief of NSDAP, "Von unserer inneren Kraft. Die Frau in Europa und US-Amerika" by Auguste Reber-Gruber, 2. Heft 1943 (Folge 3/4): BA, ZSg 3/433.
107. "Meldungen aus dem Reich," March 1, 1943: Boberach, p. 363.
108. *Tagebücher*, p. 270.
109. Cited in *"Wollt ihr den totalen Krieg?"*, p. 347 (March 16, 1943).
110. Speer, *op. cit.*, pp. 269, 553.
111. See Partei-Kanzlei II B4, "Auszüge . . ." for April 4-10, 1943: BA, NS6/414.
112. "Meldungen aus dem Reich," March 15, 1943: Boberach, p. 373.
113. Report of Gauleitung Hamburg, cited in Partei-Kanzlei II B4, "Auszüge . . ." for April 11-17, 1943: BA, NS6/414.
114. *Idem.*, period May 23-29, 1943: *ibid.* This report gains in importance because it does not come from Ohlendorf's office, who was less objective as director of the Reichsgruppe Handel. Cf. Boberach, p. xxiv.
115. Cited in Partei-Kanzlei II B4, "Auszüge . . ." for April 18-May 1, 1943: BA, NS6/414.
116. Report of Gau Mark Brandenburg. *Ibid.*
117. "Meldungen aus dem Reich," May 6, 1943: Boberach, p. 390. The same verse was not cited by SD-section Halle until July 6. BA, NS6/406, fol. 11202.
118. See Boberach, pp. 333, 341, footnote 6; 354, footnote 3; 372.
119. Partei-Kanzlei II B4, "Auszüge . . ." for April 18-May 1, 19 415.
120. Boberach, pp. 395-96. Cf. especially footnote 2.
121. See page 143 above.
122. SD section Halle, May 22, 1943: BA, NS6/406.
123. Gau Halle-Merseburg. Partei-Kanzlei II B4, "Auszüge . . ." f 1943: BA, NS6/415. Similar in thrust to Gau Mark Brandenbu
124. Gau Kurhessen, *ibid.*
125. SD section, Schwerin, June 2, 1943: BA, NS6/407, fol. 14226.
126. SD-Berichte zu Inlandfragen (the name of the "Meldungen" as of June), June 17, 1943. "Meldungen zu den letzten Terrorangriffen auf Westdeutschland": BA, R58/185. Also for the following.
127. See the *Tagesparolen* of the Reich Press Chief, BA, ZSg 109/41, fol. 71; cf. fol. 79.

128. V.I. **64**/43 of March 13, 1943: *ibid.*, fol. 43. Cf. also V.I. No. 30/43 of April 10, 1943: ZSg 109/42, fol. 19.
129. *"Wollt ihr den totalen Krieg?"*, p. 347.
130. SD section, Weimar, June 22, 1943: BA, NS6/406, fol. 14218.
131. At the start of the war Göring had sworn enemy planes would not reach Germany or his name was "Meier." In the Rhenish-Westphalian region people often referred to "Meier's French horn" when the sirens wailed. Kreisleitung Wetzlar, July 22, 1943: BA, NS Misch/1641.
132. SD section, Weimar, June 29, 1943: BA, NS6/406.
133. SD-Hauptaussenstelle Schwerin, June 29, 1943, concerning the general mood and attitude. BA, NS6/407, fol. 14251.
134. See SD-Hauptaussenstelle Schwerin, June 29, 1943: "Betrifft Aufnahme und Auswirkung der Propagandalenkung in Presse und Rundfunk." *Ibid.*, fol. 14258, 14259.
135. Boberach, p. 413.
136. *Ibid.*, p. xviii.
137. See *supra* pp. 14 f.
138. Boberach, p. 414.
139. For the development and the various types of weapons, see David Irving, *Die Geheimwaffen des Dritten Reiches* (Gütersloh, 1965) and Janssen, *op. cit.*, pp. 189 ff.
140. David Irving, *Der Traum von der deutschen Atombombe* (Gütersloh, 1967).
141. Alexander Mitscherlich & Fred Mielke, *Wissenschaft ohne Menschlichkeit*, pp. 157 ff.
142. Speer, *op. cit.*, pp. 421, 580, footnote 3.
143. See "Meldungen aus dem Reich," January 21, 1943: Boberach, pp. 340-41. Similarly, "Meldungen . . ." of May 6, 1943: *ibid.*, pp. 388-89. Cf. also Regierungspräsident Regensburg, May 10, 1943: BA, NS19/426.
144. See Partei-Kanzlei II B4, "Auszüge . . ." for April 4-10, 1943: BA, NS6/414; and RSHA III A4, June 25, 1943, to the Party Chancellory II B4 concerning SD reports: BA, NS6/41.
145. "Meldungen aus dem Reich," April 25, 1943: Boberach, p. 397. SD-Hauptaussenstelle Schwerin, June 29, 1943: BA, NS6/407. Cf. also "SD-Bericht zu Inlandfragen" of July 1, 1943: Boberach, p. 415. The Halle SD section also reported on July 6, 1943: "The screams of thousands of people in phosphorus flames sounded like the death howls of dying animals. In Wuppertal they jumped into the river, burning torches, thousands of them, to avoid a fiery death. In other cities the people also ran around like living torches; the phosphorus penetrated through cracks and other open places into the air raid shelters and engulfed and killed the people there. But this is far from the end, for the end will be a dreadful gas war which will affect the whole German Volk. . . ." BA, NS6/406, fol. 14201.
146. SD section, Weimar, July 6, 1943: *ibid.*
147. *Ibid.*
148. July 6, 1943: *ibid.*, fol. 1402.
149. SD section, Schwerin, July 6, 1943: *ibid.*, fol. 14279.
150. SD section, Halle, July 6, 1943, Allgemeine Presselenkung: *ibid.*, fol. 14205.
151. SD section, Halle, July 6, 1943, Stimmung und Haltung zur Lage: *ibid.*, fol. 14202-03.
152. SD section, Schwerin, June 29, 1943: *ibid.*, fol. 14259.

153. *Ibid.*, fol. 14266 and 14267.
154. SD section, Weimar, July 6, 1943, Allgemeine Stimmung und Lage: *ibid.*, fol. 14121. Rudolf Semmler, *Goebbels: The Man next to Hitler* (London, 1947), p. 88, reports in the diary entry of July 10, that Goebbels is the most popular of the national leaders, since he personally cared about the suffering people in the bombed western regions.
155. See *Gewalt und Gewissen. Willi Graf und die "Weisse Rose."* A Documentation by Klaus Vielhaber in cooperation with Hubert Hanisch and Anneliese Knoop-Graf (Freiburg, 1964); and Inge Scholl, *Die weisse Rose* (Frankfurt/Main, 1953).
156. "Meldungen aus dem Reich," March 15, 1943: Boberach, p. 372.
157. Partei-Kanzlei II B4, "Auszüge . . ." for April 4-10, 1943: BA, NS6/414. Cf. also SD section, Weimar, July 6, 1943: BA, NS6/406, fol. 14123.
158. See footnote 156 above.
159. *Ibid.*
160. Compendium of reports from SD-(Leit)-Abschnittsbereichen sent on July 9, 1943, to the Party Chancellory: BA, NS6/411, fol. 14061.
161. As enclosure to announcement 30/44g, Bormann on February 8, 1944, sent to all Gauleiters a "Zusammenstellung aus Unterlagen des Reichssicherheitshauptamtes über das Schicksal der deutschen Kriegsgefangenen in der Sowjetunion." BA, NS6/vorl. 350.
162. "Meldung wichtiger staatspolizeilicher Ereignisse," April 16, 1943: BA, R58/210, which concerned Leipzig. Cf. Ilse Krause, *Die Schumann-Engert-Kresse-Gruppe. Dokumente und Materialien des illegalen antifaschistischen Kampfes* (Leipzig 1943-45). (East Berlin, 1960).
163. Law against treasonable attacks on state and Party and for the protection of the Party uniform, December 20, 1943: RGBl., I, p. 1269.
164. May 29, 1943: BA, R22/3380.
165. Public prosecutor general, Bamberg, June 4, 1943: BA, R22/3355.
166. Boberach, p. 372. See also SD-Bericht zu Inlandfragen, July 8, 1943. "Meldungen über Auflockerungserscheinungen in der Haltung der Bevölkerung," July 8, 1943: *ibid.*, p. 419.
167. *Ibid.*, p. 45.
168. Goebbels on April 5, 1943, at a reception of Berlin newspapers. *Kriegspropaganda*, p. 313.
169. *"Wollt ihr den totalen Krieg?"*, p. 336 (Goebbels, February 12). See also, *ibid.*, p. 337.
170. Cf. Alexander Dallin, *German Rule in Russia 1941-1945*. A Study in Occupation Policy (New York, St. Martin's Press, 1957), p. 409.
171. For Goebbels' motives and the preparation of propaganda leaflets dealing with foreign workers, see Sonderdienst der Reichspropagandaleitung, Sonderlieferung 22/43 of May 15, 1943: Information zum Sprechabend der Partei. BA, ZSg3/1672; and *"Wollt ihr den totalen Krieg?"*, p. 341.
172. Goebbels obviously referred to the previously mentioned "Meldungen aus dem Reich" of February 15, 1943. See page 197 above.
173. *"Wollt ihr den totalen Krieg?"*, p. 340.
174. BA, ZSg3/1623 and 1627.
175. See page 163 above.
176. "Meldungen aus dem Reich," April 15, 1943. Abschnitt III Volkstum "Das Russlandbild in der Bevölkerung: Auswirkungen des Einsatzes sowjetischer Kriegsgefangener und Ostarbeiter im Reich": BA, R58/182.

177. SD-Bericht zu Inlandfragen, July 26, 1943, "Einstellung der Bevölkerung zur Propaganda über den Bolschewismus": Boberach, pp. 421-23.
178. BHStA, Abt. II, MA 106684. See also Regierungspräsident of Regensburg, April 11, 1943: BA, NS19/246; and Partei-Kanzlei II B4, "Auszüge . . ." for May 23-29, 1943: BA, NS6/415.
179. Boberach, p. 379.
180. *Tagebücher*, p. 295.
181. See Ernst Klink, *Das Gesetz des Handelns. Die Operation "Zitadelle" 1943* (Stuttgart, 1966).
182. See pp. 168, 190 above, and "Meldungen aus dem Reich," January 11, 1943: Boberach, p. 332; and Partei-Kanzlei II B4, "Auszüge . . ." for January 10-16, 1943: BA, NS6/414.
183. "Meldungen aus dem Reich," April 5, 1943: Boberach, p. 382.
184. Partei-Kanzlei II B4, "Auszüge . . ." for January 24, 1943: BA, NS6/414.
185. *Idem.*, period of April 11-17, April 18-May 1, 1943: *ibid.*
186. *Idem.*, period of April 11-17, 1943: *ibid.*
187. "Meldungen aus dem Reich," May 24, 1943: Boberach, p. 397.
188. "Meldungen aus dem Reich," February 8, 1943: *ibid.*, p. 354. Regierungspräsident for Upper and Central Franconia, May 8, 1943: BHStA, Abt. II, MA 106679. Partei-Kanzlei II B4, "Auszüge . . ." for March 26-27: BA, NS6/414.
189. Partei-Kanzlei, "Auszüge . . ." for March 21-27: BA, NS6/414.
190. RSHA to Party Chancellory, June 25, 1943, "Meldungen aus den SD-(Leit-)-Abschnittsbereichen": BA, NS6/411. See also, from Upper and Central Franconia, monthly report of Regierungspräsident dated May 8, 1943: BHStA, Abt. II, MA 106679.
191. Hitler had used the same expression. Cf. Goebbels' *Tagebücher*, p. 131.
192. RSHA "Zusammenstellung von Meldungen aus den SD-(Leit)-Abschnitten," sent to the Party Chancellory on July 9. BA, NS6/41.
193. *Idem.* Sent on July 15. *ibid.*
194. SD-Hauptaussenstelle Schwerin, July 20, 1943. BA, NS6/407, fol. 14319, 14320. Goebbels noted in his diary: "We are experiencing a kind of second Stalingrad although under very different psychological and material conditions." *Tagebücher*, pp. 327-28.
195. Cf. Partei-Kanzlei II B4, "Auszüge . . ." for January 10-16, February 14-20, March 21-27, 1943: BA, NS6/414. Boberach, pp. 335, 354, 373, 374, 376. Regierungspräsident Regensburg, April 11, 1943: BA, NS19/246.
196. Partei-Kanzlei II B4, "Auszüge . . ." for May 9-15, May 29-June 5, 1943: BA, NS6/415. Boberach, pp. 397, 415, 416. Regierungspräsident Regensburg, June 11, 1943: BA, NS19/246.
197. Ulrich von Hassell, *op. cit.*, p. 281.
198. *Tagebücher*, pp. 323 (entry of May 8, 1943), 327.
199. Partei-Kanzlei II B4, "Auszüge . . ." for May 9-15, 1943: BA, NS6/415.
200. Speer, *op. cit.*, p. 271.
201. *idem.* Period May 23-29, 1943. *ibid.*
202. Arrests increased during these weeks. When Himmler was informed that in the munitions factory in Grüneberg in Mark Brandenburg "a very bad mood" prevailed, he suggested arrest and death sentences as a warning for the "worst agitators." Reichsführer-SS Tgb. No. 39/139/439 of June 23, 1943 to the Chef der Sicherheitspolizei and the SD, Berlin. BA, NS19/neu 238.

203. "Stimmen zu den Goebbels-Artikeln im Reich" zum Bericht der SD-Hauptaussenstelle Schwerin, July 20, 1943: BA, NS6/407.
204. Personal diary of Paula Stuck von Reznicek. BA MA Slg. 106/Bd. 19, fol. 39.
205. Partei-Kanzlei II B4, "Auszüge . . ." for May 30-June 5, 1943: BA, NS6/415. See also the report of Gau Magdeburg-Anhalt, period June 13-19, 1943. ibid.; period June 20-26, 1943. ibid.
206. SD-section, Halle, "Einstellung von Frontsoldaten zur Stimmung und Haltung der Heimat (Auszüge aus Feldpostbriefen)," June 28, 1943: BA, NS6/406, fol. 14150-14153. Cf. also letters by soldiers about the poor mood at home in BA, R55/583, fol. 25, 34.
207. Cf. Boberach, pp. 356, 393-95.
208. State Secretary Backe gave the press secret information about the food situation. According to him the unfavorable development in the meat sector was based largely on the higher requirements of the military. The provisioning of fats suffered heavily from the loss of North Africa since from there France obtained 40 per cent of its domestic production. BA, ZSg 115/1942.
209. Boberach, p. 398.
210. SD section, Weimar, July 13, 1943: BA, NS6/406, fol. 14129.
211. "Zur Frage des Rückganges der Kirchenaustritte und der Wiedereintritte zahlreicher Volksgenossen in die kirchliche Gemeinschaft," addendum to "Meldungen aus dem Reich," April 22, 1943: BA, R58/182.
212. Partei-Kanzlei II B4, "Auszüge . . ." for February 14-20, 1943: BA, NS6/414. Reports about strong church activity were also furnished by the district administrations for Sinsheim, Heidelberg, Waldshut, Lörrach, Rastatt. BA, NS Misch/1846, fol. 324174, 324183, 324187, 324193, 324194, 324197. Cf. also monthly report of the Upper Bavarian government, June 8, 1943: No. 788, Die kirchliche Lage in Bayern.
213. Partei-Kanzlei II B4, "Auszüge . . ." for April 4-10, 1943: BA, NS6/414. Typical is a report from the district Villingen: "People fear the pastor more than the Party although only because of fear of dying." BA, NS Misch/1730, fol. 304213. Cf. also BA, NS Misch/1847, fol. 324374-77, 324399, about the support among the military for the Corpus Christi processions.
214. Partei-Kanzlei II B4, "Auszüge . . ." for April 4-10, 1943: BA, NS6/414.
215. Regierungspräsident for Swabia and Neuburg, June 10, 1943: BHStA, Abt. II, MA 106684.
216. "SD-Bericht zu Inlandfragen," July 8, 1943: Boberach, pp. 419-20. See also the July 8 SD report summarizing "Meldungen über Auflockerungserscheinungen in der Haltung der Bevölkerung": Boberach, pp. 416-20.
217. Letter of Himmler to Bormann, May 14, 1943: Tgb. No. 1613/43 with enclosure. BA, NS19/398.
218. Reports of the Regierungspräsidenten for Upper and Central Franconia and for Upper Bavaria. BHStA, Abt. II, MA 106679 and MA 106671.
219. "SD-Berichte zu Inlandfragen," July 29, 1943: Boberach, p. 424. "Zusammenstellung von Meldungen aus den SD-(Leit)-Abschnittsbereichen. Durch Kurier am 30. 7. 43 an Partei-Kanzlei gesandt." BA, NS6/411, fol. 14106, 14110, 14112.
220. Tagebücher, p. 375 (entry of July 27, 1943).
221. Lagebesprechungen im Führerhauptquartier. Protokollfragmente aus Hit-

lers militärischen Konferenzen 1942-1945, ed. by Helmut Heiber (Munich, 1964), p. 152.

222. *Goebbels' Tagebücher*, p. 275. There were even circles in which a certain satisfaction was registered at their own predictions and assessment of the Italian situation in contrast to that of the government. See, OLG-president Bamberg, November 27, 1943: BA, R22/3355.

223. "SD-Berichte zu Inlandfragen," August 16, 1943: Boberach, p. 430. "Zusammenstellung von Meldungen aus den SD-(Leit)-Abschnittsbereichen," to the Party Chancellory via courier, July 30, 1943: BA, NS6/41, fol. 14106.

224. *Ibid.*, fol. 14104.

225. Boberach, p. 424.

226. Regierungspräsident for Upper Bavaria, August 9, 1943: BHStA, Abt. II, MA 106671.

227. See "Zusammenstellung von Meldungen aus den SD-(Leit)-Abschnittsbereichen," to the Party Chancellory via courier on July 30, 1943: BA, NS6/41, fol. 14107, 14108.

228. *Ibid.*, fol. 14108. Cf. also "SD-Berichte zu Inlandfragen," July 29, 1943: Boberach, pp. 427, 428.

229. Boberach, pp. 427, 429.

230. Kreisleitung Gelnhausen, "Allgemeines Stimmungsbild," August 23, 1943: BA, NS Misch/1641, fol. 140856.

231. V.I. No. 181/43, July 27, 1943: BA, ZSg 109/43, fol. 124.

232. "SD-Berichte zu Inlandfragen," August 2, 1943: BA, R58/187. Similar rumors about the flight of leading figures were reported as well by the Regierungspräsidenten for Upper Bavaria and for Swabia and Neuburg. BHStA, Abt. II, MA 106671 and 10684. Cf. also "Zusammenstellung von Meldungen aus den SD-(Leit)-Abschnittsbereichen" sent to the Chancellory via courier on July 30, 1943: BA, NS6/411, fol. 14116.

233. Boberach, p. 430.

234. "SD-Berichte zu Inlandfragen," August 2, 1943: BA, R58/187.

235. "The overthrow in Italy, according to my observation, has given rise to the view and even intensified the wish among more than a few citizens that in the German Reich an internal political upheaval must also come." Landgerichtsrat Wachinger, Landshut, August 7, 1943: BA, R22/3379.

236. Ulrich von Hassell, *op. cit.*, pp. 287 ff.

237. Published in *Der Luftkrieg über Deutschland 1939-1945. Deutsche Berichte und Pressestimmen des neutralen Auslands* (Munich, 1963), p. 57.

238. "SD-Berichte zu Inlandfragen," July 29, 1943: Boberach, p. 427.

239. BA, R22/3367.

240. "SD-Berichte zu Inlandfragen," August 16, 1943. "Wie sieht das Volk die Kriegslage?": Boberach, p. 429.

241. Cf. "Zusammenstellung von Meldungen aus den SD-(Leit)-Abschnittsbereichen" sent to the Party Chancellory by courier on July 30, 1943: BA, NS6/411, fol. 14109.

242. OLG-president Bamberg, August 2, 1943: BA, R22/3355. Cf. also, OLG-president Kiel, August 30, 1943, "Meldungen zu den Terrorangriffen auf Hamburg," SD-Berichte zu Inlandfragen, August 2, 1943: BA, R58/187.

243. Cited in Rundschreiben No. 8/61/43 of the district propaganda leader for

the district of greater Frankfurt, August 5, 1943: BA, NS Misch/1648, fol. 142848. It is interesting to discover in this connection that Soviet citizens were not told of Italy's capitulation for quite a while, probably to avoid awakening exaggerated hopes and adversely affecting the fighting spirit. Cf. *La presse dans les Etats autoritaires* (Zurich, 1959), p. 24.

244. Cf. Public prosecutor general, Brunswick, September 21, 1943: R22/3357; public prosecutor general at the Berlin Supreme Court, September 25, 1943: R22/3356; public prosecutor general, Cologne, September 29, 1943: R22/3374; public prosecutor general, Naumburg, September 30, 1943: R22/3380.

245. See Bodo Scheurig (ed.), *Verrat hinter Stacheldraht? Das Nationalkomitee "Freies Deutschland" und der Bund deutscher Offiziere in der Sowjetunion 1943-1945* (Munich, 1965); and Wolfgang Leonhard, *Die Revolution entlässt ihre Kinder* (Berlin, 1955), pp. 227 ff. See also the letter by Himmler to the Foreign Office on August 3, 1943, about this event. No. 356/43g-IV A ld. AA Inland II G 32.

246. Report of August 12, 1943: BA, R58/187.

247. Letter by Paul Neukirchen of October 6, 1969.

248. Himmler also came to this conclusion on the basis of experience in Reich Labor Service camps with the discharge of the generation of 1925. For him the total result was "a clear and systematic poisoning of the youth of our Volk by Christian education." Letter to Bormann of May 14, 1943: BA, NS19/398.

249. Cf. also a letter addressed to Goebbels, dated January 28, 1944, by a wounded infantryman who had reached the same opinion after numerous conversations with young people. BA, R55/580, fol. 74-75.

250. On January 28, 1944, the public prosecutor general in Cologne mentioned these kinds of gangs having names such as "Alah," "The Avengers," "Black Hand," etc. BA, R22/3374. SD section, Koblenz, reported on June 15, 1944, on the destructive impulses of juveniles who damaged public property of all kinds and were beyond police capacity to control them. HStA Wbn *Zug* 68/67, No. 1077.

251. For the texts of songs and an exhaustive report, see *Oberstaatsanwalt* Cologne, January 16, 1944: BA, R22/3374. SD section Frankfurt also reported on "edelweiss gangs" for its region and that of Siegen on January 24, 1944, and February 14, 1944: HStA Wb *Zug* 68/67, No. 1077.

252. Hamburg had a swing-club and Kiel the league, "the golden 13." Both were in opposition to the HJ. OLG-president Kiel, April 6, 1944: BA, R22/3373. Cf. also Kaltenbrunner's Runderlass of October 25, 1944, concerning the "fight against juvenile cliques": *Aus deutschen Urkunden*, pp. 270-74.

253. Police criminal statistics for 1943, in "Vertrauliche Informationen," Folge 22, Beitrag 196 of August 5, 1944: BA, ZSg 3/1624.

254. Report of the Regierungspräsident for Upper Bavaria, September 8, 1943: BHStA, Abt. II, MA 106671.

255. Propaganda directive no. 23, issued in broadcast no. 71, August 10, 1943, 8 p.m. BA, EAP 250-a/I; fol. 10817.

256. Cf. Rundschreiben no. 8/64/43 of the district propaganda leader for greater Frankfurt, August 12, 1843: BA, NS Misch/1648.

257. Cf. Rundschreiben no. 8/68/43 of the district propaganda leader for greater

Frankfurt, August 19, 1943: *ibid.* Particularly informative of the source and nature of rumors is Rundschreiben no. 8/79/43 of September 29, 1943: *ibid.*

258. Cf. Rundschreiben 8/66/43 of the district propaganda leader for greater Frankfurt, August 14, 1943: *ibid.*

259. BA, *Sammlung Schumacher*/369.

260. "To me, at least, it seems far more serious that the critical voices unleashed by Mussolini's arrest paralyzed the Party and certain official offices in some parts. . . ." OLG-president, Nuremberg, December 2, 1943: BA, R22/3351.

261. By Rundschreiben no. 45/43g.: BA, NS 6/vorl. 345.

262. For the background to the Italian coup, see Peter Tompkins, *Verrat auf italienisch* (Vienna, 1967). For a scholarly analysis of the various fascist systems, see Ernst Nolte, *Der Faschismus in seiner Epoche* (Munich, 1963); Nolte (ed.), *Theorien über den Faschismus* (Cologne, 1967).

263. Cf. the thoughts of OLG-president, Brunswick, November 30, 1943: BA, R22/3357.

264. See *infra*, p. 229.

265. "Von der Unersetzlichkeit der Freiheit," published by the Sonderdienst der Propagandaleitung, Hauptamt Propaganda, Amt Propagandalenkung, Sonderlieferung no. 38/43 of August 26, 1943: BA, ZSg 3/1672.

266. "SD-Berichte zu Inlandfragen," September 2, 1943: BA, R58/188.

267. Cf. V.I. no. 192/43 (I. Ergänzung) of August 9, 1943; V.I. no. 196/43 of August 13, 1943: BA, ZSg 109/44, fol. 18, 27.

268. "SD-Berichte zu Inlandfragen," September 6, 1943: "Stimmen zur pressemässigen Behandlung des 5. Jahrestages des Kriegsausbruchs." BA, R58/188.

269. "SD-Berichte zu Inlandfragen," September 13, 1943: Boberach, p. 433.

270. For the text, see Domarus, 2. Halbband, vol. II, pp. 2035-39. Hitler had taped his speech.

271. BA, NS 6/358.

272. See Boberach, p. 435.

273. According to the observations of Bamberg's public prosecutor general, there was a decline in the mood from north to south. "The mood is unquestionably worse in old Bavaria than in Franconia, and worse yet in the Tirol. The primary basis is probably the differences in character of the populations, possibly also in their historical development and proximity to the theater of war considered so critical for some time." Quartering evacuees from northern Germany also had a depressive effect on the mood. See the quarterly situation report of October 5, 1943: BA, R22/3355.

274. "SD-Berichte zu Inlandfragen," September 16, 1943: BA, R58/188.

275. "SD-Berichte zu Inlandfragen," September 27, 1943: *ibid.*

276. "SD-Berichte zu Inlandfragen," September 20, 1943: *ibid.* Cf. also the report of the SD section, Koblenz, of January 15, 1944, about press propaganda: HStA Wbn *Zug* 68/67, no. 1076.

277. Public prosecutor general, Nuremberg, September 30, 1943: BA, R22/3381.

278. Opinion report of the SA, troop 25/143 Recklinghausen, September 27, 1943: BA, NS Misch/1047.

279. "SD-Berichte zu Inlandfragen," September 30, 1943: "Auswirkungen der deutschen Rückzugsbewegungen im Osten auf die Stimmung." Boberach, p. 437.

280. Gruchmann, *op. cit.*, p. 437.
281. "Meldungen über den Einfluss der Frontsoldaten auf die Stimmung in der Heimat," September 6, 1943: BA, R58/188. See also "SD-Berichte zu Inlandfragen," October 14, 1943: "Meinungsäusserungen aus der Bevölkerung zur Kriegslage." BA, R58/189.
282. Speer apparently suggested the order. Cf. Janssen, *op. cit.*, pp. 269-70.
283. Der Führer OKW/WFSt/Org. No. 007436/43g. Addendum 4 to Rundschreiben 3/45g of January 4, 1945, in BA, NS 6/vorl. 354. For regulations implementing this decree, see Oberkommando der Wehrmacht, Chef des Wehrmachtssanitätswesen, No. 2013/43, *geh* (H.S. In/Wi G CH) of December 7, 1943. Notarized copy in Bischöfl. Diözesanarchiv, Würzburg: *Nachlass Leier K I.*
284. See *supra*, p. 13.
285. See the Führer's decree of September 2, 1943, concerning the concentration of the war economy. Copy in BA, NS6/vorl. 342. Cf. also Janssen, *op. cit.*, pp. 133 ff.
286. Sonderdienst der Reichspropagandaleitung, Hauptamt Propaganda, Amt Propagandalenkung, edition A, No. 23 (October, 1943): BA, ZSg 3/1672.
287. See the results of the campaign in Sonderdienst der Reichspropagandaleitung, Hauptamt Propaganda (no date), "Aktionsplan zur Aktivierung der Partei für die Zeit vom 3.1. bis 31.3.44." BA, ZSg 3/1673.
288. Cf. Bramstedt, *op. cit.*, p. 318; and "SD-Berichte zu Inlandfragen," "Was verspricht sich die Bevölkerung von der Vergeltung?", October 18, 1943: Boberach, p. 440.
289. Domarus, 2. Halbband, vol. II, p. 2056; and "Meldungen zu Führerrede vom 8.11.43.": Boberach, pp. 442-45.
290. Kreisleitung Heidelberg, October 1, 1943: BA, NS Misch/1112, fol. 11090. Cf. also Kreisleitung Waldshut, October 23, 1943, and Kreisleitung Rastatt, September 28, 1943: *ibid*, fol. 11086, 11091.
291. RGBl. I (January 29, 1943), p. 76. For those cases transferred according to paragraph 5 of the Kriegssonderstrafrechtsverordnung see RGBl. 1939 I (August 17, 1938), p. 1455. Cf. also April 24, 1934 and April 18, 1936: RGBl. I, pp. 341, 369.
292. Compare, for example, the letter of the Kreisleiter of Bad Gandersheim (December 4, 1943) to the Gauleiter of Gau South Hanover-Brunswick, in which he protested a verdict of the Berlin Supreme Court of one and one-half years imprisonment towards which the half year of detention was counted. The accused supposedly said among other things that after Stalingrad the German greeting was no longer "Heil Hitler" but rather "Horrido." The Führer had shot his first buck—which also means 'made his first blunder.' BA, R22/3357.
293. See also the "Meldung zur strafrechtlichen Bekämpfung von Zersetzungsversuchen," December 2, 1943: Boberach, pp. 460-66.
294. Cf. Weisenborn, *Der lautlose Aufstand. Bericht über die Widerstandsbewegung des Deutschen Volkes 1933-1945* (Reinbek, 1962), pp. 265-67.
295. *Ibid.*, pp. 263-65.
296. *Ibid.*, p. 482.
297. See the report of the OLG-president Bamberg, November 27, 1943: BA,

R22/3355. Also illuminating are the comments of Nuremberg's OLG-president of December 2, 1943: "Even in the blackest areas of the Upper Palatinate the old foes no longer dare come out of their holes; the death verdicts of the People's Tribunal for seditious opinions made sure that they retire to their hiding-places." R22/3381.

298. OLG-president Jena, November 30, 1943: BA, R22/3369.

299. Cf. Public prosecutor general of Königsberg, January 26, 1944: BA, R22/3375.

300. "Das Zeitgeschehen und seine Auswirkung auf die Stimmung und Haltung der Frauen," November 18, 1943: Boberach, pp. 445-47.

301. Educational literature for May-June, 1944, "Zur biologischen Sicherung der deutschen Zukunft," even demanded a downright "revolutionary change in the progenitive habits of our Volk. . . ." BA, ZSg 3/422.

302. Dated April 13, 1944. Sent by Kaltenbrunner to Reich Treasurer Schwarz. BA, NS1/544.

303. Schwerin's OLG-president reported similar observations on April 3, 1944. BA, R22/3385.

304. Field quarters, April 27, 1944, concerning wages for women. Copy in BA, R43II/541.

305. Cf. SD section, Koblenz, January 11, 1944, concerning public media and press. HStA Wbn Zug 68/67, No. 1076; and SD section Frankfurt, end of January, 1944, concerning press propaganda. Ibid., No. 1087.

306. Public prosecutor general, Berlin Supreme Court, May 31, 1944: BA, R22/3356.

307. Speech on the occasion of Hitler's birthday. Cf. Bramsted, op. cit., pp. 225-26.

308. Order to the Party, 91/44, of April 29, 1944: BA, NS6/vorl. 346.

309. "Meldungen über die Entwicklung in der öffentlichen Meinungsbildung," February 10, 1944: Boberach, pp. 486, 487.

310. "Meldungen über Gerüchte und Kombinationen zur Vergeltung und Invasion," December 27, 1943: Boberach, pp. 472-75.

311. Information Propaganda, edition B, July 10, 1944: BA, ZSg3/1673.

312. "Zusammenfassender Bericht über Stimmung und Haltung der Berliner Bevölkerung während und nach den Grossangriffen Ende November 1943:" BA, R58/191. Cf. also the positive report on the Berliners' reaction by the public prosecutor general, Berlin Supreme Court, January 27, 1944: R22/3356.

313. Public prosecutor general, Darmstadt, January 23, 1944: BA, R22/3361.

314. Situation report of January 31, 1944: R22/3373.

315. Situation report of January 31, 1944: R22/3366. Cf. also his report on the overall situation, November 27, 1943: ibid.

316. Situation report of May 8, 1944: R22/3363. Cf. also remarks of the OLG-president, Nuremberg, April 3, 1944: R22/3381; OLG-president Kiel, April 6, 1944: R22/3373.

317. "Grundfragen der Stimmung und Haltung des deutschen Volkes; hier: Gefühlsmässige Einstellung der Bevölkerung gegenüber den Feinden." Boberach, pp. 481-85.

318. Ibid., p. 443, footnote 5.

319. BA, R55/571, fol. 71.

320. BA, R55/570, fol. 132.
321. BA, R55/603, fol. 299. The press had already once received special material regarding the matter on April 26. V.I. No. 78/44, ZSg 109/49, fol. 49.
322. See Sonderlieferung No. 24/44 of the Reich Propaganda Office, May 31, 1944: BA, ZSg 3/1673.
323. No. 66/44: BA, NS6/vorl. 350.
324. SD-Hauptaussenstelle Schwerin, May 30, 1944: BA, NS6/407.
325. Cf. BA, R55/571, fol. 88/89, 91/92, 109, 110, 116.
326. Cf. supra, footnote 324. The SD section, Frankfurt, issued a report on June 6, 1944, similar in tone, since fear had also been noted concerning reprisals against German prisoners. Goebbels' words at times were considered inept. It would have been better had he prohibited acts of vengeance. "One could still have done what one wanted." HHStA, Wbn Zug 68/67, No. 1077.
327. Cf. supra, p. 28.
328. SD section, Frankfurt, March 8, 1944. Referent SS-Obersturmbannführer Streiner, Sacharbeiter Untersturmbannführer Dr. Rieck. Also "Semesterbericht über die Lage an der Hochschule Darmstadt im Wintersemester 1943/44." February, 1944. HHStA Wbn Zug 68/67, No. 1090; 1087.
329. Hans Buchheim, Totalitäre Herrschaft. Wesen und Merkmale (Munich, 1962).
330. BA, NS1/547. Cf. also "Grundfragen der Stimmung und Haltung des deutschen Volkes, hier: Totaler Krieg." Boberach, pp. 446-72.
331. Cf. Monatsbericht des Regierungspräsidenten von Regensburg, February 10, 1944: BA, NS19/246; "Meldungen über die Entwicklung in der öffentlichen Meinungsbildung," February 10, 1944: Boberach, p. 490; Generalstaatsanwalt Bamberg, February 10, 1944: BA, R22/3355; BA, NS6/vorl. 343.
332. Cf. OLG-president, Kiel, April 6, 1944: BA, R22/3373.
333. Cf. "Meldungen über die Entwicklung in der öffentlichen Meinungsbildung" of March 16, April 6, and April 20, 1944: Boberach, pp. 493, 495, 497, 503.
334. Cf. OLG-president Karlsruhe, March 30, 1944: BA, R22/3370.
335. The strongest criticism which seems very subjective and biased came from the Frankfurt SD and was directed in particular against Goebbels. Cf. the various reports of February, March, 1944, in HHStA Wbn, Zug 68/67, No. 1087, 1075. Cf. also SD section, Koblenz, March 14, 1944. Zug 68/67, No. 1087, and Kreisobmann of the DAF, Freiburg, April 28, 1944, on critical opinions concerning the campaign "the enemy listens." BA, NS5 I/58.
336. SD section, Frankfurt, March 22, 1944: HHStA Wbn, Zug 68/67, No. 1075.
337. BA, Sammlung Schumacher/368.
338. Cf. OLG-presidents Karlsruhe, March 30, 1944; Darmstadt, April 1, 1944; Nuremburg, April 3, 1944; Kattowitz, April 11, 1944: BA, R2/3370/3361/3381/3372.
339. May 16, 1944. BA, NS6/407, fol. 13577.
340. Boberach, pp. 455-460.
341. Ibid., p. 430.
342. "Meldungen über die Entwicklung in der öffentlichen Meinungsbildung:" ibid., p. 509.

343. V.I. No. 91/44: BA, ZSg 109/49, fol. 80.
344. Bormann Rundschreiben: "Höchste Alarmbereitschaft zur Invasions-
     abwehr," No. 106/44g. BA, NS6/vorl. 350.
345. Führungshinweis No. 17 of May 17, 1944: BA, NS 6/vorl. 358.
346. Schulungs-Unterlage No. 39. Sammelsendung May-June 1944: BA, ZSg
     3/422.

IV.   THE LOST WAR

In this war, not luck
but justice will finally triumph.

Adolf Hitler

1.   ALLIED LANDING IN THE WEST,
     SOVIET SUMMER OFFENSIVE IN THE EAST

THE GERMAN PUBLIC did not learn of the start of Allied landings in the early hours of June 6, 1944, until the midday news or subsequent newspaper headlines. Only a few Party and military offices had been informed earlier, as had listeners to foreign broadcasts.[1] The press received instructions to feature the landing operations. "It is an event which stirs the German people to its very depths and requires of the German press that it electrify our people and drum into them one thought: front and homeland must smash the invaders and thus make a decisive contribution to the final victory. . . ."[2]

Although a majority of Germans had daily expected and yearned for this operation for weeks and months, it still came as a surprise: "we had hardly dared to hope for this enemy undertaking."[3] Instead of "shock or fear,"[4] a general feeling of relief circulated. As he so often had before, the Führer had "done everything right again."[5] During the first days the mood became more relaxed than it had been for years,[6] and the almost unbearable tensions and uncertainties evaporated.[7] Eternal optimists believed, with Hitler, in a turn to Germany's advantage. "Discussions about the invasion revolve mainly around the following questions: Will the invasion bring the longed-for decision? Will it produce a prolonged abatement in air raids on Reich territory? Will the invasion also finally bring revenge? Will our 'secret weapon' be used now? Where else will the Anglo-Americans land? . . ."[8]

The abatement in bomber attacks since the beginning of Allied landings was greeted with relief, and many a person told himself that the opponent's strength was also obviously limited and that he was inca-

258

pable of simultaneously commanding an invasion front and hitting German territory with his air power.[9] During the first days of the invasion the hunger for news was not stilled,[10] but soon numerous PK-reports in press and radio gave Germans at home more information. For the first time in years, the "backbone" of public opinion was the official mass media, above all the Wehrmacht report, and not personal reflection and private information from front-line soldiers, and rumors even less.[11]

The abandonment of Rome on June 4 was largely forgotten in the excitement about the invasion. For approximately eight days, the Wehrmacht report kept the public abreast of the forced northern retreat of German troops. Naturally people were disappointed and would like to have taught the Italians a lesson. Why should Roman cultural monuments be spared when the German ones lay in ruin? The Allies seemed to show less respect for them. And anyway, where were Mussolini's divisions? People were eagerly awaiting the Pope's position; most believed that he would "join the other side," since he was not regarded as "pro-German."[12]

The buoyant mood of the first days did not last long. "A large portion of the population had not reckoned on the invader's ability to form bridgeheads and join up the various landing sites." Intensive propaganda about the Atlantic wall had left the majority of Germans in the dark about its imperfections: "They had . . . 'imagined real feats of magic' and were now utterly disappointed. The question also posted with increasing annoyance was 'where have our U-boats been all this time?' People had expected their reemergence during the invasion at the very latest.' . . ."[13] In the final analysis, those U-boats that were deployed made no significant impact on the development of the war.[14] Comparisons with the decisive intervention of America in World War I were heard again.

Between the optimists and the skeptics was the majority of undecided who thought " 'that there was, at present, cause neither for joy nor fear.' They don't want to 'disillusion themselves' with exaggerated confidence, but on the other hand they do not want to be regarded as pessimists either; therefore, they prefer to wait for two or three weeks when a better assessment can be made." Optimists could again be subdivided into two groups. A larger group, apparently influenced by Goebbels and his propaganda, felt that the more enemy forces let into France, the more could be destroyed. A smaller group held the opinion that those forces which had landed should be destroyed immediately and not be given an opportunity to receive reinforcements.[15]

The doubtful and the undecided alike were suddenly roused from their skepticism and swept along by the enthusiasm of the optimists when the Wehrmacht report of June 16 announced that southern England and the urban area of London had been bombed with new explosives. News of the beginning of revenge spread like wildfire. Those long-desired 'secret weapons' were not a propaganda trick after all. "It was moving to hear simple workers expressing their joy that their unshakable faith in the Führer had now found renewed confirmation. One older worker remarked on the train on his way home from work: 'How often I've argued with my co-workers because they no longer believed in revenge, in our Führer, not even in German victory. When the terror attacks on Frankfurt were getting worse, I myself almost began to doubt, but my inner conviction kept telling me: what the Führer promises, he does. And now I am overjoyed that revenge has truly come, and I firmly believe that it will bring us victory.' . . ."[16]

Letters to Goebbels confirmed this optimism.[17] All reporters agreed: the invasion had produced a strong upswing in morale, a "soaring of the mood barometer," a "stronger trust in the leadership," enthusiasm, jubilation, but also an intense feeling of revenge.[18] General opinion was: " 'Now things will improve again,' 'Now it's our turn again,' 'Nothing can happen to us now!' etc. We have also established that such positive opinions come from *all* sectors of society; it is not only those elements who have always considered it their duty to carry along their less optimistic fellow citizens who have been animated by this upswing in the mood." People wanted to be informed as accurately as possible about the destruction that had been caused and were a bit disgruntled about inadequate explanations concerning the nature and effect of the new weapon. The conclusion drawn from comments by Fritzsche and the press was "that we have a number of other, probably still more effective, secret weapons up our sleeve. . . . Other comments are that the destruction cannot be too great; hatred for England is finally finding an outlet yearned for, for so long, a revenge without mercy or compassion. In summary, one can say: if one action of the Führer ever found an unqualified response, it is this vengeance. The only regret is 'that we cannot get even with the Americans.' . . ."[19]

Excessive exuberance of this kind had not been seen since the French campaign, but neither the dovetailing of propaganda and public opinion, the widespread unanimity of opinion, nor the buoyant mood[20] lasted long. Within a few days cracks appeared in the edifice of opinion. This was due to military developments in France, Italy, and finally also in the East. Moreover, there were renewed air attacks—particularly against Hamburg, Hanover, Wesermünde, and Bremen—as well as the gradual realization that the V-1's effectiveness was far smaller than anticipated.

The German command was unable to persuade Hitler to regroup German forces south of Cherbourg; while Germans listened to radio broadcasts about the imminent destruction of American troops, the Allies penetrated further into France, solidifying their beachheads. Rommel and Rundstedt's demands for the deployment of the V-1 had to be rejected by General Heinemann because of their wide dispersion. Meanwhile, concerted bombardment of German fuel dumps and synthetic oil plants after May, 1944, greatly interfered with German efforts to send reinforcements. According to Speer's report of June 30, the enemy had succeeded in increasing German losses of airplane fuel by 90 per cent.[21] Demolished traffic arteries and fuel shortages kept reinforcements of motorized units from reaching the action. Although the Allies were also stopped for four days by a North Sea storm, by early July they had landed a million men, 171,532 vehicles, and 566,648 tons of materiel.[22] The time had come to prepare the population for the loss of Cherbourg.[23]

The twofold disappointment over the failure to throw the Allies back into the sea and the inability to bring about a decisive turn in military fortunes through retaliatory measures produced an extraordinary fluctuation and instability in the state of public opinion. "The individual's mood often fluctuates so rapidly between high spirits and pessimism that we cannot regard it as a constant quantity within the overall morale. There are many citizens, for example, who at the start of the invasion saw an early German victory, but now judge the loss of Cherbourg as the 'beginning of the end,' 'irreplaceable,' 'proof of our advancing weakness,' and the like. It is evident that a not inconsiderable segment of our population views an initial success *by our side* as a 'guarantee for our victory,' but *by the enemy* as an 'unmistakable bad omen.' Among these citizens a moral decline is noticeable, one that can only be arrested by an uninterrupted string of German successes. . . ."[24] Overall, the situation was regarded as grave, a certain disillusionment set in, and one observation from western Germany noted "that the number of citizens who, at the beginning of the invasion and retribution, had expected a decisive turn in the shortest time is far greater than initially assumed."[25]

Beginning in July, all reports spoke of a "decline" in morale and of considerable vacillation. The country was suddenly inundated with the wildest rumors.[26] Those hoping for a "miracle" were swayed by astrologers, soothsayers, and predictions based on the numerical combination of years. The death by plane crash of General Dietl[27] gave rise to all kinds of gossip, as did the deaths of Udet, Mölders, Todt, and Hube.[28] Hitler's words at the state funeral of Dietl about his example for the whole officer corps were taken as a warning, "for people knew of many officers who were definitely not yet National Socialists."[29]

From the end of June, propaganda sought desperately to head off a skid in morale and to turn the interest of readers and listeners from individual results to the overall context. "After the failure of the enemy's political onslaught last year, aimed at the demoralization of the German people, the concentrated military attack now taking place will also be repelled and German victory achieved in the end. . . ." As encouragement, sentences were cited from Hitler's unpublished speech of June 26 to factory managers: "Another 1918 will never come; as long as I live and one of my guards lives, anyone merely thinking such thoughts will be destroyed! . . . And because that November ninth will not come again, we will win this war; for Germany has never been conquered by foreign enemies, but always in the final analysis by Germans; but those Germans who could conquer Germany are no longer here today. . . ."[30]

These words by Hitler, spoken a few days before the attempt on his life, once more show the nigh traumatic effect the November revolution had had on him. It cannot be ruled out that a few SD reports had again been put before him indicating how ephemeral the harmony between public opinion and propaganda had been and how rapidly the storm of enthusiasm had once more subsided.

By the middle of July, interest was largely centered on the Soviet summer offensive, anticipated by the German command against Army Group Northern Ukraine. All reserves and tank units were transferred south, leaving Army Group Center, where the actual attack would take place, with only thirty-eight divisions to defend its eleven hundred kilometer front. Hitler's unwillingness to shorten the front, his strategy of "firm positions," now began to work to Germany's disadvantage as it pinned down numerous divisions. On June 22 the Soviets began their attack along four "fronts" and penetrated the protruding center front, producing a complete collapse of Army Group Center. The Ninth Army was encircled near Bobruisk, the Fourth in Minsk. General Model, entrusted with command of the Army Group on June 28, pulled out what men he could, but of the Ninth Army only fifteen thousand men were rescued, and the fourth was completely scattered. Army Group Center had thus lost twenty-eight divisions and 350,000 men.

The public viewed these developments with "increasing concern." Most frightening was the speed of the Russian advance; interest in the Western theatre diminished. From all regions of the Reich came similar observations: "People cannot grasp that it was possible for the Russians to make a thrust about 250 kilometers deep along a front of approximately five hundred kilometers within fourteen days. All reports concur on the enormous shock effect of the Russian break-through. . . ."[31] In East Prussia preparations were feverishly underway to receive refugees from occupied areas. Special crossing points were established for the refugee treks, from where they were to be transported by train in order to avoid alarming the population.

On July 15, a stepped-up travel ban was introduced for East Prussia and the Gaus of Danzig-West Prussia and Wartheland. All East Prussian district leaders received orders from Gauleiter Greiser to keep only the final goal in mind; if Germans could only hold out, victory was theirs: "It is not the 'V-1' alone. Other, and for our enemy more terrible, weapons will follow. The era of their technical superiority is coming to an end. German inventiveness has not been sleeping, rather it has been working on new weapons. . . . If you do find overanxious individuals who lack political faith and strong hearts and who bring unrest into the excellent attitude of the East Prussian population, the Party and state know ways of rendering them harmless. . . ."[32]

By the second week of July, 1944, Berliners who as victims of air raids had been transferred to the eastern and southeastern border regions of East Prussia were returned to the interior: the Gaus of Halle-Merseburg, Thuringia, and the Sudetenland. Preparations were made to evacuate mothers with children and the aged from East Prussia. To avoid a further collapse of morale, the reasons cited for the evacuation were the need for more infirmary rooms, billets for soldiers, military offices, and room for Eastern refugees.[33] The East Prussian population was kept quiet in the face of mounting danger by massive propaganda and intimidation of the fearful. Only the "upper strata" used all conceivable means in an attempt to leave this exposed province.

A special source of unrest was posed by the Berliners; as early as the autumn of 1943 the president of Königsberg's appeals court had reported on the difficulty of these city dwellers in accustoming themselves to rural conditions and unfamiliar food. Above all, they "complained" far more than the quiet, reserved East Prussians.[34] With danger approaching, the restless Berliners, who disliked being bossed by Party functionaries, were considered potential trouble, and their evacuation was thus also regarded as contributing to a more stable mood. Goebbels, as Gauleiter of Berlin, was naturally incensed and protested, to which the Reich propaganda office in Königsberg replied: "The points of criticism cited by the Minister are also fully appreciated here. It isn't that Berliners were simply railed at indiscriminately or that we are overbearing in our criticism of them. In my report about them I expressed myself very carefully and guardedly. . . ."[35]

Morale in endangered areas was also boosted by the call-up of all males between the ages of sixteen and sixty-five for construction of defenses, which took people's minds off the Russian advance and gave tangible evidence of public mobilization. Königsberg's Reich propaganda office noted with satisfaction on July 15 that mobilization had not crippled economic life in the region.[36] Yet despite all these stabilizing measures, Germans were day by day more overcome "by a kind of creeping panic." Press and radio, with their messages of "confidence in victory," made less and less of an impression. Criticism of the leadership mounted, and soldiers talked about a deterioration of morale within the officer corps, according to a report from southwest Germany.[37] While Goebbels was preparing another effort to counteract slipping spirits, an event occurred which deeply stirred the entire German nation, from Nazi to critic, and forced Germans to reflect on their attitude toward the regime.

2.   JULY 20, 1944[38]

At 12:42 on July 20, 1944, a bomb exploded in a barracks in the vicinity of Rastenburg, East Prussia, in which Hitler was holding his morning briefing. It detonated too late, and its effect was incomplete. Adolf Hitler was only lightly wounded. In the ensuing days approximately seven thousand people were arrested; the major representatives of the German resistance were either shot immediately or had to submit to an elaborate show trial before the People's Tribunal before being hanged or imprisoned.

The months of 1943, psychologically opportune for an overthrow of the Nazi regime, had slipped away without any decisive action undertaken. A further assassination plan had been frustrated by a last minute change in Hitler's plans. Important members of the resistance movement, like General Oster, Dietrich Bonhoeffer, Dohnanyi, Langbehn, and finally also Admiral Canaris, had been arrested or neutralized. General Beck suffered a long illness, and surveillance by the Gestapo was further intensified so that all contacts had to be camouflaged even more painstakingly.[39]

Once preparations for the coup and the change in regimes seemed sufficiently advanced and an appropriate opportunity presented itself to Colonel Claus Schenk von Stauffenberg to carry out the assassination, the most favorable domestic and diplomatic period had passed. Germany had already lost the war militarily. The Allies therefore had no motive to negotiate for peace with the plotters. Governed primarily by considerations of caution but also due to poor contacts with the people, the resisters could not initiate the public into its plans. Germans were to be won over only after the successful assassination by revealing the criminal nature of the regime, but in the meantime the public had passed its most critical phase toward the Nazi regime and been strengthened in its will to resist and its group solidarity through the invasion and the use of the V-1 weapon. Hitler had recovered some of his tarnished prestige. Stauffenberg and his friends were fully aware that their action would be subject to misinterpretation both within as well as outside Germany. Considerations of that kind were dismissed, however, because toppling the regime seemed imperative to them.

What remains to be emphasized above all about the act of July 20 is consequently its moral significance. It serves as the only proof for the existence of a "second Germany," revealing the attitude of all those who had not taken the path of regression or those willing to leave it, if they had not already done so.

On the basis of available reports, to be looked at in more detail below, the direct impact on the public at large of this assassination attempt was a temporary bolstering of the regime—a clear sign of the isolation in which the plotters had operated. What emerges from all the early reports is that a majority of Germans, including critics of the regime and the undecided, as well as Nazis, rejected tyrannicide in the middle of a war that had turned into a struggle for survival. Condemnation of the deed seems—as far as one can rely on reports—to have been strongest among the lower and middle classes; among the former elite, from which the largest contingent of resisters was recruited, and especially among the intelligentsia, feeling ranged from comprehension of the act to agreement, but without signs of unanimous endorsement.

Party reaction was swift and predictable. With the vulgar arrogance of an *arriviste*, that same evening after the plot prepared by members of the old elite had failed, Bormann issued a directive to all Gauleiters to ignore any orders emanating from the rebels.[40] On the twenty-first, in response to a question from the Gauleiter of Graz about holding a "mass rally,"[41] a statement was issued containing the following passage: "Because of the childish insurrection attempt by a small clique of reactionary generals, smashed immediately that same (yesterday) evening with its participants punished accordingly, cities with suitable opportunity are permitted and even requested to hold mass open-air rallies expressing the joy and gratification of the people at the miraculous deliverance of the Führer. . . ."[42]

Propaganda swung into action with a radio speech by Goebbels on July 24 on the theme: "the attempted assassination and its background." The speech was the signal for a solid wave of loyalty oaths conducted in all Gaus and districts.[43] Local military units were ordered to participate; in cooperation with the German Labor Front, industries held rollcalls at which time the workers had to "express their National Socialist loyalty in a congratulatory message to the Führer." Speakers were given a list of subjects to emphasize in their speeches: 1. that only a small reactionary clique of traitors was behind the deed; 2. that they shamelessly misused their powers of command in an effort to sabotage the Nazi victory; 3. that this camarilla, out of hatred for the movement, had sought to prevent the Nazification of the military and to hinder promotion of Nazi officers; 4. and that the military, whose loyalty had repeatedly been proven during the most difficult front conditions, remains unblemished by the attempted coup.[44]

Directives to the press on July 20 reveal an initial confusion over the background of the attempted assassination. The first report by the German News Agency [*Deutsche Nachrichten-Büro* or DNB] was captioned: "Murderous Assault on the Führer—the Führer Uninjured." Newspapers were to comment "in a dignified manner" on the "dramatic report" so as to move the whole nation and turn it against the enemy. "Fate clearly watches over the life of the Führer. The German people also recognize in this attempted murder that Adolf Hitler's life-work, which has been and continues to be the protection first of Germany and then of Europe from Bolshevism, is blessed by a higher source. . . . That our enemies now resort to foul murder is furthermore a clear sign of how poor their military chances are in reality, despite present claims of success. . . ."[45]

By the next day the daily slogan from the Reich Press Chief stated, obviously in reaction to Hitler's speech that night, that it was a criminal conspiracy "of a small clique in collusion with the enemy." It must absolutely not lead to criticism of the German Wehrmacht and its officers.[46] On July 23, after public opinion had been gauged on the basis of initial opinion reports, a definitive guideline was established for the mass media in the ensuing period: "It is the task of the German press, the mouthpiece of the German people so to speak, to articulate the willingness generally observed in the German public for the most selfless mobilization of all their powers in individual labor for the sake of the military decision. This is the call of the hour and must be the lesson learned from the events of July 20. The reply to this thwarted stab in the military's back must be an inner national-socialist rededication for every German . . . the moment has finally come for a mobilization of all remaining idle reserves, the deployment of which can no longer be impeded by any saboteurs. . . ."[47]

Here, as previously at the time of the invasion and V-1 activity, propaganda and articulated majority opinion largely dovetailed. First signs of an upswing in the mood appeared as early as July 21. Stemming from the Reich Security Office, where they were compiled by von Kielpinski, or from Reich propaganda offices, these opinions were later confirmed by Party officials and the Justice Ministry as well as by letters from the public. They are so informative that a few typical excerpts merit citing.

"All reports uniformly make reference to the sudden dismay, emotional shock, deep indignation, and anger unleashed among the whole people by the report of the assassination attempt. From several cities (e.g., Königsberg and Berlin) there are reports of women bursting into tears in stores and on the streets, some completely out of control. The joy at the mild outcome was extraordinarily great. Heaving a heavy sigh of relief, the public ascertained: 'Thank God, the Führer is alive.'

"To some extent a certain despondency overshadowed the joy at the Führer's escape. Citizens were suddenly aware of a very dangerous and serious situation. After the initial shock and the first consolation that nothing serious happened to the Führer, we find a great pensiveness everywhere.

"To date not one expression has been recorded giving any indication that a single citizen approved of the attempt. On the contrary, without exception the observation is made that even elements of the population which are not out-and-out supporters of National Socialism detest the attempted assassination; for example, we find a number of such reactions from northern districts of Berlin which had stood in clear opposition before. Thus workers from the northern sections of the Reich capital exclaimed that it was a foul act to stab Hitler in the back this way. 'There is no sense in ending the war now. We have to win. For heaven's sake, no civil war now,' or 'What on earth were the assassins thinking; how would the war continue if the Führer were no longer there'. . . ." Many believed Hitler's death would mean defeat.[48]

Hamburg's propaganda office observed no trace of negative opinions;[49] Weimar made sure by holding a "spontaneous" rally of thanksgiving at noon on July 21.[50] In the ensuing period many cities held loyalty rallies as ordered and reported heavy attendance both by the public and military representatives.[51] In all reports on the above, and on public reaction in general, the key words repulsion, indignation, alarm, and shock, recurred. Nuremberg's appeals court president commented on the public's attitude as "better than ever" and attributed it to the assassination attempt.[52] Similar observations came from the court presidents of Jena, Darmstadt, Breslau, and Kiel, all stressing the public's strong condemnation of the act and relief at averting a civil war.[53] If the mood remained depressed, it was due to military developments on the Eastern front.

Even considering that the assassins' failure, fear of reprisals, and new terror mitigated against a true expression of feelings, we have to acknowledge that the act was not popular, not with the public and certainly not with the majority of combat soldiers.[54] A more complex picture emerges from the officer corps as many officers experienced deep inner conflict.[55] Obersturmbannführer von Kielpinski's assertion of July 22, 1944, seems largely accurate: "No event of the war has so deeply moved the broad masses as this murder attempt. Never has it been so evident with what *loyalty the Volk stands by the Führer*;"[56] if by broad majority Kielpinski meant 60-70 per cent of the public and included the prevailing opinion of the church, this would seem convincing. Both Churches, Catholic as well as Protestant, still condemned the tyrannicide *after* the war—not to mention in July, 1944.[57] But the fact that leading members of the resistance found the strength for this act in the Christian ethic speaks well for their responsibility toward humanity; it also says a lot about the failure of the Churches who proved unequal to the situation of conflict in which Germans found themselves. Since no moral authority made it clear to Germans that the deed could not be measured by normal standards—that it revealed more genuine patriotism than did obedience to an oath sworn to Hitler—the population was "unified in its condemnation of the crime, in its joy at the Führer's deliverance, and in its hope for radical measures . . . as it had hardly been over any event of the war. . . ."[58]

The strengthened "bond to Hitler,"[59] to use the SD's words, the rise of his popularity curve after the attempt on his life, was also registered elsewhere. The American department for psychological warfare at the Headquarters for the Supreme Allied Expeditionary Forces in Europe conducted regular interrogations of German soldiers captured in Normandy in order to gear its own war propaganda to the mentality of the German military personnel. While 5 per cent of the war prisoners expressed their confidence in Hitler during the period July 1 to 17, 1944, 68 per cent did so at the beginning of August.[60]

According to SD statements, "only in decidedly isolated cases" was the assassins' act not condemned.[61] Überlingen's Kreisleiter thought he observed that "only intellectual circles, which have always attracted undesirable attention, would likely have received the success of the coup with satisfaction. These persons cannot be watched too closely and must be curbed in their influence and positions of power." He even wanted "to radically eliminate a large percentage of them."[62]

The Kreisleiter of Schlüchtern in Hesse-Nassau told of a "noticeable indifference toward this cowardly deed . . . among all aristocratic families."[63] His use of rather vulgar language in all his reports, however, suggests strong class antagonisms—he even speaks of "blue-blood idiots" in a later opinion survey—and places the veracity of his reports in question.[64] His resentments, nevertheless, reflect a pervading hostility among the lower classes, where there was talk of the "reactionary aristocracy" and the "foul" plot of "aristocratic German officers."[65] Their mouthpiece was Dr. Ley.[66]

There is no material on the reaction among aristocrats or former ruling groups in general toward the assassination attempt. No one who was not tired of living would have expressed his feelings beyond the most intimate circle of family and friends—and even then only with caution.

Many descendants of old noble families had originally sympathized with the regime, if not collaborated closely with it. The SS could boast of an impressive number of aristocrats among its leaders. One can assume that most of them, however, and particularly those not directly involved with the system, had inwardly turned away from the Nazi regime by now—just as the Third Reich had long since begun to dissociate itself from them[68]—and secretly sympathized with the resistance, to which they stood much closer not only through ties of kinship but also in lifestyle and social bearing than to Hitler's "*parvenu* state." The same applied to some parts of big business. The support furnished to Goerdeler and the resistance movement by the Bosch firm, and the attitude of the Reusch group, are well known.[69] After Hitler's star began to sink and every clear-headed person could foresee the end of the war before long, large industrial firms, who until then had profited quite handsomely from the regime's war policy, cautiously began to convert to peacetime production and thus to a Germany without Hitler.[70] The assassination attempt had abruptly exposed this inevitable development; most opportunists now slowly began to dissociate themselves from the Third Reich.

The failure of the putsch was no doubt also lamented by former Social Democrats and Communists. Even if it had been planned and executed largely by supporters of conservative and liberal persuasion, its success would have opened the way for new leftist activities, especially since Leber and his friends had concentrated the network of socialist and trade-unionist cells in order to activate it immediately in the event of a successful military putsch. The fact that the loyalty rallies turned out to be far less impressive in Berlin, pitiful in comparison to other cities such as Vienna, may serve as one indication, a limited one to be sure, of such an attitude.[71] Somewhat more illuminating is the reference to an increase in arrests for subversive opinions, particularly the numerous cases of a Marxist-communist character where disappointment was voiced over the outcome of the assassination plot.[72]

As far as the attitude of the Catholic population is concerned, the following examples will suffice. In Catholic Paderborn, about 20 per cent of the population participated in the loyalty rally; in the neighboring district of Schaumburg, a bastion of National Socialism, the figure was 70 per cent. Nevertheless, 20 per cent surpassed all previous attendance records, according to Paderborn's Kreisleiter. Salzkotten, a purely Catholic community in the district Paderborn, recorded similar results: "at this rally many citizens participated who have not attended a political rally for years."[73] Freiburg experienced greater activity as well.[74]

To take advantage of this generally positive situation, two topics offered themselves to the regime: total war and the stab-in-the-back legend. The first SD report of July 21 mentioned the public's willingness "to shoulder all the burdens of war and 'now especially' to do their utmost for victory. Numerous citizens now want to be enlisted immediately for the war and victory. Especially among the working class (e.g., in Berlin), there are demands for true total warfare and the most extreme mobilization of those elements in particular who have largely shirked energetic cooperation (for instance the mobilization of women). One frequently confronts the wish that a 'ruthless end' now be put to the domestic enemy."[75] Press and propaganda took note of the new factors and the disposition of public opinion, successfully disseminating the issues and once more achieving a consensus among the broad masses; through a "third infusion" of the total war theme, urgently requested by Speer,[76] demands could be made for an even greater effort from Germans, and failures in the East could be charged to the stab-in-the-back legend.

The subject of treason crops up in many reports: "Again and again the retreats of our troops in the East as well as the string of accidents from Todt to Dietl are attributed to the conspiratorial clique."[77] Inherent in this treachery thesis, however, was the grave danger of discrediting the entire officer corps and, in the long run, of a decline in military discipline: "Numerous conversations among the citizenry reveal a generalized *dissonance regarding the officer corps.* Often a distinction is no longer made between reliable and devoted officers and the irresponsible elements caught up in the plot against the Führer. Some class-warfare tendencies are evident among citizens who are interpreting Dr. Ley's speech in that sense. The public from the most diverse Gaus had sharp words against the 'high and mighty,' 'swelled heads,' and 'monocle wearers'. . . ." Thoughts of this kind ultimately led to a comparison with the Stalinist purges of the thirties: "This method was in any case safer than the leniency practiced by our leadership."[78]

The people thus articulated what Hitler and intransigent Nazis had thought for some time. In the perspective of the "little man," disappointed in his socio-political expectations, the attempted assassination was a welcome confirmation of the opinion that Hitler had backed the wrong horse. It seemed to prove "that the National Socialist revolution, just like the Fascist, had been forced to stop before the 'reactionary aristocracy and former German nationalist coterie.' " Like Fascism, the Nazis had employed slogans and phrases to pacify and deceive the workers, only the consequences were far worse for Germany. Stalin was seen as the only level-headed leader in dealing with the threat from the dominant class. In the end the crucial question was posed: "Has Germany, in the final analysis, not always lost because of treason?"[79]

This question and continued agitation surrounding this subject confirm the view held then and even now by opponents of the assassination attempt, namely that a successful putsch would have prepared the way for a new stab-in-the-back legend. What this ignores is that instead of Nazi propaganda, the public would finally have learned the truth about the crimes and true character of the Nazi regime. It would have permitted Germans to settle accounts among themselves, as Stauffenberg had demanded; failure to achieve this still afflicts Germans today.

As it happened, the attack on Hitler registered as a shock. The immediate, reflex reaction was to unite resolutely as an endangered national group around its leader. Gradually, however, under the continued pressure of military events, the process of corrosion which had begun in 1942 accelerated, manifested itself strikingly in 1943, and then was temporarily checked and restrained by the suffering resulting from bombardments, the psychologically adverse Allied attitude toward Italy, and the adroit conduct of propaganda concerning the invasion and secret weapons. This process was fostered by doubts about whether the "traitors" had not been right and better informed; about whether the affairs of Germany had not been placed in the wrong hands, or whether Hitler was still up to handling events. Hitler and his cohorts were sufficiently aware of the potential danger to issue directives calling for closer Party communication with the public in order to confirm the indispensability of the Nazi leadership to the masses. This meant that leading Party officials were to conduct themselves as shining examples, their lifestyles above reproach.[80] Goebbels, appointed "Reich Plenipotentiary for the Mobilization of Total War,"[81] sent a special circular to all Party and state officials and agencies on "lifestyle during total warfare;" all unnecessary activities, from pomp to parties, were forbidden. Every action had to pass the inspection of critical public and combatant eyes, and was to "testify to our firm resolve to see this struggle through to a victorious end, whatever the costs. . . ."[82]

In an effort to brake a growing trend toward the vilification of the military leadership, Martin Bormann promptly issued an order regarding public handling of the events of July 20: "The Führer wants no one, in discussing the events of July 20, to allow himself to be carried away so as to criticize or offend *in corpore* the officer corps, the generals, the aristocracy, or military services. Instead it must be emphasized repeatedly that we are dealing with a well-defined, relatively small officer clique which participated in the putsch."[83]

But the talk of sabotage and treason would not cease. The more reports filtered down about the collapse of Army Group Center, the more the conviction took hold among the public that treason was involved. People refused to believe accounts of "headlong" retreat, "failure" on the part of officers who deserted their troops, and extremely poor morale among soldiers who in some cases would even sell their weapons,[84] because the behavior of German officers and men simply had to be above reproach. Germans had been led to believe in the superiority of their military; Blitzkrieg victories had been too easy for them to accept readily that the performance and courage of military personnel also had limits and could collapse in the face of overwhelming superiority in men and materiel. It was easier to believe in betrayal, a conviction reinforced by the news that the circle of conspirators was far greater than originally thought: "If people assumed initially that it involved a small clique of officers undertaking a cause that was hopeless from the outset, today they think that for some time the traitors have sabotaged the Führer's objectives and orders. This opinion is primarily due to an increase in written and oral reports by soldiers from the Eastern front who declare that they are now discovering the reasons for the absence of reinforcements and the often senseless shifting of units and exposure of the front." This report from northwest Germany was almost identical to one from the south, where the assassination attempt was viewed as part of a systematic plot to undermine Germany's defenses.[85]

Gradually this treason theory, at first deliberately fanned by German propaganda, boomeranged on the regime. Reports came in suggesting public doubt as to Hitler's awareness; he could not be that well informed, or such treason would have been impossible. Two trends emerged: the Hitler faithful declared that the Führer could not know everything. Moreover, so much around him was withheld from him—like the late Wilhelm II—that the situation was depicted more rosily than warranted by reality. Others, however, began to doubt in the abilities and "strategic genius" of Germany's supreme military commander and head of state.[86]

The Stuttgart section of the SD reported that except for Party activists and a small minority, no one continued to believe in victory, barring a miracle. The plot against Hitler exposed the degree to which leading officials had consistently lied to the public, claiming that time was on

Germany's side, that war production was rising daily, and that the day was fixed for a resumption of the offensive—only to have Hitler now personally admit that his policies had been sabotaged for years. In other words, time had worked against Germany. If he could be so misled, either he was no genius, or, if he had known, he blatantly lied to the people about rising war production when the enemy was right under his nose. The SD reporter from Stuttgart added: "Probably most disquieting about the whole matter is that most citizens, including those most steadfast in their belief, have now lost all faith in the Führer." Comments like these had previously been withheld because other observations contradicted them, "but now it has to be stated emphatically."[87]

This report illustrates that the assassination attempt had evoked condemnation primarily due to its shock effect; Hitler's popularity curve, which shot up after July 20, soon began to decline again rapidly.

In the late summer of 1944, public interest was focused on the proceedings against the conspirators before the People's Tribunal and on the renewed campaign for total mobilization. Reports from Reich propaganda offices, the SD, Party officials, and jurists reveal strong interest, in many places motivated by a craving for sensationalism. The trial and verdicts were received favorably by most, although a minority followed Roland Freisler's cynical proceedings and the hangings with repulsion, drawing parallels between this trial and the Moscow show trials.[88] Others clamored for even more radical measures, such as the "extermination" of the assassins' families;[89] death by strangulation seemed too humane, and they would have preferred medieval lynch law. The same sadism was manifest among them as in Hitler, who viewed films of the traitors being hanged on meat hooks.

For the Wehrmacht the assassination attempt signalled a final emasculation. The traditional military greeting was replaced by the Hitler salute. Himmler became commander of the reserve army, and political crimes were transferred from its jurisdiction to that of the People's Tribunal and special courts.[90] Membership in the NSDAP, suspended during active service by the military law of May 21, 1935,[91] now also remained in force during this period. Members of the military were made responsible "to act, on and off duty, in the spirit of National Socialist ideology and to stand up for it at all times."[92]

3. VOLKSKRIEG AND MIRACLE WEAPONS

While a small number of Nazi faithful and the mass of vacillating Germans, whose attitude shifted with military circumstances and opportunities, hoped that the elimination of the conspiratorial clique would open the way for positive developments on the Eastern front—a superficial optimism encouraged by a temporary halt in the Soviet advance—events in the West again unsettled a mood that had been stabilized only with difficulty.

By the end of July, Allied operation "Cobra," under the command of General Montgomery, had brought the enemy to Avranches and threatened to penetrate the German front. Field Marshal von Kluge, who had replaced Rundstedt that month as supreme commander West, recommended evacuation of France to the Seine in order to set up a defensive line running from the mouth of the Seine to the Swiss border. But Hitler, pursuing a strategy analogous to that in the East, ordered the defense of Brittany ports as "fortresses." At the same time the left flank of the German front was to push its way back to the sea by launching a counterattack on Avranches, thereby also cutting off Patton's army which had penetrated southward. But the German attack was stalled by the firepower of Allied fighter bombers while elements of Patton's army dashed into Brittany, reached the Channel at Vannes, and thus effectively sealed off the peninsula and German troops at St. Malo, St. Nazaire, Lorient, and Brest. On August 15 Kluge independently issued the order to lead the two trapped armies out of the pocket. Two days later he was replaced by Field Marshal Model. Contributing to Kluge's dismissal was considerable doubt as to his reliability; Bormann assumed he must have known about the traitors' plans.[93] Field Marshal von Kluge, known in the army as "clever (*kluger*) Hans," had vacillated throughout and refused to join the conspiracy. But now he feared his knowledge of the plot had come to light, and so he took poison en route to the Führer's headquarters. His farewell letter to Hitler revealed his inner confusion, calling on Hitler to end a hopeless war and yet admiring his genius and professing loyalty even in death.[94]

On the basis of Kluge's letter, Keitel pronounced in a secret military order of August 31 that Kluge "had apparently acted under the impression of serious personal responsibility for the outcome of the battle in Normandy. . . ." His burial had been conducted quietly.[95] However, on September 5, Reich Propaganda Ministry officials were in possession of a report from Dessau stating that Kluge's body had lain in state for almost fourteen days in the church at Böhne in Gau Magdeburg-Anhalt. Rumors of suicide or participation in the conspiracy of July 20 would circulate and cause public unrest. In view of mounting agitation, the Dessau Reich propaganda office called for urgent counteraction by a word-of-mouth propaganda. Goebbels was presented the information and a decision was reached: von Kluge had died of a heart attack.[96]

This excitement at the death of Kluge, still observed everywhere several weeks later,[97] was only a tiny episode in a chain of bad news. Canadian troops had penetrated to Falaise and further constricted the Normandy pocket. After they joined the Americans at Chambois, the remainder of the German troops were sealed off: forty-five thousand men, remnants of eight infantry and several tank divisions, were captured. In addition, an Allied landing was effected on August 15 in the south of France; nine days later Paris fell to Patton's forces. Hitler's order to defend Paris to the last man and to destroy all military installations and bridges, "turning Paris into a wasteland," had not been obeyed by General von Choltitz.[98]

Allied penetration into Brittany took the German population by surprise. They were now confronted with a situation deteriorating daily. "The question was often posed: 'What good is the supposedly impenetrable Atlantic Wall anyway? Is it fated to be a myth like the Maginot Line?' Again people are remembering the repeated earlier explanations in newspapers and on radio of how a withdrawal along the Eastern front was inevitable because all available troops had to be massed for the decision in the West. Now, however, it has become obvious that the divisions in the West are also insufficient. If we were to explain that it involves a deliberate strategic maneuver on our part, the immediate retort would be: we have heard enough of this kind of 'systematic' strategy of evasion during recent years, and we do not believe that the breakthrough in the West was desired by our leaders in order to force the Anglo-Americans into a great decisive battle. . . ."[99]

For the moment the mood remained "one of wait-and-see, though heavily dejected" as continued Allied successes caused more and more concern. Hopes of regaining mastery of the situation were dashed by the landings in southern France. Allied superiority was the main topic of conversation; the wish for a speedy end to the war became increasingly evident amidst this depression, sustained by the illusion that "the end will not be as terrible as they pretend." More and more people clung to the hope of newer weapons and a more effective conduct of total war.[100]

Allied landings in southern France triggered further dismay. All Reich propaganda offices reported a "new low in morale. Concern that the war could no longer be won quickly is gripping ever larger numbers of people. The assessment of our position has caused dejection and widespread helplessness as never before in five years of war. Although everyone knows that the front-line soldier is fulfilling his duty to the utmost, despite painful casualties and loss of terrain, the public has more and more come to the conclusion that even the greatest bravery cannot compensate for the enemy's numerical and materiel superiority.

"But since the public remembers almost without exception that the fate of our Volk, just like that of every individual, will be sealed by the loss of our spirit of resistance, this reversal of mood has not paralyzed the fighting morale of the individual citizen in any way. All reports show that the Volk now places its trust completely in the leadership. . . ."

The "tortuous explanations" of the press and the use of clichés such as "successful withdrawal" were noted with derision. The construction of field-works produced acidic comments. If the vaunted Atlantic Wall could not hold back the Anglo-Saxons, how could these pitiful works stop the Russian advance? But the most bitter remarks were about the failure of the Luftwaffe. If people had once believed the lack of fighter plane protection over Germany was due to their deployment at the front, talk now was "that reversals at the fronts were also attributable primarily to enemy air superiority."[101]

The fall of Paris, the rapid withdrawal of German troops from southern France following Hitler's order of August 18 to shore up the front, and now, on August 25, Rumania's defection to the enemy only darkened the mood even more. "Increasingly the public is driven to believe that unless a miracle occurs the war can no longer be won. This miracle, by which is meant new weapons having such a revolutionary impact as to turn the war around, would naturally have to happen soon. Since the enemy is nearing the Reich frontiers at an alarming pace along all fronts, it is no longer a matter of months but of weeks and days. A summary of our overall situation gives the public a shocking perspective. Even previously optimistic people remarked: 'In our hearts we will continue to believe in victory, but our minds ask, how can the situation improve?' "[102]

Criticism of the military command flared up because it had repeatedly neglected to evacuate marginal positions in time. Most did not know—or did not want to know—that Hitler was personally responsible. They preferred to blame the "generals."

Developments in Rumania "shocked the masses." Until then, German propaganda had always given the impression that this country was one of the "most loyal and energetic allies."[103] The possible loss of Rumanian oil fields severely depressed the population—and indeed, the German war economy never recovered from their loss on August 30, since Allied bombing of German fuel production plants caused heavy damage.

Credibility of official news was steadily declining; propaganda was subjected to strong criticism as more and more Germans tuned in foreign radio stations. The "fourth weapon," as Goebbels once characterized propaganda,[104] had actually suffered "a heavy blow," according to the weekly activity reports of Reich propaganda offices. In vain it attempted to suggest to the public that Germany faced no more difficult a situation today than the Russians had when German troops were just outside Moscow and at the Caucasus. "What the Russians were able to do cannot be impossible for the German people." Naturally the "outer defense line" acquired between 1939 and 1942 has to be relinquished in many places and the struggle has drawn closer to the "inner ring of defenses." "If we hold this position, nothing affecting the national existence of our Volk is lost. But our enemies' intention is to destroy it. With good reason it has been said: 'Germany has won the war if it does not lose it'. . . ."[105]

By now there was no more talk of victory. The best one could hope for was a negotiated peace. Reports of Reich propaganda offices were carefully analyzed in the Reich Propaganda Ministry and topics to be avoided or expanded were heavily underlined in blue. But despite all the regime's efforts, morale sank even lower in September: "Negatively disposed citizens, with their defeatist remarks and veiled criticism of the leadership, are increasingly gaining ground and trying to shake the faith of the large majority of our population." Germans began to concern themselves more and more with the reasons and causes for this disastrous development: Why did the invasion not proceed as planned? Why was total warfare not introduced earlier? Why was the July 20 plot not discovered sooner? With no apparent way out, there was growing talk of suicide.[106] War weariness took greater hold and indifference spread. Finland was lost as an ally on September 10, the very day V-1 bombardment of London was suspended, and Bulgaria soon saw to its own interests as well. "Rats deserting a sinking ship," people said.[107]

The evacuations of Eupen and Malmédy on September 4 and Aachen on September 11 were characterized by panic and disorganization;[108] in Aachen, Party uniforms and badges were burned and the populace was left largely to its own devices.[109] Most refused to leave their homes until civil and military police units were brought into the city. Farmers, under the leadership of the district deputy farm leader, rebelled against leaving their farms, and many barricaded themselves. Some even fired on the SA. Other elements of the population hid in the woods and elsewhere, so that the evacuation was only a partial success.[110] Seeing the end of the war approaching, people preferred taking any risk rather than to being transported into the Reich interior, where they would be given makeshift lodging and continue to vegetate under air raids and NSDAP pressure.

Troops streaming back from France left a devastating impression on the population. One report from the Gauleitung of Baden refers to ragged soldiers congregating with questionable company and wagons

loaded with booty or furniture and household belongings—pictures reminiscent of 1918.[111] The scandalous occupation life smelled to high heaven,
according to military and propaganda sources;[112] such manifestations
only intensified public fatalism and resignation: "I don't care, I don't
understand the situation anymore." This opinion was held not only by
the man in the street but increasingly also by Party members.

"Bourgeois circles hope that an occupation by the Anglo-Americans
will keep Bolshevism at arm's length. These elements automatically
assume the National Socialist regime will be removed and replaced by
pre-1933 forms of government without Germany being ruined and the
middle classes suffering any serious loss. . . ." Here there was a greater
fear of the "mob" than of the Western Allies. Critical comments concerning Hitler were aired and many people realized "that the only reason
for continued resistance is that the National Socialist government
cannot capitulate because it refuses to give up."[113]

Conventional propaganda no longer worked in this situation. In
Bochum, therefore, they resorted to the proven technique of using front-
line soldiers. Every furloughed soldier the Kreisleitung could lay its
hands on—iron cross recipients were naturally preferred—had to speak in
cinemas for six minutes before the newsreel and exhort the population
to hold out.[114]

In the evening of September 11 an American reconnaissance patrol
for the first time crossed the German frontier.[115] The first German city
had been evacuated. The Nazi leadership now felt the time had come to
call on the entire nation to wage war. That same day an article appeared
in the *Völkische Beobachter*, written by the deputy Reich Press Chief
but inspired by the highest authority, calling for a *Volkskrieg* [People's
War]. One week later Richard Hildebrandt, SS-Obergruppenführer and
General of the Police, turned to Himmler and demanded "that a German partisan war be prepared and implemented immediately." On the
basis of his experiences in the East,[116] he made various suggestions.
In all border regions of the Reich "netlike strongpoints and alternate
positions were to be established at places difficult to locate and approach," and to be supplied with weapons, ammunition, food and clothing. From among the population only "leading families from Party,
state, and Wehrmacht" were to be evacuated. All other politically non-
exposed Germans were to stay put "to give our partisan troops bases for
continued operations and to preserve the backbone of German agriculture." Command of these forces was to be in the hands of higher SS and
police leaders; for reasons of secrecy the group was to be kept as small
as possible. What also seemed important to him were the organization
of passive resistance by all professional and national groups in order to

establish a "second front," the activization of "non-German members of all border states for the struggle for freedom in their homelands," and the "propagation of a new idea of European liberty."[117]

Hitler gave the order for the population to mobilize for the final fierce struggle. "The Führer has decreed: that our conduct of war must become fanatical since the battle has touched German soil along broad sectors, and German cities and villages are being turned into battle-grounds. . . . Every bunker, every block in a German city, and every German village must be turned into a fortress against which the enemy will either bleed to death or its garrison be buried in man-to-man combat."[118]

The actual manifestation and symbol of the *Volkskrieg* was the *Volkssturm*, a Home Guard created to mobilize all German men capable of bearing arms. Its objective was twofold: to secure more men for the Reich's defense under the motto: more soldiers *and* more weapons—a demand impossible to realize in the autumn of 1944;[120] and to symbolize the participation in the war of every person, regardless of social status or rank. Here factory director stood next to unskilled worker, academic next to artisan. Apparently there were attempts to draw up the *Volkssturm* along professional and class lines, but Bormann took a strong stand against this. In his free and easy language: "A baker's *Volkssturm* is nonsense, is a *kontradicio in adjecto* [sic], is a contradiction in itself! There is no such thing as a dry cloudburst! . . ." *Volkssturm* was to unite the classes and create a sense of common bond.[121] Like the Wehrmacht, the *Volkssturm* had to swear a personal oath to the Führer to remain steadfast and prefer death to defeat.[122]

Another means of heading off growing fear and a sour mood was to employ the public in field-works. The Nazi elite had correctly observed that it was the feeling of helplessness which weighed most heavily on people's minds. On the proven principle of occupational therapy, their cares were to be diverted while the illusion was created that their personal participation could delay the enemy's advance. This diversionary tactic was only partially and temporarily successful. While Freiburg enthusiastically reported on the "true blessing" of this program which encouraged camaraderie and even excessive optimism,[123] Düsseldorf painted a far different picture of grumbling over provisioning, the use of juveniles, and inadequate protection against air attack. Organization and the role of political leaders aroused particular displeasure: one prevalent opinion was that the Party had merely engineered this operation for egotistical Gauleiters who were too cowardly to gain their military decorations at the front, yet wanted to show their involvement.[124] Kaltenbrunner informed Schwarz that many of the program's organizational problems lay with its hastily improvised nature, particularly in the West where the strafing of workers and the sudden appearance of Allied troops provoked serious public questioning of the military value of these installations.[125]

Out of fear of advancing Soviet forces in the East, after an initial enthusiastic response to the appeal for workers, a similar public reaction set in. Lack of organization, poor provisioning, and inept leadership were cited: "Bitterness was particularly aroused by the totally unsuitable male supervisory staff who apparently had the nerve to drive up to the sites in automobiles and then walk along without picking up a shovel; instead they not only controlled those who were working, men and women, in some cases elderly, but also screamed at them in quite an inappropriate tone of command. What is more, most of them are no longer convinced of the real defensibility of such hastily erected fortifications."[126] After the example of the Atlantic Wall, Germans were extremely skeptical about any fortifications; criticism of the West Wall was expressed everywhere; how long could a pathetic system of trenches hold in the East?

In the course of this third wave of total mobilization, all women were finally to be enlisted. For many people, the indiscriminate shouldering of obligations by all able-bodied women remained "the touchstone as to whether the burdens had been equitably distributed."[127] People still expected the wives of leading personalities to provide an example. The NSDAP did its utmost to find work for female labor. In a decree of August 9 to his general managers, Reich Minister Speer, the actual instigator of this new total effort, made public a list of products suitable for production at home. As of September 30, it was forbidden to produce these goods in factories.[128]

To provide Hitler with more soldiers for his war, women were also included among Wehrmacht personnel. However, this policy threatened to undermine further the official image of the German woman. The OKW thus issued a kind of verbal ruling that the " 'female soldier' is not compatible with our National Socialist concept of womanhood," and women should therefore not carry arms under any circumstances.[129] Yet women were employed not only at desks and in hospitals; a dangerous shortage of soldiers led, in October, 1944, to the manning of searchlights and other installations by one hundred thousand girls, a majority of whom came from the Reich Labor Service.[130] Shortly thereafter, arrangements were made for the induction of another 150,000 women and girls, volunteers preferred, in order to form a corps of military helpers [*Wehrmachtshelferinnen*] whose assignment would be determined by the OKW in consultation with the Party Chancellory and the Reich Plenipotentiary for Total Warfare.[131]

For the interim the most important preparations had thus been made. Germans reacted to these announcements with mixed feelings. Most feared that they would only provoke the enemy to resort to even harsher terror. Others thought: "now we are also engaged in illegal warfare, after we just recently denounced terrorism in the western regions and continue to wage a war of annihilation against guerrilla activities in various places."[132] Propaganda of press and radio was consequently changed to avoid any mention of guerrilla campaigns.

Fear of being shot as a partisan by the enemy[133] was the main reason for rejecting the *Volkssturm*. Opinion concerning this most recent Nazi creation was divided and fluctuated regionally and with the passage of time. While Breslau's Reich propaganda office talked euphemistically of impulsive crowd enthusiasm, demonstrations of support, and an unqualified endorsement,[134] the weekly summary of activity reports by propaganda offices already contained other shades of opinion. It reported that the *Volkssturm* was seen basically as an important security measure and a recognition of the "leadership's will to check the enemy's assault at all cost." On the other hand, all kinds of doubt spread within "educated" circles as to how the *Volkssturm* could be armed in so short a time, about the advisability of arming potentially unreliable elements, and whether this was not a sign of military weakness. The humorous suggestion was even heard that weapons effective in 1813 would be no match for tanks and saturation bombings.[135]

In reality, only a minority of activists and gullible Germans seemed to expect anything from this ragtag outfit of poorly armed men. The impact of the announcement on most people was more likely to be depressive.[136] Berlin reported cases of placards being torn down and attempts by many to evade service. Only a few old combatants, shelved by the state, now felt needed again.[137] The most informative and numerous opinions on the *Volkssturm* come from a report of the Stuttgart SD,[138] offering a glimpse into the public's general emotional state in the autumn of 1944. The urban proletariat questioned the sincerity and commitment of the propertied classes, while the rural population regarded the whole thing as an admission of weakness. Württembergers ridiculed the *Volkssturm* as being the V-2; others referred to it as the so-called partisan army. Besides, exhausted and overburdened men felt little interest in spending their meagre spare time performing military exercises —particularly under the direction of the Party, SA, NSKK, or other Nazi organization instead of military officers. The list of derogatory comments is too long to repeat, but one blunt report from Stuttgart-Fangelsbach bears mention: "In as restricted an area as Germany, in contrast to Russia, resistance by the population is out of the question. Even if the public will were there, this resistance would soon be broken. It must not be forgotten that we are in the sixth year of war and the population is weary." Furthermore, the SD observer felt there was little chance for resistance in the south, where many people silently hoped that the old dream of liberation from Prussia would now come true. But, as with the case of the field-works, Kreisleitung Freiburg again had positive news of a generally enthusiastic response on the part of rural and urban inhabitants—with the exception of that small bourgeois element.[139]

A slight upswing was apparently achieved by the swearing-in: "just the act of marching together in fellowship" contributed "to giving the individual inner support."[140] Two other events, Hitler's proclamation of November 9[141] and the introduction of the V-2, had a more positive and lasting effect. "The impact of the message has been very profound and enduring within all groups of the population. It has strengthened the faith and confidence of all citizens, even those beginning to grow weary. . . . The manner in which the Führer spoke of foreign and domestic treason was most effective in counteracting the opinion expressed here and there that the leadership had been caught unawares by these events. The statement that a clean sweep was being made of all saboteurs was very reassuring. The Führer's proclamation has strengthened the idea that the conduct of war, by and large, is not governed by chance but rather springs from fateful necessity. The Führer's firm will and iron determination not to capitulate under any circumstances, and the message that the Führer is busily engaged in preparations for the coming last great decisions, was received with great approval. . . ."[142]

Stripped of its usual exaggeration, this summary of Reich propaganda offices' reports reveals Hitler's continued ability to inspire trust, suggest a sense of security, and stimulate hope in the minds of the unsteady and the naive. The reason for this is probably that he himself wanted to believe firmly that, by resorting to a final large-scale offensive, he could persuade the western Allies to accept a negotiated peace. With such powers of imagination, Hitler believed what he wanted to believe and communicated this conviction to others. Many who came to him full of doubt and wanted to convince him of the hopelessness of the situation left in full confidence. And the more he could convince others of his ideas, the more real they became for him. This phenomenon of transmission is demonstrable not only on individuals but also on the masses. After the attempted assassination of July 20, his popularity curve rose abruptly and then slowly sank. Indirect confirmation of this decline is seen in the survey by American researchers of captured German soldiers. The percentage of those believing in Hitler had declined from 69 per cent in August to 42 per cent by mid-October. In the second half of November it reached 64 per cent again, coinciding with soaring hopes on the part of 51 per cent of the soldiers—the highest since the invasion—in the possibility of expelling the Allies from France.[143] Even though these figures cannot be considered representative either for the Wehrmacht or the German population, they do indicate a trend confirmed by opinion reports. Hitler's explanation for the twofold conspiracy, from outside as well as from within, was eagerly accepted; his hints of new great developments awakened new hopes. Yet disappointed voices were heard as well and there were plenty of rumors because Hitler had not personally spoken, but had allowed Himmler to read the proclamation.[144]

The introduction of the V-2, made public in early November 1—although the first rockets had hit London on September 8—reinforced the buoyancy produced by the proclamation: "The use of the new retaliatory weapon, as proven by the majority of reports,[145] has had a very favorable impact even if it did not manifest itself quite as clearly as with the introduction of the 'V-1' . . . . Those citizens are especially proud who still believed in the introduction of new retaliatory weapons because their faith has not been disappointed. By way of contrast, there is a large number of citizens who no longer believed in the deployment of further V-weapons and were shamed by the introduction of the 'V-2' . . . ."[146]

This new buoyant mood did not last long. A graphic description of the mood curve since the beginning of the sixth war year would show the following: a steady decline until the end of September, a slight improvement in the first half of October, another negative development until the first week of November, then an upward movement lasting about ten days and followed by a new rapid decline until the beginning of December when another slight improvement was registered. From this point on, as rumors of a new German offensive thickened, there is evidence of a slight but steady improvement in morale. From an overall perspective, morale was higher than in the spring and summer of 1943, and this despite the ominous military situation. Desperate attempts were also made by propaganda to give the Germans hope against all reason. Finally the Wehrmacht was called in to participate in a whisper campaign dealing with hopes for new weapons and with atrocities committed by Soviet and Allied troops.[147] After an April, 1944, report on the use of soldiers in Vienna for such a campaign, already begun in January, similar preparations were initiated in September for Breslau, Berlin, and Münster. Heavy air raids on Münster precluded its introduction there, but the action was carried out in the other two cities. After some difficulty with the Reich Propaganda Office, which in the meantime had successfully intensified its traditional word-of-mouth propaganda[148] on the advice of several regional offices,[149] a further deployment of special military units was planned for several other cities. Ultimately, however, only east Bavaria, north Germany, and Berlin were subjected to this systematic propaganda as the Reich dwindled in size. The shift in propaganda responsibility to the Wehrmacht, after Goebbels had opposed military participation for years, throws light on the public confidence in the military, whose rating was much higher than that of the Party.[150] Nevertheless, even the military had suffered a severe loss in prestige over the past months, and isolated reports on positive public response do not hide the fact that many Germans were hardly disposed to listening to slogans of encouragement from soldiers who may even have seemed suspect to them.

Excerpts from a letter by a "Private Felix" to the wife of Nazi Foreign Minister von Ribbentrop in the fall of 1944 capture better than most reports the prevailing mood of the day: "Instead of first attempting to unite all Germans in a large community, the *Volkssturm* again was placed only under the Party, the SA, SS, etc. It is clear that the consequences will not be long in coming. Who is *in charge of* the field-works in the East and West? Naturally that can only be done by a Party or SA man. Who leads a *Volkssturm* company? Only a veteran SA leader! Those persons who were not accepted into the Party because of their talents and who could have become a threat to many political leaders because of their superior abilities have no say again this time. A small minority rules while the rest have to obey." The reason for harping on the Party's military contribution is that "those on top" finally got the message that "behind this 'not being a soldier' by *many* Party members lies brazen draft-dodging. . . ."[151]

"*Over* 90 per cent of the German people is certainly inspired by glowing patriotism. What percentage of the German people is National Socialist is not easy to establish. An *honest and secret* plebiscite at this time, like the one last held in the autumn of 1933, would probably not come close to 50 per cent. In voting by secret ballot, likely about 30 per cent of all ministers and *Reichsleiter*, 60 per cent of all provincial governors and *Gauleiter*, 70 per cent of all *Kreisleiter*, 30 per cent of all county directors [*Landräte*] and 80 per cent of all local Party leaders and mayors would receive a vote of no confidence. This may be regarded as an exaggeration, but there exists no doubt whatsoever that that is exactly what would happen! The German people are fighting for their fatherland, their life, their freedom. But does the leadership really believe that the masses of former Center supporters, German Nationalists, Communists, Social Democrats, etc. actually want National Socialism? . . . . That we are responsible for the war is written in 'Mein Kampf'

. . . . Let us examine carefully whether we are not the peace-breakers of the world! Whether they believe it 'up top' or not, the German people have long ago abandoned the decision of 1933 to follow National Socialism voluntarily and no longer stand behind its policy. Why do even Party members no longer want to wear the Party badge? Why does the 'German Wehrmacht' need National Socialist leadership [*Führungsstäbe*]? As it is, soldiers are already calling them 'commissars' . . . . " . . . Do you really think we soldiers don't know what bestial murders have been perpetrated by our SS in Russia? Where, for example, are the 114,000 Jews of Lemberg? We were there in 1942-43 when they were [transported] little by little on trucks and shot not far from Lemberg. SS officers could not bear to see and hear it any longer and enlisted in the army. Why is Himmler the most despised man in Hitler's entourage? . . . ."[152]

This anonymous letter from Saxony, sent to the Security Police and the SD on November 10 for analysis, makes it clear that most Germans, including former Nazis, had rejected the regime and realized Germany's war guilt. A report of January, 1945, compiled by Stuttgart's main SD office, confirms this development;[153] reference is made to the more educated elements of society who were quoting passages from *Mein Kampf* to prove Germany's war guilt, beginning as early as September, 1944. By Hitler's own admission, Germany's policy of expanding eastward had not departed from its course one inch, and this meant war with her neighbors. The SD-Obersturmführer acknowledged that the enemy reaped advantages from quoting certain passages from *Mein Kampf*. Similar reports came from district Party leaders in the region of Lüneburg[154] and likely from the rest of Germany as well, judging from references to war guilt discussions coming from Saxony, Württemberg, and Lower Saxony. A favorite tactic of English propagandists was to exploit past utterances or writings of leading Nazis to reveal the continuity of the Nazi appetite for aggression.[155]

Aside from the patriotism cited by the anonymous writer, what accounted for the continued endurance by Germans of a Nazi leadership, in spite of mounting criticism, was fear and attrition. The Third Reich's propaganda machine capitalized extensively on the Morgenthau plan to enervate the opinion repeatedly reemerging that an occupation by the Anglo-Americans would not be so bad. If one accepts the weekly reports of the activity of Reich propaganda offices, this campaign appears to have had some success. In addition to Party functionaries and the small special military units, the Reich Propaganda Directorate especially utilized the *Volkssturm* to bring these themes to the people: "In addition to military objectives, the *Volksstürme* have to use all available means to become an important instrument of public enlightenment and propaganda. *Volksstürme* are one means of conducting a positive, large-scale word-of-mouth propaganda. . . ."[156] Likewise, Nazi operational staff officers were directed to invite soldiers regularly for a beer and impress on their minds specific propaganda slogans.[157] By mid-November the report was: "*The propaganda of the last week* has produced a change in the population insofar as it has progressively stilled the speculation concerning a lenient peace with the Western Powers through capitulation. Based on the announcements of the last week, everyone knows that the western enemies are not appreciably better than the Kremlin's armed emissaries. . . ." But this observation only applied to one segment of the population, one that is poorly defined. At least extant reports from western Germany suggest a different conclusion. Just a few days before the above mentioned report, Gottlob Berger, chief of the SS-Hauptamt, had written Himmler about observations following a personal tour of the western military districts. It seemed the "*Volksgrenadier*" divisions, called into being by Himmler in his capacity as commander of the reserve army, had not developed as anticipated despite being equipped with the latest German war materiel. Composed largely of raw recruits ill-prepared for the rigors of the front, it never formed the nucleus of a planned new Nazi "militia" [*Volksheer*]. As far as public attitude was concerned, Berger regarded it as "quite disturbing:" "This is evident in the refusal to obey evacuation procedures and in the intention of 'being caught unawares' by the war."[158]

As we have already seen, a similar attitude had been discovered at the time of Aachen's evacuation. The Americans encircled the city on October 13 and took it on the twenty-first after heavy shelling. In some cases the remaining population greeted the Americans as liberators. Himmler subsequently ordered that all those guilty of "undignified" conduct would be held accountable upon Aachen's recapture.[159]

But there was little prospect of this as the Americans continued their offensive on November 16, pushing the Germans back to the Rur (Roer) river. To the south, Patton took Metz on the twenty-second and forced German troops behind the Saar; Strasbourg and Belfort fell as Allied armies reached the Rhine north of Basel. Only a German bridgehead near Colmar prevented formation of a front line along the Rhine. Initial reports of calm[160] soon changed to fear and alarm:[161] "The last seven weeks have probably been the most dramatic to date in the war for Gau Baden-Alsace." Most had expected no further Allied advances after the front had been stabilized in France. Consequently the rapid loss of Mülhausen and finally the totally unexpected collapse of Strasbourg shocked the population profoundly. "A flood of refugees poured over to the right bank of the Rhine. This was followed immediately by heavy terror attacks on Freiburg and Karlsruhe, leaving almost another hundred thousand people homeless." Allied bombardment from the left bank, which forced the evacuation of women and children from the endangered zones, only added to the depression and feeling of defenselessness. "Confidence was utterly shattered and the question as to the causes for this catastrophe actively engaged all minds. Regrettably, an easy answer was found—even in influential circles—simply by placing the blame on the Alsatians, who were collectively accused of treason, without thought of what consequences such a general defamation of a German tribe must have had on those Alsatians in the Wehrmacht or in the Labor Service in the Reich. . . ." The reporter attributed the actual cause to a false "assessment of the enemy and his aims by the responsible military command, which still offered optimistic judgments after enemy tanks were already in Zabern." Assured of a German counterattack, the political authorities had made no preparations for evacuation and thus were caught by surprise.

Karlsruhe's supreme court president on January 2, 1945, offered the same excuse for failure to evacuate his region in time: "Optimistic situation report by the supreme military command in charge" and fear of a "loss of prestige" on the part of the Gauleiter.[162] As usual, blame was passed from one to the other: the political functionaries laid it on the military, and both accused the Alsatians, instead of admitting that their own resources were exhausted and acting accordingly. In typical fashion, the Propaganda Ministry dragged out the shopworn theme of treason, in this case that of the Alsatians, to explain why another victory had eluded the Wehrmacht.[163]

Official Nazi anti-Soviet propaganda at this stage capitalized on the bloodbath staged by Soviet troops at the end of October in the East Prussian village of Hemmersdorf, in order to spread fear and terror among the population and thus spur it on to utmost resistance. "Special importance is attached to the fact," an elaboration of the Reich Press Chief's daily slogan read, "that the DNB report on the gruesome Bolshevik crimes in East Prussia be featured prominently and effectively and commented upon with extreme severity. Monstrous Soviet lust for blood must be denounced in the layout and headings. . . ." It was to be underscored that the terror was not directed against "great landowners, stockholders, and big industrialists," but rather against simple people, and that Bolshevism was set on destroying and exterminating "the essence of the Volk."[164] Glaring sensational articles of this kind, however, fell far short of Nazi expectations. By some they were rejected as a propaganda trick,[165] among others they achieved the opposite of the desired effect. "Citizens are saying it is shameful to feature these so prominently in German newspapers. . . .

> 'What motive does the leadership have in publishing pictures like those in the *NS-Kurier* on Saturday? They must surely realize that every intelligent person, upon seeing these victims, will immediately think of the atrocities we have committed on enemy soil, yes even in Germany. Did we not slaughter the Jews by the thousands? Don't soldiers repeatedly tell of Jews who had to dig their own graves in Poland? And what did we do with the Jews who were in the KZ [concentration camp] in Alsace? After all, Jews are also human. We have only shown the enemy what they can do with us should they win."

This November 6, 1944, report to the Stuttgart SD further claimed that remarks of this kind could be heard among all strata of society. Nor was criticism confined to treatment of the Jews; the imprisonment of German citizens in concentration camps was regarded by some as atonement by the German people for Nazi crimes. "We have shown them what to do with political enemies. We can't blame the Russians for being as cruel to other races as we are to our own Germans." Why should Nazis be so incensed because the Soviets "had killed a few people in East Prussia? What does a life mean here in Germany?" The report closed by citing one remark heard with increasing frequency in some form or other: " 'The claim is always made that the Führer was sent to us by God. I don't doubt it. The Führer *was* sent to us by God, not to save Germany, but rather to ruin her. Providence has decided to destroy the German people, and Hitler is the executor of this will'. . . ."[166]

Others accused the government and the Party especially for failing to warn and evacuate the endangered East Prussian population in time,[167] thereby forcing the Propaganda Ministry to issue a denial by word-of-mouth propaganda: those directly behind the lines had naturally been evacuated. It was the sudden surge of Soviet forces which enabled its lead tanks to break through at one spot and penetrate deep into German territory where they came upon fleeing refugees. Furthermore, there was the consideration of protecting the harvest. "Since East Prussia helps to feed four million Germans in the Reich, and the bulk of potatoes and root crops are still in the ground, those fit to work—including childless women workers—had to be assigned as long as possible to areas close to the lines to bring in the harvest. The higher necessity of personal duty to the German Volk had to be placed above security of the individual. This harsh but essential principle applies today not only to soldiers at the front but to everyone."[168]

The mood was clearly not uniform, fluctuating from week to week and even from day to day. Munich's supreme court president offered an overview of dominant opinion trends for his district in late November, one that seems largely applicable to other areas as well. The dichotomy between the extremes of "a not inconsiderable number" of pessimists and "inveterate" optimists continued to prevail, though the number of believers in the efficacy of German miracle weapons was dwindling. In between were two other groups, those who believed things would not turn out as badly as predicted—even capitulation and occupation by the West would be easier to take than the horrors of war, as long as Bolshevism was stemmed, as they believed it would be—and those who were extremely concerned and felt that only resolute perseverance offered any possibility for a life worth living. The latter group as well as the optimists placed their hope in an end to Allied air superiority and terror raids before these could paralyze vital German war production. Modern German weapons and techniques would then neutralize enemy land and sea superiority, deal Allied armies crushing blows, cut off or hamper their reinforcement, and achieve that decisive shift in the military balance.[169]

As far as the front-line soldiers were concerned, the court president felt the old combat spirit was "still unshaken," with a few exceptions. This view was supported by a military report of December 15, 1944: "What are the troops talking about?"[170] Soldiers were primarily worried about their families, and there was little defeatist talk. "There is a firm conviction that the tremendous military efforts of our people will lead us to victory." The relative balance of forces gave cause for concern, but even here the troops seemed to remain relatively optimistic. On the other hand, references to numerous other reports about conditions within the western army and evidence of camp life suggest fighting morale was not that unshakable. Given the OKW order of November 28, 1944, one can assume that such incidents had more likely increased than decreased.

"According to eyewitness accounts, present measures to eradicate manifestations of camp life [Etappenerscheinungen] have met with only partial success. On the contrary, there are even reports of a proliferation of this spectacle. . . ." The harshest possible measures and inspections were ordered.[171] On December 16, Berger suggested to Himmler the naming of Nazi operational staff officers with special powers in view of mounting reports of "signs of disintegration within certain units of the air force and to some extent also within the army."[172]

Meanwhile, however, an improvement in the mood had set in at home, as already briefly indicated. As early as December 5, the weekly activity report for the Propaganda Minister was able to announce: "Almost all available reports show that last week's low morale has given way to a positive opinion. Confidence in our defensive capabilities has risen; *hope* is intensifying *for coming* developments that will bring about an improvement in our situation. Primarily, the populace believes that a change will take place in the air in the near future. Rumors of new fighter planes are presently at an all time high and every bulletin about our air force is passionately discussed. In East Prussia people were even heard expressing the opinion that the Soviets are unable to begin their offensive because of increased demoralization among their troops; comparisons are made with 1917." The report noted with satisfaction that the propaganda efforts of past weeks were beginning to have an effect. Of interest is the statement that while confidence in the leadership in general "has been severely shaken," confidence in the Führer remained steadfast.

Halle reported a more confident mood among workers than among other segments of society; at a factory meeting in one armaments plant in Dresden, the workers exclaimed: "Now we really have to get moving to rectify the imbalance in the west created by the loss of weapons and equipment."[173] Shortly before, an even more radical military determination had been displayed by armaments workers in Bochum, one of whom, [with the approval of his comrades] clubbed to death a man who had questioned the wisdom of clean-up efforts in view of impending defeat.[174] Other western regions, where troop movements and concentration of forces could not be concealed, also reported an improvement in the mood.[175] The barometer climbed further when the first news was heard on December 16 of Operation "Autumn Mist" [*Herbstnebel*], the code name for the Ardennes offensive.

4. THE LAST WINTER OF WAR

"Soldiers of the Western front!

Your hour of greatness has come. Powerful assault forces today moved against the Anglo-Americans. Nothing else needs to be said.

All of you feel it.

It's do or die. Uphold the solemn pledge to do your utmost and perform superhuman deeds for our fatherland and our Führer."[176]

With this order, Field Marshal von Rundstedt, supreme commander in the West, launched the Ardennes offensive. Since August, Hitler had carried around the plan for a major offensive in the direction of Antwerp to cut off and destroy enemy forces to the north. When Rundstedt and Model were finally informed of the ambitious plan in late October, they offered a more modest, realizable one, but Hitler wanted a breakthrough—a final, all-out effort to turn the tide. On December 11-12, after the offensive had been postponed by an Allied attack in the adjacent Ruhr and by bad weather, Hitler assembled his leading officers for one of his long monologues in the hopes of convincing them success was possible, given a fairly equal match of forces on the western front.[177] He also operated on the assumption that the enemy coalition would disintegrate at any moment. But his arguments were as much the product of his fertile imagination as the operational planning for this last major German offensive: begun on December 16, it was already evident by December 23 that it had failed.

But the mere fact that the Wehrmacht was once more actively intervening in military events affected the German population like an abundant "rainfall after a long drought."[178] There was no rejoicing, the situation was still too threatening, but people felt "as if released from a nightmare."[179] The cry, "what a wonderful Christmas present," was often heard. There were also kind words for the air force, which had been increasingly abused. "Even a minor success would be welcomed with gratitude by the population. That we are actually in a position to undertake such a military operation has all at once significantly raised confidence in the leadership and in the strength of the Reich. . . ."

The psychological impact of the offensive—as reported by the president of Rostock's supreme court, who in the meantime had withdrawn to Schwerin—could not be overestimated. "Compared with this positive effect and the consequent reversal in the mood, the critical factors have completely receded into the background."[180] There were cases of extreme optimism based on comparisons with the favorable developments of 1940.[181] Such high and illusionary expectations had to be dispelled. Therefore, from the start of the offensive Nazi propaganda leaders circulated dampening slogans by word-of-mouth in the hope of avoiding the kind of backlash they had experienced in the past.[182]

The last war Christmas, because of the Ardennes offensive, was "generally observed in good spirits and full confidence in the future . . . even if in areas endangered from the air the Christmas holidays were overshadowed by constant air-raid alarms and the depressing awareness of constant danger from the skies. Except for the children, a real Christmas spirit was naturally out of the question. . . . The German western offensive has made a profound impression even on those citizens who are outright pessimists and who have believed the leadership remained silent because it has a great deal of unpleasantness to hide; in general, the diminished trust in the Wehrmacht, in the political leadership, and especially in the NSDAP has greatly increased. . . ." Probably as a favor to the Reich Propaganda Minister, the report observed that the memory of past reversals had cautioned most Germans against excessive optimism. In its summation, however, reference was again made to "understandably high hopes," in view of such a vast military undertaking. The danger of a sharp reversal of mood was all the greater because many citizens were even toying with the idea of a quick end to the war in the west. Fears of this trend were reported from all over the Reich: Hamburg, Reichenberg, Brandenburg, Stuttgart, and Dessau.[183]

This optimism, fanned by belief in the revolutionary impact of the new weapons, was most pronounced in western, central, and northern Germany, areas far removed from the menacing grip of Soviet forces. In southeastern parts of the Reich, especially in the "newly annexed" regions, people viewed Soviet advances in Hungary with increasing alarm and restlessness. In east Germany the mood was also depressed; considering Soviet troop concentration along the German frontier, the overall confidence exhibited by eastern Germans is most astonishing from our present-day perspective.[184] Contributing to this confidence was a temporary check of Soviet advances into the Courland and along the East Prussian border. The "East Wall" also proved to be a reassuring factor.[185]

Faith in Hitler was particularly evident in the eastern regions. Wehrmacht prestige had not been seriously undermined, since the population had been spared the spectacle of headlong retreat by a demoralized occupation army, which had occurred in the west. Moreover, there was the experience of World War I. Despite the tenacity and ever greater victories of Soviet troops, despite the shifting image of Russia, the concept of a colossus with clay feet which would suddenly collapse was still predominant. The power of imagination hardly went so far as to envisage the horror of a Germany inundated by "Asiatic hordes." This danger, played upon periodically by propaganda and with increasing intensity as the war neared its end, was interpreted, because of its frequent evocation, as a "line," a trick to fire up the will to resist; it was not conceived as a reality.

The public mood, positively influenced by the western offensive, received a brief stimulus from a decrease in air raids. Although the mounting bombing terror had rather helped strengthen military morale in 1943 and during the first half of 1944 by exciting hatred against the external foe and thereby simultaneously creating a safety-valve for fermenting domestic discontent, a steady and uninterrupted attrition now gradually took effect. More and more the air war influenced life at home and became the number one topic. Nervousness and mortal fear increased daily. In most cities a normal night's rest was no longer possible. Life became makeshift. People lived for the moment and closed their eyes to the future.[186] Unhindered penetration of the German countryside by waves of bombers and fighter planes contributed substantially to a downward slide of the mood curve and helped to discredit the regime in the fall of 1944.[187]

Incessant bombardment also scattered the population all over the Reich. "Lately, cases of soldiers granted leave from the front to search for their families are on the increase. These men on leave then spend two, three, even four weeks on the train inquiring after their families in their old residences or in all conceivable receiving-Gaus. . . ." Despairing, these soldiers wandered from place to place, eventually landing at broadcasting stations where they demanded air time; by now they were so furious that they were capable of anything and phrased their demands in the most radical fashion. "They declared flatly, now a rope or a bullet was all the same—they just wanted to know whether or not they still had a family." Personal adroitness had so far prevented catastrophes.[188]

A last flicker of hope was registered at the beginning of 1945. With the exception of Hesse-Nassau, reports of all Reich propaganda offices indicated an astonishingly positive reception of Hitler's New Year's proclamation.[189] This was confirmed by the thirteenth report on "Sondereinsatz Berlin" and several reports to the Reich Justice Ministry. Hitler's certainty of victory still radiated a persuasive power, even in Berlin. The only disappointment was his failure to give details on the introduction of new weapons, on how bombings were to be checked, and on the state of the offensive.[190] But this was only of momentary consequence as propaganda disseminated the argument that it was naturally impossible to make military announcements in the present situation. Reich propaganda offices were ordered to forward reports of further repercussions of the speech as quickly as possible since they "are of fundamental importance for the direction of overall propaganda."[191]

On January 12, 1945, after a five-hour artillery barrage, the Soviet assault on Greater Germany began. German resistance was weakened by the drain of manpower for the western offensive, so that only seventy-five divisions defended a nine hundred kilometer front from the Baltic Sea to the Carpathian Mountains. According to OKH calculations, Soviet superiority in infantry was eleven to one, in tanks seven to one, and in artillery twenty to one.[192] Guderian's demands for termination of the obviously unsuccessful Ardennes offensive and transfer of forces to the east was rejected by Hitler in a desire to force a decision in the west.

Nor would Hitler consent to a sea evacuation of Army Group North, cut off in Courland, nor to a transfer of the newly created Sixth SS tank army under Sepp Dietrich from Hungary to the Oder line. His only action was to relieve commanders and take personal control of divisional operations, thereby losing strategic overview in a welter of tactical details.

After the middle of January, one can no longer speak of a uniform state of opinion in all parts of the Reich. In a Germany steadily diminishing in size, public opinion has to be divided more and more into three areas: the eastern, the western, and in between, the middle zone reaching from north to south and increasingly squeezed from both sides until finally it was severed horizontally into northern and southern sections by the forces of the East-West alliance.

In those regions not directly threatened, opinion surveyors in the latter half of January did register concern and pessimism but said nothing about pronounced despair or a disastrous mood. Many reporters were surprised by the patience and resolve shown by a majority of the people. "I am not aware of outright disobedience against the orders and agents of the state anywhere," Frankfurt's public prosecutor wrote on January 25, 1945.[193] The possibility of losing industrial Upper Silesia, the consequences of which were obvious to all, was widely discussed. But generally the propagandists and soldiers sent out among the populace effectively kept the mood within manageable bounds.[194] The sixteenth report on "Sondereinsatz Berlin" read: "Now in particular it is necessary to make a clear distinction between attitude and mood. The attitude of Berliners is good and will remain good. It makes no difference that the general mood is downcast and that many people, who are standing their ground and will continue to do so, talk as if there is hardly any hope anymore for a good outcome of the war. . . ."[195]

One observation found in numerous reports concerned the impact of the unending stream of refugees: initially it stunned and depressed the population, but then it contributed significantly to strengthening resistance, if only because it confirmed the regime's propaganda about the Bolshevik reign of terror. But stories by refugees of inadequate organization and welfare for repatriation further damaged the Party's image. However, party officials in the east were only partly to blame; much as when the Americans invaded Alsace, party offices were poorly informed on German military weakness in the area and were only issued evacuation instructions at the last minute when advancing Soviet forces were already disrupting orderly transportation. Of course there were those who had saved their families and valuables in time and then neglected those placed in their trust.[196] Catastrophic transportation and traffic conditions aggravated the situation, and "wild evacuations" endan-

gered military reinforcements, thus ultimately forcing a "Führer's decision" to halt all further evacuation. Normal evacuation procedures
had degenerated into momentary improvisation.[197] Without additional
transport facilities, flight now took the form of treks, which presented
indescribable scenes of makeshift transportation, of tie-ups, of men and
animals dying of starvation and cold. In those few trains available for
evacuations, people with lice and skin diseases were packed closely together, and between them were the dead.[198] The misery and horror inflicted on other peoples by Hitler's henchmen now reached the Germans
themselves.

Finding shelter for the refugees[199] and adequate provisions for the
Reich became a critical concern. On January 25, 1945, a reduction in
rations was announced: rations for eight weeks now had to last the
recipient nine weeks.[200] But even this meager ration scale could not be
guaranteed, with increasing disruptions and destruction of the transportation network. A despairing Kreisleiter wrote, "If the people no longer
have bread, the best meetings cannot help."[201] By the end of February
the regime resorted partially to distribution of raw grain, since the destruction of the mills cancelled flour supplies in whole regions; the Nazi
Women's League was called on to instruct housewives on how to grind
the grain with mincing machines or coffee-grinders.[202]

People were suffering increasingly under these privations.[203] A general
weariness began to spread over Germany, though in comparison to the
misery endured by refugees these sacrifices seemed slight; the sight of
these refugees helped to strengthen resolve to hold out, despite a worsen-
ing mood. Evaluation of reports by Reich propaganda offices revealed that
the collapse of the mood after the start of the Soviet offensive in January
"was of a completely different character" than that following reversals
in previous years. "This time, except for those who have always been
fickle, especially bourgeois circles, the mood does not manifest itself
in the form of a diffusion of wild rumors or spiteful name-calling or
grumbling against the leadership. Nowhere has a slackening of dogged
determination and willingness to work been observed. . . . A deep
seriousness is hanging over all citizens, without exception, but no pronounced despair. On the contrary, one hears everywhere: 'The crucial
hour has come, now only composure and unconditional commitment can
help us—all who can carry arms, to the front on the double—empty the
barracks—stop military courses—get all able-bodied men from all offices of
the Party, the state, and all other administrations'. . . . Remarks of the
sort that it is too late and that there is no longer any point to it were
only seldom heard. It is clearly shown that the Volk has become harder
as a result of the many disappointments and the many sorrows. . . ."[204]

For all the hope, there were also many bitter comments: where are the

V-weapons; why are they not being deployed against the Russians; if they and the fighter planes are not used soon, they probably do not exist. Still, the will to resist and to see it through was more strongly developed the farther east one went, the public no doubt aware of the consequences of defeat. Better to endure any privations than to accept defeat prematurely. "Faith in the Führer is so great that just a small victory would quickly change the mood of many for the better."[205] This contrasted sharply with observed defeatism in Aachen and the Saar where "everyone is awaiting the conclusion of peace."[206] "Heil Hitler" was not to be heard, not even among Party officials.[207]

Invasion of German soil by Soviet troops and the defensive attitude of large segments of the population induced the Nazi regime to make one last effort. The last reserves were to be put into action ruthlessly, all indulgence renounced, the weak and vacillating to be eliminated. This last even slightly coordinated effort by the Nazi elite reveals a thrust along three lines: intensified indoctrination of the Wehrmacht and Waffen-SS; massive terror against all cowards and deserters—and this not only within the military or the population but also within the ranks of the NSDAP; and concentrated hate- and counter-propraganda.

After Himmler was named commander of the reserve army, SS methods and the content of its ideological training were introduced into those parts of the Wehrmacht under his command and from there found their way into the army. By Gottlob Berger's order of September 22, ideological education was to be put on a par with tactical training.[208] Courses for Nazi staff officers and segments of the Waffen-SS were continued, despite the desparate need for manpower at the front and a public outcry.[209] Depending on the nature of the course, they lasted from two to fourteen weeks and included such topics as the Führer, the SS, the Jew as world parasite, the Reich as the savior of Europe, the eternal German Volk, Americanism, Bolshevism, and Hitler's social achievements. The concept "political soldier"[210] was now given greater prominence; the principle of previous ideological training had been to avoid creating political commissars, but the success and morale of Soviet troops induced the regime to examine Soviet methods of political education more closely.[211]

Soldiers and public alike were bombarded with slogans of impending horrors to strengthen their resolve. The Morgenthau plan and Allied demand for unconditional surrender offered sufficient arguments to motivate even those convinced of the futility of further warfare. They too clung to the hope that the enemy was as worn out as the Germans.[212] Countless reports by war correspondents glorifying the daily valor, privations, and hardships of the soldiers helped to instill a feeling of being betrayers among those who wanted to give up. One can only describe as tragic the sacrifice, energy, courage, and idealism squandered on a lost—and especially a bad—cause. An examination of political and military writings, and the war correspondence of students killed in action, for common militant myths and key concepts from World War I through the Weimar Republic[213] to World War II would in all probability reveal a largely unbroken continuity. During World War II, however, the ideological defense against "plutocrats" and "Bolsheviks," for whom the Jew served as common denominator, was added to the tradition of national fervor.

All reports that permitted doubts to be raised concerning conjugate plans by the Allies for the extermination of Germany—and thus ideal for awakening hopes for correct if not friendly treatment by the enemy—had to be suppressed. A confidential memorandum to the newspapers on January 11, 1945, stated: "Attention is drawn to the need for emphasizing as the propaganda line not the emerging tensions among the Allies but their continued common war aim of annihilating Germany. . . ."[214]

Preparations for the Yalta Conference (held February 4 to 11, 1945) produced fear among Nazi overlords—quite without foundation, as later events proved—that the Allies would issue a joint proclamation directed at the German people, promising them decent treatment and encouraging them to break with the regime. The press was instructed to discuss this intended foul strategy before the conference convened. "The unbending resistance of the German people has to destroy the plan of the Jewish coalition of our enemies. . . . No deceitful phrases and no hypocrisies, no matter how harmless sounding, with the transparent objective of driving a wedge between the leadership and its following, can seduce the German people to commit suicide. . . ."[215]

With their philosophy of life defined by folk-biological and folk-romantic criteria, leading National Socialists had a low regard for individual right to life, which for them only had value within the context of the Volk as a whole. Convinced that the enemy was preparing for the German people a fate analogous to the one they had intended and already partially realized for the peoples of the east—not to mention the fate of the Jews—, they preferred death in battle to languishing in a state of slavery or to a systematic elimination of the existing elite. Also worth mentioning in this context is the National Socialist concept of suicide. In an SS order of April 1, 1939, Himmler, who took a personal interest in the conjugal morals, sexual needs, alcoholic excesses, health matters, and all difficulties of SS men, had also taken up this problem. According to statistics, the order read, at most 15 per cent of all suicides "resulted from motives that might be generally acceptable, such as for instance ending one's life because of crime damaging to the community and one's own honor." The remaining 85 per cent, however, were due to motives of "fear of punishment, of an investigation, after rebuke by a superior, after an argument with parents, after breaking off an engagement, out of jealousy, due to unrequited love, etc. . . . These kinds of suicide have nothing in common with heroism or heroic-mindedness. They are regarded by us SS men as escapism, as shirking the battle and life itself. . . ." No notice was to be taken of such suicides; no member of the SS was to attend those funerals.[216]

Clearly only heroic suicide was permissible. But there were cases when it was actually required for the sake of personal honor and that of the Volk. After the capitulation of German troops in the Stalingrad pocket, Hitler remarked that Field Marshal Paulus should have let himself be shot or buried alive.[217] Martin Bormann synthesized these attitudes expressed by Hitler and Himmler in a circular of July 17, 1944: "The life of the individual belongs to the people. Therefore, he may not arbitrarily put an end to his life. If he does anyway, he violates his duty to his people. This applies particularly now during wartime."

Even where crimes were involved, to atone by gallant service and unflagging work was more courageous and more honorable. This interpretation served as justification for the creation of execution squads, Strafkommandos, and so-called suicide patrols, Himmelfahrtskommandos, such as the notorious Dirlewanger special patrol comprised of convicts, poachers, and criminals.[218]

Suicide, on the other hand, was anything but dishonorable "in those cases in which no further effort for the Volk was possible or when, in the face of impending Soviet captivity, living can become a danger for one's own Volk."[219] On March 6, 1945, Goebbels praised suicide as the final way out from the horrors of war, and the Völkische Beobachter reminded Germans that Frederick the Great had once written a philosophical treatise on the "justification of suicide."[220]

The call for a Volkskrieg was thus a logical consequence of this vision of the hero and the race, a vision inspired by a romanticized past where the hero sacrifices himself for his people and the race perishes in a final glorious battle. The false romanticism and hostility toward civilization of a Karl May, whose writings Hitler repeatedly recommended, Felix Dahn's idealized downfall of the last Goths on Mount Vesuvius, and especially the battle of the Nibelungen against Etzel had become examples to be emulated.

For the regime, appeals for unconditional obedience and strictest discipline became more urgent at year's end, as evidence of demoralization and defeatism was now also found within elements of the combat troops. Once it became apparent that Germany had lost the war, fewer and fewer Germans were willing to risk their necks in this last phase. This attitude was more widespread in the west than the east, where Soviet brutalities unleashed fear and horror.[221] If fighting morale remained relatively high, this was due less to a fanatical minority— estimated by American researchers in the west at between 10 and 15 per cent—[222] carrying the others along, than to internal cohesion based on shared experiences and the comradeship of the front as well as the example of unit commanders. But this solidarity collapsed in the face of mounting losses, retreats, separation from one's unit, and a growing concern for the fate of loved ones at home. The regime found itself compelled to introduce the strictest controls and round-ups of wandering, at times marauding and plundering soldiers. This breakdown of military discipline had a significant impact on public morale at a time when a strong interaction of the mood at the front and at home was noticeable.

Military units hastily formed by throwing together soldiers separated from their squads with low-caliber reserves lacked any inner cohesiveness and thus had little combat value, according to both American researchers and German sources from the east.[223] Soldiers performed far better when returned to their own units than in makeshift formations where the only bond was a common fear of the enemy. In those groups "no one knows the man next to him and thus abandons him if he is wounded, something he would never do to a comrade of his parent unit. . . ."[224]

Numerous evidences of troop demoralization and disintegration were also reported by other authorities. The Reich propaganda office of Schwerin received mounting complaints about the behavior of troops in areas near to the front; soldiers were seen stealing, or mailing home parts of their uniforms for dyeing and remodelling into civilian clothes. "Extreme indignation reigns in the widest public circles over this, and there is talk about symptoms of decline."[225] A week later Stettin reported on the paralyzing effect on public morale of bands of soldiers openly admitting they had deserted for lack of weapons and ammunition.[226] These were not isolated occurrences. Looting and retreating soldiers were a common sight in west Prussia, according to Danzig's Reichsstatthalter[227] and Rostock's public prosecutor.[228] The district propaganda leader of Bromberg told of a total breakdown of leadership; none of the organizations stationed there made any effort to organize collective resistance. The last train leaving Bromberg to transport refugees westward was stormed by armed soldiers who denied places to women and children, thus forcing a large percentage of the civilian population to remain behind.[229] In Silesia evacuation degenerated into a rout as the military leadership—in this case Field Marshal Schörner—again felt confident of stemming Soviet advance into the industrial region and delayed authorization for evacuation until the last minute.[230] Silesian refugees were particularly shocked by "members of the Wehrmacht plundering the abandoned homes of their own countrymen."[231] "Hornisse II," a branch of section VI of the Reich Main Security Office which took over responsibility for military counter-espionage after the arrest of Admiral Canaris and made daily reports on the military situation—of which only a few have survived—confirmed on February 16 that almost all its sources observed high-handed behavior and pillaging by troops in their areas. "The growing conscious *acceptance of personal power-lessness* constitutes the *root of nearly all demoralizing phenomena within the troops*. With the exception of new reserves and reinforcements brought up from the west, the opinion that the war is lost is widely held among rank and file troops."[232]

Added to the signs of disintegration in the Wehrmacht were those in the NSDAP: "A great number of negative indications, familiar from last summer in the west, have also appeared here. . . . Negative repercussions resulted from political leaders and public officials from Upper Silesia who refused to remain behind to fight with the *Volkssturm*—Troppau alone received 210—and instead headed west because of some marching order by an apolitically-minded superior. As explanation they usually declared that they had supervisory duties, or had to remain available to the Reich ministry, and the like. Some public officials had destinations which lay up to four hundred kilometers west of their Gau borders. . . ."[233]

There is no doubt that the increasingly desperate military situation sapped the strength and undermined the institutions of the Third Reich. Since propaganda could not arrest this trend, the regime abandoned veiled terror for naked terror. In the "Regulations concerning the conduct of officers and men during wartime," issued on January 28 by the OKW, commanders were authorized to conduct courts martial and pronounce death penalties if necessary to maintain discipline.[234] The Reich Justice Ministry followed suit on February 15 by establishing drumhead courts martial in all Reich defense districts threatened by the enemy.[235]

To illustrate that these punitive measures applied equally to the common soldier[236] and higher officials and officers, the SS Unit Leader and police director of Bromberg was shot for having left the city. Colonel von Hassenstein suffered the same fate for having evacuated positions on his own authority. Himmler, in his orders to the officers of Army Group Weichsel, announced these verdicts and stated: "It is better for a coward here and there to die than to let the idea gain ground in an otherwise brave company that we can retreat."[237]

The Reichsführer SS also mentioned the "traitor" von Seydlitz and his Committee, who were being used as tools and agents by Stalin. Their appeals, he declared, had long since been contradicted by the fate of the German people in the east. In February, 1945, the motives and actions of the National Committee for a Free Germany and the Organization of German Officers were apparently discussed by the public and especially within the military. Many soldiers were of the view that the Soviets were being commanded by German officers.[238] Reports came from Berlin, [239] as well as from the eastern zone,[240] attributing the success of the Soviet offensive to treason and infiltration of the ranks by the National Committee. There were still Germans who refused to face the truth and admit that failure, corruption, and cowardice could exist even in the German Wehrmacht. However, the evidence is so striking as to make it impossible to fabricate a stab-in-the-back legend for 1945. If anything, the antithesis of 1918 applied: the poor behavior and despondency exhibited by the troops depressed and demoralized the homeland, so that those encouraged by propaganda and still hoping against all hope were also gradually disheartened. This deglorification of the army and destruction of a myth is significant for later German developments.

General Ritter von Hengl, Chief of the NS Guidance Staff of the Army, after touring the region under the control of the supreme western commander and visiting the reserve army in early to mid March, offered the most interesting observation on Wehrmacht attitude and morale.[241] Considering the constant and tremendous pressure to which men and officers were exposed during prolonged weeks of fighting amid heavy artillery fire and saturation bombings, the general thought overall performance was high. He distinguished three types of soldiers: the old fighter with his undaunted courage and faith as well as a "marvelous youth;" the tired and apathetic soldier who was impressed neither by courts martial nor punishment and only fought when dressed down by an officer but then quickly went to pieces again; and the cowards and deserters who didn't even shoot. As an effective remedy he recommended a broad popularization of a news item which had recently appeared, "that Roosevelt intended to make German war prisoners available to the Russians as slave labor after the war. This news worked like a bombshell among some of the cowards." This apathy, weariness, and manpower shortage attributed to the regular army also applied, and doubly, to the ineffectual[242] Home Guard, which lacked the bond of common war experience, lacked the model of the officer since most leaders were poorly trained Party officials, and above all was miserably equipped. The more active elements of the *Volkssturm* therefore repeatedly requested transfers to the Wehrmacht or Waffen-SS.[243] Fear was no doubt also an important factor since, without uniforms, they might be shot as partisans.[244]

General von Hengl's tripartite division of military personnel into a small group of activists and reckless youth, a broad mass of tired and indifferent soldiers, and an indeterminate number of "cowards" corresponds to the attitude of Germans in general at this time. Evaluation of Reich propaganda office reports at the end of February, 1945,[245] produced a similar result. The following categories were differentiated:

1. The "so-called middle classes." Their attitude is characterized "by a profound lethargy and an extensive letting go. . . . These groups are watching the war 'like theatre-goers [watching] the action on the stage' without the feeling that their own necks are at stake. Common expressions go: 'Everything is lost, why go on working,' or 'In three months the war will be lost anyway.' An alternative possibility no longer exists for these people. This attitude is also embraced by certain peasant elements, especially in those areas denominationally one-sided. . . ."

2. In stark contrast "is the behavior of the working class in large factories, which continues to fulfill its responsibility in an exemplary manner. There is almost no grumbling in these circles. The work force also appears immune to all Communist attempts at demoralization—even if small Communist cells were ferreted out here and there—and is remaining faithful to the Führer despite all the privations and burdens. It is also from these circles that demands come for a final end to the consideration given to the disheartened 'bourgeoisie.' The cry for drastic action is growing louder and louder."

3. Another category cited was soldiers hanging about all over the Reich and depressing the mood of the population. Only later in the report is mention made of a group analogous to "defeatists" and military deserters: the population in areas near the front. Those who belonged to the so-called "*Kofferpatrioten*," [literally suitcase patriots], during the crisis period 1938-39, had now adopted the slogan "we're staying here," and "the hope that the fighting will pass over the west as quickly as possible. These people take comfort in the knowledge that they would not fall into the hands of the Bolsheviks but 'only' of the Anglo-Americans, who are 'more civilized' and thus also 'more humane.' "

Other reports[246] substantiate the despair and "profound lethargy" which had gripped the bourgeois-conservative masses. Yet there were also further instances of radicalism, a tenacious resolve to hold out, previously reported from Bochum[247] and now also observed in Mecklenburg, a National Socialist stronghold in 1933. Convinced that no other alternative existed, here most workers clung to Hitler and increasingly demanded ruthless action against traitors and saboteurs believed to be entrenched in the highest state and Party offices. As far as they were concerned, it was high time to purge the civil service, military, and even the Party; the Führer should finally listen to the working class. Typical worker remarks included: "Stalin did the right thing in exterminating all the brains of the old school." "We are always the dupes. We have no connections and must bear all military burdens and responsibilities." "In Russia the commissars operated quite differently, that is why they are so strong today." "We only have to be guilty of a trifle and are severely punished, and immediately at that. If it is a Frau Doktor or Frau Captain, then the matter is dragged on so long that it is finally dropped entirely. The same class distinctions exist today as before. Nothing has changed in that respect."[248]

With class antagonisms and sharp criticism of Nazi failure to reconstruct society, the only thing continuing to bind the worker and lower classes in general to Hitler's state was Hitler himself. At least one-third of all Germans still placed their confidence in him despite reversals and disappointments.[249] Otherwise more and more tribute was paid to the consistent manner in which Stalin had eliminated the former elite—and this at a time when German newspapers were filled with eye-witness accounts of Red Army brutalities and murders.[250] This was apparently accepted as "normal" behavior by the victor and the stronger, and analogous to previous German conduct.

Ephemeral hopes in that historic turn of events promised by Hitler[251] were artificially kept alive by Goebbels' propaganda. On February 28, for example, he stated: "We are like a marathon runner who has completed thirty-five of the forty-three kilometers imposed on him. He feels himself near collapse, but so does his opposition. When he has won, all this agony will quickly be forgotten and only the triumph will remain."[252] A similar comparison had just recently been applied to the military situation in the east by the chief of the propaganda staff. The propaganda line emphasized the high toll in manpower and materiel suffered by the Bolsheviks in their breakthrough into the eastern zone, thereby creating a condition in which German countermeasures had a good chance of success.[253] Subsequently the weekly activity report, which evaluated information from the SD and propaganda offices, confirmed a persistence of hope and willingness to sacrifice all for life and liberty—based on faith in the Führer.[254]

But in the west, where the British and Americans were just around the corner and commanded the skies, where it was now almost impossible to receive German radio broadcasts, and where deficiency in the equipment and arms of one's own troops could no longer be hushed up, there the "spirit of Americanism"[255] began to spread. At this time, of course, this spirit, which valued freedom and the rights of the individual higher than the nation, which the Third Reich had worshipped, manifested itself in Germany as little more than an elementary hope for survival and an infinite war weariness. A report of February 27 by an SS-Obersturmbannführer to Ohlendorf's Bureau III about conditions in Geislautern, a village in the Saar near Völklingen, clearly indicates that here the attitude of the public was not determined by political or even ideological considerations. The sight of refugees pulling their meager belongings behind them in handcarts, under air attack on clogged roads, the search for temporary lodgings, and the ever-expanding conviction that the war was lost, induced people to remain where they were. "Beyond that, they hoped that the slogan increasingly spread by the enemy side, that the population will be spared, is true. These were, without exception, citizens who no longer had any connection to the movement. Primarily church-affiliated elements of the population were involved, who, under the guidance of their clergy who had also remained behind, preferred to let the war sweep over them."

Correct treatment by the Americans, who here and there distributed canned goods, cigarettes, and chocolate to a cowed and starved population, made a deep impression. "After the liberation of Geislautern by German troops . . . officials observed that the homes in which the Americans had stayed had neither been damaged nor had anything been stolen. The general assertion here was also that they had conducted themselves better 'than our German troops.' " This report to Bureau III of the RSHA concluded: "Based on these experiences with the Americans, the populace remaining behind has the highest opinion of them. They will therefore no longer leave their homes and cellars even though, for military reasons, a renewed order for the evacuation of the Saar was issued long ago by military authorities. . . ."[256] Civilians prepared white flags, burned signs of party membership, and refused to support retreating German troops in any way.

Since the whole western population could hardly be hanged or dragged before courts-martial, oral propaganda and leaflets were used in an effort to destroy the positive image of the western enemy. Reich propaganda office Westmark worked primarily with the argument "that these Americans were combat troops whose only function was to fight; but after them come the rearguard service troops and especially the Jews, who have in all other cases acted ruthlessly against the population." Lacking sufficient examples from its own Gau, it pointed to acts in Belgium and in France.[257] To strengthen resistance among Party officials, Bormann circulated excerpts from captured American documents equating Nazis with the military and Germans in general. In his order to the twelfth Army prohibiting fraternization, General O.N. Bradley had stated: "We are engaged in a total war, and every individual member of the German people has turned it into such. If it had not been Hitler leading the Germans, then it would have been someone else with the same ideas. The German people enjoy war and are determined to wage war until they rule the world and impose their way of life on us."[258] But quotations such as these produced slim results as war weariness spread to the Party cadre, forcing Bormann to order the expulsion from the Party of all those abusing or neglecting their authority.[259]

Meanwhile a mass search action was conducted under the command of SS-Obergruppenführer Steiner, supreme commander of the Eleventh SS-tank Army, in order to seize all stragglers and roving soldiers of the Wehrmacht, Waffen-SS, and police.[260]

In view of the unchecked Soviet advance, an irresistible "general east-to-west movement" had been set in motion. A member of the Party Chancellory, driving eastward at the beginning of March, only came across one unit heading in the same direction. It was a regiment of the "Polish National Army." All others—so it seemed to the observer—were streaming westward.[261] Although he felt that "military reality may not correspond to this picture," the situation was in fact far more critical. On the previous day, March 7, 1945, the Soviets had taken Kolberg. The Red Army offensive in the first three months of 1945 brought them from the East Prussian border and the Vistula to the Oder-Neisse line and the eastern edge of the Sudeten Mountains. Once they had assembled their reserves, they concentrated their forces between the Baltic Sea and the Sudeten Mountains for the last decisive blow.

The Nazi regime now began to recruit refugees and adventurers for combat behind enemy lines. Those interested were noted by a special official in every Gau to the Party Chancellory, from where their addresses were communicated to the responsible SS authority under the code name "Werewolf."[262] But as we know, no organized resistance ever materialized, and after mid-March, with the western Allies reaching the banks of the Rhine, collapse was just a matter of weeks.

5. THE END

The capture of the intact Ludendorff railway bridge at Remagen on March 7, 1945, by an American tank division of the 1st Army under Lieutenant General Hodges was interpreted by a great many Germans as "the beginning of the end."[263] The general mood had become "despondent, and faith in victory entirely vanished." The word from a harbor pub in Hamburg was: "despair. Everyone is awaiting a report on the condition of the skies. No gas, no light, no electricity, no heating. Only beer, which no one wants to drink in the cold. One worker thereupon remarked: 'I wish the English would come and put an end to it.'"

At the railroad station in Hamburg an engineer remarked to a soldier: "No more raw materials, we cannot build anything. If the Ruhr region is lost, then goodnight." Other voices revealed indifference, open despair, fear. The western Reich propaganda offices reported: " . . . Exhortation and word-of-mouth propaganda would no longer help much and could not prevent people from burying their valuables in anticipation of enemy occupation (Bochum, South Hanover, Brunswick). Refugees from the left bank of the Rhine and from Düsseldorf as well as the flood of retreating military personnel would only reinforce this psychosis. Most devastating in its effect were the accounts by soldiers who declared that we can no longer cope with the tremendous materiel superiority and air supremacy of the enemy. Stories by fleeing Party members that, for example, Neuss, Krefeld, and other towns were a sea of white flags when the Anglo-Americans entered are being interpreted as a desire on the part of the population to express their lack of intention to resist and their unconditional surrender (Bochum). . . ."[264]

In some places, therefore, an absolute "doomsday mood"[265] prevailed, although there were still some diehards waiting for the German counteroffensive. Cologne welcomed the Americans with "white kerchiefs and Rhine wine"—the Gauleiter, it seems, had bolted in time—but far more distressing personally to Goebbels was the open welcome the Allies received upon entering his home town of Rheydt. Those pages glorifying German resistance were clearly not being written in the west, but rather in the east, as far as the public was concerned.[266]

Hurrying to Silesia to speak at Lauban and Görlitz, the Reich Propaganda Minister managed to instill some courage among the despairing, with the help of a momentary pause in the Soviet advance; like the drowning and dying, the people were desperately grasping at any straws of hope. Successful local attacks by German units fostered belief that the counter-offensive would begin here. "People expect simultaneously that, if we anticipate the Soviet offensive, the planned Bolshevik thrust against Berlin can be parried and smashed. This would bring about the great turning-point, so they believe. Citizens are being strengthened in this hope by eastern refugees who generally are firmly convinced that their proximate homelands will be liberated again before long and whose attitude thus contributes considerably to strengthening fighting morale—in contrast to the attitude of evacuees from the west."[267]

To reinforce this belief in a great turning-point in western Germany as well, Bochum's Reich propaganda office organized a campaign with about thirty "itinerant speakers" in civilian clothes. Their function was to engage people in political conversations at stations, in bunkers, in trains, etc., "leading to a positive conclusion and replying appropriately to objections, thereby strengthening and stimulating faith in the approaching turning-point. . . ."[268] The objective was to cushion what the western propaganda offices considered to be a growing influence of enemy propaganda on public opinion through their emphasis on relatively moderate treatment. The western Allies, on the basis of prisoner-of-war interrogations, did in fact concentrate on egocentric subjects like food, housing,[269] and decent treatment. Ideological questions, it was found, evoked no response. "Safe conduct passes" were dropped to ease the soldier's decision to desert and to facilitate for the bearer unhindered passage through enemy lines.[270]

According to American observations, however, the results among Wehrmacht personnel were minimal; nor, it seems, were leaflets and radio propaganda nearly as responsible for people remaining at home as war weariness and despair. Subsequent correct behavior by most American and British troops proved far more convincing than any propaganda, the more so because retreating German units behaved like wild hordes, plundering, ransacking factory canteens, and staging drinking-bouts.[271] As Americans passed through, there were also instances of looting, especially by foreign workers but with German factory workers joining in; but the Allies soon restored order and reopened industries.[272]

Between the white-flag-waving Germans in the west and the tenacious but already heavily demoralized defending troops in the east, the mood of the bulk of the population was "progressively declining, fatalistic. No matter what happens, call it quits," were the words in one report from Hamburg. Propaganda about Soviet atrocities were making no headway. People expected an improvement in hitherto intolerable conditions with the occupation by the western Allies. Reproaches against the Party and politicians of the Third Reich were mounting: "Bismarck would have seen to a quiet life for his people; he would have negotiated with Russia.

Present policies are smashing the Bismarckian Reich. The last politicians in Germany were Neurath and von Papen.*" Another spoke of "brown Party dogs"; people remembered the words: "Give me ten years and you will have airy and sunny homes, you will not recognize your cities, no one will starve or freeze." Indeed, it was impossible to recognize cities amidst all this rubble, and people were ready to welcome "Tommy," "so we can lead a reasonable and orderly life again."[273]

Similar reports of hostile comments and general defeatism came from Stuttgart[274] and Berlin.[275] While some people in Württemberg watched the rapid Allied advance with apprehension, most were evidently happy that the war was finally coming to an end. Most expected the Americans to celebrate Easter in Stuttgart. The call by the mayor and Kreisleiter of Stuttgart for a general evacuation to the rural areas in anticipation of a food shortage was heeded only by mothers with children. Talk of miracle weapons to turn back the enemy met with general derision. Public anger was directed especially against the Party, which became the main scapegoat for the deplorable conditions and the situation in which Germany found itself. In the hunt for guilty parties, some blamed Nazi functionaries for having interfered in military affairs, other accused officers of failing their responsibilities.

These attitudes were confirmed by impressions gathered by soldiers in Hamburg,[276] although there was no indication of any spirit of resistance, either against the external foe or one's own leadership. The main topics affecting the overall public mood were hunger, terror from the skies, and the military situation. A large percentage of the population was already without bread and other foodstuffs: "It is no longer a rarity for soldiers to be approached on streets and in restaurants for bread and fat ration cards." Most, including those who still believed in the Führer, predicted a catastrophe. From various sides was heard that a continuation of the war only meant a senseless slaughter of the population. The general tenor was: "Better a horrible end than horror without end."

A noteworthy survey of the population's general convictions and opinions is offered in a not completely preserved report by Kielpinski written at the end of March; it indicates that no one in the Ohlendorf

---

* Konstantin von Neurath, conservative foreign minister (1932-38) who was regarded as a constraint on Nazi radicalism by German Nationalists but quickly succumbed to Nazi enticements; later Reich Protector of Bohemia and Moravia.
Franz von Papen, dilettante aristocrat, briefly chancellor in 1932, instrumental in the backroom intrigue which brought Hitler to power. Had an inflated opinion of his ability to check Hitler in a mixed cabinet; lost his Vice-Chancellor post after the Röhm purge. (ed. note)

Bureau continued to harbor illusions about public opinion, the essential points of which were cited and then spelled out in detail:[277]

"1. No one wants to lose the war. Everyone most fervently wished that we could win it.

2. Nobody believes anymore that we will win. The hitherto reliable flicker of hope is going out.

3. According to general conviction, if we lose the war we have ourselves to blame, and by that is meant not the little man but the leadership.

4. The Volk no longer has any confidence in the leadership. It is sharply critical of the Party, of certain leaders, and of propaganda.

5. For millions, the Führer is the last support and the last hope, but even the Führer is included more and more every day in the question of confidence and in criticism.

6. Doubt about the sense of continued fighting is eating away at combat morale, the citizen's confidence in himself and in others.

Amplifying on these points, the SD cited, in reference to the first, a general awareness of an impending national catastrophe ever since Soviet forces invaded the Reich. The weight of daily worries, air attacks which disrupted normal activity, a constant stream of refugees with their tales of atrocities which reached into the farthest corners of the Reich, the sight of Germans without adequate food—these contributed to a breakdown in human relations. And yet the population continued to perform its tasks in an exemplary manner, heading to work by the thousands in bombed out cities, regardless of the fact that they were tired and homeless.

On point 2, "defeatism has become a general public manifestation if the previously employed simplistic criteria are applied." Nobody imagined that they still could or even wanted to win, with the loss of the industrial regions of Upper Silesia and the Ruhr, coupled with an overall picture of utter confusion. Enemy air raids wreaked havoc with total warfare measures; for the hundreds of thousands drafted into the labor force in past months there were no jobs. After years of all-out effort, the people were clearly tired, their energies spent. Hope still glimmered in some; either an eventual political solution or the appearance of powerful miracle weapons were considered possible if only the military fronts could be held a while longer. Utter despair could be seen in day-to-day existence, in wild carousing or thoughts of suicide. The demand for poison, a gun, or other means of self-destruction was high everywhere.

As for culpability, point 3, there was consensus that this situation could have been avoided, that it "was not necessary for us to go downhill to the point where we are sure to lose the war unless there is a last minute change." The brunt of criticism, unjust in many cases according to the reporter, was directed at the conduct of the war with special reference to the air force, diplomacy, and particularly the eastern occupation policy, for which almost no support could be found. Much of this dangerous criticism was interpreted as a reaction to the feeling of impotence in the face of the enemy's superiority. Germans were meanwhile seeking to absolve themselves from any war guilt by "pointing out that they were not responsible for the conduct of war and of politics," instead merely following orders and doing what was expected of them, be they laborers, civil servants, or soldiers.

On point 4, the last for which documentation is available, the SD stated: "Confidence in the leadership has plunged like an avalanche. . . . In good conscience, having done everything possible, the 'little man' in particular is assuming the right to voice his opinion in the most public way and with the greatest candor. He no longer minces words." Whereas before people tended to trust the leaders, or were willing to await the victorious conclusion of the war, disillusionment over Nazi realities in contrast to its propaganda now unleashed widespread resentment. Though some of this was attributable to foreign radio propaganda, the SD generally found few Germans disposed to accept enemy information or even to read its leaflets. Only as disenchantment set in, as citizens felt betrayed and cheated, as their last hopes were dashed by the western Christmas offensive, did hostile attitudes manifest themselves.

"Ever since then one can find less and less uniformity in the creation of opinion as defined by the leadership and by propaganda. Everyone is acting on his own attitudes and opinions. . . ." Publicity about Soviet atrocities still invoked fear, but it could no longer instill hatred; instead the public criticized the government for underestimating the enemy. This is not to suggest, however, that the Volk had changed in its basic loyalty to the leadership, the "idea and the Führer. The German people are patient and accustomed to discipline." Where general awareness of surveillance by the Party and its ubiquitous organizations failed to do the trick, traditional respect for the police accomplished the rest.

Little needs to be added to this condensed public opinion analysis. A further report—possibly the next one—motivated Bormann to send a sharply worded protest to the head of the RSHA on April 4, 1945, which contained arguments justifying a leadership finally forced to the defensive itself. Bormann considered this SD report, like others, to be typical, "because without any restraint whatsoever, a few isolated instances and circumstances are being generalized." He refused to recognize that the vast majority had dissociated itself from the NSDAP, and that the friction between Party and Wehrmacht was becoming increasingly obvious.

"But that is exactly what I am reproaching the SD for: assertions and criticisms being made by just any completely irresponsible persons, while those responsible are not even asked. . . . What alternative remained east of the Rhine other than halting the incipient evacuation proceedings after the enemy had so quickly reached central Germany? It is truly a mystery to me how one can construe reproaches against the leadership from this. . . ." The friendly reception given the Americans was a case in point where Bormann felt that the effects of prevalent foreign propaganda, coupled with the absence of German rallies, meetings and the like, had not been considered. If the motivation for this had been an end to the war and the bombings, Bormann, in closing his epistle, observed that "within a relatively short time a very pronounced disenchantment will set in—just like after 1918."[278]

This disapproval and simultaneous justification suggests that Hitler's remarks to Speer on March 18, that it was not necessary to preserve the foundation for the continued existence of the German people since only those of inferior value remained, as well as his "scorched earth" order of March 19, were possibly a reaction to public opinion reports. The population had turned away from him, had proven weak. Thus, if he was to go under, so should they, so should Germany. Ten days later, wavering due to the inner insecurity of his character, he rescinded his regulations for the destruction under the influence of Speer; without informing Hitler, Speer then inserted the variant "paralysis."

Roosevelt's death on April 12 seemed to all those Germans who were still hoping for a miracle to be that famous turning point. Goebbels' propaganda machine sprang into action to present this event in the correct light: "The death of Roosevelt proves that the course of the war cannot be calculated in advance and is not determined solely by material potential. Imponderable events play a decisive role which it is the duty of the warring Volk and its leadership to await with steadfastness and unyielding courage. Even if we presently refrain from political speculation about the probable implications of Roosevelt's death, it should be emphasized on the other hand that his departure has caused a breach in the American people which cannot be healed. . . ." As a precaution against "precipitous hopes and exaggerated ideas," newspapers were advised not to employ the analogy common in Hitler's circle of Czarina Elizabeth's death during the Seven Years War.[279]

If a small portion of the population still clung to ephemeral hopes,[280] the war gave them no opportunity to spin further dreams. On April 14 the encircled forces in the Ruhr were cut in two, the eastern pocket surrendering on the sixteenth with eighty thousand men, the western pocket on the eighteenth with 325,000 men. Bradley's Army Group meanwhile advanced further eastward in order to effect a union with Russian forces at the Elbe according to Eisenhower's plan. American lead tanks reached the river on April 11 near Magdeburg and established a bridgehead. They were within 120 kilometers of the Reich capital. The last major Soviet assault in the direction of Berlin began on April 16. Despite isolated pockets of fierce resistance by SS and HJ units, both armies pushed on inexorably.

Typical of propaganda during these final days[282] was the daily password of April 19: "Besides an unadorned rendering of enemy hatred and plans for the destruction of the German people and the Reich, an emphatic underscoring of recently mounting tension in the Allied camp is especially appropriate for improving the spirit of resistance and the stamina of the German people. A strengthened tenacious perseverance during the present military crisis can only hasten the outbreak of political conflict on the enemy side and thus bring about the decisive turn in the overall military picture. . . ."[283]

In an opinion report of "Sondereinsatz Berlin," dated March 31, propaganda was likened to a band on a sinking ship—merrily continuing to play.[284] These were the old melodies and familiar strains, but they reached fewer and fewer passengers on the German ship of state. In the north and south, respectively, people were already dreaming of a union with Denmark, a connection with England, and an independent Bavaria. In the west, local administrations established by the Americans were already functioning. In Bavaria, the "Bavarian Independence Movement" was founded under the leadership of Captain Gerngross in cooperation with former trade unionists and Bavarian monarchists, calling over the radio for opposition to Gauleiter Giesler's order of fanatical resistance. SS and air force units crushed the timid movement and had some of its followers court-martialed and shot. On April 30, the day Nuremberg, the "city of the movement," was taken without a final battle, Hitler put an end to his life in the Berlin bunker, turning over the sinking ship to Admiral Dönitz, supreme commander of the navy.[285]

There are no official reports on how Germans received the death of their "Führer," though previously expressed opinions and a few eyewitness accounts permit the following crystallization of basic attitudes:

1. Immediate release from an almost unbearable pressure and a subsequent tumultuous joy for which we have the examples of the explosive zest for living seen in Hitler's bunker[286] and in the area between Eutin and Plön under Himmler's command.[287]

2. Consternation and shock among dedicated, idealistic National Socialists and some of the soldiers fighting to save their skins—a majority in the east, where reports of "Soviet atrocities" were not mere propaganda but a gruesome reality.[288] Directive Thirteen, issued by the NSFO from Breslau on May 2, 1945, played on the fear of capture and deportation to Siberia; traditional faith in the Führer was translated into the belief that his heroic "sacrifice" offered a possible political turning point,[289] one that produced

3. a crescendo of hope for an understanding with the western Allies. This opinion trend was reinforced by eastern refugees seeking safety in Germany's western zones, by Himmler's peace offer via the Swedish Count Bernadotte[290] during the night of April 24-25, as well as Dönitz's policy of partial surrender and retention of an open door to the west for the stream of fleeing soldiers and civilians.

4. The broad mass of the population, however, was too preoccupied with survival, scrounging for food and shelter, and protecting their valuables from occupying troops (particularly in the Russian zone)[291] to take much notice of Hitler's departure from the world scene. At most there were denunciations of the Party and denials of co-responsibility by "obedient sheep"[292] who had faithfully followed all orders from above—the attitude characterized by Kielpinski as early as March.

5. For all those fallen gods of the NSDAP, great and small, the time of reckoning, denial, or disappearance had begun. Party badges had been disappearing for some time; those who still clung to the old symbols and refused to destroy or endanger them now buried or hid them.[293]

As for the mood and attitude among Germans in the still unoccupied northern section of the Reich during these last days, a few reports by Ohlendorf's bureau provide some insights. The first report of May 6, coming after the partial surrender of German forces in Holland, Friesland, Denmark, and Schleswig-Holstein, found the population "in no way dejected. On the contrary, a *calm and quiet attitude* prevails, marred only by a certain nervousness in view of the anticipated occupation of remaining free areas." Many could still not grasp that this represented the final military defeat of Germany and saw the present condition as "an obviously transitional situation." The end would not come until the struggle against the Soviet Union had been decided in Germany's favor, with or without foreign help. Discipline among the troops remained high, since most soldiers clearly shared the view of the civilian population. Emphasis was put on the will to rebuild and the desire of most refugees to return to their eastern homeland.[294]

The first British and American occupation troops hardly influenced the prevailing mood. "Anglo-Americans are seldom still regarded as enemies; their entry is observed more with curiosity than apprehension, but in general with caution. More often than not an inquisitive crowd gathers. What seems to be determinant for this attitude is that the population is becoming more and more used to the idea that Germany and the Western Powers will jointly turn against Bolshevism in the near future. . . ." The public failed to draw more profound observations and consequences from the existing situation, which was natural enough, in view of their preoccupation with daily cares. Their outward tranquility portrayed an inability on their part to comprehend the extent of the fate which had engulfed them so suddenly.[295]

News of the unconditional surrender "abruptly changed the population's mood and inner state of mind for the worse. . . . Even among those elements of the population who had previously assessed the situation calmly and patiently, the announcement of the surrender had a shocking and crushing effect." Refugees were hit harder than Flensburgers since it spelled the end of an alliance against Russia. Utterly shaken, some threatened to kill their children if forced to return to a homeland under Soviet occupation. A large number saw their hopes of returning to the old homeland vanish: "The East is lost to us forever." Criticism of the new regime, which had initially been regarded with a wait-and-see attitude, now became more vocal as discussions of the reasons for Germany's collapse focused on the Party and its bosses. Dönitz, in his address to the people on May 8, had declared an end to the unity of Party and state without, however, officially dissolving the Party. It soon disbanded helter-skelter; the Hitler Youth burned Party literature and defaced posters, much to the disapproval and anger of Party leaders.[296]

The Party's end was inglorious. While the Third Reich's last head of state strove to lend a semblance of order and propriety to its demise and to facilitate the transition to a new system, this was soon made impossible by his arrest and that of his colleagues who had been too closely tied to the past regime. The German people were left to cope for themselves with their victors. Long deprived of their majority, they continued to be passive recipients of orders. Horrified by the flood of news and descriptions about the inhumanity and crimes of the Nazi regime, they closed they eyes and ears and protested their innocence to all who would listen. Germans, it seems, still failed to grasp Montgomery's dictum that a guilty nation not only has to be condemned, it also has to realize its guilt. There were complaints over the order prohibiting fraternization. " 'We feel as if we are not worth being spoken to,' said one Hamburg businessman, and another declared to a British officer: 'If you persist, you will lose our friendship yet'. . . ."[297]

But hardly anyone attached much importance to German friendship. And so they grimly and assiduously began to clear away their rubble and rebuild, to find their families and to forget the horror.

The Germans had stumbled unwillingly into the war, they had endured it more or less reluctantly, and now they unwillingly accepted the accusations of the enemy. These three stages reveal the degree of immaturity, the flight from personal responsibility, which has so long characterized the political thinking of Germans. Several of the opinion configurations of that time are still discernible today. Some people still hope to return to their lost homeland, some still harp upon doing one's duty without accepting joint responsibility. For many, a hierarchical structure is still the best safeguard for order and security—two concepts which contributed substantially to the election of Hitler and which, for many, not only still serve today as a justification for their former behavior but also continue to be interpreted as positive aspects in assessing Adolf Hitler as a statesman.[298] Yet many of the old wishes and longings have lost their force. The myth of disciplined Germans, conscious of their duty, is vanishing; authority and the father figure are increasingly being dethroned. What remains for many Germans is merely the "strange image of a being that I used to be."[299]

NOTES

1. "Meldungen über die Entwicklung in der öffentlichen Meinungsbildung," June 8, 1944: Boberach, p. 514.
2. Vertrauliche Information, No. 111/44 of June 6, 1944: BA, ZSg 109/50, fol. 9.
3. SD section Schwerin, June 6, 1944: "Erste Stimmen zum Beginn der Invasion." BA, NS6/407. fol. 13662.
4. Kreiswirtschaftsberater Dinkelsbühl, June 8, 1944: BA, NS Misch/1858.
5. BA, NS6/407, fol. 13663, 13704.
6. SD main section Schwerin, June 12, 1944: BA, NS6/407, fol. 13702, 13705.
7. Boberach, p. 511. All reports of OLG presidents and public prosecutors confirm this observation.
8. Boberach, p. 512.
9. Von Hassell also noticed the easing of tension due to the invasion and abatement in air attacks: op. cit., p. 314. The Party and Bormann particularly had expected intensified air attacks, sabotage and the need to close civilian travel. See Boberach, p. 513.
10. SD main office, Schwerin, June 13, 1944: BA, NS6/407, fol. 13702.
11. Boberach, p. 512.
12. Ibid., pp. 517, 518.
13. BA, NS6/407, fol. 13703.
14. See Gruchmann, op. cit., pp. 286-87.
15. BA, NS6/407, fol. 13703-13705.

16. SD section, Frankfurt, June 17, 1944: HHStA Wbn, *Zug* 68/67, No. 1075.

17. See BA, R55/572, fol. 156, 159.

18. Cf. SD section, Frankfurt, June 29, 1944; SD section Koblenz, June 20, 1944: HHStA Wbn, 1077/1078; summary of reports from SD sections, June 19, 1944: BA, NS6/411, fol. 13929-13933.

19. SD-Hauptaussenstelle Schwerin, June 30, 1944: BA, NS6/407, fol. 13716-13718.

20. See V.I. No. 120/44 of June 18; V.I. No. 126/44 of June 24, 1944: BA, ZSg 109/50, fol. 26, 44.

21. Cf. Steinert, *op. cit.*, p. 83; Janssen, *op. cit.*, p. 239.

22. Gruchmann, *op. cit.*, pp. 293-94.

23. BA, *Sammlung Schumacher*/368.

24. SD section, Schwerin, June 27, 1944: BA, NS6/407, fol. 13728-13730.

25. "Zusammenstellung von Meldungen aus den SD-(Leit)-Abschnitten" of June 28, 1944: BA, NS6/407, fol. 13949. Cf. also "Meldungen über die Entwicklung in der öffentlichen Meinungsbildung," June 29, 1944: BA, NS6/41, fol. 80-85.

26. Cf. "Einfluss der Gerüchte und militärisch-politischen Kombinationen auf die Stimmung und Meinungsbildung der Bevölkerung seit Beginn der Invasion:" Boberach, pp. 518-25.

27. See Jürgen Thorwald, *Die ungeklärten Fälle* (Stuttgart, 1950), 2. ed., pp. 52-79.

28. Weekly activity report of propaganda offices to Goebbels on July 4, 1944: BA, R55/601, fol. 26.

29. SD section Schwerin, July 4, 1944: BA, NS6/407, fol. 13742.

30. V.I. No. 128/44, 2. add. of June 28, 1944: BA, ZSg109/50, fol. 54, 57.

31. "Meldungen aus den SD-(Leit)-Abschnittsbereichen," sent to the Party Chancellory on July 14, 1944: BA, NS6/41, fol. 13487. This report came from northwestern Germany; those from other regions sounded similar. See also "Meldungen über die Entwicklung in der öffentlichen Meinungsbildung," July 13, 1944: Boberach, pp. 525, 527.

32. Transmitted to the Reich Propaganda Ministry on July 11, 1944: BA, R55/616, fol. 100, 101.

33. Propagandaparole No. 66 of July 13, 1944, sent to all Gauleiters, heads of propaganda offices and propaganda leaders. *Ibid.*, fol. 1.

34. November 29, 1943: BA, R22/3375.

35. The unpopular situation report was No. 3004 of July 14, 1944. The reply to Goebbels' protest was sent on July 17, 1944 (No. 3009): BA, R55/616, fol. 107, 110.

36. Meldung No. 3002: *Ibid.*, fol. 109.

37. "Meldungen aus den SD-(Leit)-Abschnittsbereichen," sent to the Party Chancellory on July 22: BA, NS6/411, fol. 13514-13524.

38. Numerous documents and monographs have been published on the attempted assassination and the German resistance. Among the most noteworthy:
20. Juli 1944. Revised edition of the special edition by the weekly "Das Parlament:" "Die Wahrheit über den 20. Juli 1944." Edited by Hans Royce and published by the Bundeszentrale für Heimatdienst, Bonn (n.d.)
"SS-Bericht on July 20: "Aus den Papieren des SS-Obersturmbannführers Dr. Georg Kiesel," *Nordwestdeutsche Hefte*, No. 1/2 (1947), pp. 5-34.
Spiegelbild einer Verschwörung. Die Kaltenbrunner-Berichte an Bormann

und ehemaliges Reichssicherheitshauptamt (Stuttgart, 1961). For a critique of this documentation and edition, see Hans Rothfels, "Zerrspiegel des 20. Juli," *VJHZ*, No. 1 (January, 1962), pp. 62-67.
Harold C. Deutsch, *The Conspiracy against Hitler in the Twilight War* (Minneapolis, 1968).
Heinrich Fraenkel & Roger Manvell, *The July Plot* (London, Bodley Head, 1964).
Annedore Leber (ed.), *Das Gewissen entscheidet. Berichte des deutschen Widerstandes von 1933-1945 in Lebensbildern* (Berlin, 1957).
Roger Manvell & Heinrich Fraenkel, *The Canaris Conspiracy. The Secret Resistance to Hitler in the German Army* (London, 1969).
Gerhard Ritter, *The German Resistance: Carl Goerdeler's Struggle Against Tyranny* (New York, 1958).
Hans Rothfels, *The German Opposition to Hitler* (London, Wolff, 1963).
Ger van Roon, *Neuordnung im Widerstand. Der Kreisauer Kreis innerhalb der deutschen Widerstandsbewegung* (Munich, 1967).
Hans Buchheim & W. Schmitthenner (eds.), *Der deutsche Widerstand gegen Hitler. Vier historisch-kritische Studien* (Cologne, 1966).
Peter Hoffmann, *Widerstand, Staatsstreich, Attentat. Der Kampf der Opposition gegen Hitler.* (Munich, 1969).

39. Goebbels wrote in his diary on November 8, 1943, that Himmler had informed him of a circle of traitors to which Halder and Popitz belonged. He considered "these dilettantish attempts as basically harmless." Himmler will see to it that no major damage is done. *op. cit.*, p. 469.
40. Führer headquarters, 21.40 hours. BA, *Sammlung Schumacher*/242.
41. BA, R55/614, fol. 4.
42. BA, *Sammlung Schumacher*/242. See also, Wheeler-Bennett, *The Nemesis of Power*: The German Army in Politics, 1918-1945 (New York, 1953), pp. 674 f.
43. No. 68. BA, R55/614, fol. 26-28. Cf. also fol. 29-33. For instructions on how to stage the oath ceremonies, see Rundspruch No. 203 of July 24, 1944, 12.40 hours: *ibid.*, fol. 42-45.
44. Rundschreiben of state secretary Dr. Naumann to all Gauleiters, heads of Reich propaganda offices and Gau propaganda leaders, dated July 23, 1944: BA, *Sammlung Schumacher*/242.
45. V.I. No. 149. No. 149/44: BA, ZSg 109/50, fol. 105.
46. V.I. No. 150/44: *ibid.*, fol. 107/108.
47. V.I. No. 151/44 (1. add.): *ibid.*
48. Chief of the Security Police and SD, July 21, 1944: "Erste stimmungsmässige Auswirkungen des Anschlags auf den Führer." Published in *Spiegelbild einer Verschwörung*, pp. 1-3. See also the report from the same office that day concerning the disgust and grief at the assassination attempt, *ibid.*, pp. 4, 5.
49. BA, R55/614, fol. 13. (Reich propaganda office, Hamburg, July 21, 1944).
50. *Ibid.*, fol. 14.
51. Cf. reports of Reich propaganda offices in Brunswick, Hanover, Stuttgart, Stettin, Nuremberg, and Königsberg: *ibid.*, fol. 10-20.
52. OLG-president Nuremberg, August 1, 1944: BA, R22/3381.
53. OLG-president Jena, July 28, 1944; OLG-president Darmstadt, August 1, 1944; OLG-president Breslau, August 1, 1944; OLG-president Kiel, August 4, 1944: BA, R22/3369, 3361, 3358, 3373.
54. Cf. army field mail in R55/575, fol. 204, R55/577, fol. 68, and the SD

report of October 31, 1944, about "Die Verschwörer vom 20.7.44 und die Wehrmacht:" *Spiegelbild einer Verschwörung*, pp. 475-476; cf. also MGFA, H34/1 with censor reports from the Wehrmacht.

55. Hoffmann, *op. cit.*, pp. 520 ff.
56. *Spiegelbild einer Verschwörung*, p. 6.
57. Cf. Zahn, *op. cit.*, p. 185; and *Der deutsche Widerstand gegen Hitler*, p. 243.
58. Chief of the Security Police and SD, July 24, 1944: "Stimmungsmässige Auswirkungen des Anschlages auf den Führer:" *Spiegelbild einer Verschwörung*, p. 8. Cf. Stimmungsbericht, July, 1944: BA, NS Misch/1047, fol. 107340.
59. "Meldungen über die Entwicklung in der öffentlichen Meinungsbildung" by Kaltenbrunner, sent to Bormann on July 28, 1944: BA, NS6/411, fol. 13529.
60. M. J. Gurfein & Morris Janowitz, "Trends in Wehrmacht Morale," *Public Opinion Quarterly* (Spring, 1946), p. 81.
61. *Spiegelbild einer Verschwörung*, p. 10. Cf. also public prosecutor general, Berlin Supreme Court, October 1, 1944: BA, R22/3356.
62. Stimmungsmässiger Überblick, July 24, 1944: BA, NS Misch/1674, fol. 148528. See also the report from Kreis Büdingen; BA, NS Misch/1634, fol. 139288.
63. Stimmungsbericht for district Schlüchtern, November 27, 1944: BA, NS Misch/1634, fol. 139260.
64. His report of August 2: *ibid.*, fol. 139234.
65. Cf. the report of Ortsgruppe Hüningen-St. Ludwig Ost, related by RPA Baden on July 28, 1944: BA, R55/602, fol. 2.
66. Reference to Ley's speech is made in "Stimmungsmässige Auswirkungen des Anschlags auf den Führer," Chief of the Security Police and SD, July 24, 1944: *Spiegelbild einer Verschwörung*, p. 10.
67. In 1938 they constituted 18.7 per cent of the SS-Obergruppenführer, 9.8 per cent of the SS-Gruppenführer, 14.3 per cent of the SS-Brigadeführer, 8.8 per cent of SS-Oberführer and 8.4 per cent of SS-Standartenführer: BA, *Der Adel im deutschen Offizierskorps*, p. 10, cited by Höhne, p. 127.
68. As early as May, 1943, in discussions concerning the successor to Lutze as head of the SA, Hitler had objected to any more aristocrats, a feeling reinforced after Italy's defection. *Goebbels Tagebücher*, pp. 331, 401.
69. Cf. Ritter, *op. cit.*, and *Widerstand und Erneuerung*.
70. Cf. the correspondence of SS-Sturmbannführer Backhaus, personal adviser to the acting Reich Minister for Food and Agriculture, Backe, of August 26, 1944, to the personal adviser of the Reichsführer-SS, SS-Standartenführer Brandt: BA, NS19/neu 830.
71. Cf. letter of the Deutschen Propaganda-Atelier to the Reich Minister for Enlightenment and Propaganda, concerning "Treuekundgebungen für den Führer": BA, R55/614, fol. 162.
72. RSHA, Amt IV, Meldung wichtiger staatspolizeilicher Ereignisse, No. 1, of September 1, 1944: BA, R58/213.
73. Meldung 9505 of the Münster RPA, August 8, 1944: BA, R55/614.
74. "Stimmungsmässiger Überblick über die gesamtpolitische Lage der Gauleitung Baden," August 5, 1944: BA, NS Misch/1823, fol. 313529.
75. *Spiegelbild einer Verschwörung*, p. 3. See also p. 5.
76. Cf. Janssen, *op. cit.*, p. 268.

77. *Spiegelbild einer Verschwörung*, p. 7.

78. *Ibid.*, pp. 10-11. Cf. also the weekly activity report of the head of the propaganda division, RMVP, August 7, which includes the following: "Today one has to say that it would have been wiser if we had also cleansed and politicized our military at the same time. Stalin thereby once again showed how to do it. . . ." BA, R55/601, fol. 70.

79. See *supra*, footnote 65.

80. See Anordnung des Leiters der Partei-Kanzlei 167/44, August 1, 1944, concerning the behavior of the Party leadership: BA, NS6/vorl. 347; also, Rundschreiben des Leiters der Partei-Kanzlei 171/44, August 8, 1944: *ibid.*

81. Cf. Führer decree of July 25, 1944, concerning total war mobilization. *ibid.*

82. Dated August 1, 1944, Anlage zu OKW/WZA/Ag WZ (II). NSF of August 12, 1944: BA/MA Wi I F 5/3211.

83. No. 170/44, July 24, 1944: BA, NS6/vorl. 347.

84. Cf. Special SD report about "Starke Beunruhigung der Bevölkerung in Ostdeutschland durch Erzählungen von Soldaten über die Verhältnisse bei den jüngsten Rückzügen im Mittelabschnitt der Ostfront": sent by Kaltenbrunner to Reichsleiter Schwarz on August 7, 1944: BA, NS1/544.

85. "Meldungen über die Entwicklung in der öffentlichen Meinungsbildung," sent by Kielpinski to the Party Chancellory on August 12, 1944: BA, NS6/411, fol. 13548, 13549. For treason slogans, see also Kreisleitung Buchen/Odenwald, August 15, 1944: BA, NS Misch/1672, fol. 148499, and the reports of OLG-president, Rostock, August 5, and public prosecutors general, Schwerin and Hamm of October 14, 17, 1944: BA, R22/3385, 3379, 3367.

86. Weekly activity report of the deputy chief, division propaganda within the RMVP, target date September 18, 1944: BA, R55/601, fol. 124.

87. Führungsbericht of August 8, 1944, quoted in *Aus deutschen Urkunden*, p. 264.

88. Weekly activity report, deputy chief of the propaganda division, RMVP, August 15, 1944: BA, R55/601, fol. 79.

89. Kreisleitung Säckingen, August 10, 1944: BA, NS Misch/1832, fol. 316346. These observations as well as those of the two previous reports are in Kielpinski's report of August 20, 1944: "Stimmungsmässige Auswirkung der Verhandlung vor dem Volksgericht gegen die Attentäter des 20. 7. 44."

90. Decree of the Führer about the prosecution of political crimes committed by members of the Wehrmacht, Waffen-SS and Police of September 20, 1944.

91. RGBl. I, p. 609.

92. 1. Law for the revision of the military law of September 29, 1944: RGBl. I, p. 317.

93. Aktenvermerk für Pg. Friedrichs, Pg. Klopfer, Pg. Schütt, August 17, 1944: BA, *Sammlung Schumacher*/242.

94. KTB/OKW vol. IV, 2. Halbband, pp. 1574-76.

95. No. 63/64. Copy in BA, *Sammlung Schumacher*/242.

96. *Ibid.*

97. Cf. weekly activity report of the head of the propaganda division in the RMVP, target dates September 11, October 2, 1944: BA, R55/601, fol. 115, 146.

98. Dietrich von Choltitz, *Soldat unter Soldaten. Die deutsche Armee in Frieden und Krieg* (Zurich, 1951), p. 256.

99. Weekly activity report, head of the propaganda division, RMVP, August 15, 1944: BA, R55/601, fol. 75/76.

100. "Meldungen über die Entwicklung in der öffentlichen Meinungsbildung," August 17, 1944: BA, NS6/411, fol. 13561/13562. Cf. Speer's testimony concerning the systematic fostering of belief in the miracle weapons. IMT, XVI, p. 581, and Speer, op. cit., pp. 417-18, 579, footnotes 25, 26.

101. Weekly activity report by the head of the propaganda division, RMVP, August 22, 1944: BA, R55/601, fol. 81-86.

102. idem, August 28, 1944: ibid., fol. 92-100.

103. "The treason of King Michael of Rumania was received with great dismay and paid more attention than the treason of Badoglio and Victor Emmanuel in their day." Monatsbericht des Regierungspräsidenten Regensburg, September 9, 1944: BA, NS19/246.

104. On June 25, 1940. Kriegspropaganda, p. 405.

105. V.I. No. 186/44 of August 29, 1944: BA, ZSgl09/51, fol. 60.

106. Weekly activity report of the head of the propaganda division, RMVP, target date September 4, 1944: BA, R55/601.

107. Kreisleitung Kreis Oberwesterwald: BA, NS Misch/1634, fol. 139292. Cf. also BA, R55/575, fol. 140; weekly activity report of the head of the propaganda division, RMVP, target date September 11, 1944: BA, R55/575, fol. 116.

108. SS-Gruppenführer and Lieutenant-General of the Waffen-SS, Professor Dr. K. Gebhardt, to Himmler, September 5, 1944: BA, Sammlung Schumacher/ 366.

109. Letter of an SA man to Goebbels, September 16, 1944: BA, R55/575, fol. 116. Cf. also the report of the public prosecutor of Cologne, September 30, 1944: BA, R22/3374, and of Gauleiter Grohé of September 28, 1944, according to which some 71,823 inhabitants of a total of ca. 73,000 were transported, at times only with police pressure. BA, R58/976.

110. Abschlussbericht über die Räumungsaktion im Kreise Aachen-Land durch das Sonderkommando der Kreisleitung Hansestadt Köln: BA, R58/976.

111. Stimmungsmässiger Überblick über die Gesamtpolitische Lage vom 9. 9. 44. BA, NS Misch/1761, fol. 306775.

112. Cf. the assessment of General Hengl for the period September 22 to October 3, 1944, dated October 5, 1944: BA, NS19/neu 1858; cf. also reports of the Reich propaganda offices, September 18, 26, 1944: BA, R55/601, fol. 125, 135; and soldiers' letters: BA, R55/581, fol. 103-117, 73, 140; R55/581, fol. 37.

113. Weekly activity report of the head of the propaganda division, RMVP, target date September 18, 1944: BA, R55/601, fol. 122.

114. Ibid., fol. 130.

115. Bullock, op. cit., p. 755.

116. Cf. here KTB/OKW, vol. IV, II, pp. 1062, 1113.

117. Tgb. No. 784/44g. BA, NS19/36.

118. Addendum to Rundschreiben 255/44 of September 21, 1944, signed Heil to our Führer! by Field Marshal von Rundstedt. Copy in BA, NS6/vorl. 348.

119. Decree concerning the creation of the Volkssturm, September 25, 1944: RGBl. I, p. 253.

120. Cf. Janssen, op. cit., pp. 271 ff. concerning the dispute between Speer,

who demanded more weapons, and Goebbels, who favored mobilization of the masses.

121. Rundschreiben 353/44, October 27, 1944: BA, NS6/vorl. 348.

122. Rundschreiben 354/44, October 27, 1944: *ibid.*

123. Stimmungsmässiger Überblick über die gesamtpolitische Lage, September 30, 1944: BA, NS Misch/1719, fol. 302164.

124. Sicherheitsdienst des Reichsführers SS, SD-Leitabschnitt Düsseldorf, September 27, 1944: BA, R58/976. See also the reports of Reich propaganda offices, target date October 2, 1944: BA, R55/601, fol. 149.

125. III A 3-905-1-4628/44 of October 28, 1944: BA, NS1/544. Cf. also the negative report of the Düsseldorf SD section, April 8, 1944: BA, R58/976, and public prosecutor general, Hamm, of October 17, 1944: BA, R22/3367.

126. Public prosecutor general, Kattowitz, October 6, 1944: BA, R22/3372.

127. "Meldungen über die Entwicklung in der öffentlichen Meinungsbildung," August 17, 1944: BA, NS6/411, fol. 13563.

128. Cf. here the circular by Bormann, No. 192/44 of August 23, 1944: BA, NS6/vorl. 341.

129. Az 26/27 AWA/Ag WV2 (III) of September 5, 1944. Copy in BA, NS6/vorl. 351, No. 1649/44 geh.

130. Cf. Bormann's circular 303/44, 330/44 and 366/44 of October 7, 17, November 2, 1944: BA, NS6/vorl. 348 and 349.

131. Rundschreiben 421/44 of November 30, 1944 and the second instruction for the implementation of total warfare of November 29, 1944: BA, NS6/vorl. 349.

132. Weekly activity report by the head of the propaganda division, RMVP, target date October 9, 1944: BA, R55/601, fol. 160.

133. Cf. 5th report on "Sondereinsatz Berlin" for the period November 4 to 12, 1944: Berghahn, "Meinungsforschung im Dritten Reich," *loc. cit.*, p. 96.

134. No. 14501 of October 20, 1944: BA, R55/602, fol. 111.

135. Target date October 23, 1944: BA, R55/601, fol. 184-185.

136. Cf. Kreisleitung Wertheim, October 25, 1944: BA, NS Misch/1732.

137. Cf. the reports on the Sondereinsatz Berlin of October 25, November 3, 27, 1944: MGFA WO 1-6/368.

138. "Stimmen zum Erlass des Führers über die Bildung des Deutschen Volkssturmes," November 8, 1944: HStA Stuttgart K750/59 and BA, NS Misch/443. For other reports see BA, R22/3366 and 3869; Meldung des RPA Westmark, December 5, 1944: R55/603, fol. 57.

139. Stimmungsmässiger Überblick über die gesamte politische Lage, November 14, 1944: BA, NS Misch/1719, fol. 302155.

140. Weekly activity report, target date November 14, 1944: BA, R55/601, fol. 219.

141. Text of the speech in Domarus, vol. II, 2. Halbband, pp. 2160 ff.

142. BA, R55/601, fol. 22, 222. Cf. also the report of November 21, 1944: *ibid.*, fol. 228.

143. M. J. Gurfein, Morris Janowitz, *loc. cit.*, p. 81.

144. Sixth report on the Sondereinsatz Berlin, November 21, 1944: MGFA WO 1-6/368; the seventh report in Berghahn, "Meinungsforschung im Dritten Reich," p. 99.

145. There were also those who thought the population was not particularly im-

pressed. Cf. 5th report about Sondereinsatz Berlin for the period November 7-12, 1944: *ibid.*, p. 95.

146. Weekly activity report of the head of the propaganda division, RMVP, target date November 14, 1944: BA, R55/601, fol. 217-218. See also Kreisleitung Freiburg report of November 14, 1944: BA, NS Misch/1719.

147. For its beginnings, development, expansion and scope see Berghahn, "Meinungsforschung im Dritten Reich," *loc. cit.*, pp. 83 f.

148. Weekly report, propaganda division, target date October 30, 1944: BA, R55/601, fol. 197.

149. Cf. *idem*, target date October 23, 1944: *ibid.*, fol. 185-187.

150. Cf. report of Oberstleutnant Wasserfall, MGFA WO1-6/368.

151. In a letter to Goebbels of November 11, 1944, from Berlin-Steglitz, similar comments were made: "They always talk of victory because the whole Volk yearns for it as soon as possible. But when they send children and grandpas to the front and leave Party members at home (those gentlemen who wear warm uniforms all day), the whole mobilization is called in question. . . ." BA, R55/577, fol. 41.

152. AA Inland II A/B 80/3.

153. *Aus deutschen Urkunden*, pp. 276-78.

154. Cf. Weekly activity report of the head of the propaganda division in the RMVP, target date November 7, 1944, December 19, 1944: BA, R55/601, fol. 209, 257-258. Cf. also *Parole* 28, NSDAP *Sprechabenddienst*: BA, ZSg 3/1540.

155. Cf. Bramsted, *op. cit.*, pp. 296 f.

156. Weekly activity report, RMVP, BA, R55/601, fol. 188.

157. *Ibid.*, fol. 187.

158. Letter of November 17, 1944: BA, *Sammlung Schumacher*/366.

159. RF/BU 39/60/44g., October 18, 1944: BA, NS19/neu 751.

160. Weekly activity report, RMVP, November 21, 1944: BA, R55/601, fol. 226.

161. No. 2005, concerning report on the conduct of propaganda in Gau Baden: BA, R55/602, fol. 4,5.

162. BA, R22/3370.

163. See BA, R55/608, fol. 226 and R55/601, fol. 239.

164. V.I. No. 237/44: BA, ZSg 109/52, fol. 44.

165. Weekly activity report, target date October 30, 1944: BA, R55/601, fol. 197.

166. *Aus deutschen Urkunden*, pp. 275-76.

167. Weekly activity report, target dates October 30, November 7, 1944: BA, R55/601, fol. 197-199, 210.

168. Dated November 7, 1944: BA, R55/608, fol. 29.

169. Dated November 28, 1944: BA, R22/3379.

170. F. St. VI/Ia-Org. Kö/Bo. BA, *Sammlung Schumacher*/367.

171. Party Chancellory, Bekanntgabe 19/45, January 24, 1945: BA, NS6/vorl. 354.

172. *Ibid.*, and NS19/neu 750.

173. Weekly activity report, target date December 5, 1944: BA, R55/601, fol. 237.

174. Reich propaganda office report, Westphalia-South, from Bochum, November 14, 1944: BA, R55/602, fol. 142.

175. Cf. reports by OLG-presidents Jena (December 2, 1944), Breslau (December 3, 1944): BA, R22/3369 and 3358. Cf. also "Zusammenfassende

Berichterstattung über die militärische Entwicklung, hier: Deutsche Gegenoffensive im Westen" of December 20, 1944, to the RSHA, Amt III (IIID): BA, R58/976.

176. Copy in BA, R58/976.
177. *Lagebesprechungen im Führerhauptquartier*, pp. 292, 294.
178. Weekly activity report, target date December 28, 1944: BA, R55/601, fol. 261.
179. Weekly activity report, target date December 19, 1944: *ibid.*, fol. 249. The same for the following.
180. Report of December 19, 1944: BA, R22/3385.
181. OLG-president Kiel, January 29, 1944; public prosecutor general, Nuremberg, January 31, 1944: BA, R22/3385 and 3381.
182. Weekly activity report, target date December 19, 1944: BA, R55/601, fol. 250.
183. Weekly activity report, Komm. Leiters Pro. und Chef des Propagandastabes, target date December 28, 1944: *ibid.*, fol. 261, 262.
184. Cf. report by the Security Police and Special SD Commando-7b, dated December 28, 1944, to the supreme commander of the Fourth Army, General Hossbach: BA, R58/976.
185. Report by OLG-president, Kattowitz, December 20, 1944: BA, R22/3372.
186. Cf. for example articles in *Morgon Tidningen*, July 10, 1944—excerpts translated and summarized in *Der Luftkrieg über Deutschland, 1939 bis 1945*, pp. 244-47.
187. See OLG-president, Karlsruhe, BA, R22/3370; weekly activity report, head of propaganda division, target date December 19, 1944; December 28, 1944: BA, R55/601, fol. 253, 265.
188. Leiter, Rundfunk Abteilung, to State Secretary in the RMVP, betr. Suchmeldungen im Rundfunk, January 4, 1945: BA, R55/616, fol. 24-25.
189. A complete volume of the RMVP holdings are devoted to this report, compiled January 2 by Pro. Min.Rat Imhoff: BA, R55/612.
190. See Berghahn, "Meinungsforschung im Dritten Reich," *loc. cit.*, p. 101; OLG-president Kiel, report of January 29, 1945: BA, R22/3373. Cf. also Karlsruhe, January 2, 1945: R22/3370; public prosecutor general, Frankfurt, January 25, 1945: R22/3364.
191. Schnellbrief, head of the propaganda division, to all Reich propaganda offices: BA, R55/612, fol. 20, 38.
192. Gruchmann, *op. cit.*, pp. 414 ff. Also for the following.
193. BA, R22/3364. Cf. also public prosecutor general, Kiel, January 29, 1945: R22/3373.
194. Cf. 15th report on "Sondereinsatz Berlin" for the period January 1 to 21, 1945: MGFA WO1-6/368.
195. February 1, 1945: *ibid.*
196. Cf., for example, the situation report by the public prosecutor general, Hanseatic supreme court, of January 30, 1945, detailing a number of excesses. BA, R22/3366.
197. Report by Kommissarischen Leiters, propaganda division, January 26, 1945: BA, R55/616, fol. 153.
198. "Lagebericht in der Evakuierung" by head of propag. div. to the State Secretary, February 8, 1945, and also subsequent reports: *ibid.*, fol. 166-235.
199. *Ibid.*, pp. 183, 209, 250.

200. "Ernährungslage. Stichtag 25. 1. 45" and Fernschreiben an die Landesbauernführer, January 25 (copy provided by H. J. Riecke); Rundschreiben 72/45 of the head of the Party Chancellory, February 10, 1945: BA, NS6/vorl. 353.
201. BA, NS Misch/1858.
202. Rundschreiben 99/45 by the head of the Party Chancellory, February 23, 1945: BA, NS6/vorl. 353.
203. Cf. the 16th report on "Sondereinsatz Berlin," February 1, 1945: MGFA, WO1-6/368; public prosecutor, Hamburg, January 30, 1945: BA, R22/3366.
204. Activity report by the head of propag. div., RMVP, target date January 24, 1945: BA, R55/601, fol. 274, 275.
205. 17th report on "Sondereinsatz Berlin" for the period from January 29 to February 2, 1945: MGFA, WO1-6/368.
206. *Ibid.*
207. Fernschreiben, Himmler to Bormann, December 26, 1944: BA, *Sammlung Schumacher*/366.
208. BA, NS19/neu 750.
209. Cf. Hitler decree of November 27, 1944; addendum to Rundschreiben 25/45g. of January 24, 1945: BA, NS6/vorl. 354. For more information on the courses, cf. Dienstanweisungen für die Abteilung VI . . . of September 22, 1944; *ibid.*, and *Die NS-Führungsstäbe der Wehrmacht*: BA, *Sammlung Schumacher*/367. According to OKW statistics of December 20, 1944, there were 1,074 fulltime NSFO, including 255 in the air force, 43,000 parttime with the army, 3,432 with the air force, and 9,000 with the navy. Not all were Party members (89.24 per cent with the army, 72.97 per cent with the navy). Cf. also directive of Gottlob Berger, February 12, 1945: BA, NS19/neu 750.
210. Under this title, *Der politische Soldat*, the NS Guidance Staff issued a political and cultural information service for unit commanders. Individual issues in MGFA OKW 820.
211. BA, NS19/neu 750.
212. Cf. here Anne Armstrong, *Unconditional Surrender*. The impact of the Casablanca Policy upon World War II (New Brunswick, 1961), pp. 109-167. Also, Albert Kesselring, *Soldat bis zum letzten Tag* (Bonn, 1953), p. 410; Jay W. Baird, "La campagne nazie en 1945," *Revue d'Histoire de la deuxième guerre mondiale* (July, 1969), No. 75, pp. 71-92. Baird, however, overestimates the effect of propaganda at this point and fails to differentiate sufficiently between the various groups of public opinion. The role of Nazi ideology is also overestimated.
213. For the wide-reaching consequences of the war experiences and their central themes, see Kurt Sontheimer, *Antidemokratisches Denken in der Weimarer Republik. Die politischen Ideen des deutschen Nationalismus zwischen 1918 und 1933* (Munich, 2nd ed., 1964), pp. 115-33.
214. V.I. No. 9/45: BA, ZSg 109/53, fol. 94. This warning was repeated near the end of the month. Cf. V.I. No. 22/45 of January 27, 1945: *ibid.*, fol. 130.
215. V.I. No. 27/45 (I. Erg.) Nachtrag zur Parole des Reichspressechefs vom 2. 2. 45: BA, ZSg 109/45, fol. 6. Even after these directives the tenor of the press was apparently not yet aggressive enough. Cf. Speer, *op. cit.*, p. 426.
216. Tgb. No. 35/69/39. Rf/pt CH SS-HA/2K/Az. B 4 c. April 1, 1939. Copy in StA Bamberg, Rep. K17/XI. No. 398.
217. Warlimont, *op. cit.*, p. 320.

218. Cf. BA, NS19/neu 1, 189 F102.
219. Rundschreiben 166/44g. concerning suicide, July 17, 1944: BA, NS6/vorl. 351.
220. Hagemann, *op. cit.*, p. 489.
221. Examples in BA, NS19/neu 2068.
222. Gurfein, Janowitz, *loc. cit.*, p. 82.
223. Edward A. Shils and Morris Janowitz, "Cohesion and Disintegration in the Wehrmacht in World War II," *The Public Opinion Quarterly*, XII (1948), No. 2, pp. 281 ff.
224. Hornisse II, No. 98, dated March 9, 1945: BA, NS19/neu 2068.
225. BA, R55/603, fol. 97.
226. *Ibid.*, fol. 114.
227. Report of January 31, 1945: BA, R22/3360.
228. Report from Schwerin of February 6, 1945: BA, R22/3385.
229. Report of January 26, 1945: BA, R55/616, fol. 143-148.
230. Cf. report by OLG-president and public prosecutor general of Kattowitz from Neisse, dated February 1, 1945: BA, R22/3372.
231. Letter of Kreisleitung Liebenwerda to Gauleitung in Halle, February 22, 1945: BA, R55/616, fol. 47. Cf. also the sixteenth report on "Sondereinsatz Berlin" for the period February 14 to 20, 1945: Berghahn, "Meinungsforschung im Dritten Reich," *loc. cit.*, p. 108.
232. Hornisse II, No. 53: BA, NS19/neu 2068.
233. Report from Troppau, January 29, 1945 (additions in pencil): BA, R55/603, fol. 113. Cf. also a report from Weimar about conditions in the Warthegau, dated February 7, 1945: *ibid.*, fol. 122.
234. Copy in BA, NS6/vorl. 354.
235. *Dokumente der Deutschen Politik und Geschichte von 1848 bis zur Gegenwart*, ed. by Johannes Hohlfeld, vol. V: *Die Zeit der nationalsozialistischen Diktatur 1933-1945* (Berlin, 1953), pp. 519-20.
236. Steinert, *op. cit.*, p. 32.
237. BA, NS19/294.
238. 19th report on "Sondereinsatz Berlin" for the period from February 14 to 20, 1945: Berghahn, "Meinungsforschung im Dritten Reich," *loc. cit.*, p. 111.
239. 17th report on "Sondereinsatz Berlin" for the period from January 29-February 4, 1945: MGFA WO1-6/368.
240. Hornisse II, No. 47, February 15, 1945: BA, NS19/neu 2068.
241. Chief of the NS Guidance Staff of the Army, No. 304/45 GKdos, March 19, 1945: MGFA III W 129 (OKW 183).
242. See the report of the Chief of the NS Guidance Staff, addendum 1. *Ibid.*
243. Hornisse II, February 24, 1945: BA, NS19/neu 2068.
244. Twentieth report on "Sondereinsatz Berlin" of March 3, 1945: MGFA WO1-6/368.
245. Weekly activity report of the head of propaganda division, target date February 21, 1945: BA, R55/601, fol. 284-288.
246. Cf. for example, "Merkpunkte zur Versammlungsaktion Februar/März 1945:" BA, R55/610, fol. 182.
247. See *supra*, p. 290.
248. Report, "Stimmung und Haltung der Arbeiterschaft," signed by SS-Obersturmbannführer von Kielpinski and sent to SS-Brigadeführer Dr. Naumann, state secretary in the Propaganda Ministry, on March 19, 1945: BA, R55/620, fol. 129, 132.
249. Of those war prisoners in the west who were questioned, 30 per cent still

had faith in Hitler in March, 1945—and here the percentage of "defeatists" was far higher than in the east or among refugees. Gurfein and Janowitz, *loc. cit.*, p. 81.

250. Cf. Hagemann, *op. cit.*, pp. 483, 484. The first sworn eyewitness accounts were published in February.

251. Cf. Report of the Halle-Merseburg Reich propaganda office, cited in the weekly activity report of the head, propaganda div., target date March 21, 1945: BA, R55/601, fol. 296. Cf. also the twentieth report on "Sondereinsatz Berlin" of March 3, 1945: MGFA WO1-6/368, and Hornisse II, No. 95 of March 7, 1945: BA, NS19/neu 2068.

252. Hagemann, *op. cit.*, p. 487.

253. Dated February 17, 1945: BA, R55/608, fol. 35.

254. Dated March 21, 1945: BA, R55/601, fol. 285.

255. Cf. a letter to the Hauptschriftleiter of the magazine, "Front und Heimat" of March 7, 1945, which states that this spirit had already unconsciously penetrated many segments of society and continued to spread. BA, *Sammlung Schumacher*/367.

256. BA, R55/602, fol. 148, 150. Cf. similar reports cited in Fernschreiben No. 367 of Reichsleiter Keitel to Bormann (March 19, 1945): BA, *Sammlung Schumacher*/369. References are made to Mayen, Bingen, and the Rhine-Mosel area.

257. Letter to the RMVP of March 16, 1945: BA, R55/602, fol. 149.

258. Addendum to Rundschreiben 62/45 (February 8, 1945): "Auszug aus der Handmappe des an der Westfront gefallenen USA-Leutnants R. D. Underwood:" BA, NS6/vorl. 353.

259. Anordnung 98/45 of February 23, 1945: BA, NS6/vorl. 353. A few examples of expulsions and transfers are mentioned in the addendum to Bekanntgabe 61/45 of February 8, 1945: *ibid.*

260. BA, *Sammlung Schumacher*/366.

261. Notation for Pg. Walkenhorst by Dr. Metzner, March 8, 1945: *ibid.*

262. Rundschreiben 128/45 g. Rs. of March 10, 1945, concerning "Durchführung von Sonderaufgaben im Rücken des Feindes:" BA, NS6/vorl. 354.

263. Activity report No. 1 for the period March 8-14, 1945, by the deputy chief command X. A. K. IIa/W/Pro No. 39/45 GKdos. regarding action "MPA:" MGFA WO1-6/368. (It concerned a word-of-mouth propaganda campaign carried out in Hamburg with the help of a special section of soldiers). Applies to subsequent remarks.

264. Weekly activity report, head of propag. div., target date March 21, 1945: BA, R55/601, fol. 298.

265. *Ibid.*, fol. 296.

266. Wilfried von Oven, *Mit Goebbels bis zum Ende* (Buenos Aires, 1950), II, p. 267.

267. Weekly activity report by head of propaganda div., target date March 21, 1945: BA, R55/601, fol. 299.

268. *Ibid.*, fol. 386.

269. Sargent & Williamson, *op. cit.*, p. 521.

270. Shils & Janowitz, *loc. cit.*, p. 313.

271. See, for example, the report in the archives of Gute-Hoffnungshütte in Oberhausen: "Betrifft Kampflage and Besetzung von Oberhausen" (handwritten comment Napp-Zinn. Hist. Archiv May 22, 1945, NZ), sgd. Dr. Hilbert: HA/GHH No. 400,1016/3.

272. Cf. "Die Zeche Franz Haniel während den Kriegshandlungen in der Zeit vom 24. März bis 15. April," sgd. Buschmann; and "Bericht über den Verlauf einiger kritischer Tage in der Verkaufsanstalt II der Gutehoffnungshütte (Knappstrasse) kurz vor und nach der Besetzung Oberhausens durch die Amerikaner," of April 23, 1945, sgd. Hermann Holz: *ibid.* Cf. also a memorandum on the last days in the east by the Kreisleiter of Küstrin-Königsberg to Martin Bormann, dated April 5, 1945, in the Bericht vom Gaubefehlsstand in Potsdam: BA, *Sammlung Schumacher*/366.

273. Stellv. Generalkommando X A.K. II a/W Pr O No. 44/45 GKdos. Activity report No. 2 of March 22, 1945: MGFA WO1-6/368.

274. Report to the SD section, Stuttgart, of March 27, 1945: HStA Stuttgart, K 750/58.

275 25th report on "Sondereinsatz Berlin" of April 10, 1945: MGFA WO1-6/368. Cf. also the previous report of March 31, whose trend is a bit less pessimistic. Berghahn, "Meinungsforschung im Dritten Reich," *loc. cit.*, pp. 113-19.

276. Stellv. Generalkommando X. A. K. II a/W PrO. No. 49/45 GKdos. concerning action "MPA," activity report No. 4 of April 5, 1945: MGFA, WO1-6/368.

277. USNA T-77, microfilm 873 (OKW 2345), No. 5620871-620887.

278. NSDAP Parteikanzlei 8000171 Bo/UR: BA. R58/976.

279. Confidential—not for duplication, April 13, 1945: BA, ZSg101/42.

280. See the report by Gauleitung Bayreuth to the Party Chancellory, April 18, 1945, which states that a decisive turn of events was still expected on Hitler's birthday: BA, *Sammlung Schumacher*/368.

281. Cf. telephone messages by the deputy Gauleiter of Nuremberg, Holz, of April 16, 17: BA, *Sammlung Schumacher*/248.

282. See the *Tagesparole* of April 18, 1945: BA, ZSg 101/42, fol. 126.

283. *Ibid.*, fol. 127.

284. Berghahn, "Meinungsforschung im Dritten Reich," *loc. cit.*, p. 114.

285. Cf. Steinert, *op. cit.*, and Reimer Hansen, *Das Ende des Dritten Reiches. Die deutsche Kapitulation 1945* (Stuttgart, 1966).

286. Hugh R. Trevor-Roper, *The Last Days of Hitler* (London, 1947), p. 165 ff.

287. Steinert, *op. cit.*, p. 141.

288. "We didn't inquire as to why, we had no time to reflect and worry about the future; we knew about the enemy before us, the comrade next to us, and quite simply did our duty. How things really stood with our Fatherland, how few of us knew that! . . . ." Gerhard Boldt, *Die letzten Tage der Reichskanzlei* (Hamburg-Stuttgart, 1947), pp. 54-55. (Boldt was Guderian's adjutant).

289. *"Festung Breslau." Documenta obsidionis. 16. II. bis 6. V. 1945.* Editerunt praefatione et indicibus instruxerunt Karolus Jonca et Alfredus Konieczny (Warsaw, 1962), p. 266.

290. Folke Bernadotte, *Das Ende* (Zurich, 1945), pp. 17-87; Walter Schellenberg, *Memoiren*, ed. by Gita Petersen (Cologne, 1959), pp. 353-57 and 360-64; Felix Kersten, *Totenkopf und Treue. Heinrich Himmler ohne Uniform* (Hamburg, 1952), pp. 9-13, 244-46, 358-81.

291. Margret Boveri, *Tage des Überlebens. Berlin 1945* (Munich, 1968).

292. *Ibid.*, p. 63.

293. Führungshinweis des Stellv. Gauleiters Ost-Hannover, April·12, 1945: BA, NS Misch/1857.

294. "Haltung und Meinungsbildung der Bevölkerung:" MGFA, OKW/112.

295. Tagesmeldung No. 4: "Haltung und Meinungsbildung der Bevölkerung," May 7, 1945: *ibid.*
296. Tagesmeldung No. 7, May 8, 1945: *ibid.*
297. Nachrichtenbüro der Reichsregierung, Abt. Funkerfassung, No. 48, Blatt 15: May 22, 1945: *ibid.*
298. Cf. Erich Peter Neumann and Elisabeth Noelle, *Antworten. Politik im Kraftfeld der öffentlichen Meinung* (Allensbach/Bodensee, 1954), pp. 29 f., and 42 f.; cf. also *l'Express*, June 9-15, 1969, p. 69, interview by Michael Salomon with Elisabeth Noelle-Neumann, from which emerges that Hitler would still receive the attribute of great statesman from 40 per cent if he had not dragged the country into war.
299. Boveri, *op. cit.*, p. 29.

CONCLUSION

THE EXISTENCE of a *Publikumsmeinung* (public's opinion) in totalitarian states, assumed at the beginning of this study, has been substantiated for National Socialist Germany by the evidence presented. It seems fair to assert that the phenomena of *öffentliche Meinung* (public opinion) seen in democratic states resemble those of *Publikumsmeinung* in totalitarian states. Both systems have one, two or more segments of opinion, rumors, complex stereotypes, and rigid series. The opinions themselves are frequently "irresponsible, often harmfully self-confident, and changeable."[1] The widely held view that in totalitarian states opinion is conditioned almost exclusively by official propaganda also seems to be untenable. Numerous other sources of influence exist, particularly historical myths and images, which have proven extremely enduring. Then there are leading figures within primary and secondary groups, and above all the evidence of personal observation, which can often be in direct conflict with state propaganda. In the overall balance, however, it is undeniable that daily one-sided propaganda exercises a decisive influence over a wide range of opinion, all the more so as the level of education and the objective information of the masses are circumscribed. A survey concluded by the Institute for Public Research in October, 1952, revealed that almost two-thirds, 63 per cent, of the adult population of the Federal Republic could be classified as uninformed or underinformed. One quarter of the women questioned were unable to answer even one of the questions posed.[2] One cannot assume that an appreciably different degree of awareness existed in the Third Reich. This fact alone is startling for the light it sheds on the widespread ignorance, the stupidity, and the chronic indifference to politics which make it so easy for any active minority to gain power, provided it masters the keyboard of emotions to which every people is more or less attuned. This relative ignorance within the political sector is not an exclusively German phenomenon, but it applies more generally to problems of foreign policy in western democratic countries, where the degree of awareness on questions of domestic policy is higher.[3] For many totalitarian states and third world countries, results of such a poll should prove even more unfavorable.

Let us now turn to the three questions posed in the introduction. First, to what extent was German *Publikumsmeinung* differentiated, independent, or genuine, and to what extent was it uniform, manipulated, or directed?

If one surveys the period under examination, from September, 1939, to May, 1945, examples can be found in support of both sides of the argument. Contradictory and multi-dimensional opinions with a critical emphasis are exemplified particularly by views concerning the regime's social and church policies. Here a trend which already existed in the prewar period is intensified by privations and sacrifice during the war years. They combined with disappointment over the defeats of Stalingrad and Tunisia and with Mussolini's fall to produce a broad reversal of opinion in 1943. The pressure to fashion majority opinions made itself felt adversely if not dangerously for the regime in 1941, in contrast to developments during the years 1933 and 1938-39. The efficiency of the Nazi leadership, both in domestic and foreign affairs, was called into question by a majority of the population.

The decrease in space devoted to the conflict with the denominations in opinion reports of the last war years should not obscure the fact that the churches steadily gained in popularity and prestige, becoming the focal point for numerous criticisms of the Third Reich. As the horrors of war came closer to home, as impending death became a daily concern for every family, more and more people were in need of consolation and reassurance. Few Party officials were in a position to supply these; their much-criticized lifestyle contrasted sharply with that of church leaders. Clichés about Germanic heroes and the mysticism of the blood proved powerless against hopes for a hereafter and an eternal life. A chance for forgiveness of sins soothed tormented consciences more than exoneration in the name of an increasingly remote greater Germany. If the influence and activity of Christian churches occupied less space in the opinion reports of the final war years and thus also in our inquiry, which has focused on the substantive topics in the reports for the various phases of the war, this is principally because more dangerous developments threatened Hitler's Germany from outside and from within and diverted attention from this sector. The same applies to the provisioning of foodstuffs. From an objective standpoint it deteriorated rapidly during the last years, but less attention is paid to complaints and irritation concerning the food supply.

The reaction of youths and women[4] to Nazi reality is symptomatic of a general attitude on the part of the population. Only a small fraction of the teenagers developed a political consciousness: the vast majority blindly obeyed the commands and regulations of the Hitler Youth or took refuge in a youth league romanticism. The female population remained apolitical; displeasure was registered only in the form of complaints, a listlessness in employment, and an emphasis on amusement.

The working and middle classes remained divided. In each case only small organizations conducted underground opposition to the regime; the only real attempted overthrow was led by members of the former ruling elite. A great many workers, relatively well paid and supplied with bonuses, had largely assimilated into the middle class and apparently continued to support the regime at a point when the dominant element of the bourgeoisie and the peasantry had already distanced themselves from it or rejected it.

Both the opportunities and limitations of massive manipulation of opinion are most clearly evident in the stereotyped images of friend and foe. Here we confront the astonishing results of, as well as the far-reaching immunity to, the most tenacious propaganda efforts. Historically conditioned national images proved to be extraordinarily difficult to undermine. But where no collective experience existed, propaganda found it relatively easy to impart the desired images to the broad masses. However, where the opportunity existed for the development of independent attitudes and opinions, the artificially created pictures were demolished—and even discredited their originators. No amount of praise, however lavishly heaped on the Italian allies by Goebbels' opinion makers, could destroy the mistrust stemming from World War I. The fall of Mussolini and the surrender of the Axis partner were noted almost with satisfaction, since they confirmed the ingrained stereotype and left the average German with the pleasant feeling of having been smarter than the "little Doctor." The exact opposite applied to Japan, where the absence of a well-defined stereotype enabled Nazi propaganda—with some acrobatics over the race question—to project an image of the "Super-Teuton of the East," one which was to boomerang on its authors when these supermen came off better than the German Teuton.

Quite revealing, and decisive for certain political options in the postwar period, is the transformation of the stereotype of France. In the

Blitzkrieg against this arch-enemy, we see for the first and only time during World War II an atmosphere of lightheartedness; all hatred quickly dissipated after the shame of 1918 had been revenged. No amount of maneuvering by Goebbels could stem growing pro-French sympathies, intensified by years of occupation and a greater familiarity with French "savoir vivre"—in stark contrast to life in Nazi Germany. Ultimately a new wave of resentment and mounting indifference to the fate of this neighbor was unleashed when Germans, unaware of the deep bitterness and contempt harbored by Frenchmen against the conqueror, did not hear a responsive echo from the French side. This fluctuation in the image of France—with further variations within Germany between the traditionally more anglophile north and francophile south—found symbolic expression in the shift from an original admiration of Marshal Pétain to indifference and disapprobation based more on disappointment than on genuine antipathy.

The national stereotype of the Englishman also proved difficult to modify. There had been anti-English feeling during Wilhelm II's reign, as evidenced especially by Imperial Germany's naval policy; Anglo-German relations, however, were often inspired, on the German side, by a subliminal feeling of inner kinship and admiration which, like unrequited love, could suddenly turn to hatred. Hitler's fundamental international perspectives, his notion of the Germanic sister nation, should be interpreted as an expression of these currents. This friend-foe concept also largely governed the image of England held by the German public during World War II. After the September 3 declaration of war, a wave of disappointment broke, reinforced by the Third Reich's propaganda of an "encirclement policy"; but this was still far from the "claustrophobia"[6] experienced before and during the First World War because of the crucial role played by the pact with the Soviet Union. After some expressions of hatred, skillfully stimulated by propaganda, a kind of grudging admiration for the tenacity of the English emerged, reaching its high point after the failure of the war over Britain in the autumn of 1941. Then the intensification of the air war, especially the area bombardment of German cities as well as the low-level attacks by English fighters, unleashed that hatred which Goebbels' propaganda machine had tried in vain to ignite.

In the ensuing period there was a tendency to amalgamate the images of England and America, expressed in the more global term of Anglo-Saxon or Anglo-American, until the concept of a powerful USA as actual victor in the west increasingly emerged. The image of the American, who had quickly departed after World War I and disappeared from sight, was originally vague and diffuse, but near the end of the war took shape as the humanitarian antipode to Bolshevik terror. All of the Propaganda Minister's skills failed when confronted with compelling reality: American conquerors proved more correct and humane than Germany's own Wehrmacht or even the often cowardly and corrupt Party functionaries. In place of the hatred preached by National Socialism, a hope for decent treatment and an end to this unpopular war appeared. The image of America that had slowly evolved since the Allied landing in western Europe was deepened in the postwar period by the occupation and Berlin blockade and became a key factor in West Germany's new political orientation.

Most interesting but also most tragic is the development of the German view of Russia. Old fighters and ardent Nazis, impressed by the confrontations of the twenties, accepted the pact with Stalin only with extreme reservation and as a tactical maneuver. Rank and file Germans, inundated with anti-Bolshevik propaganda for years, were nevertheless more inclined to interpret this agreement positively because fear of a two-front war and of an onslaught from the east was more deeply rooted than ideological antipathy. Bismarck remained the ideal of the gifted statesman, which Hitler was not beginning to approach. The rupture of the agreement and the attack on Russia could only be made acceptable to the broad masses by using the argument of an inevitable military confrontation between Bolshevism and National Socialism and by playing on atavistic fears. Thus the picture of Asiatic "sub-humans" (*Untermenschen*) was incessantly drummed into the public. As early as the winter of 1941-42, however, cracks appeared in this artificial caricature, and doubt began to creep in as to its authenticity. Men who fought so doggedly for their fatherland and their political system, who were able to bring such military potential into play, could not operate exclusively under the lash of their commissars and be completely primitive. The daily contact with the eastern worker, who showed himself to be intelligent, technically talented, and likeable, caused the real breach in this carefully created image of the enemy. Collective stereotype and personal experience clashed increasingly, and despite all official propaganda efforts the fear of Bolshevism vanished, especially among certain strata of the working class and among those who had nothing more to lose as respect grew for the tremendous accomplishments of the eastern foe. The view began to spread that it was only the establishment—old and new—which had to fear for its existence, and not the mass of the working people. However, the Red Army's conduct on German soil painfully confirmed Goebbels' worst invectives concerning the "Asiatic hordes." Towards the end of the war this almost-vanished fear of eastern savagery, combined with the concept of a despotic Bolshevik system in comparison to which National Socialism seemed downright benign, emerged stronger than ever. The wretched mass of refugees became the vehicle for this terror and now had to atone vicariously for the Teutonic mania and German atrocities. Next to the repercussions of renewed totalitarian developments in East Germany, these people remained the strongest motive force of a rapidly spreading anti-Communism in West Germany during the postwar period.

Orchestrated collective stereotype and personal opinion also diverged frequently over the Jewish question. Even if the Jew was a popular and widely accepted cliché as the source of all failures—especially since his prowess and intelligence, with which he outmaneuvered many a German, were viewed with envy—almost every German knew what Hannah Arendt called his "first-rate Jew." People therefore welcomed economic discrimination but were prepared to intervene for their Jewish friends —as long as their own existence was not threatened. But in most cases it was. Thus began this deplorable period, the acknowledgment of which is so bitter that Germans still tend to suppress it.

The pictures of other peoples remained vague and unimportant. There were the courageous Finns, the not quite trustworthy Hungarians, and similar stereotypes. Interest in and understanding for these remained ephemeral, however, so that Nazi propaganda had a relatively easy time achieving desired results. Taken in its entirety, the outcome of National Socialist demoscopy confirms observations made by René Rémond as to the effective preferences of all peoples for certain countries and regions.[7]

The limitations of the manipulation of public opinion and its relative range of control become all the more evident in the problem of euthanasia, the Jewish question, the critique of Party leaders' lifestyles, even the military news service.

Indirect influence using the film "I accuse" and a pacifying word-of-mouth propaganda campaign by the NSDAP proved ineffectual in the face of honest human outrage over the administrative murder of the aged, the infirm, and the weak. Here the position of the churches unquestionably played a very important role in crystallizing opinion. The pressure of *Publikumsmeinung* was so great that Hitler called a halt to the action and only permitted its later continuation in closed, remote camps under the aegis of the SS. In the case of the organized murder of Jews, the reaction of public opinion at home and abroad was given far greater consideration. The chaotic executions in Poland and Russia were presented either as retaliation for crimes against ethnic Germans or as a response to partisan activity, whereby the Jews were deliberately declared from the beginning to be the principal enemy. Their "extermination" thus seemed like a modern variant of the concept of annihilation increasingly accepted since Clausewitz' time.[8] In the face of mounting opposition from the churches and the public, and massive counter-propaganda notwithstanding, Martin Bormann issued the statement in 1943 that the deportation of the Jews was purely for labor purposes in the east. With only a few exceptions, the public knew nothing about the organized gassings. If rumors to this effect emerged, the public relegated such incredible horrors to the realm of slander or simply refused to listen, in accordance with the mental process described by Freud, whereby perception is restricted to the desirable. We should also remember that during those years when the gassings reached greatest dimensions and news could have slipped through, the German population was itself exposed to severe terror tactics by enemy air raids, so that their receptivity to events beyond their immediate sphere of activity was significantly limited. In addition there was the fear and anxiety over the fate of loved ones in the field. The lot of the Jews thus interested only those elements of the population with personal friendly ties to Jews, or those who were always prepared to place humanism above the nation. The masses, engrossed in daily cares and mounting fear for their lives, hardly realized what was happening outside their narrow vocational and familial atmosphere. What was criticized above all was what could be personally observed and was regarded as unjust or scandalous. The best example is seen in the growing censure of the sumptuous lifestyle of many Party leaders and the undignified, luxurious living of functionaries and officers in occupied areas. The regime found itself forced to adopt sharp measures to counter such corruption if it wanted to retain a minimum of respect for its "accomplishments" among the population. If initial lapses could be excused as growing pains, it was clear that defects still existed and threatened the relationship of the Party to the Volk; leaders admitted that the goal of the NSDAP as the true elite of the people was still far off in 1942 and that the Party had to win over the nation as it had during the "period of struggle."

Yet national disintegration was prevented not only by intensified efforts by the Party and forced indoctrination and domestic terror, but by mounting danger from the outside. In times of external danger every social group undergoes a process of internal concentration—national cabinets and slogans of national unity are common manifestations. Domestic disputes and feuds are temporarily shelved in favor of what is perceived as a vital common defense. Such a process, which can be characterized by the motto attributed to the English, "my country, right or wrong," occurred in Germany from late autumn of 1943 to the spring of 1945. As an ideology, National Socialism played a diminishing role and was tolerated because it was German and because it advocated the preservation of Germany. The more it proved a failure in this regard, the more it was discredited. Had the Allies capitalized on the fall of Mussolini to treat Italy fairly and to offer a non-Nazi Germany reasonable peace terms, a majority of Germans in all probability would have welcomed such an initiative. The time was ripe for revolution. The only effective obstacle was the bond with Hitler. Only the disclosure of crimes committed under his direction could destroy the Hitlerian image. The strictest surveillance, isolation from the public, technical mishaps, and the heavy mental strain of undertaking a domestic revolt during a period of gravest external danger account for the fact that the active German resistance group missed the opportune moment for a coup d'état. From the autumn of 1943 on, when the fate of the former Italian ally became known, the masses eagerly grasped any straws of hope held out to them by the Nazi regime. This explains the tremendous success of the propaganda campaign about miracle weapons and the slogans of revenge —a critical situation in which the ordinary German was more concerned with surviving than with asking questions about who was responsible for this crisis; accounts could be settled later. The regime was invulnerable as long as it could keep alive the belief in a favorable decision for Germany, in a new technical weapon and in the ultimate superiority of the German soldier. Piecemeal proof of the V-1 and V-2 and finally the Ardennes offensive were instrumental in maintaining and stimulating such hopes.

Thus propaganda, which responded to hopes for a positive turn of events and an end to the war, was successful only because it conformed to a deep longing on the part of a population suffering helplessly under terror from the skies. When this became evidently just a final propaganda trick, a bluff by the regime, "defeatism [became] . . . a general public manifestation."[9] Even if it had been possible up to this time to sustain the belief of many Germans in the brilliant and decisive military capabilities of the German soldier, the Wehrmacht itself shattered this image: technical and numerical enemy superiority often made the bravest military act seem pointless. Ultimately, discipline and front-line solidarity became the Wehrmacht's strongest cohesive factor. And here confidence in the Führer survived the longest, if only to give some meaning to the fighting. This applied particularly to the eastern army and to the refugees, for whom no sacrifice seemed too great. However, there were signs of increasing dissolution and demoralization within noncombative units, particularly in rearguard areas and in the West. Goebbels' propaganda finally appealed only to those who had nothing more to lose and everything to gain: the small, hard core of ardent Nazis, those troops fighting against the Soviets, and the refugees.

In answer to the question of the genuineness of *Publikumsmeinung* or its absolute manipulation, we must say that perfection in influencing the population of the Third Reich was never achieved. The degree of manipulation was great in cases of a strong agreement between established stereotypes, popular longings, and political objectives—when there was a very low level of information without opportunity for personal observation or opinion. As soon as information, be it direct or indirect in nature, could be obtained independent of official news and propaganda sources, the possibility of manipulation and thus the credibility of propaganda in general fell. Just as injurious in the long run was the constant repetition of the same themes, which led not only to a dulling of the senses but to a downright aversion to official news policy and thus provoked either complete lack of interest in politics[10] or a more intense desire for an independent formulation of opinion. Simultaneously, prospects increased for the most absurd rumors and combinations. Every method of indoctrination proved difficult to sustain when confronted with firmly rooted, historically conditioned stereotypes.

Turning to the second question posed in the introduction, namely what factors influenced German *Publikumsmeinung*, it is clear that military events dominated in capturing public attention. What is striking is that this interest waned as quickly as it soared; as the tide turned, military events no longer diverted attention from everyday worries and the realities of daily routine. Socio-political and material discontent contrasted sharply with military victories and were only briefly neutralized. For an ardent Nazi, this grumbling, arising from daily events, stood in lamentable contrast to the "greatness of the times." The dimension which this discontent assumed in the SD reports of the early period, next to the activity of the churches, is partly a reflection of this disappointment. Dissatisfaction and unrest naturally existed, but they were hardly relevant politically, since social frustrations were cushioned by national satisfaction. The turning point was the Russian campaign. Domestic discontent could barely be balanced by external results. In 1943, disappointment over military failures brought socio-political unrest and criticism of the Party to a dangerous head; former enemies from the left and the right, combined with a disillusioned center, represented a potentially broad opposition to the regime. But this coalition collapsed again in the face of mounting air terror and the absence of an alternative to that struggle for national existence preached by the regime. Apathy and resignation were the result.

Aside from the "social" and "national" factors with strong economic tendencies and the constellation of opinion created by propaganda, there was a deep-seated syndrome arising from geographical location and sociological as well as historical development, which manifested itself in a certain stoicism toward authority and fate. If conjectural factors expressed themselves in the rapidly shifting mood from "jubilation to utter depression," the long range factors manifested themselves in "attitude." Perhaps these components are best illustrated in the behavior of Berliners. Was there anything significantly different between their perseverance during the blockade of 1948-49, which evoked admiration from a large part of the world, and the courage and patience during the hail of enemy bombs? The will to survive and the ability to cope with buffeting fate have only a limited connection with politics.

In a detailed study of the opinion phenomena, one thus arrives at a view different from that of the Nazis: it was not "Weltanschauung," resting on the guiding principle of blood ties, that determined the attitude with which the Volk endured the Nazi regime and the war. Stalin's words, that Hitlers come and go but the German people remain, touch on a far more profound truth, even though it was clouded by the distinction which separated Hitler from the reality of National Socialism in the eyes of the German people. This state which Hitler had created, the Party which carried him, and the ideology which justified them had long been repudiated by the people, while, in an almost schizophrenic manifestation, their author continued to be the object of adulation. "Trust in the Führer," the personification of the ego ideal, was the bond which, in addition to group consciousness, foreign and domestic pressures, and the hopes sustained by propaganda, held state and people together.

Hitler's influence on the behavior and thought of Germans must be rated high, even at the risk of once more placing him in the foreground in exoneration of individual and collective culpability. If one weighs him against factors such as national, social, and economic frustrations, the weight of tradition, education, and experience, then his is the role of catalyst or, even stronger, that of detonator. If the geographical situation, the economic configuration, the class structure of society, historical experience and resulting cultural peculiarities constituted the so-called infrastructure, the frustrations of the twenties are the conjectural element which compressed these factors into an explosive mixture. Hitler's charismatic, profoundly frustrated, and aggressive authoritarian personality represents the spark which ignited this highly inflammable mixture. That this constellation will recur in Germany is highly unlikely, since in both the eastern and the western sectors profound economic and social changes are in progress and have lifted the German question out of its isolation. Economic depressions and charismatic personalities should, therefore, hardly be in a position again to bring about an analogous development.

In this connection, Dahrendorf's observation that it was Hitler who first effected that transformation of German society that permitted a free, democratic form of government to function has to be taken up once more and rejected. The Third Reich neither destroyed the old social structure nor extinguished class consciousness. To argue the opposite would be easier. The bourgeoisie remained as committed to their ideals and habits, after brief enthusiasm for the novelty which the Nazi regime seemed to represent, as did the class-conscious workers. Though many were seduced for a time by slogans of consensus and nationalism, the realities of everyday Nazi life soon taught them that basically nothing had changed other than the fact that the citizen had less power than before. Even though Hitler styled himself as the spokesman for the lower classes,—for example the "poor worm," as he characterized the simple soldier,—though he promised everyone a three-room dwelling and garden, improving the lot of the poor was far down on his list of priorities. Hitler never regarded himself as representative of a class, only of the nation. Egalitarian utopias were foreign to him. On the contrary, he had elitist ideas which were based not on traditional privileges but on ostensible racial factors with corresponding specific inherent abilities. But even Hitler had to admit to himself that the German Volk "represents no racial unity but rather a racial conglomerate."[11] For him the value of a nation lay in its "racial kernels," and the duty of the government was to employ everyone in proper accordance with his abilities based on his racial assessment. The top positions naturally fell to members of the Nordic race, to which he ascribed a "constructive" and especially an aggressive disposition, while the basic Slavic race, in his view, was musically inclined. Intermarriage of the two could produce, so he thought, great composers such as Beethoven, Wagner, and Bruckner.

For Hitler only one thing was determining: "That we gradually bring each racial kernel to the place in our community where it seems most suitable for the work required at that place." Hitler's concept was therefore a variant of the Saint-Simonian maxim, built on a racial foundation, according to which everyone is employed on the basis of his abilities and paid according to his needs, a formula which underwent the most diverse modifications at the hands of nineteenth-century utopian socialists[12] and reappeared with Lenin. Like Lenin, Hitler operated on the premise that only a minority in any nation is fit for political leadership. In his biologically fixated world scheme it had to come from an order of both the strong and the warrior, since only these had a chance to survive. Not everyone was to become part of this new world order, "only a specific kernel from the Volk, namely the kernel possessing iron and steel; the others I didn't want." He emphasized his preference for fighters over intellectuals and the bourgeois, but these fighters were not to be dull and brutal peasants, but rather rational and deliberate warriors. Terror was not a mindless instrument; it required intellect and judgment. The military instrument was for him nothing more than "spiritualized terror." "The soldier especially must understand that terror can only be broken by terror and nothing else." It was this concept which lay at the root of warfare in the east and the creation of "political officers."

But instead of an order of brilliant warriors, the NSDAP's leadership corps was a motley crew of dull troopers, frustrated petty bourgeoisie, and half-educated dreamers. Highly qualified men were a rarity in the first generation of National Socialists. To carry out his national program, Hitler was therefore forced to fall back on those classes with proven abilities, and the former elite offered its services. It is typical that Hitler, for example, admiringly stressed the homogeneity of the English governing elite. In it he saw the product of talent and training which he had in mind for a future Nazi establishment. Collaboration with those prominent in the economy and with the heads of the Wehrmacht thus reflected not only the opportunism of the early hours but also the conviction that the right man must be assigned to the right place. However, as soon as his partner showed signs of weakness, Hitler jumped in and assumed the post himself or gave it to his deputies. In this manner many a former pliable bastion was penetrated, but the actual social structure and regional peculiarities remained and proved extraordinarily resistant.

A comparison between the main geographical electoral centers in 1933 and in the postwar period in the Federal Republic reveals amazing continuities of the left, right, and rural particularities. One must, of course, take into account advancing industrialization and its effects, as well as the existence of a left wing within the CDU, a right wing within the SPD, the non-existence of the KPD, and the large numbers of displaced persons, in order to discover this constant in opinion centers right up to the present day in the west. In Hitler's state, plurality of opinion, particularism, and consequent inevitable antagonisms were resolved only briefly in a national intoxication and in the case of extreme threat from outside. The survival of the old social structure and potent regionalism, conditioned by the lateness of national unification and an industrial revolution directed from above, stands in strange contrast to the longing for an end to this diversity (to what extent a new totalitarian system, elimination of the old elite's power and advancing industrialization have produced *real* integration in the East is difficult to say). For many, Hitler was—and is—regarded as the man who brought order to this confusion.

But in actuality, Hitler neither wanted to, nor did, eliminate pluralism in society. Uniformity only applied to the political sphere, not in the interest of a class but rather that of a national elite based on "racial" superiority. Hitler's utopia foundered. And it is not Hitler's Reich that caused both a social and political transformation. On the contrary, a total catastrophe was necessary to initiate a reorientation which is still far from completed. This slow transformation of German society now underway cannot be explained in terms of an indigenous German development but rather as the consequence of two universal historical developments: industrialization with its inherent equalizing and levelling tendencies, and the incorporation of Germany into two ideologically hostile blocs. The German "contribution" to the existence of a largely permeable and democratic, pluralistic society in the West remains relatively modest, as does the socialist, totalitarian system in the East and its at least outwardly egalitarian society. Political immaturity continues to prevail in some areas of public life.

There remains the answer to the last question: what was the extent of the influence exerted by public opinion in the Third Reich? We have seen that Hitler's decision to wage war against Poland and the idea of war *per se* were largely unpopular in Germany, and that the depressed population received grudgingly the decision made by the head of state and supreme commander of the Wehrmacht. Acceptance of the war and an aggressive policy were facilitated, however, by propaganda which rationalized the war as a seemingly necessary "police action" in response to Polish "atrocities" and by a strong current of opinion favoring a revision of the eastern boundaries fixed by Versailles. Most, like Hitler, also anticipated a short, localized campaign. This miscalculation of British intentions and resolve plunged German into a world war. The influence of German *Publikumsmeinung* on this expansion of the war was nil. In this area—that of foreign policy, especially in regard to the decision between war and peace—the impotence of the public in totalitarian systems is most apparent. While limited opportunities for influencing the domestic scene through personal pressure, the creation of factions within the state party, demonstrations, whisper campaigns, passive and active resistance, etc., continued to exist as a reflection of diverse social and political interests, the foreign policy domain remained the absolute prerogative of the leadership. The public played no role here, even though decisions were ostensibly made in its name. Little difference exists here between the practices of the "ancien régime" and those of totalitarian systems.

In western-oriented democracies the ultimate decision on war and peace also rests with the executive. But its decisions can only be made in harmony with broad segments of the organized and unorganized public. Roosevelt's preparation of Americans for entry into the war, his fight against isolationism, is one of the best examples in support of this thesis.[13] Cases also exist where the pressure of public opinion has forced a government to adopt or abandon a policy. Chamberlain's negotiations with Soviet Russia for an alliance in the summer of 1939 resulted from pressure by Parliament and the press in Great Britain.[14] By contrast, the Hoare-Laval pact of late 1935 could not be implemented because of public outrage.[15] There are numerous examples illustrating the potentialities and limitations of public influence on government policy. Two more revealing examples from the recent past are the decisive role played by public opinion in the Saar in reorienting French policy regarding this territory,[16] and Soviet disregard of the Czech public will, confirming the impotence of public opinion in the socialist bloc.

The increasing acceptance of public opinion polls, the results of which influence more and more the kinds of programs and positions adopted by the major parties, is the best index of the mounting influence of public opinion—and not only in western democracies. More and more states in all corners of the globe use open or secret opinion surveys. This fact is in itself, as J. B. Duroselle observed, "a historical phenomenon."[17] In parliamentary regimes as in totalitarian states, the aim of the leadership is to achieve as broad a consensus as possible. The methods used vary considerably and the result is seldom perfect.

The limitations of manipulating public mood and attitude were summed up previously. Beyond them is where the possibilities of *Publikumsmeinung* begin. The Germans did not become aware of the power inherent in public opinion and neglected to employ this weapon against the abuses of an increasingly intolerant system. Their expressions of displeasure usually occurred within the margins tolerated by the regime and seldom overstepped the dimension referred to by Goebbels as the "faeces of the soul."[18] In those few cases where criticism of the regime's policies assumed more violent proportions, Hitler and his cadre were forced either to halt or to moderate and conceal their intentions and crimes.

Blind trust in Hitler, lack of imagination, indifference, and ignorance of the most elementary rules of politics were the essential reasons why such protests did not occur more frequently or with more direction. But as long as a people does not understand what a powerful weapon it has in *Publikumsmeinung*, as long as no effort is made to raise its level of information as much as possible in order to apply its criticism more pointedly and effectively, the people will remain a prisoner of the various manipulative processes, from disguised seduction to massive indoctrination.

NOTES

1. Hofstätter, *Psychologie der öffentlichen Meinung*, p. 15.
2. Neumann and Noelle, *Antworten*, p. 85.
3. Cf., for example, Gabriel A. Almond, *The American People and Foreign Policy* (New York, 1960), p. 138, who distinguishes between the general public, the attentive public, and the informed public. Or, Paul F. Lazarsfeld, Bernhard Berelson and Hazel Gaudet, *The People's Choices: How the voter makes up his mind in a presidential campaign* (New York, 1960); or Pierre de Bie, "Quelques aspects psychologiques du Beneluz," *Bulletin International des Sciences Sociales*, II, No. 3 (1951), pp. 582-92.
4. In his psychology of social classes, Henry Lefebvre rightly emphasizes that the general psychic class and family characteristics are reflected in the social role and attitude of the woman. "Psychologie des classes sociales," *Traité de sociologie*, II, (1960), p. 379.
5. Cf. Pauline R. Anderson, *Background of anti-English Feeling in Germany, 1890-1902* (New York, 1967).
6. Fritz Stern, "Bethmann Hollweg und der Krieg: Die Grenzen der Verantwortung," *Recht und Staat in Geschichte und Gegenwart* (Tübingen, 1968), No. 351/352, p. 12.
7. Rémond calls this phenomenon, not very aptly, "sentimental geography:" "Options idéologiques et inclinations affectives en politique étrangère," *L'élaboration de la politique étrangère*, published by Léo Hamon (Paris, 1969), pp. 85-93.
8. Cf. the introduction by Alfred von Schlieffen to the 8th edition of General von Clausewitz' *Vom Krieg* (Berlin, 1914), p. v.
9. See *supra*, p. 309.
10. These kinds of reactions are also known to Soviet leaders. In late 1953, Khrushchev tried to put an end to the monotony of newspapers. During the following years of 'liberalization,' criticism of the uniform news policy took on major proportions. In 1956 and 1957 one could even read in *Pravda* that Soviet newspapers were "insipid, without life, deathly boring and difficult to read." *La presse dans les Etats authoritaires* (Zurich, 1959), p. 15.
11. "Ansprache des Führers an die Feldmarschälle und Generale am 27. 1. 1944 in der Wolfsschanze:" BA, *Sammlung Schumacher*/365. Also for subsequent quotations.
12. Sebastien Charlety, *Histoire du Saint-Simonisme (1825-1864)*, 2nd ed. (Paris, 1931); and Harry W. Laidler, *History of Socialism. A comparative survey of Socialism, Communism, Trade Unionism, Cooperation, Utopianism and other systems of Reform and Reconstruction* (London, 1968).
13. William Langer & Sarell Everett Gleason, *The Challenge to Isolation, 1937-1940* (New York, 1964); and *The Undeclared War, 1940-1941* (New York, 1953). Wayne S. Cole, *America First*. The battle against intervention 1940-1941 (Madison, 1953).
14. William R. Rock, "Grand alliance or daisy chain. British opinion and policy toward Russia. April-August 1939," *Power, Public Opinion and Diplomacy. Essays in Honor of Eber Malcolm Carroll* (Durham, N.C., 1959), pp. 297-337.
15. Cf. Jean-Baptiste Duroselle, "Der Einfluss der Massen auf die Aussenpolitik," *Masse und Demokratie* (Zurich, 1957), pp. 85 f.

16. Cf. Jacques Freymond, *Die Saar 1945-1955* (Munich, 1961).
17. J. B. Duroselle, "De l'utilisation des sondages d'opinion en histoire et en science politique," I.N.S.O.C., 1957, No. 3.
18. *Goebbels Tagebücher*, p. 171.

BIBLIOGRAPHY

DOCUMENTS

a) UNPUBLISHED

I. *Reports on Public Mood and Attitude*

1. The most important holdings are those of the *Sicherheitsdienst* in the Reichssicherheitshauptamt: "Berichte zur innerpolitischen Lage," "Meldungen aus dem Reich" and "SD-Berichte zu Inlandfragen" located in the Federal Archives (Bundesarchiv), Koblenz, R58, No. 144-194.[1] Numbers 1094, 1095, and 1096 in holdings R58 include photocopies of the RSHA's annual report for 1938, and No. 717 has the first-quarter report for 1939.

In terms of content the following sources also apply: "Zusammenstellungen von Meldungen aus den SD-(Leit)-Abschnittsbereichen," the "Meldungen über die Entwicklung in der öffentlichen Meinungsbildung" and a series of reports from SD-Hauptaussenstellen to be found in BA, NS6, as well as special reports by Kaltenbrunner, head of the RSHA, to Reichsleiter Schwarz in BA, NS1; there are also the reports of SD section Leipzig in the Imperial War Museum (Foreign Documents Center), London, holding 271/46 CIOS 4233 and FD 332/46, as well as those unpublished reports of various SD-Unterabschnitte and SD-Aussenstellen compiled by the British Foreign Office shortly after the war, contained in *Aus deutschen Urkunden 1939-1945*;[2] then the reports of SD sections Frankfurt and Koblenz for the year 1944 in the Hessische Hauptstaatsarchiv, Wiesbaden, Zug. 68/67; two reports of the SD-Leitstelle Stuttgart and the Rundschreiben of the SD-Leitstelle Stuttgart, Hauptstaatsarchiv Stuttgart, holding K750, and the reports on the "Stimmungsmässigen Auswirkungen des Anschlages auf den Führer" published in *Spiegelbild einer Verschwörung*.[3]

2. A further block of materials, though far more fragmentary, is composed of the reports of Party officials from the various regions of the Reich, especially the "Auszüge aus Berichten der Gaue u. a. Dienststellen" compiled by the

345

Party Chancellory, of which only those for January-July, 1943, exist, thus raising the question whether they could not be compiled regularly because of arbitrariness on the part of some Gaue and were possibly only prepared periodically; then there are fragmentary holdings of situation reports by the most diverse Nazi organizations. All these documents are located in BA: NS Misch, NS6, NS22 and NS5 I. A few supplementary documents are located in the Niedersächsische Staatsarchiv, 277-10/2, the Bischöfliche Ordinariatsarchiv, Würzburg, *Nachlass Leier*, and the Staatsarchiv Bamber, *Rep. M* 31, *Rep.* K 9/*Verz.* XV and *Rep.* K 17/XI.

3.   Aside from the reports of the Sicherheitsdienst, Gauleiter, Kreisleiter, and various Nazi organizations, there are three further significant groups of documents relevant for studying public opinion in the Third Reich:

A.   The reports of Oberlandesgerichtspräsidenten and Generalstaatsanwälte to the Reich Justice Ministry from 1940 to the beginning of 1945 in BA: R22, No. 3355-3389.

B.   The compilations by the head of the propaganda division in the Reich Ministry for Propaganda and Public Enlightenment of activity reports of Reich propaganda offices, which not only referred to the effects of propaganda in all Gaue but also reported on the mood of the population. The Bundesarchiv has the reports from March 15, 1943, to March 21, 1945, as well as a few isolated reports and additional information in R55, No. 600-603 and 620.

C.   Monthly reports of Regierungspräsidenten for the Bavarian governing districts of Upper Bavaria, Lower Bavaria, Upper Palatinate, Palatinate, Swabia and Neuburg, Lower Franconia, Central Franconia, and Upper Franconia for the period from July, 1937, to September, 1943, supplemented by the monthly reports of the police department of Augsburg from October, 1934, to October, 1943, located in the Bavarian Hauptstaatsarchiv, Division II (Geheimes Staatsarchiv), Munich, MA 106671, 106673, 106674, 106676, 106678, 106679, 106681, 106683. In addition, a few reports of the Regierungspräsident in Regensburg for the years 1943 and 1944 are located in the Bundesarchiv, NS19/246. The reports by Bavarian Regierungspräsidenten were supplemented by individual files of the secret state police and a few Landrat offices from divisions I (Allgemeines Staatsarchiv) and V (Staatsarchiv für Oberbayern) of the BHStA.

4.   Further information on public opinion can be found in typical individual remarks contained in letters, notes, or diaries. Here the following were drawn upon: BA, R54, containing the Office of the Reich President, later Präsidialkanzlei, and the previously mentioned R55, No. 570-599, 610, and 618, Reich Propaganda Ministry; the highly personal diary notes of Paula Stuck von Reznicek *Slg.* 106/Bd. 19, located in the Military Archives, and individual reports of the last days of the war from the Historical Archive of Gute-Hoffnungshütte as well as printed diaries and letters.[4]

5.   There are also some reports on the mood in the holdings of the Wehrmacht, WO1-5 and WO1-6 of the Militärgeschichtliches Forschungsamt, now the Militärarchiv of the Bundesarchiv. Add to these the holdings H34/1 with censor reports about the views of military personnel concerning the attempt on Hitler's life, July 20, 1944, and III W 129 containing a situation report of the head of

the NS-Führungsstab of the Army from the western front in March, 1945. See also the documents of Schriftgutverwaltung Himmler, BA, NS19 and *Sammlung Schumacher*.

II. *Propaganda Measures and Control Tactics of the Nazi Regime*

1. The most revealing source is that of the ministerial conferences of the Reich Propaganda Minister, published and edited by Willi A. Boelcke,[5] effectively amplified by the "Vertrauliche Informationen," "Sonderinformationen" (Tagesparolen des Reichspressechefs) collected by the former main editor of the *Weilburger Tageblatt*, Oberheitmann. The collection belongs to the Institut für Publizistik in Münster and forms holdings ZSg 109 of the Bundesarchiv. In addition, there are the "Anweisungen" from the press conferences, "Informationsberichte" and "Vertrauliche Informationen" collected by the former editor of "Korrespondenz Brammer" in BA ZSg 101, and the "Sammlung Sänger," notes by journalists of the *Frankfurter Zeitung* until 1943 in ZSg 102 as well as the economic press conferences (Nadler) from 1939 to 1942 in BA, ZSg 115.

2. Besides the activity of the Propaganda Ministry, there was that of the NSDAP in the area of "public enlightenment," found in BA, ZSg 3 with a wealth of material. Very illuminating is the Information of the Party Chancellory to all Gauleitungen as of January 30, 1941, called "Vertrauliche Informationen" (No. 1620-1624 and 2095) because it frequently presented a reaction to opinion reports. See also the educational material (No. 420-425, 432, and 433), "Der Schulungsbrief," edited by the Reich Organization Leader (No. 1537-1540), the "Mitteilungen zur Weltanschaulichen Lage" (No. 3109, 1688-1692) and the holdings, following the reorganization, in NS Misch, NS22 and NS6 (Stellvertreter des Führers/Partei-Kanzlei der NSDAP, No. 228-232, 329-358, 406-408, 409-412).

3. For propaganda and censor activity by the Wehrmacht, see holdings WO1-6, and isolated information in WO1-5 as well as III W 129 and OKW 1652, 1654, 820 of MGFA, i.e., BA/MA, and copies in BA, NS6.

Also used as supplement and annotation: a few files of R58, *Sammlung Schumacher*, Schriftgutverwaltung Himmler, NS 19, the holdings WI/IF 5.1043 and 5.357 of the Military Archiv, FD 4809/45 file 2 (Übersicht über die wirtschaftliche Gesamtlage, aus Görings Dienststelle des Vierjahresplanes, vom 28. 2. 1940 bis 20. 8. 1941) in the Imperial War Museum, London, the *Rep.* 501/IV F, 12 of the Institut für Zeitgeschichte, Munich, as well as a few files of *Inland ID*, *Inland II A/B* and *Inland IIG* of the Political Archives of the Foreign Office, Bonn.

b) PUBLISHED

1. *Official*

Actes et Documents du Saint Siège relatifs à la Seconde guerre Mondiale. 4 Vols. Città del Vaticano, Libreria editrice Vaticana, 1965-67.

Akten zur Deutschen Auswärtigen Politik 1918-1945. Series D: 1937-45. Baden-Baden: Imprimerie Nationale; and Frankfurt a.M.: Keppler Verlag, 1950 on, vol. I-XI.

Auswärtiges Amt. *Dokumente zur englisch-französischen Politik der Kriegsausweitung.* Berlin: Zentralverlag der NSDAP, 1940 (1940 No. 4).

Auswärtiges Amt. *Dokumente zur Vorgeschichte des Krieges.* Berlin: Carl Heymanns Verlag, 1939 (1939, No. 2).

Auswärtiges Amt. *Weitere Dokumente zur Kriegsausweitungspolitik der Westmächte. Die Generalstabsbesprechungen Englands und Frankreichs mit Belgien und den Niederlanden.* Berlin: Zentralverlag der NSDAP, 1940 (1940, No. 5).

Auswärtiges Amt. *Urkunden zur letzten Phase der deutschpolnischen Krise.* Berlin: Carl Heymanns Verlag, 1939 (1939, No. 1).

Die Berichte des Oberkommandos der Wehrmacht. 3 vols. Berlin: Wiking Verlag, 1941-1943.

Aus Deutschen Urkunden 1933-1945 (compiled by the Foreign Office in 1945, not for publication).

Documents on German Foreign Policy 1918-1945. Series D. Washington: U.S. Printing Office.

In acht Kriegswochen 107mal gelogen! Dokumente über Englands Nachrichtenpolitik im gegenwärtigen Kriege. Compiled by Fritz Reipert. Zentralverlag der NSDAP, n.d.

Nazi-Soviet Relations 1939-1941. Documents from the Archives of the German Foreign Office, ed. by James Sontag and James Stuart Beddie. Washington: Department of State, 1948.

The Trial of the Major War Criminals before the International Military Tribunal. Nuremberg: November 14, 1945, to October 1, 1946. Published in 1947, 42 vols.

U.S. Strategic Bombing Survey. *The effects of Strategic Bombing on German Morale.* Washington: Government Printing Office, 1947.

Verhandlungen des Reichstags. *Stenographische Berichte.* Berlin: Reichsdruckerei.

2. Documentary Publications

Anatomie des Krieges: neue Dokumente über die Rolle des deutschen Monopolkapitals bei der Vorbereitung und Durchführung des Zweiten Weltkrieges. Edited with introduction by Dietrich Eichholtz and Wolfgang Schumann. Berlin: VEB Deutscher Verlag der Wissenschaften, 1969.

Archiv der Gegenwart. Vienna: Siegler Verlag, n.d.

Die Beziehungen zwischen Deutschland und der Sowjetunion 1939-1941. Aus den Archiven des Auswärtigen Amtes und der Deutschen Botschaft in Moskau. Edited by Dr. Alfred Seidl. Tübingen: H. Laupp'sche Buchhandlung, 1959.

Die Briefe Pius XII. an die deutschen Bischöfe 1939-1944. Edited by Burkhart Schneider. Mainz: Matthias Grünewald Verlag, 1961 (Publication of the

Kommission für Zeitgeschichte bei der Katholischen Akademie in Bavaria, editor Konrad Repgen, series A. Sources, vol. 4).

Domarus, Max. *Hitler, Reden und Proklamationen 1932-1945.* 2 vols. With commentary by a German contemporary. Munich: Süddeutscher Verlag, 1965.

Dokumente der Deutschen Politik. Der Kampf gegen den Osten 1941. Prepared by Dr. Hans Volz. Berlin: Junker und Dünnhaupt Verlag, 1944 (Series: Das Reich Adolf Hitlers).

Dokumente der Deutschen Politik von 1848 bis zur Gegenwart. 8 vols. Edited by Johannes Hohlfeld. Berlin: Dokumenten Verlag Dr. Herbert Wendler Cie., 1951-1956.

Entscheidungsschlachten des Zweiten Weltkrieges. Edited by Hans-Adolf Jacobsen and Jürgen Rohwer. Frankfurt a.M., 1960.

"Festung Breslau." Documenta obsidionis. 16. II.-6. V. 1945. Editerunt praefatione et indicibus instruxerunt Karolus Jonca et Alfredus Konieczny. Warsaw: Panstowe Wydawnictwo Naukowe, 1962.

Gewalt und Gewissen. Willi Graf und die "Weisse Rose." A Documentation by Klaus Vielhaber in cooperation with Hubert Hanisch and Anneliese Knoop-Graf. Freiburg: Herder Verlag, 1964.

Heyen, Franz Josef. *Nationalsozialismus im Alltag. Quellen zur Geschichte des Nationalsozialismus vornehmlich im Raum Mainz-Koblenz-Trier.* Boppard am Rhein: Harald Boldt Verlag, 1967.

Hitlers Weisungen für die Kriegsführung 1939-1945. Dokumente des Oberkommandos der Wehrmacht. Edited by Walter Hubatsch. Frankfurt a.M.: Bernard and Graefe Verlag für Wehrwesen, 1962.

Jacobsen, Hans-Adolf. *Der Zweite Weltkrieg. Grundzüge der Politik und Strategie in Dokumenten.* Frankfurt a.M.: Fischer Bücherei, 1965.

Die kirchliche Lage in Bayern nach den Regierungspräsidentenberichten 1933 bis 1943. I. Regierungsbezirk Oberbayern; II. Regierungsbezirk Ober- und Mittelfranken. Compiled by Helmut Witetschek. Mainz: Matthias Grünewald Verlag, 1966 and 1967 (Publication of the Kommission für Zeitgeschichte bei der Katholischen Akademie in Bavaria, editor Konrad Repgen, vols. 3 and 8).

Kriegspropaganda 1939-1941. Geheime Ministerkonferenzen im Reichspropagandaministerium. Edited by Willi A. Boelcke. Stuttgart: Deutsche Verlagsanstalt, 1966.

Krause, Ilse. *Die Schuman-Egert-Kresse-Gruppe. Dokumente und Materialien des illegalen antifaschistischen Kampfes (Leipzig, 1943-1945).* East Berlin: Dietz-Verlag, 1960.

Kriegsbriefe gefallener Studenten 1939-1945. Edited by Walter Bähr and Dr. Hans W. Bähr. Tübingen: Rainer Wunderlich Verlag Hermann Leins, 1952.

Kriegstagebuch des Oberkommandos der Wehrmacht (Wehrmachtsführungsstab) 1940-1945. 4 vols. By Helmuth Geiner and Percy Ernst Schramm. Frankfurt a.M.: Bernard and Graefe Verlag für Wehrwesen, 1961-1965.

Lagebesprechungen im Führerhauptquartier. Protokollfragmente aus Hitlers militärischen Konferenzen 1942-1945. Edited by Helmut Heiber. Munich: Deutscher Taschenbuch Verlag, 1963.

Letzte Briefe aus Stalingrad. Gütersloh: Sigbert Mohn Verlag, n.d.

Die letzten hundert Tage. Das Ende des Zweiten Weltkrieges in Europa und Asien. Edited by Hans Dollinger. Munich, Vienna, Basel: Desch-Verlag, 1965.

Der Luftkrieg über Deutschland 1939-1945. Deutsche Berichte und Pressestimmen des neutralen Auslandes. Based on the "Dokumenten deutscher Kriegsschaden" published by the Bundesminister für Vertriebene, Flüchtlinge und Kriegsgeschädigte, compiled and introduced by Erhard Klöss. Munich: Deutscher Taschenbuch Verlag, 1963.

Meldungen aus dem Reich. Auswahl aus den geheimen Lageberichten des Sicherheitsdienstes der SS 1939-1944. Edited by Heinz Boberach. Neuwied: Luchterhand Verlag, 1965.

Der Nationalsozialismus. Dokumente 1933-1945. Edited by Walther Hofer. Frankfurt a.M.: Fischer Bücherei, 1957.

Die Niederlage 1945. Aus dem Kriegstagebuch des Oberkommandos der Wehrmacht. Edited by Percy Ernst Schramm. Munich: Deutscher Taschenbuch Verlag, 1962.

Picker, Henry. *Hitlers Tischgespräche im Führerhauptquartier 1941/42.* New edition by Percy Ernst Schramm in cooperation with Andreas Hillgruber and Martin Vogt. Stuttgart: Seewald Verlag, 1963.

Poliakov, Léon, and Josef Wulf. *Das Dritte Reich und seine Denker.* Berlin: arani Verlag, 1959.

Poliakov, Léon, and Josef Wulf. *Das Dritte Reich und seine Diener.* Berlin: arani Verlag, 1956.

Poliakov, Léon, and Josef Wulf. *Das Dritte Reich und die Juden.* Berlin: arani Verlag, 1955.

Reichsführer! Briefe an und von Himmler. Edited by Helmut Heiber. Stuttgart: Deutsche Verlags-Anstalt, 1968.

Spiegelbild einer Verschwörung. Die Kaltenbrunner-Berichte an Bormann und Hitler über das Attentat vom 20. Juli 1944. Geheime Dokumente aus dem ehemaligen Reichssicherheitshauptamt. Published by the Archiv Peter für historische und zeitgeschichtliche Dokumentation. Stuttgart: Seewald Verlag, 1961.

Staatsmänner und Diplomaten bei Hitler. Vertrauliche Aufzeichnungen über Unterredungen mit Vertretern des Auslandes 1939-1941. Edited with commentary by Andreas Hillgruber. Frankfurt: Bernard and Graefe Verlag für Wehrwesen, 1967.

Volksopposition im Polizeistaat. Gestapo- und Regierungsberichte 1934-1936. Edited by Bernhard Vollmer. Stuttgart: Deutsche Verlags-Anstalt, 1957 (Quellen und Darstellungen zur Zeitgeschichte, vol. 2).

"Wollt ihr den totalen Krieg?" Die geheimen Goebbels-Konferenzen 1939-1943. Edited by Willi A. Boelcke. Stuttgart: Deutsche Verlags-Anstalt, 1967.

1939-1945. Der Zweite Weltkrieg in Chronik und Dokumenten. Edited by Hans-Adolf Jacobsen. Darmstadt: Wehr- und Wissen-Verlagsgesellschaft, 1959.

3.   *Writings of leading National Socialists*

Hitler, Adolf. *Mein Kampf.* Munich: Zentralverlag der NSDAP, 1942 (ed. 733-741).
Hitlers Zweites Buch. Ein Dokument aus dem Jahre 1928. Stuttgart: Deutsche Verlags-Anstalt, 1961.
Rosenberg, Alfred. *Der Mythus des 20. Jahrhunderts. Eine Wertung der seelisch-geistigen Gestaltenkämpfe unserer Zeit.* Munich: Hoheneichen-Verlag, 1933 (11th ed.).

4.   *Diaries, Memoirs, Notes*

Andreas-Friedrich, Ruth. *Schauplatz Berlin. Ein deutsches Tagebuch.* Munich: Rheinsberg Verlag Georg Lentz, 1962.
Bernadotte, Folke. *Das Ende.* Zurich, New York: Europa-Verlag, 1945. Published in English as *The Curtain Falls,* 1945.
Boldt, Gerhard. *Die letzten Tage der Reichskanzlei.* Hamburg-Stuttgart: Rowohlt Verlag, 1947. Published in English: *In the Shelter with Hitler,* London: 1948.
Boveri, Margret. *Tages des Überlebens.* Berlin 1945. Munich: Piper and Co. Verlag, 1968.
Choltitz, Dietrich von. *Soldat unter Soldaten. Die deutsche Armee in Frieden und Krieg.* Constance, Zurich, Vienna: Europa-Verlag, 1957.
Delmer, Sefton. *Die Deutschen und ich.* Hamburg: Nannen Verlag, 1962. From the 2 vol. *Autobiography:* 1. *Trailsinister* and 2. *Black boomerang.* London: Secker and Warburg, 1961-62.
Dietrich, Otto. *12 Jahre mit Hitler.* Munich: Isar-Verlag, 1955. Published in English: *The Hitler I Knew.* London: Methuen, 1957.
Der Generalquartiermeister. Briefe und Tagebuchaufzeichnungen des Generalquartiermeisters des Heeres, General d. Art. Eduard Wagner, mit Beiträgen früherer Mitarbeiter. Munich, Vienna: Olzog-Verlag, 1963.
Goebbels Tagebücher aus den Jahren 1942 bis 1943. Edited by Louis P. Lochner. Zurich: Atlantis-Verlag, 1948. In English as *The Goebbels Diaries 1942-1943.* Westport, Conn.: Greenwood Press, 1970.
Granzow, Klaus. *Tagebuch eines Hitlerjungen 1943-1945.* Bremen: Carl Schünemann Verlag, 1965.
Halder, Franz. *Kriegstagebuch.* 3 vols. Edited by Hans-Adolf Jacobsen. Stuttgart: W. Kohlhammer Verlag, 1964.
Hassell, Ulrich von. *Vom anderen Deutschland. Aus den nachgelassenen Tagebüchern, 1938-1944.* Frankfurt a.M., Hamburg: Fischer Bücherei, 1964. In English, *The Von Hassell Diaries, 1938-1944.* London, 1948. Originally by Atlantis-Verlag, Zurich, 1946.
Hohenstein, Alexander. *Wartheländisches Tagebuch aus den Jahren 1941/42.* Stuttgart: Deutsche Verlags-Anstalt, 1961.
Keitel, Wilhelm. *Generalfeldmarschall Keitel. Verbrecher oder Offizier? Erinnerungen, Briefe, Dokumente des Chefs OKW.* Edited by Walter

Görlitz. Göttingen: Musterschmidt-Verlag, 1961. In English, *The Memoirs of Field-Marshal Keitel.* London: W. Kimber, 1965.

Kersten, Felix. *Totenkopf und Treue. Heinrich Himmler ohne Uniform.* Hamburg: Robert Mölich-Verlag, 1952. In English, *The Kersten Memoirs, 1940-1945.* London: Hutchinson, 1956; New York: Macmillan, 1957.

Kesselring, Albert. *Soldat bis zum letzten Tag.* Bonn: Athenäum-Verlag, 1953. In English, *The Memoirs of Field-Marshal Kesselring.* London: W. Kimber, 1953.

Kleist, Peter. *Zwischen Hitler und Stalin 1939-1945. Aufzeichnungen.* Bonn: Athenäum Verlag, 1950.

Klepper, Jochen. *Überwindung. Tagebücher und Aufzeichnungen aus dem Kriege.* Stuttgart: Deutsche Verlags-Anstalt, 1959 (1958).

Klepper, Jochen. *Unter dem Schatten Deiner Flügel. Aus den Tagebüchern der Jahre 1932-1942.* Stuttgart: Deutsche Verlags-Anstalt, 1965.

Kommandant in Auschwitz. Autobiographische Aufzeichnungen des Rudolf Höss. Edited by Martin Broszat. Munich: Deutscher Taschenbuch Verlag, 1963. In English, *Commandant of Auschwitz.* London; New York: World, 1960.

Leber, Annedore (ed.). *Das Gewissen entscheidet. Berichte des deutschen Widerstandes von 1933-1945 in Lebensbildern.* Berlin: Mosaik-Verlag, 1957.

Leber, Annedore. *Das Gewissen steht auf. 64 Lebensbilder aus dem deutschen Widerstand 1933-1945.* Frankfurt: Europäische Verlagsgesellschaft m.b.H., 1966. In English, *Conscience in Revolt.* Westport, Conn: Associate Booksellers, 1957.

Leonhard, Wolfgang. *Die Revolution entlässt ihre Kinder.* Berlin: Ullstein-Verlag, 1966 (Cologne, Berlin: Kiepenheuer and Witsch, 1955). In English, *Child of the Revolution.* Chicago: Henry Regnery Co., 1958.

Ludendorff, Erich. *Meine Kriegserinnerungen 1914-1918.* Berlin: Ernst Siegfried Mittler and Sohn, 1919. In English, *My War Memoirs 1914-1918.* London: Hutchinson and Co., 1919.

Manstein, Erich von. *Verlorene Siege.* Bonn: Athenäum-Verlag, 1955. In English, edited as *Lost Victories.* Chicago: H. Regnery, 1958.

Oven, Wilfred von. *Mit Goebbels bis zum Ende.* 2 vols. Buenos Aires: Dürer-Verlag, 1949-1950.

Reck-Malleczwen, Friedrich Percival. *Tagebuch eines Verzweifelten. Zeugnis einer inneren Emigration.* Stuttgart: Goverts Verlag, 1966. In English, *Diary of a Man in Despair.* New York: Macmillan, 1970.

Rosenberg, Alfred. *Das politische Tagebuch Alfred Rosenbergs 1934/35 und 1939/40.* Edited by Hans Günther Seraphim. Munich: Deutscher Taschenbuch Verlag, 1964 (Musterschmidt-Verlag, Göttingen, 1956). In English, *Rosenberg's Memoirs.* Edited by Serge Lang and Ernst von Schenck. New York: 1949.

Schlabrendorff, Fabian. *Offiziere gegen Hitler.* Zurich: Europa-Verlag, 1951 (1946). In English, *Revolt against Hitler.* London, 1948.

Scholl, Inge. *Die Weisse Rose.* Frankfurt: Verlag der Frankfurter Hefte, 1953.

Semmler, Rudolf. *Goebbels the Man next to Hitler.* London: Westhouse, 1947.

Shirer, William L. *Berlin Diary. The Journal of a Foreign Correspondent 1934-1941.* New York: Alfred A. Knopf, 1941.

Shirer, William L. *End of a Berlin Diary.* New York: Alfred A. Knopf, 1947.

Speer, Albert. *Erinnerungen.* Frankfurt a.M.: Ullstein-Verlag; Berlin: Propyläen Verlag, 1969. In English, *Inside the Third Reich. Memoirs.* New York: The Macmillan Co., 1970.

Thomas, Georg. *Geschichte der deutschen Wehr- und Rüstungswirtschaft 1918-1943/45.* Boppard am Rhein: Harald Boldt Verlag, 1966.

Zhukov, Georgi K. *The Memoirs of Marshal Zhukov.* London: Cape, 1971. The German edition, *Erinnerungen und Gedanken.* Stuttgart: Deutsche Verlags-Anstalt, 1969.

SECONDARY SOURCES

Adler, H. G. *Die Juden in Deutschland. Von der Aufklärung bis zum Nationalsozialismus.* Munich: Kösel Verlag, 1960.

Adorno, Theodor W., Else Frenkel-Brunswik, Daniel J. Levinson, & R. Nevitt Sanford. *The Authoritarian Personality.* New York: Harper Brothers, 1950 (The American Jewish Committee—Studies in prejudice. Ed. by Max Horkheimer and Samuel H. Flowerman).

Albig, William. *Modern Public Opinion.* New York, Toronto, London: McGraw-Hill Book Co. Inc., 1956.

Allen, William Sheridan. *The Nazi Seizure of Power. The Experience of a Single German Town 1930-1935.* Chicago: Quadrangle Books, 1965.

Allport, Gordon, and Leo Postman. "The basic psychology of rumor," in *The Process and Effects of Mass Communication.* Edited by Wilbur Schramm. Urbana: University of Illinois, 1954.

Almond, Gabriel. *The American People and Foreign Policy.* New York: Harcourt, Brace and Co., 1950.

Anderson, Pauline Relyea. *Background of anti-English feeling in Germany, 1890-1902.* Washington, D.C.: The American University Press, 1939.

Arendt, Hannah. *Eichmann in Jerusalem. A Report on the Banality of Evil.* London: Faber and Faber Co.; New York, Viking, 1963.

Armstrong, Anne. *Unconditional Surrender. The impact of the Casablanca Policy upon World War II.* New Brunswick, N.J.: Rutgers University Press, 1961.

Der Aufstieg der NSDAP in Augenzeugenberichten. Edited with introduction by Ernst Deuerlein. Düsseldorf: Karl Rauch Verlag, 1968.

Baird, Jay W. "La campagne de propagande nazie en 1945." *Revue d'Histoire de la deuxième guerre mondiale.* 19ᵉannée, juillet 1969, no. 75, pp. 71-92.

Ball-Kaduri, Kurt Jakob. *Das Leben der Juden in Deutschland.* Frankfurt: Europäische Verlagsanstalt, 1963.

Bartz, Karl. *Die Tragödie der deutschen Abwehr.* Salzburg: Pilgram-Verlag, 1955. In English, *The Downfall of the German Secret Service.* London: W. Kimber, 1956.

Berghahn, Volker R. "Meinungsforschung im Dritten Reich. Die Mundpropaganda-Aktion der Wehrmacht im letzten Kriegshalbjahr." *Militärgeschichtliche Mitteilungen*, 1/67, pp. 83-119.

Berghahn, Volker R. "NSDAP und 'geistige Führung' der Wehrmacht 1939-1943." *VJHZ*, January 1969, No. 1, pp. 15-71.

Bethge, Eberhard. *Dietrich Bonhoeffer. Theologe-Christ-Zeitgenosse.* Munich: Chr. Kaiser Verlag, 1967. In English, *Dietrich Bonhoeffer. Theologian, Christian, Contemporary.* London: Collins, 1970.

Bleuel, Hans Peter. *Deutschlands Bekenner. Professoren zwischen Kaiserreich und Diktator.* Munich: Scherz Verlag, 1969.

Böhme, Hermann. *Der deutsch-französische Waffenstillstand im Zweiten Weltkrieg.* I. Teil: *Entstehung und Grundlagen des Waffenstillstandes von 1940.* Stuttgart: Deutsche Verlags-Anstalt, 1966 (Quellen und Darstellungen zur Zeitgeschichte, Vol. 12, part 1).

Bracher, Karl-Dietrich. *Adolf Hitler.* Bern, Munich, Vienna: Scherz Verlag, 1964.

Bracher, Karl-Dietrich. *Die deutsche Diktatur. Entstehung-Struktur-Folgen des Nationalsozialismus.* Cologne, Berlin: Kiepenheuer and Witsch, 1969. In English, *The German Dictatorship.* New York: Praeger, 1970.

Bracher, Karl-Dietrich, Wolfgang Sauer and Gerhard Schulz. *Die nationalsozialistische Machtergreifung. Studien zur Errichtung des totalitären Herrschaftssystem in Deutschland, 1933/1934.* Cologne-Opladen: Westdeutscher Verlag, 1960.

Bramstedt, Ernest K. *Goebbels and National Socialist Propaganda 1925-1945.* London: The Cresset Press, 1965.

Broszat, Martin. *Nationalsozialistische Polenpolitik 1939-1945.* Stuttgart: Deutsche Verlags-Anstalt, 1961.

Broszat, Martin. *Der Staat Hitlers. Grundlegung und Entwicklung seiner inneren Verfassung.* Munich: dtv., 1969 (dtv-Weltgeschichte des 20. Jahrhunderts vol. 9).

Buchheim, Hans. *Anatomie des SS-Staates.* 2 vols. Gutachten des Instituts für Zeitgeschichte. Olten/Freiburg: Walter Verlag, 1965. In English, *Anatomy of the SS State.* New York: Walker, 1968.

Buchheim, Hans. *Totalitäre Herrschaft. Wesen und Merkmale.* Munich: Kösel Verlag, 1962. In English, *Totalitarian Rule. Its Nature and Characteristics.* Middletown, Conn.: Wesleyan University Press, 1968.

Bullock, Alan. *Hitler. A Study in Tyranny.* New York: Harper and Row, rev. ed., 1964.

Burgelin, Henri. *La société allemande 1871-1968.* Paris: Arthaud, 1969.

Carsten, Francis L. *The Rise of Fascism.* Berkeley: University of California Press, 1967.

Carell, Paul. *Unternehmen Barbarossa. Der Marsch nach Russland.* Frankfurt a.M., Berlin, Vienna: Ullstein-Verlag, 1963. In English, *Hitler's War on Russia: The Story of the German Defeat in the East* (English edition, London: Harrap, 1964); *Hitler moves east 1941-1943.* (American edition, Boston: Little, Brown and Co., 1964).

Charlety, Sébastien. *Histoire du Saint-Simonisme (1825-1864).* Paris: Paul Hartmann, 1931.

Clausewitz, Karl von. *Vom Kriege.* Berlin: B. Behr's Verlag, 1914. Published as *On War* in numerous editions.

Cole, Wane S. *America First. The battle against intervention 1940-1941.* Madison: The University of Wisconsin Press, 1953.

Compton, James V. *The Swastika and the Eagle. Hitler, the United States and the origins of the Second World War.* London, Sydney, Toronto: The Bodley Head, 1968.

Conquest, Robert. *The Great Terror. Stalin's purge of the Thirties.* London, Melbourne: Macmillan, 1969.

Conway, John S. *The Nazi Persecution of the Churches, 1933-1945.* London: Weidenfeld and Nicolson, 1968.

Czichon, Eberhard. *Wer verhalf Hitler zur Macht? Zum Anteil der deutschen Industrie an der Zerstörung der Weimarer Republik.* Cologne: Pahl-Rugenstein Verlag, 1967 (Stimmen der Zeit, 5).

Dahms, Hellmuth Günther. *Geschichte des Zweiten Weltkrieges.* Stuttgart, Zurich, Salzburg: Sonderausgabe Europäischer Buchklub, 1965 (c. Rainer Wunderlich Verlag Hermann Leins, Tübingen, 1965).

Dahrendorf, Ralf. *Gesellschaft und Demokratie in Deutschland.* Munich: R. Piper and Co. Verlag, 1965. In English, *Society and Democracy in Germany.* New York: Doubleday, 1967.

Dallin, Alexander. *German Rule in Russia, 1941-1945. A Study of Occupation Policies.* New York: St. Martin's Press, 1957.

Demeter, Karl. *Das deutsche Offizierskorps in Gesellschaft und Staat 1650 bis 1945.* 4th rev. ed. Frankfurt a.M.: Bernard and Graefe Verlag für Wehrwesen, 1965. In English, *The German Officer-Corps in Society and State, 1650-1945.* New York: Praeger, 1965.

Debie, Pierre. "Quelques aspects psychologiques du Benelux." *Bulletin International des Sciences Sociales,* 1951, III, No. 3.

Deutsch, Harold C. *The Conspiracy against Hitler in the Twilight War.* Minneapolis: University of Minnesota Press, 1968.

Diehl-Thiele, Peter. *Partei und Staat im Dritten Reich. Untersuchungen zum Verhältnis von NSDAP und allgemeiner innerer Staatsverwaltung 1933-1945.* Munich: C. H. Beck, 1969 (Münchener Studien zur Politik, vol. 9).

Deutsches Geistesleben und Nationalsozialismus. Eine Vortragsreihe der Universität Tübingen. Edited by Andreas Flitner. Tübingen: Rainer Wunderlich Verlag, 1965.

Die deutsche Justiz und der Nationalsozialismus. Vol. I. Stuttgart: Deutsche Verlags-Anstalt, 1968.

Der deutsche Widerstand gegen Hitler. Vier historisch-kritische Studien. Edited by Werner Schmitthenner and Hans Buchheim. Cologne: Kiepenheuer and Witsch, 1966.

Dovifat, Emil. *Zeitungslehre I.* Vols. 1 & 2: *Theoretische Grundlagen—Nachricht und Meinung. Sprache und Form.* Berlin: Walter de Gruyter and Co., 1937 (Sammlung Göschen).

Dulles, Allan Welsh. *Germany's Underground.* New York: Macmillan, 1947.

Duroselle, Jean-Baptiste. "Der Einfluss der Massen auf die Aussenpolitik."

Masse und Demokratie. Erlenbach-Zurich, Stuttgart: Eugen Rentsch Verlag, 1957, pp. 55-70 (Volkswirtschaftliche Studien für das Schweizerische Institut für Auslandsforschung, Ed. Albert Hunold).

Duroselle, Jean-Baptiste. *De l'utilisation des sondages d'opinion en histoire et en sciences politiques.* Brussels: INSOC, 1957.

Eibl-Eibesfeld, Irenäus. *Grundriss der vergleichenden Verhaltensforschung. Ethologie.* Munich: R. Piper and Co., 1967.

Eich, Hermann. *Die unheimlichen Deutschen.* Düsseldorf, Vienna: Econ Verlag, 1963. In English, *The unloved Germans.* London: Macdonald, 1965.

Erbe, René. *Die nationalsozialistische Wirtschaftspolitik 1933-1939 im Lichte der modernen Theorie.* Zurich: Polygraphischer Verlag, 1958.

Evans, Richard J. "Personal values as factors in anti-Semitism." *Journal abnorm. soc. psychol.,* XLVII, 1952, pp. 794-96.

Fraenkel, Heinrich, and Roger Manvell. *The July Plot: the attempt in 1944 on Hitler's Life and the men behind it.* London: Bodley Head, 1964.

Free, Lloyd A., and Hadley Cantril. *The political beliefs of the Americans. A study of public opinion.* New Brunswick, N.J.: Rutgers University Press, 1967.

Freund, Michael. *Der Zweite Weltkrieg.* Gütersloh: Bertelsmann Verlag, 1962.

Freymond, Jacques. *The Saar Conflict, 1945-1955.* London: Stevens; New York: F. A. Praeger, 1960.

Friedländer, Saul. *Auftakt zum Untergang. Hitler und die USA 1939-1941.* Stuttgart: Kohlhammer Verlag, 1965. In English, *Prelude to Downfall: Hitler and the United States, 1939-1941.* New York: Knopf, 1967.

Friedländer, Saul. *Kurt Gerstein ou l'ambiguité du bien.* Paris: Castermann, 1967. In English, *Kurt Gerstein, The Ambiguity of Good.* New York: Knopf, 1969.

Friedländer, Saul. *Pius XII. und das Dritte Reich. Eine Dokumentation.* Reinbek b. Hamburg: Rowohlt GmbH., 1965. In English, *Pius XII and the Third Reich. A Documentation.* New York: Knopf, 1966.

Fromm, Erich. *Escape from Freedom.* New York, Toronto: Holt, Rinehart and Co., Inc., 1941.

Gamm, Hans-Jochen. *Der braune Kult.* Hamburg: Rütten and Loening, 1962.

Gamm, Hans-Jochen. *Der Flüsterwitz im Dritten Reich.* Munich: List Verlag, 1963.

Gehlen, Arnold. *Die Seele im technischen Zeitalter. Sozialpsychologische Probleme in der industriellen Gesellschaft.* Hamburg: Rowohlt GmbH., 1957 (rowohlts deutsche enzyklopädie).

Genschel, Helmut. *Die Verdrängung der Juden aus der Wirtschaft im Dritten Reich.* Göttingen: Musterschmidt-Verlag, 1967.

Gerlach, Heinrich. *Odyssee in Rot. Bericht einer Irrfahrt.* Munich: Nymphenburger Verlagsbuchhandlung, 1966.

Gersdorff, Ursula von. *Frauen im Kriegsdienst 1914-1945.* Stuttgart: Deutsche Verlags-Anstalt, 1969 (Beiträge zur Militär- und Kriegsgeschichte, vol. 11).

Gilbert, G. M. *The psychology of dictatorship, based on an examination of the leaders of Nazi Germany.* New York: The Ronald Press Co., 1950.

Gisevius, Hans Bernd. *Adolf Hitler. Versuch einer Deutung.* Stuttgart: Europäischer Buchklub, Sonderausgabe, n.d. (c. Rütten and Loening, Munich, 1963).

Glaser, Hermann. *Eros und Politik. Eine sozialpathologische Untersuchung.* Cologne: Verlag Wissenschaft und Politik, 1967.

Glaser, Hermann. *Spiesser-Ideologie. Von der Zerstörung des deutschen Geistes im 19. und 20. Jahrhundert.* Freiburg: Rombach Verlag, 1964.

Glum, Friedrich. *Der Nationalsozialismus. Werden und Vergehen.* Munich: C. H. Beck'sche Verlagsbuchhandlung, 1962.

Göhring, Martin. *Alles oder Nichts. Zwölf Jahre totalitärer Herrschaft in Deutschland.* Vol. I: *1933-1939.* Tübingen: Verlag J. C. B. Mohr (Paul Siebeck), 1968.

Görlitz, Walter. *Der Zweite Weltkrieg 1939-1945.* Stuttgart: Steingrüben Verlag, 1952.

Graml, Hermann. "Die deutsche Militäropposition vom Sommer 1940 bis zum Frühjahr 1943." *Vollmacht des Gewissens.* Frankfurt: Metzner Verlag, 1965, Vol. II, pp. 411-74.

Greiner, Helmut. *Die oberste Wehrmachtführung 1939 bis 1943.* Wiesbaden: Limes-Verlag, 1951.

Gross, Johannes. *Die Deutschen.* Frankfurt: Scheffler Verlag, 1967.

Gruchmann, Lothar. *Der Zweite Weltkrieg. Kriegsführung und Politik.* Munich: Deutscher Taschenbuch Verlag, 1967 (dtv Weltgeschichte des 20. Jahrhunderts, Vol. 10).

Gurfein, M.I., and Morris Janowitz. "Trends in Wehrmacht-Morale." *Public Opinion Quarterly,* 1946, No. 10, pp. 78-84.

Hagemann, Walter. *Publizistik im Dritten Reich. Ein Beitrag zur Methodik der Massenführung.* Hamburg: Joachim Heitmann and Co., 1948.

Hammen, Oscar. "German Historians and the advent of the national socialist state." *The Journal of Modern History.* XIII, June, 1941, No. 2, pp. 161-88.

Hansen, Reimer. *Das Ende des Dritten Reiches. Die deutsche Kapitulation 1945.* Stuttgart: Klett Verlag, 1966 (Kieler Historische Studien, Vol. 2).

Heer, Friedrich. *Gottes erste Liebe. 2000 Jahre Judentum und Christentum. Genesis des österreichischen Katholiken Adolf Hitler.* Munich: Bechtle Verlag, 1967. In English, *God's first Love. Christians and Jews over two thousand years.* London: Weidenfeld and Nicolson, 1970.

Heiber, Helmut. *Walter Frank und sein Reichsinstitut für Geschichte des neuen Deutschlands.* Stuttgart: Deutsche Verlags-Anstalt, 1966 (Institut für Zeitgeschichte, Quellen und Darstellungen zur Zeitgeschichte, Vol. 13).

Heiden, Konrad. *Adolf Hitler. Eine Biographie.* 2 vols. Zurich: Europa-Verlag, 1936-37. In English, *Hitler, A Biography.* London: Constable and Co., 1936.

Henkys, Reinhard. *Die nationalsozialistischen Gewaltsverbrechen. Geschichte und Gericht.* Stuttgart: Kreuz-Verlag, 1964.

Herzog, Bodo. *60 Jahre deutsche U-Boote 1906-1966.* Munich: J. F. Lehmanns Verlag, 1968.

Hilberg, Raoul. *The Destruction of the European Jews.* Chicago: Quadrangle Books, 1961.

Hillgruber, Andreas. *Deutschlands Rolle in der Vorgeschichte der beiden Welt-*

kriege. Göttingen: Vandenhoeck and Ruprecht, 1967 (*Die deutsche Frage in der Welt*, Vol. 7).

Hillgruber, Andreas. *Hitlers Strategie. Politik und Kriegsführung 1940 bis 1941.* Frankfurt a.M.: Bernard and Graefe Verlag für Wehrwesen, 1965.

Hoch, Anton. "Das Attentat auf Hitler im Bürgerbräukeller." *VJHZ*, October 1969, No. 4, pp. 383-413.

Hoffmann, Peter. *Widerstand—Staatsstreich—Attentat. Der Kampf der Opposition gegen Hitler.* Munich: R. Piper & Co. Verlag, 1969.

Hofstätter, Peter. *Psychologie der öffentlichen Meinung.* Vienna: Wilhelm Braumüller, 1949 (*Erkenntnis und Besinnung*, Vol. 13).

Hofstätter, Peter. *Einführung in die Sozialpsychologie.* Stuttgart, Vienna: Humboldt-Verlag, 1954.

Höhne, Heinz. *Der Orden unter dem Totenkopf. Die Geschichte der SS.* Gütersloh: Sigbert Mohn Verlag, 1967. In English, *The Order of the Death's Head: The Story of Hitler's SS.* London: Secker and Warburg, 1969.

Homze, Edward L. *Foreign Labor in Nazi Germany.* Princeton: Princeton University Press, 1967.

Hubatsch, Walter. *"Weserübung." Die deutsche Besetzung von Dänemark und Norwegen.* Göttingen: Musterschmidt-Verlag, 1960.

Hüttenberger, Peter. *Die Gauleiter.* Bonn, 1967 (dissertation).

Inkeles, Alex. *Public Opinion in Soviet Russia. A study in mass persuasion.* Cambridge: Harvard University Press, 1958.

Irving, David. *The Destruction of Dresden.* New York: Ballantine Books, 1963, rev. 1966.

Irving, David. *The Mare's Nest.* London: W. Kimber, 1964; Boston: Little, Brown, 1965. In German, *Die Geheimwaffen des Dritten Reiches.* Gütersloh: Sigbert Mohn Verlag, 1965.

Irving, David. *The German Atomic Bomb. The history of nuclear research in Nazi Germany.* New York: Simon & Schuster, 1967.

Isaac, Jules. *Genesis des Antisemitismus.* Vienna, Frankfurt a.M., Zurich: Europa-Verlag, 1968 (Europäische Perspektiven).

Jäckel, Eberhard. *Frankreich in Hitlers Europa. Die deutsche Frankreichpolitik im Zweiten Weltkrieg.* Stuttgart: Deutsche Verlags-Anstalt, 1966.

Jäckel, Eberhard. *Hitlers Weltanschauung. Entwurf einer Herrschaft.* Tübingen: Rainer Wunderlich Verlag Hermann Leins, 1969. In English, *Hitler's Weltanschauung. A blueprint for power.* Middletown, Conn.: Wesleyan University Press, 1972.

Jacobsen, Hans-Adolf. *Fall Gelb. Der Kampf um den deutschen Operationsplan zur Westoffensive 1940.* Wiesbaden: Steiner Verlag, 1957 (Institut für europäische Geschichte, Mainz, Vol. 16).

Jacobsen, Hans-Adolf. *Nationalsozialistische Aussenpolitik 1933-1938.* Darmstadt: Metzner Verlag, 1969.

Jacobsen, Hans-Adolf. *Zur Konzeption einer Geschichte des Zweiten Weltkrieges 1939-1945.* Frankfurt a.M.: Bernard & Graefe Verlag für Wehrwesen, 1964 (Schriften der Bibliothek für Zeitgeschichte. Weltkriegsbücherei, Stuttgart, No. 2).

Janssen, Gregor. *Das Ministerium Speer. Deutschlands Rüstung im Krieg.* Berlin, Frankfurt a.M., Vienna: Ullstein-Verlag, 1968.

Jong, Louis de. "Die Niederlande und Auschwitz." *VfZG*, January, 1969, No. 1, pp. 1-16.

Katz, Elihu, and Paul F. Lazarsfeld. *Personal Influence. The part played by people in the flow of mass communications.* Glencoe, Ill.: The Free Press, 1955.

Klempner, Benedicto Mario. *Priester vor Hitlers Tribunalen.* Munich: Rütten and Loening, 1966.

Klein, Burton H. *Germany's Economic Preparation for War.* Cambridge: Harvard University Press, 1959.

Klineberg, Otto. *Social Psychology.* Rev. ed. New York: Holt, Rinehart and Winston, 1966.

Klink, Ernst. *Das Gesetz des Handelns. Die Operation "Zitadelle" 1943.* Stuttgart: Deutsche Verlags-Anstalt, 1966 (Schriftenreihe des Militärgeschichtlichen Forschungsamtes, Vol. VII).

Klose, Werner. *Generation im Gleichschritt. Ein Dokumentarbericht.* Oldenburg, Hamburg: Stalling Verlag, 1964.

Klotzbach, Kurt. *Gegen den Nationalsozialismus. Widerstand und Verfolgung in Dortmund 1930-1945.* Hanover: Verlag für Literatur und Zeitgeschehen, 1969.

Knackstedt, H. "Der 'Altmark' Zwischenfall!" *Wehrwissenschaftliche Rundschau*, 1959, pp. 391-411, 466-86.

Knapp, Robert H. "A psychology of rumor." *Public Opinion Quarterly*, VIII, 1944, No. 1, pp. 22-37.

Kosthorst, Erich. *Die deutsche Opposition gegen Hitler zwischen Polen- und Frankreichfeldzug.* Published by the Bundeszentrale für Heimatdienst, Bonn, 1957 (3rd ed.).

Krannhals, Hanns von. "Die Judenvernichtung in Polen und die Wehrmacht." *Wehrwissenschaftliche Rundschau*, No. 10, 1965, pp. 570-81.

Krannhals, Hanns von. *Der Warschauer Aufstand 1944.* Frankfurt: Bernard and Graefe Verlag für Wehrwesen, 1963.

Krausnick, Helmut. "Hitler und die Morde in Polen." *VfZG*, 1963, No. 2, pp. 196-209.

Krausnick, Helmut. "Vorgeschichte und Beginn des militärischen Widerstandes gegen Hitler." *Vollmacht des Gewissens.* Vol. I. Frankfurt a.M.: Metzner Verlag, 1960, pp. 177-348.

Krausnick, Helmut, and Hermann Graml. "Der deutsche Widerstand und die Alliierten." *ibid.*, Vol. II, 1965, pp. 475-522.

Laidler, Harry W. *History of Socialism. A comparative survey of socialism, communism, Trade unionism, cooperation, utopianism and other systems of reform and reconstruction.* London: Routledge and Kegan, Paul, 1968.

Lange, Karl. *Hitlers unbeachtete Maximen. "Mein Kampf" und die Öffentlichkeit.* Stuttgart: Kohlhammer Verlag, 1968.

Langer, William, and Sarell E. Gleason. *The Challenge to Isolation 1937 to 1940.* New York: Harper and Row, 1964 (c. 1952).

Langer, William. *The Undeclared War 1940-1941.* New York, Harper, 1953.

Lazarsfeld, Paul F., Bernhard Berelson and Hazel Gaudet. *The Peoples' Choices. How the voter makes up his mind in a presidential campaign.* New York: Columbia University Press, 1960 (c. 1944).

Lefebvre, Henri. "Psychologie des classes sociales." *Traité de Sociologie,* publié sous la direction de Georges Gurvitch. Paris: Presses Universitaires de France, 1960, T. II, pp. 364-86.

Leiser, Erwin. *Mein Kampf. Eine Bilddokumentation.* Frankfurt: Fischer Bücherei, 1963 (Fischer Bücherei Vol. 411).

Leon, Abraham. *La conception materialiste de la question juive.* Paris: Etudes et Documentation internationales, 1968. In English, *The Jewish Question, a Marxian interpretation.* New York: Pathfinder Press, 1970.

Lewy, Guenther. *The Catholic Church and Nazi Germany.* New York: McGraw-Hill, 1965.

Lippmann, Walter. *Public Opinion.* New York: The Free Press, 1965 (c. 1949).

Lochner, Louis P. *Tycoons and Tyrant. German industry from Hitler to Adenauer.* Chicago: H. Regnery Co., 1954.

Lorenz, Konrad. *Das sogenannte Böse. Zur Naturgeschichte der Aggression.* Vienna: Barotha-Schöler, 1964. In English, *On Aggression.* London: Methuen, 1966.

Manvell, Roger and Heinrich Fraenkel. *The Canaris conspiracy. The secret resistance to Hitler in the German army.* London: Heinemann, 1969.

Massenwahn in Geschichte und Gegenwart. Ein Tagungsbericht. Edited by Wilhelm Bitter. Stuttgart: Ernst Klett Verlag, 1965.

Meinecke, Friedrich. *Die deutsche Katastrophe.* Wiesbaden: E. Brockhaus Verlag, 1946. In English, *The German Catastrophe.* Cambridge: Harvard University Press, 1950.

Messerschmidt, Manfred. *Die Wehrmacht im NS-Staat. Zeit der Indoktrination.* Hamburg: R. von Deckers Verlag, 1969.

Milward, Alan S. *The German Economy at War.* London, New York: Oxford University Press, 1965.

Mitscherlich, Alexander and Margarete. *Die Unfähigkeit zu trauern. Grundlagen kollektiven Verhaltens.* Munich: R. Piper and Co., 1968.

Mitscherlich, Alexander and Fred Mielke. *Wissenschaft ohne Menschlichkeit. Medizinische und eugenische Irrwege unter Diktatur, Bürokratie und Krieg.* Heidelberg: Verlag Lambert Schneider, 1949. In English, *The Death Doctors.* London: Elek Books, 1962.

Mommsen, Hans. *Beamtentum im Dritten Reich.* Stuttgart: Deutsche Verlags-Anstalt, 1968 (Schriftenreihe der Vierteljahreshefte für Zeitgeschichte, No. 15).

Mommsen, Hans. "Der nationalsozialistische Polizeistaat und die Judenverfolgung von 1938." VJHZ, 1962, January, No. 1, pp. 68-87.

Mommsen, Wolfgang J. "L'opinion allemande et la chute du gouvernement Bethmann Hollweg en juillet 1917." *Revue d'histoire moderne et contemporaine,* XV, January-March, 1968, pp. 39-53. Appeared in German: "Die öffentliche Meinung und der Zusammenbruch des Regierungssystems Bethmann Hollweg im Juli 1917." *Geschichte in Wissenschaft und Unterricht,* 19, 1968, pp. 656-667.

Mommsen, Wolfgang J. "Die Regierung Bethmann Hollweg und die öffentliche Meinung 1914-1917." *VfZG*, 1969, April, No. 2, pp. 117-159.

Mosse, George L. *Nazi Culture. Intellectual, cultural and social life in the Third Reich.* New York: Grosset and Dunlap, 1966.

Müller, Klaus-Jürgen. *Das Heer und Hitler. Armee und nationalsozialistisches Regime 1933-1940.* Stuttgart: Deutsche Verlags-Anstalt, 1969 (Beiträge zur Militär- und Kriegsgeschichte, Vol. 10).

Müller-Claudius, Michael. *Der Antisemitismus und das deutsche Verhängnis.* Frankfurt a.M.: Verlag Josef Knecht, Carolus Druckerei, 1948.

Murawski, Erich. *Der deutsche Wehrmachtsbericht 1939-1945. Ein Beitrag zur Untersuchung der geistigen Kriegführung. Mit einer Dokumentation der Wehrmachtberichte vom 1. 7. 1944 bis 9. 5. 1945.* Boppard/Rhein: Verlag Harald Boldt, 1962.

Neumann, Erich Peter and Elisabeth Noelle. *Antworten. Politik im Kraftfeld der öffentlichen Meinung.* Allensbach: Verlag für Demoskopie, 1954.

Nolte, Ernst. "Ebenen des Krieges und Stufen des Widerstandes." *Probleme des Zweiten Weltkrieges.* Cologne: Kiepenheuer and Witsch, 1967, pp. 203-211.

Nolte, Ernst. *Der Faschismus in seiner Epoche.* Munich: R. Piper and Co., 1963. In English, *The Three Faces of Fascism.* New York: Holt, Rinehart and Winston, 1966.

Nolte, Ernst. *Die faschistischen Bewegungen.* Munich: Deutscher Taschenbuch Verlag, 1966 (dtv-Weltgeschichte des 20. Jahrhunderts, Vol. 4).

Nolte, Ernst (ed.). *Theorien über den Faschismus.* Cologne: Kiepenheuer and Witsch, 1967.

Nyomarky, Joseph. *Charisma and Factionalism in the Nazi Party.* Minneapolis: University of Minnesota Press, 1967.

O'Neill, Robert J. *The German Army and the Nazi Party 1933-1939.* London: Cassell, 1966.

Parkes, James W. *Antisemitism.* Chicago: Quadrangle Books, 1964.

Pavlov, Dmitrii W. *Leningrad 1941: The Blockade.* Translated from the Russian by J. C. Adams. Chicago: University of Chicago Press, 1965.

Perrault, Gilles. *L'orchestre rouge.* Paris: Favard, 1968. In English, *The Red Orchestra.* London: Barker, 1968.

Petzina, Dieter. *Autarkiepolitik im Dritten Reich. Der nationalsozialistische Vierjahresplan.* Stuttgart: Deutsche Verlags-Anstalt, 1968 (Schriftenreihe der Vierteljahreshefte für Zeitgeschichte No. 16).

Platen-Hallermund, Alice. *Die Tötung Geisteskranker in Deutschland.* Frankfurt a.M.: Verlag der Frankfurter Hefte, 1948.

Plessner, Helmuth. *Die verspätete Nation. Über die politische Verfügbarkeit bürgerlichen Geistes.* Stuttgart: W. Kohlhammer Verlag, 1959.

Pohle, Heinz. *Der Rundfunk als Instrument der Politik. Zur Geschichte des deutschen Rundfunks von 1923-1939.* Hamburg: Verlag Hans Bredow Institut, 1955.

Poliakov, Léon. *Le bréviaire de la haine.* Paris: Calman-Lévy, 1951. In English, *Harvest of Hate. The Nazi program for the destruction of the Jews of Europe.* N.Y.: Syracuse University Press, 1954.

Poliakov, Léon. *Histoire de l'antisémitisme.* Vol. I: *Du Christ aux Juifs de la*

Cour. Paris: Calman-Lévy, 1961 (1955). In English: *The History of anti-Semitism.* New York: Vanguard Press, 1965.

La presse dans les Etats autoritaires. Publié par l'Institut international de la Presse, Zurich, 1959.

Prittie, Terence. *Germans against Hitler.* London: Hutchinson, 1964.

Probleme des Zweiten Weltkrieges. Edited by Andreas Hillgruber. Cologne: Kiepenheuer and Witsch, 1967.

Reichmann, Eva G. *Hostages of Civilization: the social sources of national socialist anti-semitism.* Boston: Beacon Press, 1951.

Reitlinger, Gerald. *The Final Solution. The Attempt to Exterminate the Jews of Europe, 1939-1945.* London: Valletine; New York: Beechhurst Press, 1953. German: *Die Flucht in den Hass.* Berlin: Colloquium Verlag, 1956.

Reitlinger, Gerald. *The House Built on Sand: the conflicts of German policy in Russia, 1939-1945.* New York; Viking Press; London: Weidenfeld and Nicolson, 1960. In German as *Ein Haus auf Sand gebaut.* Hamburg: Rütten and Loening, 1962.

Les relations germano-soviétiques de 1933 à 1939. Recueil d'études sous la direction de Jean-Baptiste Duroselle. Paris: Colin, 1954 (Cahiers de la Fondation Nationale des Sciences Politiques 58).

Remarque, Erich Maria. *Die Nacht von Lissabon.* Cologne, Berlin: Kiepenheuer and Witsch, 1962. In English, *The Night in Lisbon.* New York: Harcourt, Brace and World, 1964.

Remond, René. "Opinions idéologiques et inclinations affectives en politique étrangère." *L'élaboration de la politique étrangère.* Publié par Léo Hamon. Paris: Presses Universitaires de France, 1969, pp. 85-93.

Renouvin, Pierre. "L'opinion et la guerre en 1917." *Revue d'histoire moderne et contemporaine,* XV, January-March, 1968, pp. 4-23.

Ritter, Gerhard. *Carl Goerdeler und die deutsche Widerstandsbewegung.* Munich: Deutscher Taschenbuch Verlag, 1964 (c. Deutsche Verlags-Anstalt Stuttgart, 1954). In English, *The German Resistance. Carl Goerdeler's Struggle against Tyranny.* New York: Praeger; London: Allen and Unwin, 1958.

Robbins, Keith. *Munich 1938.* London: Cassell, 1968.

Robertson, Edwin H. *Christians against Hitler.* London: SCM Press, 1962. In German, *Christen gegen Hitler.* Gütersloh: Gütersloher Verlagshaus Gerd Mohn, 1964.

Rock, Williams. "Grand Alliance or Daisy Chain. British opinion and policy toward Russia, April to August 1939." *Power, Public Opinion and Diplomacy. Essays in Honor of Eber Malcolm Carroll.* Durham, N.C.: Duke University Press; London: Cambridge University Press, 1959, pp. 297-337.

Rohwer, Jürgen. *Die U-Boot-Erfolge der Achsenmächte.* Munich: J. F. Lehmanns-Verlag, 1968.

Roon, Ger van. *Neuordnung im Widerstand. Der Kreisauer Kreis innerhalb der deutschen Widerstandsbewegung.* Munich: Verlag R. Oldenbourg, 1967. In

English, *German Resistance to Hitler. Count von Moltke and the Kreisau Circle.* London, New York: Van Nostrand Reinhold, 1971.

Rosenau, James N. *Public Opinion and Foreign Policy. An Operational Formulation.* New York: Random House, 1961.

Rothfels, Hans. *Die deutsche Opposition gegen Hitler. Eine Würdigung.* Frankfurt a.M., Hamburg: Fischer Bücherei, 1958. In English, *German Opposition to Hitler.* Chicago: Regnery, 1962; London: Wolff, 1963.

Rothfels, Hans. "Zerrspiegel des 20. Juli." *VfZG,* 1962, January, No. 1, pp. 62-67.

Rothfels, Hans. "Zur 25. Wiederkehr des 20. Juli 1944." *VfZG,* 1969, July, No. 3, pp. 237-53.

Ryan, Cornelis. *The Longest Day: June 6, 1944.* New York: Simon and Schuster, 1959. In German, *Der längste Tag.* Gütersloh: Sigbert Mohn Verlag, 1959.

Sargent, Stephen Stansfeld, and Robert Clifford Williams. *Social Psychology.* New York: The Ronald Press Comp., 1966 (3rd ed.).

Schabrod, Karl. *Widerstand an Rhein und Ruhr. 1933-1945.* Published by the Landesvorstand der Vereinigung der Verfolgten des Nazi-Regimes Nordrhein-Westfalen. Herne, 1969.

Schaffner, Bertram. *Fatherland.* New York: Columbia University Press, 1948.

Scheffler, Wolfgang. *Judenverfolgung im Dritten Reich 1933-1944.* Berlin: Colloquium Verlag, 1960.

Scheurig, Bodo. *Der 20. Juli—Damals und heute.* Hamburg: Holsten-Verlag, 1965.

Scheurig, Bodo (ed.). *Verrat hinter Stacheldraht? Das Nationalkomitee "Freies Deutschland" und der Bund deutscher Offiziere in der Sowjetunion 1943-1945.* Munich: Deutscher Taschenbuch Verlag, 1965. In English, *Free Germany: the National Committee and the League of German Officers.* Middletown, Conn.: Wesleyan University Press, 1969.

Scheurig, Bodo. *Claus Graf Schenk von Stauffenberg.* Berlin: Colloquium Verlag, 1964.

Schmidt, Paul. *Statist auf diplomatischer Bühne 1923-1945.* Bonn: Athenäum-Verlag, 1953.

Schneider, Franz. *Politik und Kommunikation.* Drei Versuche. Mainz: v. Hase and Koehler Verlag, 1967.

Schoeck, Helmut. *Der Neid. Eine Theorie der Gesellschaft.* Munich: Karl Albert Verlag, 1966. In English, *Envy. A theory of social behavior.* New York: Harcourt, Brace & World, 1969.

Schoenbaum, David. *Hitler's Social Revolution: Class and Status in Nazi Germany 1933-1939.* New York: Doubleday and Co., 1966. In German, *Die braune Revolution.* Cologne, Berlin: Kiepenheuer und Witsch, 1968.

Scholder, Klaus. "Die evangelische Kirche in der Sicht der nationalsozialistischen Führung bis zum Kriegsausbruch." *VfZG,* 1968, January, No. 1, pp. 15-35.

Schorn, Hubert. *Der Richter im Dritten Reich. Geschichte und Dokumente.* Frankfurt: Vittorio Klostermann, 1959.

Schorn, Hubert. *Die Gesetzgebung des Nationalsozialismus als Mittel der Machtpolitik.* Frankfurt: Vittorio Klostermann, 1963.

Schröter, Heinz. *Stalingrad. ". . . bis zur letzten Patrone."* Lengerich, Westphalia: Kleins Druck- und Verlagsanstalt, n.d. In English, *Stalingrad.* New York: Ballantine Books, 1958.

Schwabe, Klaus. *Wissenschaft und Kriegsmoral. Die deutschen Hochschullehrer und die politischen Grundfragen des Ersten Weltkrieges.* Göttingen, Zurich, Frankfurt: Musterschmidt-Verlag, 1969.

Schweitzer, Arthur. *Big Business in the Third Reich.* London: Eyre and Spottiswoode, 1964.

Sendtner, Kurt. "Die deutsche Militäropposition im ersten Kriegsjahr." *Vollmacht des Gewissens.* Vol. I. Frankfurt a.M.: Metzner Verlag, 1960, pp. 385-532.

Shils, Edward A., and Morris Janowitz. "Cohesion and disintegration of the *Wehrmacht* in World War II." *Public Opinion Quarterly,* XII (1948), pp. 280-315.

Shirer, William L. *The Rise and Fall of the Third Reich.* New York: Simon and Schuster; London: Heinemann/Secker and Warburg, 1960.

Smith, Bradley F. *Adolf Hitler. His family, childhood and youth.* The Hoover Institution on War, Revolution and Peace. Stanford: Stanford University Press, 1967.

Sontheimer, Kurt. *Antidemokratisches Denken in der Weimarer Republik. Die politischen Ideen des deutschen Nationalismus zwischen 1918 und 1932.* Munich: Nymphenburger Verlagsanstalt, 1964 (2nd ed.).

"SS-Bericht über den 20. Juli. Aus den Papieren des SS-Obersturmbannführers Dr. Georg Kiesel." *Nordwestdeutsche Hefte,* 1947, No. 1-2, pp. 5-34.

Staff, Ilse (ed.). *Justiz im Dritten Reich. Eine Dokumentation.* Frankfurt: Fischer Bücherei, 1964.

Steinert, Marlis G. *Die 23 Tage der Regierung Dönitz.* Düsseldorf, Vienna: Econ Verlag, 1967. In English, *23 Days. The Final Collapse of Nazi Germany.* New York: Walker, 1969.

Stern, Fritz. "Bethmann Hollweg und der Krieg: Die Grenzen der Verantwortung." *Recht und Staat in Geschichte und Gegenwart.* J. C. B. Mohr (Paul Siebeck), 1968 (No. 351-352).

Stoetzel, Jean. *L'étude expérimentale des opinions.* Paris: Presses Universitaires de France, 1943.

Stoetzel, Jean. "La conception de la notion d'attitude en psychologie sociale." *Sondages,* 1963, No. 2, pp. 5-20.

Strobel, Ferd. *Christliche Bewährung.* Olten: Walter Verlag, 1946.

Thayer, Charles W. *The unquiet Germans.* New York: Harper, 1957. In German, *Die unruhigen Deutschen.* Bern, Stuttgart, Vienna: Alfred Scherz Verlag, 1958.

Thorwald, Jürgen. *Die ungeklärten Fälle.* Stuttgart: Steingrüben, 1950.

Tippelskirch, Kurt von. *Geschichte des Zweiten Weltkriegs.* Bonn: Athenäum-Verlag, 1954.

Tompkins, Peter. *Italy betrayed.* New York: Simon and Schuster, 1966. In German, *Verrat auf italienisch.* Vienna: Molden Verlag, 1967.

Treue, Wilhelm. "Die Einstellung einiger deutscher Gross-industrieller zu Hitlers Aussenpolitik." *Geschichte in Wissenschaft und Unterricht*, 1966, No. 8, pp. 491-507.

Trevor-Roper, Hugh H. *The Last Days of Hitler*. New York: Macmillan, 1947. In German, *Hitlers letzte Tage*. Frankfurt a.M., Berlin, Ullstein-Verlag, 1965.

Tschuikow, Marschall Wassilij. *Das Ende des Dritten Reiches*, Munich: Wilhelm Goldmann, 1966.

Uhlig, Heinrich. "Der verbrecherische Befehl. Eine Diskussion und ihre historisch-dokumentarischen Grundlagen." *Vollmacht des Gewissens*. Vol. II. Frankfurt: Metzner Verlag, 1965, pp. 287-410.

Der ungekündigte Bund. Neue Begegnung von Juden und christlicher Gemeinde. Edited by Dietrich Goldschmidt und Hans-Joachim Kraus. Stuttgart: Kreuz-Verlag, 1962.

Von Versailles zum Zweiten Weltkrieg. Vorträge zur Zeitgeschichte. Edited by Erhard Kloess. dtv-Dokumente. Munich: Deutscher Taschenbuch Verlag, 1965.

Warlimont, Walter. *Im Hauptquartier der deutschen Wehrmacht 1939-1945. Grundlagen. Formen. Gestalten.* Frankfurt a.M.: Bernard & Graefe Verlag für Wehrwesen, 1962. In English, *Inside Germany's Headquarters, 1939-1945*. New York: F. A. Praeger, 1964.

Webster, Sir Charles and Noble Frankland. *The strategic air offensive against Germany, 1939-1945*. 4 vols. London: Her Majesty's Stationery Office, 1961.

Weisenborn, Günther (ed.). *Der lautlose Aufstand. Bericht über die Widerstandsbewegung des Deutschen Volks 1933-1945.* Hamburg: Rowohlt, 1953.

Werner, Karl Ferdinand. *Das NS-Geschichtsbild und die deutsche Geschichtswissenschaft.* Stuttgart: Kohlhammer, 1967.

Werth, Alexander. *Russia at War, 1941-1945.* London: Pan; New York: Avon, 1965. In German, *Russland im Kriege 1941-1945*. Munich, Zurich: Droemersche Verlagsanstalt Th. Knaur Nachf., 1965.

Wheeler-Bennett, John W. *The Nemesis of Power. The German Army in Politics, 1918-1945.* New York: The Viking Press, 1962. In German, *Die Nemesis der Macht*. Düsseldorf: Droste-Verlag, 1955.

Widerstand und Erneuerung. Neue Berichte und Dokumente vom inneren Kampf gegen das Hitler-Regime. Edited with introduction by Otto Kopp. Stuttgart: Seewald Verlag, 1966.

Wulf, Josef. *Aus dem Lexikon der Mörder—"Sonderbehandlung" und verwandte Worte in nationalsozialistischen Dokumenten.* Gütersloh: Sigbert Mohn Verlag, 1963.

Wulf, Josef. *Literatur und Dichtung im Dritten Reich.* Gütersloh: Sigbert Mohn, Verlag, 1964.

Zahn, Gordon C. *German Catholics and Hitler's Wars; a study in social control.* London: Sheed, 1963. In German, *Die deutschen Katholiken und Hitlers Kriege*. Graz, Vienna, Cologne: Verlag Styria, 1965.

Zeller, Eberhard. *Geist der Freiheit. Der 20. Juli.* Munich: Hermann Rinn, n.d.

Zipfel, Friedrich. *Kirchenkampf in Deutschland 1933-1945. Religionsverfolgung und Selbstbehauptung der Kirchen in der nationalsozialistischen Zeit.*

Berlin: Walter de Gruyter and Co., 1965 (Veröffentlichungen der Historischen Kommission zu Berlin beim Friedrich-Meinecke-Institut der Freien Universität Berlin).

Zeman, Z. A. B. *Nazi Propaganda*. London: Oxford University Press, 1964.

Der 20. Juli 1944. Published by the Bundeszentrale für Heimatdienst. Bonn: Köllen Verlag, 1953.

NOTES

1. A selection of these have been published by Heinz Boberach with a detailed criticism of the sources. For the citation, see published documents below.
2. One copy in IWM, see published documents below.
3. See published documents, below.
4. See printed documents, published documents and notations, below.
5. *Kriegspropaganda 1939-1941* and *"Wollt ihr den totalen Krieg?"*; see printed documents.

INDEX*

* Footnotes have not been indexed unless they amplify or elaborate on the text. *Ed.*